Becoming Aware

A Text/Workbook for Human Relations and Personal Adjustment

Eighth Edition

VELMA WALKER
Tarrant County College

LYNN BROKAW
Portland Community College

KENDALL/HUNT PUBLISHING COMPANY
4050 Westmark Drive   Dubuque, Iowa 52002

You Can Be Whatever You Want To Be

There is inside you all of the potential to be whatever you want to be—all of the energy to do whatever you want to do.

Imagine yourself as you would like to be, doing what you want to do, and each day, take one step . . . toward your dream.

And though at times it may seem too difficult to continue, hold on to your dream.

One morning you will awake to find that you are the person you dreamed of—doing what you wanted to do—simply because you had the courage to believe in your potential and to hold on to your dream.

Cover images courtesy of PhotoDisc and Corel.

ISBN 0-7872-7678-2

Printed in the United States of America.
10 9 8 7 6 5 4 3 2 1

 # Brief Contents

Chapter 1: Getting acquainted with ourselves and others
Relationships are the source of our greatest pleasures and pain throughout our lives. We will discover the process of understanding our inner "self" and getting acquainted with others throughout this chapter.

Chapter 2: Self-awareness
Understanding the "self" and discovering how you evolved into the person you are will be addressed in this chapter.

Chapter 3: Who's in control?
Learning to take control of your life and change your behavior will be addressed in this chapter.

Chapter 4: Dealing with emotions
The full spectrum of human feelings, from love and excitement to anger and despair, is discussed. New research on emotional intelligence—learning to achieve a balance between emotional expression and control—is also addressed in this chapter.

Chapter 5: Interpersonal communication
This chapter focuses on effective communication skills for establishing and maintaining more satisfying relationships with others.

Chapter 6: Developing close relationships
The evolution of a relationship—finding friends, becoming intimate, and discovering love will be addressed throughout this chapter.

Chapter 7: Resolving interpersonal conflict
In this chapter, we learn to approach interpersonal conflict differently—there doesn't have to be a winner and a loser.

Chapter 8: Managing stress and wellness
Various stressors are identified in this chapter, as well as effective ways of coping with stress. The interaction of thoughts, feelings, and negative self-talk is also addressed.

Chapter 9: Meaning and values
Prioritizing individual values—what is important in life—and finding meaning and purpose in life are discussed in this chapter.

Chapter 10: Where do I want to go with my life?
Taking risks and developing a plan of action for success are emphasized in this chapter. New research on the secret of happiness is also discussed.

 Contents

4 Dealing with Emotions   175

5 Interpersonal Communication   227

6 Developing Close Relationships   279

 # Preface

You will discover that the new eighth edition of *Becoming Aware: A Text/Workbook for Human Relations and Personal Adjustment* will assist you in the process of becoming more aware of yourself and others through the most interactive learning process you have found in any textbook.

Since ancient times, folk wisdom, and philosophy, have told us that the greatest amount of learning takes place when the student is an active participant in a critical thinking process. We have carefully designed our new edition to help students apply psychological principles, to develop the ability to think critically, to better understand themselves, and improve their relationships with others through an interactive process.

We're excited about the new eighth edition of *Becoming Aware: A Text/Workbook for Human Relations and Personal Adjustment,* and we hope you will be too.

This new edition, is a text/workbook that will give you, the student, the opportunity to become an active learner in the process of learning about Human Relations and Personal Adjustment. Learning should be a "hands on" experience. We have carefully designed this new edition to help students explore, experiment, test, and apply the theories and ideas within the world of Human Relations and Personal Adjustment. This text/workbook will allow the learner to think critically, work through problems logically, and make connections with the real world and thus become an active learner. The more you become actively involved within the subject matter of Human Relations and Personal Adjustment, the more you will learn. This new edition will give you and the students within the class many new opportunities to get actively involved in learning about yourself and others.

What is more important to us than our own personal adjustment and our relationships with other people? We have tried in every way possible to make this a personal book. This new edition is written for college students of all ages and for all others who wish to explore the world of self-awareness and discover new avenues for personal growth and adjustment and the development and continuance of personal relationships.

Life is a journey and this book will guide you in the process of self-discovery and self-understanding. Relating with others is an art to be learned and practiced. This new edition will provide you with many new ideas and new activities that will allow you to gain a better understanding of yourself and others.

The self is the foundation of all relationships. One of the goals of this book is to guide us in the active process of getting acquainted with others and ourselves. As we continue this process, we will gain a better understanding of our emotions and resolving interpersonal conflict.

Because human beings interact and relate to one another through interpersonal communication, another goal of this book is to help us learn how to communicate positively. We believe human beings have the capacity to change and

The art of teaching is the art of assisting discovery.

Mark Van Dorem

adapt, and to effectively cope with stressful circumstances in our lives. This new edition will facilitate the process of allowing you to gain control of your life with a better understanding of learning theory and personality theory.

As we learn to relate to others, we will discover the value of friends and intimate partners. As they say, "love is a many splendored thing," and we hope we will all discover through this book and throughout life what love is and the importance of a loving relationship. As we continue through our journey of life, we will discover what is important to us in life and the importance of life planning.

ABOUT THE BOOK

Our approach in *Becoming Aware* is humanistic and personal; that is, we stress the healthy and effective personality and the common struggles we all have in developing a greater awareness of self and establishing more meaningful relationships with others. We especially emphasize taking risks in accepting personal responsibility for achieving a greater awareness of self and deciding whether and how we want to change our life.

We wrote this book for students who were looking for a practical course: one that dealt with issues in everyday living and would also provide a catalyst for their own personal growth. Many previous students have found this book so valuable in their own lives, they have added this book to their own personal library and have read it many different times and have also bought their friends copies as gifts.

Becoming Aware has been adopted in courses dealing with the psychology of adjustment, human relations, applied psychology, personal growth and awareness, communication, etc. We have also been fortunate to have had numerous adoptions from technical and vocational programs, ranging from nursing to electronics. In addition, instructors in teacher-training courses, as well as management development courses, have found *Becoming Aware* a practical guide for their students.

It has been our experience that active, open, practical, and personal participation in these courses has led to greater self-awareness, enhanced relationships with others, and increased control over choosing direction for one's life.

We hope that this book will make your journey more fulfilled as you travel through life.

ORGANIZATION OF THIS NEW EDITION

We have tried in every way possible to make this a personal interactive book. Within each chapter, we encourage the reader to examine relevant ideas and issues pertaining to their understanding of self and their relationships with others.

This book is designed to be a personal workbook as well as a classroom text. Each chapter has a minimum of five activities for the reader to pause and reflect on the personal application of the concepts and theories presented in the chapter. Most of the activities will allow the reader to get personally and individually involved in completing the tasks, while a few of the activities will require each person to get involved in a small group process in order to complete the task. We believe that it is important for all students to participate in individual projects as well as group activities. In today's world of business we all have to learn to function as a team (within groups) and as individuals. The better we learn to do it now, the better we will survive in the world of business.

As we have all discovered, the more we get personally involved in any subject the more we learn. It is the intention of the authors and this book to get the reader more involved within the subject matter and thus learn more about themselves and their relationships than they ever have before.

Each chapter also contains a Learning Journal that will allow the reader to write and assess the personal value or meaning gained from the concepts presented. The activities, as well as the Learning Journals, have perforated pages, specifically designed for more convenient classroom participation of work outside of class that can be used for evaluation and assessment. Additionally, there are over 200 thought-provoking quotations, from well-known sources, and over 25 short poems designed to further promote insightful awareness.

The learning process is an important aspect of this book. We are attempting to get the reader more involved within the subject matter of the text through the use of chapter review questions, which will allow the student to relate directly to the important concepts and ideas within each chapter.

Chapter discussion questions are designed to help students to develop critical thinking skills and work through problems logically. The activities at the end of each chapter will allow each individual to get personally involved, not only individually, but also within groups which allow for interaction and teamwork

WHAT'S NEW IN THIS EDITION?

The eighth edition of *Becoming Aware* reflects significant updating. Each chapter has been extensively reviewed and updated to give the reader the most current research available in the search for self-exploration. In fact, over eighty new 1999 and 2000 references are included in this new edition.

We are fortunate to have received some excellent suggestions from reviewers for this edition and have incorporated many of their suggestions in this new edition.

MAJOR REVISIONS AND ADDITIONS

A major emphasis on active learning is emphasized throughout the text. We have revised some of the previous activities to make them more meaningful and to allow the reader to get more individually involved. Many of the activities may be completed individually and then personally assessed. Each student will also have the opportunity to participate within the group process in order to facilitate the understanding and application of the theories and concepts discussed in each chapter.

We have changed the titles of three chapters in order to make them more relevant to the student and to carefully blend the theories and concepts discussed in each chapter.

To emphasize the need for critical thinking skills, we have highlighted many of the important concepts and ideas through use of additional boxes and tables that are titled—"Think about this"—"Check this out"— and "How to." A variety of new pictures and illustrations have been added and each chapter is highlighted with many new quotations.

The sociocultural perspective within the field of human relations and personal adjustment is having a much greater impact on our lives, and we believe it needs to be emphasized more and more. We have expanded our emphasis on diversity, including additional information on ethnicity, along with culture and gender. You will note the additional emphasis on the headings and boxes titled "Focus on Diversity" and "Focus on Gender."

Updates to Each Chapter:

Chapter One
- New section on Living Together Lonely (LTL);
- New information on having a confidant;
- Additional tips on overcoming shyness;
- New information on physical attractiveness;
- New emphasis on Diversity and You;

Chapter Two
- A new information on mid-life transition and mid-life crisis;
- A new section on the Big Five Dimensions of Personality;
- A new box on The Big Five Factors;
- Greater emphasis on personality development;
- Additional information on individualism and collectivism;
- Additional emphasis on self-esteem;
- A new activity; Human Relations Position Paper;

Chapter Three
- Additional information on being an External or an Internal?
- New section on Taking Control of Your Life;
- New information on optimism and pessimism;
- A new section on Classical Conditioning;
- A new table on how classical conditioning applies to our own life;
- A new Student Story on classical conditioning;

Chapter Four
- New chapter title—Dealing With Emotions
- Expanded information on what are emotions and living with problem emotions
- New information on Emotional Intelligence;
- Updated section on aggression
- Additional tips on grief and bereavement

Chapter Five
- New information in *focus on diversity*
- Expanded section on listening
- Revised styles of responding
- New emphasis on empathy
- Revised gender and communication activity

Chapter Six
- New chapter title—Developing Close Relationships;
- Additional information on friends, dating and mating;
- A new section on Do You Flirt?

- New information on the theory of love, the cultural influence of love and different types of love;
- New statistics on marriage and divorce;
- New information on jealousy;
- Additional Quotes;

Chapter Seven
- Expanded section on what is conflict
- Additional information on the realities of conflict
- Updated research on personal problem solving

Chapter Eight
- Additional emphasis on what is stress and the causes of stress
- New research on type A personality
- Additional information on the power of self-talk
- New research on the effects of stress
- New tips for managing stress
- Revised the social readjustment scale activity

Chapter Nine
- New chapter title—Meaning and Values
- Revised introduction to the chapter
- Additional information on how values develop
- New research on the importance of meaning and purpose

Chapter Ten
- New information on learning to take risks
- Updated research on ways to be happy

Features and Learning Aids

Included in this eighth edition are several helpful features and pedagogical tools to enhance understanding and allow you to directly apply concepts that will further develop your awareness of yourself and your relationship with others.

To enhance the learning environment and to facilitate the process of getting the reader more involved within the subject matter, the authors have included a variety of learning aids within this new edition. They are:

- INSIDE COVER . . .
  FRONT . . . The Art of Getting Along
  BACK . . . The Rules for Being Human
- INTRODUCTION . . . briefly gives highlights of each chapter.
- CONSIDER THIS . . . each chapter begins with questions or a vignette to heighten awareness of the concepts to be discussed in the chapter.
- PHOTOS . . . new photos throughout text to add interest to the chapter content.
- QUOTES/POEMS . . . relate directly or indirectly to textual context.
- TABLES . . . interesting, non-threatening tables to clarify textual concepts.
- CHECK THIS OUT-OR-THINK ABOUT THIS . . . short vignettes or questions to make students pause and reflect upon issues addressed in the chapter.

- FOCUS ON DIVERSITY . . . issues dealing with diversity which are meant to heighten awareness of diversity issues.
- GENDER AND YOU . . . serves to highlight the differences that gender plays on our roles in life.
- TIPS FOR . . . STRATEGIES FOR . . . practical effective strategies are provided to aid students in accomplishing various goals.
- HOW TO . . . these boxes explain practical methods of dealing with everyday issues.
- END OF CHAPTER SUMMARY . . . bulleted listings of important chapter concepts.
- REVIEW QUESTIONS . . . designed to aid students to review, in their own words, important aspects of the chapter.
- DISCUSSION . . . questions designed to enhance class participation and encourage critical thinking about chapter concepts.
- KEY TERMS . . . located at the end of each chapter to provide a review of terms and concepts covered in the chapter.
- GLOSSARY . . . alphabetical listings of important words and phrases for use as a quick reference.
- INDEX . . . provides easy access to important concepts and terms in the text.
- REFERENCE SECTION . . . listed by chapter at the end of the text.
- LEARNING JOURNAL . . . personalized evaluation of knowledge gained from each chapter.
- APPLICATIONS . . . five or more activities at the end of each chapter allows many different opportunities to become involved in the subject matter individually and within groups.
- INSTRUCTOR'S MANUAL . . . has been updated with revised materials and new test questions.

# Acknowledgments

We are grateful for the insightful suggestions and innovative ideas received from David Stanton of Tarrant County College, Pam Gasper of Portland Community College, Tobin Quereau of Austin Community College, Rich Reiner of Rogue Community College, and Carol Shapiro of South West State University.

We are also indebted for those who reviewed the earlier editions and made suggestions that have been included in this revision: Dr. Mary Jane Dickson, Eddie Sandoval, and Mary Ann Lee, Tarrant County College; George Vaternick, Portland Community College; Jo Carolyn Miller, in private practice in Dallas, Texas; Minister and former Human Relations Professor, J. D. Phillips; and Jeannene Cox Ward, a Licensed Professional Counselor.

Also, we would like to thank our families, Danny, David, Judy, Chad, and Brett, who endured the irritating and constant sounds of keyboards and printers, patiently tolerated the late-night hours of work and research, and who always gave us their moral support and encouragement.

Finally, we would like to acknowledge those individuals and publishers who kindly gave us their permission to reprint their materials. In several instances, we regret that even after diligent searching, we have not been able to properly credit material being used. Some of our material has been used for many years in classes and workshops with the result that proper identification has been lost, or we no longer are able to provide source information as we would like. Because the material has proved to be of great value, we have included it in our book. We trust that eventually we will be able to credit these authors with proper recognition for their work.

Velma Walker

Lynn Brokaw

 # Introduction

If you cannot become your best, you cannot be happy,
If you cannot risk, you cannot grow,
If you cannot grow, you cannot become your best,
If you cannot become your best, you cannot be happy,
If you cannot be happy, what else matters?

David Viscott, M.D.
(from Risking, 1988)

Thank you for joining us as we explore avenues to new and greater beginnings in our lives. The title, *Becoming Aware: A Text/Workbook for Human Relations and Personal Adjustment,* is descriptive. The basic element in this class is you and your relationship with others. Therefore, it is important that we begin this book with you as the subject.

You are probably varied and complex. You have needs and wants, feelings and fears, problems and anxieties, goals and ambitions, prejudices and priorities, and accomplishments and potentials.

You are also constantly adapting to changes. Life, then, requires a continuous adjustment. Adjustment is perhaps synonymous with coping and adapting to change, which are significant parts of the process of growth and development. Therefore, adjustment might be referred to as the process of achieving a satisfactory relationship between oneself and one's environment.

You are also a unique individual, but at the same time, you share a common struggle of wanting to be a healthy, happy, and more fully functioning individual. What does this mean? What kind of person are you trying to become?

Psychologists Abraham Maslow and Carl Rogers have devoted much of their lives researching and describing a healthy, happy, and more fully functioning individual. Carl Rogers calls this person "the fully functioning person" whereas Maslow calls this person "the self-actualizing person" and the "fully-human person." Do these individuals have common characteristics? Let us see.

A MODEL FOR PERSONAL GROWTH

Throughout this book, there will be frequent references to "growth as a person," and much will be said about the necessity of self-awareness and interpersonal encounter as a means to this growth. We will also be emphasizing that each individual has to grow into his or her own person and not become "like" anyone else. While it is difficult to describe what "growth as a person" really means, we have tried to focus the contents of this book around the following common characteristics of healthy, happy, and more fully functioning individuals: (1) an ability to accept oneself and others, (2) an efficient perception of reality, (3) close, caring interpersonal relationships, (4) autonomy and independence, (5) a strong ethical sense, and (6) willingness to continue to grow as a person. We will now explain these characteristics more fully.

1. **An Ability to Accept Oneself and Others**

   Happy, healthy individuals like themselves—they have a positive self-concept. Feeling good about themselves, they can also accept others, even when they are different. Healthy individuals tend to view themselves as people who are acceptable and capable of making a valuable contribution to the world in which they live.

2. **An Efficient Perception of Reality**

   Having a good self-concept, happy and healthy individuals do not have to hide behind a mask through which they filter reality. They see the world as it really is rather than the way "it ought to be," and they see people as they really are, rather than the way "they ought to be."

3. **Close, Caring Interpersonal Relationships**

   Happy and healthy individuals are not afraid to be open and let others see how they feel. Because they feel good about themselves they can afford to have deep human relationships with others. These strong ties however, are usually to only a few people, for a deep involvement with even one person takes considerable time.

4. **Autonomy and independence**

   They trust themselves and rely on their own insights about what is right, what is wrong, and about what should be done in a given situation. Thus, happy and healthy individuals are independent in thought and action, relying more on their own standards of behavior and values rather than overemphasizing what others expect of them.

5. **A Strong Ethical Sense**

   They are as much concerned with the rights of others as they are with their own rights. They believe in honesty for all, kindness for all, and respect for all, regardless of nationality, race, religion, political beliefs, or whether relative, friend, or enemy.

6. **Willingness to Continue to Grow as a Person**

   Happy and healthy people tend to understand that being alive means allowing oneself to grow and to change, rather than reaching some end point and standing there. They tend to know where they are going, and consequently, have developed a sense of meaning or mission in their life. Thus, they enjoy and appreciate the fullness of life.

It is important to emphasize that the characteristics above represent a guide in our own search for happiness and fulfillment. It is also important to note that personal growth and development is a life-long process. We don't suddenly arrive at a certain point and then relax and quit. Rather, we are on a never-ending journey, with each day offering new experiences, contacts with new people, and new opportunities for personal enrichment.

Therefore, personal growth, as well as meaningful relationships, does not just happen. We must be aware of the dynamics involved in acquiring the awareness and skills necessary to develop and expand our lives. We must be willing to take some risks to incorporate what we have learned into our own unique personalities. It is to this end that we, the authors, commit the contents of this book.

ORGANIZATION OF BECOMING AWARE

Using the above characteristics of healthy, happy, and more fully functioning individuals as a model for this book, we have attempted to include concepts which we hope will assist you in becoming the person you want to be. We have chosen to explain a brief overview of the book by asking you some thought-provoking questions.

Chapter 1: Am I an Open or Closed Person?

In order for growth to take place and for effective relationships to be established, you must be willing to share your thoughts, feelings, and values with others. You must be open with what you love, hate, feel, desire, and what you are committed to. If you are feeling lonely in spite of being surrounded by people, it may be possible that you are keeping your real self hidden from others. Are you ready to take some risks and explore some avenues for learning to be more open and honest about yourself?

If you have the desire to form special, close relationships with others, the prerequisite is knowing, accepting, and appreciating yourself.

Chapter 2: Who Am I?

Obviously, all growth begins with self-acceptance. The more we approve and accept ourselves, the less concerned we are whether others will approve and accept us. We are then able to be ourselves with confidence. In order to connect with others, we must have a clear sense of who we are, what we want, our strengths and weaknesses, likes and dislikes, our values and priorities in life. A strong identity is part of the foundation of intimate relationships. Are you ready to take the risks necessary to discover Who Am I?

After you have developed a personal identity and a deeper appreciation for yourself, you are then more equipped to exercise control over your life.

Chapter 3: Am I in Control of My Life?

Fortunately, life is filled with both the freedom and the opportunity to make choices. Some people feel that they are in control of their own destinies. They believe that what happens to them and what they achieve in life are due to their own abilities, attitudes, and actions. These people are happier, more fully functioning people. Some people, however, see their lives as being beyond their control. They believe that what happens to them is due to fate, luck, or even other people. Consequently, such people never really actualize their potential. Are you ready to take the risk in learning to accept the responsibility for shaping your own destiny?

Not only do happier and healthier people have control over their behavior and what they become, they also have control over what they "do with their emotions."

Chapter 4: How Do I Express My Emotions?

As we go through adulthood, we have the opportunity to experiment with a full range of behaviors and a full range of emotions. Emotional health includes experiencing the full spectrum of human feelings from love and excitement to anger and despair. The ability to express feelings rather than squelching them is also important. Stored-up hurt, fear, or anger may result in emotional numbness, shutting off positive as well as negative feelings. Are you ready to take some risks in learning how to achieve a balance between emotional expression and control?

The full and free experience and expression of all our feelings is necessary for personal peace and meaningful relationships. Happy, healthy people realize the tremendous benefits of being able to communicate what they are feeling.

Chapter 5: How Well Do I Communicate?

A significant part of the entire growth process is learning effective communication skills. In fact, communication is extremely important in almost every aspect of our lives. We need to become aware of the conditions that are interfering with the communication process and make an attempt to modify our behavior in such a way that real meaning and understanding are communicated. This can lead to establishing and maintaining more satisfying relationships with others, which is the basic goal of communication. Are you ready to take the risk of learning how to communicate more effectively?

It is through communication that we begin the process of becoming acquainted with others. It is also through communication that special relationships are formed.

Chapter 6: What Is the Role of Love in My Life?

As we begin to openly and honestly share ourselves with others, we find that others will begin to share themselves with us. This will be the beginning of beautiful friendships and intimate relationships. There is an inescapable law built into human nature that reads: We are never less than individuals but we are never merely individuals. No man is an island. Fully functioning people have learned to move the focus of their attention and concern from themselves to others. They care deeply about others. Are you ready to take the risks of learning how to "move out of yourself" into genuine love relationships?

As we develop special relationships and learn to deal with our emotions, we will inevitably experience some interpersonal conflicts.

Chapter 7: How Can I Solve My People Problems?

There is really no end to the numbers and kinds of disagreements possible since people are different, think differently, and have different needs and wants that sometimes do not match. Likewise, there are a wide range of feelings and emotions that accompany conflict. How you resolve your interpersonal conflicts is the single most important factor in determining whether your relationships will be healthy or unhealthy, mutually satisfying or unsatisfying, friendly or unfriendly, deep or shallow, intimate or cold. Are you ready to take some risks in learning how to approach your interpersonal conflicts differently—do you realize that there does not have to be a winner and a loser?

Sometimes interpersonal conflicts, as well as some of the adjustments we have to make in life, become difficult situations for us to deal with.

Chapter 8: How Am I Coping with the Stress in My Life?

It is a fact of life that everyone experiences stress at one time or another. There are potentially negative and positive effects that can result from stress. Therefore, it is extremely important, not only that we recognize stress, but that we learn how to handle it, live with it, and make it work for us. Frequently, our stress is created by our own thoughts and feelings. You will recall from our earlier discussion that one of the characteristics of fully functioning people is that they accept reality for what it is rather than what it "ought to be." Are you ready to take some risks in learning to identify your stressors, as well as finding the level of stress at which you are most comfortable?

When you have learned how to manage the stress in your life, you are then free to prioritize your values and develop a lifestyle with meaning.

Chapter 9: What Is Important to Me?

A well-defined value system is basic to personal motivation, self-determination, and a lifestyle with meaning. Fully alive people are committed to a cause in which they can believe and to which they can be dedicated. Their value system is the control point of their lives, helping them to choose their direction in life. When we can control the direction of our lives, rather than allowing them to be controlled by forces and values outside ourselves, a feeling of self-affirmation is created. Are you ready to risk clarifying your values, and in return, find meaning and a sense of mission to which you can direct your life?

You are now ready to deal with where you want to go with your life.

Chapter 10: Where Do I Want to Go with My Life?

As we experience growth and depth in our personal life and in our relationships, we begin to plan where we want to go with our life. Effective life planning begins with an answer to these questions: What are my needs? What are my wants? What are my priorities? Once we have arrived at the answer, a well-defined, implemented course of action is essential—keeping in mind that life is a process and we must remain open to change as we move through our daily experiences. Are you ready to risk getting in touch with your needs and wants and begin exploring ways in which you can meet them?

A LAST THOUGHT

If you are going to become a happier, healthier, and more fully functioning individual, you'll have to take risks. There is simply no way you can grow without taking chances. Because your personal growth and development are important to us, we have created personalized activities in each chapter for the sole purpose of encouraging you to begin taking risks. As you read each chapter, we encourage you to think about how the different concepts presented relate to you in your search to become a healthier, happier, and more fully functioning individual. Then we ask you to reflect on what you have learned in your personal *Learning Journal.* Our desire is that you will risk and grow in your understanding of self and how you relate with others.

We hope to motivate you with these words from Leo Buscaglia (1982), taken from several pages of his writings in *Living, Loving, & Learning*.

Risk—The Key to Change

To laugh is to risk appearing the fool.
To weep is to risk appearing sentimental.
To reach out for another is to risk involvement.
To expose feelings is to risk exposing your true self.
To place your ideas, your dreams, before a crowd is to risk their loss.
To love is to risk not being loved in return.
To live is to risk dying.
To hope is to risk failure.
But risks must be taken, because the greatest hazard in life is to risk nothing.
The person who risks nothing, does nothing, has nothing, and is nothing.
They may avoid suffering and sorrow, but they cannot learn, feel, change, grow,
    love, live.
Chained by their attitudes, they are a slave;
They have forfeited their freedom.
Only a person who risks is free.

It is now time to begin your journey to a happier, healthier, and more fully functioning individual. Are you ready to become free to be the person you want to be?

About the Authors

Dr. Velma Walker is a professor of psychology at Tarrant County College, Northeast Campus in Hurst, Texas. Although she has specialized in human relations courses for over 29 years at the college level, she has also been a counselor and coordinator of student job placement and career information. She has a bachelor's degree in business administration/education; a master's degree in counseling and psychology, and a doctor of education degree, with emphasis in counseling, psychology, and administration. Dr. Walker is also a certified mediator for conflict resolution.

Dr. Walker owns her own consulting company and has given human relations training seminars in the areas of communication, motivation, stress management, time management, and personality lifestyles for educators and business and professional groups for over 25 years. She has also served as a teacher consultant for the Educational Division of the Zig Ziglar Corporation. Dr. Walker is a Multiple Year Honoree in *Who's Who Among America's Teachers* and is included in the 2000 edition.

Lynn Brokaw is a professor of psychology at Portland Community College, specializing in human relations courses. He has been teaching at the university and community college level for over 30 years. He received a bachelor's degree in social sciences/education, a master's degree in counseling and psychology, and an education specialist degree (EDS) in counseling and psychology from the University of Northern Colorado. He has conducted many seminars and workshops for educators and corporations in psychology and human relations. He has received recognition for his teaching ability.

He not only teaches, he also "practices the principles that are being taught." He has experience in private counseling and in college administration. He is president of a corporation and is active in the real estate industry.

CHAPTER 1

Getting Acquainted with Ourselves and Others

Me–A Question

Am I afraid to be me?
Why?
Why am I afraid to be the only thing I can be?
Am I afraid that if I am me, if I find out who me is
I will be disappointed?
Am I afraid that the person I think is me is someone else?
Why?
Why don't I know who the real me is?
Why?
Why have I tried to fool so many people that
I have fooled myself?
Who?
Who is me?
I am me.
How?
How will I find me? By looking.
When?
When will I find me? Now.
Why?
Why must I find me? To be free.

Dorothy Dickson

(Written in 1968, at the age of nine. Dorothy completed her PhD. in Clinical Psychology in 1992).
Used with permission of Dorothy Dickson Rishel, Gulfport, MS.

occur. Others may perceive you based on their own interpretation rather than on information you give them.

*If I expose my naked-
ness as a person to you,
do not make me feel
shamed.*

John Powell

- **Knowing Yourself.** As you disclose information about yourself, you can get deeper insight and understanding about the kind of person you are. You also give others the opportunity to give you feedback.
- **Getting Acquainted.** Talking about yourself and letting other people talk about themselves gives each of you the opportunity to understand and know the other as an individual. Each is given the opportunity to understand and trust the other.
- **Developing Intimacy.** As you begin to share and receive, a deeper feeling of trust and understanding will evolve and a mutual feeling of closeness will develop.

Sidney Jourard (1971) has investigated the process of self-disclosure in detail. In *The Transparent Self,* he writes:

> You cannot collaborate with another person towards some common end unless you know him. How can you know him, and he you, unless you have engaged in enough mutual disclosure of self to be able to anticipate how he will react and what part he will play? Self-disclosure, my communication of my private world to you, in language, which you clearly understand is truly an important bit of behavior for us to learn something about. You can know me truly only if I let you, only if I want you to know me. Your misunderstanding of me is only partly your fault. If I want you to know me, I shall find means of com-

FOCUS ON DIVERSITY

Respect Diversity in Relationships

Just as individuals differ, so do relationships. There is tremendous variety in what people find comfortable, affirming, and satisfying in interpersonal interaction. It is counterproductive to try to force all people and relationships to fit into a single mode. For example, you might have one friend who enjoys a lot of verbal disclosure and another who prefers less. There is no reason to try to persuade the first friend to disclose less or the second one to be more revealing. Similarly, you may be comfortable with greater closeness in some of your relationships and more autonomy in others. The differences between people create a rich diversity of relationships we can experience.

People from various cultures, including ones within the United States, have learned different communication styles. What Westerners consider openness and healthy self-disclosure may feel offensively intrusive to people from some Asian societies. The dramatic, assertive speaking style of many African Americans can be misinterpreted as abrasive within a Western Caucasian perspective. The best way to understand what another's behavior means is to ask. This conveys the relational message that they matter to you, and it allows you to gain insight into the interesting diversity among us.

municating myself to you. If you want me to reveal myself, just demonstrate your goodwill—your will to employ your power for my good and not for my destruction.

Before we can engage in self-disclosure, there must be an atmosphere of goodwill and trust. An individual is not likely to engage in much self-disclosure if the situation involves too much personal threat, or even a threat to anyone with whom he or she is closely associated. Jourard feels that it sometimes takes a form of self-disclosure to stimulate goodwill in other people. For example, a little self-disclosure establishes your goodwill which encourages the other person to some self-disclosure, thus establishing his or her goodwill, which reassures you about further self-disclosure, and so on.

Do You Need To Disclose? *Self-disclosure* usually involves the sharing of private information, and it is generally of such a nature that it is not something you would normally disclose to everyone who might inquire about it. Therefore, you are not expected to bare the innermost secrets of your soul to casual acquaintances—you can save that information for the significant others in your life. However, if you are to communicate effectively with others, some degree of self-disclosure is required.

> No one can develop freely in this world and find a full life without feeling understood by at least one person.
>
> Paul Tournier

WOMEN TALK MORE THAN MEN

If you are a female, please do not be offended, this is a positive statement. According to research, it is to a woman's benefit that she is more open and willing to disclose than man. (Cline, 1986) Women tend to have more friends and closer relationships than men. These friendships tend to provide her with more social support.

Within families, parents tend to disclose more to their daughters than to their sons (Daluiso, 1972). Since we learn through modeling, females would be more likely to be open and share their feelings with others. Males are socialized not to disclose and so build up more tension and anxiety in their daily lives and thus would be more likely to experience stress related problems—ulcers, heart attacks, early death, etc. Women tend to have fewer stress related problems.

Males tend to disclose more to strangers than females do, and are more willing to disclose superficial things about themselves, such as their work, accomplishments, attitudes, and opinions. Males are also less intimate and less personal than females. Males are expected not to disclose; it's not "manly." Men are socialized to compete, and sharing private information can seem to be incompatible with winning (Lewis, 1978). One finding is that both men and women generally prefer self-disclosure with members of the opposite sex (Rosenfeld 1981). Women say to the men, "let's talk." Men communicate to women by "telling" them what to do and giving directions. As many of you have discovered, this creates communication problems within many male-female relationships.

Men need to learn to talk more, it will improve their relationships with members of both sexes.

Gender & You

What Kind of Things Can You Reveal to Another Person? A few examples might be:

- Likes and dislikes
- Fears and anxieties
- Feelings and reactions about something another person has said or done
- Attitudes and opinions
- Tastes and interests
- Ideas about money
- Work perceptions
- Personality choices
- Feelings and reactions about events that have just taken place
- Perceptions of self and others

There are some disadvantages to self-disclosure as well, particularly if there is too much of it (Wortman, et al. 1976). Talking too much about ourselves early in a relationship may not facilitate the development of friendship. People might attribute your high self-disclosure as an indication that you are too immature, insecure, or phony, or even that you tell everyone such things. Other people like to think that they are special to you.

What Is the Greatest Risk of Self-Disclosure? *Self-disclosure involves taking risks. The greatest risk is one of rejection—not being liked or accepted.* This may cause us to hide behind a mask—a *facade*—and try to be something we know we are not. In this state, effective communication cannot occur and the growth and maintenance of those deep, special, and meaningful relationships with friends and spouses cannot occur. Risk nothing, gain nothing. You have a choice—to withdraw from honest encounters, to hide your feelings, to falsify your intentions—or to be transparent, open, and real through self-disclosure.

> What does the baby chicken know which we overlook? The shell around us won't crack at its own accord.
>
> Anonymous

What Are the Advantages of Self-Disclosure? Self-disclosure has the potential to improve and expand interpersonal relationships, but it serves other functions as well. One advantage is that **Self-disclosure improves relationships.** We prefer to be with people who are willing to disclose to us and we are more willing to be open with them. Self-disclosure is a reciprocal process. Disclosure leads to trust and trust leads to more disclosure and thus, the relationship will grow and develop into a mature and long lasting, loving interaction. There is a strong positive correlation between self-disclosure and marital satisfaction (Miller and Lefcourt, 1982). Research has shown that the more a couple is willing to disclose about themselves, the greater the marital satisfaction and the greater the chance the marriage will last over a longer period of time.

Self-Disclosure Promotes Mental Health. The second advantage is that *self-disclosure promotes **mental health.*** Withholding important information can create stress and thus lead to less-effective functioning and even possible physical problems (Jourard, 1971). We all need a release and for many of us "talking-out" our feelings, problems, and thoughts will relieve us of the stresses and anxieties that are interfering with our everyday functioning. *This release of emotional tension through talking is known as a catharsis.* As many of you have discovered, you feel relieved after sharing your problems with another person. This is the reason counseling and therapy are so effective for many individuals.

Self-Validation. Another advantage of self-disclosure is that periodically we need *self-validation.* If we disclose information such as "I think I may have made a mistake . . ."—with the hopes of obtaining the listeners agreement, you are seeking validation on your behavior—confirmation of a belief you hold about yourself. On a deeper level, this sort of self-validating disclosure seeks confirmation of important parts of your self-concept (Adler & Towne, 1999).

Social Control. Another possible advantage of self-disclosure is *social control.* Revealing personal information may increase your control over other people and sometimes over the situation in which you and the other person find yourself. For example, you tell your partner that someone else is showing interest in you, your partner may begin to show more interest in you. You tell your boss that another firm has offered you a job, you probably will have an increased chance of getting a raise and improved working conditions. Could this type of disclosure also lead to a negative reaction? What else could happen?

Impression Management. Many people reveal personal information in order to project a specific image. This is a form of *impression management.* You may tell your prospective employer that on your last job that you were selected as "employee of the year," or that you are a member of the "Million Dollar Club," in order to get others to have a positive impression of you. This is a way we attempt to market ourselves.

As we have discussed, there are many reasons for self-disclosure and each reason varies from situation to situation depending on several factors. The results may be positive or negative, so you need to analyze each situation before you begin the process.

We all need to discover new ways to communicate our feelings and thoughts to others. One way to illustrate how self-disclosure operates in communication is to look at Figure 1.1 (The Johari Window).

THE JOHARI WINDOW

The Johari Window (1969), developed by and named after psychologists Joseph Luft and Harry Ingram, can be looked upon as a communication window through which you become more aware of yourself and your potential as a communicator, as you give and receive information about yourself and others. In order for a relationship to develop into a quality relationship, there needs to be trust and mutual sharing of information and feelings, also known as *openness.* An *open* communicator is one who is willing to seek feedback from others and to offer information and personal feelings to others. Open communication involves both giving and receiving. According to the Window, a person's communication behavior can be viewed by looking at the size of each of the four windowpanes—Open, Hidden, Blind, and Unknown.

Figure 1.1 is the "Total You," everything there is to know about you. Figure 1.2 is divided into two squares, the left half is everything that you are aware of regarding yourself (Known to Self). The right half is your unconscience—everything about you that you are not aware of (Not Known to Self). Figure 1.3 is divided into a top half and a bottom half. The top half is everything that others are aware of about you (Known to Others). The bottom half is the part of you that others are not aware of about you (Not Known to Others). As you look at Figures

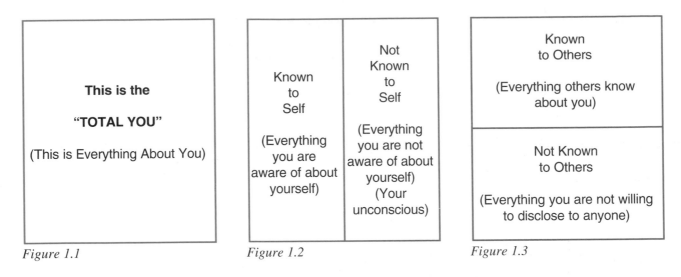

Figure 1.1

Figure 1.2

Figure 1.3

1.2 and 1.3 you will notice that as you now put the whole window together you will observe that the window is divided into four sections or windowpanes as shown in Figure 1.4. These four quadrants, illustrated in Figure 1.4, represent the whole person in relation to others.

The *Open Self (I know, others know) represents information, feelings, and opinions that you know about yourself and that others know about you.* This area also includes feelings that others have about you, perhaps a mutual friend of yours and another person, of which you are aware. Communication in this open area is free and open.

The *Blind Self (Others know, I don't know) represents information about you of which you are unaware but is easily apparent to others.* An example would be a mannerism in speech or gesture of which you are unaware but that is quite obvious to others, such as constantly saying, "you know" or constantly "playing with your keys." Communication in this area is not free and open.

The *Hidden Self (I know, others don't know) represents information and personal feelings that you keep hidden from others.* Consequently, communication in this area is restricted. The only way others can learn of this information is if you decide to participate in self-disclosure. This area is quite large with a new acquaintance because we do not feel safe in revealing our true selves and feelings.

The *Unknown Self (I don't know, others don't know) represents information about you that is unknown to self or others.* For example, you may have an aptitude or skill of which you and others are completely unaware. Communication in this area is impossible, since it is totally unknown. Information in this area may take years to be known. However, as you try to gain insight into your *real, true* self, you may be able to add to this area.

Can the Size of the Windowpane Change? The size of each windowpane varies depending on your communication behavior and the quality of your relationship. When you first meet someone, the area of common knowledge is minimal. Likewise, your communication with that individual would be represented by a small open windowpane and a large unknown area. Also, if you find it difficult to share your ideas and feelings with others, as well as to receive feedback from others, you would tend to have a small open windowpane, as illustrated in Figure 1.5.

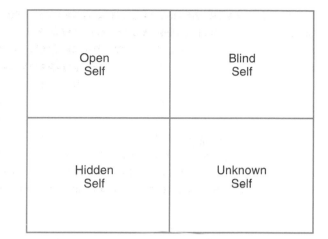

Figure 1.4

Figure 1.5

Figure 1.6

Figure 1.7

Figure 1.8

(Adapted from Joseph Luft, OF HUMAN INTERACTION, by permission of Mayfield Publishing Co., Copyright 1969 by the National Press.)

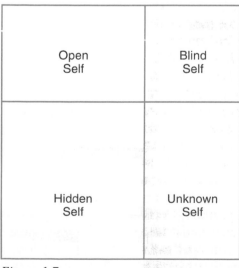

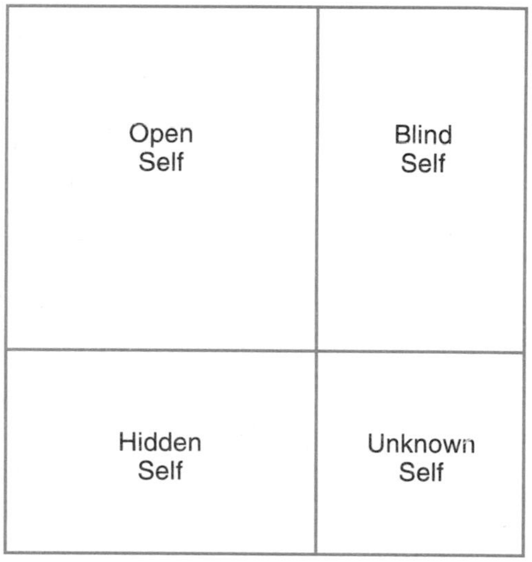

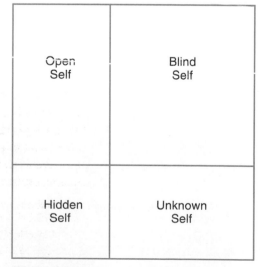

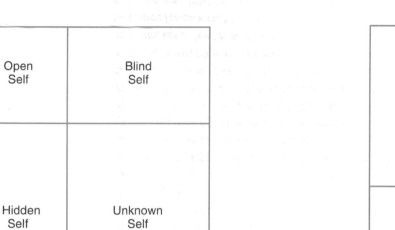

As a relationship grows and the trust level increases, you will be more likely to share more information and feelings. Consequently, others will respond by giving you more feedback. Therefore, your communication behavior should be represented by a much larger open windowpane and a smaller unknown pane. See Figure 1.6.

If you are receptive to feedback but are basically unwilling to share information and feelings with others, your communication behavior will be represented by a fairly large hidden pane and a smaller open pane, as illustrated in Figure 1.7.

On the other hand, you may find it very difficult to receive criticism or suggestions from others, but it may be easy for you to share information and feelings with others. Consequently, your communication behavior would be represented with a large blind pane, as illustrated in Figure 1.8.

As we can see, interpersonal communication of any significance is virtually impossible if the individuals involved have little or no open windowpane. Ideally, we strive to make the open window the largest area, which would indicate the extent to which two or more persons can give and take, work together, and enjoy experiences together. By improving the use of feedback in our communication with others, we begin to expand our open windowpane.

Some people may get along fine with others without insight or awareness. Such lack of awareness, however, inhibits our communication effectiveness and thus impedes our personal growth.

Now that we understand the importance of self-disclosure in the development of a relationship, we need to understand why relationships are so important. We are all social beings and seek social relationships. We all have a need for other people. Relationships satisfy needs. We are motivated not only to seek the company of others, but to form close and lasting relationships. Many people have difficulty forming relationships and do not seem to have any friends. What happens to these people?

LONELINESS

Have you ever felt lonely? What causes loneliness? Answer the following questions before you continue to read this section.

The lack of relationships creates *loneliness. Loneliness occurs when a person has fewer interpersonal relationships than desired or when the relationships are not as satisfying as desired.* Loneliness is one of the most serious problems in our society today. Harry Stack Sullivan (1953) considered loneliness to be the worst emotional experience imaginable. He stated that the deepest problems for people are *loneliness, isolation,* and *difficulty with self-esteem.* Research has shown that loneliness leads to depression and depression can cause psychological and physiological problems.

In national surveys, roughly one American in four says he or she has felt very lonely or remote from other people in the past two weeks (Perlman & Peplau 1998). Most of you have observed many of your friends and rela-

Being lonely is not the same as being alone.

☞ CHECK THIS OUT . . .
What Do You Know About Loneliness?

True or False?

_____Loneliness is more predominant during adolescence.

_____Loneliness varies with the time of day and day of the week.

_____Loneliness may be a sign of personal problems.

_____Loneliness may be the cause of depression, suicide, and other mental disorders.

_____The elderly are less lonely than most groups of individuals.

_____Loneliness is not the same as aloneness.

_____Most people assume other people have more friends than they do.

All of the above questions will be answered in the following discussion. Based on research and literature all of the above statements are mostly true.

─── ☜

lives going through some form of transition in their life—the breaking-up of a long term relationship or marriage, death of a loved one, etc., that has caused them to be in a state of need. Most of us at one time or another in our lives have also experienced this feeling, that something is lacking in our life and there does not seem to be anything to live for. What is this feeling? It is the feeling of loneliness. *Loneliness is a feeling of longing and emptiness that is caused by the lack of emotional attachment and/or social ties.*

Can People Be Lonely In the Presence of Others? The answer is a resounding **yes**, and the feeling can be dreadful. Mara commented, "You can be in the center of a crowd and be dreadfully lonely." Some people can feel lonely even when surrounded by others. Debbi, whose husband had left her, said, "I have periods of loneliness now, but it's nothing compared to how lonely I felt when my husband was sitting in the same room with me. In fact, living together loneliness (LTL), *the results of a perceived discrepancy between expected and achieved contact has been identified* (Kiley, 1989). More than one-fourth of married people, the majority of them females, suffer from LTL.

Being lonely is not the same as being alone. Some people prefer solitude and are content with fewer social interactions. Many of us have a need to be alone at times in order to maintain our mental health. Loneliness is a highly subjective and personal feeling.

Are the Elderly More Lonely than Other Groups of People? Loneliness is most prevalent among teenagers, unmarried young adults, the divorced, and the widowed. Recent research speculates that the modern emphasis on self-fulfillment and the instability of relationships and commitment to others are "loneliness-provoking factors."

Loneliness makes a person vulnerable to many different situations. This may include the use of drugs, alcohol, suicide, sexual promiscuity, mental illness, and negative relationships. Very lonely people, especially women in the 18–20 age

> Happiness may be had only by helping others to find it.
>
> Napolean Hill

group are more at risk of becoming alcoholics than the general population (Page & Cole, 1991). People who are extremely lonely have higher blood pressure than do their nonlonely peers, less effective immune systems, more sleep and eating disturbances, headaches, nausea and other health problems (Goldstein, Edelberg, Meier, and Davis, 1991). Maintaining that love and intimacy are instrumental in protection from disease and in the maintenance of wellness, a medical doctor believes that emotional support, the opposite of loneliness, is essential (Ornish, 1998).

Loneliness is something that will affect most of us at one time or another in our life. What can we do to help ourselves and others to prevent this feeling of loneliness from taking over our lives? Robert Weiss (1974) has found that satisfying *two relationship needs* will help us overcome feelings of loneliness. These are: 1) *the need for emotional attachments and; 2) the need for social ties.* If one or both of these needs are not satisfied, loneliness will exist. What are these needs and why do we really need relationships?

> Relationships with others lie at the very core of human existence.
>
> Ellen Berscheid and Lettia Peplau

WHAT SHOULD A RELATIONSHIP PROVIDE?

Why do our society and many other cultures put so much emphasis on marriage? Why are there clubs for single people, escort services, single's bars, dating services, and more recently, people advertising for partners in local newspapers, and using 1-900 telephone services to meet new people? Why—because people are lonely. We have a strong need for relationships. The following needs must be satisfied in order to have a fulfilling life and overcome feelings of loneliness.

Emotional Attachments. *We all need to know that no matter what the situation is or whatever we do, good or bad (for better or worse, in sickness or in health), that there will be someone around to take care of us or help us out.* As long as we know this, we feel comfortable and secure. A child who knows that mother or father is available whenever he or she needs one of them will feel secure enough to explore the world around them. They will be willing to take some chances and risks in life. A child who is insecure and not sure if the parents will be available when needed, will be clinging and unsure of other people. How would you feel if you were told by your parents, "If you ever get in trouble with the law," or "If I ever hear about you taking drugs," or "If you ever get someone pregnant or get pregnant, don't step a foot back in this house?" Most people who have been told this when they were young feel very insecure and lonely since they are not sure anyone will be there in a time of need.

Think about this...

Feeling Lonely

Excluded—to feel excluded from a group you would like to belong to

Unloved—to feel unloved or uncared about by those around you

Constricted—to feel constricted and unable to share your private feelings with anyone

Alienated—to feel alienated or different from those around you

Will You Be My Friend?

Will you be my friend?
There are so many reasons why you never should:
I'm sometimes sullen, often shy, acutely sensitive,
My fear erupts as anger, I find it hard to give,
I talk about myself when I'm afraid

And often spend a day without anything to say.
But I will make you laugh
And love you quite a bit
And hold you when you're sad
I cry a little almost every day
Because I'm more caring than the strangers ever know,
And if at times, I show my tender side
(The soft and warmer part I hide)
I wonder, will you be my friend?
A friend
Who far beyond the feebleness of any vow or tie
Will touch the secret place where I am really I,
To know the pain of lips that plead and eyes that weep,
Who will not run away when you find me in the street
Alone and Lying mangled by my quota of defeats
But will stop and stay—to tell me of another day
When I was beautiful.

Will you be my friend?
There are so many reasons why you never should:
Often I'm too serious, seldom predictably the same,
Sometimes cold and distant, probably I'll always change.
I bluster and brag, seek attention like a child,
I brood and pout, my anger can be wild,
But I will make you laugh
And love you quite a bit
And be near when you're afraid.
I shake a little almost every day
Because I'm more frightened than the strangers ever know
And if at times I show my trembling side
(The anxious, fearful part I hide)
I wonder,
Will you be my friend?
A friend
Who when I fear your closeness, feels me push away
And stubbornly will stay to share what's left on such a day,
Who, when no one knows my name or calls me on the phone,
When there's no concern for me—what I have or haven't done—
And those I've helped and counted on have, oh so deftly, run,
Who when there's nothing left but me, stripped of charm and subtlery,
Will nonetheless remain.

Will you be my friend?
For no reason that I know
Except I want you so.

Where Do We Get Emotional Attachments? Most people will receive their *emotional attachments* from their parents, especially during their early years of development. And if you think about it, many individuals continue to rely on their parents for this support for most of their lives. This is why you will hear stories about married couples who, when they are having marital problems, either the husband or wife will go back to their parents' home, because parents still provide that individual with the feeling of security. As we tend to mature and start to "cut the apron strings," becoming more independent, we begin to find this emotional support from others—our best friend, boyfriend, girlfriend, spouse, pastor, etc. For some people, their dog or cat will provide them with this feeling of security. Having a **confidant**, *a significantly close personal friend with whom one can safely share one's deepest concerns and joys*, is related to higher levels of well-being, health, satisfaction, and lowered distress (Ornish, 1998). One of the earlier studies on confidants found that older people who had a confidant lived longer than those who didn't.

Why do we need friends?

Inanimate objects can also be a source of security. Items such as teddy bears, dolls, or imaginary companions are examples. Other sources could be certain belief systems, religious beliefs, or a philosophy of life, and even confidence within one's self may satisfy the need for *emotional attachments* for some people. A young child's blanket or teddy bear is a source of security for some. As you know, if you take the blanket or bear away from some children even for a short time just to be washed, the child will go into a rage and become very insecure and lonely.

What happens to a person who has been relying solely on their spouse for the satisfaction of this need, especially when the spouse announces that the relationship is over? This person will become insecure, lonely, and vulnerable. A newly divorced or separated individual who has lost his or her emotional support is very open and vulnerable to another person or belief system that tends to show support for the individual. This is why many individuals will possibly end up in a negative relationship, some type of cult, or so-called religion, or gang that purports to provide emotional support.

Whosoever is delighted in solitude is either a wild beast or a god.

Francis Bacon

What about Teenagers? Teenagers are another group of people who are very vulnerable. Teenagers are attempting to become independent and no longer want to rely on their parents for emotional support. They seek satisfaction of this need through other means—peer group, boyfriend or girlfriend, drugs, religion, cults, gangs, etc. They will continue to seek emotional support until it is satisfied. Most individuals will satisfy this through positive means, but others may end up in negative situations, such as becoming a member of a gang or cult, or using drugs.

As you can see, satisfaction of the emotional attachment need is vital to us in order to overcome loneliness. We have also discovered another need that must be satisfied in order for us to overcome the feeling that something is missing in our life. What is it?

Social Ties. *Social ties provide us with the feeling of belonging—a feeling that we are part of a group and have an identity.* During early childhood this feeling of belonging and developing an identity is, for most children, provided by their parents. This is expressed with statements like, "I'm a member of the Smith family or Adams family or Sanchez family." Later in childhood the peer group becomes more important to them than the family, especially during adolescence. Special groups, clubs, teams, and religious organizations such as Boy Scouts, Bluebirds, Indian Guides, Little League, church youth groups, pep clubs, gangs, and fraternal organizations provide many young people with a feeling of identity. Have you ever observed a child walking down the street in their scout uniform or team uniform? They really think they are "special." The uniform makes them feel like they are part of a group and they have an identity. We all need an identity.

Our lives today are in greater transition than in the past. We are traveling more, leaving friends and family for "greener pastures." Job related mobility makes for fewer long-term family and social ties and increased loneliness (Dill & Anderson, 1998).

How does the person feel who is not able to join a club or be a member of a team? This person feels "left-out" and feels that there is something missing in their life. They will do whatever it takes to satisfy this need. The end result of not having this need satisfied is the same as for those whose emotional attachment needs are not satisfied. This person will feel lonely, depressed, and vulnerable.

How Can We Satisfy This Need? *Social ties* may be satisfied through positive as well as negative means. Social ties may be satisfied through marriage—a legal bond that makes you feel like you belong to another person and have a recognized identity. A person's job or career may also give some people a feeling of identity or belonging. Ask a person the question, "Who are you?" and the response is generally, "I'm a student, a banker, a plumber, a salesperson, an attorney," etc. These titles give the individual an identity and the organization the person works for gives the person a feeling of belonging.

During the high school and college years a person's identity may be found in many different ways. Some students find their identity by being on an athletic team, by being an excellent student, playing in the band or orchestra, dating a cheerleader, or being in a sorority or fraternity. If a student does not find his or her identity or feeling of belonging through "normal" or acceptable means, he or she will attempt to satisfy this need through other means, such as drugs, bizarre clothing, a unique hairstyle, promiscuous behavior, gang activity or delinquent behavior.

Emotional support and social ties are not only important to young people, but they are vital to all of us and will continue to be important throughout our lives. We will be in a constant state of stress and anxiety if our emotional support and social ties change too much. Divorce, death of a loved one, changing jobs or being fired from a job, retirement, breaking up with a boyfriend or girlfriend, or a serious illness may be the cause of our needs changing.

Ask Yourself the Following Questions. Where do you get emotional support? Who or what provides you with an identity or feeling of belonging? Most of you have heard the stories about couples who have been married for twenty-five or more years and suddenly one of the two dies, and within a few hours or days the other one dies. A similar situation is when a long-term employee retires from a firm and within a year passes away. What has happened in both of these situations? For many individuals their spouse becomes their sole emotional support and identity and when their needs are no longer being satisfied they become lost. The person becomes lonely, insecure, and depressed and says, "What's there

People are lonely because they build walls instead of bridges.

Joseph Newton

Man never reasons so much and becomes so introspective as when he suffers since he is anxious to get at the cause of his sufferings.

Luigi Pirandello, 1922

to live for?" and just *gives-up.* In a retirement situation, the same thing happens; the job becomes the individual's security and identity, and all of a sudden when the individual retires, both needs are lost, and the person *gives up psychologically and physiologically.*

These examples should demonstrate to all of us that we should not rely only on one person or one source for the satisfaction of our emotional needs. We all need to work at developing a good support system. We also need to make sure our loved ones, including children, parents, spouses and friends, have a good support system that satisfies all of their needs.

Now that we understand the need for relationships, many of us still find it difficult to get to know other people and develop good relationships. Why do we fear getting acquainted?

THE FEAR OF GETTING ACQUAINTED

Meeting people and forming relationships should be fun, but for a lot of people it is a difficult process full of stress and anxiety. "It seems so easy for other people, but for me, it's one of the most difficult things I do in life." Because of the complexity of our society we have made the process of getting acquainted and developing relationships an involved process. "How can I make meeting people and forming relationships more fun and less stressful? Why do I feel so uncomfortable meeting people?" You may want to answer the questions in the following box.

Am I Shy? How did you answer the questions above? If your answer to any of the questions is that you feel uncomfortable, anxious, inhibited, and excessively cautious, then you showed signs of shyness. Do not feel bad—shyness is universal. You have lots of company. Nearly one of two Americans claim to be shy. What is more interesting, the incidence is rising, and the use of the computer and technology may be turning our society into a culture of shy people (Carducci & Zimbardo, 1995). It affects the young and old, men and women, celebrities and people like you and me. It is a very common problem. A study by Phillip Zimbardo (1987, 1990) indicated that 40 percent of the respondents were currently troubled by shyness and that 80 percent had reported being shy during some stage in their lives. Most shy people reported that they do not like being shy. Shy people find it difficult to make friends and they tend to be sexually inhibited. They also tend to be lonelier and more depressed than others. Loneliness and shyness are closely related. Shyness leads to loneliness and loneliness leads to shyness.

What Is Shyness? Shyness involves *feelings, physical reactions, and thoughts,* that create a state of anxiety, discomfort, and inhibition. Let's discuss each one.

- **Feelings.** Feelings associated with shyness include anxiety, insecurity, stress, loneliness, mistrust, embarrassment, tension, fear, and confusion.
- **Physical reactions.** Physical reactions associated with shyness include nausea, butterflies in the stomach, shaking, perspiring, pounding heart, feeling faint, and blushing.
- **Thoughts.** Thoughts associated with shyness include: "I'm not an interesting person," "I'm not as good as they are," "They won't like me," "I lack self-confidence," or "I don't have the social skills."

Having enjoyed the friendship of many people in many places for many years—I have learned that, in the main, people are as we choose to find them.

Doris Schary

A man who talks only of himself and thinks only of himself is hopelessly uneducated.

Murray Butler

What Are the Consequences of Shyness? **For some people shyness may become a "mental handicap" that is as crippling as the most severe of physical handicaps. Its consequences can be devastating. What are the consequences of shyness? (Zimbardo, 1990) (Carducci & Zimbardo, 1995).**

Why doesn't anyone like me?

1. *Shy people become preoccupied with themselves and thus become self-conscious.* Because of this, they are not aware of other people's feelings and needs. For example, if this person has a facial blemish or their hair is not "just right," they know everybody will notice so they will not go to school or to a party.

2. *Shyness makes it difficult for us to become acquainted with new people and thus make new friends.* At a party these people would not introduce themselves to others, but would say to themselves, "Nobody is interested in me, I must be a boring person, nobody would want to get to know me anyway."

3. *Shyness keeps us from experiencing new situations.* A new experience is a risk that may result in failure, so it seems easier not to take the chance.

4. *Shyness prevents people from standing up for their own rights and as individuals, keeps them from expressing their own feelings and beliefs.* If other people do not know how you feel and what you want, how do you expect them to make decisions that will benefit you?

5. *Shy people tend not to demonstrate their personal strengths and capabilities and thus, prevent others from making positive evaluations.* If you have two employees, equal in all abilities except that one is shy and the other is not shy, which of the two would you promote? In most situations the non-shy person would be promoted because we are more aware of his or her potential than that of the shy person.

As you have observed, shyness can have some very negative effects.

Mutual confidence is the foundation of all satisfactory human relationships.

Napolean Hill

How Do You Feel in the Following Situations?

✓ Meeting people for the first time.
✓ Asking someone for a date.
✓ Giving a talk in front of a group of people.
✓ Going to a party.
✓ Asking someone for help—for example, your boss or professor.
✓ Being interviewed.
✓ Situations requiring assertiveness—for example, asking for your money back.
✓ Participating in a discussion group.
✓ Showing your body in a nonsexual context.
✓ Going to a dance or nightclub.

How to . . .

. . . Overcome Shyness

Analyzing Your Shyness

1. Try to pinpoint exactly what social situations tend to elicit your shy behavior.

2. Try to identify what causes your shyness in that situation. Use a diary or journal to keep track of the times you experience this feeling.

3. Have a friend or relative give you feedback. Discuss how you interact with others and how you can improve.

Building Self-Esteem

1. Recognize that you ultimately control how you see yourself.

2. Set your own standards. Do not let others tell you how to live your life.

3. Set realistic goals. Do not set your goals too high or too low. Many people demand too much of themselves.

4. Talk positively to yourself. Tell yourself that you can do it and that you are a good person.

5. Learn to take rejection. Rejection is one of the risks everyone takes in social interactions. Try not to take it personally; it may have nothing to do with you.

Improving Your Social Skills

1. Follow a role model. Select someone you respect and observe how they interact. Imitate their behavior.

2. Learn to listen.

3. Smile.

4. Reinforce yourself for each successful interaction.

5. Use your imagination. Rehearse in your mind new situations—how you will respond.

6. Practice with a friend—interviews, dating situations, etc.

7. Find your comfort zone. Not all social situations are for everyone. Go where your interests are. You might be happier at an art gallery, book club, or on a volleyball team than you are at a cocktail party or bar.

(Zimbardo, 1987)

What Is the Difference Between a Shy and Non-Shy Person? It may come as a surprise to many of you that the major difference between the two individuals is a matter of *self-evaluation.* How do you compare yourself to others? Do you see yourself as capable, intelligent, or as attractive as the person next to you? If the answer is no, then would you interact with them? Or, if you did have to interact with them, how would you feel? Would you feel inferior or inadequate? Many people would feel this way. Why? As we stated earlier, *shyness is a matter of self-evaluation*—how you compare yourself with others. Actually this should tell you how ridiculous shyness really is, since we are all capable human beings. Just because the other person is a doctor, lawyer, teacher, or engineer does not mean that person is superior to you. The other person may have more formal education than you or more money than you, but you may have more common sense, or *real-life* education. You are just as good as the other person.

What Causes Shyness? There seems to be many different causes of shyness. One of the major causes of shyness is *competition*. We live in a very competitive society and because of that we have a high incidence of shyness as compared to

Strategies to . . .

OVERCOME SHYNESS

- **Get Your Feet Wet:** Nothing breeds success like success. Set up a non-threatening social situation that has a high probability of success and build from there. Call a radio talk show with a prepared comment or question. Interact in small group activities.
- **Smile and Make Eye Contact:** When you smile you project a positive image. People will be more likely to notice you and smile back. If you continue to frown or look down at your feet, you project a negative image. Always maintain eye contact while interacting with others; it signals that you are listening and interested.
- **Compliment:** The shortest route to social success is through a compliment. It is a way to make other people feel good about themselves and about talking to you. Compliment someone everyday.
- **Stop Assuming the Worst:** In expecting the worst of every situation, shy people undermine themselves—they get nervous, start to stutter, and forget what they wanted to say. Chances are that once you throw yourself into that dreaded interaction it will be much easier than you thought. Only then will you realize how negative your predictions are.
- **Face to Face Interaction:** Start a casual, quick exchange with someone you are next to, in class, on the bus, in an elevator, in the supermarket, wherever you are. Since half the battle is having something to say, prepare—think of things you can say now in each of the above situations. Practice different scenarios, role play, and imagine in your mind what might happen in these different situations.
- **Find Your Comfort Zone:** Not all social situations are for everyone. Go to places where you feel comfortable and to places that relate to your interests. You might be happier at an art gallery than at a bar.
- **Stop Whipping Yourself:** Quit telling yourself how stupid you sound and how nobody really likes you. No one judges your performance as harshly as you do. Search for evidence to refute your beliefs about yourself. Focus on the positive

Do not overgeneralize your social mishaps. You may have made a fool of yourself in one situation, but that does not mean you will the next time.

(Zimbardo, 1990)

other cultures. Beginning at birth people start comparing us: "Why don't you act like your sister?" or "Why don't you get good grades like your brother?" Since people compare us with others, we begin to compare ourselves with others and what do we discover? There is always someone we perceive as better than us. Thus, we begin to feel inferior and then begin to act inferior. Consequently, shyness is created.

Once we begin to see ourselves as shy, we begin to act shy and now the *self-fulfilling prophecy* begins. Later in this chapter we will see how the *self-fulfilling prophecy* influences us. Recent research also indicates that shyness may be inherited or biologically influenced, but many people learn to overcome this tendency and become rather outgoing (Carducci & Zimbardo, 1995). Fifteen to twenty percent of infants are born shy and others seem to have a neurobiological influence that tends to cause shyness. Since most of us have what we would call developmental shyness, let's look at some ways in which we can overcome shyness.

Overcoming Shyness. **How can a person overcome shyness? It would be na-ive to pretend that shyness can be overcome easily. It is important, however, to emphasize that shyness can be overcome successfully. There are three steps in the process of dealing with shyness (Zimbardo, 1987). These steps are: 1) Analyzing your shyness, 2) Building your self-esteem, and 3) Improving your social skills.**

Overcoming Shyness Is an On-Going Process. **It takes time to change. Do not expect to overcome shyness overnight, it is a gradual process.**

Many of the projects at the end of the chapter will help you in this process. The Self-Change Project in the Learning chapter of overcoming shyness could be used to help a person overcome shyness. If shyness is creating a problem in an individual's life, we recommend that the individual consult a professional counselor at your local college or workplace who may be able to provide some new insights into helping you overcome shyness.

The Future of Shyness. **The future of shyness is bleak—it is not going to dis-appear and there are many reasons to expect the numbers of shy people to climb. Technology is continually redefining how we communicate. We are not engaging in as many face-to-face interactions on a daily basis. How often do you call a friend or colleague when you know they are not in so you can leave a message on their machine? How often do you see a bank teller or gas station attendant? Voice mail, faxes, bank machines, and E-mail give us an illusion of being "in touch," but what is to touch but the keyboard? Some people no longer even have to go to the office, they telecommute. Many individuals do not get to practice their social skills on a daily basis. Technology is ushering in a culture of shyness and it is the perfect environment for the shy. The danger is that technology will be-come the hiding place for those who dread social interactions (Carducci & Zimbardo, 1995). We need to be aware of this and hopefully stay "in-touch."**

As we begin to reach out and meet new people in the process of overcoming shyness, we attempt to sift through the millions of people in the world to select the individuals that will eventually become our friends and lovers. How do we do this? We begin the process of getting acquainted and finding friends through *perceptual awareness*.

Perception refers to how we mentally organize and interpret the world around us. Because we all have different backgrounds and experiences, we perceive the world around us in different ways—and thus many of us misinterpret

Most of us feel that others will not tolerate emotional honesty in communication. We would rather defend our dishonesty on the grounds that it might hurt others; and having rationalized our phoniness into mobility, we settle for superficial relationships.

John Powell

and misunderstand the people around us. We need to increase our perceptual awareness.

PERCEPTUAL AWARENESS

How can we prevent misunderstandings due to the inaccuracy of our own perceptions? Serious problems can arise when people accept their misinterpretations as if they were a fact of life while we tend to get upset with others when they jump to conclusions about our own behavior.

A friend says, "You really look tired today!" (You were feeling great until they said that.)

"What's the matter with you today?" (Who said anything was wrong?)

"Why are you mad at me and not talking to me?" (You are concerned about your final exam that you are not prepared for.)

How can we become more aware of our misinterpretations and make people more aware of their personal perceptions? The *perceptual awareness process* will provide us with a technique that will help us deal with these misperceptions. What is this process?

The perceptual awareness process will help us understand others more accurately instead of assuming that our first impression is correct. Our goal is a mutual understanding and acceptance of others—the perceptual awareness process will allow us to do this.

How to . . .

. . . Become Perceptual

1. Make note of the behavior you are observing. Describe the behavior.

2. Interpret the behavior. Why is that person acting that way? (Write down at least two interpretations.)

3. Ask yourself what you would do in the same situation. Put yourself in the other person's "shoes."

4. Ask for clarification about how to interpret the behavior. Do not jump to conclusions. Ask the person why they are acting that way or ask someone else how they would interpret the situation.

Now, let us take a closer look at how we perceive the people we meet and interact with on a regular basis through the process called *people perception*.

PEOPLE PERCEPTION

Imagine yourself alone at a large party that you are attending. You look around and see nothing but unfamiliar faces. As you look at each individual, you

Don't Be Fooled By Me

Don't be fooled by me.

Don't be fooled by the face I wear

For I wear a thousand masks, masks that I'm afraid to take off, and none of them are me.

Pretending is an art that's second nature with me, but don't be fooled, for God's sake don't be fooled.

I give the impression that I'm secure, that all is sunny and unruffled with me, within as well as without, that confidence is my name and coolness my game; that the water's calm and I'm in command, and that I need no one.

But don't believe me.

Please.

My surface may seem smooth, but my surface is my mask.

Beneath this lies no complacence.

Beneath dwells the real me in confusion, in fear, and aloneness,

But I hide this. I don't want anybody to know it.

I panic at the thought of my weakness and fear of being exposed.

That's why I frantically create a mask to hide behind, a nonchalant, sophisticated facade to help me pretend, to shield me from the glance that knows.

But such a glance is precisely my salvation. My only salvation.

And I know it. That is if it's followed by acceptance, if it's followed by love. It's the only thing that will assure me of what I can't assure myself, that I am worth something.

But I don't tell you this. I don't dare. I'm afraid to.

I'm afraid you'll think less of me, that you'll laugh at me, and your laugh would kill me.

I'm afraid that deep-down I'm nothing, that I'm no good, and that you will see this and reject me.

So I play my game, my desperate game, with a facade of assurance without, and a trembling child within.

And so begins the parade of masks. And my life becomes a front.

I idly chatter to you in the suave tones of surface talk. I tell you everything that is really nothing, and nothing of what's everything, of what's crying within me; so when I'm going through my routine do not be fooled by what I'm saying. Please listen carefully and try to hear what I'm not saying, what I'd like to be able to say, what for survival I need to say, but what I can't say.

I dislike hiding. Honestly!

I dislike the superficial game I'm playing, the phony game.

I'd really like to be genuine and spontaneous, and me, but you've got to help me. You've got to hold out your hand, even when that's the last thing I seem to want.

Only you can wipe away from my eyes the blank stare of breathing death.

Only you can call me into aliveness. Each time you're kind and gentle, and encouraging, each time you try to understand because you really care, my heart begins to grow wings, very small wings, very feeble wings, but wings. With your sensitivity and sympathy, and your power of understanding, you can breathe life into me. I want to know that.

I want you to know how important you are to me, how you can be the creator of the person that is me if you choose to.

Please choose to. You alone can break down the wall behind which I tremble, you alone can remove my mask.

You alone can release me from my shadow-world of panic and uncertainty, from my lonely person. Do not pass me by. Please . . . do not pass me by.

It will not be easy for you. A long conviction of worthlessness builds strong walls.

The nearer you approach me, the blinder I strike back.

I fight against the very thing I cry out for.

But I am told that love is stronger than walls, and in this lies my hope.

Please try to tear down those walls with firm hands, but with gentle hands, for a child is very sensitive.

Who am I, you may wonder. I am someone you know very well.

For I am every man you meet, and I am every woman you meet.

CONSIDER THIS . . .
Application of the
Perceptual Awareness Process

Your roommate Stephanie, has been quiet for the last two days and has not been talking to you (behavior). You are sure that she is mad at you (first interpretation). She may have had a fight with her boyfriend (second interpretation). Why would I be acting that way? (Put yourself in that situation.) Ask Stephanie, "Why have you been so quiet recently?" (request for mclarification).

Jim stomped out of the room and slammed the door (behavior). Jim must have not liked what I said and got mad (first interpretation). Jim sure must be in a hurry and accidently slammed the door (second interpretation.) "Why would I have acted that way?" (Put yourself in that situation). "Jim, how did you feel when you left the room yesterday?" (request for clarification).

Think of some situations you have been in and go through this process.

immediately make a judgment of what you think each person is like. Your perception of each individual is based on many things, such as your past experiences, prejudices, and stereotyping. Since your past experiences, prejudices, and stereotypes are different from those of others, your perception of each individual will be different from other people's interpretations. You may perceive someone as serious and studious while someone else may perceive the same individual as depressed and slow intellectually. Sometimes we discover that our perception is not always accurate. Some recent psychological studies indicate that our perception may be distorted at the time of perception because we are using, our own past experiences, prejudices, and stereotyping to make the interpretation.

As we encounter people daily, we form an impression or perception of them. The term *social perception describes the way we perceive, evaluate, categorize, and form judgments about the qualities of people we encounter.* These *social perceptions* have a critical influence on our interactions. In fact, they are more important in guiding our feelings, thoughts, and behaviors than the actual traits or attitudes of the people around us. The factors that seem to influence our *social perceptions are first impressions, stereotyping, and prejudices.*

First Impressions. First impressions can have a tremendous influence on our perception of others. The initial impression we have of another person may have a strong impact on our future interactions with them. If you go to a party and see someone that looks just like the boss that fired you last week, what is your impression of that person? What is the likelihood of you approaching that person? You will most likely avoid that person even though they seem to be very friendly and not at all like your boss. The *primacy effect occurs when the first impression carries more weight than any subsequent information.* That first impression of the person that looks like your previous boss will be difficult to change even if you see them in a new and different situation.

Our first impressions are formed quite rapidly—often within a matter of seconds (Berscheid & Graziano, 1979). Research indicates that negative first impressions are often quickly formed and hard to overcome. This is why they say "getting off on the wrong foot" may be particularly damaging to a person. The opposite tends to be true of positive first impressions, which are often hard to earn but easily lost (Rothbart & Park, 1986). If the person you are going out with for the first time is late, what is your first impression? Would you think that he or she is unreliable and must be a flake—a negative first impression? Many of you would feel this way and this impression will be difficult to change. If your new date is on time are you willing to say that this person is reliable and conscientious? Most of us will take more time to make that judgment even though the first impression was positive.

What Do You Notice First? While you are walking down the street one day, notice a person that you have never seen before. In your mind you immediately form an impression of what you think this person is like. What had the greatest impact on the formation of your opinion? Was it the way the person was dressed, their hairstyle, their size or shape, their facial expression, or their physical attractiveness? A recent survey indicated that women are most impressed by the way a man dresses, while men seem to be influenced most by the physical attractiveness of women. Overall, we seem to be influenced more by **physical appearance** than anything else. This may be due to the fact that mass media puts too much emphasis on these factors and thus, has a great influence on our perception of the world.

Other factors that seem to have an impact on our first impressions of others include what the individual is doing *(their behavior)* at the time you perceive them and what the *interactional possibilities* are with that person (whether or not they would be a good date, tennis partner, or study partner). If you see someone acting weird the first time you see them, what kind of person do you think he or she is? What will you think of that person the next time you see them? Most of us would continue to perceive them as weird, because of what we observed them doing the first time we saw them. If you see someone who you think would be fun to date, will you approach them? If you think the person sitting in the corner would help you study psychology, will you ask them to help you? If you perceive someone as "stuck-up," or with an "attitude," will you approach them? Based on your first impression of these individuals you have already determined how you will respond or not respond to them. You are making your decision based on how you perceive the *interactional possibilities*.

When you go to a rock concert and look at all the different people attending, what other factors are influencing your perception of them? Are you making judgments about each individual without knowing anything about them because of the way they are dressed, or their hairstyle, or their race? Or, could it be that you have preconceived beliefs about people who attend rock concerts? Are you prejudiced or is it that you are stereotyping people? Prejudices and stereotyping have a great influence on our perception of others.

Prejudices. Our perception of other people may be influenced and distorted by our prejudices. Prejudices predispose us to behave in certain ways toward other people and groups. *Prejudice is when we prejudge a person or group of people prior to having all known information and facts.* Being prejudiced does not always have a negative meaning, it can also be positive. You see someone dressed as a nurse. You automatically perceive that person as kind and generous, even though you do

Over the years, I learned to choose from the best opinions. Chinese people had Chinese opinions. American people had American opinions. And in almost every case, the American version was much better.

It was only later that I discovered there was a serious flaw with the American version. There were too many choices, so it was easy to get confused and pick the wrong thing.

Amy Tan—
The Joy Luck Club,
1989

The Color Black!

What does the color black mean to you? Cornell University psychologists Mark Frank and Thomas Gilovich (1988) noticed that in virtually all cultures from the Orient to Central Africa to South America to the Arctic, the color black connotes evil. It is a black day if we get "black-balled" or "black mailed." In movies and TV the people in the black hats are the bad guys. As Frank and Gilovich noticed, the phenomena that black garb suggests evil, cues us to perceive people dressed in black as evil and cues those who wear black to act out their evil image. Frank and Gilovich discovered that we perceive teams that wear black uniforms as more aggressive and mean (the bad guys). When the Pittsburgh Penguins switched to black uniforms during the middle of the 1979–1980 season, their penalties increased from an average of eight minutes per game to twelve minutes.

What do you think about this?

FOCUS ON DIVERSITY

not know anything else about the individual. It is too bad that most of us allow our prejudices to affect our interaction with others negatively.

Stereotyping. Many people think people with red hair have hot tempers, that all police officers are mean, that all Irish people drink a lot, that all Japanese are intelligent, and that all Jewish people are rich. These are all *stereotypes—preconceived, inaccurate, rigid beliefs about individuals or groups of people.* The habit of stereotyping people is so common that almost any personal characteristic leads to the formation of stereotypes. For example, what are your feelings about overweight people, people who wear glasses, short people, black people, women, or homosexuals?

Did you know that tall people are more apt to get hired first and get paid more than short people? Did you know that attractive students tend to get better grades than less attractive students? Are you aware that women are paid sixty-five percent of what men are paid for doing the same job? Is this because tall people are better qualified than short people, attractive students are more intelligent than the less attractive students, women are not as good employees? No, it is because we have allowed our prejudices and stereotyping to influence our behavior. We must learn to overcome these influences and accept people as they are and not how we learned to perceive them. We must work together to reduce prejudices and break down the assumptions that one group is better than or inferior to others. We must work toward developing positive interactions among all individuals—no matter what size, shape, or color the person is.

Do Our Social Perceptions Influence our Attitudes and Behaviors Toward Prejudice and Stereotyping? *Social perception involves the creation of images of ourselves and of others.* Our cultural background and past experience have a tremendous impact upon how we interpret our daily experiences. A prejudice is a negative **attitude** toward members of a group while, discrimination involves your behavior toward members of a group. Prejudice, is a negative cognitive set;

discrimination, is negative behavior (unfair treatment). For example, a store owner has a strong prejudice toward everyone from Mexico, yet treats them like everyone else because she needs their business. This is an example of prejudice without discrimination. Can discrimination happen without prejudice? It is less common, but it can happen. A restaurant manager who has a handicapped child has empathy for all handicapped people but still will not hire them at his restaurant.

Inaccuracy in Social Perceptions. This is both a cause and an effect of prejudice. We will examine a few sources of inaccuracy that we discussed earlier that contribute to prejudice in important ways.

- **Stereotyping.** Stereotyping seems to contribute more than any other factor in determining our prejudices. Many people subscribe to derogatory stereotypes of various groups. Although recent studies suggest that racial stereotypes have declined over the last fifty years, they are still not a thing of the past (Dovidio & Gaertner 1986). The most prevalent stereotypes in America are those based on gender, age, and ethnicity (Fiske, 1993). The following box will demonstrate to you the impact of how our perception effects our thinking.

  As you can see from this example, the selectivity of a person's perception makes it likely that people will see what they expect to see when they actually come in contact with minorities they view with prejudice.

- **First Impressions.** One of the problems with the power of first impressions is that many people's first impressions of minorities come not from actual interactions, but from disparaging remarks made by parents, neighbors, and others. Thus, many impressionable children develop unfavorable opinions toward Hispanics, African-Americans, homosexuals, the handicapped, etc., before they have any opportunity for rewarding interactions with members of these groups. Even though these negative first impressions may eventually be overridden by contradictory experiences, the primacy effect probably contributes to prejudice. Judging a book by its cover is a pervasive consequence of our initial reactions to other people—reactions that encourage often inaccurate stereotypes about races, and ethnic groups other than our own, women, old people, overweight people, and many other negatively stigmatized social groups (Pingitore, et al. 1994).

You can see a lot by observing. . . .

Yogi Berra

- **Categorizing.** People frequently categorize others on the basis of age, sex, race, sexual orientation, weight, height, and so forth. *In-group-out-group bias explains the tendency to hold less favorable opinions about groups to which we do not belong (out-groups), while holding more favorable opinions about groups to which we do belong (in-groups).* We perceive people like ourselves to be members of the "in-group" and those who are different to be part of the "out-group." We tend to have more favorable attitudes toward "in-group" members than "out-group" members. We tend to explain the behavior of people in the "out-group" on the basis of their membership in the group. Jamie is slow, not very athletic, and obese, so Jamie must be just like all fat people. In contrast, my best friend, Larry, is slow and also obese, but I do not categorize him into the "out-group," because I perceive Larry to be a unique person. Therefore, he's part of my "in-group." We need to learn to avoid categorizing people.

● ***Attribution Error.*** When we observed Juan for the first time he was studying by himself in the cafeteria using a laptop computer. What is our first impression of Juan? He must be a loner. He must be an intellectual. He must be a "nerd." Are we right about our perception of Juan? The next day we are walking by the soccer field and we notice a very fast aggressive player scoring a goal and we discover that it is Juan. Was our first impression of Juan correct? We then further discover that Juan is also a very outgoing individual with lots of friends. We definitely made an error based on our first impression. Remember, a person's behavior at a given time may or may not reflect their personality—but we tend to assume that it does.

Inaccuracy in our perceptions tend to persist because first impressions can be very difficult to overcome. Evidence tends to demonstrate that we tend to see what we expect to see in our interpersonal interactions. Now that you are more aware of how your perceptions are influenced, we hope that you can now begin to accept people as they really are.

As we continue the process of people perception, we discover that it is common for us to make many mistakes and errors in our perceptions of others (Buckhout, 1980). We have found that our prejudices and our stereotypes often lead to unfair treatment of others. Take a look at one characteristic that seems to have the greatest impact on our perception of others without substantial evidence to support its accuracy—another distortion in perception.

Physical Attractiveness. Are you more likely to seek out an attractive person as a friend or someone who is perceived as less attractive? If you were an employer, would you be more likely to hire the most attractive applicant? Do you perceive physically attractive people to be more poised, likeable, sexy, competent, happy, interesting and socially skilled than people of average or unattractive appearance. Many of you would answer no to these questions, but when it comes time for you to act on these questions it could be a different story. Research indicates that physical attractiveness has a profound influence on our impression of others and our interactions with them (Dion & Berscheid, 1974; Baron, 1986; Dion & Dion, 1987; Solomon, 1987).

Put Yourself in the Other Person's Shoes

When thinking about sensitive ethnic, cultural, and gender issues, it is important to consider different sides of the issue in a contemplative, analytical way as we explained in the perceptual awareness process. We need to see things from many points of view. Unless we can mentally represent information about sociocultural issues from more than one point of view, we may rely on inadequate information to draw conclusions. If we do not seek alternative explanations and interpretations of problems and issues, our conclusions may be based solely on our own expectations, prejudices, stereotypes, and personal experiences.

FOCUS ON DIVERSITY

How do you determine whom to date?

In general, people tend to believe that what is beautiful is good. (Eagly et al., 1991) This stereotype seems to start early in life. When preschool children were asked to pick whom they liked best and who they thought was the best behaved in their class, they selected both categories of their classmates with the same group of children adults judged to be the most attractive physically (Dion & Berscheid, 1971).

We have all been told, "beauty is only skin deep, it's what's inside the person that counts." A person's character and behavior are more important than looks. Most of us would probably agree that physical attractiveness should not be a major factor in interpersonal attraction. Then, why is physical beauty such a powerful influence in attracting us to others?

One reason is that we all want to be accepted and liked and we perceive attractive people as being more friendly, liked more by others, and thus, if we hang around them more we will also be perceived in the same way. People tend to see themselves as being more similar to attractive people than to unattractive people. Another reason is that beginning early in life we have been told that beautiful things are good and that ugly things are bad, so we have generalized this belief to include our perception of people. Later, we discover that attractive people tend to receive more positive reinforcement than less attractive individuals and thus they will be more likely to feel good about themselves. Finally, if they feel good about themselves, other people will also perceive them as more positive and they will continue to receive more and more reinforcement. As a result of such cultural conditioning, most people do associate physical attractiveness with a wide variety of desirable characteristics (Feingold, 1992: Eagly, et al. 1991).

Attractiveness judgments are relative. They depend on the accepted standards of beauty in one's place and time. In an attempt to look attractive, people in different cultures have pierced their noses, ears, tongues, navels, lengthened their necks, bound their feet, dyed their skin and hair, eaten to achieve a full figure or liposuctioned fat to achieve a slim one, strapped on leather garments to prevent their breasts from growing, or stuffed their breasts with silicone to make them larger. In North America, the ultra-thin ideal of the "Roaring Twenties" gave way to the soft, voluptuous Marilyn Monroe type of the 1950's to be replaced by the lean, athletic ideal of the 1990's. Again, "beauty is in the eye of the beholder."

People's attractiveness is surprisingly unrelated to their self-esteem (Major, et al. 1984). One reason may be that, except after comparing themselves with superattractive people, few people view themselves as unattractive (Thornton & Moore, 1993). As time goes by, we become accustomed to our own face and perceive it on a positive basis.

Personal beauty is a greater recommendation than any letter of introduction.

Aristotle
Apothegems, 330 B.C.

What about Dating? When selecting a date, does physical attractiveness influence your selection? Research has shown that people desire to date the most attractive person possible. But when given the opportunity to choose a date people tend to choose someone of attractiveness nearly equal to their own (Berscheid et al., 1971). We may desire the more attractive date but we are afraid that they would reject us. In order to maintain a positive self concept, we are more likely to select someone we think would be more likely to say "yes." That person will most likely be someone whom we perceive as equal to us in physical attractiveness. ***The matching hypothesis*** *proposes that people of similar levels of physical attractiveness gravitate toward each other.* There seems to be evidence to support this in regard to selecting friends, dating partners, and marriage partners. Look around you, look at your friends and mates. Are they similar to you?

What Traits Are Important to You? Your best friend wants to get you a date. Your friend asks you to list the three most important characteristics you would like that date to have. What are the three characteristics you would list? Take a minute and write down the three characteristics that are most important to you in a date. Most people would say *intelligence, friendliness,* and *sincerity* are the most important qualities. But when you actually make your selection, you base your selection on physical appearance.

Are attractive people really better adjusted, smarter, or more assertive than unattractive people? After analyzing dozens of studies, psychologist Alan Feingold (1992) found that there were actually very few personality differences between beautiful people and their plainer counterparts. Physical attractiveness is not correlated with intelligence, mental health, or even self-esteem. But, we still discover that physical attractiveness has a persuasive influence on us in our perception of others.

The more aware we are that characteristics, like physical attractiveness, influence our perceptions of others, the less chance that these characteristics will have on influencing our perceptions of others. Thank goodness that *beauty is in the eye of the beholder* and what is beautiful to one person is not considered beautiful to another person. This gives all of us a fair chance.

Perception is an interesting subject. The better we get to know someone the more beautiful he or she becomes in our eyes. We often perceive the people we love as being beautiful, regardless of what anyone else may think.

Another important aspect of *people perception* is the judgment we make about why people behave as they do. Our responses to other people are strongly influenced by these judgments, and we are constantly attempting to understand the reasons for other people's behavior. This leads us to the *attribution process.*

> The only way to live happily with others is to overlook their faults and admire their virtues.
>
> David Goodman

What Is the Attribution Process? Attributions allow us to make sense out of other people's actions, figure out their attitudes and personality traits, and ultimately to gain some control over subsequent interactions with them through our increased ability to predict their behaviors. To keep our world predictable and controllable, we do not need to ask "why" questions all the time. Many of our casual attributions are virtually automatic, implicit in the impression we form of other people and situations as we have seen (Krull & Dill, 1998).

What would you do and think in the following situation? Class is over and you are walking to your next class and you see your boyfriend or girlfriend on the other side of campus talking to a member of the opposite sex. Many of you would feel your emotions take control of your mind and body and react aggressively toward your partner and accuse them of flirting with the other person. Are you jealous? What would you say when your boyfriend or girlfriend finds you talking to a member of the opposite sex? It tends to be a different story when the *shoe is on the other foot,* doesn't it? Why? ***Attribution theory*** *shows that we frequently over-estimate the influence of a person's personality and under-estimate the impact of the situation he or she is in.* In the situation above, you attributed your girlfriend's or boyfriend's behavior to his or her personality and not being a trustworthy per-

> Treasure life in yourself and you will give it to others, give it to others and it will come back to you. For life, like love, cannot thrive inside its own threshold, but is renewed as it offers itself. Life grows as it is spent.
>
> Ardis Whitman

Who would you hire? What impressions are these two individuals projecting?

their students. The teacher expected certain students to do well and as a result they did better than the low-expectation students. To put this phenomenon in context with self-concept, we can say that when a teacher communicates to a student the message "I think you're bright," the student accepts that evaluation and changes their self-concept to include it. In contrast, we realize that the reverse is also true for students whose teachers send the message "I think you're stupid." Can you think of some examples of this type of self-fulfilling prophecy that you have observed.

- A coach telling a player he is not sure if he will make the team.
- A parent telling his daughter that she is a brat.
- A doctor telling her patient that he may not live much longer.
- A teacher telling his student that he is not college material.
- A coach telling a player that she is too short to play basketball.

How would these comments influence a person's behavior?

The second category of *self-fulling prophecy* is the self-imposed prophecy that occurs when your own expectations influence your own behavior.

Expectations Are the Basis of the Self-Fulfilling Prophecy. We find that expectations are the foundation of our success, but they can also be the basis of our failure. If we believe that we can succeed, we can do it. If we believe that we are incompetent and not capable, we will be a failure. Which do you want to become—a failure or a success? This type of self-fulling prophecy becomes a vicious circle (Schultz & Oskamp, 2000). A thought about self is carried out in behavior, which then brings about an even stronger confirming thought. You, a shy person, will fulfill your own prophecy. If the descriptor is a positive one which increases your self-esteem, the self-fulfilling prophecy is a friend. Too often,

☞ CHECK THIS OUT . . .

Student Story

When I was in elementary school I was a quiet, shy kid. I wasn't very popular, but I wanted to be. I wanted to be like the popular kids, but whatever I did it didn't seem to make any difference.

In middle school I observed the older students and identified the ones I would most like to be like. The students I observed were the student leaders involved in student government. I decided to imitate (model) the behavior I thought that made them popular. I also set a goal, I decided that I wanted to be student-body president in two years.

I tried to project a favorable image. I started to be more friendly to others and show more interest in them. And to my surprise more people started to show more interest in me.

I joined some of the school clubs and activities. I was starting to have fun.

It took a lot of work, but I continued to work on my image.

To make a long story short, two years later I was elected student-body president.

This proved to me two things: 1) I can change if I want to; and 2) If I set a goal that is important to me, I know I can achieve it.

This is the self-fulfilling prophecy at work.

---

though, our thoughts are limiting and serve as our enemy. Figure 1.9 demonstrates this vicious circle.

Self-fulfilling prophecies are powerful. They can have a positive or negative impact on our self-concept, or they can influence us in the business world, or in how our family operates. What kind of effect has the self-fulfilling prophecy had on you?

CAN I CHANGE MY IMAGE?

Can I change how others perceive me? Can I change my expectations? It is not easy but you can change. How can you do this? You are constantly projecting yourself to others as being a capable, good, bad, inferior, successful, dumb, happy, sad, depressed, or superior type of person. Do you like the way others perceive you as a person? You can change your image through *impression management*.

Impression Management. There is a strong correlation between the *self-fulfilling prophecy* and *impression management*. If you project yourself as being a successful person others will perceive you as being successful, and if they expect you to be successful you become more successful. *Impression management refers to our conscious effort to present ourselves in socially desirable ways.*

Have you ever been interviewed for a job? How did you dress? Did you project yourself in a positive way? Did you relate to this person differently than you do with your friends? Most of you would dress differently for the interview. You would make sure that you say the "right" things and respond positively to the interviewer. You are doing what we call *impression management*. You are at-

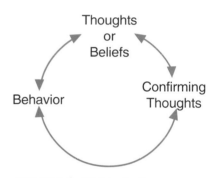

Figure 1.9. Person to Person: Positive Relationships Don't Just Happen, 2/E by Sharon L. Hanna, © 1995. Adapted by permission of Prentice-Hall, Inc., Upper Saddle River, NJ.

How to . . .

. . . Make Favorable Impressions

How can you influence the impressions you make on others? Most of us make a conscious effort to influence the way others think of us. When we present ourselves to others, we usually try to make ourselves look better than we really are. We spend billions of dollars rearranging our bodies, our faces, our minds, and our social skills.

Here are a few recommendations to help you make favorable impressions on others:

1. **Use behavioral modeling.** This simply means to do what the other person is doing. When you are with a quiet person, behave in a quiet way. When you are with a modest person, behave in a modest way.

2. **Use positive nonverbal cues.** We can influence what others think of us not only by our words but also by a number of nonverbal cues—smile more, walk erect, and look directly at people as they speak to you.

3. **Presenting a favorable self-image.** If you expect someone to like you, it certainly helps to portray yourself as likable. In some situations you may need to be non-aggressive even though you are an aggressive person.

4. **Conform to situational norms.** Dress for the occasion. Do not wear shorts to the job interview for a management position. Do not ride your bike in the library.

5. **Show appreciation of others and flatter them.** People like to be complimented. Do something nice for another person. Look for something nice you can say about the other person. Be sincere.

6. **Be consistent.** People trust and like those who behave in accordance with their professional beliefs.

7. **Be creative.** Write down as many additional ways as you can think of to manage the impressions that you have on others.

Remember that first impression techniques that work in one cultural setting may not work in another. For example, the non-verbal "thumbs up" gesture, which means in the U.S. that everything is OK, or that we would like to hitch a ride, means something very different in Greece—an insult similar to a raised finger. In the Native American culture of the Sioux, it is considered courteous to open a conversation with a compliment. In some Eastern European countries, if one person expresses great admiration for another's wristwatch, courtesy dictates that the watch be given to the admirer. When interacting with people from different backgrounds and different cultures you need to remember that they may be interpreting the situation or event differently than you.

Our values can also color "the facts." Our preconceptions can bias our observations and interpretations. Sometimes, we see what we are predisposed to see. Even the words we use to describe a person or an event can reflect our values.

tempting to portray yourself in a way that you think the interviewer expects you to be. *Impression management* is necessary if we want people to like us, respect us, hire us, or buy something from us.

How can you influence the impressions you make on others.

What Kind of Image Do You Project? How do others perceive you? Remember, if you do not like how others are perceiving you, you can change the image. You can change the way you dress, the way you act, your hairstyle, your posture, whatever it takes to change the image. You can do it.

As we begin to understand the process of people perception we are now ready to begin the process of getting acquainted. What are the stages in the development of a friendship?

Life is now in session. Are you present?

B. Copeland

DEVELOPING NEW RELATIONSHIPS

Unfortunately, it is not easy to meet or get acquainted with others. If we wait for others to initiate the encounter, we may become very lonely. It is up to you, and only you to initiate the encounter and get the ball rolling in order for your friendships to grow and develop into long-lasting relationships.

If we understand the steps that are involved in initiating new relationships, we will be more likely to begin to incorporate them into our everyday life. What are these steps?

☞ CHECK THIS OUT . . .
Student Story

One of my students came to my office one day for counseling. He said he was depressed and that he did not have any friends. He said that there was something missing in his life. I asked him about his daily activities. He had an early morning class where he sat in the front corner seat. After class he went to the library to study, then on to his next two classes where he also sat in the front corner seat. Next, he would go to his job and finally go home. This was his daily routine. Was he giving himself the opportunity to meet new friends? No wonder he was lonely and depressed. We discussed some alternatives to his daily routine. What would you recommend?

Some alternatives would be for him to sit near other students, go to where the other students socialize between classes and expose himself to other students. It took some effort on his part but he slowly started to reach out to and get acquainted with others. To his surprise, within one week, he began to make new friends.

Steps in Initiating New Relationships.
Here are four steps you can take to initiate new relationships.

1. **Communication** underlies all relationships, but in order to communicate with others we must first make contact with them. Whatever the nature of

Each day you either
get better or worse.
The choice is yours.

Byrd Baggett

the situation, an encounter will usually begin with some communicative act that invites a response from another person. In order to do this, we must develop good communication skills. We find that the people who seem to have lots of friends also seem to have good communication skills. These skills can be learned. The Communication chapter will help you learn these skills.

2. ***Exposing yourself*** may give you the opportunity to get acquainted with someone you would like to get to know. When we say *exposing yourself,* we do not mean by showing parts of your body. We mean, by allowing the people you want to get to know you to see you more often. The more familiar you become with someone the more apt you are to interact with that person. The first time you walk by a stranger what do you do? Most of us would ignore the stranger. The next time you walk by the stranger you may smile. The next time you see one another you say, "Hi," and from then on the more you encounter this person the more you begin to interact. All of a sudden— you're friends.

Have you heard the story about people marrying the person next door? You are constantly being *exposed* to that person. You see each other on a regular basis and without any real effort on your part, all of a sudden you are friends and begin dating. The more we see someone the less we will be influenced by first impressions.

Where Did You Meet Your Friends? Was it school, church, near where you live, at your place of employment, the grocery store, or at the athletic club? Research reveals that most people are more likely to like and even marry, an individual who lives, works, or goes to school within close proximity to them. *Proximity—geographical nearness—*is perhaps the most powerful predictor of friendship. Of course, *proximity* also provides opportunities for fights, assaults, rapes and murders. But much more often it instigates liking.

A study of college students living in a dormitory found that students were more likely to become friends with the person next door than with the person who is living two doors down the hall. And further that they were more likely to become friends with the person living two doors away from them than with the person living on the floor above them (Priest & Sawyer, 1967).

What about the saying, *absence makes the heart grow fonder?* As long as you isolate yourself from other prospective dates or mates, the saying is accurate. But, for most of us the saying goes, *"Absence makes the heart grow fonder for someone else."* There is another saying that is appropriate here, *"When I'm not with the one I love, I love the one I'm with."* What happens when friends and lovers move away? Eventually most of these relationships will slowly dissolve to nothing more than a periodic phone call or card.

Does Familiarity Breed Contempt? Evidence shows that familiarity does not breed contempt, it breeds fondness. The more we are exposed to novel stimuli— a new person or new product, our liking for such stimuli will increase. This phenomenon, called the *mere-exposure effect,* explains in part, why we are attracted to people in close proximity to us (Brooks-Gunn & Watkins, 1989; Moreland & Zajonc, 1982). Richard Moreland and Scott Beach (1992) demonstrated this by having four equally attractive women silently attend a 200-student class for 0, 5, 10, 15 class sessions. At the end of the class, the students were shown slides of each woman; the students rated the ones they had seen as most attractive. The phenomenon will come as no surprise to the young Taiwanese who wrote over 700 letters to his girlfriend, urging her to get married. She did—to the mail carrier (Sternberg, 1993). If it seems as though you are having difficulty getting acquainted with others you may want to join a single's club, try a dating service, join an exercise club, take a special interest class, or even advertise in a newspaper. These are only a few of the possibilities of exposing yourself to others. Be careful when joining a club or dating service, check their references. How long have they been established? How much will they cost you? Talk to others who have joined or used their services. You want to make sure that you can benefit from their services and not let them take advantage of you.

> Become acquainted with your other self; it may be better than the one you know best.
>
> Napolean Hill

3. ***Social Skills*** enable you to create situations to meet new people and to maintain their friendship. How can you learn these skills? Practice makes perfect. Practice the skills you observe other people using that enables them to interact well among others. Practice role playing with a friend—your friend will also be able to provide you with beneficial feedback that will enable you to change. Practice different situations in your mind. Picture yourself asking someone out for a date or imagine yourself being interviewed for a job. The more you practice, the better you will be able to handle the situation. Practice verbal and non-verbal skills. Another idea would be to have someone video tape you in different situations. This is a lot of fun and provides great feedback when you watch yourself on film.

4. ***Classes*** in communication skills, human relations, or acquiring assertiveness skills will provide you with new techniques and skills that you can apply in developing new relationships while improving your present relationships.

Strategies to . . .

DEVELOP A FRIENDSHIP

- **Awareness.** We become aware of each other in a social setting—first impressions. Without talking or letting the other person know we are interested in them, we begin to evaluate them. What are the interactional possibilities? If we think there are possibilities, we are ready for the next step.
- **Breaking the Ice.** This is a difficult step for most people. Talk about the weather, hobbies, school, new movies in town, politics, or other relatively superficial issues. As we begin to get to know each other we will begin to disclose more and more information about ourselves. Disclosure leads to trust, trust leads to disclosure, and it all leads to discovering more about each other.
- **Mutuality.** As the relationship evolves, we disclose more about our personal lives and we begin to share our hopes, dreams, and fears with each other. If we discover that we have some common interests and desires, the relationship will continue to develop (Levinger & Snoek, 1972).

Think of several people you have met recently. Did you go through these stages?

These are just a few steps you can use in initiating new relationships. There are many other techniques that will facilitate the process that are included throughout this text. We hope they will work for you.

As many of you have discovered, the world, including the area where you are living, is becoming more racially mixed. As we begin to meet and interact with people from different cultures we do not always feel comfortable in knowing how to react and relate with one another. It is important now and more so in the future that we learn to successfully interact with one another. Here are a few ideas on how we can successfully learn to relate to people from different cultures.

How We Can Have Successful Interactions with People from Other Cultures. In the world today, it is important that we learn to relate successfully with people from other cultures. We need to move beyond prejudicial thinking that affects our interactions with different types of people. We all want to experience success in our efforts in developing intercultural relationships. How can we do this?

In order to be successful when engaging in extensive intercultural interactions, the following four conditions must be met:

When I meet someone from another culture, I behave in the way that is natural to me, while the other behaves in the way that is natural to him or her. The only problem is that our "natural" ways do not coincide.

Raymonde Carroll

1. **People must feel that they are having successful relationships with people from other cultures.** They must show respect, seek out activities of mutual interest, work cooperatively on projects, spend part of their free time with others, and so forth. In short, relationships should be warm and cordial, and people should look forward to their intercultural interactions.

2. **These feelings must be perceived as positive and be reciprocated by those culturally diverse individuals.** Some people report that they have many friends and that these friends are gracious and cordial, but others report that those same people are abrasive, unfriendly, and should be avoided.

3. **We discover that most intercultural interactions often involve tasks of some kind.** The tasks that people want to accomplish while interacting with people from other cultures involve such things as; community projects, completing a degree in school, wanting to start or maintain a joint venture, completing forms that have to be filled out, visiting a foreign country and finding your way to a strange location, communicating with someone you cannot understand, dealing with government agencies, medical facilities, or legal hassles. These tasks need to be accomplished in an efficient manner and within a reasonable amount of time.

4. **People should also experience minimal stress due to the fact that they are dealing with individuals from other cultures rather than from their own culture.** Life is stressful enough and successful intercultural relations suggest that there should be no additional stress brought on by the fact that the others with whom people work and/or interact with are from a different cultural background (Brislin, 1997).

If you have the desire to form special, close relationships with other people, remember that the prerequisite is knowing, accepting, and appreciating yourself.

You can learn to make your social life rich and rewarding by taking an active role in changing yourself. Your knowledge and beliefs about relationships will influence your ultimate enjoyment. You learn from experience, so take charge of your life, take a few risks and chances. Enjoy life and appreciate each and every relationship you have.

Chapter Review

Our greatest pleasures and our most traumatic experiences have evolved around relationships.

- Self-Discovery—To get to know yourself and to get to know another person requires a shared giving and taking regarding what we know about ourselves.
- The revealing of the inner-self is called self-disclosure.
- The evolution of a relationship is based on how much you are willing to disclose about yourself and how much the other person is willing to disclose about themselves to you—the process called self-disclosure.
- Good self-disclosure skills are fundamental to relationships for many reasons: defining yourself, knowing yourself, getting acquainted, developing intimacy.
- The greatest risk of self-disclosure is rejection.
- There are many advantages of self-disclosure: improves relationship, promotes mental health, self-validation, social control, impression management.
- The Johari Window illustrates how self-disclosure operates and will allow you to become more aware of yourself and your potential as a communicator.
- The size of the window pane in the Johari Window may vary depending on your communication behavior and the quality of your relationship.
- Loneliness is one of the most serious problems in our society today—it is a feeling of longing and emptiness that is caused by the lack of emotional attachments and social ties.
- Loneliness is most prevalent among teenagers, unmarried young adults, the divorced, and the widowed.
- Loneliness makes a person vulnerable to many different situations, including the use of drugs, alcohol, suicide, medical problems, sexual promiscuity, mental illness, and negative relationships.
- What should a relationship provide? Emotional attachments and Social ties must be satisfied in order to have a fulfilling life and overcome the feeling of loneliness.
- Most people will receive their emotional attachment from: parents, relatives, mates, friends, pastor, animals, teddy bear, etc.
- Social ties provide us with the feelings of belonging, a feeling that we are part of a group and have an identity.
- Shyness is universal; it involves feelings, physical reactions, and thoughts that create a state of anxiety, discomfort, and inhibitions.
- The consequences of shyness may be devastating.
- The major difference between a shy person and a non-shy person is a matter of self-evaluation.
- There are three steps in the process of overcoming shyness—1) Analyzing your shyness; 2) Building your self-esteem; 3) Improving your social skills.
- The perceptual awareness process will help us understand others more accurately instead of assuming that our first impressions are correct.
- When thinking about sensitive ethnic, cultural, and gender issues, it is important to consider different sides of issues in a contemplative, analytic way as the perceptual awareness process explains.
- Social perception describes the way we perceive, evaluate, categorize, and form judgments about the qualities of people we encounter.
- The factors that influence our social perceptions are: first impressions, stereotyping, and prejudices.
- First impressions can have a tremendous influence on our perceptions of others. The initial impression we have of another person may have a strong impact on our future interactions with them. The primacy effect occurs when the first impression carries more weight than subsequent information.
- The inaccuracy of social perception is both the cause and effect of prejudice. Stereotyping seems to contribute more than any other factor in determining our prejudices.
- The attribution process allows us to make sense out of other people's actions, figure out their attitudes and personality traits, and ultimately, gain some control over subsequent interactions with them through our increased ability to predict their behaviors.

- The self-fulfilling prophecy is a powerful force in our life that, not only determines how you see yourself in the present, but can actually influence your future behavior and that of others (We see what we want to see; we become what others expect of us).
- You can change. Impression management allows you to consciously present yourself in socially desirable ways.
- Developing new relationships is not always an easy process. The steps involved in initiating new relationships include communication and exposing yourself. The mere-exposure effect explains why we are attracted to those we are in close proximity to.

You can learn to make your social life rich and rewarding by taking an active role in changing yourself. Your knowledge and beliefs about relationships will influence your enjoyment. You learn from experience, so take charge of your life, take a few risks and chances. Enjoy life and appreciate each and every relationship you have.

??? **Questions** ???

1. Describe the risks involved in getting acquainted with others?
2. Describe what a person can do to overcome shyness?
3. Why do we need to study self-disclosure? Why is self-disclosure important in a relationship?
4. What are the greatest risks of self-disclosure? Explain.
5. What are the advantages of self-disclosure? Explain.
6. What is the purpose of the Johari Window? How can the Johari Window be of benefit to you?
7. What is loneliness? What effects will loneliness have upon an individual?
8. How can a person overcome the effects of loneliness?
9. Define emotional attachments and social ties and explain their importance in relationship to loneliness.
10. Explain what shyness is and discuss the consequences of shyness.
11. What would you tell someone to help them overcome shyness?
12. Explain the perceptual awareness process.
13. Why do we need to study people perception?
14. Explain how first impressions, stereotyping, and prejudices influence our perception of others.
15. How does physical attractiveness influence our perception of others?
16. Explain the attribution process.
17. What is the self-fulfilling prophecy? What influence can it have on a person?
18. Explain how you can change your image. Why should we study impression management?
19. What are the qualities necessary to have a close, personal relationship with another person?
20. Explain the three steps in initiating new relationships.
21. How can we have successful interactions with people from other cultures?

Key Terms

Attribution Error
Attribution Theory
Categorizing
Catharsis
Confidant
Emotional Attachments
Expectations
First Impressions
Impression Management
In-Group—Out-Group Bias
Interactional Possibilities
Johari Window
   Open Self
   Blind Self

Hidden Self
   Unknown Self
Living Together Loneliness
   (LTL)
Loneliness
Matching Hypothesis
Mere-Exposure Effect
Open Communicator
People Perception
Perceptual Awareness Process
Physical Attractiveness
Prejudice
Primacy Effect

Proximity
Self-Disclosure
Self-Discovery
Self-Evaluation
Self-Fulfilling Prophecy
Self-Validation
Shyness
Situational Shyness
Social Comparison
Social Control
Social Perception
Social Ties
Stereotyping

??? Discussion ???

1. Discuss the risks involved in getting acquainted with others?
2. Describe what a person can do to overcome shyness?
3. Why is self-disclosure so important in a relationship and what are the advantages of self-disclosure?
4. What is the purpose of the Johari Window? How can the Johari Window be of benefit to you?
5. What effects will loneliness have upon an individual?
6. How can a person overcome the effects of loneliness?
7. What is the self-fulfilling prophecy? What influence can it have on a person?
8. What are the qualities necessary to have a close, personal relationship with another person.
9. If you knew someone was moving to a new town and did not know anyone in that town, what would you tell this person about meeting and getting to know others? Explain the three steps in initiating new relationships.
10. Describe Impression Management and give examples of how it can be used. How have you applied it in the past?
11. Give some examples of how first impressions have influenced your interactions with others? Were they accurate or inaccurate?
12. How can we have successful interactions with people from other cultures?

Name _____ Date _____

Getting to Know You

Purpose: To provide an opportunity for participants to get to know each other in a unique way.

Instructions: Students need to ask other students in the class individual questions from the list and then have them sign the appropriate space. At a specified time (approximately ten minutes), have the students stop and do a more intense interview with the person they are questioning at that specific moment. Interview each other. In addition to this you may want to have each student introduce the person they have just interviewed to the rest of the class and tell the class something interesting about the person.

Name	Item

1. _____ Find a person who was born in a different state.

2. _____ Find a person who enjoys country-western music.

3. _____ Find a person who has a female boss (employer).

4. _____ Find a person of the opposite sex who has the same color eyes as yours.

5. _____ Find a person who really enjoys the opera.

6. _____ Find a person who enjoys playing a sport. Which sport?

7. _____ Find a person who owns a dog. What kind?

8. _____ Find someone who will not walk under a ladder.

9. _____ Find someone who has three or more brothers and sisters.

10. _____ Find someone who owns a Ford Motor Company product.

11. _____ Find someone who regularly attends church.

12. _____ Find a person who is in love.

13. _____ Find a person who likes to eat sushi.

14. _____ Find a person who has traveled to Europe. Where?

15. _____ Find a person who speaks another language.

Interview Questions:

1. Where would you like to be in five years and what kind of career would you like to have?
2. What are your hobbies or leisure activities?
3. Why are you going to school?
4. Tell me something interesting or unique about yourself.
5. What makes you happy?
6. What accomplishments are you most proud of in your life?
7. Ask any question about the person that you or other people would like to know about.

Name _____ Date _____

Getting Acquainted Interview

Purpose: To interview another person in order to get to know them well enough to introduce them to the rest of the group.

Instructions:
1. Each individual should make a list of 10 interview questions that you would like someone to ask you.
2. Choose a partner and exchange your list of questions with the person.
3. During the next 10 to 20 minutes you have in which to interview each other, each of you should write out your partner's answer as you ask them questions.
4. At the end of interview time, you and your partner join the larger group (if the group is larger than 20, you may want to divide into smaller groups). Each individual will introduce their new friend to the rest of the group using the information you received in the interview. Each partner may correct or modify the information.

Discussion

1. What was the value of this activity?

2. What did you learn about your partner that you did not know prior to the interview?

3. How is an interview different from an ordinary discussion?

4. Do you believe that the information you have gained from your partner is accurate? Is this the same impression you had of your partner when you first saw this person?

5. Were your answers honest or were you attempting to impress your partner? Explain.

6. Because of this experience in class, will you be willing to talk with this person in the courtyard, sit with this person in the cafeteria or do something social with this person outside of school?

Who Am I Collage

Purpose: To help students put their concept of self-image into a more definite form and enable each person to know something about all the other people in the class—including the teacher.

Instructions:
    I.   Construct out of class a self-image collage by pasting or gluing fragments, pictures, or words torn out of magazines, newspapers, and so on, on a large piece of poster board (or other chosen object) to form an abstract "picture" or composition. This will represent your view of the self.

    II. Each individual is asked to compose the collage around the following ideas:
        A. Use at least three people who are the most influential in your own life.
        B. Use hobbies and interests you have.
        C. Use three words you would like to have said about you.
        D. Use the part of your personality that you are the most proud of.
        E. Use the part of your personality that may create difficulties in your relationship with others.
        F. Use an accomplishment you are most proud of.
        G. Use your likes and dislikes.
        H. Use the goals and values you have for your life.
        I. Use your background, family, and friends.
        J. Use any other pertinent information.

    III. Show your collage to the rest of the class, commenting on the various pictures, or meanings reflected, or write a brief statement that explains your collage and turn it in along with your collage.

    IV. The instructor may wish to give the class members a pad of small sheets of paper to write individual comments on the members of the class as they give their collage. This feedback should be based on how the class members see each other in their presentation.

Discussion

1. If you were to do your collage again, what changes would you make?

2. What was the most difficult part of this assignment? Why?

3. What did you learn about yourself from this project?

Do I Know You?
Do You Know Me?
A Lesson in "First Impressions"

Purpose: To utilize feedback in discovering how accurate your judgments are about people. To discover how first impressions influence our perceptions of others.

Instructions:

1. Without speaking—select a person you do not know in the class and sit together.

2. Complete the form, "About Other," based on guesses you make about your partner from observation only. Do not speak to each other or signal each other in any way.

3. Complete the second form, "About Self," estimating what you think your partner has written about you.

Interests:

____Sports	____Politics	____Golf	____Writing
____Camping	____Basketball	____Artistic	____Cooking
____Movies	____Civic Activities	____Music, what type?	
____Gourmet food	____TV	____Reading, what type?	
____Dancing	____Gambling	____Travel	

Other: _____

This Person Is:

____Enthusiastic	____Quiet	____Follower	____Shy	____Patient
____Optimistic	____Confident	____Aggressive	____Impatient	
____Pessimistic	____Insightful	____Leader	____Rigid	
____Extrovert	____Depressed	____Happy	____Assertive	
____Outgoing	____Passive	____Generous	____Empathetic	

List any other characteristics that describe this person

_____

Name _____ Date _____

About Self

This sheet is to be used for your estimate of how you think your partner observed you.

Your willingness to participate in this activity:

Not very ____   Little ____   Moderate ____   Very ____

Degree of anxiety about participating in this exercise:

None ____   Little ____   Moderate ____   Much ____

Age: _____   Place of birth: _____

Month of birth _____

Marital status:

Married ____   Separated ____   Divorced ____   Single ____   Widowed ____

Children: Yes ____   No ____   How many? ____

Estimated Education: Did not complete high school ____   Completed high school ____

Some college ____   College degree ____

Nationality: _____

Occupation: _____

Interests:

____Sports   ____Politics   ____Golf   ____Writing

____Camping   ____Basketball   ____Artistic   ____Cooking

____Movies   ____Civic Activities   ____Music, what type?

____Gourmet food   ____TV   ____Reading, what type?

____Dancing   ____Gambling   ____Travel

Other: _____

I am:

____Enthusiastic   ____Quiet   ____Follower   ____Shy   ____Patient

____Optimistic   ____Confident   ____Aggressive   ____Impatient

____Pessimistic   ____Insightful   ____Leader   ____Rigid

____Extrovert   ____Depressed   ____Happy   ____Assertive

____Outgoing   ____Passive   ____Generous   ____Empathetic

List any other characteristics about you that is not listed:

_____

Discussion

1. Compare your impressions of each other. Discuss the similar and different impressions of each other. What are the similarities? What are the differences? Explain.

2. Were you surprised by any of your partner's observations of you? Why?

3. How easy/difficult was this activity for you? Explain.

4. How does this apply to your everyday interactions with others?

5. How can we change our impressions of others?

Name _____ Date _____

Where Does It Come From?

Assessing Your Emotional Attachments and Social Ties

Instructions: Refer to the definitions of Emotional Attachments and Social Ties in the chapter and then look at the following list. If the item provides you with no support put a "0." If the item provides you with minimal support put a "1" in the appropriate space or if you feel that the item provides you with a lot of support put a "2" in the appropriate space. For example, for Significant Others, you may have a 2 under Emotional Attachment and a 1 or 0 under Social Ties.

You may also want the people who are important to you to take this inventory and review their means of emotional attachment and social ties. If you have young children you may want to review the inventory for them to make sure they have adequate means of support.

	Emotional Attachment	Social Ties
Significant Others—boy or girlfriend, husband or wife, parents, etc.	_____	_____
Friends—school-mates, co-workers, close friends, neighbors, etc.	_____	_____
Extended Family—aunts and uncles, grandparents, brothers and sisters, in-laws, etc.	_____	_____
Support Groups—singles clubs, men's groups, women's groups, 12 step groups, etc.	_____	_____
Teams—sport teams, hobby groups, singing groups, athletic club members, square dance groups, etc.	_____	_____
Service Groups—Rotary, Kiwanis, Sororities and Fraternities, Elks, Masons, Scouts, etc.	_____	_____
Racial, ethnic, and nationality groups—associations, clubs, and so on.	_____	_____
Vocational Groups—Unions, Firefighters, Police assoc., etc.	_____	_____
Religious Organizations—church, Bible study group, men's or women's groups, etc.	_____	_____
Community Groups—neighborhood associations, protection groups, etc.	_____	_____
Total	_____	_____

Scoring: Add your total points under each column. You should have a score of at least five in each column. The higher the score the better. If your score is below a five in either column you may want to seek help in adding to your means of emotional attachments and/or social ties.

Discussion

1. Explain where you receive your emotional attachments from. How important are these sources to you?

2. Explain where you receive your social ties from. How important are they to you?

3. What would you tell a friend, who is lonely, how to change in order to find emotional attachments and social ties?

Name_____   Date_____

Draw Your Own Window

Purpose: To gain a better understanding of yourself and examine the degree of overall "openness" of your communication. To understand self-disclosure as a situational concept—you respond (communicate) differently in different situations. To provide insight into your "open self," "blind self," "hidden self," and "unknown self."

Instructions: Draw your own Johari Window for each of the following situations:
1. When you are with your closest friend.

2. When you are with your parent or parents.

3. When you are in this class.

4. When you are at a social gathering with people you do not know very well.

In addition to the above activity you may want to explain the purpose of the Johari Window to the following individuals: your best friend, one of your parents, another member of this class, and a new acquaintance, and have them draw the Johari Window as they perceive you. This will give you an idea of how others perceive you.

Discussion

1. Compare your windows in the different situations. Do they differ? Why?

2. How could you become a more "open" communicator?

3. How do others perceive you? Do you agree with their perception of you?

4. What could you do to change other people's perception of you?

Self-Awareness

Learning Journal

Select the statement below that best defines your feelings about the personal value or meaning gained from this chapter and respond below the dotted line.

- I learned that I . . .
- I realized that I . . .
- I discovered that I . . .

- I was surprised that I . . .
- I was pleased that I . . .
- I was displeased that I . . .

. . . .

continue on reverse

CHAPTER 2

Self-Awareness

The Man in the Glass

When you get what you want in your struggle for self,
And the world makes you king for a day,
Just go to a mirror and look at yourself,
And see what the man has to say.

For it isn't your father, or mother, or wife,
Whose judgment upon you must pass;
The fellow whose verdict counts most in your life,
Is the one staring back from the glass.

He's the fellow to please, never mind all the rest,
For he's with you right up to the end,
And you've passed your most dangerous difficult test,
If the man in the glass is your friend.

You may fool the whole world down the pathway of years
And get pats on the back as you pass,
But your final reward will be heartaches and tears,
If you've cheated the man in the glass.

Think about this...

My "Self-Image"

In my memories of when I was a "little" kid, between the ages of two and four, it seemed like everything I would attempt would be a "No, No," "No" to this, and "No" to that, and "No" to everything. For awhile I almost thought my name was "NoNo." I soon learned that my life was much easier if just sat and watched television.

Life was not much fun because I was afraid to try anything since I thought I would get in trouble. I didn't think I was a very good kid since most of the people around me kept telling me that I wasn't capable of doing anything. I thought it was because I was "no good" and "inferior," but in reality I just wasn't old enough to do what I wanted to do. I didn't realize that.

When I turned six, I was excited because it was time to go to school like the "big kids." It was a new life and I needed a change. It didn't take long for me to realize that I was not as good as the rest of the kids. They laughed at my overalls and shiny shoes. When it came time to select teams, I was the last to be picked since I was short, skinny, and wore glasses.

I wanted to be liked by the other students and my teachers, so I became the "class clown." I needed attention and I got it, but it was the wrong type of attention. I became depressed and felt inferior to the people around me, so I withdrew into my own little world and isolated myself as much as I could. I would sit in the corner at school and at home I would go to my room and draw.

My early school years were not fun. In middle school I got mixed up with the "wrong crowd." I wanted to be accepted, so I thought I had to be like everyone else. I wanted to be part of a group with an identity so I got involved in a gang. In the meantime I tried a few drugs and got in trouble. It wasn't a happy time in my life.

In ninth grade, I registered for an art class, not knowing what art was all about. The teacher asked the students to draw a picture. I turned mine in and the teacher thought it was great. The teacher thought that I had talent, but I knew better. I have been told that I am "dumb, inferior and not capable of accomplishing anything," so why try. My teacher encouraged me and kept telling me how good I really was, so I kept trying. All of a sudden the other students were also telling me that I was good and I began to believe it. I became motivated to succeed in the field of art. I overcame my depression, set some goals, found some friends that accept me for being me and not because of my size or looks.

I am now a professional artist and feel good about myself and my life. I like people and accept them as they are and will allow them the freedom to grow and develop as an individual. I hope you will too.

"SELF-IMAGE" DEVELOPMENT

Reviewing the story above, we realize that people acquire a sense of self throughout their life. It is an ongoing process that evolves from our experiences and interactions with others within the environment. Significant adults in our life also provide us with feedback as to who we are. This is the beginning of *self-image development*. In this chapter you can learn ways in which you can identify and better understand your *real self* and learn strategies to improve your self-esteem.

Who am I?

Was I Born This Way? Are you born with a self-image or is it acquired? Most psychologists say that it is acquired. During infancy, early emotional experiences form the basis for its development (Eder & Mangeldorf 1997). Our *self-image* is affected by all the experiences we have had—successes and failures, compliments and "put downs," happy times and sad times, personal thoughts and experiences, our own expectations and others' expectations of us, and the way other people have reacted to us, especially in our early adulthood. As you can see, a person's self-concept is not a singular mental self-image, but a multifaceted system of related images and ideas (Hermans, 1996).

Who Are You? How many times have you asked yourself that question? Before we go on, take a few minutes and try to answer the question by writing twenty brief statements that begin with ***I am*** _____. After you have completed your list, examine it to find ways that your self-image has evolved. It may have developed from your social world with statements such as: I am a Roman Catholic, I am a student, I am an adult, I am a mechanic; or it may refer to the nature of your interactions with others with statements such as: "I am a friendly person," "I am a shy person," "I am a family oriented person," "I am a political activist." Still other statements may refer to traits that you attribute to yourself either because other people have attributed them to you or because you have seen that you stand out in those ways in comparison to other people: "I am short," "I am good at math," "I am conscientious." You probably will not find any self-statements in your list that do not stem in one way or another from your social environment. We will now begin to explore many of the theories and ideas of how you have become the person you are. Let us take a look at how other people influence our feelings about ourselves.

SIGNIFICANT OTHERS

We learn who we are from the way we are treated by the important people in our lives. Harry Stack Sullivan (1953) calls these important people *significant others.* Sullivan goes to the extent of saying that *"a person is nothing more than the reflected appraisal of significant others."* From the verbal or nonverbal communication of these *significant others,* we learn whether we are liked or disliked, accepted or unaccepted, worthy of respect or disdain, a success or a failure. If we are to have a strong self-concept, we need love, respect, and acceptance from the *significant others* in our life. In essence, our self-image is shaped by those who have loved—or have not loved us.

Who Are the Significant Others in Your Life? How have they affected your *self-image?* Who are you a *significant other* to? Think about the kind of influence you are having on their *self-image.* Is it a positive or negative effect? You may be surprised to find that if you are a parent, a spouse, a boyfriend or girlfriend, a teacher, a son or daughter, a brother or sister, or a person that can have any impact on another individual, you are a significant other.

The living self has one purpose only: to come into its own fullness of being, as a tree comes into full blossom, or a bird into spring beauty, or a tiger into lustre.

D.H. Lawrence

A man has to live with himself, and he should see to it that he always has good company.

C.E. Hughes

A parent says to a child, "You better not try that, I don't think you can do it." You tell your husband, "Can't you ever do anything right?" A teacher tells a student, "Everyone else in the class understands it, what's wrong with you?" A son tells his mother, "You're a 'rotten' parent, you made me this way." Have you heard any of these comments? If we hear these comments too often, we soon begin to believe them, especially if the person saying them is important or significant to us.

From all of these numerous experiences, we construct a mental blueprint of the sort of person we believe we are. Once an idea or belief about ourselves goes into this mental picture, it becomes "true" as far as we are personally concerned. We generally do not question its validity, but proceed to act upon it as if it were true. Most of our actions, feelings, responses, and even our abilities are consistent with this contracted self-image. If we see ourselves as incapable when we enter a math class, we will most likely experience difficulty and failure. If you view yourself as well qualified and capable as you are interviewed for a job, the interviewer will evaluate you on a positive basis, and this will improve your prospects of getting the job. Do you remember from Chapter one what this process is called? This is often called the *self-fulfilling prophecy*. For further discussion on the self-fulfilling prophecy refer to Chapter one.

Do you ever compare yourself to other people? How does this comparison influence your feelings about yourself?

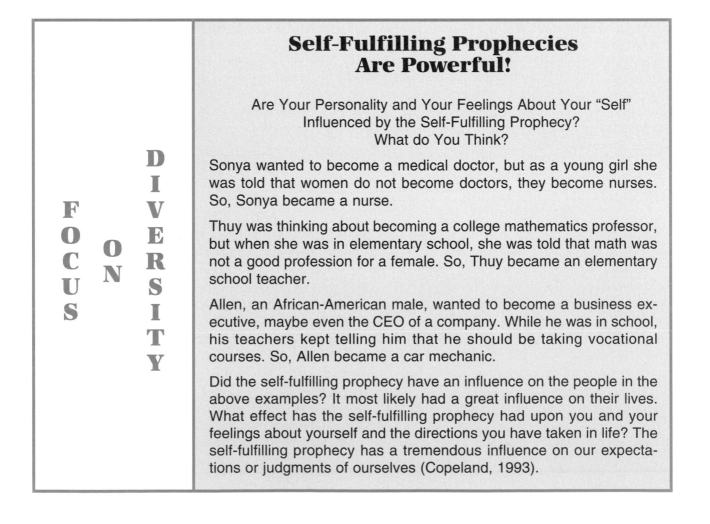

FOCUS ON DIVERSITY

Self-Fulfilling Prophecies Are Powerful!

Are Your Personality and Your Feelings About Your "Self" Influenced by the Self-Fulfilling Prophecy? What do You Think?

Sonya wanted to become a medical doctor, but as a young girl she was told that women do not become doctors, they become nurses. So, Sonya became a nurse.

Thuy was thinking about becoming a college mathematics professor, but when she was in elementary school, she was told that math was not a good profession for a female. So, Thuy became an elementary school teacher.

Allen, an African-American male, wanted to become a business executive, maybe even the CEO of a company. While he was in school, his teachers kept telling him that he should be taking vocational courses. So, Allen became a car mechanic.

Did the self-fulfilling prophecy have an influence on the people in the above examples? It most likely had a great influence on their lives. What effect has the self-fulfilling prophecy had upon you and your feelings about yourself and the directions you have taken in life? The self-fulfilling prophecy has a tremendous influence on our expectations or judgments of ourselves (Copeland, 1993).

Gaining Self-Knowledge from Our Perceptions of Others: Social Comparison. How many times have you asked yourself such questions as, "Am I as good looking as Jake?" "Can I play tennis as well as Anne?" "Am I as smart as Marti?" We gain self-knowledge from our own behavior; we also gain it from others through **social comparison,** *the process in which individuals evaluate their thoughts, feelings, behaviors, and abilities in relation to other people.* Social comparison helps individuals evaluate themselves, tells them what their distinctive characteristics are, and aids them in building an identity. Some years ago Leon Festinger (1954) proposed a theory of social comparison. He stressed that when no objective mean is available to evaluate our opinions and abilities, we compare ourselves with others. Festinger believed that we are more likely to compare ourselves with others who are similar to us than those who are dissimilar to us. We tend to compare ourselves with others of our own sex; males compare themselves to other males and females compare themselves to other females. Social comparison allows us a way to decide if we are the *same or different, inferior or superior.*

Same or different? How did you learn about your ethnicity or that you are male or female? A child that is told that he is a different color than his school mates begins to see himself as different. A 6'4" female student compares herself with her female school mates and perceives herself as weird. "All my friends are from Viet Nam just like I am and this makes me feel like I'm part of the group, I'm the same as they are." This perception of sameness or difference in relation to others has a great influence on how we perceive ourselves.

Inferior or superior? We tend to decide whether we are superior or inferior by comparing ourselves to others. Are we attractive or ugly? A success or failure? Intelligent or dumb? It depends on those against whom we measure ourselves. In school we compare ourselves with other students, "I'm not as smart as Jose," or "I'm more intelligent than Gretchen." In sports we tend to compare ourselves with other athletes, "I'm a better racquetball player than Steve," or "Ben's a better quarterback than I am." Take the Social Comparison test on the next page and see how you compare yourself to others.

Social comparison theory has been modified over the years and continues to provide an important rationale for why we affiliate with others and how we come to know ourselves.

The Importance of Self-Concept. When our *self-concept* is intact and secure, we feel good. When it is threatened, we feel anxious and insecure. When it is adequate and one that we can be wholesomely proud of, we feel self-confident. We feel free to be ourselves and to express ourselves. When it is inadequate and an object of shame, we attempt to hide it rather than express it—we withdraw inside ourselves. If we have strong, positive feelings about ourselves, we want and feel that we deserve a good loving relationship, or a good job, and even a feeling of freedom—whatever we think of as the highest good for us. On the other hand, if we have a poorly developed, negative, or inferior self-image we may expect very little for ourselves. We may settle for second or third best because we feel that is all we deserve. In

> If the only tool you have is a hammer, you tend to see every problem as a nail.
>
> Abraham Maslow

> There are three things extremely hard, Steel, a Diamond, and to know one's self.
>
> Benjamin Franklin

Do you compare yourself with others?

essence, we project to others the way we feel about ourselves. If we cannot like and respect ourselves, how can we ever hope other people will see us as worthy individuals who have something to contribute to the world in which we live?

To gain a better understanding of how the self-image evolves over a life span, we need to study some of the traditional theories of personality that will provide us with a foundation of how we become aware of who we really are.

> Retrospectively, one can ask "Who am I?" But in practice, the answer has come before the question.
>
> J.M. Yinger

PERSONALITY DEVELOPMENT

Throughout our lives we will be attempting to understand other people, such as our boyfriends or girlfriends, our bosses, our husbands or wives, or our teachers. In addition, we will also be attempting to understand ourselves. The following theories will help us gain an understanding of ourselves and the people around us. We will consider a variety of theories that will help you in the journey of finding yourself and answering the question, *who am I*.

The theory that has had the greatest impact on the field of psychology was developed by Sigmund Freud. This theory has created a lot of controversy, not only within the realm of psychology, but also within our everyday lives—in literature, movies, child-rearing practices, the feminist movement, etc. Let us take a look at some of Freud's ideas.

Sigmund Freud. Freud's theory of personality development provided the foundation for many other personality theories. Freud (1920) states that a per-

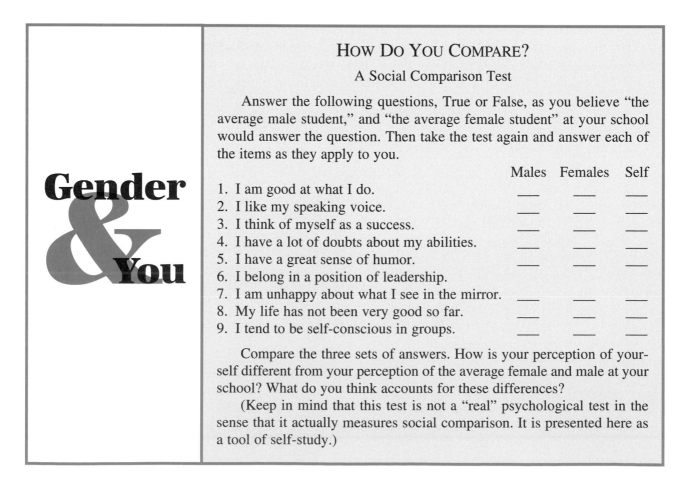

Gender & You

HOW DO YOU COMPARE?

A Social Comparison Test

Answer the following questions, True or False, as you believe "the average male student," and "the average female student" at your school would answer the question. Then take the test again and answer each of the items as they apply to you.

	Males	Females	Self
1. I am good at what I do.	___	___	___
2. I like my speaking voice.	___	___	___
3. I think of myself as a success.	___	___	___
4. I have a lot of doubts about my abilities.	___	___	___
5. I have a great sense of humor.	___	___	___
6. I belong in a position of leadership.	___	___	___
7. I am unhappy about what I see in the mirror.	___	___	___
8. My life has not been very good so far.	___	___	___
9. I tend to be self-conscious in groups.	___	___	___

Compare the three sets of answers. How is your perception of yourself different from your perception of the average female and male at your school? What do you think accounts for these differences?

(Keep in mind that this test is not a "real" psychological test in the sense that it actually measures social comparison. It is presented here as a tool of self-study.)

son's personality is made up of three distinct but interrelated parts: the id, ego, and superego.

What Is This Thing Called an Id? The *id* is composed of the basic biological drives that motivate an individual. This includes the hunger drive, the thirst drive, sexual impulses, and other needs that assure survival and bring pleasure. The *id* operates according to the pleasure principle, which demands immediate gratification of its urges. Many of Freud's supporters feel that this could be the reason some people resort to drugs, alcohol, or some form of sexual gratification. They do not think about what they are doing, they just look for immediate gratification. The *id* engages in primary process thinking, which is primitive, illogical, irrational, and fantasy-oriented. The *id* is present at birth and remains an active force throughout our life. We are not consciously aware of the actions of our *id*. As many of you have heard, Freud has received much of his criticism because of the emphasis he puts on the sexual impulses, pleasure drives, and their control over our behavior.

When Does the Superego Develop? The *superego* begins to develop after the age of four and is acquired from the environment around us. It consists of our values, morals, religious beliefs, and ideals of our parents and society. Another name for the superego would be our *conscience*. The superego tells us what is right and wrong, what we should do and should not do—the *ideal-self* rather than the *real-self*. This is the part of our personality that makes us feel guilty and experience anxiety. The superego attempts to limit the sexual and aggressive impulses of the id. As you can observe, the id and the *superego* are in conflict. Each characteristic is trying to take control of your life. You could use the following analogy—the id is the "devil" and the superego is "God," each attempting to control your life. If the id or the super-ego takes control of your life you may develop some form of personality disorder.

The Ego to the Rescue. Thank goodness for the *ego* and the fact that it develops before the *superego*. The *ego* begins to develop after the first year of life and begins to moderate and restrain the *id* by requiring it to seek gratification of its impulses through realistic and socially acceptable means. The *ego* is the rational, logical, and realistic part of your personality that attempts to maintain balance between the id and superego. The conflict between the *id* and the *superego* causes anxiety, which in turn, leads the ego to create defense mechanisms to control the anxiety. Defense mechanisms will be discussed in Chapter eight.

Freud's theory has had a major impact in the field of psychology. As you have observed, his theory has created a lot of controversy, but that is not at all bad. Many people became so upset with his ideas that they began doing serious research in the field of psychology and since that time many new theories have evolved. As you take additional psychology classes you will study Freud's theory and many of these other theories in more depth. We will take a brief look at a few of these theories in the following pages.

Most psychologists today think that Freud put too much emphasis on the biological drives, specifically the sex drive—the *id*. Erik Erikson, an original follower of Freud, realized that the biological drives are important, but that the effects of the environment on us and our development are as important, if not more important. Let's take a look at Erikson's theory. Erikson's first five stages correspond closely with Freud's stages of development but with extra emphasis on the environment.

I do the very best I know how, the very best I can, and I mean to keep on doing it to the end.

Abraham Lincoln

I am not what I think I am, I am not what you think I am. I am what I think you think I am.

Aaron Blieberg and Harry Leubling

Becoming is superior to being.

Paul Klue

Eric Erikson: Erikson (1993) has identified *eight stages of psychosocial development* that each individual experiences through his or her life. Each stage is characterized by specific tasks that must be mastered. If these tasks are not satisfied an unfavorable outcome throws us off balance and makes it harder to deal with later crises. As each stage is completed, we continue to build toward a positive, healthy development and a satisfying life. Those who are plagued with unfavorable outcomes will continue to face frustration and conflict while striving to develop as a person. A brief description of Erikson's eight stages of psychosocial development follows.

> Caring sometimes hurts, but not as much as the alternative.
>
> Anonymous

ERIKSON'S EIGHT STAGES OF PSYCHOSOCIAL DEVELOPMENT

1. **Trust vs. Mistrust.** During the first years of life, a child is completely dependent on others for the satisfaction of his or her needs. If these needs are satisfied on a consistent basis, the child will feel comfortable and secure. If the child's needs are not satisfied on a regular basis, *mistrust* will develop and this may become the core of later insecurity and suspiciousness. This child will become *mistrusting* and fearful of others and have difficulty developing close, trusting relationships with others in the future.

2. **Autonomy vs. Doubt.** During ages from one through three, a child is attempting to become more independent. He or she is learning to walk, talk, explore, and become toilet trained. The people around him or her, especially the parents, help the child to develop a sense of independence and autonomy by encouraging him to try new skills and by reassuring him or her if he fails. Consistent discipline is also important during this time. If the parents are inconsistent, overprotective, or show disapproval while the child is attempting to do things on his or her own, he or she will become doubtful, unsure, and ashamed of himself or herself. If a child is told by a *significant other* that he should be able to read or be toilet trained, s/he may wonder, "What is wrong with me? My parents say I should be able to do that but I can't do it." This child will feel doubtful and shameful of himself or herself and thus feel negative about his or her capabilities. A child that has accomplished some of these tasks and is given encouragement and positive reinforcement will feel confident and independent.

> Caring in an adult relationship is helping each other grow by receiving and not denying each other's authentic feelings . . . caring thus is encouraging someone to do, not what you want him to do—encouraging him to act the way he feels, not the way you think he should feel.
>
> Nena & George O'Neil

3. **Initiative vs. Guilt.** During the ages of three through five, the child moves from simple self-control to an ability to take control. This is the *questioning and exploring stage* when a child wants to try anything and everything. The child becomes very curious about the world around himself or herself. If s/he is encouraged to take the *initiative* and explore the world, the child will feel good about himself or herself and will continue to be curious in the future. If the parents inhibit the child's activities and curiosity, the child will feel *guilty* whenever he or she takes the initiative and thus cause the individual to become passive. Why try to do something if your parents keep showing disapproval?

4. **Industry vs. Inferiority.** Assume that the child is between the ages of six and eleven and is excited about life and motivated to solve problems and accomplish tasks. These are the early school years when the child should be making new friends, joining clubs and teams, and succeeding in school. When a child has a task to complete, such as a homework assignment, or

cookies to sell, or a wood car to make, the child should attempt to accomplish the task with encouragement from others. The parents should not intervene and complete the task for the child. Otherwise, the child will quickly learn that the parents will always complete the task, so why try? Or possibly the child will feel inferior and incapable because his or her parents always ended up completing the tasks for them. Many parents feel like they are being responsible parents by helping their children learn, but in reality, they are hindering their development. During this stage the child is becoming involved in the outside world, and other people such as teachers, classmates, and other adults can have a great influence on the child's attitude toward himself or herself.

5. **Identity vs. Role Confusion.** Between the ages of twelve and eighteen a person is caught between childhood and adulthood. The major task to accomplish during this stage is to answer the question, "who am I?" Adolescence is a turbulent time for many individuals. Mental and physical maturation brings on new feelings and new attitudes that people are unsure of. Should these new feelings and attitudes be expressed or inhibited—especially, one's new found sex drive?

    Our identity evolves from our self-perceptions and our relationships with others. People need to see themselves as positive, capable, and lovable individuals as well as having the feeling that they are accepted by others. Otherwise, they will experience *role confusion, an uncertainty about who they are and where they are going. Role confusion* may lead to a constant searching for acceptance and a feeling of belonging. This search can lead people to unhealthy relationships and to alternatives such as drugs and gangs. To look at the importance of identity formation and the reason some people end up joining gangs review the "Focus on" Identity Formation box.

The Beginning of the Adult Years. Freud did not put much emphasis on the adult years, but Erikson noticed that we continue to go through different stages as we age.

6. **Intimacy vs. Isolation.** Now that we feel good about ourselves and have an *identity*, we are ready to form meaningful relationships and learn to share with others. During the young adult years we must develop the ability to care about others and express a willingness to share experiences with them. Marriage and sexual intimacy does not guarantee these qualities. Failure to establish intimacy with others leads to a deep sense of *isolation*. The person feels lonely and uncared for in life. A person that satisfies this stage is capable of developing close intimate, and sharing relationships with others and feels comfortable and secure in these relationships.

7. **Generativity vs. Self-Absorption.** Until middle age we seem to be preoccupied with ourselves. Even the intimacy stage is primarily for the self to prevent loneliness. Now, we are ready to look beyond the self and look to the future, not only for ourselves, but also for others. This seems to be the best time to establish a family because we are concerned about the development and welfare of others. This is the time in our life when we feel productive and are concerned for the benefit of humankind.

    What about the individual who does not feel productive and also feels like he or she is not accomplishing any goals in life? This person feels trapped. Life loses its meaning and the person feels bitter, dreary, unfulfilled,

Think about this...

Identity Formation

A number of studies on identity formation indicate a relationship between status and behavior. People who have achieved their identity have higher grade point averages, perform better under stress, are better at engaging in intimate interpersonal relationships, and are more self-assured.

Most studies on identity formation have been carried out on middle-class people. Is the process different for individuals in other subcultures in our society?

Who Becomes Members of Urban Gangs?

Urban gangs have become an increasingly visible feature in our cities. It is estimated that Los Angeles alone has 750 gangs with up to 100,000 members (Majors & Billson, 1992). Because of the prevalence of gangs, some researchers have studied this culture by interviewing gang members, and in some cases, participating in gang activities. Why do people join gangs? Virgil (1988) found that youths attracted to gang life were the most deprived in terms of home life and school achievement. Their poor home life—often characterized by parental fighting or by a single mother overwhelmed by too many children to care for—pushes them into the street, where they face the realities of street violence. The threat of violence and the presence of gang members on the street encourages some to join the neighborhood gang. Thus, the gang provides protection (emotional support) and a sense of belonging (social ties). The gang may also provide a substitute for the absent father. Older members serve as male role models, and street fighting provides a way to affirm maleness by being tough. To affirm their identification as strong males, these adolescents identify themselves as gang members by adopting the street style of manners and dress; such as baggy, low-hung pants, a special scarf, a shaved head, tattoos, etc. The gang, according to Virgil, takes on the responsibility of "doing what the family, school, and other social agencies have failed to do—provide mechanisms for age and sex development, establish norms of behavior, and define and structure outlets for friendships, human support, and identity formation."

What can we do to solve this problem?

---

and stagnant. This person becomes preoccupied with the self, personal needs, and interests.

8. **Integrity vs. Despair.** Old age should be a time of reflection, when a person should be able to look back over the events of a lifetime with a sense of acceptance and satisfaction. This is the type of person who has tried to live life to its fullest. The individual who wished he or she could live life over again, and also feels cheated or deprived of any of the breaks in life, will live a life of regret and failure. This is the person that keeps saying, "What if . . .?" or "If I would have taken that opportunity" and because of this, feels depressed and will be unhappy the rest of his or her life.

As most people continue through this stage, they re-evaluate the meaning of life for themselves and ideally find a new meaning that will help reduce fear and anxiety and help prepare them for facing death.

> Life is an echo. What you send out—Comes back. What you sow—You reap. What you give—You get. What you see in others—Exists in you.
>
> Zig Ziglar

As you observe these eight stages, you notice that there is a positive and negative aspect of each stage. Are you able to identify the stage you are in right now? Are you able to identify the stages some of your friends are in? Erik Erikson was one of the first psychologists to put some emphasis on the fact that we continue to go through developmental stages throughout our lives. Freud emphasized that the first six years of life were the most important years.

STAGES OF ADULT DEVELOPMENT

Most psychologists ignored the adult years until Daniel Levinson (1986) did an intensive study of the lives of forty men. Levinson's study indicates that we all continue to go through developmental stages our entire lives. Some of these stages we experience may be as traumatic as some of the stages we experienced earlier in life, such as in adolescence. The stages seem to alternate between relatively stable periods and periods of transition. Levinson's study begins between the ages of seventeen and twenty-two while the individual is still struggling with his or her identity. This is a continuation of the ***adolescent identity stage*** where the individual is still striving to become independent. During this age range the individual is attempting to break the apron strings between the self and the parents. This is easier for some individuals than for others.

A Continuation of the Identity Stage. This is a period of time for searching, not only for your own personal identity, but also for your career and social identity. Money seems to be an important factor in developing independence. Not until a person feels economically independent will he or she feel like an independent individual.

Getting Established. As people become comfortable with their "self" and their own identity they are ready to enter the adult world. For most individuals this stage takes place between the ages of twenty-two and twenty-eight. This is the time where the individual is getting established in the "game of life." During this period the individual finds his or her first real job, the one that has the potential for a future career. Permanent relationships are being formed, including marriage and the beginning of a family. This seems to be a good period of time for most individuals. They feel like they are really "getting established" and they are on the road to success.

According to Levinson, during this phase a young adult begins to shape a "dream"—a vision of what he or she would like to become and accomplish as an adult. At first the dream may be vague and unrealistic, such as simplistic visions of becoming a TV star, rising to the position of CEO of the company, or finding a cure for cancer. Men's dreams tend to center on career goals. Women are likely to have "split dreams" that include both career and family goals (Roberts & Newton, 1987).

Levinson (1986) calls early adulthood the "era of greatest energy and abundance and of greatest contradiction and stress." In terms of our physical development we are at a peak during our twenties and thirties, and we are apparently willing to work hard to maintain that physical condition. On the one hand, young adulthood is a season for finding our niche, for working through aspirations of our youth, and for raising a family. On the other hand, it is a period of stress, finding the "right" job, taking on parenthood, and maintaining a balance among self, family, job, and society at large. Now look at the next stage of life.

Do not be too timid and squeamish about your actions. All life is an experiment.

Ralph Waldo Emerson

☞ CHECK THIS OUT . . .

There's a Revolution Going On!
(Many changes have taken place in the last 20 years)

There is a revolution going on in our "life-cycle" development. People are leaving childhood sooner, but they are taking longer to grow up and much longer to die. Look at some of the "happenings" that we have been hearing about.

- Nine year old boys carrying a gun to school
- Nine year old girls developing breasts and pubic hair
- 16 year olds divorcing their parents
- 35 year old men still living at home with their parents
- 40 year old women are just getting around to pregnancy
- 50 year old men are forced into early retirement
- 55 year old women can have egg donor babies
- 65 year old women receive their doctorate degrees
- 70 year old men reverse aging by 20 years with human growth hormones
- 80 year olds run marathons
- 85 year olds remarry and still enjoy sex
- More and more people are reaching the age of 100

There seems to be a shifting of all the stages of adulthood—by at least ten years. Adolescence is being prolonged, especially for the middle and upper class. Adulthood begins around 30. Most baby-boomers do not feel "grown up" until they are into their forties. When our parents turned 50, we thought they were old! Fifty is what 40 used to be; 60 is what 50 used to be. Middle age has already been pushed far into the 50's (Sheehy, 1995). So what's next?

--- ☜

> You have no idea what a poor opinion I have of myself, and how little I deserve it.
>
> W.S. Gilbert

We Begin to Ask Questions about Life. During the previous two stages of life, most people have been setting goals for the future. Some of these goals are realistic and others are unrealistic fantasies. During the ages of twenty-eight and thirty-three, we begin to evaluate what we are doing and where we are going. We begin to ask ourselves some questions such as, "Is this the type of job and career I want to be involved in the rest of my life?" or "Is this the person I want to be married to the rest of my life?" After evaluating yourself and your life, you need to make some major decisions that may affect you the rest of your life. This is not an easy period for many people since many decisions need to be made.

This is why this period is considered the ***wavering and doubt stage.*** "Should I change jobs, or should I get a divorce, or should I do this or should I do that? If I made this decision, what will the end result be?" We keep wondering whether or not we are making the right decision. Some individuals will make major transitions during this stage, such as changing careers or getting divorced. Life becomes more serious, now it is for real. Other individuals evaluate their lives during this period and decide that they are happy with their career and their marriage and will continue to be motivated to succeed in both.

Are We Ready to Settle Down? We are now ready to establish a place for ourselves in society, to solidify our family life, and to succeed in the world of work. We are between the ages of thirty-three and forty and are striving to reach the goals that we have set for ourselves and our family. We are interested in making the world a better place to live, especially for our immediate family. We are willing to join service clubs, be on the school board, run for political office or do what it takes to help make the world a better place to live. We are finally **getting settled** in what society has been telling us to do for the last thirty-some years. We now want to establish roots and make sure we live in an area that is "best" for our family and our career. We are beginning to feel good about our life and the direction it is going.

As we approach the age between forty and forty-five we begin to ask ourselves questions about our lives (Feldman 2000). We realize that life is half over. We ask ourselves, "What have I accomplished so far in my life? Have I reached the goals I have set for myself? Am I going to be president of the corporation?" This is a time for re-evaluation of our life and what we want out of it. According to Levinson, if people do not go through a **mid-life transition,** they will live a life of *staleness and resignation.*

Is It a Crisis or a Transition? This is the time in life when individuals may experience a major transition or they may decide that they like what they are doing and are happy with the relationships they are involved in and become re-motivated to succeed in what they are doing. Some of the transitions that are common during this time are changes in career and marriage. Some individuals experience a painful and disruptive struggle which is called the **mid-life crisis.** This is similar to the *adolescent identity crisis* where the individual seeks a new identity. Since these individuals have not satisfied their goals that they had set for themselves, they experience frustration.

In order to overcome this frustration and depression they attempt to find their identity through radical and extreme means. Some will quit their jobs, divorce their spouse, and attempt to start all over again. Some men will leave their wives, sell the family station wagon, buy a sports car and start dating twenty-year old women. They are trying to prove to themselves that they are still capable as a "man." Recent studies indicate that the mid-life "crisis" occurs in only a small minority (2%–5%) of subjects (McCrea & Costa, 1990). Thus, it's clear that the mid-life crisis is not universal or typical. Of course, this doesn't mean that people don't make changes in mid-life. Nearly everyone knows someone who has embarked on a new career or committed relationship during middle age, but we also know other individuals who have experienced major transitions at younger ages as well as older ages. So, nonetheless, researchers find that such changes in directions are more often caused by unexpected events (divorce, death, job transition, serious illness) than by mid-life events, such as menopause or becoming a grandparent.

Do Women Experience a Mid-Life Transition or Crisis? During the *mid-life transition* years, the female is not as concerned about her sexual capacity as the male. For women, who have primarily been mothers, this is a time for an emerging identity, as their children are becoming adults and more independent. It is a *bittersweet* time in which a woman who has not established a career or other outside interest, begins to experience the empty-nest syndrome and at the same time begins to look available options for redirecting her talents and energy. As the woman continues through this stage, depression and listlessness are common but temporary feelings. These vulnerable feelings may be followed by or coincide with the menopausal years and thus become a particularly trying period.

Life is a grindstone. Whether it grinds us down or polishes us up depends on us.

Thomas Holdcroft

The future belongs to those who believe in the beauty of their dreams.

Eleanor Roosevelt

The career oriented woman who postpones motherhood, or who decides not to have children, may experience similar feelings, either, guilt for not having children and being unfulfilled as a woman, or anxiety to reaffirm her work identity. As an extreme example consider a woman between forty- and fifty-years of age who has two children age twenty and eighteen respectively. Both children are becoming independent and the mother is no longer feeling needed. Twenty years ago she was told by society that her goal in life was to get married and have children. She has done both and now what is there left for her to do? Her body is beginning to change and she can no longer reproduce. She may feel as though she is no longer attractive to the opposite sex. Because of the culture she grew up in and the physiological changes that are taking place, she becomes depressed. She feels worthless as a person, she has reached her goals, and she feels that she is no longer a "sexual being." She has no identity. This is generally a temporary condition and after adjusting to the physiological changes within her body, and after re-evaluation of her life, she sets new goals and begins to strive toward them.

Times Are Changing. Women's lives seem to be much more complex than men (Levinson, 1996). Recent research indicates that women may not experience a mid-life transition as the men do. Whereas some men experience their mid-life transition at age forty as a last chance to hold on to their youth, many women see it as a time to reassess, refocus, and revitalize their creative energies. When

Table 2.1 Stages of Development	
Erikson's Eight Stages of Psychosocial Development	**Levinson's Stages of Adult Development**
Trust vs. mistrust Ages 0–1	Identity formation Ages 18–22
Autonomy vs. doubt Ages 1–3	Getting established Ages 22–28
Initiative vs. guilt Ages 3–6	Wavering & doubt Ages 28–32
Industry vs. inferiority Ages 6 to puberty	Getting settled Ages 32–40
Identity vs. role confusion Ages puberty to 18	Mid-life transition or mid-life crisis Ages 40–45
Intimacy vs. isolation Young adulthood	Commitment to tasks Ages 45–50
Generativity vs. self-absorption 40's to 60's	Questioning and modification Ages 50–55
Integrity vs. despair Late 60's and up	Facing retirement and fulfillment Ages 60 and up

(Erikson, 1993 & Levinson, 1996)

women near the age of 40, they tend to focus on changes in personal identity, such as becoming more self-reliant, rather than on a reassessment of career-related goals (Levinson & Levinson, 1996). At fifty, many women become suddenly aware of their aging due to physical changes in their bodies—especially declining fertility—and this creates still a different type of "crisis" (Jarrett & Lethbridge, 1994).

Many people go through the transition stage without any real problems and will be able to adjust to these problems without experiencing a major crisis. Other individuals will experience major transitions that result in positive changes, while others will have negative experiences that could result in such things as depression and suicide.

All of us need to continue to evaluate our lives on a regular basis. As long as we do this we will not experience any traumatic transitions that will disrupt our lives.

Following a mid-life transition, the middle years of adulthood are often a time of satisfaction and happiness (MacArthur Foundation, 1999).

Are We Getting Older and Better? Life's options for people in their fifties and sixties and older are changing radically. There are now whole new passages leading to stages of life that are nothing like what our parents experienced. The fifties are a continuation of middle age and the age of mastery. The sixties have changed just as dramatically. Only ten percent of Americans age sixty-five and over have a chronic health problem that restricts them from carrying on major physical activity. Clearly, the vast majority of American men and women now in their sixties have reached the stage where maximum freedom coexists with a minimum of physical limitations. And another passage looms: the one from mastery to integrity. Experts in gerontology make a clear distinction between passage aging and successful aging. To engage in successful aging is actually a career choice—a conscious commitment to continuing self-education and the development of a whole set of strategies.

The major predictable passage in this period for most people is retirement, though many consider part-time work to help pay for their longer lives and perhaps to handle other family cares like aged parents or the needs of grandchildren. The younger the retiree, the harder the transition.

Surviving the Seventies. Those who thrive into their seventies and beyond "live very much in the present, but they always have plans for the future." The seventy-something's need to master the art of "letting go" of their egos gracefully, so they can focus their attention on a few fine-tuned priorities.

The Age of Integrity is primarily a stage of spiritual growth. Instead of focusing on time running out, we should make it a daily exercise to mark the moment. The present never ages. And instead of trying to maximize our control over the environment, we must cultivate greater appreciation and acceptance of that which we cannot control.

Humans are in a constant state of transition, emerging, evolving, and becoming. Every experience is a learning experience. Make the most of your life, enjoy everyday to its fullest.

It is time to review the different stages of development as we have already discussed. (See Table 2.1.)

Tell Me About Him. Your friends ask you to tell them about your brother. You tell them he tends to be domineering, anxious, optimistic, intelligent, and athletic. Are these terms you have used to describe other people? Many of us use terms like moody, smart, stupid, restless, impulsive, passive, careful, aggressive, quiet, reliable, shy, outgoing, etc. to describe people. The words you use to describe other people (and yourself) are called **traits,** relatively stable and consistent personal characteristics. Trait theorists are interested in measuring how people differ (which key traits best describe them), and then in measuring how much they differ (the degree of variation in traits within the individual and between the individuals).

The Big Five. Because trait and type theories, developed by well-known psychologist, such as Gordon Allport, Raymond Cattell, and Hans Eysenck, follow a common sense approach, researchers today still find them attractive. However, rather than speaking of hundreds of traits or of a few types, many theorists agree that there are five broad categories. These five major dimensions of personality have become known as the **Big Five** (McCrae & Costa, 1987). (You can easily remember the five factors with the following mnemonic device by using the first letters of each of the Big Five traits, which spells OCEAN.)

Many researchers are now convinced that the best way to describe personality and individual differences is to find where people stand on the following dimensions: (1) openness, (2) conscientiousness, (3) extraversion, (4) agreeableness, and (5) neuroticism. Like Cattell, McCrae and Costa maintain that personality can be described adequately by measuring the basic traits that they've identified. Their bold claim has been supported in many studies by other researchers, and the five-factor model has become the dominant conception of personality structure in contemporary psychology (Ozer & Reise, 1994). This is indicated, in part, by the fact that these dimensions are ones to which most people in many different cultures refer in describing themselves.

Table 2.2   The "Big Five" Personality Factors

Trait	Description
Openness	Imaginative versus retiring Preference for variety versus preference for routine Independent versus conforming
Conscientiousness	Organized versus disorganized Careful versus careless Disciplined versus impulsive
Extraversion	Sociable versus retiring Fun-loving versus sober Affectionate versus reserved
Agreeableness	Soft-hearted versus ruthless Trusting versus suspicious Helpful versus uncooperative
Neuroticism	Calm versus anxious Secure versus insecure Self-satisfied versus self-pitying

Source: adapted from McCrae & John, 1992

The Self-Accepting Person*

The self-accepting person is a participant in life rather than a spectator.

He is inclined to be objective, spontaneous, emotional, and intellectually honest.

He tries to understand the interpersonal and environmental problems he faces, but he also accepts his limitations in gaining true insight concerning them.

He works out the best adjustment to life of which he is capable, often without fully understanding all that is involved.

However, he is willing to experience the pleasures and discomfort of self-revelation: i.e., he accepts the mixed pain and joy that accompanies each change in his attitude and feeling toward himself and others.

His claims on life are, for the most part, reasonable. If he wants to be a member of the Country Club and yet cannot afford it, he finds other social and recreational outlets in keeping with his budget.

The self-accepting person without special talent or ability is able to emotionally share in the gifts of others without undue regret about his own inborn deficiencies.

He does not brood about missed opportunities, lost causes, errors, and failures. Rather, he looks on them for what they can contribute to his doing things differently or better in the future.

He does not get stuck in the rut of irrational feelings of love, hate, envy, jealousy, suspicion, lust, and greed, because he lets each feeling spell out its special message for him.

*From SELF-ACCEPTANCE by McDonald, Smith and Sutherland. Copyright by The Hogg Foundation for Mental Health. The University of Texas, Austin, Texas.

If you think about it, many of us are constantly applying these dimensions to others as soon as we meet them (first impressions). Researchers have conducted several studies in which strangers met and interacted briefly, then rated each other on measures of the big five dimensions. When the researchers compared these ratings by strangers with ratings by other people who knew the participants very well (e.g., their parents or best friends), they found a substantial amount of agreement on at least some of the big five dimensions. For instance, strangers who met each other for a few minutes were quite accurate in rating one another with respect to the dimensions of extraversion and conscientiousness. While this may seem surprising, it actually fits quite well with our informal experience. Think about it: If someone met you for the first time, could he or she tell right away whether you are friendly and outgoing or shy and reserved? Whether you are neat and orderly or impulsive and disorganized? The answer offered by research findings is clear. They probably could!

New tests have thus been developed to specifically measure these broad traits (McCrae & Costa, 1992). The results of these tests may be helpful in helping us understand ourselves and others. They may also be helpful in career and vocational counseling. But, we do need to be careful not to use these categories to stereotype individuals.

Trait theories allow us to describe personality, but they do not help us understand how we developed these traits. Many of the other theories that we study in this chapter will help us understand how we have evolved into the individuals we are today.

CARL ROGERS: SELF-THEORY

Carl Rogers (1995) defines the development of the self-concept in terms of *self-actualization, which is defined as the fulfillment of one's own completely unique potential.* The key to self-actualization is the self-concept. Rogers maintains that the way we regard ourselves depends largely on the kind of regard given by others. In the ideal situation love is given freely and does not depend on any specific aspects of behavior. Rogers calls this *"unconditional positive regard."* Unconditional acceptance leads to unimpaired growth and the development of positive characteristics. Individuals who have received *unconditional positive regard* have a positive realistic self-concept, high self-esteem and feelings of self-respect. Rogers believes that a fully functioning person lives totally in the present and is continually changing to make full use of their potential.

How do I become self-actualized?

The difficulties in functioning are caused by a lack of *unconditional acceptance* by others starting at birth. Many parents make their affection and approval conditional on certain kinds of behavior. If the child does what the parent says, the parent will love the child. If the child does not live up to parental expectations the parent may show disapproval and withhold affection. Consequently, the child attempts to live up to his parents' expectations but cannot always be successful. This is the beginning of an unrealistic self-concept.

In order to become a *self-actualized* individual, we must accept ourselves as we are, the positive and the negative, with the potential to grow as a person and to accept others as they are, rather than wishing that they were somehow different. We all need to learn to place a high value on the individuality and uniqueness of ourselves and others.

VIKTOR FRANKL: SEARCH FOR MEANING

Viktor Frankl (1998) states:

> As humans, we are capable of *self-awareness* which allows us to reflect and to decide. With this *awareness,* we become free beings who are responsible for choosing the way we live and thus influence our own destiny.

This awareness of freedom and responsibility gives rise to existential anxiety, which is a basic human condition. Whether we like it or not, we are free, even though we may seek to avoid reflecting on this freedom. The knowledge that we must choose leads to anxiety. Facing the inevitable prospect of eventual death gives the present moment significance, for we become aware that we do not have forever to accomplish our projects.

Our task is to create a life that has *meaning* and *purpose*. (Meaning, purpose, and self-actualization will be discussed in more detail in Chapters nine and ten). As humans, we are unique in striving toward creating purposes and values that give meaning to living. To help you live life to its fullest read the following strategies.

Strategies to . . .
LIVE LIFE TO THE FULLEST

- We are finite and we do not have an unlimited time to do what we want to do with our life.
- We have the potential to take action or not to act; inaction is a decision.
- We choose our actions, and therefore we can partially create our own destiny.
- Meaning is not automatically bestowed on us but is the product of our searching and of our creating a unique purpose.
- Existential anxiety, which is basically a consciousness of our own freedom, is an essential part of living; as we increase our awareness of the choices available to us, we also increase our sense of responsibility for the consequences of those choices.
- We are subject to loneliness, meaninglessness, guilt, and isolation.
- We are basically alone, yet we have an opportunity to relate to other human beings.

This is an existential view of human nature that states that the significance of our existence is never fixed once and for all. Rather, we continually recreate ourselves through our goals. Humans are in a constant state of transition, emerging, evolving, and becoming. Being a person implies that we are discovering and making sense of our existence.

VIRGINIA SATIR: SELF-WORTH

Virginia Satir (1988) indicates in her writing that the crucial factor in *interpersonal relations—what happens inside people and between people—is the picture of the individual worth that each person carries around.* A person who can appreciate his or her own self worth will be able to see and respect the worth of others. She describes a human being who is living humanly, as a person who understands, values, and develops his or her body, finding it useful and beautiful. This is a person who is honest about himself or herself and others, who is willing to take risks, to be creative, embrace change, who is feeling, loving, playful, authentic, and productive. She says that the person who is living humanly can stand on his or her own two feet, can love deeply and fight fairly and effectively, and can be on equally good terms with both his or her tenderness and his or her toughness.

Get plenty of psychological sunshine. Circulate in new groups. Discover new and stimulating things to do.

David Schwartz

Self-worth is learned and the family is where it is basically acquired. There is always hope that your life can change because you can always learn new things. Human beings can learn, grow, and change all their lives. Every person has a feeling of worth, positive or negative. The question is, which one is it—***positive or negative?***

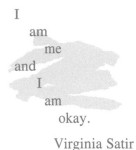

I
am
me
and
I
am
okay.

Virginia Satir

Do You Have High or Low Self-Worth? If you have *low self-worth* or know someone with *low self-worth,* you can change or help the other person change. Do not blame other people for your problems or faults. You are already that way, but you can change. Look to the future. For others to change, a nurturing environment needs to be provided; and for you to change a new environment is also needed. You will be able to develop and grow in an atmosphere where individual differences are appreciated, mistakes are tolerated, communication is open, and rules are flexible— this is a nurturing environment. Satir describes the main points that help human beings change and grow:

1. Communication of feelings: all feelings are honorable—Express your feelings—no one knows how you feel if you do not disclose your feelings to them.
2. Belief that a person is able to grow and change—If you believe you can change, you can.
3. Restoring the use of the senses—take in the world and see freely, touch freely, and hear freely.

What is in the Pot of Self-Worth? Finally, it is essential that people are able to be in contact with themselves on a *human* basis. Unfortunately, people are often dominated by some kind of idea of "what is right" that is actually *not right.* Satir uses a big pot that was used on her farm when she was a child as an analogy. There were times when the pot was used for soup, soap, and fertilizer. There were always two questions one had to ask about that pot to find out if you could use it or whether you wanted to put your energy into cleaning it out: 1) What is it full of? and 2) How full is it? Satir uses this *"pot concept"* to refer to how you feel about yourself, your *self-worth.*

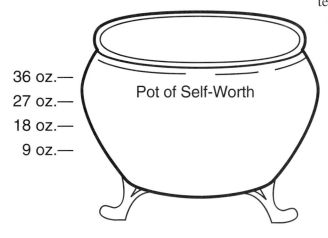

36 oz.—
27 oz.—
18 oz.—
9 oz.—

Pot of Self-Worth

What will it take to fill your pot?

Suppose your *"pot"* is full of a feeling you have had since childhood, such as hostility toward one of your parents because they abused you. Your inner thoughts say, "I must be a bad person since my parents always beat me. I'm no good. I must have deserved the abuse." *Your pot of self-worth is low* because of your past experience. You are experiencing "self-defeating" thoughts. You can learn to change these feelings. You can change your "self-talk," and tell yourself that you are a "good person." You can read a good self-help book that may help you or you may seek professional counseling.

Does Your Pot of Self-Worth Change? Your *self-worth pot* is constantly changing. One day you get an "A" on a test and you feel great, your *pot of self-worth* is full of good feelings. The next day you call someone on the phone for a date and you get turned down. Now your *pot of self-worth* is low—it has a lot of negative feelings in it. Knowing that you are a "good" person no matter what happens to you, will help you maintain a full pot of good feelings and help you succeed in life.

You must learn to free yourself of any rule decreeing that some feeling you have is not a human feeling. Then you are free to function fully and free to make choices about what you want for your life.

HOW DO OUR THOUGHTS AND OUR ENVIRONMENT RELATE TO THE DEVELOPMENT OF OUR PERSONALITY?

In Chapter three we will discover how learning theory relates to the development of our personality, but in the meantime we will discover how our thoughts and our relationships with other people interrelate.

HOW DID I GET TO BE THE PERSON I AM TODAY?

"I'll never get picked to play on the team." What would you tell this boy when he says this?

Cognitive theories of personality point out that there are important individual differences in the way people think about and define situations. Cognitive theories stress the mental processes through which people turn their sensations and perceptions into organized impressions of reality. They emphasize that people actively choose their own environments to a great extent. People choose to enter those situations that they expect to be reinforcing and to avoid those that are unsatisfying and uncertain. As many of you have observed, some members of minority ethnic groups "stick together" on college campuses. Often times it is that these members are uncertain about whether they would be accepted if they ventured into different ethnic friendships. Most of us tend to avoid relationships that we anticipate as unsatisfying by not attempting to start them and by continuing with familiar ones instead.

The cognitive emphasis to personality is the interaction of a person's thoughts and behavior. It considers the uniqueness of human beings, especially, of their thought processes. It also assumes that human beings are decision makers, planners, and evaluators of their own behavior. Many contemporary researchers claim that people can change their behavior, their conception of themselves, and their personalities in a short time if they are willing to change their thoughts. More often than not, we hope our cognitions are rational and sensible, thus enabling us to live and make decisions in emotionally healthy ways. But many times, our cognitive processing is irrational and nonsensible, and we may be totally unaware of it.

One can smile and smile and still be a villain.

William Shakespeare

Talk to Yourself. Use positive self-talk. It has been said that there is nothing wrong with talking to yourself, but if you should ever start answering back, then it is time to be concerned. Although going around talking to yourself in public may cause people to wonder about you, holding a dialogue is not only very useful, but also quite normal.

In fact, the inner conversations we have with ourselves can have a powerful effect on our emotional well-being and our motivation. Developing an awareness of precisely what we are saying to ourselves and about ourselves can help us understand why we react the way we do to various people and events in our lives.

Building self-esteem is easier with the help of positive self-talk (Self-talk is discussed in depth in Chapter Eight). You may have discovered that negative self-talk can have a tremendous influence in the development of someone's feelings about themselves—a poor self-concept.

> Each person has a mental picture of his or her ideal self. Moving towards that mental picture is what makes people feel good about themselves. The need to feel good about ourselves is the basis of human motivation.
>
> Harry Levinson, Ph.D.

Strategies to . . .

MONITOR YOUR SELF-TALK

1. Periodically during the day, ask yourself, "What am I thinking at this moment?" Then write down your thoughts along with a few notes about your situation and your feelings at the time. Do not censor your thoughts or feelings when you write them down.
2. Try to pinpoint specific thoughts and identify the feelings as accurately as possible. "Do I feel depressed, anxious, angry, happy, excited, or whatever?"
3. Are your thoughts appropriate for the situation you are experiencing? Do you have the right to feel angry in this situation? Should you feel guilty for what you did? Are you really inferior to other people?
4. We tend to have a subjective view of our own thoughts. It would be helpful to enlist the assistance of your friends and relatives. Using a friend or possibly a therapist who is objective, to discuss your assessment of your thoughts, can help you to identify the ways in which your self-talk is distorted and might be improved. An accurate perception of reality is the best path to positive adjustment.
5. Replace negative self-talk with positive self-talk.

Thinking Positively and Optimistically. You may recall the words of a popular song by Bobby McFerrin, "Don't worry, be happy" and it continues, "Cause when you worry, your face will frown and that will bring everything down." Does this kind of thinking influence your behavior? Indeed it does. A positive mood improves our ability to process information more efficiently, increases optimism, and raises self-esteem. A positive attitude enhances our sense of controlling our environment, and acting on this optimism can actually lead to more control over our circumstances. Since many of us are not positive thinkers and are more pessimistic than optimistic, how can we change this behavior?

Let's take a brief look at what is called *cognitive restructuring—the process of modifying thoughts, ideas, and beliefs*. Cognitive restructuring can be used to increase positive and optimistic thinking. This is also known as *self-talk—the non-verbal, mental speech we use when we think about something, solve problems, and make plans*. Self-talk is very helpful in cognitive restructuring. Positive self-talk will allow you the freedom to build the confidence you need in order to reach your potential. Take a look at what you may be saying to yourself in Table 2.3.

Is there a relationship between the self-fulfilling prophecy and positive self-talk? When you keep telling yourself, "I'm no good," "I'll never amount to anything," "I'm a liar," "Nobody likes me," "Nobody will ever love me," "I will never be able to pass math," etc, you will discover that it unconsciously effects your attitude and behavior. This is why it is so important to monitor your self-talk.

Table 2.3 What Do You Tell Yourself?	
Positive Self-Talk	**Negative Self-Talk**
I sure am a good person.	I am not a very good person.
I know I can do it.	I can not do anything right.
I am smarter than most people think.	I sure am stupid.
I know, if I try hard enough, I can pass that math class.	I will never be able to pass math.
If I do not ask I will never know if Cassandra will go out with me.	Cassandra would not want to go out with me.
I sure feel good.	I feel depressed.
Sabi and Angie are two of my good friends.	Nobody likes me.

What can you say to yourself to make you feel more confident?

You need to become aware of your self-talk. Several strategies are listed on the previous page that will help you monitor and fine tune your self-talk.

Mental health experts have discovered that this process has had a tremendous influence on the development of positive self-esteem for many people. Our thoughts have a great influence on our behavior, but we also need to look at the importance of external events and see how they are interrelated.

COGNITIVE AND SOCIAL-LEARNING THEORIES

Two somewhat different theories combine an emphasis on cognitive processes and a focus on social-learning processes. Some psychologists believe that we learn many of our behaviors either by conditioning or by observing others and modeling our behavior after them. Like cognitive and social psychological theorists, they emphasize the importance of mental processes: How we think and feel about the situations we are in affects our behavior. So instead of focusing solely on how our environment controls us (learning theory), social-cognitive theorists focus on how we and our environment interact: How do we interpret and respond to external events? How do our schemas, our memories, and our expectations influence our behavior patterns?

Human beings are driven by neither inner forces nor environmental factors, but rather by monitoring the impact of their behavior on other people, on the environment, and on themselves. We learn from our own experience and also learn vicariously by observing other people. We can also evaluate our own behavior according to personal standards and provide ourselves with reinforcers, such as self-approval or disapproval. You expect to get at least a "B" in your psychology class, but the night before the final exam you go to a party instead of studying. You only get a "C" for your grade. You tell yourself how dumb you were for not studying and feel disappointed in yourself.

Self-respect is the best means of getting the respect of others.

Napolean Hill

☞ CHECK THIS OUT . . .
Personal Influences on Behavior

The following categories of cognitive variables may have a tremendous influence on your behavior. Can you identify how these relate to your life?

1. **Expectancies.** What we have learned from our past experience leads us to form different expectations that help to determine our reactions to future events. You expect that your marriage will be the perfect relationship. When you discover that your spouse does not live up to your expectations, how do you feel? You expect to get a "D" in your calculus class, and you receive a "C." How do you feel? Think back on some of your experiences. How have your expectations affected your life?

2. **Competencies.** Each of us have a different combination of abilities and skills that shape our responses to events. Juan and Kyla are both asked to give a speech at a local event. Juan thinks he is a good speaker, so he accepts, but Kyla does not feel competent as a public speaker, so she refuses the offer. What are your competencies and how have they influenced your behavior?

3. **Personal Values.** Our sense of priorities and values also shape our decisions and actions. You refuse the offer for a job in a store where they sell pornographic magazines, but accept the job as a sales clerk in a store that sells religious goods. Your values influenced your decision.

4. **Encoding Strategies.** We also have different ways of perceiving and categorizing experiences that shape our responses. One mother gets very angry at her teenager when she sees his messy room, while another mother takes it in stride and realizes that it is a stage most teenagers go through.

5. **Self-Regulatory Systems.** We also formulate goals, plans, and strategies that influence our actions. You decide to take a physics class because you are majoring in science, and even if you decide to drop science as your major, physics will help you in your other future pursuits. Another student decides that physics would be a waste of time and would not be beneficial. (Mischel, 1993).

─────────────────────────────── ☜❚

What is reciprocal determinism?

Bandura's (1996) theory explains the complex interaction of individual factors, behavior, and environmental stimuli. Each factor can influence or change the others, and the direction of change is rarely one-way; it is reciprocal or bidirectional. This is an interactive, reciprocal perspective that has inspired researchers to study how the environment shapes personal factors, such as self-control and self-concept, and how these in turn influence behavior.

What Is Reciprocal Determinism? We have repeated this statement many times, but we cannot recall who we should credit for it: "We react to others as others react to us; others react to us as we react to them." "Behavior, in-

How can I find my "true self"?

ternal personal factors, and environmental influences all operate as interlocking determinants of each other" (Bandura, 1996). *Reciprocal determinism is the interacting influences between person, behavior, and environment.* You respond to a new acquaintance as a happy, positive person and they respond back to you on a positive basis. Your new acquaintance sees you as a friendly, happy person and you feel good about yourself because they responded back to you on a positive basis. You have a new friend. You were reinforced positively for being friendly and in the future you will most likely respond positively to other new acquaintances. Your younger sister would like to be just like you, a friendly, happy person. Everytime she tries to be nice and friendly to new people she seems to be rejected. She feels bad and thinks that people must think she is ugly or inferior, so she withdraws from people and becomes shy. She was not reinforced positively for being friendly and she interpreted that response as an indication that she must be inferior or inadequate. Her behavior is being influenced by her environment and she interprets the situation as positive or negative. Someone else may have interpreted the situation differently. They may say to themselves that those other people were sure weird, and do not perceive their reaction as a negative response. Figure 2.1 will demonstrate how reciprocal determinism influences our behavior.

Don't sell yourself short, Conquer the crime of self-deprivation. Concentrate on your assets. You're better than you think you are.

David Schwartz

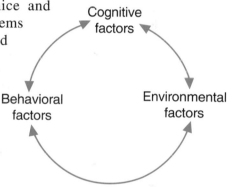

Figure 2.1. Reciprocal Determinism

How Do Environments and People Interact? We are both the products and the architects of our environment. Let's take a look at some specific ways in which people and environments interact.

1. Our personalities shape how we interpret and react to events. A shy person is most likely to interpret a frown on someone's face as a negative response, even though the person is not feeling well.
2. Our personalities help create situations to which we react. You think your roommate is mad at you and you respond negatively to your roommate and thus, your roommate responds angrily toward you. Now you are being reinforced correctly for your response, you think. Originally your roommate was not mad at you, but because of your response your roommate now is mad. Has this ever happened to you?
3. Different people choose different environments. The type of party you go to, the friends you associate with, the music you listen to, the type of shows you watch on television, the places you hang-out, the reading you do for pleasure—all are environments that you have chosen based on your beliefs, attitudes, and moods. The son of one of our colleagues was trying to decide which college to attend. He made his choice based on his liberal

Myself

I have to live with myself, and so
I want to be fit for myself to know,
I want to be able, as days go by,
Always to look myself straight in the eye;
I don't want to stand, with the setting sun,
And hate myself for things I have done.

I don't want to keep on a closet shelf
A lot of secrets about myself,
And fool myself, as I come and go,
Into thinking that nobody else will know
The kind of man I really am;
I don't want to dress myself in shame.

I want to go out with my head erect,
I want to deserve all men's respect;
But here in the struggle for fame and self
I want to be able to like myself.
I don't want to look at myself and know
That I'm bluster and bluff and empty show.

I can never hide myself from me;
I see what others may never see;
I know what others may never know,
I never can fool myself, and so.
Whatever happens, I want to be
Self-respecting and conscience free.

Edgar A. Guest

A good man just doesn't happen.
They have to be created by us women.
A guy is a lump like a doughnut.
So, first you gotta get rid of all the stuff his mom did to him.
And then you gotta get rid of all that macho crap that they pick up from beer commercials.
And then there's my personal favorite, the male ego.

Rosanne

political beliefs. Most of the students attending that college will have similar political beliefs and will thus reinforce each other for having that belief. A person with a conservative orientation would not feel very comfortable at that college.

As you continue to read this book you will see how your thoughts, behavior, and environment interact to influence your behavior. You may want to refer to locus of control, self-efficacy, and social learning theory in Chapter three.

We now have some insight into how our personalities have evolved over a period of time. We have looked at a variety of theories that contribute to our development. What theory do you feel has had the greatest influence on you or do you think that each theory has some valid points that you could use to justify how your personality developed? An interesting project would be for you to write your own personality theory that best describe your development.

Now we need to take a look at the importance of the "self"—your self-concept, self-image, and self-esteem. What kind of influence do these have on your behavior and how does the "self" develop?

THE SELF

There is new thinking about the self! The *self* is one of psychology's most vigorously researched topics. Every year it is amazing to see all the new studies that appear on "self-esteem," "self-awareness," and "self-monitoring."

One example of new thinking about the self is the *concept of "possible selves."* Your possible selves include your visions of the self you dream of becoming—the rich self, the thin self, the educated self, the successful self, and the admired self. They also include the self you fear becoming—the unemployed self, the addicted self, the failure self, and the unloved self. Such selves motivate us by laying out specific goals to pursue and the energy to work toward them. As they say: "Those who dream most, achieve most."

The Nature of the Self. One of the main factors differentiating humans from other animals is awareness of *"self."* As human beings, we can think, feel, and reflect on who we are. We form an identity and attach a value to it.

- Who are YOU?
- Where are you headed?
- Does it make a difference that you exist?

Over 2,000 years ago, the Greek philosopher Socrates advised all seekers of wisdom to, *"know thyself."* What Socrates realized and we have discovered since is the most vibrant, compelling, and baffling reality that we can know is, *the self.* It is difficult to define and even more difficult to measure or even investigate. Yet, such awareness of *self* is vital in knowing how people adjust to life.

Many ideas about *the self* have sprung from the humanistic-existential perspective. Carl Rogers (1995) has summarized a number of important characteristics of the self as follows:

> The greatest discovery in our generation is that human beings, by changing the inner attitudes of their minds, can change the outer aspects of their lives.
>
> William James

Ethnicity, Self, and Self-Esteem

Previous research indicated that African Americans, especially African American children, have a more negative self-concept than whites. More recent research, however, suggests that African Americans, Mexican Americans, and Puerto Ricans have equally positive self-concepts and perhaps even a higher self-esteem than Anglo-Americans (Allen & Majidi, 1989).

During the 1960's "Ethnic pride" was one of the positive movements to spring out of social turmoil. Its emphasis on the richness and diversity of various cultures appears to have improved the self-esteem of ethnic minority groups. Ethnic pride, however, has both positive and negative aspects. One obvious benefit is a sense of cultural identity (such as being African American, Mexican American, Hispanic, or Native American), with clearly defined cultural roles as to what is expected of a competent person. How can we help individuals discover and maintain a positive identity (a feeling of self) in such a diverse world in which we live? What would you suggest?

FOCUS ON DIVERSITY

1. It is organized and consistent.
2. It includes one's perceptions of all that comprises "I" or "me."
3. It includes the relationship among I or me and other people and features of life, as well as the value and importance of these relationships.
4. *The self* is available to consciousness (we can become aware of it) but it is not always conscious at any given moment.
5. The shape of *the self* is constantly changing, yet always recognizable.

We are human. We wrestle with our humanness. Some of us struggle with insecurity or inferiority, some deal with emotional problems, while others face mental or sexual problems. Poverty, illness, and physical disability can also test us. Many feel the pain of gender, racial, or ethnic prejudice. It is as if each of us is given a special task or challenge to work on as part of life and part of what will enhance our growth as an individual. It is the joy of discovering ourselves as human beings, our personal growth, sharing our love with others, and the contribution we make to others' lives that makes the process of life so exciting. The journey inward is life. Each of us must find our own way.

FIND YOUR REAL SELF

The Personal Self Image is the part of self that includes physical, behavioral, and psychological characteristics that establish uniqueness. It also includes gender, racial or ethnic identity, age, and status. Your *Personal Self Image,* who you think you are, is literally a package you put together from how others have seen and treated you and from your conclusions as you compared yourself to others. Your *sense of identity* is the end result of the interaction between your uniqueness and how others have reacted to it. It is the package you call *me.* But it is not the *Real Self.*

It is never who you are that hangs you up, but rather who you *THINK* you are. To discover your *Real Self* it is important to separate the *Real You* from your *Personal Self Image.* Lining up your self picture to fit the "real you" is of the utmost importance. There is probably no more exciting journey than that of *Real Self* discovery. Once your *self belief system* is accurate, you are free of the low self-esteem trap. You are free to be the *Real You.*

Where Did Your "Personal Self-Image" Come From? Your *personal self-image* includes past teachings about yourself. As a child, you build your *sense of self* based on what others told you about you. If you were exposed to large doses of *put downs* and *belittlers,* your *personal self-image* does not feel very pleasant. If you grew up in a very positive climate, your *me* package feels good to live in. *Your personal self image* is simply a belief system you have constructed about yourself. These past learnings jell into a *self* which may or may not be accurate. But once past learnings are part of your *self-image,* you see the package you have put together as accurate, regardless of the facts.

Tom, for instance, was repeatedly told as a child that he was dumb because he was slow to learn to read. Because he bought that label, he ignored or denied any evidence of his academic ability and creativity. "Dumb" and "smart" do not mix, they are mutually exclusive. Tom held onto those negative messages he received from significant

I often marvel that while each man loves himself more than anyone else, he sets less value on his own estimate than on the opinions of others.

Marcus Aurelius, A.D. 121–180 Meditations

people in his life, such as his parents and teachers. He also ignored any contrary evidence because it did not fit the "dumb" profile.

As an adult, Tom's past learning limited the accuracy of his "Personal Self-Image." He saw only evidence of being academically inferior. Years later, despite a college degree and a successful career, Tom still sees himself as "dumb."

Each of us identifies whatever qualities we learn to place after the words *I am.* Like Tom, we see such traits as truths about ourselves. These truths or *self-beliefs* literally screen out any messages to the contrary. In this way, past teachings can limit our options. If your *self-worth* is low or shaky, you are still believing things about yourself that are untrue negative ideas programmed into you about *You.*

> There was a prisoner who spent years in his cell totally unaware that the door was unlocked. At any point he could have walked out. But because he assumed there was a lock on the door, he remained trapped. His false belief limited his behavior.

Becoming Aware of the Self. Once you become aware that you are not locked into a prison of self-doubt, a whole new set of choices will open up. You become aware of new ways to see yourself, new ways you can behave, and new ways to relate. Of course, such choices and behaviors have been available to you all along. The problem has been you did not fully appreciate your capabilities and potential.

Lack of awareness, of course, is the same as having no choice. It is up to you to increase your awareness about the *Real You* so you can experience inner freedom. By increasing your awareness about yourself, you increase your choices in life. Carl Rogers (1995) described such a person as a *fully functioning person* who feels inwardly free to move in any direction. Being a *fully functioning person* can be a reality for you. If you strive to such an inner freedom, little can hold you back.

What about people from different ethnic groups and cultural backgrounds? Will this difference have an influence on an individual's self-concept?

> Accept human differences and limitations. Don't expect anyone to be perfect. Remember, the other person has a right to be different. And don't be a reformer.
>
> David Schwartz

HOW WE GET OUR SELF-IMAGE FROM OTHERS

There is no doubt about it, kids come into this world with different personalities.

> Take my youngest, sweet good natured boy, he would give you the shirt off his back. But the oldest will not part with a dime. He is a 'born miser'.

> I know what you mean. I've got one at Princeton, and another who'll be lucky if he gets out of high school. He'll never be a student that's for sure. I've told him, 'You're not stupid, just lazy.'

> You should meet my daughters. You wouldn't know they are related. The little one is graceful, moves like a ballerina. The big one can't walk into a room without knocking something over. We call her 'the klutz.'

If I were able to express myself, I could have told them:

Dear Friends, what you are making jokes about is no laughing matter. Children see themselves primarily through their parents' eyes. They look to us to tell them not only who they are, but what they're capable of becoming. They depend on us for a larger vision of themselves, and for the tools to implement that vision.

I also could have given them the following quote by an anonymous writer:

There is no such thing as a child who is selfish. There is only a child who needs to experience the joys of generosity. There is no such thing as a child who is lazy. There is only a child who is unmotivated, who needs someone to believe that he can work hard when he cares enough. There is no such thing as a child who is clumsy. There is only

FOCUS ON DIVERSITY

What Is Your Cultural Orientation?

Answer the following questions Yes or No: Yes   No

1. I like to live close to my good friends and family.   ___   ___

2. To be superior, a person must stand-up for
   herself or himself.   ___   ___

3. I enjoy meeting and talking to my neighbors
   everyday.   ___   ___

4. If the group is slowing me down, it is better to
   leave it and work alone.   ___   ___

5. The larger the family, the more family problems
   there are.   ___   ___

6. It is reasonable for a son to continue his father's
   business.   ___   ___

7. I can count on my relatives for help if I find myself
   in any kind of trouble.   ___   ___

8. In the long run, the only person you can count on
   is yourself.   ___   ___

9. There is everything to gain and nothing to lose for
   classmates to group themselves for study and
   discussions.   ___   ___

10. If you want something done right, you have to do
    it yourself.   ___   ___

If you answered "yes" to questions #1,3,6,7, and 9, you are more than likely from a collectivist orientation. If you answered "yes" to #2,4,5,8, and 10, you are more than likely from an individualistic orientation. What does this mean?

a child who needs to have his movements accepted and his body exercised. Children—all children—need to have their best affirmed and their worst ignored or redirected.

SELF-ESTEEM

How to Appreciate Your True Self. This chapter began with a description of the *nature of self.* Remember that as human beings, we have the ability to reflect on who we are. We are aware of a unique *identity.* But we are not only aware of *ourself,* we attach a value to that *self.* So we can decide whether we will accept or reject our *self,* whether we are *OK* or *not OK,* whether we are good or bad. You are either a *self-hater, self-doubter,* or a *self-affirmer.*

So this unique human ability we have—the ability we have to attach a value to our self—can lead to self rejection and tremendous emotional pain. The term *self-esteem refers to the overall evaluation of oneself, whether one likes or dislikes who one is, believes or doubts oneself, and values or belittles one's worth.* How you evaluate yourself is crucial to your psychological adjustment.

Does your cultural orientation influence your self-esteem?

INDIVIDUALISM VS COLLECTIVISM

Over the years, social scientists have observed that cultures differ to the extent to which they value individualism and the virtues of independence, autonomy, and self-reliance, or collectivism and the virtues of interdependence, cooperation, and social harmony. In a collectivist society, a person is first and foremost,

> To love oneself is the beginning of a life long romance.
>
> Oscar Wilde

> There is as much difference between us and ourselves, as between us and others.
>
> Michel de Montaigne
> Essays, 1588

Table 2.4 Individualism vs. Collectivism

	Individualism	Collectivism
Concept of self	Independent (identity from individual traits)	Interdependent (identity from belonging)
Relationships	Many, often temporary or casual; confrontation acceptable	Few, close and enduring; harmony required
Attribution	Behavior reflects one's personality and attitudes	Behavior reflects social norms and roles.
Coping methods	Changes reality	Accommodates to reality
Morality	Defined by individuals (self-based)	Defined by the group (duty-based)
Life task	Discover and express one's uniqueness	Maintain connections, fit in
What matters	Me-personal achievement and fulfillment; rights and liberties	We-group goals, and solidarity; social responsibilities and relationships

Source: Adapted from Myers (1995), Triandis (1994).

a loyal member of a family, team, company, church, state, and other groups. In an individualist culture, however, personal goals take priority over group allegiances. In what countries are these different orientations most extreme? The United States, Australia, Great Britain, Canada, and the Netherlands, in that order, are the most individualistic. While people from Venezuela, Colombia, Pakistan, Peru, Japan, Taiwan, and China are the most collectivistic (Triandis, 1994).

Individualism and collectivism are so deeply ingrained in a culture that they mold our very self-conceptions and identities. Take a brief look at the following table and see how each culture may influence your personality and self-esteem.

The Benefits of Self-Esteem. How we feel about ourselves is important. Research studies reveal the benefits of positive self-esteem and the hazards of self-righteous pride. High self-esteem—a feeling of self worth—pays dividends. People who feel good about themselves have fewer ulcers, fewer sleepless nights, succumb less to pressures to conform, are less likely to use drugs, are more persistent at difficult tasks, and are just plain happier (Brown 1991).

A study in 1951 by Leaky showed that when a student's self-esteem changed, so did performance. A later study found a positive correlation between self-esteem and grade-point average. Self-esteem was also related to teacher rat-

---

Table 2.5   High Self-Esteem vs. Low Self-Esteem

High Self-Esteem Traits	Low Self-Esteem Traits
Perceives Reality	Avoid Reality to Avoid Anxiety
Relatively Undefensive	Defensive
Spontaneous	Reserved
Natural	Plays a Role
Task Centered	Self-Centered
Enjoys Being Alone	Oriented Toward Approval of Others
Self Reliant	Dependent
Feels Kinship with Humankind	Us vs. Them
Relationships are Intimate	Relationships are Casual
Non-judgmental of Others	Critical of Others
Acceptance	Strives to Be Perfect and Avoid Mistakes
Well Developed Value System	Values not Clarified
Philosophical Sense of Humor	Hostile
Creative	Creativity Perceived as Risky
Cooperative with Others	Views Self as Different from Others
Makes Growth Choices	Makes Fear Choices
Dares to Be Unpopular	Conforming
Experiences without Self-Consciousness	Considers What Others Think

(Brown, 1991)

ings of students and observations of classroom behavior. Students with higher levels of self-esteem generally performed at higher academic levels and got along more positively in the classroom. In terms of academic performance, a student's IQ score may not be as important as the self-esteem rating. "Self-confidence permits a child to perform; whereas brilliance may be trapped in low self-esteem" (Briggs, 1975).

Briggs also stated that "self-esteem is the mainspring that slates every child for success or failure." Self-esteem has a direct influence on the feeling of self-worth, on human relations, productivity, integrity, stability, and uncertainty. "Self-esteem is the armor that protects a person from the dragons of life: drugs, alcohol, unhealthy relationships, and delinquency" (McKay & Fanning 1987).

Another benefit of self-esteem is the ability to accept criticism and rejection. Those with high self-esteem tend to view criticism as constructive. They do not interpret a "no" as rejection. Instead, these individuals usually learn and "return with a more polished act" (Zimbardo, 1977).

Clearly, self-esteem influences all aspects of life; in fact, it is the foundation upon which happiness and well-being are built.

The Costs of Low Self-Esteem. Low self-esteem exacts costs. People who do not feel good about themselves are vulnerable to depression and failure. Those whose self-image falls short of what they think they ought to be are vulnerable to anxiety. Most counselors will agree that most of the clients that they encounter that are unhappy, frustrated, and in a state of despair are individuals that have

My Declaration of Self-Esteem

I am me.

I was uniquely created by God. There's not another human being in the whole world like me—I have my very own fingerprints and I have my very own thoughts. I was not stamped out of a mold like a Coca-Cola top to be the duplicate of another.

I own all of me—my body, and I can do with it what I choose; my mind, and all of its thoughts and ideas; my feelings, whether joyful or painful.

I own my ideals, my dreams, my hopes, my fantasies, my fears.

I reserve the right to think and feel differently from others and will grant to others their right to thoughts and feelings not identical with my own.

I own all my triumphs and successes. I own also all my failures and mistakes. I am the cause of what I do and am responsible for my own behavior. I will permit myself to be imperfect. When I make mistakes or fail, I will know that I am not the failure—I am still OK—and I will discard some parts of me that were unfitting and will try new ways.

I will laugh freely and loudly at myself—a healthy self-affirmation.

I will have fun living inside my skin.

I will remember that the door to everybody's life needs this sign:
Honor Thyself.

I have value and worth.

reluctant to acknowledge your positive side. Critical parents often punish children for speaking well of themselves. Also, while growing up
children experience hundreds and hundreds of interactions like these:

Heather: "I got a 100 on my spelling test."
Dad: "Great. But what are you going to do about that D in
            Math?"
Jason: "I made my own bed."
Mom: "Yes, but it is hard to tell. Your room is such a mess."
Mike: "I came in second place at the district track meet and got
            my best time."
Dad: "Who came in first?"

As a result of cultural and parental conditioning, you may find it anxiety provoking to give yourself credit for your assets. It is now time, however, to toot your own horn. Get a BIG piece of blank paper. List all your
strengths. Think of all parts of your *Real Self-Image.*

- Your physical appearance
- How you relate to others
- Your personality
- How others see you
- Your work/school/daily task performance
- Your mental functioning
- Your sexuality

It takes a concentrated effort to make this list. If you are having difficulty thinking of strengths, think of how your best friend would describe you
in each of these areas. Your list of strengths will be long if you are willing
to put forth the effort and willing to experience the anxiety. Once you have
listed many of the qualities in yourself you appreciate, that does not mean
you will remember them. Remembering your strengths, particularly at the
times when you feel most down on yourself requires a system. The following three strategies may help you really believe in your positive qualities:

A.   Daily affirmations. Write affirmations for yourself each day. Make them
     believable, comforting, and supportive.
B.   Reminder signs and notes. Many people who post positive messages re-
     port they reinforce and strengthen their personal sense of adequacy.
C.   Active Integration. Recall specific examples and times when you clearly
     demonstrated your strengths. Transform your strengths into specific
     memories. This process will help to convince you that your list of posi-
     tive qualities actually applies to you.

4. **List Your Faults.** There is nothing wrong with having faults. Every human being has them. The problem is not with your faults, but how you
   overrate them. The problem is that people use their faults for destructive self attack and to condemn themselves. There are four basic rules
   to acknowledging weaknesses:

   A.   *Use non-pejorative language*—language that does not make a bad
        situation worse. Go through your list and eliminate all the words
        that have negative connotations. Banish certain words from your
        self descriptive vocabulary; for example; fat, ugly, dumb, blabber-
        mouth, etc.

That you may retain
your self-respect, it is
better to displease the
people by doing what
you know is right, than
to temporarily please
them by doing what
you know is wrong.

William J.H. Boetcker

    B. *Use accurate language.* Confine yourself to the facts.

    C. *Be specific rather than general.* Eliminate words such as always, never, anything, etc.

    D. *Find exceptions or corresponding strengths.* This is essential for any item you feel particularly bad about.

5. **Listen to Your Inner Voice.** We pay attention to other people so that we can learn best how to gain their acceptance, love, respect and protection, and at the same time avoid their rejection. As a result, we tend not to pay enough attention to our inner voices. Abraham Maslow (1971) suggests that one way to promote our own growth is to pay attention to our own values and tastes. Carl Rogers (1961) tells us to trust ourselves. We must trust our ability to live our own life, to discover and follow our own standards. He reminds us that it is all right to become more like the person we want to be. If we value our own judgments more highly, and become more self directing, we will become more self confident.

6. **Make the Growth Choice Rather Than the Fear Choice.** Reject rigidity. Take responsibility to direct your own life. If you are dissatisfied with your life as it is now, be willing to accept change. You promote your growth or fail to do that every time you make a decision. We are constantly making decisions whether to be honest or to lie, to try new things or be safe, to be open or be defensive. If you make each decision a choice for growth you manifest courage.

7. **Shed Perfectionistic Demands.** Realize that you are human and that you do have faults. Do not expect always to live up to your own ideals or those of others. By accepting your faults you can begin to examine them without being afraid of what you might find. Come to grips with the fact that everyone can not like you, or you will spend your life trying to please others. Although there is nothing wrong with pleasing others, you must first of all be true to yourself.

8. **Becoming More Synergistic.** Maslow describes *this as being involved with others*. Become involved with other people and your work and leisure time will become more valuable to you. Make a commitment. Alfred Adler (1927) points out that we greatly promote our health and functioning by cooperation with others.

9. **Do Not Overburden Yourself with Work.** Take time for the pleasures in life. Enjoy the present and expand it. Plan for the future but do not live it.

10. **Keep a Diary.** Record what you enjoy about your day. You may be doing things out of habit rather than because you enjoy them. By keeping a diary you may discover that some of your activities do not make you happy. If this is the case, then you can actively make the attempt not to do these things any longer.

11. **Keep a Sense of Humor.** Laugh easily, enjoy a good joke, get fun out of life. Some of us do not know how to play. We take our life and ourselves too seriously. Perhaps we grew up in families in which there was not much fun and happiness. Remember to keep a balance in your life between work and play.

> People can be terribly brutal with themselves. Out of the whole animal kingdom, only humans are endowed with this capacity to make themselves miserable.
>
> S.A. Bower & Gordon G. Bower

> We are free to go where we wish and to be what we are.
>
> Jonathan Livingston Seagull

- Viktor Frankl states that our task is to create a life that has meaning and purpose.
- Virginia Satir's Self-Worth theory indicates that what happens inside people and between people—is the picture of the individual worth that each person carries around.
- Cognitive theories of personality point out that there are important individual differences in the way people think about and define situations.
- Building self-esteem is easier with the help of positive self-talk, thinking positively, and optimistically.
- Cognitive restructuring, the process of modifying thoughts, ideas, and beliefs, can be used to increase positive and optimistic thinking.
- Self talk—the non-verbal, mental speech we use when we think about something, solve problems, and make plans. Positive or negative self-talk may have an influence on your self-concept.
- Reciprocal determinism is the interacting influences between person, behavior, and environment.
- Your personal self-image is the part of the self that includes physical, behavioral, and psychological characteristics that establish uniqueness.
- There are many benefits to positive self-esteem, including better health, feeling happy, etc.
- There are many costs to low self-esteem, poor health, not as happy, more frustration, poorer work performance, etc.
- The self-serving bias is a person's tendency to evaluate his or her own behavior as worthwhile, regardless of the situation.
- Individualistic societies value independence, autonomy, and self-reliance. Collectivistic societies value interdependence, cooperation, and social harmony.
- Individualism and collectivism are so deeply ingrained in a culture that they mold our self-concepts and identities.
- There are many strategies to improve self-esteem, including:

  1. Recognize that you are in control,
  2. Accept your physical appearance—just the way you are,
  3. Affirm your strength,
  4. List your faults,
  5. Listen to your inner voice,
  6. Keep a sense of humor,
  7. Do not be afraid to make mistakes, etc.

Personal growth and self-awareness involve accepting ourselves and enjoying our relationships with others. Only "you" can make the choice whether you will live an enjoyable and fulfilling life or one of stagnation.

??? Questions ???

1. Why do we need to study about the development of the "self"?
2. Explain how significant others influence a person's self-image.
3. Define and explain the following concepts of Freud: id, ego, super-ego.
4. Describe Erikson's Eight Stages of Psychosocial Development.
5. Briefly explain Levinson's Stages of Adult Development.
6. Explain how the Big Five Model of Personality has influenced your perception of others using the "Big Five" Traits.
7. Describe how Carl Roger's Self-Theory influences the development of your personality.
8. Describe, briefly, Viktor Frankl's Search for Meaning theory.
9. Briefly describe Virginia Satir's theory of Self-Worth.
10. Define Reciprocal Determinism and explain how our thoughts and our environment influence the development of our personality?
11. Explain how cognitive and social-learning theories influence your self-image.

12. Describe the cognitive variables that influence your behavior.
13. Define collectivism and individualism and explain how they may influence an individual's self-concept.
14. What are the costs of low self-esteem? Explain.
15. What are the benefits of having high self-esteem? Explain.
16. Define the Self-Serving Bias and explain how it influences your behavior.
17. Briefly explain the twelve strategies that will help you improve your self-esteem.

🔑 Key Terms 🔑

Adolescent Identity Crisis Stage
Agreeableness
Autonomy vs. Doubt
Cognitive Restructuring
Cognitive Theory
Collectivism
Conscientiousness
Ego
Extraversion
Generativity vs. Self-Absorption
Getting Established Stage
Getting Settled Stage
Id
Individualism

Industry vs. Inferiority
Initiative vs. Guilt
Integrity vs. Despair
Interpersonal Relations
Intimacy vs. Isolation
Mid-Life Crisis
Mid-Life Transition
Neuroticism
Openness
Personal Self-Image
Pot of Self-Worth
Real-Self
Reciprocal Determinism
Search For Meaning
Self-Awareness
Self-Esteem

Self-Image
Self-Perception
Self-Serving Bias
Self Theory
Self-Worth
Significant Others
Social Comparison
Social-Learning Theory
Stages of Psychosocial Development
Super-ego
Trait
Trust vs. Mistrust
Unconditional Positive Regard
Wavering and Doubt Stage

??? Discussion ???

1. Do we have a choice in determining who we become? Explain.
2. How do our interactions with others help in discovering who we are?
3. Who are the significant others in your life? What impact have they had on your life? Were they a good influence or a bad influence?
4. How does striving for perfection lead to emotional pain?
5. How does social comparison influence our self-image?
6. How has the id, ego, and super-ego influenced your behavior?
7. Discuss the relationship between your life and Erikson's Stages of Development.
8. Discuss the stages of adult development and how they relate to your development or to the development of someone older than you.
9. Why is it so difficult to make changes in our self-concept?
10. Discuss the cultural influences on a person's development.
11. What theory of personality has had the greatest influence on your development?

Who Do You Think You Are?

Purpose: To help you identify your own self-concept.

Instructions:

    I. For each category below supply three words or phrases that best describe you.

    II. After filling in the spaces within each category, organize your responses in Part B so that the most fundamental characteristic is listed first, with the rest of the items following in order of descending importance.

Part A: *Identifying the elements of your self-concept*

1. What moods or feelings best characterize you (cheerful, considerate, optimistic, etc.)?

    a. _____

    b. _____

    c. _____

2. How would you describe your physical condition and/or your appearance (tall, attractive, weak, muscular, etc.)?

    a. _____

    b. _____

    c. _____

3. How would you describe your social traits (friendly, shy, aloof, talkative, etc.)?

    a. _____

    b. _____

    c. _____

4. What talents do you possess or lack (good artist, lousy carpenter, competent swimmer, etc.)?

    a. _____

    b. _____

    c. _____

5. How would you describe your intellectual capacity (curious, poor reader, good mathematician, etc.)?

    a. _____

    b. _____

    c. _____

6. What beliefs do you hold strongly (vegetarian, Christian, passivist, etc.)?

    a. _____

    b. _____

    c. _____

7. What social roles are the most important in your life (brother, student, friend, bank teller, club president, etc.)?

    a. _____

    b. _____

    c. _____

8. What other terms haven't you listed so far that describe other important things about you?

    a. _____

    b. _____

    c. _____

Part B: *From Part A list the self-concept elements in order of importance*

1. _____   10. _____

2. _____   11. _____

3. _____   12. _____

4. _____   13. _____

5. _____   14. _____

6. _____   15. _____

7. _____   16. _____

8. _____   17. _____

9. _____   18. _____

19. _____   22. _____

20. _____   23. _____

21. _____   24. _____

III. Give this list (Part **B**) to another person (classmate). This list will describe to your partner how you perceive yourself as a person.

Discussion

A. Does this list describe you as a person? If not, tell your partner more information about you that describes the *real* you.

B. Tell your partner what you like about yourself as a person. Use the characteristics from your list.

C. Tell your partner what element or elements you listed that you would like to change.

D. Discuss with your partner how important a person's self-concept is and how a person's self-concept affects his or her personality.

E. Discuss with your partner what you learned about yourself from this activity.

Name _____ Date _____

Accepting Myself

Purpose: To demonstrate the value of feeling positive about yourself and to demonstrate the value of accepting yourself with your strengths and your weaknesses.

Instructions:

   I. Divide into groups of three to five participants.

  II. All participants answer the following questions.

    a. *Three* things I like about myself.

    _____

    _____

    _____

    b. *Two* things I would like to change about myself.

    _____

    _____

  III. When the participants have completed the questions, share the answers with your group. Give examples so that your partners will understand you better.

  IV. Your partners will ask at least two questions about each of your statements. Then, each partner will have a turn to share and be asked questions.

   V. Group members might want to discuss how they feel each other might change the aspects of themselves that they feel need some modification.

Discussion

A. Which answer was harder for you to reveal? Why?

B. Discuss the following statement: Accepting ourselves means to accept our strengths and our weaknesses and make every effort to change the weaknesses into strengths, if *possible* and *desirable* to the individual.

Name _____ Date _____

I Am a Person Who Conveys

Purpose: To become more aware of how you are perceived by others and how accurate you are in your perceptions of others.

Instructions:

   I. Each person responds to the first scale by circling the number on the continuum that indicates the way you convey yourself to others. Do not mark this the way you see yourself but the way you feel you come across to others.

  II. Give the second form to a friend and have him or her evaluate you.

 III. Looking at both scales, identify any discrepancies between the two. Ask your friend to discuss the discrepancies in terms of: "I see you this way because. . ."

I Am a Person Who Conveys . . .

Personal warmth	1 2 3 4 5 6 7 8 9	Aloofness, coldness
Neat appearance	1 2 3 4 5 6 7 8 9	Careless appearance
Cheerful disposition	1 2 3 4 5 6 7 8 9	Unhappy disposition
Sincerity, genuineness	1 2 3 4 5 6 7 8 9	Insincerity, artificiality
Insecurity in behavior	1 2 3 4 5 6 7 8 9	Confidence in behavior
Reluctancy to talk with others	1 2 3 4 5 6 7 8 9	Eagerness to talk with others
Desire to listen	1 2 3 4 5 6 7 8 9	No interest in listening
Primary concern for self	1 2 3 4 5 6 7 8 9	Primary concern for others
Ability to express ideas and feelings	1 2 3 4 5 6 7 8 9	Difficulty in expressing ideas and feelings
Awareness of what is happening	1 2 3 4 5 6 7 8 9	Lack of awareness of what is happening

| Difficulty in making other people comfortable | 1 | 2 | 3 | 4 | 5 | 6 | 7 | 8 | 9 | Ease in making other people comfortable |

| Talk too much | 1 | 2 | 3 | 4 | 5 | 6 | 7 | 8 | 9 | Talk too little |

| Not intelligent | 1 | 2 | 3 | 4 | 5 | 6 | 7 | 8 | 9 | Intelligent |

| Excitement, enthusiasm | 1 | 2 | 3 | 4 | 5 | 6 | 7 | 8 | 9 | Dullness, apathy |

_____ IS A PERSON WHO CONVEYS . . .

Personal warmth	1 2 3 4 5 6 7 8 9	Aloofness, coldness
Neat appearance	1 2 3 4 5 6 7 8 9	Careless appearance
Cheerful disposition	1 2 3 4 5 6 7 8 9	Unhappy disposition
Sincerity genuineness	1 2 3 4 5 6 7 8 9	Insincerity, artificiality
Insecurity in behavior	1 2 3 4 5 6 7 8 9	Confidence in behavior
Reluctancy to talk with others	1 2 3 4 5 6 7 8 9	Eagerness to talk with others
Desire to listen	1 2 3 4 5 6 7 8 9	No interest in listening
Primary concern for self	1 2 3 4 5 6 7 8 9	Primary concern for others
Ability to express ideas and feelings	1 2 3 4 5 6 7 8 9	Difficulty in expressing ideas and feelings
Awareness of what is happening	1 2 3 4 5 6 7 8 9	Lack of awareness of what is happening
Difficulty in making other people comfortable	1 2 3 4 5 6 7 8 9	Ease in making other people comfortable
Talk too much	1 2 3 4 5 6 7 8 9	Talk too little
Not intelligent	1 2 3 4 5 6 7 8 9	Intelligent
Excitement, enthusiasm	1 2 3 4 5 6 7 8 9	Dullness, apathy

111

Discussion

1. Many times we feel we convey a particular characteristic to others because that is the way we see ourselves. What does this activity show us about our awareness and honesty in conveying our true self to others?

2. Did you have a realistic perception of yourself as compared to how the other person perceived you? Discuss the differences between your perceptions and the other person's perceptions.

3. Discuss how our perceptions of another person affect our interactions with them.

Adjective Checklist

Purpose: To provide an opportunity for the class members to reveal themselves to the other group members and to receive feedback on how the other group members perceive them.

Instructions:

I. Review the list of words and place a (+) next to the adjectives you think best describes you and a (–) next to the adjectives which are least descriptive of you.

II. Divide into groups of three or four.

III. Each member then shares, with the group, at least four adjectives most descriptive and least descriptive of them.

IV. Another option is to make a copy and ask a friend to place a (+) next to the adjectives he or she thinks best describes you and a (-) next to the adjective which are least descriptive of you.

_____ accepting	_____ sarcastic	_____ insensitive
_____ self-accepting	_____ dreamy	_____ nervous
_____ anxious	_____ silly	_____ loving
_____ aggressive	_____ selfish	_____ ambitious
_____ original	_____ carefree	_____ authoritative
_____ happy	_____ determined	_____ calm
_____ vain	_____ spontaneous	_____ conforming
_____ controlling	_____ tense	_____ confident
_____ irritable	_____ certain	_____ Intelligent
_____ worried	_____ sentimental	_____ observant
_____ rigid	_____ unpredictable	_____ obsessive
_____ brave	_____ patient	_____ relaxed
_____ responsible	_____ extroverted	_____ intuitive
_____ simple	_____ hostile	_____ serious
_____ proud	_____ questioning	_____ modest
_____ adaptable	_____ remote	_____ mature
_____ dependent	_____ shy	_____ unsympathetic
_____ effervescent	_____ warm	_____ immature
_____ thoughtful	_____ withdrawn	_____ objective
_____ lazy	_____ bitter	_____ religious
_____ dependable	_____ independent	_____ organized
_____ mystical	_____ naive	_____ unorganized
_____ inconsiderate	_____ complex	_____ sympathetic
_____ understanding	_____ sensitive	_____ temperamental

Discussion

1. What did you find out about yourself as a result of this activity?

2. What is the one adjective that causes you the greatest amount of difficulty in relationships with other people? Explain.

Name_____   Date_____

Do Gender Roles Still Exist?

Purpose: Discover how you and others perceive gender roles and issues.

Instructions: In the spaces below, list ten characteristics and behaviors that you associate with being male and female in our society.

   I. You may either do this activity individually or with a partner. An interesting alternative would be to divide your pairs by sex; males with males and females with females. This will help the class see whether there is a distinct perceived difference or not.

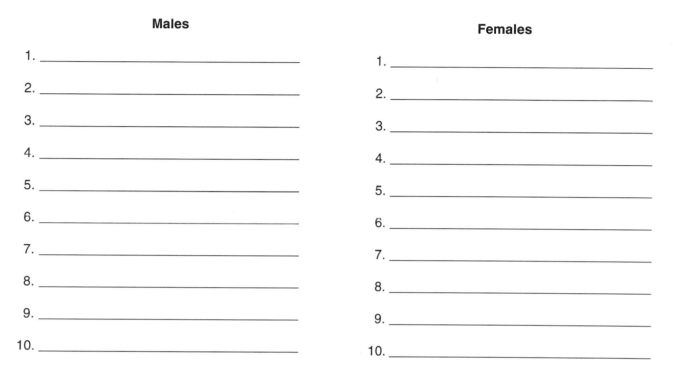

Males

1. _____
2. _____
3. _____
4. _____
5. _____
6. _____
7. _____
8. _____
9. _____
10. _____

Females

1. _____
2. _____
3. _____
4. _____
5. _____
6. _____
7. _____
8. _____
9. _____
10. _____

   II. Before you go on, make two copies of the list and set them aside for now.

   III. Look at the list of the 20 different characteristics, both male and female, and circle the ones that best apply to you. You may discover that you identify with some characteristics of the opposite sex. How many of them did you select?

   IV. Divide into small groups of 3–5 individuals and answer the following questions.

Discussion

1. Did the females in the group circle more of the male characteristics than males circled of the female characteristics? If so, why?

2. Are there some characteristics of the opposite sex that you wish could be attributed to members of your sex? Which ones are they? Why would you like them attributed to your sex?

3. Do you feel our definitions of gender roles are preventing you from behaving or developing in the ways you would prefer? Explain.

4. How has gender role influenced your personality development?

5. How could we best eliminate the effects of gender role development in our society?

   V. Now, give the copy of the list that you previously made, and give it to someone that knows you well and ask them to circle the characteristics that best apply to you, using both male and female characteristics. When they have completed the list, compare your list with theirs. How we see ourselves is not always how others see us. How close did your list compare with your friends? What might the difference tell you about yourself?

   VI. Give the other copy of the list to someone who knows you well that is at least ten years or more older or younger than you, and do the same as in previous question. Is there a difference because of age? If there is a difference, why?

Human Relations Position Paper

Purpose: To analyze your present position, based upon your past experiences and learning, in order to have a better idea of the direction in which you want to move in the future.

Instructions:

I. A Human Relations Position Paper should represent a critical analysis of those factors that have brought you to this point in your life and have made you what you are. It should also include your plans for the future.

II. No one but you and your instructor will read your position paper unless, of course, you choose to show it to someone else. Your instructor considers it completely confidential.

III. As a guide for preparing your position paper, the following outline is suggested. This is intended only as a guide, and you may add or delete whatever items you choose.

IV. Anything that helps you arrive at your *position* and chart your course of action (from poetry to pictures to words) is acceptable.

V. Your instructor will determine the length of this paper. We suggest five pages.

Human Relations Position Paper Outline

I. The Person I Am (Include the influential factors which have contributed to making you what you are).

  A. Influence of Family Background
   1. Relationship with parents
   2. Relationship with siblings
   3. Socioeconomic setting
   4. Family's expectations
   5. Other

  B. Adolescence
   1. School experience
   2. Peer group (left out/included—Why?)
   3. Successes/Failures and their effect
   4. Influential adults other than parents
   5. Other

  C. Personal Sexuality
   1. Dating experiences and its effect
   2. "Facts of life" information or misinformation and its effect
   3. My "role" as a man/woman
   4. My attitudes toward the opposite sex
   5. Other

  D. Goals for Future
   1. How have I arrived at my goals?
   2. Occupational choice—Why?
   3. Feelings of personal adequacy or inadequacy
   4. Degree of flexibility
   5. Influential people
   6. Other

II. Where Do I Go From Here?

    A. Summary of Present Position
        1. How do I see myself/how do others see me?
        2. How well do I communicate?
        3. Value system
        4. Relationships with others (OKness)
        5. My view of a meaningful occupation
           a. What I expect
           b. What's expected of me
           c. My chances for success
        6. How I view my sexuality
           a. In relation to marriage
           b. "Role" expectations
           c. Understanding of needs

    B. Plans for Future
        1. What is the Good Life for me?
           a. How I will achieve it
           b. How it relates to my value system
           c. How it relates to my chosen occupation
        2. What are my priorities for future?
        3. Do I want to "go it alone" or build relationships with others?
           a. How I will do this
        4. Do I want to share my life with someone else in marriage?
           a. My responsibilities
           b. What I expect of others
        5. What will my biggest problems be?

Self-Awareness

Learning Journal

Select the statement below that best defines your feelings about the personal value or meaning gained from this chapter and respond below the dotted line.

- **I learned that I . . .**
- **I realized that I . . .**
- **I discovered that I . . .**

- **I was surprised that I . . .**
- **I was pleased that I . . .**
- **I was displeased that I . . .**

. . . .

continue on reverse

CHAPTER 3

Who's in Control?

Children Learn What They Live

If a child lives with criticism, He learns to condemn.
If a child lives with hostility, He learns to fight.
If a child lives with ridicule, He learns to be shy.
If a child lives with shame, He learns to feel guilty.
If a child lives with tolerance, He learns to be patient.
If a child lives with encouragement, He learns confidence.
If a child lives with praise, He learns to appreciate.
If a child lives with fairness, He learns justice.
If a child lives with security, He learns to have faith.
If a child lives with approval, He learns to like himself.
If a child lives with acceptance and friendship, He learns to find
    love in the world.

Dorothy Law Nolte

Think about this...

- "How am I ever going to stop smoking?"
- "I've tried hundreds of times to lose 15 pounds. I lose 5 pounds then gain back 10 pounds. How can I lose weight and make sure that I can keep it off?"
- "I need to study more. My grades aren't too good. How can I get myself to sit down and study more?"
- "I would sure like to have more dates, I haven't had a date for two months. How can I get more dates?"
- "I've been married for three years and the relationship is not as exciting as it was before. What can I do to improve the relationship or is it time to get out?"
- "My boss is always so critical. Why can't she be more positive?"

Most of us have either asked one or more of these questions or we have heard many of our friends ask them. Now the question is "If I want to change, can I?" "Am I in control of my own behavior or is someone or something else in control of me?" "How can someone change?" As we all know, change is not easy.

B.F. Skinner (1972), a well known psychologist, has indicated in much of his writing that all of our behavior is controlled and that there is no such thing as "free will." Do you agree? This is a philosophical question that people have been discussing for years. We will not attempt to answer this question in this book, but we will be referring to it, directly or indirectly, throughout the book.

Who is in control? You? Me? Someone else? Our environment? Psychologists have come up with a number of theories to explain how we can develop the capacity to control our own behavior and to develop the capacity to influence other people's behavior. Many psychologists believe that learning theory is the answer to all our questions. Learning theory underlies all relationships, good, bad, happy, and sad ones.

SELF-CONTROL OR EXTERNAL CONTROL

Self-control is often considered the opposite of external control. In self-control, the individual sets his or her own standards for performance, and will then reward or punish themselves for meeting or not meeting these standards. On the other hand, in external control, someone else sets the standards and delivers or withholds the rewards or punishment.

Both Angie and Beth took a Psychology test last Friday. Angie studied two hours every night for the last five nights and it paid off for her, she received an "A" grade. Angie knows that she earned her grade; it took a lot of work. On the other hand, Beth only studied two hours total for her test and she also received an "A" for her grade. Beth knows how hard she really studied and that she was really lucky to receive such a good grade. How hard will Beth study for her next test? Who will be more motivated to study, Beth or Angie? Which person will be most likely to succeed in school and every day life?

Perceived Locus of Control. People differ markedly in their feelings about their capacity to control life situations. Some people feel that they are in control

> Nothing said to us, nothing we can learn from others, reaches us so deep as that which we find in ourselves.
>
> Theodore Reik

of their own destinies. Their general expectancy about what happens to them and what they achieve in life is due to their own abilities, attitudes, and actions. In contrast, other people see their lives as being beyond their control. They believe that what happens to them is determined by external forces whether it luck or fate, other people, "Mother Nature," or the stars. According to Julian Rotter (1966), these two types of people are said to be identified as having either an *internal* or an *external* "locus of control." Angie would be said to have an *internal locus of control* and Beth would have an *external locus of control.*

Internals perceive that their efforts make a difference when they are facing a difficult situation, so they try to cope with it. They take whatever action that seems appropriate to solve the problem.

Externals perceive that their efforts will not make a difference, so naturally they do not attempt to cope with threatening situations.

The difference in perceived locus of control is important for personal adjustment to the world. People who believe they can control events in their environment will respond to stress quite differently from those who believe the opposite. Rotter indicates that these attitudes are learned from experience prior to the age of nineteen. If you discover that your efforts are repeatedly rewarded, you will believe that you will be able to exert control over your outcomes in the future. If you discover that your efforts are to no avail, you will become resigned to the lack of control.

Internals are more apt to become *activists* because they feel their efforts will have an effect on the outcome. Smokers who successfully quit smoking have been found to be more *internal* than those who were unsuccessful (James, Woodruff, & Werner, 1965). Externals who attempt to stop smoking are apt to say, "It's no use, I'm hooked and there is nothing I can do about it."

> Luck is a matter of preparation meeting opportunity.
>
> Oprah Winfrey

> O God give us the grace to accept with serenity the things that cannot be changed, courage to change the things which should be changed, and the wisdom to distinguish the one from the other.
>
> Reinhold Niebuhr
> The Serenity Prayer, 1943

ARE YOU AN INTERNAL OR EXTERNAL?

What implications does research on the locus of control have for you? The most important point is that there is a link between your beliefs about locus of control and your behavior. If you believe your experience is beyond your own control, you may expend less effort than you could. You may not try as hard as you are able, because you believe that your efforts will not make a difference. You may satisfy yourself with poor performance, figuring there is nothing you can do to improve the situation. Certainly some situations are more out of your control than others are, but your overall attitude about challenging situations will affect every aspect of your life.

To help you assess your own locus of control, we suggest that you identify who or what controls different aspects of your life by doing the exercise at the end of the chapter, **What Controls Your Life?**

Are Internals or Externals More Successful? *Internals* seem to be more successful in more aspects of life than externals. Although an internal locus of control does not ensure success, those who believe they can influence the events in life tend to be the best life managers. This is true for several reasons. For one

Am I an Internal or External?

thing, these people are more likely to consider the possibility of doing something differently in their lives than people with an external orientation.

Internals are more curious than externals about ways to improve their lives. They see that education and knowledge is personal power. They are more likely to read about problem areas in their lives and attend workshops and classes related to solving these problems. Internals are also better listeners than externals (Lefcourt, et al. 1985). They are more likely to ask questions, give others time to speak, and accurately interpret what others are saying. Internally oriented individuals tend to get better grades and score higher on standardized academic tests than externals (Mayer & Sutton, 1996).

Concerning relationships, internals tend to fare better than externals, especially considering the fact that internals tend to be better listeners and are more willing to work at improving their relationships. During stressful times in life, internals are more likely to seek social support than externals (Lefcourt, 1982). Numerous studies have found that having an internal locus of control is positively associated with higher psychological functioning and better mental health (Osterman, 1999). Take a look now at the following "Consider This" box.

> For the weak, it is impossible.
> For the fainthearted, it is unknown.
> For the thoughtful and valiant, it is ideal.
>
> Victor Hugo

PERCEIVED CONTROL OR LACK OF CONTROL

Jeff continues to call his girlfriend to find out what he can do to get her back. He sends her gifts, pleads with her, etc., but his efforts are to no avail. Whatever he does, does not seem to have any effect on her. He does not have any control over the situation.

Wanda seems to understand that she has no control over her boyfriend's behavior, but she does have control over her own life. She accepts the fact that the relationship is over and she needs to get on with the rest of her life.

CONSIDER THIS . . .
Internals and Externals

How Would You Respond in this Situation?

Event

Wanda's boyfriend and Jeff's girlfriend just announced to each of them that the relationship is over.

Cognitive Response

Jeff's response: "What did I do wrong?" "What can I do to get her back?" "Why doesn't she like me anymore?" "I'll do anything for her." "My whole life is ruined."

Wanda's response: "My boyfriend has sure been depressed lately," "He sure has changed in the past few months," "I really like him, but I could tell that things weren't going well between us recently," "I know it will be tough, but I know I can get along without him."

Imagine what you would say to yourself if your mate were to tell you today that your relationship is over?

OUTCOME

Jeff develops a negative feeling about himself and his life. He sees himself as no good, not worthy, and that nobody will ever love him, so what is the use of living. He becomes depressed, passive and develops *learned helplessness*.

Wanda's not happy with the situation, but realizes that she does not have any control over her boyfriend, so she looks to the future. She sets new goals and actively begins to work to achieve them ("There are other fish in the sea").

WHO'S IN CONTROL?

We would define Jeff as an "external" because he feels that he is not in control of his own destiny, that outside forces are determining his fate, and that whatever effort he puts into it, will not make any difference.

Wanda would be defined as an "internal," since she perceives herself as in control of her destiny and her success is dependent upon her efforts and not on others. She also realizes that she does not have control over other people's behavior.

Again, how would you respond in this and other similar situations?

Are you an internal or an external?

Personal Control versus Learned Helplessness. Helpless, oppressed people often perceive that control is external and this perception may deepen their feelings of resignation. This is what Martin Seligman (1975, 1998) and others found in experiments with both animals and humans. When dogs are strapped in a harness and given repeated shocks, with no opportunity to avoid them, they learn a sense of helplessness.

When later placed in a situation where they could escape the punishment by merely leaping a hurdle, they remained idle and without hope. In contrast, animals that escape shock in the first situation learn personal control and easily escape shock in the new situation. When people are faced with repeated traumatic events over which they have no control, they too, will come to feel helpless, hopeless, and depressed. You can see the importance of parents teaching their children to have the feeling of some control over their lives and their behavior.

Is Your Life Out of Control? *Learned helplessness* is the passive behavior produced by the exposure to unavoidable aversive events. For example, in concentration camps, prisons, work environments, colleges, or nursing homes where people are given little control, they will experience a lowering of morale, a feeling of increased stress, depression, and a feeling of helplessness. Increasing control—

Who's in control of my life?

allowing workers to have some participation in decision making, allowing inmates to make decisions when they want to watch TV or exercise, letting nursing home patients make choices about their environment—noticeably improves morale along with mental and physical health. Perceived control is vital to human functioning (Langer, 1983). Thus, for young and old alike, we should create an environment that enhances a sense of control and self-efficacy.

Are you an *internal* or an *external?* Which of these do you want to be? Can you change your behavior? Who's in control?

How Can We Take Control? In the following paragraphs we will give you some helpful hints on taking control of your life. In order to increase the probability of you developing an internal locus of control, you will want to work on the following items:

1. *Considering changing aspects of your environment.* Ask yourself some of the following questions: What types of people in my life contribute to my locus of control beliefs? What is it about school or my job that contributes to my belief that I am not in control of my life? How do my current friends, acquaintances, and other people in my life contribute to my locus of control? What can you do about these situations in order to take control of your life?
2. *Try new activities rather than the usual safe and secure ways of doing things.* Take some risks, do something different, try a new restaurant, do not travel the same route home or to school each day, try new food, wear dif-

---

Table 3.1   Characteristics of Externals and Internals

Externals	Internals
More susceptible to depression.	Not very susceptible to depression.
Not likely to vote in elections.	More likely to vote and get involved in politics.
Not too likely to complete school, or college.	Likely to complete high school, college, and graduate school.
Not too likely to change habits.	Willing to take action to change bad habits.
Tend to be susceptible to anxiety.	Not too susceptible to anxiety.
Does not adapt well to stress.	Copes better with stress.
Gives up easily.	Willing to continue trying in spite of failure, persistent.
Will not spend much time on a task.	Willing to work on a task for a long time.
Does not like new challenges and does not handle them well.	Willing to meet new challenges and handles the pressure.
Tends to just let things happen and not too curious.	Will seek out information to help solve problems.
Does not earn as much money as an internal.	Tends to be more successful and earns more money.

(Seligman, 1998)

ferent clothes, or anything that will help you break old habits. Externals have difficulty trying something new and breaking old habits. Trying and enjoying something new will help you see that you can control aspects of your life.

3.   *Begin to assume more responsibility for tasks at home, work, and school.* Volunteer to do things that you do not usually do. Join a committee, volunteer to help someone, offer to take responsibility for some tasks to be completed. Start slow and then keep adding on responsibilities. You will feel much better about yourself and see that you are in control.

Read Table 3.1 to decide whether you want to become an external or internal.

As you continue to read this chapter you will discover new ways to take control of your life. One of the ways that you will discover to take control of your own life is by developing a high level of *self-efficacy.*

What Is Self-Efficacy? *Self-Efficacy is our belief about our ability to perform behaviors that should lead to expected outcomes.* Believing that you can control your behaviors is fundamental to self-management. Individuals having high self-efficacy for particular behaviors or skills are likely to work longer and try more strategies to develop these skills than those with low self-efficacy (Bandura, 1997). When self-efficacy is high, we feel confident that we can execute the responses necessary to earn reinforcers. When self-efficacy is low, we worry that the necessary responses may be beyond our abilities.

Perceptions of self-efficacy are subjective and specific to different kinds of tasks. For instance, you might feel extremely confident about your ability to handle difficult social situations, but very doubtful about your ability to handle academic challenges. Perceptions of self-efficacy can influence which challenges we tackle and how well we will perform them. Because people can think about their motivation and even their own thoughts they can effect changes in themselves, persevere during tough times and do better at difficult tasks (Stajkovic & Luthans, 1998).

Gender and Self-Efficacy. Men and women develop differently, both physiologically and socially. This difference affects their self-efficacy. As children, girls are more likely than boys to play in small groups in which interpersonal awareness is more likely to be heightened. In contrast, boys are more likely than girls to play in large groups where opportunities for discussion are minimized. In addition, boys more than girls, may be encouraged to become involved in competitive, achievement-related activities (Cohn, 1998). Research that has manipulated a person's view of performance on various tasks shows that a person's sense of self-efficacy is related to the person's fulfillment of culturally mandated, gender appropriate norms (Joseph, Markus, & Tafarodi, 1992). Men more than women focus on independence and distinctiveness; women more than men focus on interdependence and good relationships. From these different focuses, both men and women derive a sense of self-efficacy. Can you identify any culturally mandated gender appropriate norms that have been expressed to you in your environment?

Increasing your self-efficacy about behaviors you wish to change is very much tied to the recall of past successes. The more successes you recall, the more likely you are to believe that you can change other behaviors. On the other

What one single ability do we all have? The ability to change.

L. Andrews

☞ CHECK THIS OUT . . .
Rate Your Self-Efficacy

Do you ever find yourself in any of these situations: Nervous on a first date; annoyed at a friend for not doing what they promised; or emotionally strained when too many demands are placed upon you? You might have serious concerns about your ability to perform in such situations. Or, you may feel totally confident about your ability to cope. To assess your self-efficacy, your degree of confidence that you can perform adequately at a particular task, consider the following situations. For each situation try to imagine how you might feel, whether you might feel relaxed or tensed. On a scale from 1-10, estimate your degree of self-confidence.

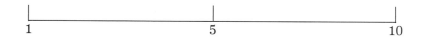

1 = You don't think you can perform the task.
5 = You are moderately confident that you can perform the task.
10 = You are completely confident you can perform the task.

Task	**Rating**
In the library, asking other students you do not know who are sitting next to you, to quiet down.	_____
While waiting in line for a movie, asking someone who cuts in line to go to the back of the line.	_____
When returning a purchase that you are dissatisfied with and insisting on seeing the manager.	_____
Complaining about bad service to a waiter or waitress.	_____
Sending a meal back at a restaurant because the food is not hot enough when served.	_____
Complaining about a professor who is a lousy teacher and seems to be unfair in his or her grading policy.	_____
At a social gathering, discussing controversial issues (such as abortion, AIDS, religion, discrimination, and so on) with people who strongly disagree with you.	_____
Going to a party where you do not know anyone.	_____
At a social gathering, approaching a group of people you do not know and introducing yourself.	_____
Going to a party where you know only the host.	_____
At a social gathering, joining in on a conversation with a group of strangers.	_____
Total	_____

Add up your total score. The higher your score, the more likely it is that you will successfully complete the tasks and have a high level of self-efficacy (self-confidence). A low score may indicate that you may want to consider taking an assertiveness class, reading some self-help books, or doing some of the exercises mentioned in this book.

hand, recalling failures is very debilitating to self-efficacy (Lefton, 2000). Having a sense of self-efficacy is important in taking the active approach to life for successful adjustment.

You Can Take Control! To realize your aims, you should try to exercise control over the events that affect your life (Bandura, 1997). You have a strong incentive to act if you believe that control is possible—that your actions will be effective. Perceived self-efficacy, or belief in your personal capabilities, regulates human functioning in three major ways:

1. *Mood or affect:* The amount of stress or depression a person is experiencing in threatening or difficult situations depends largely on how well they think they can cope in that situation. People with high self-efficacy are able to relax, divert their attention, calm themselves, and seek support from friends, family, and others.
2. *Motivational:* Motivation will be stronger if individuals believe they can attain their goals and then adjust them based on their progress. People motivate themselves by forming beliefs about what they can do, anticipating likely outcomes, setting goals, and planning courses of action.
3. *Cognitive:* People with positive thoughts, feelings, beliefs, and high aspirations will have high self-efficacy. They will meet challenges and will believe they can overcome any challenge. They guide their actions by visualizing successful outcomes instead of dwelling on personal deficiencies or ways in which things might go wrong

Optimism is necessary for accomplishment and a sense of well being. In a world full of impediments, adversities, and frustrations, people with a robust sense of personal efficacy are more likely to succeed. Optimism as it relates to stress will be discussed in Chapter 8.

Optimism versus Pessimism. Everyone experiences defeat, rejection, or failure at some point in their lives. Yet despite repeated failures, rejections, or defeats, some people persist in their efforts, while others give-up. Psychologist Martin Seligman (1998) believes that how people characteristically explain their failures and defeats makes the difference. People who have an *optimistic explanatory style* tend to use internal, stable and global explanations for negative events. *Optimism* is defined as a generalized tendency to explain positive outcomes. In contrast, people who have a *pessimistic explanatory style* use external, unstable and specific explanations for negative events. *Pessimism* is defined as a general tendency to envision the future as unfavorable. Pessimists are inclined to believe that no amount of personal effort will improve their situation. Not surprisingly, pessimists tend to experience more stress than optimists.

Are you an optimist or a pessimist? Do you look at the bright side and expect good things to happen, or do you tend to believe that if something will go wrong, it will? Let's take a look at the two explanatory styles in action in the following scenario.

Optimism is a remarkable predictor of achievement and resilience. For example, studies have found that optimistic life insurance agents sell more insurance than pessimistic agents, and optimistic Olympic-level swimmers recover from defeat and later swim even faster, whereas pessimistic swimmers, following defeat get slower (Seligman, 1998). When faced with serious problems—such as deciding about a risky operation, coping with traumatic events, or over-

The charm of fishing is that it is the pursuit of what is elusive but attainable, a perpetual series of occasions for hope.

Scottish author
John Buchan,
1875–1940

Are you an Optimist or a Pessimist?

Pat Pessimist and Otis Optimist were invited to a social function. Both are single and looking for a date. Pat sees an attractive person across the room and decides to approach the person and introduce himself and see what it could lead to. As he approaches her, she notices him approaching and immediately looks the other direction. Pat immediately interprets this as rejection and thus turns away and goes to the bar for a drink. Otis notices a different female and approaches her. She sees him coming toward her and she immediately turns away and begins a conversation with another person. Otis decides that she must not want to meet him and he heads to the bar.

If you were in this situation what would you say and do? Let's see what Pat and Otis did.

Pat Pessimist: I guess I'll just have a couple more drinks and then go home and watch TV alone. (After rejection, becomes passive and withdraws)

Otis Optimist: Wait a minute, there's another good looking one over there, why not try her. (After rejection, persevere, don't stop trying)

Pat Pessimist: Women just don't seem to be interested in me. I don't know what to say and they don't like the way I dress. It must be my hair. (Global, pervasive explanation)

Otis Optimist: I bet she's engaged anyway. She's probably shy and not too interesting. (Specific explanation)

Pat Pessimist: I just have to accept the fact, I am boring and not very attractive, why would she want to talk to me. (Stable, permanent explanation)

Otis Optimist: I should have ironed my shirt, I just don't look too good today. (Unstable, temporary explanation)

Pat Pessimist: She must have seen me when I spilled my drink and thinks I'm clumsy. (Internal explanation; Pessimists blame themselves)

Otis Optimist: She must have a problem. (External explanation; Optimists blame other people or external circumstances)

Are you an Otis or a Pat?

- -

coming drug abuse or alcoholism—optimists tend to focus on what they can do rather than on how they feel. They keep their sense of humor, plan for the future, and reinterpret the situation in a positive light. When researchers followed a sample of survivors in Florida, who had suffered devastating losses as a result of Hurricane Andrew, they found that pessimism was a significant predictor of continued distress six months after the disaster, whereas loss of resources was not (Carver, et al., 1993).

Optimists by definition, expect to eventually recover from adversity, and they expect to be successful at whatever they do, so they work much harder to

The Bottom Line

Face it, nobody owes you a living.

What you achieve or fail to achieve in your lifetime, is directly related to what you do, or fail to do.

No one chooses his parents or childhood, but you can choose your own direction.

Everyone has problems and obstacles to overcome, but that too is relative to each individual.

Nothing is carved in stone, you can change anything in your life, if you want to badly enough.

Excuses are for losers: Those who take responsibility for their actions are the real winners in life.

Winners meet life's challenges head on, knowing there are no guarantees, and give all they've got.

And never think it's too late or too early to begin. Time plays no favorites and will pass whether you act or not.

Take control of your life. Dare to dream and take risks . . . Compete.

- -

reach their goals than pessimists do. Thus, another self-fulfilling prophecy is created.

Optimistic thinking tends to lead us to a more successful, happier, and healthier life. According to Seligman, people can train themselves to make optimistic explanations by the following three steps: 1) think about situations of adversity (being turned down for a date, doing poorly on a test, losing a sports competition, 2) consider the way you normally explain these events, and if it is pessimistic (Nobody likes me, I'm not very smart, I really choked in the game), then 3) dispute these explanations by looking closely at the facts (She probably had plans with her family, I need to spend more time studying, my opponent played a great game). Practice this exercise over and over again. You may find that changing pessimistic explanatory style is like breaking a bad habit.

The recipe for well being requires neither positive nor negative thinking alone, but a mix of ample optimism to provide hope, a dash of pessimism to prevent complacency, and enough realism to discriminate those things we can control from those we cannot (Myers, 1993).

Children need models more than they need critics.

Joseph Joubert
Pensees, 1842

How did you become an internal or external? Where did your high level or low level of self-efficacy come from? How did you learn to become a pessimist or optimist? How can you take control of your life? These are not easy questions to answer. In order to understand yourself better and to discover different ways to improve your life, psychologists have developed many different theories. Many of these theories evolve from or revolve around learning theory.

SOCIAL LEARNING THEORY

Albert Bandura is one of several behaviorists who have added a cognitive flavor to learning theory. Bandura points out that humans obviously are conscious, thinking, and feeling beings. He feels that some psychologists like B.F. Skinner ignore these cognitive processes. An important aspect of *social learning theory* that may have an important impact on our lives is *observational learning*. The fact that much of personality is learned in social situations through interactions with and observations of other people, including family members (Mischel & Shoda, 1998).

Observational Learning. *This occurs when an individual's behavior is influenced by the observation of others, who are called models.* Observational learning requires that you pay attention to someone who is *significant* to you, a parent, or a friend, etc. You observe their behavior and understand its consequences, and then store this information in your memory.

Some role-models are more influential than others. Children and adults tend to imitate people they like and respect more so than people they do not. We also are especially prone to imitate the behavior of people that we consider attractive or powerful, such as rock stars, movie stars, sports heroes, or politicians. It is a bit scary to discover that we are also more likely to model after the individual who is the most aggressive, especially if that aggression leads to positive reinforcement. If you observe your mother yelling at your father in order to get him to do something, and he does do it, you are more likely to yell at someone the next time you want something. Prior to that experience you most likely would have not yelled at someone in order to get your way. A five-year old boy goes to the store with a seven-year old. The older boy picks up a candy bar and does not pay for it and on the way home shares it with his friend. Did he get positive reinforcement for stealing? What is the likelihood of the younger boy attempting to pocket a

> Never try to teach a pig to sing. It wastes your time and annoys the pigs.
>
> Mark Twain

CONSIDER THIS . . .
Who Are You Likely to Imitate?

Factors that Increase the Likelihood of Imitation

You are more likely to imitate:

- Significant Others.
- Warm, nurturing people.
- People you perceive as having higher social status.
- If you lack confidence in your own abilities in a particular situation.
- If you observe people being rewarded for their behavior—even if the behavior is improper, illegal, or immoral.
- People who are similar to you in terms of age, sex, and interests.
- If the situation is unfamiliar or ambiguous.
- If you have been rewarded for imitating the same behavior in the past.

Who are you likely to imitate?

Adapted from Hockenbury & Hockenbury, 1999.

candy bar the next time he goes to the store? What we learn through modeling is not always positive. That is why our parents keep saying, "Do what I say, not what I do."

According to *social learning theory,* modeling has a great impact on personality development. Children learn to be assertive, conscientious, self-sufficient, aggressive, fearful, and so forth by observing others behaving in these ways.

Many of you are familiar with the cartoon TV program called *The Simpsons.* Matt Groening, the creator, decided it would be funny if the Simpson's eight-year-old daughter Lisa played the baritone sax. Do you think this would have an influence on the audience of this program? Sure enough, across the country little girls began imitating Lisa. Cynthia Sikes, a saxophone teacher in New York, told the *New York Times* (January 14, 1996) that when the show started, I got an influx of girls coming up to me saying, "I want to play the saxophone because Lisa Simpson plays the saxophone." Groening says his mail regularly includes photos of girls holding up their saxophones. Can you think of other ways that the media has influenced your behavior?

What are some of the other theories of learning that may have an impact on my relationships? You will now get a chance to understand how learning theory applies to you and your life.

HOW DOES LEARNING THEORY INFLUENCE YOUR LIFE?

When you do something you enjoy, what is the likelihood that you will do it again?

If you try something and fail at it, what are the chances that you will attempt it again?

If you ask someone out for a date five times and the answer is "NO" each time, are you going to ask again?

If you make a comment to a member of the opposite sex who responds by slapping you, will you make that comment next time?

If someone you do not know very well embarrasses you in front of a large group, are you going to avoid that person in the future?

If you drink something that tastes good, will you drink it again?

You hate green peas because you were forced to eat them as a kid. Do you eat them now?

All of these situations can be explained by learning theory.

In order to understand learning theory, we need to define the term **learning**. *Learning is defined in psychology as a relatively permanent change in behavior as a result of experience or practice.*

Before you can begin the process of learning, you have to pay attention. Are you aware of all the different types of stimuli that get your attention?

WHAT GETS YOUR ATTENTION?

You are concentrating on reading a book and the phone rings. What do you do? A person enters the room that you perceive as being attractive. Do you notice that person? What gets your attention? Before you can learn something, you have to pay attention to it. Attention is the most important aspect of learning because we have to pay attention to something before we can respond. Another aspect of attention that may surprise you is that you can only pay attention to one thing at a time. You can not watch TV and study at the same time. Again, what do you pay attention to? We find that there are three kinds of stimuli that attract our attention. They are *novel stimuli, significant stimuli, and conflicting stimuli.* We find that these three different kinds of stimuli are not only important to learning, but also vital to our relationships with others.

Novel Stimuli. We tend to pay attention to people, places, or things that are new, different, unique, or original. You tend to pay more attention to the student who is new to your school than a student who has been going to your school for the past few years. When reading the newspaper, you tend to notice an advertisement that is in color more than in black and white, because the color ad is unique. The person with a mohawk haircut will generally be noticed before someone with a "normal" hairstyle. A person wearing the latest in fashionware will tend to get more attention than someone wearing last year's style of clothing. Why? Because it is unique, different or *novel.* The more familiar we become with the "new" person, the "unique" hairstyle, or the "latest" fashionware the less we are apt to pay attention. We tend to begin to take them for granted. When you begin to date someone you tend to give the individual a lot of special attention, but what happens after you have been dating that same individual for years? Many times you find that you begin to habituate or get bored with that individual when the novelty wears off and you no longer pay as much attention to him or her.

How Can We Apply This to the Classroom? Teachers need to consider this while they attempt to get students to learn. A teacher needs to make material unique or *novel* to the students in order to get their attention so they can learn. A salesperson needs to market his or her product in a unique way in order to get the customer to pay attention to their product and not their competitor's product.

Eventually, the *novelty* or uniqueness of people or things will tend to fade away and we pay less attention to them. Now, what can we do to continue to keep someone's attention and thus get people to learn? What else gets your attention?

Significant Stimuli. So, you like to listen to music? Do you like ice cream? Are you interested in sex? Do you like money? If your answer to all of these questions is yes, then all of these things are *significant* to you and you will pay attention to them. If you are a teacher and want to get your students to learn, you better make sure the material is *significant* to your students. Otherwise, you may find it difficult to keep your student's attention. You need to make the material relate directly to your students' needs, wants, interests, and desires, and if you do this, you will be surprised to discover that your students are paying attention and learning.

How Important Is This in a Relationship? When you first start dating someone, do you consider your date's needs, wants, interests, and desires when deciding where to go and what to do? If you do, you will find that your date will respond more positively to you and you both will be much happier. If you send your mate flowers for the first time and he or she likes them, will you receive more attention? Are the flowers *significant?* Are the flowers *novel?* Since they are both

I was born a human being. I had to learn what being human is all about.

Rabbi Abraham
Heschel

novel and *significant,* they should increase the attention paid to you by your friend. You reinforce your mate and your mate reinforces you. It tends to make life more interesting to you and your friends.

If you want a relationship to continue on a positive basis over a long period of time, you must make sure that you provide *novel* and *significant* stimuli in the relationship—otherwise the relationship will become stale and boring. This is why that old saying is appropriate here, *The grass always looks greener on the other side of the fence.* You wonder why your boyfriend, girlfriend, husband, or wife is always looking at members of the opposite sex? You wonder why students are not paying attention to the teacher? Could it be that the other people are novel and maybe even more significant?

Would kids enjoy Halloween as much if they went trick-or-treating every day?

A Birthday Surprise. Not too long ago a colleague of mine told me it was her husband's birthday. This couple have been married about ten years. The morning of her husband's birthday she packed a picnic-type lunch; cheese, wine, etc. She put on her coat and nothing else, went to his office building at noon, went into his private office and closed the door. She set up the picnic lunch and opened up her coat and said, "Happy Birthday, Dear!" Is this significant? Is it novel? It most definitely is, and if these two people continue to provide novel and significant stimuli in their relationship, it will continue on a positive basis for a long time. You do not have to do what this woman did, but you do need to continue to provide novel and significant stimuli in your relationships with others; otherwise, you may discover that your friends and partners become bored with the relationship and then they tend to start to form other relationships that will meet their needs and be more exciting. Is there anything else that seems to get our attention? When you have an argument with your mate, do you pay attention to them? Of course you do, but why?

Conflicting Stimuli. What if we were to tell you that, "All of your behavior is controlled!"; "There is no 'God'!"; "It is all right to steal!"; and "It's okay to cheat on your spouse, boyfriend, or girlfriend?" Are these statements in conflict with any of your beliefs?

We have discovered that you will not only pay attention to *novel* and *significant* stimuli, but also to anything that is in conflict with your values, needs, or morals. It has been found that in many relationships the only time that two people pay attention to one another is when they are in conflict—arguing, fighting, etc. We do not recommend this form of stimuli in order to get attention because it can create more problems than it solves. If this is the only time you find that you and your partner pay attention to one another, you might want to change this by seeking counseling, reading a good self-help book, or changing your behavior in order to provide more novel or significant stimuli in your relationships.

With all the technology and equipment we have today and with all the activities available to us, many of us still get tired of just sitting around. We get bored with life, why?

Are You Bored? Have you ever heard someone say, "I sure am bored, there's nothing to do?"

We have TVs, VCRs, computers, video games, cable TV, the latest table games and there is still nothing to do. After playing a video game for two hours

The quality, not the longevity, of one's life is what is important.

Martin Luther King, Jr.

without any additional challenge, a person will finally get bored with the game. Your family has owned a full sized pool table for the last eight years and you no longer get excited about playing pool, but when your friends come to visit you, all they want to do is play pool. Playing pool is boring to you since it is always available, but to your friends, playing pool is exciting, it is novel and also significant.

Make Life More Exciting! We all seek change in our lives. Kids get bored, teenagers get bored and adults get bored. If you take your kids to the zoo every Saturday, eventually they will not enjoy going any longer. If you take your date to the movie every Friday night, it just is not as exciting as it used to be. You have your favorite dessert, a hot fudge brownie sundae, every night for two months. Believe it or not, even that sundae will not be enjoyed as much as it was when you could have it only once a month. Using novel and significant stimuli in your life will help you and those around you have an exciting, non-boring life.

We learn throughout life. We all need to change in order to adapt to the world that we must live in. What we have learned in the past is not always the best for us in the future. Consider using novel and significant stimuli and sometimes conflicting stimuli as you relate to others in business situations, in relationships, in family situations, and in teaching-learning environments—which is the laboratory of life. If you do, you will discover that your life and the life of the people around you will improve.

Now that we have your attention, it is time to learn.

LEARNING THEORY

Learning is the eye of the mind.

Thomas Drake

Why study learning theory? Learning theory is the basis of all interactions—we are applying it constantly and it is constantly being applied on us, most of the time without our knowledge. Learning theorists believe that our behavior, including our personality, is shaped through classical conditioning, operant conditioning and observational learning. If you have a better understanding of learning theory, it will help you understand the relationships you have with others and hopefully you will be able to improve the relationships you are involved in and help you acquire new relationships.

An understanding of learning theory will also allow you to understand yourself as well as others. You will learn how to manage your own behavior as well as discover ways in which you can influence other people's behavior. Most aspects of learning begin with *classical conditioning*, but as learning evolves, classical conditioning develops into another form of learning—*operant conditioning*. Let's take a look at these processes.

WHY DO I HATE PEAS?

When I was a baby I was feed peas. At that time I tolerated them since I really didn't have a choice. As I got a little older I could decide what I like and dislike, but at the dinner table I was told that I had to "clean" my plate and eat every one of the peas. I hated the taste of them, but I had to eat them anyway. Every time I took a bite of them I thought I was going to get sick and a time or two when I did eat them I did get a little ill. I always associated the feeling of sickness with the peas. Twenty years later I will still not eat peas. Now, when I look at them, I

☞ CHECK THIS OUT . . .
We Are All Teachers!

- Parents teach children
- Children teach parents
- Husbands teach wives
- Wives teach husbands
- Teachers teach students
- Students teach teachers
- Employers teach employees
- Employees teach employers
- All behavior is taught
- You are a teacher!
- **Remember, Everyone is a Teacher!**

Think for a moment—what are you teaching others? Is it positive or negative?

---

still get a weird feeling in my stomach. Why do I still dislike peas? You will discover that this was learned through classical conditioning.

Originally, as a baby I tolerated peas and didn't feel ill when I ate them. Later, as I was forced to eat them I felt ill. Over time I associated the feeling of illness with the taste of peas and later with the sight of peas. This was a learned response. I was conditioned to dislike peas. This was learned through classical conditioning.

It's amazing how classical conditioning has created many of our emotions, including fears, phobias, likes, dislikes, attractions, and bonding experiences.

CLASSICAL CONDITIONING

How Does Classical Conditioning Work?

Ivan Pavlov, a Russian physiologist is considered the founder of *classical conditioning*. To make a long story short, Pavlov was experimenting with the salivary response of dogs. At first a bell was rung and the dog emitted no response or an irrelevant response, such as the ears perking up. When the food was placed in the dog's mouth, the dog would automatically salivate. Food is called the *unconditional stimulus* because it is the cause of the salivation, the *unconditional response*. After ringing the bell a few times prior to feeding the dog, Pavlov noticed that the dog was salivating in response to the bell, before the food was brought in. The bell now becomes the *conditioned stimulus* and causes the dog to salivate, the *conditioned response*. Was there a change in the dog's behavior as a result of its experience? If the answer is yes, then learning has taken place and the dog has been conditioned. Do you salivate to the sight of food? This is a conditioned response. Table 3.2 outlines the classical conditioning process.

As most of you know, when a child goes to the clinic for the first time for an injection, the child is *not* hesitant to go. Again, as you know the injection, the *unconditioned stimulus*, causes pain, the unconditioned response. Will the child willingly go to the clinic next time? The answer is most likely, NO WAY!! As

Life's greatest achievement is the continual remaking of yourself so that at last you know how to live.

W. Rhodes

Table 3.2   Classical Conditioning

Before conditioning: The unconditioned stimulus automatically elicits the unconditioned response. (This is an unlearned reaction.)

UNCONDITIONED STIMULUS (U.C.S.) (FOOD)	UNCONDITIONED RESPONSE (U.C.R.) (SALIVATION)

NEUTRAL STIMULUS (N.S.) (BELL)	NO RESPONSE

During Conditioning: The neutral stimulus is paired with the unconditioned stimulus.

After Conditioning: The neutral stimulus alone elicits the response: the neutral stimulus is now a conditioned stimulus: and the response to it is a conditioned response. (This is a learned reaction.)

CONDITIONED STIMULUS (BELL) (C.S.)	CONDITIONED RESPONSE (SALIVATION) (C.R.)

soon as the child sees the clinic or smells the odor in the clinic the child will get very upset and attempt to get away from there as quickly as possible. The sight of the clinic, or the odor is the *conditioned stimulus* that causes the child to try to avoid the pain of the injection, the *conditioned response*. Do you now understand why many children don't want to go to the clinic or doctor's office? They have been *classically conditioned* to fear these situations.

Has This Ever Happened to You? Did you ever drink too much of a specific kind of alcohol one evening and then later that night get very sick? As many of you know, since that night, you have never touched that kind of alcohol and most likely never will again, but you will still drink other forms of alcohol. Why? You associated getting sick with a specific kind of alcohol, not alcohol in general. This one experience conditioned you to dislike that specific kind of alcohol. Sometimes you can be conditioned very quickly as many of you have learned.

Have You Heard about Albert? Most fears and phobias are learned through the process of *classical conditioning*. The famous experiment of John B. Watson and Rosalie Rayner (1920) demonstrates how fears and eventually phobias are easily learned.

An eleven month old boy named Albert was classically conditioned to fear a variety of furry things. Before the experiment Albert enjoyed playing with a white rat. One day as the rat was handed to Albert the experimenters made a loud terrifying noise that startled Albert and made him cry. They continued to do this six more times, until Albert showed a strong fear of the rat, crying and shrinking away whenever the rat was placed near him. As the experiment continued, the experimenters presented Albert with other objects that were similar to the white rat, such as a white stuffed animal, a furry white blanket, and a Santa Claus mask. To their surprise Albert showed the same fear response to the different furry objects as he did the white rat. This process is called *stimulus generalization*. A day later, Albert was released from the hospital where the experiment took place. So, if you are walking down the street one day wearing your white fur coat and a seventy year old man starts yelling and running the other way, say, "Hi Albert." Albert should have gone through a reconditioning process called *desensitization* in order to extinguish him of the fears.

Table 3.3 gives you some additional examples of classical conditioning.

Classical conditioning helps explain the formation of fears, attitudes, prejudices and feelings that may seem quite irrational. For example, you don't understand why you have such an uneasy feeling around your red-haired boss. You can't think of any logical, rational reason for this feeling. You have also noticed that you feel uneasy around other red-haired individuals. One day while you were reminiscing about elementary school, you remembered that your second-grade, red-haired teacher slapped your hands with a ruler everytime you made a mistake. At this time, this was a very painful embarrassing experience to be hit in front of all your friends. This one early experience, that you repressed, is still having an effect upon your present life, especially your interactions with red-haired individuals. You were conditioned to dislike red-haired individuals. Prior to second grade you liked people with red hair, but since this one experience, red-haired individuals have become the *conditioned stimulus* for your fear (uneasy feeling), the *conditioned response*. Have you ever had an experience like this?

Table 3.3 Classical Conditioning: Learning Through Associations					
	Neutral Stimulus	**Pleasant or Painful Stimulus**	**Before Conditioning**	**Conditioning**	**After Conditioning**
Pavlov's Experiment	Bell	Food	Bell elicits no response	Bell is paired with food which elicits salivation	Bell alone without food elicits salivation
McDonald's Advertising goal	Golden arches	Food	Arches elicit no response	Arches are paired with tasty food, which elicits salivation	Arches alone without sight of food elicits salivation
A child learning	Dog	Dog-bite	Dog elicits pleasant response	Dog-bite is paired with pain	Sight of dog instills feeling of fear and avoidance

Student Story

It was my first year of college and living five hundred miles away from home. I didn't know anybody at the college. I decided to go to Starbucks for a cup of coffee. I walked in the door and smelled the aroma of fresh coffee. At that moment an attractive young woman approached me and asked if she could help. As I looked at her I could feel my heart beat faster and I began to perspire. I stuttered and finally said, "Yes, I would like a cup of coffee." The next day I returned to the coffee shop and again walked in and smelled the coffee and then noticed the young women, and again my heartbeat increased and I began to perspire.

As time went by I finally got the "guts" to ask her out and she said yes. We went out for about six months, until she finally broke up with me.

During the six months, we had a great time. We went skiing, went bungee jumping and a number of other emotionally arousing encounters. It was a great time while it lasted. It has now been four years since we broke up and still, every time I walk into a coffee shop and smell the odor of fresh coffee, my heart begins to beat a little faster and I think of my ex-girlfriend. For some reason I can't forget her. Why?

When this fellow first went into the coffee shop and smelled the coffee, his increased heartbeat and thoughts of the female were not present. As he continued going to the coffee shop, seeing her and experiencing the physiological reaction as he smelled the coffee, he unconsciously made the association of the odor of the coffee with thoughts of her and the increased heartbeat. This is an example of classical conditioning.

So you now understand how fears, prejudices, phobias, dislikes, stereotypes and uneasy feelings can be learned through classical conditioning? Each one of these can have a negative effect upon our relationships with others. The more we are aware of how these feelings develop, the greater the chance we have to un-learn them through the same conditioning process. Most aspects of learning be-gin with classical conditioning, but as learning evolves, classical conditioning develops into another form of learning—*operant conditioning* (Weiten & Lloyd, 2000).

No law or ordinance is mightier than understanding.

Plato

WE LEARN FROM OUR EXPERIENCE

Operant Conditioning. Why do you work? The authors work because we en-joy what we are doing and we also earn money for working. If we did not enjoy working and did not earn money for doing it, do you think we would still be work-ing? Why do you continue going out with the person you are dating? Why do you still have certain friendships that remain strong over the years and other friend-ships that have waned? You receive positive reinforcement for working, so you continue to work. Your date satisfies your needs, so you continue to date that person. Your friends satisfy some of your other needs and in return you reinforce them and the friendship continues, while the relationships that are not reinforcing or satisfying will wane over a period of time. All of these interactions involve operant conditioning.

Operant conditioning is based on the premise that we are controlled by the consequences of our behavior. Many psychologists will say that most of our behavior is learned through operant conditioning. If you cry and then get what you want, are you going to cry the next time you want something? The cry was reinforced and the reinforcement will increase the probability of you crying the next time you want something. The class clown gets attention for acting out in

Positive reinforcement is very effective.

class, even though it is considered by most of us as negative attention, so the individual continues acting out. If this person did not get any attention, would he or she continue to be the class clown? Most likely, this individual would not. If you change your hair style and receive a lot of compliments, will you continue to wear it that way? If you receive a lot of stares or negative comments on your new outfit, will you wear it again? You will tend to like people who compliment you more than people who ignore you or make negative comments. These are all examples of operant conditioning. You make a response and the consequences of that response determines whether or not you make that response again.

WHAT ARE THE CONSEQUENCES?

Reinforcement. In behavioral terminology, pleasant or unpleasant stimuli that strengthens a behavior are called *reinforcers,* and their effect is called *rein-*

> Failure is positive reinforcement.
>
> Anonymous

 CONSIDER THIS . . .

Grandma's Rules

What Kind of Reinforcement Is Grandma Using?

"You can play ball when you finish your homework."

"Eat your vegetables and then you can have some pie."

"Clean your room and then you can play the video game."

"Take your bath and then you can have some cookies and milk."

"When everyone is seated at the table and quiet, Grandpa will say Grace and we can eat."

"You can go out and play after you take out the trash."

First You Work, Then You Play

To teach a person to carry out his or her responsibilities, requires that the less preferred activity should come before a more preferred activity (fun).

Is Grandma using positive reinforcement?

forcement. The simplest type of reinforcer, called ***primary reinforcer,*** is a pleasant or unpleasant one to which we respond automatically without learning (food, drink, heat, cold, pain, physical comfort or discomfort). For example, a kiss is a *primary reinforcer,* it can be pleasant or unpleasant, depending on who is doing the kissing, your sweetheart, or Dracula. The vast majority of our reinforcers, however, are not primary reinforcers, but *conditioned or secondary reinforcers—* stimuli to which we have attached positive or negative value through association with previously learned conditional reinforcers. For example, money is a secondary reinforcer. When you were a youngster and someone gave you a dollar bill what did you do with it? Most likely you tried to eat it or make an airplane out of it. In order for the dollar to gain reinforcing value you had to take it to the store and trade it for candy or food and at that time you realized it had reinforcing value. Other secondary reinforcers would be a smile, a grade you receive in school, or a trophy, etc.

Reinforcers act to strengthen behavior through two different types of consequences. These two consequences are *positive reinforcement* and *negative reinforcement.* Consequences can also weaken or eliminate a behavior through the use of *punishment.*

Positive Reinforcement. *This is anything that increases a behavior by virtue of its presentation.* If you help a stranger who responds by giving you five dollars, what is the chance of you helping other strangers?

You were given five dollars (positive reinforcement) for helping the stranger and that five dollars will increase the probability of you helping other strangers in the future. If you had not received the money, you are not as likely to help in the future. A child cries at the store and the father gives the child a candy bar to be quiet. Now the father discovers that the child cries everytime they go to the store. What is happening here? The father is giving the child positive reinforcement for crying. We need to be careful about what behaviors we are reinforcing.

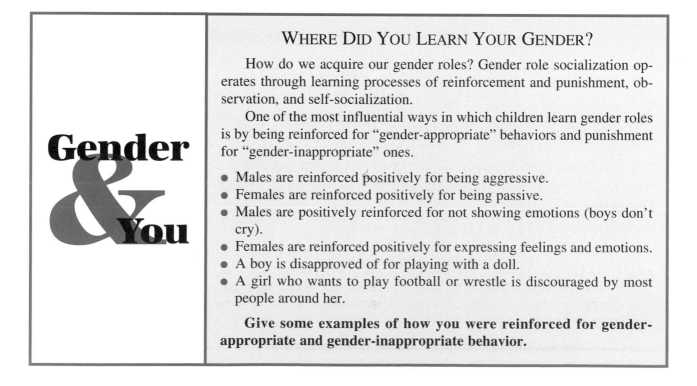

Where Did You Learn Your Gender?

How do we acquire our gender roles? Gender role socialization operates through learning processes of reinforcement and punishment, observation, and self-socialization.

One of the most influential ways in which children learn gender roles is by being reinforced for "gender-appropriate" behaviors and punishment for "gender-inappropriate" ones.

- Males are reinforced positively for being aggressive.
- Females are reinforced positively for being passive.
- Males are positively reinforced for not showing emotions (boys don't cry).
- Females are reinforced positively for expressing feelings and emotions.
- A boy is disapproved of for playing with a doll.
- A girl who wants to play football or wrestle is discouraged by most people around her.

Give some examples of how you were reinforced for gender-appropriate and gender-inappropriate behavior.

Guidelines for Punishment

1. **Punishment should be timely.** It should take place as soon after the incident as possible. A delay undermines the impact. The old saying, *Wait until your father gets home,* is not an effective means of using punishment. Quick punishment highlights the connection between the prohibited (inappropriate) behavior and its negative outcome (consequences).

2. **Punishment should be just severe enough to be effective.** Although more severe punishments tend to be more effective in eliminating and suppressing unwanted behavior they also increase the likelihood of undesirable effects, such as aggression. Thus, it is best to use the least severe punishment that seems likely to have some impact.

3. **Punishment should be explained.** A person needs to know the reason why they are being punished. Explain, as fully as possible, the reason for the punishment. The more a person understands why they are being punished, the more effective the punishment tends to be.

4. **Punishment should be consistent.** If you want to eliminate an undesirable behavior, you should punish it each and every time it occurs. Inconsistency creates confusion.

5. **Make an alternative response available and reinforce it.** One shortcoming of punishment is that it only tells a person what not to do. A person needs to know what they can do. Most undesirable behaviors have a purpose. If you make another behavior available that leads to positive reinforcement, doing so should weaken the response being punished. For example, the class clown (mentioned earlier in the chapter), should receive positive reinforcement for being quiet and paying attention and thus, the need for clowning around will decrease.

6. **Physical punishment should be kept to a minimum.** A minimum amount of physical punishment may be necessary when children are too young to understand a verbal reprimand or the withdrawal of privileges. A light slap on the hand or bottom is adequate. Otherwise, physical punishment tends to lead to aggressive responses by the person being punished.

7. ***Do not* apply punishment to consummatory responses!** Consummatory responses (eating, drinking, sleeping, sex, studying, etc.) are very sensitive to punishment. When rats were shocked while they were consuming food, the experimenters were "shocked" to discover that the rats would never eat again and starved to death. Could this be the cause of some eating disorders? Parents who force their child to study may be causing that child to hate school. The child may interpret the force as punishment. A person who is raped may never enjoy sex again if they perceived the raping as being punished for having sex. Be careful if you use punishment.

Everything should be made as simple as possible, but not simpler.

Albert Einstein

I expect to pass through this life but once; therefore if there be any kindness I can show or any good thing that I can do for any fellow being, let me do it now, not defer, or neglect it, for I shall not pass this way again.

Anonymous

8. **Punishment suppresses behavior.** Research has demonstrated that when the punisher is not around or available, the person receiving the punishment will most likely start emitting the negative behavior again. While individuals are in prison for committing a crime, they cannot commit the crime again. Being in prison would be defined as punishment. But, as soon as the prisoners are released, we find that many of them commit the same crime again. Was punishment effective? If you did not think the police officer would catch you speeding, would you speed again?

· ·

(Axelrod & Apshe, 1985)

As you can see, it is easy to reinforce improper behavior. Your spouse may ask you very nicely to do a favor for them, and you ignore the request. Later, when your spouse yells and screams at you to do something, you immediately respond and do it. What is happening here? *You are positively reinforcing your spouse for yelling.* And, now you wonder why your spouse is always yelling at you. Remember, positively reinforce the good responses not the bad ones.

Negative Reinforcement. *This is anything that increases a behavior by virtue of its termination or avoidance.* My employer yells at me for not producing enough work, so now I work harder to produce more in order to avoid being yelled at. In this situation, the yelling would be defined as *negative reinforcement.* I received a ticket for speeding once, and now I find that I am obeying the speed limit more often in order to avoid getting anymore tickets. The ticket is negative reinforcement. We avoid people who are not nice to us and avoid classes we have difficulty with because of negative reinforcement. Negative reinforcement may have positive consequences because it allows us to avoid painful and dangerous situations. Can you think of any examples?

Punishment. *This is anything that decreases a behavior by virtue of its presentation.* A child runs across the street and then gets spanked. Now, the child no longer runs across the street. The spanking stopped or decreased the number of times the child runs across the street, so the spanking would be defined as *punishment.* You drink too much scotch one evening and get very sick. To your amazement, you do not ever want to drink scotch again. Getting sick is the punishment for over drinking.

Punishment is considered to be the most effective, but not the best means of stopping a response, and that is why so many of us continue to use it so often. We get positive reinforcement for using punishment. You spank your child for damaging your new stereo. Since the spanking the child has not touched your stereo. The spanking is then defined as punishment and you discover you are spanking your child more often because it stops or decreases the child from emitting negative, unwanted responses. You, the punisher, are receiving positive reinforcement for punishing (spanking) your child.

Should You Use Punishment? Psychologists suggest that you do not need to use punishment as a means of disciplining your children, because positive reinforcement is the most effective and best mean of controlling someone's behavior. But, if you find it necessary to use punishment, make sure you use some type of alternative form of behavior that will lead to a positive reinforcement. If your child knows that it is wrong to run across the street, but still does it, you may use some form of punishment. In order for the punishment to be effective, however, you must make sure the child knows that he or she will receive some type of positive reinforcement. Otherwise, the child will have no real reason to stay on your side of the street.

As you already know, we do not recommend using punishment, but many people do use it and many abuse it. The guidelines on the previous page summarize research on how to make punishment effective while minimizing its side effects (Axelrod & Apsche, 1983).

WHAT KIND OF REINFORCEMENT DO YOU USE?

Many facets of your personality have been developed through operant conditioning. When children are being good nobody pays attention. When children "act out" they get a lot of attention. They like attention so they "act out" more and we wonder why they are so "bratty." This behavior then becomes part of their personality. How was your personality formed? What kind of reinforcement did other people use on you? What kind of reinforcement are you using on other people? Is it effective? How does it effect your relationship with other people? Is there a chance that you learned to be male or female by the way others reinforced you?

Positive reinforcement is generally much more effective than any other form of reinforcement. You will discover that if you use positive reinforcement on yourself and in your relationships with others you will be much happier and those around you will be much happier. Your own life, your business relationships, and your personal life will be richer and much more positive and effective.

SELF-CONTROL IN EVERYDAY LIVING

All of us are engaged in a variety of everyday activities simply to survive. We must eat, drink, sleep, and take care of basic biological needs. It turns out that all of these activities can pose challenges to successful personal adjustment to our environment, and we must be careful to control them and not let them control us. For some people their eating habits, drug use, sleeping habits, or alcohol use controls their life.

What other challenges do we have that seem to control our everyday lives? Do any of you need to study more? Would you like to stop smoking?

Would you like to exercise more? Do you watch TV too much? Are you shy? Would you like to make more friends? These and many of your other habits that you would like to change can be modified. You can do it! Find out how.

Psychologists have devised a number of different theories to explain how we develop the capacity for self-control. We have found one technique that has been very successful for many individuals. This technique includes the application of learning theory to improve your self-control. If you stop and think about it, self-control—or the lack of it—underlies many of the personal challenges that we struggle with in everyday life. *What we learn can be unlearned.*

A SELF-CHANGE PROGRAM

Identify the Behavior To Be Changed. The first step in any systematic program in self-modification is to identify the specific behavior that you would like to change. Many of us tend to be vague in describing our problems and identify-

Strategies for . . .

SELF-CONTROL

A Five Step Program

Step 1:   Identify the behavior to be changed.
Step 2:   Observe the behavior to be changed.
Step 3:   Set your goal.
Step 4:   Design your program.
Step 5:   Monitor and evaluate your program.

ing the exact nature of the behavior we want to change. You must be specific and clearly define the overt behavior to be changed. For example:

Not everything that is faced can be changed, but nothing can be changed until it is faced.

James Baldwin

- I want to lose weight
- I want to stop smoking
- I need to spend more time studying
- I want to exercise more
- I would like to have more dates
- I need to stop procrastinating

Which of the statements above is too vague and would not be easy to observe? Can you measure and observe how much exercise you do? Definitely. But, can you observe yourself procrastinating? You need to identify what things you are not doing, so you can get them completed in a timely manner.

Drug abuse, physical abuse, eating disorders, and other serious negative habits that are detrimental to your health can be changed through this process of self-modification—with a lot of willpower. But, we have found that it is easier to change these serious habits with the benefit of professional help. So, please seek professional help, or if you know anyone else having a serious problem, please help him or her find professional help. Talk to your instructor, counselor, pastor, or therapist.

Observe the Behavior to Be Changed. The second step in your self-modification project is to observe the behavior to be changed in order to discover your *operant level* (baseline), *the number of responses prior to beginning the project.* People are often tempted to skip this step and move ahead. In order to evaluate your progress you must not skip this step. You need to know the original response level, the starting point. You can not tell whether your program is working unless you have a baseline for comparison. While observing your behavior in order to find your *operant level,* you need to monitor these three things: 1) the initial response level of the target behavior, 2) the events that precede the target behavior, 3) the typical consequences (reinforcement or punishment).

Wonder is the beginning of understanding.

Greek Proverb

1. **Initial Response Level.** You need to keep track of each and every response of the targeted behavior that occurs within a specified period of time—usually five to seven days. Write down on a piece of paper attached to your cigarette package each and every cigarette you have each day for a week. Keep a diary of the number of dates you have within a three week period,

the amount of time you study each day for five days, the number of times you yell at your kids, the amount of time you spend exercising each day for six days, or whatever the targeted behavior happens to be. As soon as you can identify a *pattern of behavior,* you are ready for the next step. If you discover that you do not exercise, there is nothing to observe, you are ready to begin. Your *operant level* for exercise is "0," no responses prior to conditioning. You may discover that your *operant level* for cigarette smoking is "23 cigarettes" per day, "42 minutes" of studying each day, "3,100 calories" each day, or "2 dates" per month. Now to the next step.

2. **Events That Precede the Target Behavior.** The events that precede the target behavior can play a major role in governing your target response. Where you study may affect how much time you actually study. When you study at the library, you find that you study more than when you study at home on the kitchen table or on your bed. You discover that you smoke more when you drink coffee. You may find that you may have to give up coffee in order to stop smoking because coffee seems to create the urge to smoke. You find that you eat the greatest number of calories late at night after you have a couple of beers; the beers seem to stimulate the hunger drive. Once you are able to pinpoint the events that seem to cause the behavior, you can design your program to circumvent or break it down.

3. **Consequences.** Finally, you need to identify the reinforcement that is strengthening the targeted behavior or the punishment that is decreasing or suppressing it. We eat because we like food—the food becomes reinforcing within itself, just like smoking, we enjoy it. It is easier not to study than to study. Bad habits are self-reinforcing. I do not have to worry about being turned down for a date, if I do not ask anyone out. Most of the behaviors we would like to change are being reinforced and are very difficult to change.

Set Your Goal. The most important factor in the third step is that when you set your goal, make sure that it is a realistic goal that can be accomplished. Losing twenty pounds in four weeks is not realistic, but four to five pounds could be realistic. Studying five hours a day, seven days a week is not realistic for many students, but studying three hours a day five days a week would most likely be accomplished by most students, depending on how many courses you are taking and how many hours you work per week.

Try to set behavioral goals that are both challenging and realistic. You want your goals to be challenging, so that they lead to improvement in your behavior. Setting unrealistically high goals—a common mistake in self-modification—often leads to unnecessary discouragement.

Designing Your Program. Now that you have identified the targeted behavior to be changed, found your operant level, and set your goal, you are ready to design your program.

You have now discovered that many of your bad habits and behaviors that you have identified to change are self-reinforcing. In order for you to change you must find something that is more reinforcing to you than the previous reinforcement. You must find something that will motivate you and make you want to change. If you intend to reward yourself for increasing a response, you need to find an effective reinforcer. What is reinforcing to one individual may not be reinforcing to another. Your choice will depend on your unique personality and situation. How can you discover what is reinforcing to you?

Life's greatest achievement is the continual remaking of yourself so that at last you know how to live.

W. Rhodes

 **CONSIDER THIS . . .**

A Sample Contract

Target behavior: I want to lose five pounds in the next six weeks.
Contract between: Sally Sane
                       Amy Abler (roommate of Sally Sane)

Agreement: Sally Sane—I agree to stop eating candy bars and drinking pop between meals. I will write down each and every candy bar and soda pop that I consume for the next seven days. I will weigh myself each day and record it. After the observation period, for the following two weeks, I will eat only one candy bar each day and two cans of pop. During the second two weeks, I will eat one candy bar every other day and one soda pop each day. On the final two weeks, I will have only one candy bar and one soda pop every three days. From that day following I will substitute pieces of fruit and vegetables and glasses of water for my snacks between meals.

Agreement: Amy Abler—I agree to help Sally Sane lose five pounds and stop eating candy bars and drinking pop between meals. I will review her program with her weekly and do whatever I can to help her reach her goal.

Consequences: Sally Sane—For each week that I reach my goal, I will buy myself a new tape or CD. If I fail to reach my goal during the week, I do not get the new tape or CD and I will have to clean the apartment without Amy's help. When I reach my final goal, I will receive two tickets to the concert that I have been wanting to attend.

Consequences: Amy Abler—I will praise Sally for keeping her schedule and offer encouragement. I will review her program with her weekly and give her feedback. If she reaches her goal by the end of the six weeks I will clean the apartment the next two weeks without Sally's help.

Signed: _____

_____

Date: _____

> Change is the law of life; and those who look only to the past or the present are certain to miss the future.
>
> John F. Kennedy

Selecting Reinforcers. What is reinforcing enough to you to motivate you to change? Is it money, sex, free time, compact discs, concert tickets, praise, or tickets to the ball game? An easy way to discover what is reinforcing to you is to observe your own behavior for awhile.

- Observe what you enjoy doing for a few days.
- Observe what you spend your money on each week?
- What kind of praise do you like to receive: from yourself and from others?
- What are your major interests?
- What do you do for fun?
- What people do you like to be with?
- What do you like to do with those people?

- What would be a nice present to receive?
- What makes you feel good?
- What would you like to do for your next vacation?
- What would you buy if you had an extra $20? $50? $100? (Watson & Tharp, 1997).

Any or all of the above could be used as reinforcers to motivate you to change.

Administering the Reinforcers. Receiving the reinforcement has to be contingent upon you first making the appropriate response. Once you have chosen the reinforcer, you then have to set up reinforcement contingencies. Your reinforcement contingencies will describe the exact behavioral goals that must be met and the reinforcement that may then be awarded. Do not administer too much reinforcement and receive it too often. If you receive too much of something or receive it too often, you soon get bored or habituate to it. If a chocolate milk shake was used as reinforcement five times a day for three weeks, you would soon get tired of having milkshakes and habituate to them. They will soon lose their reinforcing value.

Generally, rapid reinforcement works better than delayed reinforcement. If we delay reinforcement, we discover that we do not realize what behavior is being reinforced. You may find it easier to have a friend or relative administer the reinforcement. It may also commit you more to your project if you make up a behavioral contract for you to sign and give to your friend.

Trying to modify behavior is a difficult task. Sometimes it helps to have someone we can talk to or who might assist us to do this. It is difficult to change some of our actions by ourselves. We might benefit from a person who can offer advice or encouragement. Or, we might need another person to know about our plan because it keeps us honest and committed to our project. It is sometimes easy to fool yourself about your progress, but another person may not be as easily deceived.

JUST DO IT!

Monitor and Evaluate Your Program. Now that you have designed your project, you are ready to "do it." As you begin the project, you need to monitor your progress as you begin to achieve your goal. Monitoring your progress will allow you to assess if your plan is working. Start with your operant level (baseline) and continue to accurately record the frequency of your targeted behavior so you can evaluate your progress. If your behavior shows improvement, keep up the good work; however, if there is no improvement or you begin to regress, you need to reevaluate your reinforcers, since they do not seem to be motivating you to improve. You may need to strengthen your reinforcement or the delay between the time you emit the behavior and the time you receive the reinforcement may be too lengthy. Do not reward yourself when you have not actually earned it. Many people end up giving themselves the reinforcers no matter what they do. They rationalize it by saying, "I needed that new dress anyway" or "I just need a vacation, even though I'm not going to stop smoking." Another problem you may have in not reaching your goal is that you are trying to do too much too quickly by setting unrealistic goals.

When set into action, self-modification programs often need some fine-tuning. So do not be surprised if you need to make a few adjustments. Often, a small revision or two can turn a failing program around and make it a success. Don't give up!

A Happy Ending. Often a new and improved pattern of behavior becomes self-maintaining. When you feel good about yourself and know that you are successful, it becomes self-reinforcing. Responses such as eating right, not smoking, exercising regularly, or studying diligently may become habitual so that they no longer need to be supported by an elaborate program. But you may find it important to periodically reinforce yourself for *doing the right thing* and not slipping back to your old patterns of behavior. You did a good job, keep up the good work!

Once you learn to apply this process to yourself, you will discover that it can also be used in many different situations. Parents may apply it to their children. Teachers use it in the classroom. An employer may use these principles in the workplace. A wife may use it on her husband. Can you explain how it can be applied in these situations? Positive reinforcement is very motivating. Make sure it is applied appropriately.

Chapter Review

We learn throughout life. What we learn is not always positive, but we have also learned that we can take the negative and turn it into a positive and rewarding experience.

- B. F. Skinner states that "all of our behavior is controlled and that there is no such thing as free will." Other psychologists state that we are in control of all our behavior, while others state that both the environment and our thoughts are equally important in the control of our behavior.
- Self-control is the opposite of external control.
- In self-control, the individual sets his or her own standards for performance, and will then reward or punish themselves for meeting or not meeting these standards. On the other hand, in external control, someone else sets the standards and delivers or withholds the rewards or punishment.
- People differ markedly in their feelings about their capacity to control life situations.
- People who perceive that their efforts make a difference when they are facing a difficult situation and take whatever action that seems appropriate to solve the problem are referred to as Internals.
- People who perceive that their efforts do not seem to make a difference and they seem to be controlled by such things as luck or fate are referred to as Externals.
- Learned helplessness is the passive behavior produced by the exposure to unavoidable aversive events.
- Self-efficacy is our belief about our ability to perform behaviors that should lead to expected outcomes.
- According to Social Learning Theory, modeling (imitation) has a great impact on personality development.
- Learning is defined as a relatively permanent change in behavior as a result of experience or practice.
- Before you can begin the process of learning, you have to pay attention. We find that there are three kinds of stimuli that attracts our attention. 1) Novel stimuli, 2) Significant stimuli, and 3) Conflicting stimuli.
- Why study learning theory? Learning theory is the basis of all interactions—we are applying it constantly and it is constantly being applied to us, most of the time without our knowledge.
- Many of our emotions, feelings (love, hatred, etc.), biases, phobias, and fears are learned through classical conditioning. Classical conditioning is a type of learning in which a neutral stimulus acquires the capacity to evoke a response that was originally evoked by another stimulus.
- In most of our daily interactions, we are using operant conditioning. Operant conditioning is based on the premise that we are controlled by the consequences of our behavior.
- Reinforcers strengthen behavior. A primary reinforcer is a pleasant or unpleasant stimulus that has immediate reinforcing value: food, water, heat, pain, etc. A secondary reinforcer is a stimulus to which we attach positive or negative value through association with previously learned conditioned reinforcers.
- Positive reinforcement, negative reinforcement, and punishment all have a tremendous impact on our life. Positive reinforcement is defined as anything that increases a behavior by virtue of its presentation. Negative reinforcement is defined as anything that increases a behavior by virtue of its termination or avoidance. Punishment is anything that decreases a behavior by virtue of its presentation.
- If you decide to use punishment, make sure you use the guidelines for punishment in order to minimize its side effects.
- We can change! We all have bad habits and things that we would like to change. If you apply the Self-Change Program to your daily life, you will discover that you will be able to modify your behavior.

Who is in control? You are in control! Take the "steering wheel" of your own life and head it in the right direction.

??? Questions ???

1. Define "perceived locus of control" and explain the difference between an internal and an external.
2. Explain what learned helplessness is and how it can influence someone's life.
3. What are the recommended "helpful hints" mentioned in the text for developing an internal locus of control?
4. What is self-efficacy and explain how you can increase your self-efficacy?
5. Define optimism and pessimism and explain how optimistic explanatory and pessimistic explanatory styles can influence someone's behavior.
6. Define Social Learning Theory and explain the importance of imitation (modeling) in a person's development.
7. Explain the importance of novel, significant, and conflicting stimuli in our life.
8. Why is it important to study learning theory in relation to understanding yourself and in your relationships with others? Explain.
9. Define classical conditioning and give an example of how it has influenced your life.
10. Define operant conditioning and how it applies to our life.
11. What are primary and secondary reinforcers?
12. Define positive reinforcement, negative reinforcement, and punishment and explain their influence on our behavior.
13. Discuss the pro's and con's of using punishment and the guidelines for the use of punishment.
14. What is a self-change program? What are the steps involved in a self-change program? Explain.

🗝 Key Terms 🗝

Behavioral Contract
Conflicting Stimuli
Classical Conditioning
Conditioned Response (CR)
Conditioned Stimulus (CS)
Consequences
Desensitization
External Locus of
   Control
Initial Response Level
Internal Locus of
   Control
Learned Helplessness
Learning

Modeling
Negative Reinforcement
Neutral Stimulus (NS)
Novel Stimuli
Observational Learning
Operant Conditioning
Operant Level
Optimism
Optimistic Explanatory Style
Pessimism
Pessimistic Explanatory Style
Positive Reinforcement
Primary Reinforcers
Punishment

Reinforcement
Reinforcers
Secondary Reinforcement
Secondary Reinforcers
Self-Change Program
Self-Control
Self-Efficacy
Significant Stimuli
Social Learning Theory
Target Behavior
Unconditioned Response
   (UCR)
Unconditioned Stimulus
   (UCS)

??? **Discussion** ???

1. Why do you think it is important to study learning theory in regards to human relations?
2. Do you agree with B. F. Skinner that all of your behavior is controlled? Explain your answer.
3. What are the benefits of having an internal locus of control? What are the benefits of having an external locus of control?
4. What do you think determines whether you become an internal or external?
5. What is self-efficacy and how can you increase your self-efficacy?
6. Discuss the benefits of being an optimist as compared to being a pessimist.
7. Who has been a role model in your life? What influence have they had on you?
8. Are there any positive role models in our society? Who are they and what characteristics do they have that make them a positive role model?
9. Name some negative role models and what influence are they having on our youth today?
10. Give some examples of how classical conditioning has influenced your life.
11. Explain how positive reinforcement, negative reinforcement and punishment has affected your life.
12. What can you do to your relationships to make them more interesting and exciting?
13. If you were a teacher, what would you do in order to keep your students attention?
14. Using operant conditioning, how would you change one of your bad habits? Explain.

Name _____   Date _____

What Controls Your Life?

Purpose: This is a device to measure your attitudes toward rewards and punishments: Do you feel that they come as a result of your own behavior or from outside sources? We have reproduced this device below so that you can measure yourself and determine your own beliefs. Read each set of two statements and decide which statement seems to you more accurate and place a check mark next to it. Read and answer carefully. There are no right or wrong choices. They are based on your *personal* judgments. Try to respond to each pair of statements independently, apart from your responses to other pairs of statements.

1. _____ a. A great deal that happens to me is probably a matter of chance.
   _____ b. I am the master of my fate.

2. _____ a. It is almost impossible to figure out how to please some people.
   _____ b. Getting along with people is a skill that must be practiced.

3. _____ a. People like me can change the course of world affairs if we make ourselves be heard.
   _____ b. It is only wishful thinking to believe that one can really influence what happens in society at large.

4. _____ a. Most people get the respect they deserve in this world.
   _____ b. An individual's capabilities often pass unrecognized no matter how hard he or she tries.

5. _____ a. The idea that teachers are unfair to students is nonsense.
   _____ b. Most students do not realize the extent to which their grades are influenced by accidental happenings.

6. _____ a. If you do not get the right opportunities, one cannot become a good leader.
   _____ b. Capable people who fail to become leaders have not taken advantage of their opportunities.

7. _____ a. Sometimes I feel that I have little to do with the grades I get.
   _____ b. In my case the grades I make are the results of my own efforts; luck has little or nothing to do with it.

8. _____ a. Heredity plays the major role in determining one's personality.
   _____ b. It is one's experiences in life that determine what one is like.

9. _____ a. It is silly to think that one can really change another person's basic attitudes.
   _____ b. When I am right I can convince others.

10. _____ a. In my experience I have noticed that there is usually a direct connection between how hard I study and the grades I get.
    _____ b. Many times the reactions of teachers seem haphazard to me.

11. _____ a. The average citizen can have an influence in government decisions.
    _____ b. This world is run by the few people in power, and there is not much the little guy can do about it.

12. _____ a. When I make plans, I am almost certain that I can make them work.
    _____ b. It is not always wise to plan too far ahead because many things turn out to be a matter of good or bad fortune anyhow.

13. _____ a. There are certain people who are just no good.
    _____ b. There is some good in everybody.

14. _____ a. In my case, getting what I want has little or nothing to do with luck.
    _____ b. Many times we might just as well decide what to do by flipping a coin.

15._____ a. Promotions are earned through hard work and persistence.
_____ b. Making a lot of money is largely a matter of getting the right breaks.
16._____ a. Marriage is largely a gamble.
_____ b. The number of divorces indicates that more and more people are not trying to make their marriages work.
17._____ a. In our society a person's future earning power is dependent on their ability.
_____ b. Getting promoted is really a matter of being a little luckier than the next person.
18._____ a. Most people do not realize the extent to which their lives are controlled by accidental happenings.
_____ b. There is really no such thing as luck.
19._____ a. I have little influence over the way other people behave.
_____ b. If one knows how to deal with people, they are really quite easily led.
20._____ a. In the long run, the bad things that happen to us are balanced by the good ones.
_____ b. Most misfortunes are the result of lack of ability, ignorance, laziness, or all three.
21._____ a. With enough effort, we can wipe out political corruption.
_____ b. It is difficult for people to have much control over the things politicians do in office.
22._____ a. A good leader expects people to decide for themselves what they should do.
_____ b. A good leader makes it clear to everybody what their jobs are.
23._____ a. People are lonely because they do not try to be friendly.
_____ b. There is not much use in trying too hard to please people—if they like you, they like you.
24._____ a. There is too much emphasis on athletics in high school.
_____ b. Team sports are an excellent way to build character.
25._____ a. What happens to me is my own doing.
_____ b. Sometimes I feel that I do not have enough control over the direction my life is taking.

Scoring Key for Project: For each of the responses below, give yourself 1 point.

Item #	Response	Item #	Response	Item #	Response
1	a	10	b	19	a
2	a	11	b	20	a
3	b	12	b	21	b
4	b	13	a	22	b
5	b	14	b	23	b
6	a	15	b	24	a
7	a	16	a	25	b
8	a	17	b		
9	a	18	a		

Total Points _____

Your total number of points indicate the degree to which you view control as external or internal. The higher the score (above 15), the more you perceive control as external. The lower the score (below 15), the more you perceive control as internal. Now that you have totaled your score, you may want to refer back to the chapter discussion on Internal and External controls in order to interpret your results.

Discussion

1. What are the benefits of being an Internal?

2. What are the advantages of being an External?

3. If you decided that you would rather be an Internal rather than an External, how would you go about changing yourself?

4. What did you learn from this activity?

Self-Change Project

Purpose: To understand how learning theory applies to your life.

Instructions: Review the chapter on Learning Theory, specifically the Self-Change Program. This program will explain how you can apply this to your life.

1. Identify the behavior you would like to change.

   _____

2. Observe the target behavior for five to seven days to get the baseline (operant level). (Make a record every few hours of the behavior you are changing)

   Day 1 _____

   Day 2 _____

   Day 3 _____

   Day 4 _____

   Day 5 _____

   Day 6 _____

   Day 7 _____

3. What is your goal and the date to be completed?

   _____

   _____

4. Identify your reinforcers, long-term reinforcement and short-term reinforcement. What will motivate you to change?

   _____

   _____

5. Make a plan. What are you going to do to change the behavior.

_____

_____

_____

_____

_____

_____

6. Change the behavior. (This can take anywhere from one to six weeks.) Keep records of the daily activity relating to the project. Record the daily activity in a separate notebook.

7. What are the results?

_____

_____

_____

_____

Suggestion to Instructors: The authors suggest that this Self-Change Project be a major out-of-class assignment and that on completion, the projects are shared with the class or small group and the questions below are to be discussed.

Discussion

1. What kinds of changes would you like to make yourself?

2. What is motivating (reinforcing) enough to get you to change your behavior?

3. What could people use as reinforcers in order to facilitate the behavior change?

4. How could you apply the methods of the self-change project to other aspects of your life (job, children, spouse, mate, and so on)?

What Kind of Reinforcement Do You Use?

I. **Purpose:** To learn the value of reinforcement.

II. **Instruction:**

    A. You can either answer the following questions individually or with a partner. After you have completed the questions, get into larger groups and answer the discussion questions.

    B. Put yourself in the following roles and state how you think each form of reinforcement and/or punishment will influence the person involved.

        1. Parent—Discuss how you would use or if you would use the following forms of positive reinforcement, negative reinforcement, and punishment in the training and education of your child. What impact will it have on your child?

           Money

           Hugs and kisses

           Spanking

           Compliments

           Gifts

           Allowance

           "Time-out"

Video games and TV

Encouragement

Special outings—zoo, miniature golf, science museum, movie theater, etc.

2. If you are a teacher, what kind of positive reinforcement, negative reinforcement, and punishment would you use? What effect do you think each of these would have on your students? Would it be motivating for the student or would it have a detrimental effect? Explain how or if you would use the following:

Compliments

"Time-out"

Sitting them in the corner

The "star" or "point" system

Taking away recess time

Encouragement

Negative comments

"Student of the Week"

Grades

Sending them to the Principal's office

No after school activities

a. Which of the above would have the greatest effect on your students' motivation, positive and negative? Explain.

3. If you were an employer, what would be the best way to motivate your employees? How would you use the following:

A plaque for accomplishments:

A salary increase; how much is needed in order to motivate them? 1%, 5%, 10% or more?

Positive comments

Larger work area

New job title

Extra time off

Flex-time

Special commendations

Criticism

Feedback on undesirable behavior

Bonus

Commission

Fines

Probation

a. Which of the above do think would motivate your employees the most. Explain.

b. Which of the above would be most detrimental to your employees' motivation and morale? Explain.

Discussion

1. Considering all of the above situations:

    a. Which forms of reinforcement seem to be most effective? Explain.

    b. Which forms of punishment seem to be most effective? Explain.

    c. Which forms of reinforcement do not seem to be very effective? Explain.

2. Can you think of any types of reinforcement and/or punishment that could be used in any of the above situations that would be more effective than what has been previously mentioned? Explain what it is and in what situation it would be most effective.

3. Some people say that punishment is the best way to control another person's behavior. Other people say that punishment should never be used. What do you think?

Attention!!!
Attention!!!
Attention!!!
Attention!!!

Purpose: To understand the importance of attention in a learning situation and in relationships.

Instructions:

1. Review the section of your text in this chapter, *What Gets Your Attention.*

2. Put yourself in the role of the following individuals and discuss how you would apply the following concepts:

   a. If you were a fourth-grade teacher, you are getting ready to teach a lesson on history and you know it is a boring topic, what can you do to make it fun to teach and also interesting for your students? Remember, in order for learning to take place, you must have their attention. How are you going to get your students attention? How would you apply the following to your class?

      Novel stimuli

      Significant stimuli

      Conflicting stimuli

   b. If you just met Stephanie (or Mark) in your music class and would like to get to know her/him better and possibly ask her/him out for a date, how would you apply the use of each of the following in this situation?

      Novel stimuli

      Significant stimuli

      Conflicting stimuli

c. Imagine, if you can, that you have been married to the same person for fifteen years. You are still in love, but not enjoying the relationship as much as you did the first few years of marriage. What can you do to enhance this relationship with the use of the following:

Novel stimuli

Significant stimuli

Conflicting stimuli

d. You were just hired to develop a 30 second TV commercial for a client. Why do you need to consider using the following concepts? How would you apply them in this situation?

Novel stimuli

Significant stimuli

Conflicting stimuli

Discussion

1. Were you able to apply the use of conflicting stimuli in each of the situations above? In which of the situations should conflicting stimuli be used and which situations should you avoid applying it? Explain.

2. Why is it important to understand the use of novel, significant, and conflicting stimuli in all aspects of life? Explain.

3. Can you think of some other situations where the application of novel stimuli, significant stimuli, and conflicting stimuli should be applied? Explain.

Can You See It?

(Observation of Learning Theory)

Purpose: To observe learning theory in action. This is a great opportunity to observe the application of many of the theories and ideas discussed in this chapter.

Instructions: This activity may be done individually or with a partner. We would recommend it to be done with a partner.

1. Visit one of the following:
   a. Preschool class
   b. Junior high school class or Middle school class
   c. High school class

2. Recognize and record one or all of the following concepts:
   a. The use of positive and negative reinforcement and punishment.
   b. The use of novel, significant, and conflicting stimuli.
   c. The use of positive and negative reinforcing behaviors toward female and male students.

3. Make a chart to record the situation and the type of reinforcement or stimuli being used by the teacher. (You may use the chart included here or make one that applies to your specific situation).

4. Make sure you get permission from the school administrator and classroom teacher to observe the student/teacher interaction. The students involved in the activity will attempt to remain unobtrusive in the classroom.

5. When the teacher responds to a student, make a note as to whether it is a male or female student, what the circumstances are, whether it is positive or negative reinforcement or punishment, how the teacher gets and keeps the students attention with the use of novel, significant or conflicting stimuli, etc.

6. If you have time, it may benefit you to observe a second class and teacher in order to compare the difference in application of these concepts.

Observation Chart

Name: _____

Place of Observation: _____

List the type of reinforcement or punishment applied and state what effect it had on the receiver:

_____

_____

_____

_____

_____

_____

_____

_____

Make a record of how novel, significant, and conflicting stimuli were applied:

_____

_____

_____

_____

_____

_____

_____

_____

Did the teacher reinforce females different than males? Make a record of the different types of reinforcement for each gender and how the reinforcement was applied.

_____

_____

_____

_____

_____

_____

_____

_____

_____

Discussion

1. Did the teacher respond differently to females than males. Explain. (Typically, boys receive more reinforcement, both positive and negative, than do girls in the same classroom setting.) Could the difference in reinforcement have an influence on a student's sense of self-esteem and/or learning ability? What do you think you would do differently in this situation?

2. How and when did the teacher apply positive and negative reinforcement and punishment? What affect do you think each type has had on the interactions of the students in the classroom and on their learning ability? How do you think you would respond in the same situation?

3. Describe how and when the teacher applied novel, significant, and conflicting stimuli in the learning environment. Do you think it was used effectively? Explain.

4. If you were the teacher in the class you observed what would you do different from the teacher you observed? Explain.

Who's in Control

Learning Journal

Select the statement below that best defines your feelings about the personal value or meaning gained from this chapter and respond below the dotted line.

- **I learned that I . . .**
- **I realized that I . . .**
- **I discovered that I . . .**

- **I was surprised that I . . .**
- **I was pleased that I . . .**
- **I was displeased that I . . .**

. . . .

continue on reverse

CHAPTER 4

Dealing with Emotions

The fully human being is aware of the vitality of his senses, emotions, mind, and will; and he is neither a stranger to, nor afraid of, the activities of his body and emotions. He is capable of the whole gamet of emotions: from grief to tenderness. What I mean, is that the fully human being experiences the fullness of his emotional life; he is in touch with, attuned to his emotions, aware of what they are saying to him about his needs and his relationships with others.

Carl Rogers
("On Becoming a Person," 1972)

Think about this...

How would you feel in these situations?

- It has finally happened! You have found that special person, and the two of you are discussing marriage. You are "soo—" in love.
- Once again, your boss said some critical, unfair things to you today. You are "really" angry.
- The telephone rings, and you learn that one of your best friends has been killed in an accident. You are "filled" with sadness and grief.
- Your spouse has just come in and told you, quite unexpectedly, that he or she wants a divorce. You are "very, very" hurt. No! Maybe you're angry.

Would your feelings and emotions be similar to the feelings and emotions that other people have when they are having the same experiences? How do you feel when you are in love? Can you easily verbalize the words: "I love you?" Do you verbally express your anger, or do you save your "bad" feelings and explode at a later date? Could you talk about your feelings if your best friend or someone very close to you died? How would you deal with your feelings if your spouse walked out?

We know that our emotions play an important part in making our relations with other people pleasant and joyful, or sad and painful. We also know that what we respond to emotionally is learned. For example, we learn what situations or people stimulate our feelings of anger; we learn what situations produce stress or anxiety for us; we learn what kinds of situations leave us with a sense of guilt; and we learn which experiences help us to feel joyful and pleasant.

Because emotional responses and expressions are learned, we can learn how to change emotional patterns that are self-defeating or harmful to our growth towards self-actualization. We can also learn how to develop ways to become more emotionally expressive.

In our society, people often experience alienation or lack of ability to express emotions. And it sometimes appears that many of us have almost forgotten how to cry or laugh or express genuine feelings for ourselves and others. Therefore, we hope this chapter will help you become a more emotionally mature person and help you better understand the reasons behind some of your emotional reactions to certain people or situations. And we hope that you will be able to get ideas about ways you can manage emotional patterns that are giving you trouble in living with yourself and others.

WHAT ARE EMOTIONS?

If someone asked you to explain *emotions,* what would you say? In all probability, you would say, "They are the different feelings I have." You might even give these feelings a label such as anger, love, hate, and so on. Now, suppose someone asked you to explain the term *feelings.* Would you be likely to say, "They are the different emotions I have?" And, you might even give these emotions a label, such as anger, love, or hate. The point is, it is quite difficult to separate the two; therefore, we will use the two interchangeably.

Actually, Dr. Daniel Goleman (1995), author of *Emotional Intelligence,* defines emotion in this way:

"I take emotion to refer to a feeling and its distinctive thoughts, psychological and biological states, and range of propensities to act." Richard Carlson (1997), in the New York Times bestseller, *Don't Sweat the Small Stuff . . . and it's all small stuff*, says: Your *"feelings act as a barometer, letting you know what your internal weather is like."* Therefore, we are going to think of *emotions as feelings that are experienced.*

Without emotions, we would be little more than drab, color-less machines that run the same way day after day. We would not know the happiness of success or the pangs of disappointment. We would not experience joy from the companionship of others and would feel no grief at their loss. We would neither love nor hate. Pride, envy, and anger would be unknown to us. We would not even be able to understand the joys and sorrows of others. Roger-John and McWilliams (1994), in their book, *Life 101,* summarize the impact of emotions with these thoughts: *"We experience life's pains and pleasures through our emotions."*

Fortunately, we are not machines; we are humans. Therefore, each of us, young or old, male or female, is capable of having and express-ing many different emotions. Although it is true that individuals expe-rience and express their emotions in many different ways, psychologists generally agree that emotions are very complex experiences, with at least four common characteristics: physiological or internal changes, be-havioral expressions, cognitive interpretations, and motivational tendencies (Wood and Wood, 1999). We will now look more closely at these characteristics, as well as briefly discuss the effect our moods have on our emotional reactions.

Emotions are feelings that are experienced. What feelings do you think are being experienced in this photo?

CHARACTERISTICS OF EMOTIONS

Physiological or Internal Changes. Let us assume that you are walking alone at night when suddenly a large object jumps in front of you. Would your neck muscles tighten? Would your stomach possibly feel "funny"? Would you be able to hear the sound of your heartbeat, even when you later discovered that the "large object" was just a box blowing in the wind? Would you still be breathing faster? What would be happening inside of you? How do you feel inside when you are nervous, frightened, or angry?

As the question suggests, a main characteristic of emotional states is that they involve physiological changes.

When our emotions are aroused, there are physiological changes over which we have no control. In strong fear and anger, you do not tell your adrenal glands to pump adrenaline into the bloodstream so that you will have extra energy. These physiological changes in the nervous system are nature's way of preparing you to react faster, harder, and for longer periods of time. In essence, your whole body is mobilized for action—you are physiologically ready to run or fight.

When you experience strong feelings, the internal changes in your body con-tribute to your feelings. For example, in grief or depression, there is a reduction of pulse rate, breathing, and muscular strength. Consequently, you feel tired.

Behavioral Expressions. Even though emotions are felt internally, they of-ten lead to observable expressions. These expressions may come in the form of a

The feelings or emo-tional aspects of life lie pretty close to the value and significance of life itself.

J. B. Watson

TYPES OF EMOTIONS

At this point, you may be asking, "Just how many emotions are there?" We really do not know the answer to this question, because our emotions include many subjective factors and individual differences. Our language is rich with words to describe our emotions. Table 4.1 gives a partial list of some common emotions we experience.

In a way, this list only represents labels we give to our feelings. Perhaps we need to explain these labels further. One way we can do this is to identify emotions or feelings as either primary, mixed, mild, or intense.

Primary and Mixed Emotions. Psychologists who study emotions have made up lists of certain basic emotions. Robert Plutchik (1996) identified eight *primary emotions:* joy, acceptance, fear, surprise, sadness, disgust, anger, and anticipation. The emotion wheel (See Figure 4.1) illustrates that these *primary emotions are inside the perimeter of the circle.* He suggests that these primary feelings can combine to form other *mixed emotions, some of which are listed outside the circle:* love, submission, awe, disappointment, remorse, contempt, aggressiveness, optimism, etc.

Emery and Campbell, however, (1987) indicate that there are only four basic emotions: mad, sad, glad, and scared. They go on to suggest that all the other emotions we experience are just derivatives of these basic four. For example, too much sadness becomes depression, too much gladness becomes mania, too much fear becomes panic, and too much anger becomes rage.

Although you may not agree with the specific primary and secondary emotions just identified, you would probably agree that it is possible to experience

---

Table 4.1   Some Emotions: How Do You Feel Today?

accepted	envious	insecure	sad
afraid	exhilarated	intimidated	sentimental
aggravated	fearful	isolated	self-reliant
angry	friendly	jealous	shy
annoyed	frightened	joyful	sincere
anxious	glad	lazy	sorry
ashamed	grieving	lonely	supported
bitter	guilt-free	loved	surprised
calm	guilty	loving	tense
cautious	happy	optimistic	terrified
cheerful	helpful	out-of-control	tired
comfortable	hopeless	overcontrolled	trusting
confident	hostile	pessimistic	uneasy
confused	humiliated	powerful	unsure
contented	hurried	powerless	uptight
defeated	hurt	puzzled	vulnerable
defensive	impatient	regretful	wanted
depressed	inadequate	relieved	weak
embarrassed	incompetent	resentful	worried
energetic	inferior	restless	

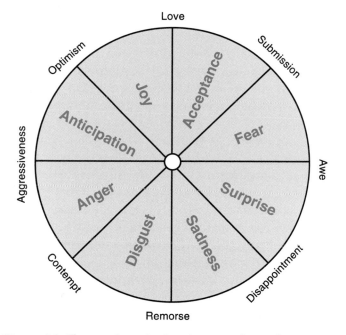

Figure 4.1 The emotion wheel: primary and mixed emotions.

several different emotions at the same time. For example, consider the following example.

> You are going to have some friends over for hamburgers. Your date is going to help you get ready for your guests and also act as a host for the evening. An hour before your date is due at your house, you get a call that he has an unexpected guest from out-of-town arriving and will be unable to join you and your friends. Your date tells you that this is just an "old friend" he used to date, and she is only going to be in town for the evening.

Now, would you just be angry? No, you would probably be hurt, jealous, and even embarrassed that you are the only one without a date. The point is, an emotional event can create a wide range of feelings. We generally communicate only one feeling, however, usually the most negative one. In this case, it would probably be your anger. Could your anger become a problem for you? Let's see!

Intense and Mild Emotions. We have discussed that it is human to have and express emotions and that our emotions have a lot to do with how much pleasure and enjoyment we get out of life. Our emotions can have negative effects, however, and cause problems for us. For example, strong emotions such as fear, depression, anger, and hate can disrupt our functioning and ability to relate to other people.

Generally, our emotions begin to have negative effects when they are viewed as being excessive in *intensity* and *duration*. For example, if intense emotions linger, your ability to get enjoyment from life may be increasingly decreased. It is perfectly normal to be sad when someone close to you dies. However, if you are still depressed about this three years later, this sustained, intense emotion may be a problem for you. For example, other people may want to avoid being with you, because you are so sad and probably feeling sorry for yourself!

Our perceptions about the causes of anger can be affected just by talking about them and deciding on an interpretation.

Carol Tavris

How do you deal with feelings of loneliness?

How about another example? Have you ever had to get up in front of a group and give a speech? How did you feel? A "little bit" of anxiety before a speech can help you prepare and do a more effective job in delivery. Total fear, however, will probably cause you to be unable to concentrate on preparing adequately for the speech. In some cases, intense anxiety can cause you to stammer and forget important aspects of your speech.

Now, let us answer the question concerning your date who did not show for dinner: When could your anger become a problem for you? It would be normal for you to be angry if you were left in this situation. If this anger becomes so bad that you awoke for "nights on end" and "stewed" about your anger, or even tried to harm your date and his "guest," then your intense anger or rage would be a problem for you.

Consequently, we say that when mild, emotions can be *facilitative*—they assist us in preparing for the future, solving problems, and in doing what is best for us. However, intense, sustained emotions can be *debilitative* —they disrupt our overall functioning (Gaylin, 1989). For example, we may experience difficulty in performing certain tasks, such as passing a test or giving a speech, and in solving problems— "stewing" over that date who did not show up for dinner.

What are we trying to say? Essentially, emotions can serve a purpose in one situation and in other situations may serve as a hindrance. Specifically, what emotions cause us the most difficulty?

LIVING WITH PROBLEM EMOTIONS

Some emotions cause more difficulties than others: fear, anxiety, anger, guilt, grief, and love are such emotions which are experienced often and with mixed reactions.

Fear

We all experience the emotion of fear. It can take many forms, serve many purposes, and create many different responses. It is important to distinguish *fear* from *anxiety* (Ellis, 1999).

A specific situation or object elicits *fear*, whereas *anxiety* is objectless. Therefore, we speak of *fear* when we think we know what we're afraid of and *anxiety* when we're unsure.

Where fear is, happiness is not.

Seneca

Types of Fear. You may feel the emotion of fear as a type of warning that danger is near (Beck, 1991). This warning may take the form of an external "cue," or it may reflect your learning. For example, if you walked into your house and a burglar carrying a gun met you in the hallway, you would feel frightened. This feeling of fear was caused by an external force. Sometimes fear reactions are learned through past associations. You might be afraid of thunderstorms because your father had a tendency to believe that lightning could result in a tornado. After all, his mother had been killed in a tornado when he was quite young.

Although most of the above examples reflect physical dangers, we also have fears of being left out of the crowd, of being ridiculed, of being a failure, or of

How much anxiety would you feel if you were giving this speech or presentation?

being rejected. For example, if you have ever been rejected in a relationship, you may be afraid of getting involved in another relationship again. Actually, this is a good example of where you are really experiencing mixed emotions. Is it fear you are feeling, or is it hurt? Could it be that you want to protect yourself from getting hurt again? This type of fear/hurt is one that takes time to work through. After all, do you really want your "bad feelings" from one relationship to "rob" you of the opportunity to have a healthy and satisfying relationship with someone else?

Some people have a personal fear of failure. Have you been wanting or at least considering a financial, personal, or scholastic risk? What is the worst that could happen if you did experience a disappointment? Could you cope with that? Remember that even if you do fail, some good can come from it. How did you learn to walk? You did not just jump up from your crib one day and waltz gracefully across the room. You stumbled and fell on your face and got up and tried again. David Burns (1999) makes some valid points in the following thoughts:

> At what age are you suddenly expected to know everything and never make any more mistakes? If you can love and respect yourself in failure, worlds of adventure and new experiences will open up before you, and your fears will vanish.

We will have more to say on the fear of failure and learning to take risks in Chapter ten.

How do you handle your fears? Because fear and anxiety are closely related, we have included some suggestions on the next page for dealing with these emotions. First of all, let us get a clearer picture of the sometimes troublesome emotion of anxiety.

Anxiety

As we mentioned earlier, when the basis for our fear is not understood, we are experiencing anxiety. Actually, *anxiety* is an unpleasant, threatening feeling that something bad is about to happen. Rollo May (1967) in his book, *Man's Search for Himself,* states:

> Anxiety is the feeling of "gnawing" within, of being "trapped and overwhelmed." Anxiety may take all forms and intensities, for it is the human being's reaction to a danger to his existence, or to some value he identifies with existence. . . . It is the quality of an experience which makes it anxiety rather than the quantity.

Types of Anxiety. Many times the basis of our anxiety is so vague it is very difficult to explain what we are really feeling. As Rollo May suggests above, anxiety may occur in slight or great intensity. It may be mild tension before going for an important job interview; or it may be mild apprehension before taking an examination in your educational endeavors. These are common examples of *preparation anxiety, which help us get energized to deliver our best.*

The emotional tension that we commonly refer to as anxiety also functions as a signal of potential danger. For example, "I better study for that test, or I will flunk!" However, when the quality of the threatening experience is blown way out of proportion to the actual danger posed, and to the point that our anxiety hinders daily functioning, it becomes *"neurotic" anxiety.* A common example of this is when a student loses his "cool" over a test: "I can't do it—I just know I am going to flunk." and *goes totally blank.* Is this normal anxiety or neurotic anxiety?

I believe that courage is all too often mistakenly seen as the absence of fear. If you descend by rope from a cliff and are not fearful to some degree, you are either crazy or unaware. Courage is seeing your fear in a realistic perspective, defining it, considering the alternatives and choosing to function in spite of risk.

Leonard Zunin

How to . . .
. . . Face Your Fears and Anxieties

1. **Admit your fears.** It is one thing to mask your anxieties with physical and creative activities; but if these activities become avoidance techniques, anxiety eventually increases.

2. **Take risks.** Fear does not go away unless you take chances to make your dreams come true. You will gain new strength and improved self-esteem with each accomplishment.

3. **Acknowledge the positive.** Anxious people tend to overlook their own strengths. When you are scared, make a conscious effort to remember some past positive experiences instead of focusing on your failures.

4. **Avoid catastrophic thinking.** Ask yourself what the worst possible outcome of the situation could be. Having faced the worst possibility makes it easier to deal with what does come.

5. **Stay in the present.** Much anxiety is the result of projecting yourself into future situations. Stay focused in the present—here and now—because that is all you can control anyway.

6. **Have patience.** If you are overwhelmed at the thought of confronting an anxiety triggering situation, take it one step at a time. Do not get in a hurry.

Worry is also a form of anxiety. For example, it is normal for people to worry about future events they are going to be involved in and whose outcome they are uncertain about. However, some people worry and lose sleep, lose sleep and worry even more, over "things" that never happen. Does this ever happen to you?

The difference in normal and "neurotic anxiety" may be in one's ability to handle or cope with the anxiety-producing situation. Just ask yourself, "Am I in control of this situation, or is the anxiety controlling how I react to this situation?"

Anger

Anger is a signal that tells us that we do not like what is going on. *Anger* refers to a feeling of extreme displeasure, usually brought about by interference with our needs or desires. Ultimately, your anger is caused by your belief that someone is acting unfairly or some event is unjust. The intensity of the anger will increase in proportion to the severity of the maliciousness perceived and if the act is seen as intentional (Larsen, 1992).

Therefore, anger can range from mild to very strong. Carol Tavris (1989) has identified several forms of anger:

- **Hate** may be thought of as intense anger felt toward a specific person or persons.
- **Annoyance** is used to describe a mild form of anger.
- **Rage** describes intense anger and implies that the anger is expressed through violent physical activity.
- **Hostility** is a mild form of anger/hate directed to a specific person or group; often it is unintentionally conveyed to others either verbally or nonverbally.
- **Resentment** is chronic anger that may be entirely subjective. It is a combination of the emotions and actions and thought patterns resulting from our unresolved anger at an injustice. *Resentment comes from anger just as smoke comes from fire.*

Anger does not go away if we ignore it, deny it exists, or fail to resolve it. Instead, it goes "underground" where it makes "sneak attacks" on our health and interpersonal relationships. Buried anger can also surface the next time an emotional crisis comes along, intensifying the impact of that crisis on us.

Anger most often begins with a loss or the threat of a loss, such as (Lerner, 1997):

- **Loss of self-esteem.** We get angry when we think we have failed or "let ourselves" down.
- **Loss of face.** Public exposure of one's failures or inadequacies can be both humiliating and infuriating.
- **Threat of physical harm or violence.** Anger helps activate our instinct for self-preservation.
- **Loss of valued possessions, skills, or abilities.** Regardless of who is to blame, losing something we are proud of can cause both hurt and anger.
- **Loss of a valued role.** If we lose a part of our life, such as a job, that is important to our identity, we may feel angry at having the role removed.
- **Loss of valued relationships.** Anger is often a response to the loss of an important relationship.

> Worry does not empty tomorrow of its sorrow; it empties today of its strength.
>
> Corrie Ten Boom

> Anger is the emotional response to real or perceived injustice.
>
> Earnie Larsen

Now stop and think for a moment about the times you have experienced genuine anger. Do you agree that your anger began with some loss or even the threat of a loss you incurred? Which type of loss just described were you dealing with?

From these losses then, there are four *psychological reactions* to anger. They are:

1. seeing yourself as a victim
2. feeling discounted or ignored
3. feeling powerless
4. looking for justice and revenge.

In dealing with these psychological reactions to anger, it is important to remember three characteristics of anger (Williams & Williams, 1998).

- **Anger is neither right nor wrong.** Everybody gets angry. Haim Ginott (1985) confirms this but provides some limits, too:

  You have the right to get angry, but you do not have the right to attack other people or their character traits.

- **Anger can be released in a right or wrong way.** It is important to remember that anger released in inappropriate ways destroys relationships. This most often occurs when we *displace* our anger toward important people onto other relationships. In this way, anger at a boss gets deflected onto our spouse; anger at a spouse onto our child, and so on. Because we trust them to accept us as we are, we often unconsciously choose our strongest relationships as a "dumping ground" for our anger.

- **You are vulnerable when angry.** You may say or act in ways that are totally uncharacteristic of you. Sometimes anger causes more anger. Uncontrolled anger leads to bitterness, hatred, and even violence. If your local newspaper carries a brief synopsis of the daily police reports, we encourage you to take notice of the assaults and even murders that occur because people are angry and lose control of their emotions. Sometimes people even strike out at others with aggressive behavior.

Aggression. *Aggression* is any behavior that is intended to hurt someone, either verbally or physically (Weiten, 1999). Curses and insults are much more common than shootings or fistfights, but aggression of any kind can be a real

Do not permit the body to act out your desire to attack.

Hugh Prather

If you are patient in one moment of anger, you will escape a hundred days of sorrow.

Chinese Proverb

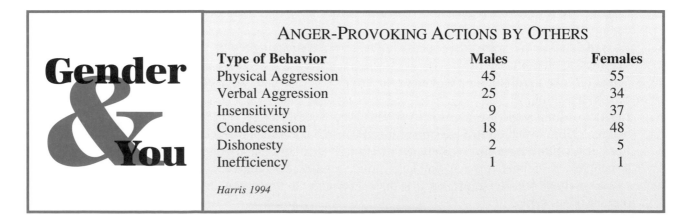

Gender & You

ANGER-PROVOKING ACTIONS BY OTHERS		
Type of Behavior	**Males**	**Females**
Physical Aggression	45	55
Verbal Aggression	25	34
Insensitivity	9	37
Condescension	18	48
Dishonesty	2	5
Inefficiency	1	1

Harris 1994

How to . . .

. . . Control Your Anger

Anger Do's and Don'ts

Do speak up when an issue is important to you.

Do take time out to think about the problem and clarify your position.

Do speak in "I" language.

Do try to appreciate the fact that people are different.

Do recognize that each person is responsible for his or her own behavior.

Do try to avoid speaking through a third party.

Don't strike while the iron is hot.

Don't use "below-the-belt" tactics.

Don't make vague requests.

Don't tell another person what she or he thinks or feels or "should" think or feel.

Don't participate in intellectual arguments that go nowhere.

Don't expect change to come about from hit-and-run confrontations.

(Lerner, 1997)

problem. Why do people behave in such fashion? Most psychologists believe that aggression is largely learned in humans. It is well known that aggression is higher in groups and subcultures that condone violent behavior and grant high status to aggressive members (Dishion, 1990). Albert Bandura (1976) indicates that aggressive models in the subculture, the family, and the media all play a part in increasing the level of aggression in our society. In fact, the glorification or revenge in real life and in the entertainment industry are influences that cannot be denied (Begley, 1999).

Gender and anger. What actions, precisely, do people find provoking? Several studies have investigated this issue. One that points to important gender differences in responses to provocation has been conducted by Harris (1994). She asked several hundred students (both males and females) to describe the most anger-provoking behavior that a man or woman of their own age could display toward them. Physical and verbal aggression by another person were identified by both males and females as the most anger-provoking behaviors they could encounter.

Interesting gender differences emerged, however, with respect to several other potential causes of anger. For example, females reported being much more likely than males to be angered by condescending actions—ones in which the other person showed arrogance or suggested that he or she was superior in some manner. Similarly, females reported being more likely than males to be angered by actions in which someone hurt someone else and by actions involving insensitivity—behaviors in which their feelings were ignored by another person. As noted by Harris (1994), these differences seem to reflect prevailing gender stereotypes: females should be kind, nurturant, and sensitive to others' feelings. In view of such stereotypes, it is not surprising that they find behavior contrary to these supposed traits to be especially annoying.

Expressing Anger. The question now might be: How do I express my anger? Carol Tavris (1989) suggests that we have been told if we ventilate our anger, we will experience the following:

- improved communication and closeness with the target of our anger,
- have physiological relief and catharsis,
- solve problems instead of brooding about them, and
- we will just feel better because we got "rid" of the anger.

A clear understanding of the significance of our misdeeds is emotionally healthier than hopeless misery afterward.

Dr. Theodore Reik

Tavris goes on further to say that sometimes we get the benefits of this list, but most frequently, we get exactly the opposite:

- decreased communication and feelings of closeness with the target of our anger,
- physiological arousal and even higher blood pressure,
- the problem becomes worse, and
- we frequently just rehearse the anger and get angrier.

The question then is, how can I ensure the benefits and avoid the "exact opposites?" Psychologist Harriet Lerner (1997) feels that the expression of anger provides maximum results when the *Do's and Don'ts* on the previous page are followed. Also, you will find the discussion dealing with resolving interpersonal conflict through the use of "I" messages in Chapter seven helpful in dealing with your anger.

Anger is a very powerful emotion and one that requires a balance between spontaneous expression and rational control. It is helpful to remember that when you are angry at someone, you are the one with the problem; therefore, you must be the one to correct the problem.

Guilt

Another powerful emotion that can rule our lives is that of *guilt*. David Burns (1999) indicates that *"guilt is anger directed at ourselves—at what we did or did not do."* We feel a sense of guilt when we have violated our conscience, our internalized standards of good and bad (Atwater, 1998). Guilt, in its simplest form, is the realization of sorrow over having done something morally, socially, or ethically wrong. Experts in human behavior report that unjustified, excessive guilt can sour our enjoyment of living, disrupt our social and business lives, worry, dishearten, and even humiliate us. It can cause fears and anxieties and even torment a person to the point of suicide. As you can see, tragedy and much human suffering have been triggered by needless feelings of guilt.

Consider the following example given by a 32-year-old mother and student of one of the authors:

> The marriage of this student and her lawyer-husband ended in divorce after ten years. The legal papers said "mental cruelty" but they both knew the real reason was her sexual coldness. Yet, there was another deeper layer. Two years before their marriage, during a relationship with another man, she had become pregnant and undergone an abortion—but she never told her husband about it. Guilt over an act she considered deeply shameful, worsened by harboring a secret she felt he

should know, made her feel unworthy of him. She was unable to respond freely and joyously to his lovemaking. Quarrels erupted that in time eroded the foundation of their union.

Without question, guilt can literally paralyze us, making us totally unable to function as human beings. Is guilt all bad, however? Sidney Jourard (1973) has an answer for us:

> Guilt itself is a desirable human emotion in the sense that it enables us to recognize what we have done wrong, when we have violated our own consciences and the mores of our society. Most of us have been brought up to believe that all guilt is harmful, unnecessary, and should be eradicated. That's as wrong as saying all germs are bad. If we never felt guilt, we would not learn in school, do our jobs properly, obey traffic rules, feed and clothe our children, work for our families, have good relationships with loved ones, or live in harmony within our communities or with one another. In short, guilt is our society's regulator.

How to ...

... Deal with Guilt

Examine why you feel guilty. Take a long inward look, seeking the reason for your feelings. It is important to remember that powerful guilt feelings are sometimes pushed far beneath the layers of our conscious thinking. In such cases, professional help may be needed to help bring them to the surface. The point is to find out exactly why you feel guilty.

Determine whether you really need to feel guilty. Reappraise all the rules that have been set down for you during your lifetime. Take a whole new look at the principles, not created by yourself, but prescribed by parents, friends, society, and others. Are these principles realistic and valid for you at your stage of life and relevant in the society in which you now live and work?

Do what is right for you. Make decisions that sound "good" to you. No one can tell you how you should live your life. You must make your own decisions about what is right and what is wrong. Do not live your life by listening to what other people say you should or should not do. Obviously, you will have to accept the consequences of your choices, but be your own person.

Forgive yourself. Learn to accept the fact that perfection is an unattainable ideal. Mistakes happen. If you have done something morally or ethically wrong, accept it and forget it. Apologize if you can or correct the misdeed in whatever way is proper. Say nothing if you will hurt someone else grievously, recognizing that "telling all" is actually asking for punishment to ease your sense of guilt. It is possible to feel sorry about something without feeling guilty. The point is that you will need to tell yourself and also internalize, that you have done something wrong, that it was wrong, and that it is now behind you.

> Guilt is feeling bad for what you have done or not done, while shame is feeling bad for who you are, measured against some standard of perfection or acceptability.
>
> Harold Kushner

behaviors. Yet, the most healthful approach to grief is to heal it, you have to feel it. You have to go through the wilderness (Labi, 1999).

The four previous steps in a grief reaction do not always fall in quite that order, and a person may skip back and forth between these stages. However, the final step of acceptance must be reached to eventually get through a grief reaction (Dickenson and Johnson, 1993).

Grief-work, the process of freeing ourselves emotionally from the deceased and readjusting to life without that person, takes time. You will need a strong support system of family and friends to aide you in your progress. People who are fortunate to work out that grief may eventually find it becomes a positive growth experience—sometimes called *good grief* (Welshons, 1999).

Sometimes we have to experience grief to really appreciate others. In the process of reaching this awareness, we may tend to value those friends and loved ones who are still living. Furthermore, grief helps us to put our own lives into perspective. We may realize how short life really is and how important it is to do what is meaningful to us before it is too late. As Judith Viorst (1998) explains in her book, *Necessary Losses:*

> And in confronting the many losses that are brought by time and death, we become a mourning and adapting self, finding at every stage—until we draw our final breath—opportunities for creative transformations.

Love

Countless volumes have been written about the subject love. Yet do we really understand the true meaning of love? You will have the opportunity to explore love as it relates to more intimate relationships in Chapter 6. Therefore, our discussion in this chapter will be limited to the learned attitudes that interfere with our ability to give and receive love, as well as the use and misuse of love.

Learned Attitudes. Certainly, our ideas about love are shaped by childhood experiences. If your parents hug you and tell you how great you are, hugs and praises become a part of your vocabulary of love. If they slap you and tell you you are stupid, however, you may conclude that in some odd way, abuse is part of a loving relationship. Why would you do this? From a child's perspective: "These people are my parents; parents love their children; therefore, the way my parents love me is loving behavior."

We also grow up assuming that others will find the same things lovable that our parents did. For example, if we are lucky, our parents love us unconditionally and continue to love us even when they do not love our behavior or when we disagree with them. Consequently, we grew up believing that we deserved to be loved just because we are who we are.

If, however, our parents loved us only when we were compliant and undemanding, we may have mistakenly learned that compliance was loving behavior. Therefore, we assume that we should not make demands on those we love. In essence, our parents' loving us only when we pleased them taught us that we must always be pleasing or risk losing love.

Use and Misuse of Love. There are also problems we encounter through the misuse of the emotion, love. Because love is such a powerful and yet complicated

The only path away from suffering is to embrace the suffering.

M. Scott Peck

Whatever things make your life most meaningful, plan to do them before it's too late. The greatest lesson we may learn from the dying is simply LIVE, so you do not have to look back and say, "God, how I wasted my life."

Elisabeth Kübler-Ross

Letting Go

To **let go** does not mean to stop caring, it means I can't do it for someone else.

To **let go** is not to cut myself off, it's the realization I can't control another.

To **let go** is not to enable, but to allow learning from natural consequences.

To **let go** is not to care for, but to care about.

To **let go** is not to fix, but to be supportive.

To **let go** is not to judge, but to allow another to be a human being.

To **let go** is not to be in the middle arranging all the outcomes, but to allow others to affect their own destinies.

To **let go** is not to be protective, it's to permit another to face reality.

To **let go** is not to deny, but to accept.

To **let go** is not to regret the past, but to grow and live for the future.

To **let go** is to fear less and love more.

- -

emotion, we may even have a tendency to "smother" other people because we "love" them. Do we love them in the appropriate manner?

Psychiatrist Dr. Foster Cline (1998) makes an interesting comment about the misuse of love: *"Love becomes a problem when it gets in the way of our allowing individuals the right to experience the consequences of their choices."* For example, what about the countless hours spent in enabling a child or spouse who has a drug or alcohol problem? Why do we find it difficult for those we love to suffer the consequences of their choices? The answer is simple: We love them, and we do not like to see those we love suffer—we want to spare them their pain.

Remember, to let go is not to care for, but to care about.

The reality is that love can mean letting go of the responsibility we sometimes impose on ourselves to "take care" of those we love. It is in the best interest of those we love to let them assume the responsibility for making their choices and the consequences of those choices. When we jump in and smother them, we take away their choices and their freedom to be self-sufficient human beings. In essence, we have done them a major injustice, quite the opposite of what we really believe we are doing. This is extremely difficult for people to accept, and it takes a great deal of time to work through this emotional understanding of the true meaning of love.

Another misuse of love is when we find ourselves or others using love as a control agent—"If you loved me, you would do this . . . , or you wouldn't do this." Do we really understand what we are saying? This is obviously a strong form of manipulation and can totally destroy whatever love and caring there may be in a relationship.

Although there are many definitions of love, in the final analysis, love may truly be the desire to see another individual become all he or she can be as a person—with room to breathe and grow; and it may be caring as much about another person's well being as we do our own. This is true whether our love be for a spouse, friend, child, or co-worker.

How to . . .

. . . Expand Your Ability to Love

Express yourself. You have positive feelings, so put them into words: "Our relationship means a lot to me," "I like being with you," "I love you."

Love yourself. Self-love is the opposite of selfishness, not the same thing. If you do not love yourself, you can not love someone else.

Be tolerant. You can love and be loved without sharing exactly the same opinions, values, and personality traits. Do not make constant agreement your main criterion for love. This is unrealistic.

Hang in there. You are vulnerable and there is always the risk of hurt, but do not give up at the first sign of trouble. Relationships can be difficult but rewarding.

Learn to be alone. You cannot be happy until you can be happy being alone. Do not ask another person to be your "security blanket." If you love someone, give the person room to breathe and grow while you keep your distance.

Grow up. Immature love says, "I love you because I need you"; or "I love because I am loved." Mature love says, "I need you because I love you"; or "I am loved because I love."

Practice. The more you practice developing a loving attitude, the more love you will attract. The more frequently you say, "I really care about you," "I love you," the more comfortable you will become in expressing these loving words.

From The Art of Loving *(Fromm, 1956) and* Living, Loving and Learning *(Buscaglia, 1982).*

Joe, never feel guilty about having warm feelings toward anyone.

Ben Cartwright
"Bonanza"

Expressing Love. Certainly, there are many types of love relationships. Depending upon the relationship involved, the true meaning of love will be expressed in various ways. Some people have trouble saying the words, "I love you!" Instead, they show their love by buying presents or doing nice things for those they love. Obviously, for one who says, "I love you" frequently, it is difficult to understand why another person can not "spit" the words out. People, however, express their emotions in different ways. Although it is true that adults who did not know love as a child have a greater difficulty learning how to express love, it is never too late to develop or expand our ability to love.

Now that we have a better idea of how some of our more common emotions affect us, we will discuss how we got to be feeling persons. The chapter concludes with a discussion on learning how to express emotions, as well as the benefits to be derived in achieving a balance between emotional expression and emotional control.

DEVELOPMENT OF EMOTIONS

From early infancy, human beings display tendencies toward responding emotionally. Most authorities agree that heredity does predispose us towards fairly specific emotional tendencies (Jung, 1923). For example, one child develops a natural tendency to react calmly to most emotional stimuli, whereas another shows a tendency to react quickly and intensely to all emotional stimuli.

An infant's first emotional expression is crying. For several months, babies will continue to show their excitement by crying when they feel like doing so. After a few weeks, they have learned to distinguish and respond to two basic emotions—*distress* and *delight*. Bodily discomfort (a wet diaper or hunger) brings forth the earliest unpleasant reaction, known as *distress. Delight,* the earliest pleasant reaction, appears several weeks after distress, in the form of smiling, gurgling, and other babyish sounds of joy.

Soon, we become more aware of the world within us and the world outside us. Consequently, we learn from others and our own experiences other emotional responses such as love, anger, frustration, fear, jealousy, and so on. We learn which emotions will bring us rewards and those that will bring us punishment.

Through our family, school, and social experiences, we learn various ways of dealing with our emotions. We also receive messages on how to express and deal with some of our emotions. For example, we may hear: "Don't make a scene by crying"; "There is nothing to be afraid of"; "Don't let everybody see how angry you are"; "Cheer up, there is no reason to feel bad"; "Be strong and endure your pain"; or even, "Control yourself; don't let others know how excited you are." It is even possible that you heard the statement, "Big boys don't cry." Consequently, we may grow up thinking that girls and women can cry, but boys and men must not do so. This is an example of how sexist behavior is learned and can be unlearned in the same manner.

With modeling and messages from our parents, society, and our peers, is it any wonder that we grow up confused about *what to do with our feelings?*

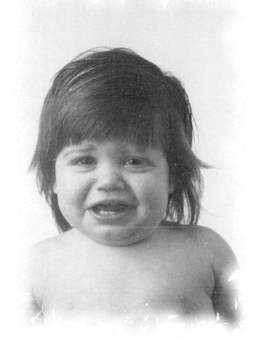

"It's okay for girls to cry but boys don't." How do we learn such sexist beliefs?

EMOTIONAL INTELLIGENCE

Have you ever wondered why some people with high academic IQs are "poor pilots of their private lives," while those with modest academic IQs may do surprisingly well? Why do some "really bright people" make disastrous choices in business and in their personal lives? Are we either emotional beings or rational beings? Could it be possible to have an intelligent balance of the two, whereby the head and heart are in harmony with each other? Most people understand what academic or intellectual intelligence means, but what does it mean to use emotion intelligently?

Daniel Goleman (1995) draws upon groundbreaking brain and behavioral research done by Yale psychologist, Peter Salovey, and the University of New Hampshire's John Mayer (1990) to reveal a different way of being smart—one he terms *emotional intelligence*. What abilities are involved?

1. **Knowing one's emotions.** If there is a cornerstone of emotional intelligence on which most other emotional skills depend, it is a sense of *self-awareness*, of being smart about what we feel. Feelings have a major influence on all our decisions. Formal logic alone can never work as the basis for deciding

To be loved because of one's merit, because one deserves it, always leaves doubt; maybe I did not please the person whom I want to love me, maybe this or that—there is always a fear that love could disappear. Furthermore, "deserved" love easily leaves a bitter feeling that one is loved for oneself, that one is loved only because one pleases, that one is, in the last analysis, not loved but used.

Erich Fromm

whom to marry, or trust, or even what job to take; these are realms where reason without feeling is blind.

2. **Managing emotions.** The goal is balance, not emotional suppression: every feeling has its value and significance. What is wanted is *appropriate* emotion, feeling proportionate to circumstance. It is important to be able to calm oneself, to shake off widespread anxiety, gloom, or irritability. People who have weaknesses in this ability are constantly battling feelings of distress, while those who excel in it can bounce back far more quickly from life's setbacks and upsets.

3. **Motivating oneself.** A strong work ethic translates into higher motivation, zeal, and persistence. Emotional self-control—delaying gratification and stifling impulsiveness—underlies accomplishment in any area. People are more productive and effective in whatever they undertake when they have been able to get in the "flow" state—that delicate zone between boredom (too little demand) and anxiety (too much demand).

4. **Recognizing emotions in others.** *Empathy,* another ability that builds on emotional self-awareness, is the fundamental "people skill." People who have no idea what they feel themselves are at a complete loss when it comes to knowing what anyone else around them is feeling. They are emotionally tone-deaf. People who are empathic are more attuned to the subtle social signals that indicate what others need or want.

5. **Handling relationships.** Handling emotions in someone—the fine art of relationships—requires the maturity of two other emotional skills: *self-management* and *empathy.* With this base, the "people skills" mature. These are the social competencies that allow one to shape an encounter, to mobilize and inspire others, to thrive in intimate relationships, to persuade and influence, and to put others at ease. Deficits here lead to inefficiencies in the social world or repeated interpersonal disasters.

People differ in their abilities in each of these domains; some of us may be quite skilled at handling our own anxiety, but relatively inefficient at soothing another person's upsets. Emotional intelligence is not fixed at birth; however, these abilities can be nurtured and strengthened in all of us. We are *both* emotional and rational beings, and we need an intelligent balance of the two (Gibbs, 1995). Be sure and review The Criteria of Emotional Maturity on the following page for additional insights into Emotional Intelligence.

THE COSTS OF DENYING EMOTIONS

What kinds of messages did you get about expressing or controlling your emotions? Were you taught to express your emotions openly, or did you grow up believing that you should "stop showing" your emotions, even though you continued to experience them. That is right! As long as you live, you continue to experience emotions. Why? You already know the answer: you are a human, not a robot or a machine. You will be given several opportunities in the activities at the end of this chapter to review how you express your emotions.

How, then, do people deal with the emotional aspects of their life? There are only two choices: *deny* them or *express* them. Because overcontrol poses our biggest problem in expressing emotions we will begin by looking at two common ways we deny our emotions.

The Criteria of Emotional Maturity*

HAVING the ability to deal constructively with reality
HAVING the capacity to adapt to change
HAVING a relative freedom from symptoms that are produced by
tensions and anxieties
HAVING the capacity to find more satisfaction in giving than
receiving
HAVING the capacity to relate to other people in a consistent
manner with mutual satisfaction and helpfulness
HAVING the capacity to sublimate, to direct one's instinctive hostile
energy into creative and constructive outlets
HAVING the capacity to love

William C. Menninger, M.D.
1899–1966

*Courtesy of William C. Menninger, M.D. Copyright 1966, © The Menninger Foundation,
Topeka, Kansas.*

Repression. The most common form of overcontrol is repression. In *repression*, the self automatically excludes threatening or painful thoughts and feelings from awareness. By pushing them into the subconscious, we are able to manage the anxiety that grows out of uncomfortable situations.

Perhaps the most destructive aspect of repression is that although we realize we are hurting when we have repressed our true feelings, we do not know why. We have hidden the source of pain in the "dungeon" of the subconscious. Repressed emotions unfortunately do not die. They refuse to be silenced and continue to influence our whole personality and behavior. For example, when we repress guilt feelings we are forever, though subconsciously, trying to punish ourselves. We will not allow ourselves success or enjoyment because we are so unworthy. For example, rather than accepting compliments, we "qualify" them or quickly give all the credit to someone more deserving than us!

Repressed fears and angers may be acted out physically as insomnia, headaches, ulcers, and so on. If such fears and angers had been consciously accepted and expressed, however, there would be no necessity for the sleeplessness, the tension headaches, or ulcers. In his book *The Language of Feelings*, David Viscott (1990) indicates that feelings always follow a predictable pattern when you suffer one of three major kinds of loss: *1) the loss of someone who loves you or the loss of their love or your sense of lovability; 2) the loss of control; 3) the loss of self-esteem.* The predictable pattern then becomes:

When a loss threatens, you feel anxious.
When a loss occurs, you feel hurt.
When hurt is held back, it
becomes anger.
When anger is held back, it
creates guilt.
When guilt is unrelieved,
depression occurs.

> When feelings are avoided, their painful effects are often prolonged, and it becomes increasingly difficult to deal with them.
>
> Andrew Salter

Viscott goes on to say that if you take care of your fear, hurt, and anger, the guilt and depression will take care of themselves. In other words, they will be nonexistent, just like the sleeplessness, the tension headaches, or ulcers. When a person is especially sensitive to one type of loss, however, he or she tends to bury the unpleasant feelings associated with the loss.

What is the result of these buried feelings? John Powell (1995) makes a profound statement about the costs of repressed feelings:

> Buried emotions are like rejected people; they make us pay a high price for having rejected them. Hell hath no fury like that of a scorned emotion.

When you deny what is real,
When you hide from life's pains,
When you shut out the world,
Only fantasy remains.

David Viscott

Suppression. Sometimes people suppress rather than repress their emotions. In *suppression* people are usually conscious of their emotions, but deliberately control rather than express them. For example, you might say, "I'll never let her know that I'm jealous." Why would you say this? You might be afraid that your emotional admissions could be used against you; maybe she would bring it up later. Then you would probably always wonder if she might distance herself from you because of the feelings you confided. Obviously, these are all threats to your self-esteem, so why take the risk? After all, what you do not say can not be used against you.

Although suppression of emotions is a healthier way of handling feelings than is repression, habitual suppression may lead to many of the undesirable effects of repression. Furthermore, chronic suppression of feelings interferes with rational, problem-solving behavior. When people have unexpressed feelings that are "smoldering" within, they cannot think clearly. Consequently, they may have difficulty studying, working, or even socializing with others. More importantly, when you consistently suppress your emotions, you may eventually explode and do things or say things totally uncharacteristic of you. Obviously, this makes the problem(s) much, much worse. As you can see, chronic suppression can be just as unhealthy as repression (Atwater, 1998).

You have the right to get angry; but you do not have the right to attack other people or their character traits.

Now, we are left with the other choice of dealing with our feelings—expressing them. But, is not this difficult when we have been holding them back for so long? Let us see.

GETTING OUT OF EMOTIONAL DEBT

Everybody gets into emotional debt from time to time. Gary Emery and James Campbell (1987) define *emotional debt* as a condition of imbalance in which feelings are trapped instead of expressed. As we have already stated, keeping feelings from being expressed naturally employs defenses and drains energy. The more feelings are held in, the less energy you have to be yourself. Obviously, this interferes with your ability to interact with others.

Accepting and learning to handle and express emotions are the marks of maturity. You are a feeling being. If you are to have the joy of positive emotions, you also must accept the reality of your negative emotions without guilt, self-condemnation, or repression of the emotion. Do you want to begin to learn how to express your emotions? Before we discuss the steps involved, we ask you to internalize the words of John Powell (1995):

> When you are ready to stop telling your emotions what they should be, they will tell you what they really are.

Now, are you ready to uncover your lost emotions?

GUIDELINES FOR DEALING WITH YOUR EMOTIONS

Emotions are a fact of life, and communicating them certainly is not a simple matter. It is obvious that showing every feeling of anger, frustration, and even love and affection could get you in trouble. However, withholding emotions can be personally frustrating and certainly affect your relationships. Therefore, the following suggestions can help you to decide when and how to express your emotions (Adler and Towne, 1999).

Listen to Your Body. What is happening inside of you? What are those butterflies in your stomach telling you? Why is your heart pounding? Remember, physiological changes are a part of your emotions and what you are feeling. Those internal changes speak to you very clearly; do not ignore them.

Identify Your Feelings. Just ask yourself, "What am I really feeling?" Is it fear, anger, frustration, etc? Give your feelings a label if you can. If you have difficulty with an exact label, use the techniques in the next suggestion to help you express your feelings. Remember to name all the feelings you are having. Try to identify your primary feeling and then your secondary feeling. Above all, do not deny or suppress your feelings.

Personalize Your Feelings. There are times when you can name the feeling: "I'm feeling hurt," "I love you," "I'm angry." There are times, however, when it is easier to describe the *impact* the feelings are having on you: "I feel like I'm being dumped on," "I feel used," "I feel he cares for me." Metaphors with a *colorful description* such as "I'm sitting on top of the world," "I feel like my world has caved in," "I'm down in the dumps," can be used. Feelings can also be expressed by describing what action you feel like taking: "I feel like giving up," "I feel like telling him off," "I just want to jump for you."

Own Your Feelings. Your feelings are yours; no other person can cause or be responsible for your emotions. Of course, we feel better assigning our emotions to other people: "You made me angry," "You frightened me," "You made me jealous." The fact is that another person can not make you *anything*. Another person can only stimulate the emotions that are already in you, waiting to be activated. The distinction between *causing* and *stimulating* emotions is not just a play on words. The acceptance of the truth involved is critical. If you think other people can make you angry, when you become angry you simply lay the blame and pin the problem on them. You can then walk away from your emotional encounter learning nothing, concluding only that the other people were at fault because he or she made you angry. Then, you do not have to examine your

The greatest lesson I ever learned was to accept complete responsibility for what I was feeling.

George B. Shaw

Life is like an onion. You peel it off one layer at a time, and sometimes you weep.

Carl Sandburg

own feelings because you gave all the responsibility for your feelings to the other people.

Decide What You Will Do with Your Feelings. This is oftentimes very difficult, because there are many factors to consider. Careful consideration of the following suggestions may be of assistance to you:

- **Timing and Appropriateness of Place.** We are all familiar with the thought: *there is a time and a place for all things.* This is particularly true when expressing emotions because you want to get your message across. You also want your message to be heard, and you hope your message is understood. As we will discuss in Chapter 5, your receiver will probably be more receptive to your message if he or she is not distracted by outside stimuli and if the receiver has the energy and time to listen.

- **How Much Emotion to Express.** Young children may squeal with delight or cry with anguish in the grocery store, at church, or wherever they so please. Adults, however, are expected to exert control over their emotional expressions. This does not mean that adults should not express emotion spontaneously. Instead, it means that adults feel an emotion, understand it, and decide how intensely to express it. For example, regardless of how intensely an adult feels he or she wants to laugh and get excited in church, this is just considered taboo, if you are the only one laughing. Also, regardless of how sad you feel that your daughter is marrying this "certain" boy, it might not be a good idea to cry loudly and profusely through the entire wedding. A quiet sob would be much more appropriate.

- **Significance of Relationship.** There is some risk involved in expressing feelings. In an encounter with a store clerk, an acquaintance, or a distant relative, expressing your feelings may do nothing more than relieve tension. In other words, you might be able to get away with "telling this person off." If you value another person's friendship, however, you may want to carefully consider just "telling this person off." You may find that this relationship means so much to you, you need to be very careful in expressing your feelings. Maybe, you can soften your approach. After all, you want the net effect to be a closer, more meaningful relationship. It is important to realize you are going to be interacting with this person in the future; you can avoid the store clerk if you so choose.

- **Words and Mannerisms.** You already know some ways to personalize your feelings. You will also want to consider the appropriate verbal and nonverbal techniques to use in getting your message across. This will be discussed in more detail in Chapter 5. Careful selection of words means that you use tact and deal with facts instead of interpretations, judgments, or accusations.

- **Recognize the Difference Between Feeling and Acting.** At times you may be so angry that you feel like "punching someone in the nose." In this instance, it would be more constructive to talk about your feelings, rather than act upon your feelings. One point should be made clear: Allowing ourselves the freedom to feel and observe our emotions does not necessarily mean that we should act on those emotions. As a small child, you might punch someone in the nose when you get angry. Although this is not necessarily appropriate, you might just get a spanking or a "time out" period. As an adult, however, if you "punch" someone in the nose, you might get a ticket to jail

An emotion without social rules of containment and expression is like an egg without a shell: a gooey mess.

Carol Tavris

or even get killed in extreme cases. To live effectively in our world requires that we be sensitive to situations and adjust our emotional expression accordingly. Remember, we used the term *adjust,* not *deny.*

Although it is true that people express their emotions differently and respond to situations differently, the truth is that sometimes, as we have stated above, it is just not possible to openly express what you really feel. In these instances, you need to choose some indirect ways to express your feelings. As you already know, feelings do not just go away. Here are some suggestions for these times:

1.   Ventilate or share your feelings with someone you trust.
2.   Choose some type of physical or creative activity to help release your "pent-up" emotions.
3.   Work to maintain a positive or realistic perspective of the situation.
4.   As much as possible, keep a sense of humor.

You are probably thinking or saying to yourself, "I'll never remember all these guidelines." If this is true for you, perhaps the "shorthand technique" developed by Gary Emery and James Campbell (1987) and illustrated in the "Consider This" box on the next page will be a quick way for you to remember the key concepts in expressing your feelings.

> Do you collect emotional trading stamps—that is, collecting feelings, rather than dealing with them?
>
> Ann Ellenson

UNDERSTANDING CULTURE AND EMOTION

Research shows that certain basic emotions are experienced by people around the world. The ability to feel and recognize happiness, sadness, surprise, anger, disgust, and fear seems to be universal, regardless of a person's background or where he or she is born (Gudykunst and Young, 1996; and Ekman, 1992a). Culture plays a key role in moderating our expression of emotion and in helping us cognitively appraise situations in appropriate ways. Paul Ekman (1992b) found that different cultures have different display rules: norms about when, where, and how much we should show emotions. The "Focus on Diversity" box on the following page gives examples of some of these culture display rules (Ekman 1992b), (Adler and Towne, 1999), (Wallace and Goldstein, 1999).

We are emotional human beings. Understanding our emotions, how they affect us, and developing ways of handling them can be beneficial for all of us. Understanding how different cultures express emotions can certainly eliminate some potential communication problems. Learning to constructively express and utilize our emotions is a life-long process; we learn by doing.

BENEFITS OF EXPRESSING YOUR FEELINGS

Many emotional responses feel good to us. Feelings of love, tenderness, and warmth toward other people give us a sense of well-being. Emotions involved in our anticipation of some good news we are momentarily expecting feel good. Emotional responses involved in happy or joyful experiences in life are also enhancing to us, as are emotional responses found in humor or laughter that tend to help us feel good about being alive.

However, the real benefit of having good feelings can only be found if one chooses to truly experience emotions and share them with others.

CONSIDER THIS . . .
Feel–The Shorthand Technique

F   Focus on your feelings.
E   Express them constructively.
E   Experience them.
L   Let them go.

(Emery & Campbell, 1987)

> The things that most clearly differentiate and individuate me from others are my feelings and emotions.
>
> John Powell

As we have stated several times in this chapter, strong feelings that are not expressed or dealt with rarely go away. Instead, you may begin to collect your feelings and cash them in at a later date for a free mad, temper tantrum, or an angry outburst at someone else. Also, bottled-up anger may "leak out" in the form of a lack of cooperation, silence, coldness, cynicism, or even sarcasm. Obviously, none of us would really want these types of behaviors to occur.

The authors believe after you have carefully considered your options and the consequences involved in expressing your feelings, and *choose to take the risk,* you are likely to derive several long-term, positive benefits. We will name three, although there are many others.

1. **You Will Develop Positive Feelings about Yourself.** You can not possibly understand that part of yourself which you deny or repress. Furthermore, you

FOCUS ON DIVERSITY

Cultural Display Rules

● The Ifaluk culture severely restricts expressions of happiness because they believe that this emotion often leads people to neglect their duties.

● Japanese culture emphasizes the suppression of negative emotions in public.

● African-Americans display emotion with more liveliness than whites, showing more changes in facial expression, voice pitch, and body movements.

● If you see someone eating a hamburger, you are not likely to respond emotionally, unless you are in India where cows are sacred.

● In Native-American culture, emotions ranging from expressing affection, being curious, or even expressing unhappiness are much less public than in Anglo cultures. For example, expressing love is displayed by helping and caring for people they love. You do not see much hugging and kissing, and people rarely say "I Love you" to one another.

How might these differences in display rules lead to communication problems?

can not possibly appreciate yourself when you know you are not being honest with yourself and others. Once you begin to openly and honestly deal with your feelings in a constructive way, you will automatically experience increased feelings of self-esteem. People who feel good about themselves are not afraid of their emotional responses. That is, they trust themselves and their emotions. Obviously, this type of dual trust, leads to a sense of inner harmony and freedom—you do not have to *pretend* any longer.

2. **Your Relationships Will Grow Stronger.** The expression of feelings is vital to effectively building meaningful relationships. How can others know what you are feeling if you never tell them? How can another person really get to know you if you only talk about the "weather" or "surface" type issues?

Other people may have dark hair as you do or drive a Ford as you do, but others will not experience fears, frustrations, love, and joy in the same way as you do. So, you must tell others how you feel, what your "gut" is saying, if you really want to establish and maintain meaningful relationships.

Often, when you begin expressing your feelings, others will be more likely to express some of their own. Consequently, you each know more about each other. When two people can share their feelings in an open, honest, and caring way, their relationship will deepen, even if these feelings are sometimes negative.

3. **Pressure Is Relieved.** Experts in psychosomatic medicine believe that the most common cause of fatigue and actual sickness is the repression of emotions. We all experience frustrations and anxieties in our daily lives. For example, our goals may be thwarted, our self-esteem and integrity may be threatened, and our abilities to handle situations may seem overwhelmed. As we have seen, our health and our relationships are negatively affected when we deny "what we are really feeling." When we are able to express what we have kept "bottled up" inside us, we normally feel better. Consequently, we naturally reduce some of the stress we are feeling. We will discuss stress and its effects more fully in Chapter eight.

Sometimes in the process of expressing and dealing with our feelings, we even go through a healing process, known as *Forgiveness*. Let us see what this process involves.

FORGIVENESS—THE HEALING PROCESS

Have you ever been hurt or experienced a painful injustice from:

- Parents
- Lovers
- Children
- Spouses (former and present)
- Brothers and sisters
- Grandparents
- Friends
- Co-workers
- Employers

> The top eight hits on the "hurt parade": disappointment, rejection, abandonment, ridicule, humiliation, betrayal, deception and abuse.
>
> Sidney and Suzanne Simon

> I was angry with my friend:
> I told my wrath, my wrath did end.
> I was angry with my foe:
> I told it not, my wrath did grow.
>
> William Blake

- People of the opposite sex, other races, or religions
- Ourselves
- Whole systems (schools, government, criminal justice system, the media)

Do you harbor bitter, angry, resentful feelings toward these people? Have you tried to "even the score" with any of these people or wished that harm would come to those who have hurt you?

Actually, we have all experienced some hurts and had some painful past experiences. Many of these no longer influence our life. On the other hand, there may be some hurts that we still hang on to. We have not forgiven the people who hurt us, but more important, we have not let go of the pain. Sidney and Suzanne Simon (1991), authors of the book, *Forgiveness: How to Make Peace with Your Past and Get On with Your Life,* explain that the pain has not let go of us:

> Many of us wake up each morning and fill an enormous suitcase with pain from our pasts. We stuff it with grudges, bitterness, resentment, and self-righteous anger. We toss in some self-pity, envy, jealousy, and regret. We load that suitcase with every injury and injustice that was ever done to us; with every memory of how others failed us and how we ourselves have failed; and with all the reminders of what we have missed out on and what we can never hope to have. Then, we shut that suitcase and drag it with us wherever we go.

Throughout our lives, we have all heard the following statements:

> forgive and forget,
> let bygones be bygones,
> turn the other cheek, and
> kiss and make up.

However, it is oftentimes very difficult to forgive the people who caused us real pain. Instead, we believe that the people who hurt us should pay for the pain they caused—they *deserve to be punished, not forgiven.* Sometimes we may even say, "I'll work at forgiving when they say they are sorry. I will work at forgiveness when somehow they communicate to me that they realize and regret what they have done."

In all probability, the people who hurt you have not made up for what they did to you, and even if they wanted to, they probably could not really do that. Furthermore, no amount of *punishment* they may have endured could relieve your pain or evaporate your resentment. What if they never apologize? What if they are never sorry? What if they are never even capable of knowing what they did to you? Then what? Then what do you do? Do you continue to let them dictate the quality of your life (Larsen, 1992)?

Forgiveness Has Nothing to Do with Them. It's natural and certainly tempting to blame others or unfortunate circumstances for feelings of anger, guilt, depression, anxiety, shame or insecurity. But look at the word *blame.* It is just a coincidence that the last two letters spell the word *me.* Other people or unfortunate circumstances may have caused you to experience some pain but only *you control whether you allow that pain to go on.* You may not have had any power or control over what happened to you when you were five, ten, or fifteen years old,

Forgiveness is a way of reaching out from a bad past and heading out to a more positive future.

Marie Balter

but you do have a choice now whether you are going to keep on carrying that hurt and resentment with you. If you want those feelings to go away, you have to say: "It's up to me" (Freeman and DeWolf, 1993).

What can you do to make those feelings go away? What can you do to get those people who hurt you off your *blame list?* Forgiveness is not done as a favor to the people who hurt you or because someone once told you that forgiving was the good or right thing to do. Forgiveness is something you do for *yourself*, for your own health, happiness and emotional well-being. You forgive so that you can let go of the pain and finally get rid of the excess emotional baggage that has been weighing you down and holding you back.

Rabbi Harold Kushner (1994, 1997), author of *When Bad Things Happen to Good People* and *How Good Do We Have to Be*, explains what is meant by carrying around emotional baggage that has been weighing one down:

> When I would counsel a divorcee still seething about her husband's having left her for another woman years ago and having fallen behind on child support payments, she would ask me, "How can you expect me to forgive him after what he's done to me and the children?" I would answer, "I'm not asking you to forgive him because what he did wasn't so terrible; it was terrible. I'm suggesting that you forgive him because he doesn't deserve to have this power to turn you into a bitter, resentful woman. When he left, he gave up the right to inhabit your life and mind to the degree that you're letting him. Your being angry at him doesn't harm him, but it hurts you. It's turning you into someone you don't really want to be. Release that anger, not for his sake—he probably doesn't deserve it—but for your sake, so that the real you can re-emerge."

The key to forgiveness is the realization that the price we are paying for the hurt and resentment is simply too high. The goal is to refuse to pay this price any longer. That is why we forgive. It is for ourselves; it is not about them. It is about our own quality of life (Larsen, 1992).

University of Wisconsin's Robert Enright (1996), head of the recently established International Forgiveness Institute, reminds people that forgiving does not mean letting the guilty party off the hook. It is not excusing, forgetting or even reconciling—it is giving up resentment to which you are entitled. The paradox, he says, is that *"by giving this gift to the other, it is the gift-giver who becomes psychologically healed."*

Forgiveness is possible if and only if you commit yourself to an ongoing healing process. The "Consider This" box on the next page outlines the main components of the healing process.

Six Stages of Healing. Even though we move through the healing process in our own way and in our own time, we all will pass through six stages of healing (Simon and Simon, 1991). These are the stages:

1. **Denial.** This is the stage where we tend to play down the impact or importance of painful past experiences and bury our thoughts and feelings about those experiences.
2. **Self-blame.** While in this stage, we try to explain what happened to us by assuming we were somehow responsible for the injuries and injustices we suffered. Our self-esteem is at an all-time low.

> It's a simple truth that even the most begrudging grudge-holder must one day admit: hard feelings are often hardest on those who cannot—or will not—forgive. That is why those who have hurt us seem to have moved on, leaving us mired in our blame, anger, and bitterness.
>
> Sidney and Suzanne Simon

> We will probably never understand why we were hurt. But forgiving is not having to understand. Understanding may come later, in fragments, an insight here and a glimpse there, after forgiving. But we are asking too much if we want to understand everything at the beginning.
>
> Lewis Smedes

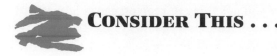

CONSIDER THIS . . .

The Healing Process

Healing is a personal process, influenced by:

- the specific ways you were hurt, when, and by whom;
- how you reacted to the injuries and injustices you experienced—including what you came to believe about yourself and what you did because you were hurt;
- your present circumstances—both the positive and negative aspects of your life today, the problems you may be experiencing and the insight, resources, and emotional support you have right now;
- your own personal vision of inner peace and what you want your life to become.

Simon & Simon, 1991

Human pain does not let go of its grip at one point in time. Rather it works its way out of our consciousness over time. There is a season of sadness, a season of anger, a season of tranquility, and a season of hope.

Robert Veningo
Gift of Hope: How To Survive Our Tragedies

3. **Victim.** In this stage, we recognize that we did not deserve or ask for the hurt we received. We are well aware of how we were damaged by painful past experiences, so much so that we wallow in self-pity and expect little of ourselves. Earnie Larsen (1992) states that *"being a victim usually equals an unwillingness to take responsibility for our own lives."*

4. **Indignation.** In this stage, we are angry at the people who hurt us and at the world. We want the people who hurt us to pay and to suffer as we have. Our self-righteousness is at an all-time high.

5. **Survivor.** Finally, at this stage, we recognize that although we were indeed hurt, we did, in fact, survive. Our painful past experiences took things away from us but gave us things as well. We become aware of our strengths and realize that, all things considered, we did the best we could.

6. **Integration.** In this stage, we are able to acknowledge that the people who hurt us may have been doing the best they could, too; that if we are more than our wounds, they must be more than the inflictor of those wounds. With this knowledge, we can release them from prison and reclaim the energy we used to keep them there. We can put the past in perspective—without forgetting it—let go of the pain, and get on with our lives unencumbered by excess emotional baggage.

It is important to note that you do not necessarily move from one stage to the next stage in a linear fashion. Healing happens in fits and starts, when you are standing still as well as when you are taking giant leaps forward. It also involves moving backward at times, to a former stage. It is a journey of hard work. And, *you will know that forgiveness has begun when you recall those who hurt you and feel the power to wish them well* (Smedes, 1996).

Chapter Review

We would all agree that emotions are a crucial part of being human. Indeed, we experience life's pains and pleasures through our emotions.

- Emotions are feelings that are experienced, with at least four common characteristics: physiological or internal changes, behavioral expressions, cognitive interpretations, and motivational tendencies.

- Although authorities do not always agree on the exact number of basic emotions, there appear to be both primary and mixed emotions. Primary and mixed emotions suggest that many feelings need to be described in more than a single term.

- Generally, our emotions begin to have negative effects when they are viewed as being excessive in intensity and duration. When mild, emotions can be facilitative—they increase our functioning. When emotions are intense, or sustained, they are debilitative—they disrupt our overall functioning.

- Some emotions cause us more difficulty than others. Some of these are fear, anxiety, anger, guilt, grief, and love.

- Although there are gender differences with respect to several potential causes of anger, both males and females report physical and verbal aggression as the most anger-provoking behaviors they could encounter.

- Anger most often begins with a loss or the threat of one, such as: loss of self-esteem, loss of face, threat of physical harm or violence, loss of valued possessions, skills, or abilities, loss of a valued role, or loss of valued relationships.

- Four psychological reactions to anger are: 1) seeing yourself as a victim, 2) feeling discounted or ignored, 3) feeling powerless, and 4) looking for justice and revenge.

- Three characteristics of anger are: 1) anger is neither right nor wrong, 2) anger can be released in a right or wrong way, and 3) you are vulnerable when angry.

- Some fairly common stages people go through in coping with a loss are denial, replacement or searching activity, anger, depression, and acceptance. Grief-work is the process of freeing ourselves emotionally from the deceased and readjusting to life without that person.

- With modeling and messages from our parents, society, and our peers, it is not surprising that we grow up confused about what to do with our feelings.

- We are both emotional and rational beings, and we need an intelligent balance of the two. Using emotion intelligently means having qualities such as self-awareness and impulse control, persistence, zeal and self-motivation, empathy and social deftness that mark people who excel in real life.

- Because overcontrol poses our biggest problem in the expression of emotions, there are two common ways we deny our emotions—repression and suppression.

- It is helpful to remember the following suggestions when deciding when and how to express your emotions: Listen to your body, personalize your feelings, identify your feelings, own your feelings, and decide what you will do with your feelings.

- Different cultures have different display rules—norms about when, where, and how much we should show emotions. These differences, if not understood, can lead to communication problems.

- Several long-term, positive benefits can be derived from learning to express emotions: You will develop positive feelings about yourself, your relationships will grow stronger, and pressure is relieved.

- Sometimes in the process of expressing and dealing with our feelings, we may even go through a healing process, known as forgiveness. Forgiveness is something you do for yourself, for your own happiness and well-being: It is not done as a favor to the person(s) who may have hurt you.

As we go through adulthood, we have the opportunity to experiment with a full range of behaviors and full range of emotions. Hopefully, we learn to express our emotions in constructive ways and to control those emotions and expressions that might be destructive to ourselves and others.

??? **Questions** ???

1. What are emotions, and explain their four characteristics?
2. Describe the cognitive-physiological theory of emotion.
3. What are the eight primary emotions? What is the difference in primary and mixed emotions?
4. Differentiate between mild (facilitative) and intense (debilitative) emotions? When do our emotions begin to have negative effects?
5. What is the difference in fear and anxiety? Define preparation anxiety and neurotic anxiety?
6. Anger most often begins with what kinds of losses or threats?
7. What are the four psychological reactions to anger? What are the three characteristics of anger? What are at least six do's and don'ts to remember in the expression of anger?
8. What seems to be three causes of aggression in our society? Explain the gender similarities and differences in anger-provoking actions by others?
9. Discuss the common stages people go through in coping with a loss?
10. Compare and contrast the importance of intellectual IQ and emotional intelligence. List and define the components of emotional intelligence?
11. Name and define the two common ways we deny our emotions.
12. List and discuss the five guidelines for dealing with your emotions. What is the shorthand technique for dealing with emotions?
13. Define the term "culture display" rules and be able to give examples of some ways these rules are expressed in different cultures.
14. Discuss the three common benefits of learning to express emotions.
15. Why do we need to consider going through a forgiveness process? List and discuss the six stages of healing in the forgiveness process.

🗝 **Key Terms** 🗝

Aggression	Emotions	Mild emotions
Anger	Facilitative emotions	Mixed emotions
Annoyance	Fear	Moods
Anxiety	Forgiveness	Neurotic anxiety
Cognitive-physiological	Good grief	Preparation anxiety
theory of emotion	Grief and bereavement	Primary emotions
Cultural display rules	Grief work	Rage
Debilitative emotions	Guilt	Repression
Delight	Hate	Resentment
Distress	Hostility	Stages of grief work
Emotional debt	Intense emotions	Suppression
Emotional intelligence	Love	

??? **Discussion** ???

1. Why do our emotions often color our point of view and affect our opinions?
2. How were you taught to express and deal with your emotions?
3. Do you believe that feelings follow a predictable pattern when we suffer a loss? If so, explain the process for you.
4. Of the problem emotions discussed, which one(s) present the greatest problem for you?
5. Which one of the four psychological reactions to anger is the most difficult for you to deal with?
6. What can be done to decrease aggression in our society?
7. Which component of emotional intelligence do you feel is the most important?
8. Discuss any "cultural display rules" you have experienced.
9. How do you deal with forgiveness in your life?

Name_____ Date _____

Taking an Emotional Inventory of Yourself

Purpose: To analyze some of the patterns in your emotional life.

Instructions:

I.   At the end of every day for a week, write down your emotional reactions through various periods of the day. (You may want to carry a small notepad with you and record these reactions every three or four hours.) You can begin by making a list of the positive emotions (love, happy, helpful, optimistic, energetic, and accepting, or other positive emotions discussed in this chapter) and negative emotions (sad, fear, anger, hurt, guilt, and anxiety, or other negative emotions discussed in this chapter.) You may want to review Table 4.1 for a list of some common emotions. Pay attention to any physiological or behavioral indicators you may have had throughout the day. These indicators often reveal corresponding emotional states.

II. Record the strongest emotion/s you felt for each day and complete the chart below. If you cannot put your finger on one event or person, or perhaps you are not sure why you were angry or anxious; in that case, put down "unknown" for the cause.

Day	Emotion(s) Feeling(s)	Situation/Cause Person(s)

Discussion

1. What percentage of your daily life is used in the expression of negative emotional expression? What percentage in positive expression?

2. Are your emotional reactions appropriate to the situation? Were you justified in feeling angry, for example, in the situation that produced this response?

3. How many of your emotional responses are caused by unknown or possible unconscious factors?

4. Do you tend to use one or two kinds of emotional responses consistently, or is there variety in your emotional responses?

5. As you review your week in general, do you believe you used your emotional responses with intelligence? If not, explain why you were unable to do so.

6. Explain what you can do to improve so that you use emotions/feelings intelligently?

Name _____ Date _____

How I Learned to Express My Feelings

Purpose: To review the different messages received during childhood on how to express emotions.

Instructions:

I. Below is a list of common feelings and/or emotions. Remember and record what you learned or were told as a young person about how you were to express (what were you supposed to do) with these emotions. For example, Resentfulness: "I was told to grin and bear it."

II. Next, what did you learn as a result of what you were told. For example, Resentfulness: "I learned to keep my feelings inside."

Feelings	What I Was Told as a Child	What I Learned as a Child
Love		
Anger		
Grief/Crying		
Loneliness		
Happiness		
Guilt		
Anxiety/Fear		
Jealousy/Envy		

Discussion

1. In general, how does/did your father express his emotions?

2. In general, how does/did your mother express her emotions?

3. What one emotion would you like to learn to express in a different way? How can you learn to do this?

4. What do you plan to tell your children about expressing their emotions?

Name _____ Date _____

Identifying Feelings

Purpose: To determine how you deal with various feelings and emotions.

Instructions: Complete the "feelings" survey below by circling the number which expresses how well you deal with each feeling listed.

1. Can express easily and completely in any situation
2. Can express most of the time
3. Can express some of the time—with difficulty
4. Can express rarely—with reservation
5. Cannot express this emotion

Caring	1 2 3 4 5	Love	1 2 3 4 5
Concern	1 2 3 4 5	Sadness	1 2 3 4 5
Depression	1 2 3 4 5	Fear	1 2 3 4 5
Anger	1 2 3 4 5	Tension	1 2 3 4 5
Disappointment	1 2 3 4 5	Hurt	1 2 3 4 5
Excitement	1 2 3 4 5	Pride	1 2 3 4 5

Complete the sentences below:

1. I very much care about _____

2. The thing which depresses me most frequently is _____

3. I feel tense when _____

4. The thing that hurts me most is _____

5. I am excited about _____

6. I take pride in _____

7. I am disappointed with _____

8. The thing that frightens me most is _____

9. I get angry when _____

10. I am concerned about _____

11. I feel sad when _____

12. Love is a feeling _____

Discussion

1. Is there a feeling that you absolutely cannot deal with? If so, what?

2. Which feeling do you think you deal with most successfully? Why?

3. How important are feelings to you in your interactions with others?

4. How can you learn to express your emotions in a positive way?

Name _____ Date _____

How I Express My Feelings

Purpose: To identify how you personally express a variety of emotions/feelings.

Instructions: Being as spontaneous as possible, complete the following sentences:

1. When I'm angry, I express it by

2. When I'm worried, I express it by

3. When I'm sad, I express it by

4. When I'm depressed, I express it by

5. When I feel like a failure, I express it by

6. When I'm afraid, I express it by

7. When I feel successful, I express it by

8. When I feel affectionate, I express it by

9. When I feel guilty, I express it by

10. When I feel lonely, I express it by

11. When I feel hurt, I express it by

12. When I feel rejected, I express it by

Discussion

1. Which of these feelings would you like to be able to express in a different manner?

2. Explain what steps you would take to learn how to express the feelings identified in question 1?

3. Which of these feelings are the most difficult for you to express?

4. Which of these feelings are the easiest for you to express? Why?

Anger Inventory

Purpose: To learn how you confront and/or handle your anger.

Instructions: Complete these questions as quickly as you can. Your first response is usually going to be the best.

1. I concern myself with others' opinions of me more than I like to admit.   T   F
2. It is not unusual for me to have a restless feeling on the inside.   T   F
3. I have had relationships with others that could be described as stormy or unstable.   T   F
4. It seems that I wind up helping others more than they help me.   T   F
5. I sometimes wonder how much my friends or family members accept me.   T   F
6. At times I seem to have an unusual amount of guilt even though it seems unnecessary.   T   F
7. At times I prefer to get away rather than to be around people.   T   F
8. I realize that I do not like to admit to myself how angry I feel.   T   F
9. Sometimes I use humor to avoid facing my feelings or to keep others from knowing how I really feel.   T   F
10. I have a problem of thinking too many critical thoughts.   T   F
11. Sometimes I can use sarcasm in a very biting way.   T   F
12. I have known moments of great tension and stress.   T   F
13. When I feel angry I sometimes find myself doing things I know are wrong.   T   F
14. I like having times when no one knows what I am doing.   T   F
15. I usually do not tell people when I feel hurt.   T   F
16. At times I wish I had more friends.   T   F
17. I find myself having more bodily aches and pains.   T   F
18. I have had trouble in the past in relating with members of the opposite sex.   T   F
19. Criticism bothers me a great deal.   T   F
20. I desire acceptance by others, but fear rejection.   T   F
21. I worry a lot about my relationships with others.   T   F
22. I believe I am somewhat socially withdrawn.   T   F
23. I believe I am overly sensitive to rejection.   T   F
24. I find myself preoccupied with my personal goals for success.   T   F
25. I often have felt inferior to others.   T   F
26. There are times when I like to convince myself that I am superior to others.   T   F
27. Even though I do not like it, I sometimes am phony in social settings.   T   F
28. I do not seem to have the emotional support I would like from my family or friends.   T   F
29. I would like to tell people exactly what I think.   T   F
30. My concentration sometimes seems poor.   T   F

31. I have had sleep patterns that do not seem normal.   T   F

32. I worry about financial matters.   T   F

33. There are times when I feel inadequate in the way I handle personal relationships.   T   F

34. My conscience bothers me about things I have done in the past.   T   F

35. Sometimes it seems that my religious life is more of a burden than a help.   T   F

36. There are times when I would like to run away from home.   T   F

37. I have had too many quarrels or disagreements with members of my family.   T   F

38. I have been disillusioned with love.   T   F

39. Sometimes I have difficulty controlling my weight, whether gaining or losing too much.   T   F

40. At times I feel that life owes me more than it has given me.   T   F

41. I have had trouble controlling my sexual urges.   T   F

42. To be honest, I prefer to find someone to blame my problems on.   T   F

43. My greatest struggles are within myself.   T   F

44. Other people find more fault with me than they really should.   T   F

45. Many of the nice things I do are done out of a sense of obligation.   T   F

46. Many mornings I wake up not feeling refreshed.   T   F

47. I find myself saying things sometimes that I should not have said.   T   F

48. It is not unusual for me to forget someone's name after I have just met him/her.   T   F

49. It is difficult for me to motivate myself to do things that do not have to be done.   T   F

50. My decisions are often governed by my feelings.   T   F

51. When something irritates me I find it hard to get calmed down quickly.   T   F

52. I would rather watch a good sporting event than spend a quiet evening at home.   T   F

53. I am hesitant for people to give me suggestions.   T   F

54. I tend to speak out when someone wants to know my opinions.   T   F

55. I would rather entertain guests in my own home than be entertained by them.   T   F

56. When people are being unreasonable I usually take a strong dislike to them.   T   F

57. I am a fairly strict person, liking things to be done in a predictable way.   T   F

58. I consider myself to be possessive in my personal relationships.   T   F

59. Sometimes I could be described as moody.   T   F

60. People who know me well would say I am stubborn.   T   F

Total _____

Scoring & Evaluation

Go back and count the number of "T's" you circled. This will tell you how great your need is to confront your anger. For example:

I. **Less than 15:** You probably have pretty good control over your anger (or else you were using a lot of denial). Look back over the questions you responded to with a "T" and you will be able to focus on those items as areas for further improvement.

II. **Between 15 and 30:** You are probably in the normal range. You are willing to admit that you have anger within you and you know you have plenty of room to grow. You will need to be careful as you learn to handle your anger in more effective ways.

III. **Between 31 and 40:** You have probably experienced more than your share of problems. Chances are you have had more dissatisfying moments than you would like to admit.

IV. **Greater than 41:** You probably need to work diligently at keeping your anger under control.

Discussion

1. Do you agree with the description of how you confront your anger? Why or why not?

2. As you analyze your results, what do you think you need to do to confront and/or handle your anger?

Your Letter

Discussion

1. How do you feel now that you have written your letter?

2. What is the difference in forgetting and forgiving?

Dealing with Emotions

Learning Journal

Select the statement below that best defines your feelings about the personal value or meaning gained from this chapter and respond below the dotted line.

- **I learned that I . . .**
- **I realized that I . . .**
- **I discovered that I . . .**

- **I was surprised that I . . .**
- **I was pleased that I . . .**
- **I was displeased that I . . .**

. . . .

continue on reverse

CHAPTER 5

Interpersonal Communication

Communication, the art of talking with each other, saying it clearly, listening to what the other says and making sure that we're hearing accurately, is by all indication the skill most essential for creating and maintaining meaningful, loving relationships.

Leo Buscaglia
("Loving Each Other," 1984)

> # Think about this...
>
> - Friends say, "We can't communicate anymore. We aren't even on the same wavelength."
> - Kids say, "I can't talk to my parents. They just don't understand me."
> - Parents say, "I can't talk to my kids. They won't even listen to me."
> - Marriage partners say, "We can't talk to each other. We just don't have anything meaningful to talk about."
> - Students say, "We can't discuss our lack of understanding with Mr. Jones. He thinks he has explained the chapter perfectly well. There is no use in us trying to talk to him."
> - An employer learns that his secretary is leaving and just can't believe she didn't tell him she was so unhappy. She replies, "I've tried to many times in the past, but we just can't communicate."

Have you ever said to another person, "We just can't communicate?" Has another person ever said that to you? Actually, you were both communicating at some level, but you were not *connecting*. What, then, is communication?"

Miller and Wackman (1981) indicate that to communicate means to make known, to give to another; to interchange thoughts, feelings, and information; to participate; to share; to form a connecting link. How important is this?

The foundation of all relationships is based on communication. Because communication underlies all relationships and the process of communication is such a complex topic, we want to begin by providing some organizational structure for our discussion. The first half of the chapter deals with the communication process, including the verbal and nonverbal aspects of communication. The remaining part of the chapter is devoted to learning how to improve our listening and responding skills.

WHY DO WE NEED TO COMMUNICATE?

Without communication, we, as humans, would not be able to survive. We need to find out about the world we live in; we need to know how to interpret the experiences we have; we need to release tension; we need to find out about other people; we need to know how to get information from others; we need to know how to let others know what is going on inside of us.

Communication has been described as the process of conveying feelings, attitudes, facts, beliefs, and ideas between individuals, either verbally or non-verbally. On the surface, then, communication appears to be such a simple act. After all, our daily lives are filled with one communication experience after another.

We have all heard the statement that a relationship is only as good as its communication. When we are with other people who are aware of our presence, it is impossible not to communicate. No matter what we do, we send out messages that say something about ourselves.

This points to the fact that communication is perhaps the most important factor in determining the kinds of relationships we have with others. Furthermore, communication is the way relationships are created, maintained, and destroyed. The ability to send clear messages and to be heard is central to any ongoing rela-

We have developed communication systems to permit man on earth to talk with man on the moon. Yet, mother often cannot talk with daughter, father to son, black to white, labor with management, or democracy with communism.

Hadley Read

tionship—husband and wife, parent and child, employer and employee, friends, siblings. In his book *People Skills,* Robert Bolton (1986) confirms this:

> Communication is the lifeblood of every relationship. When open, clear, sensitive communication takes place, the relationship is nurtured. When communication is guarded, hostile, or ineffective, the relationship falters. When the communication flow is largely obstructed, the relationship quickly deteriorates and ultimately dies. Where communication skills are lacking, there is so much lost love— between spouses, lovers, friends, parents, and children. For satisfying relationships, it is essential to discover methods that will help us to at least partially bridge the interpersonal gaps that separate us from others.

However, as much communicating as we do, most of us are not all that efficient in performing this simple act. Perhaps, the trite, but true statement—*keep the communication channels open*—indicates the complexity, rather than simplicity of communication.

WHY IS COMMUNICATION DIFFICULT?

Do you generally communicate what you mean or intend? Do you generally interpret messages in the same way the sender intended? Think about the following statement: When two people talk, six possible messages can get through:

1.   What you mean to say.
2.   What you actually say.
3.   What the other person hears.
4.   What the other person thinks he hears.
5.   What the other person says about what you said.
6.   What you think the other person said about what you said.

We are all concerned with the ability to communicate real meaning and understanding. Some people think that communication is really the sending and receiving of messages, because both elements must be present for communication to take place. They think that communication originates with the sender, and they believe that the message sent is the one that is received. They expect their listeners to act in accordance with the intentions of their message, and they are often bewildered, hurt, or angry when their listeners do not do so.

As we can see, the fundamental transaction of the message sent and received does not presuppose that communication has occurred. In essence, if I speak and you listen, I may be transmitting information, but that is all. If I speak, however, and you listen, and we understand, then we are communicating effectively. Therefore, effective communication exists between two people when the receiver interprets the sender's message the way the sender intended it (Johnson, 2000).

Effective communication is not just an event, but a process—a process that requires the cooperation and understanding of both parties. What kind of cooperation are we talking about?

Whether clear or garbled, tumultuous or silent, deliberate or fatally inadvertent, communication is the ground of meeting and the foundation of community. It is, in short, the essential human connection.

Ashley Montagu

Some people talk to a person, at a person, or with a person. Which one do you do?

WHAT IS INVOLVED IN THE COMMUNICATION PROCESS?

In any given situation, there are three commonly accepted parts to the communication process. There is always 1) *a sender of the message,* 2) *a receiver of the message* and 3) *the content of the message.* The message can be either verbal or nonverbal. Could it be possible that there are really more than three parts to the communication process (De Vito, 1997; Hamilton, 2000)?

Let us look at a simple diagram (see Figure 5.1) of what is involved in a communication transaction. Assume that Jill wants to inform John, her husband, that she would like to remodel the house.

Step One: The Idea. Here the sender creates an idea or chooses a fact to communicate. Jill says to herself, "I think I'll ask John if we can remodel the house."

Step Two: Encoding. The sender, in attempting to get his or her message across, forms a mental picture of that message and then organizes and translates this picture into symbols that will make the sender's idea receivable. Symbols involve such things as the selection of words, tone and pitch of voice, nonverbal method, or even types of supportive materials. Jill says, "John, there is something I would like to talk to you about after dinner and when the children are in bed." Later, Jill says, "I would like for us to remodel the house this summer."

Step Three: Transmission. This refers to the means by which the encoded communication is to be made, or the channel through which the message must pass from the sender to the receiver. *Communication channels* can be a face-to-face discussion, something in writing, the telephone, or even radio or television. In this instance, Jill chose to talk to John face-to-face.

Step Four: Receiving. John can only receive the message if he is attentive to Jill. He must not be reading the newspaper or watching the news.

Communication is perhaps the most important factor in determining the kinds of relationships we have with others.

Step Five: Decoding. This is done by the receiver. The message that has been transmitted by the sender must be interpreted and translated into meaning. By decoding, the listener has now formed his or her own mental picture of what the sender said. In our example, decoding is not complete until John hears the whole message. The opening comment, "John, there is something I would like to talk to you about," is a good way to get John's attention and help him listen for the whole message. John hears the complete message from Jill.

Step Six: Understanding. If the receiver has decoded accurately, the mental picture he or she has formed of what the sender said will match. Consequently, the message has been understood correctly. In our example, John does not have any trouble understanding that Jill wants to remodel the house this summer.

There is always the possibility that the listener may have misinterpreted the speaker's words, however, thus forming a totally different mental picture. This would mean that communication did not properly take place. Too often, this type of communication breakdown occurs, resulting in all sorts of problems, ranging from not knowing what to study for an exam to painful relationship situations.

There is a means of preventing, or at least reducing this type of communication problem, by checking a decoding for accuracy and thus improving the quality of your communication. This method is called feedback.

Step Seven: Feedback. *Feedback,* the process by which the sender clarifies how his or her message is being received and interpreted, is really the only means for determining whether there is mutual understanding between the sender and receiver.

In our example, John understands Jill's request, but he does not agree. He acts, or gives feedback, by telling Jill that she will have to wait six more months until his promotion and salary increase will become effective. Jill understands John's position and tells him, "Okay, but I am counting on us starting November 1." As you can see from this illustration, as well as in Figure 5.1, *feedback* becomes a message, and the sender and receiver switch roles (Garrison and Bly, 1997).

I see communication as a huge umbrella that covers and affects all that goes on between human beings. Once a human being has arrived on this earth, communication is the largest single factor determining what kinds of relationships he makes with others and what happens to him in the world about him. How he manages his survival, how he develops intimacy; how productive he is, how he makes sense, how he connects with his own divinity—all are largely dependent on his communication skills.

Virginia Satir

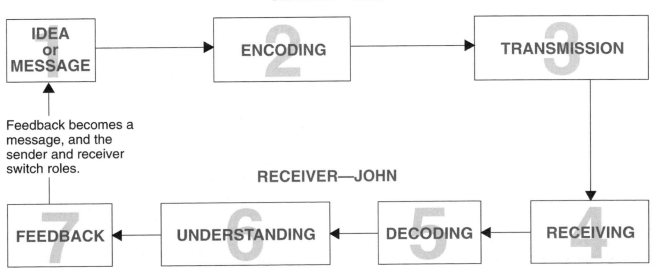

Figure 5.1. Communication Process

ONE- AND TWO-WAY COMMUNICATION

As we have just discussed, since there are so many sources of error or distortion in a message, it is wise for both the sender and receiver to provide adequate feedback to one another in an effort to gain understanding and rapport. This completes the process of *two-way communication,* with the *key element being feedback.* One-way communication frequently results in our making inaccurate inferences or assumptions (Garrison and Bly, 1997).

One-way communication is sometimes referred to as *passive listening,* because there is an *absence of verbal feedback.* Examples of one-way communication might be a class you may be taking which is *strictly* lecture oriented, or a certain person you know who tends to dominate and control conversations, with little interest shown in your ideas or concerns. Even written messages can become avenues for two-way communication. For example, "I'll follow-up with a phone call to you within a week to hear your ideas on this proposal," or "Send me your ideas on this proposal, and then we will get together for lunch and discuss our mutual concerns."

> It takes two to make communication.
>
> Irving Lee

CONSIDER THIS . . .
Is It Our Money or Your Money?

Monologue Between Wife and Husband

"Dick, I thought of something when I signed the joint income tax form the other day. Although all our assets are shared by state law, our three banking accounts are in your name. Why is that? Don't you trust my judgment about financial matters?"

"Why are you complaining about a technical detail like that? It's the husband's job to protect his wife from having to worry about things like bank accounts. That's what my father did for my mother. What's for dinner?"

"The whole thing doesn't sound quite right to me. I feel left out of things."

"You find the pickiest things to complain about."

Dialogue Between Wife and Husband

"Dick, I thought of something when I signed the joint income tax form the other day. Although our assets are shared by state law, our three banking accounts are in your name. Why is that? Don't you trust my judgment about financial matters?"

"It sounds like you're discontented about the way I have arranged things financially. Maybe you feel you should have equal input in these matters."

"Exactly. Your having total control over the bank accounts makes me feel like a second-class citizen in our marriage."

"My intent was not to make you feel like a second-class citizen. It's just been a long-held belief of mine that only one person in a marriage should be in charge of the bank accounts. How would having separate accounts appeal to you?"

"Maybe that would be a good compromise. I appreciate your understanding how I feel about the whole topic."

One-way communication sometimes takes place even when the second party responds to the first party. In such instances, the second party is not responding to what the other person is *really* saying. Two-way communication usually requires that the parties respond to each other's feelings. Another way of looking at the same issue is to examine the difference between a monologue and a dialogue. In a dialogue, the parties understand what each other is *really* saying. The "Consider This" box on the previous page illustrates the difference between a monologue *(one-way communication)* and a dialogue *(two-way communication)*.

Without a doubt, many of the difficulties that arise in communication stem from the fact that we fail to remember that communication is really a two-way process. Open two-way communication facilitates understanding in communication, which in turn helps such things as developing a fulfilling relationship and being able to work together effectively (Johnson, 2000).

After having reviewed the complete communication process, it becomes apparent that "breakdowns" can occur at any step. Sometimes these "breakdowns" are caused by *barriers*—something that stops, blocks, prevents, or hinders. In communication, we may be hindered by a number of barriers that seem to arise from natural human differences and others that are the result of personal habits or attitudes. All or most can be eliminated, changed, or minimized. Review Table 5.1 for a partial listing of barriers to interpersonal communication. Which barriers sometimes prevent you from achieving clear, open communication?

The remaining sections of this chapter will discuss ways to minimize these barriers and reduce communication "breakdowns." We will begin with a discussion of nonverbal communication.

> What you are speaks so loudly, I cannot hear what you say.
>
> Ralph Waldo Emerson

NONVERBAL COMMUNICATION

The science or study of nonverbal communication, called *kinesics,* composes a great deal of the meanings between people. Most experts on the subject of nonverbal communication agree that more than 60 percent of our communication is by nonverbal means. Randall Harrison (1970), a prominent authority on nonverbal behavior, claims that a mere 35 percent of the meaning of communication derives from words; the remainder comes from body language. Albert Mehrabian

Table 5.1   Barriers to Interpersonal Communication

Background and experience	Hidden agendas
Health and physical condition	Stereotyping
Feelings and emotions	Physical environment
Word meaning and usage	Preoccupation
Listening only for words	Closed mind
Jumping to conclusions	Being self-centered
Making snap judgments	Failure to listen
Failure to seek clarification	Unclear messages
Disregarding feedback	Highly charged, emotion-laden words
Status of relationships	Talking too fast
Incongruent verbal and nonverbal behavior	Generalizations
Lack of eye contact	Language level

What nonverbal message is being communicated between these two people?

(1980), a psychologist who has studied nonverbal communication, claims that in situations he examined, only 20 percent of the impact was verbal—the remaining 80 percent was nonverbal.

The authors may not go to that extreme, but we do agree that nonverbal communication is an extremely important medium of communication. Actually, nonverbal communication relates to verbal communication in three ways:

1. Nonverbal communication can reinforce the verbal message.
2. Nonverbal communication can replace the verbal message.
3. Nonverbal communication can contradict the verbal message.

When the nonverbal message contradicts the verbal message, a *double bind* exists. Usually, however, the nonverbal message is more accurate and is believed over the verbal message.

Do you know how you communicate nonverbally? Do you know how other cultures communicate nonverbally? Let's look at some possible ways.

Facial Expressions and Eye Contact. More than any other nonverbal factor, facial expressions can communicate more emotional meaning more accurately. For example, the face:

● Communicates evaluative judgment.
● Reveals the level of interest or lack of it.

Facial Expressions and Eye Contact

Researchers indicate we can move people from culture to culture and they know how to make and read the same basic expressions: anger, fear, sadness, disgust, surprise and happiness. The six appear to be hardwired in our brains. Embarrassment, some suspect, may be the seventh (Blum, 1998). Would it surprise you to know that smiles, the most recognizable signal of happiness in the world, are so important that we can see them far more closely than any other expression—even at 300 feet, the length of a football field (McNeill, 2000)?

White Americans consider a reluctance to make eye contact as rude, disrespectful, and hostile, as well as conveying disinterest. However, looking someone in the eye is often perceived as a sign of disrespect or rudeness by people from many Asian, Latin American, and Caribbean cultures. Many African-Americans, especially from the South, observe this custom, too (Baruth and Manning, 1998).

FOCUS ON DIVERSITY

- Can exhibit the level of intensity of the emotions.
- Reveals the amount of control we have over our expressions.
- Shows whether we understand or not.

Through our facial expressions, we reveal a great deal about our feelings and responses to other people as we nonverbally convey shock, sadness, anger, happiness, worry, and so on. This is confirmed by researchers, Paul Eckman and Wallace Friesen (1984):

> The rapid facial signals are the primary system for expression of emotion. It is the face you search to know whether someone is angry, disgusted, afraid, sad, etc. Words cannot always describe the feelings people have; often words are not adequate to express what you see in the look on someone's face at an emotional moment.

The eyes are the most expressive part of the face and have considerable effect on communication. We may use eye contact in a positive way to:

- Invite interaction with another by looking directly at them.
- Show friendship and positive regard by extended mutual eye contact.
- Demonstrate believability or honesty.
- Demonstrate interest by extended eye contact.
- Signal turn-taking in normal conversation.

Many times we avoid eye contact when we want to hide feelings, when we are tense, when we are interacting with someone we dislike, or when attempting to end social contact. However, it is important to note here that nonverbal expressions have different meanings in various cultures. Therefore, it is wise to be careful about assigning your culture's meanings for eye behavior to all people. (See Focus on Diversity on the previous page.)

Vocal Qualities. *Paralinguistics* is the study of vocal cues such as pitch, rate, tone, fluency, etc. Almost everyone distinguishes meanings by noting differences in vocal qualities. For example, the statement "What a vacation I had" can have at least two different meanings, depending on the tone of voice of the

I suppose it was
  something
you said
That caused me to
  tighten
and pull away.
And when you asked,
"What is it?"
I, of course, said,
"Nothing."
Whenever, I say,
"Nothing,"
You may be very
  certain
there is something
The something is a
  cold,
hard lump of
Nothing.

        Louis Wyse

Vocal Qualities

White Americans often use a loud voice and a warm, hearty greeting when they meet each other. However, Asian Americans are more likely to greet each other calmly and quietly. Native-Americans speak more softly and at a slower rate than white Americans do (Halonen and Santrock, 1999).

FOCUS ON DIVERSITY

Are your posture, facial expressions, and eye contact effective or distracting as you converse with others?

speaker. The ambiguous phrase might mean that it was a most enjoyable weekend. With different qualities, however, the listener would assume that it was quite unpleasant.

Len Sperry (1975) suggests that the voice characteristics described in Table 5.2 are likely to have the meanings described in the right-hand column.

With practice, we can all learn to notice the pitch and timbre of a person's voice, the rhythm of speech, and the rapidity of expression. These vocal qualities help us to tune into the mood of the speaker, as well as to understand how different cultures use vocal qualities in their communication.

Gestures and Other Body Movements. Because movements and gestures of other parts of the body are also closely tied to culture, it is extremely misleading to isolate a single body movement (such as crossing the arms) and give it a precise meaning. Regardless of your intentions, however, your gestures and body movements may be given specific meanings by others.

For example, the way a person stands may indicate self-confidence, status, friendliness, or enthusiasm. Various types of gestures may be used to indicate feelings of restlessness, nervousness, or perhaps the need to emphasize a meaning. Frequent hand movements, for example, often communicate a positive, enthusiastic attitude. However, movements such as the constant pencil tapper or the doodler may indicate nervousness and boredom. Even weak or overly strong handshakes will be given some significance by many people. They can communicate enthusiasm, or they can communicate uneasiness.

You will be given an opportunity in one of the exercises in this chapter to evaluate your gestures and body movements. Pay very close attention to what you learn about yourself.

Touching. Some people use the language of touch more easily and readily than others. Actually, *one of the most meaningful methods* of nonverbal communication can be that of touching. There are times in our lives when it is difficult to express our feelings through words. We may use a hug, a pat on the shoulder, or a clasp of the hand to communicate meaning without words. Touching is risky,

Table 5.2   Voice Characteristics and Probable Meanings

Paralanguage	Probable Feeling/Meaning
Monotone voice	Boredom
Slow speed, low pitch	Depression
High voice, emphatic pitch	Enthusiasm
Ascending tone	Astonishment
Abrupt speech	Defensiveness
Terse speed, loud tone	Anger
High pitch, drawn-out speech	Disbelief

Sperry, 1975

F
O
C
U
S

O
N

D
I
V
E
R
S
I
T
Y

Gestures and Other Body Movements

Gestures are not universal (Cohen & Borsoi, 1996). For example, white Americans view a firm handshake as a sign of strength and power. However, Native-Americans view a firm handshake as aggressive and disrespectful (Everett, Proctor, and Cartmela, 1997). Furthermore, the sign shown in Figure 5.2, which in our culture usually means "OK," has other meanings in other cultures. In Japan, it can mean "coins." In France, it means "worthless" (as in "zero worth"). In Greece, it is a hostile allusion to body parts.

Another example of how a simple gesture can be subject to misunderstanding and offense is noted in Figure 5.3. The sign of the University of Texas football team, the Longhorns, is to extend the index finger and the pinkie. In Italy and other parts of Europe, this gesture means a man's wife has been unfaithful to him—a serious insult (Tavris and Wade, 1999)! Without a doubt, tourists should be very careful about their gestures.

Figure 5.2 In many cultures, but not all cultures, the circle made with the thumb and forefinger means everything is "OK."

Figure 5.3 Be careful where you make this gesture.

however, because this form of nonverbal communication may violate the personal space of others. Because there is indeed a complex language of touch, researchers Heslin and Alper (1983) have suggested a number of factors to consider:

- What part of the body does the touching
- What part of the body is touched
- How long the touch lasts
- How much pressure is used
- Whether there is movement after contact is made
- Whether anyone else is present
- The situation in which the touch occurs
- The relationship between the persons involved

Kenneth Blanchard (1993) confirms the ideas of Heslin and Alper: *"There is a very simple rule about touching—when you touch, don't take."*

Think for just a moment and respond to these questions. How do you feel when a friend touches you on the shoulder? How do you feel when your boss touches you on the shoulder? How do you feel when a family member touches you on the shoulder? How do you feel when a stranger touches you on the shoulder?

We would guess that you will have many different answers to these questions, which just illustrates that we feel differently and interpret differently the language of touch.

> Too often we underestimate the power of a touch, a smile, a kind word, a listening ear, an honest compliment, or the smallest act of caring, all of which have the potential to turn a life around.
>
> Leo Buscaglia

Touching

There are cultural and gender differences in the language of touch. For example, there is a strong taboo against strangers touching in Japan, which is reflected in the sufficient distance maintained by most Japanese in public. Latinos tend to touch one another while communicating, whereas white Americans tend not to touch one another while communicating (Halonen and Santrock, 1999).

How does this "tidy" desk compare with your desk at home or work?

Personal Space and Distance. Our own personal space is an invisible bubble around us that allows us to feel safe. As we said earlier, if this bubble is violated, we are uncomfortable and may become defensive. Usually, only intimates can violate the space without making us uncomfortable. Sometimes, violation of this space by another can demonstrate that person's dominance of the situation.

Many times you can tell how people feel toward one another by observing the distance between them. Anthropologist Edward T. Hall (1992) defined four distances that we use in our everyday lives. These are:

- *Intimate distance, which begins with skin contact and ranges out to about 18 inches.* This is reserved for close friends and loved ones, or other people you feel affectionate to.
- *Personal distance, from 18 inches to 4 feet.* This is where you may carry on a friendly conversation or sometimes even a heated argument.
- *Social distance, from 4 to 12 feet.* This is reserved for social interactions that are businesslike or impersonal.

Personal Space and Distance

French people maintain very small personal spaces in trains, buses, cafes, and even in their homes, and they increase their involvement with other people by using more direct body postures and eye contact. In consequence, when Americans visit Paris, they are sometimes shocked when strangers approach so closely and stare right into their eyes. Furthermore, when Americans attempt to protect their invaded personal space, Parisians interpret their retreat as a lack of good manners (Dresser, 1996).

- *Public distance, ranging out from 12 feet.* This is reserved for speaking to a large audience.

Hall is careful to note that these distances pertain to Americans only and may be quite different for people raised in other cultures.

Hall feels that we choose a particular distance, according to the way we feel toward the other person at a given time, and that by reading the selected distance, we can get insight into the other person's feelings.

How would you describe the person who works at this desk?

Physical Environment and Territory. What characteristics in a physical environment make you feel comfortable or uncomfortable? What do you think your room, house, or car communicates to others? Do you prefer a neat and "tidy" room, house, or car, or do you prefer the more "lived-in" look? What meaning do you give to a spotless house or to a friend's constantly clean car? How about your desk at home or work? Is it free of papers, or does it look like *someone works there every minute of the day and night?* Interestingly enough, physical environments not only reveal characteristics of the owner of the territory but also actually affect how a person communicates. Psychologist Mehrabian (1980) found that each person reacts emotionally to the environment with "approach" (positive) or "avoidance" (negative) behaviors.

 Word Power

Words can comfort
  or they can hurt.
Words can compliment
  and they can also insult.
Words can motivate
  just as they can hinder.
They can inspire
  and they can reject.
Words can express feelings
  or they can verbalize reactions.
Words, carelessly or angrily spoken
  can be as destructive a force as the fiercest storm.
And once the damage has been done
  it takes much more than words to mend or rebuild that
  which in the moment of thoughtlessness received the
  crashing blow. . . .
  of piercing, crushing Words.

Delyn Dendy Harrison

When you come closer than an arm's length to me, I may feel uncomfortable. When I'm comfortable with you and want to be closer to you, I will invite you to invade my personal space.

M. Hankins

Delyn Dendy Harrison, Some Things Are Better Said in Black and White (Fort Worth, Texas: Branch Smith, Inc., 1978) p. 13. Used with permission.

How to . . .
. . . Improve Nonverbal Communication

Have a video tape made of you conversing with another person. There is a great deal you can learn from seeing yourself as others see you. Are your gestures, facial expressions, and eye contact effective or distracting as you converse with others? Do you have any annoying mannerisms?

Role-play with a friend. Select a topic you feel comfortable with and practice various forms of nonverbal communication. Experiment with various forms of posture, tone and voice inflection, gestures, and so forth. Then, ask the other person to comment on the effectiveness of your nonverbal behavior.

Decide what changes you want to make. After reviewing your total body language, you can begin to make a conscious effort to eliminate the gestures and mannerisms that distract from the effectiveness of your communication endeavors. Do not forget to practice the gestures and mannerisms that will make your verbal communication come alive.

Beginning with the verbal initiation of hello, language nourishes or starves whatever grows between two people.

S. Miller

Clothing and Personal Appearance. What we wear and how we groom ourselves are also important means of nonverbal communication. We send messages about our economic level, level of success, social position, educational background, moral character, and sometimes just our personal preferences. We also may send messages that suggest, "notice me." For example, there is a tremendous amount of pressure in schools to wear the "in" brand of jeans, shoes, dress and so on.

Although it is natural to make assumptions about clothing and personal appearances, it is equally important to note that this area of nonverbal communication is filled with ambiguity. A stranger, wearing worn, ill-fitting clothes might normally be a stylish person or even a millionaire. Maybe today he or she is on vacation, going to do some "dirty" work, or just wants to be comfortable. This points to the fact that as we get to know others better, the importance of clothing and personal appearance decreases.

What kind of messages do you think you send about the clothing you wear and the manner in which you groom yourself?

Silence. Silence is *communication.* Silence may convey relaxation, contentment, fatigue, anxiety, frustration, uncertainty, shyness, avoidance, or thoughtful analyses. Sometimes, what we do not say has more impact than what we do say. For example, silence can be used to convey negative messages such as "I'm angry with you," "I'm not OK," or positive messages of, "It is nice just to be alone," "I understand."

Nonverbal communication, everything in the communication context except the actual words being uttered, is sometimes very clear and unambiguous. At times it can be difficult to decipher. Julius Fast (1988), author of *Body Language,* reminds us that as we become aware of nonverbal messages in our everyday lives, we need to think of them not as facts, but as clues that need to be checked out. Furthermore, we can be more effective in communicating messages if we support words with appropriate forms of nonverbal communication.

VERBAL COMMUNICATION

Verbal communication—words and language—is generally considered the primary means of communication. We gather, share, give, and receive information through words, and establish, continue, or terminate relationships through words. Words can make us feel good or miserable; they can make us lose our tempers or keep our cool; they can persuade us to take action or convince us not to move; they can be clear and concise or ambiguous and confusing; more importantly, *they cannot be unsaid once they are said.*

Is communicating by E-mail and the Internet a positive or negative technological advancement?

Actually, the way we use words may communicate much more than the actual words used. As we have already discussed, our tone of voice and the emphasis placed on our words may reveal far more than our choice of words. As we can see, it is the meaning and understanding behinds words that is the essence of communication. And, *meanings are in people—not words.* Let us look at some barriers or ways that meanings can go astray.

Semantics. *Semantics* is the study of meaning and changes of meanings in words. It is virtually impossible to communicate effectively if the people conversing do not understand the same terminology, or if they hold different meanings for the same word. For example, consider the common expressions:

> I'll be back in a little while.
> I'll be back in a few minutes.
> I'll be back about 5:00 P.M.

What or when is *a little while* or *a few minutes*? Do we mean a little late, or do we mean 5, 10, or 30 minutes? Does "about 5:00 P.M." mean exactly 5:00 P.M., or does the expression mean between 5:00 and 6:00 P.M.? What do you mean when you use these expressions?

Also, certain occupations have their "jargon" too: realtors talk about going after "listings"; computer programmers talk about "Pascal" language; individuals working in finance and credit talk about a "class 2-A credit rating." Do you know what all of these statements mean? Any profession, avocation, or field of specialization will develop such word usages. This often splits persons inside the group from those outside the group in that they will use the same language terminology to mean different things.

Certain age groups have a language all their own. Teenagers talk about a "cool" party or an "awesome" date. What are they really saying?

Even countries have different meanings for the same word. For example, in the United States, "Let us *table* that motion," means "Let us put it aside." In England, the same phrase means, "Let us bring it up for discussion."

Maybe the meaning only rests in the "eyes of the beholder." The beholder leaves the listener to guess what he or she means, while the beholder operates on assumptions that he or she is, in fact, communicating. The listener, in turn, proceeds on the basis of what he or she guesses. Mutual misunderstanding is an obvious result.

That words are powerful may seem obvious, but the fact is that most of us, most of the time, use them lightly. We choose our clothes more carefully than we choose our words, though what we say *about* and *to* others can define them indelibly.

Joseph Telushkin

Assumptions. To *assume* is to accept as fact without any evidence of proof (Milliken, 1997). Often, we make the mistake of assuming that others will understand more than we actually say to them. "If it is clear to me, it must be clear to you also." This assumption is one of the most difficult barriers to successful human communication. In personal relationships, for example, we may expect our intimates to be able to read our minds because they know us so well. "She ought to know how I feel," you may say to yourself, even though you have said nothing about your feelings.

A story is told of a family ruckus that occurred when the father sent his son to the lumber yard for a *longer* board. The young man thought he knew what his father wanted—but the longer board he brought back was still three feet too short. His father became angry and accused the boy of being stupid and not listening. The father had simply assumed that since he knew what he meant by *longer,* his son would also know. Could it be possible that Dad had not bothered to make himself clear or to check his meaning with his son?

Self-Concept. The most important single factor affecting our communication with others is our self-concept. Chapter 2 showed that a strong self-concept is necessary for healthy and satisfying interactions. On the other hand, if we have a weak self-concept we may feel inadequate and lack the confidence to converse with others. As a result, we feel our ideas are not worth communicating and we become guarded in our communication attempts.

In circumstances where we feel insecure or unsafe, it is extremely easy for us to feel that our self-image is being threatened. As a result, our defenses are immediately aroused. It is so easy to take an innocent remark and reply with, "What did you mean by that?" We may distort questions into accusations. Our replies become immediate justifications.

For example, a husband may ask his wife, "Did you happen to get my blue shirt from the cleaners?" His intention may be informational. If the wife feels insecure, she may respond as if the issue was her inability to meet his needs. She may say, "No, I didn't. I can't think of everything, you know, when I've got the kids with me and time is getting short, and I can't even find a decent roast that we can afford. I suppose you think my getting your shirt is more important than preparing a good meal." The wife assumes an accusation is made. This accusation may be seen as an "intended putdown." Does the husband really mean to cut the wife down, or does the wife have her feelings on her shoulders?

Emotion-Packed Phrases. As we can see, words stated may not be as important as the way in which we *catch* these words. Because it is highly possible for us to operate on different mood levels, an experience we have had during the day may cause us to react with words that we really do not mean. Sometimes, our mood level, combined with certain emotion-packed phrases, really sets us off. Some of these emotion-packed phrases are as follows (Hoffman and Graiver, 1983):

After all I've done for you . . .
I wish you would say what you mean . . .
After you have been here as long as I have . . .
When I was your age . . .
Do you know what you are doing? . . .

How to . . .
. . . Improve Verbal Communication

Speak with enthusiasm

Enunciate

Use inflection

Avoid antagonistic words

Use short simple sentences

Adjust the volume of your voice to the situation

Adjust your speaking rate to the situation

Keep the door open for feedback

You aren't upset, are you? . . .
Talk to me later . . .
Do you understand me? . . .
I wouldn't do that . . .
You wouldn't understand . . .
Are you sure that's right? . . .
Any very opinionated statement . . .

Have you ever reacted to one of these emotion-packed phrases? It takes a great deal of practice to learn to listen, to not be distracted by emotion-packed phrases. The key here is to *respond* to the statement and not *react* to the statement. After all, when you *respond,* the rational, thinking, logical part of you is communicated, but when you *react,* the emotional, feeling, irrational part of you is communicated. Sociolinguist professor Deborah Tannen (1992) in her powerful communication book, *That's Not What I Meant,* offers some helpful advice:

> The most important thing is to be aware that misunderstandings can arise and with them tempers, when no one is crazy and no one is mean and no one is intentionally dishonest. We can learn to stop and remind ourselves that others may not mean what we hear them say.

As we can see, there are numerous ways that words can go astray. Have you ever had a discussion with a friend, spouse, or someone about a particular topic and later realized that your communication attempts fell short of your desires?

GENDER AND COMMUNICATION

For a moment, review Table 5.3 Different Languages, adapted from the research and writings of Deborah Tannen (1992) and John Gray (1992). Do you agree or disagree with these differences? Tannen (1992) offers some helpful hints on learning how to deal with these differences. For example, men may need to understand why many women like to talk about the details of their personal lives,

> The real art of conversation is not only to say the right thing in the right place but to leave unsaid the wrong thing at the tempting moment.
>
> Dorothy Nevell

COMMUNICATION

We also need to remember that men and women often use different styles in communication. Consider the following exchange:

> A couple are in their car on a long-distance journey. The woman asks her husband, "Would you like to stop for a cup of coffee?" "No," he says, and they do not stop. He was later upset to learn that his wife was annoyed because she had wanted to stop for coffee. He asked, "Why didn't you just say what you wanted? Why did you play this game with me?" She explained that she was upset not because she did not get her way, but because her preference had not even been considered. From her point of view, she had shown concern for her husband's wishes, but he had shown no concern for hers.

Different Languages

In the national best-seller, *You Just Don't Understand: Women and Men in Conversation,* Deborah Tannen (1991) contends that males and females are typically socialized in different "cultures." That is, males are likely to speak and hear a language of "status and independence" while females are likely to speak and hear a language of "connection and intimacy." Stated in another way, men use language to challenge others, to achieve status in a group, to convey information, and to keep from getting pushed around. On the other hand, women use language to achieve and share intimacy with others, to promote closeness and equality in a group, and to prevent others from pushing them away. It is not so much that men want to dominate women as that they simply have different ways of communicating.

John Gray's (1992) practical guide for improving communication in relationships, *Men are From Mars, Women are From Venus,* confirms these differences:

> Not only do men and women communicate differently but they think, feel, perceive, react, respond, love, need, and appreciate differently. They almost seem to be from different planets, speaking different languages and needing different nourishment. When you remember that your partner is as different from you as someone from another planet, you can relax and cooperate with the differences instead of resisting or trying to change them.

and women need to understand that most men do not have this need. In addition, both women and men need to extend their communication strategies by adding aspects of the other style to their own. Some men may need to learn to feel more comfortable talking about their personal lives, while some women could benefit by talking more about impersonal topics and talking in a more assertive manner.

Sometimes, our communication attempts go astray because we fail to listen. We will now discuss the skills of listening and the qualities essential for improving person-to-person communication.

Table 5.3 Different Languages	
Men . . .	**Women . . .**
Talk about sports, money, facts, business, and events	Talk about feelings, relationships, people, and psychological states
Use commands to get what they want	Use requests
Use and respond to actions more than words in communicating	Rely on and respond to words in communicating
Communicate to persuade, argue, control, or impress	Communicate to share, inform, or support
Language is factual and action oriented	Language is emotional and evaluative
Emphasize talking rather than listening in conversations	Emphasize listening and sharing in conversations
Use pauses in conversation for emphasis	Use "intensifiers" like *really, terrifically, tremendously,* (for emphasis)
Speak mostly in a monotone	Use a variety of tones of voice to convey emotion and meaning
Express feelings indirectly	Verbalize feelings directly
Interrupt more in conversation	Are interrupted more
Speak authoritatively regardless of subject	Speak in tentative terms
By understanding one another's "language," men and women can communicate more easily and effectively.	

(Tannen, 1992 & Gray, 1992)

LISTENING (WHAT DID YOU SAY?)

How many times have you had a conversation with people and not heard a word they said? Do you sometimes ignore others when they are talking? How many times have you had a conversation with someone, and you felt they were not paying attention to you? Actually, listening is a form of *paying attention,* which is an active process involving much more than hearing and seeing.

According to Stephen Covey (1990), when another person speaks, we are usually "listening" at one of four levels. We may be *ignoring* another person, not really listening at all. We may practice *pretending.* "Yeah. Uh-huh. Right." We may practice *selective listening,* hearing only certain parts of the conversation. Or we may even practice *attentive listening,* paying attention and focusing energy on the words that are being said. Very few of us ever practice the fifth level, however, the highest form of listening, *empathetic listening*—listening with the intent to *understand.* We will discuss listening with the intent to understand in greater detail later in the chapter.

Communication experts describe listening as our primary communication activity. According to one study, college students spent an average of 14 percent of their communication time writing, 16 percent speaking, 17 percent reading and 53 percent listening. Of the 53 percent listening time, mass communication (radio and television) accounted for 21 percent of the students' communication time. Likewise, of the 53 percent listening time, face-to-face messages ac-

Many people perceive a style difference as the other person's personal failing. If we could see style differences for what they are, then a lot of blaming and negative feelings could be eliminated. Nothing hurts more than being told your intentions are bad when you know they are good, or being told that you are doing something wrong when you know you're just doing it your way.

Deborah Tannen

Listen

When I ask you to listen to me and you start giving advice, you have not done what I asked.

When I ask you to listen to me and you begin to tell me why I shouldn't feel that way, you are trampling on my feelings.

When I ask you to listen to me and you feel you have to do something to solve my problems, you have failed me, strange as that may seem.

Listen! All I asked was that you listen, not talk or do—just hear me. And I can do for myself; I'm not helpless.

When you do something for me that I can and need to do for myself, you contribute to my fear and weakness.

But when you accept as simple fact that I do feel what I feel, no matter how irrational, then I quit trying to convince you and can get about the business of understanding what's behind this irrational feeling.

And when that's clear the answers are obvious and I don't need advice.

Irrational feelings make sense when we understand what's behind them. So, please listen and just hear me, and if you want to talk, wait a minute for your turn, and I'll listen to you.

> The worst sin towards our fellow creatures is not to hate them, but to be indifferent to them; that's the essence of inhumanity.
>
> George Bernard Shaw

counted for 32 percent of the students' communication time (Barker, et al. 1981). In the world of work, listening is just as important. Studies show that most employees of major corporations in North America spend about 60 percent of each workday listening to others (Wolvin and Coakley, 1991).

Unfortunately, few people are good listeners. Researchers claim that *75 percent of oral communication* is ignored, misunderstood, or quickly forgotten (Bolton, 1986). It just seems that the speaker's words go *in one ear and out the other.* Yet, the quality of your friendships, the closeness of your family relationships, and your effectiveness at work depend to a great extent on your ability to listen.

Is there really a difference in hearing and listening? *Hearing* says John Drakeford (1967) is a word used to describe the physiological sensory process by which auditory sensations are received by the ears and translated to the brain. *Listening,* on the other hand, is an intellectual and emotional process that integrates physical, emotional, and intellectual inputs in a search for meaning and understanding.

> We have been given two ears but a single mouth, in order that we may hear more and talk less.
>
> Zeno of Citium

In short, you can hear what another person is saying without really listening to him. How can this be possible?

BARRIERS TO LISTENING

Do you have any habits, attitudes, or desires that may screen out what is really said? Are you ever too busy to really listen? What kinds of things prevent you from really listening? Let us examine some possible barriers to listening.

Internal Psychological Filter. Each of us has an internal psychological filter through which we process all the information we receive. This filter consists of prejudices, past experiences, hopes, and anxieties. Everything that we hear, see, or read is interpreted through this filter. For example, the style of a speaker's clothing, facial expressions, posture, accent, color of skin, mannerisms, or age can cause you to make prejudgments and tune him or her out—all because of what is in your filter.

The further we go through life, the more clogged that filter can get. Regardless of what we intend to say, what is ultimately heard depends on what is in the filter of the listener. If your filter contains memories of many painful past experiences, then you may perceive hurt where none is intended. If your filter contains a reservoir of unexpressed anger from the past, then you may hear anger in what others say, regardless of their intent. In *Principle Centered Leadership,* Stephen Covey (1992) summarizes the *root* of most communication problems as being *perception problems:*

> None of us see the world as it is but as we are, as our frames of reference or "maps" define the territory. And our experience-induced perceptions greatly influence our feelings, beliefs, and behavior.

Hidden Agenda. Sometimes we enter a conversation or situation with a special interest in mind, a grudge which we are wanting to bring into the open, or even a "chip on our shoulder." Consequently, we may hear the message in accordance with our own needs. Either consciously or unconsciously, we may sabotage a meeting or direct a conversation in such a way as to further our own needs and motives.

Preoccupation. The communication failures arising from the gap between what the sender meant does not usually arise from word usage or lack of verbal ability. Many times we are so preoccupied that we just do not listen to what others are saying. We may allow our mind to wander while we are waiting for the speaker to make his or her next thought. Perhaps, we need to remember, that the *rate of speech* is about 100–150 words per minute and the *rate of thought* is about 400–500 words per minute. Also, we may be so preoccupied with what we have to say that we listen to others only to find an opening to get the floor to say what we want to say. Sometimes, our fast-paced lifestyle contributes to our not taking the time to really listen to others.

A story is told of a very busy business executive who every morning rushed through the office and asked his secretary, "How are you?" She always said, "Fine, thank you." After all, is not that what we expect others to say to such a question? Rushing through the office, the executive replied, "That is great." One day, the secretary decided to really "test" the executive's ear. When the usual question came the next morning, the secretary said, "Terrible, terrible, thank you." The executive, still rushing into his office replied, "That is great." The executive's ear had really been tested.

Noise. Noise includes anything that interferes with communication and distorts the impact of the message. *External noise* includes such elements in the physical environment as temperature, a show on television, music on a stereo, loud traffic, or any other external event or distracting influences. *Internal noise* includes such things as a headache, lack of sleep, daydreaming, preoccupation

Our frame of reference is the filter through which we integrate, evaluate, and interpret new persons, events, and ideas.

John Powell

How to . . .

. . . Improve Listening Skills

Be receptive and attentive
Allow the speaker to speak freely
Listen to the speaker and ignore distractions
Avoid preoccupation with your own thoughts
Use verbal following or minimal encourages
Avoid all judgments, initially
Try to listen for more than just the spoken words
Use feedback and reflect on what the speaker said

with other problems, or even a preconceived idea that the message is going to be unimportant or uninteresting (Hamilton, 2000).

It seems as though the capacity to listen effectively is a "natural gift" for some people. This "natural gift" has been referred to as *sensitivity*. However, the ability to listen can be cultivated by anyone who wants to develop this capacity. It requires a conscious alertness that can become a *habit* with practice.

> One of the best ways to persuade others is with your ears—by listening to them.
>
> Dean Rusk

STYLES OF RESPONDING

How do you respond when others want to discuss their problems or innermost feelings with you? Do you ask a lot of questions? Are you judgmental, or supportive? Do you ever criticize?

Noted psychologist, Carl Rogers (1995) indicates that a major barrier to building close relationships is the very natural tendency we have to *"judge and evaluate the statements made by others."*

There are several ways of responding to others. Thomas Gordon (1990) devised a comprehensive list that he calls the "dirty dozen" communication spoilers. Review the 21 Communication Spoilers for an expanded list. Which style gives you the most difficulty in responding to others?

Sometimes we overuse one style, rely on the style too early in the conversation, or fail to know when and how to use a style that will be of most benefit to

Ernest Roy's Short Course in Human Relations

The six most important words:	*"I admit I made a mistake"*
The five most important words:	*"You did a good job"*
The four most important words:	*"What is your opinion"*
The three most important words:	*"If you please"*
The two most important words:	*"Thank you"*
The one most important word:	*"We"*
The least most important word:	*"I"*

the sender and thereby create a better relationship. Let us discuss six of the more common styles of responding: 1) Evaluative or Judging, 2) Advising, 3) Interpretative, 4) Supportive, 5) Questioning, and 6) Understanding (Adler, Rosenfeld, and Towne, 1998).

Evaluative or Judging. *This type of response shows that the receiver is making a judgment about the motive, personality, or reasoning of the sender.* The evaluation indicates the sender's statement is either "right" or "wrong." The response may be positive, "You're right on target," or unfavorable, "You shouldn't feel that way." In both cases, the receiver appears to be qualified to suggest to the sender what he or she might or ought to do.

Since evaluative or judgmental responses often lead to defensiveness, it is best to begin your responses with "I feel . . .", rather than "You are. . . ." Evaluative or judgmental responses are best accepted when you have been specifically asked to make a value judgment and when you want to disclose your own values

> Don't judge any person until you have walked two moons in their moccasins.
>
> American Indian Proverb

CONSIDER THIS . . .
21 Communication Spoilers

"I'm sick and tired of being hassled." How would you respond? Some typical responses are listed below:

FEELING	RESPONSES
Threatening	Feeling like that will get you in trouble.
Lecturing	You should be glad it's not worse.
Moralizing	You ought to be trying harder.
Blaming	Maybe you're just getting what you deserve.
Advising	If I were you, I'd do something about it.
Sympathizing	It's too bad you're always getting picked on.
Questioning	Who's hassling you?
Kidding	You don't look like you're being hassled.
Sarcastic	Why would anyone want to hassle a nice person like you.
Praising	They're just hassling you because they're jealous.
Name-calling	Don't be such a baby.
Ordering or Commanding	Don't give me any of that garbage.
Criticizing	Feeling like that isn't going to get you anywhere.
Analyzing	You just have a persecution complex.
Diverting	Oh, why don't you just have a cold drink and forget it?
Rejecting	I can't do anything about it.
Counterattacking	Well, how many people have you hassled?
Placating	Well, everybody gets hassled at some time in their life.
Overidentifying	I know what you mean, I get hassled all the time too.
Shifting Focus	What does your teacher think about that?
Ignoring	(No response is a response.)

(Gordon, 1990)

and attitudes. In the early stages of relationships, it is generally best to avoid evaluative or judgmental responses.

Criticizing. Even though criticizing is often a part of the evaluative or judging response, it is also a commonly used and even misunderstood response pattern. Therefore, we have decided to discuss it separately. Sometimes, you may want to give someone some constructive feedback, but you are afraid they will perceive it as criticism. After all, have not you perceived feedback as really just criticism? Criticism often has a negative connotation and may not be pleasant, but it can be helpful when it leads to productive changes. If you want to give constructive criticism or feedback, rather than destructive criticism or feedback, it is wise to remember these points (Groder, 1997):

- **Emphasize Behavior Rather than Personalities.** Concentrate on what a person does or says rather than who you think the person is. The use of choice adjectives oftentimes leads to labeling the person rather than the behavior. This causes defensiveness. There is a big difference between saying, "John is lazy" and in "John works slowly."
- **Refrain from Using "You" Messages.** The use of "You" messages creates a feeling of blame and accusation. It is more appropriate to say, "I felt hurt today when . . ." rather than use, "You were cruel today when . . ."
- **Focus on Actual Observations Rather than Judgments.** Reporting what actually occurred is giving objective feedback. However, reporting on what you think about what actually occurred is giving subjective, value-laden feedback. It is one thing to say, "I really liked the house better the way it was decorated," and quite another to say, "The house looks terrible now."
- **Do Not Criticize When You Are Angry or Upset.** Other people will hear only your anger and not your message. "Cool down" until you can express yourself with facts. It is acceptable to say, "I need to think this through and get back with you later."
- **Concentrate on Sharing Ideas Rather Than on Giving Advice.** It is less threatening to say, "Here are some ideas for you to think about . . ." rather than, "Well, you would be wise to do. . . ." Sharing ideas gives options to others; advising implies, "My solution is the best way."

You have the right to get angry, but you do not have the right or the license to attack another person or their character traits.

Haim Ginott

When others respond to you with criticism, it is easier to handle if you can learn to deal with it *intellectually* and not *emotionally*. *Remember to respond and not to react.* Rather than hearing criticism as a personal attack, it might be helpful to remember some suggestions from Lynn Weiss and Lora Cain (1991):

- **Listen.** Do not panic and get defensive when someone criticizes you. Calm listening helps you think clearly.
- **Analyze.** Is the criticism factually correct or is the critic mostly venting anger? If the critic is really just ventilating, you can sympathize with his or her feelings without accepting the content of what they say.
- **Decide What to Do.** If the criticism is accurate, what can you do to remedy the situation and prevent recurrences? If you decide to change your behavior as a result of the criticism, let your critic know.
- **Practice.** Make an honest effort to consistently practice the new routine or behavior until it feels natural or becomes a habit.

Advising. *This is responding to others by offering a solution.* Sometimes this type of response is helpful and sometimes it is not. For example, we may have the tendency to tell others how we would behave in their place. They may not want to hear what we would do; they may just want us to listen to their thoughts. Giving advice also means that you may get blamed if the advice is followed and *does not work. In giving advice, it is helpful* to remember to be sure: 1) your advice is correct, 2) the other person really wants your advice, 3) the other person is willing to accept the responsibility for choosing to follow your advice.

Foster Cline (1998) a nationally known psychiatrist, frequently suggests two magic sentences that will help you from appearing dogmatic when offering advice:

> I wonder if it would be helpful to . . . rather than, If I were you, I would . . .

> Do you think it would be beneficial to . . . rather than, You really should . . .

When giving advice, it is important to remember some advice from Paula Englander-Golden and Virginia Satir (1990):

> We maximize our chances of being heard when we express our caring friendship and support while expressing our hopes, wishes, and a specific suggestion that our friend can consider.

Interpretative. *In this response, the receiver tries to tell the sender what his or her problem really is and how the sender really feels about the situation.* The receiver implies what the sender might or ought to think. Consider these statements:

Criticism, like rain, should be gentle enough to nourish one's growth without destroying one's roots.

The Best of Bits & Pieces

At its worst, advice represents an "interferiority" complex.

Robert Bolton

Criticism is like fertilizer—the right amount does wonders, but too much is fatal.

I don't think you really mean to say that.
Maybe you are really feeling . . .
It sounds to me that what is actually bothering you is . . .

Giving an interpretative response can often offer a person another way of looking at his or her situation. It can produce great insight. Interpretative responses are best received when they are made as suggestions rather than as absolutes and when they are offered with integrity and empathy.

Supportive. *This response shows the receiver's intent is to reassure, comfort or minimize the intense feelings of the sender.* There is an implication that the sender not feel as he or she does. Statements such as, "Now, it is okay. It is all going to be better," or "Mary, you don't have anything to worry about. I know you can pass your test," are examples of supportive responses. Consider this exchange:

Sender: I could die here, and no one would even notice.
Receiver: Now, now, it's okay. It's all going to be better. I will help you.

This reply may not have acknowledged the content or emotion of the original statement and may get you involved in a situation you wished you had avoided. It might be more helpful to simply say, "Let's talk about why you feel this way."

Supportive statements are best received when they are sincere and help others to feel accepted and motivated to try and solve their problems. Sometimes, supportive statements can be made in a joking manner and result in the sender feeling "put down" and "worse off" than before.

Questioning. *This response indicates that the receiver wants to probe the sender for additional information and to discuss the issue further.* The receiver often implies that the sender might benefit from discussing the issue in more detail. Typical statements might be:

- What is your understanding of why your husband lost his job?
- How do you feel about that?

Questioning is a way to get additional information so that you can understand the situation in more detail. Actually, if you do not understand the situation, it is extremely important that you try to ask questions for clarification before you respond to the situation. We have a tendency to ask questions that often fail to give us adequate information. Let us distinguish between two types of questions: *closed questions and open questions. Closed questions* often result in yes, no, or a very short response. *Open questions,* on the other hand, provide space for the speaker to explore his or her thoughts.

Let us look at a typical example between a boss and an employee who have been having conflict with a valued customer. The employee enters the boss's office, and the boss replies:

Closed question: Do you want to see me about the Smith account?
Open question: What's on your mind, Linda?

> The greatest compliment that was ever paid me was when one asked me what I thought, and attended to my answer.
>
> Henry David Thoreau

In short, closed questions are like multiple choice or true/false test questions, whereas open questions are like essay questions.

It is also important that you ask questions about the issue raised, rather than asking questions about irrelevant issues. You do not want to lead the sender to possibly more problems and forget the original issue.

Another important aspect of questioning is to remember to avoid *interrogating and manipulating* the other person. Too many questions do precisely that.

If you have reviewed the Communication Spoilers and given some thought to the styles of responding discussed above, you may be thinking to yourself, "I am confused, it seems that all these responses can spoil my attempts at listening and communicating. Is there another type of response that will be more effective for me?"

Understanding. *This response indicates that the receiver is seeking to fully understand what the sender is actually saying.* Stephen Covey (1990), author of *The 7 Habits of Highly Effective People,* believes that understanding is the key to achieving effective interpersonal communication. Covey makes a profound point about understanding:

Sometimes our fast-paced lifestyle contributes to our not taking the time to really listen to others.

> If I were to summarize in one sentence the single most important principle I have learned in the field of interpersonal relations, it would be this: Seek first to understand, then to be understood.

Because this is the most effective way of responding to others and requires the specific skills of active listening, sometimes referred to as empathetic listening, we will now discuss the meaning and development of these skills.

ACTIVE LISTENING—EMPATHETIC LISTENING

In *active listening* you see the expressed idea, attitude, or problem from the other person's point of view, to sense how it feels to the sender, and to achieve the sender's frame of reference in regard to the thing he or she is talking about. This really means that you are listening with the whole body and that you are paying careful attention to the person who is talking. How is this achieved?

As a vehicle of communication, listening must focus on the other person, not just on what the other person is saying. This has been referred to as *listening with the third ear.* The third ear hears what is said between the lines and without words, what is expressed soundlessly, and what the speaker feels and thinks. It is listening in such a way that creates an atmosphere of communication; others will be able to hear us because they feel we have heard them, that we are in touch with them and not just what they are saying. How can you learn to listen with the third ear?

Robert Bolton (1986) and Thomas Gordan (1990) have written extensively about the requirements of active listening. We will now discuss four of these: 1) develop a posture of involvement, 2) make use of door openers, 3) keep the other person talking with minimal encourages, and 4) respond reflectively.

The reality of the other person is not in what he reveals to you, but in what he cannot reveal to you. Therefore, if you would understand him, listen not to what he says but rather to what he does not say.

Kahlil Gibran

Develop a Posture of Involvement. This means you practice the habit of inclining your body toward the speaker rather than leaning back in the chair or slouching around on the floor or on the sofa. It also means you position yourself at a comfortable distance from the speaker so that you can have close eye contact. Usually, about three feet is a comfortable distance in our society. Effective eye contact expresses interest and a desire to listen. You will also need to turn the TV or stereo off and remove any environmental distractions. Remember to actively listen means to move with the speaker.

Make Use of Door Openers. This is really just an invitation for the other person to say more. These responses do not communicate any of the listener's own ideas or judgments or feelings; they merely invite the other person to share his own ideas, judgments, or feelings. Some examples might be:

> Tell me more about that . . .
> Let's talk about it . . .
> Go ahead, I'm listening . . .
> Sounds like you have a lot of feelings about that . . .
> This seems like something that is important to you . . .
> I'd like to hear some more about that . . .
> Can you tell me what's going on . . .
> Sounds like this is difficult for you to talk about . . .

Most people feel encouraged to talk with the use of door openers. More importantly, people feel worthy, respected, significant, and accepted when we invite them to share their feelings and ideas.

Keep the Other Person Talking with Minimal Encourages. Minimal encourages are brief indicators to the other person that you are still listening. Some examples you can use are:

- "Mm-hmmm."
- "Really."
- "You did, huh."
- "How about that."
- "Go on."

- "I see."
- "Oh."
- "And."
- "Interesting."
- "I hear you."

Another way to use minimal encourages is to repeat the last word or two of the speaker's comment. When the speaker says, "I just don't know what to do; I guess I'm confused," the listener may respond, "Confused?" Generally, the speaker will then express more about his or her confusion.

Respond Reflectively. Thomas Gordon (1990) explains responding reflectively in this way:

> In active listening, the receiver tries to understand what the sender is feeling or what his message means. Then, he puts his understanding into his own words and feeds it back for the sender's verification. The receiver does not send a message of his own—such as an evaluation, opinion, advice, logic, analysis, or question. He feeds back only what he feels the sender's message meant—nothing more, nothing less.

I can never tell you what you said, but only what I heard. I will have to rephrase what you have said, and check it out with you to make sure that what left your mind and heart arrived in my mind and heart intact and without distortion.

John Powell

As you can probably see, when you use active listening, you really respond reflectively in two ways. *First, you paraphrase or state the essence of the other's content in your own words, focusing on facts and ideas rather than the emotions the sender is expressing.*

Paraphrasing responses usually begin with phrases such as:

> What I hear you saying is . . .
> Correct me if I'm wrong . . .
> Do I understand you correctly that . . .

Let us look at this exchange:

Sender: "My psychology professor is really piling the assignments on, and I'll never get caught up. Does she think psychology is the only course I am taking?"

Receiver: "Do I understand you correctly that she is giving you too much work and doesn't realize you have three other college courses?"

Sender: "Oh she knows I have other courses, but it is just the end of the semester, and she is shoving it all in at the last minute."

Receiver: "It doesn't seem fair, is that it?"

Sender: "It really isn't, but I'll just have to buckle down and get the work done. I need this course on my degree plan."

> I wish that you would take the time to try and understand why I think the way I think, and why I feel the way I feel.
>
> David Augsburger

Sometimes people confuse paraphrasing with parroting. However, parroting means to repeat exactly the speaker's words.

Secondly, when possible, mirror back to the speaker the emotions which he or she is communicating. The most difficult part of learning to respond reflectively is to listen for the feeling of the other person. The format is simple when you learn to listen for feeling words. For example:

"You
sound_____ about _____."

- angry
- frustrated
- worried
- upset
- excited

- this
- that
- the other
    thing
- . . . . . .
- . . . . . .

Let us look at some examples:

Sender: "I could die here, and no one would even notice."
Receiver: "You sound really frustrated."
Sender: "Oh, I just get to thinking that no one really cares about me."
Receiver: "So, maybe you aren't frustrated, but just a little angry."
Sender: "Yea, I suppose I am a little angry. I just wish I knew how my family really cares about me."

You will note that in both of these examples, the receiver actively demonstrates that he or she genuinely wants to understand the sender and to hear more of the problem. The receiver does not make evaluative or judgmental responses regarding either the sender or the content. Instead, the receiver just paraphrases

Next to physical survival, the greatest need of a human being is psychological survival—to be understood, to be affirmed, to be validated, to be appreciated.

Stephen Covey

or mirrors back what the sender has said. By maintaining an objective stance, the active listener encourages a sharing of ideas and paves the way for a freer exchange of other points of view.

Active listening is an excellent tool to use in "heated discussions." The next time you get into an argument with your wife, husband, friend, or a small group of friends, just stop the discussion for a moment and, for an experiment, generate Carl Rogers' (1995) communication rule: *Each person can speak up only after he or she has restated the ideas and feelings of the previous speaker accurately and to that speaker's satisfaction.* This is the heart of active listening.

Do you see what this would mean? It would simply mean that before presenting your point of view, it would be necessary for you to achieve the other speaker's frame of reference—to understand his or her feelings so well that you could summarize them for him or her. Sounds simple, does not it? If you try it, however, you will discover that it is one of the most difficult things you have ever tried to do. Nevertheless, once you have been able to see the other person's point of view, your own comments will have to be drastically revised. You will also find that with this type of listening and response, there is an attitude of open, two-way communication.

WHICH STYLE OF RESPONDING DO YOU USE?

Of the styles of responding we have discussed in this chapter, how often do people use each response? Carl Rogers (1995), a noted psychologist, conducted a series of studies on how individuals communicate with each other in face-to-face situations. *(You will note that Rogers studied five styles, whereas we included six in our discussion. That is because Rogers considered the advising response style to be closely related to the evaluative or judging style.)* He found that the categories of evaluative or judging, interpretative, supportive, questioning, and understanding statements encompass 80 percent of all the messages sent between individuals. The other 20 percent of the statements are incidental and of no real importance. From his observations of individuals in all sorts of different settings—business, home, people at parties and conventions, and so on—he found that the responses were used by individuals in the following frequency: 1) *evaluative or judging* was most used, 2) *interpretative* was next, 3) *supportive* was the third most common response, 4) *questioning* the fourth, and 5) *understanding* was the least used style in human communication. Finally, he found that if a person uses one category of response as much as 40 percent of the time, then other people see him as *always* responding that way.

Although we would classify this last statement as a process of oversimplification, the question to ask yourself is, What style of responding to others do I use most often? Obviously, depending on various situations, you use all of the styles as you constantly interact with others. It would be beneficial to pay careful attention and become aware of how you respond to others. Then, you be the judge: are you pleased with the way you respond to others?

PERSON-TO-PERSON COMMUNICATION

How do we integrate all that we have discussed in this chapter to improve our communication with those with whom we live and work? In the late 1950's, psychologist Carl Rogers (1957) hypothesized that there were three qualities essential to constructive communication: *genuineness, acceptance and respect of others, and empathy*. Since then, numerous research studies have been conducted which support Rogers' theory. Summarizing empirical data, Bolton (1986) reports the outcomes in several different types of relationships where high levels of these key attitudes are demonstrated (review the "Consider This" box below). Let us look at each of these qualities in more detail.

Genuineness. This means being honest and open about one's feelings, needs, and ideas. Genuineness means being what one really is without front or facade. The authentic person experiences feelings and is able to express those feelings when appropriate. A genuine person can spontaneously be himself with another so they know him as he truly is: "What you see is what you get." Being a genuine person involves the search and constant improvement directed toward self-awareness, self-acceptance, and self-expression. Robert Bolton (1986), a human performance and communication skills consultant in New York, summarizes genuineness in this way:

> Genuineness is essential to all vital relationships. To the degree that I lack authenticity, I am unable to relate significantly to any other person. I must dare to be me to be able to relate to you.

Acceptance and respect of others. This refers to the decision to offer an atmosphere largely uncontaminated by evaluations of the other's thoughts, feelings, or behaviors. In a way, it can even be described as attitude of neutrality toward another person or persons. It also means that we respect the other person's capac-

> To be persuasive, we must be believable; to be believable, we must be credible; to be credible, we must be truthful.
>
> Edward Murrow

CONSIDER THIS . . .
Improved Communication in Relationships

Researchers and theorists in the behavioral sciences have identified the following improvements in relationships when the qualities of *genuineness, acceptance, and respect of others, and empathy* are practiced (Bolton, 1986):

- Teachers who model these qualities foster greater student achievement than teachers who are deficient in them.
- Physicians and nurses can facilitate a patient's return to health through the expression of these characteristics as well as by their surgical and pharmaceutical techniques.
- Managers with these attitudes elicit greater motivation and less resistance from their employees
- Salespersons with these qualities tend to have customers who are more satisfied, and this is reflected positively in sales volume.
- Therapists who demonstrate these qualities have constructive relationships with clients.
- Fulfilling marriages and constructive parent-child relationships result from the expression of these characteristics.

- The understanding style requires the specific skills of active listening, sometimes called empathetic listening—seeing the expressed idea, attitude, or problem from the other person's point of view. The requirements of active listening or empathetic listening are to develop a posture of involvement, make use of door openers, keep the other person talking with "minimal encourages," and respond reflectively.
- Researchers and theorists in the behavioral sciences have identified three qualities or attitudes, when communicated to others, that foster improved relationships with people. These qualities are genuineness, acceptance, and respect of others, and empathy.

We need to become aware of the conditions that are interfering with the communication process and make an attempt to modify our behavior in such a way that real meaning and understanding are communicated. This can lead to establishing and maintaining more satisfying relationships with others, which is the basic goal of communication.

??? **Questions** ???

1. Define communication. Why do we need to communicate?
2. What are the three commonly accepted parts to the communication process? What is involved in a communication transaction?
3. Define feedback and why is it so important. Describe the difference in feedback in one-way and two-way communication.
4. What are the three ways nonverbal communication relates to verbal communication? When the nonverbal message contradicts the verbal message, which message is usually more accurate?
5. What are at least five different types of nonverbal communication? Which form of nonverbal communication communicates more emotional meaning more accurately? Define paralinguistics and give at least two examples in sentence form. Define the four distances Edward T. Hall discovered in his research.
6. Give at least five examples of cultural differences in nonverbal communication.
7. Explain at least four barriers or ways that meanings can go astray in verbal communication.
8. What are some examples of emotion-packed phrases? What is the key to remember in dealing with these phrases?
9. Compare and contrast at least six differences in the communication styles of men and women.
10. What is the difference in listening and hearing? List and discuss the five different levels of listening we may employ when another person speaks.
11. What are the barriers to listening? What is the difference in external and internal noise?
12. Give at least four techniques for improving nonverbal communication, verbal communication, and listening skills.
13. Define and give examples of the six common styles of responding to others. What is the most used responding style in human communication? What is the least used responding style in human communication?
14. What are the suggestions to remember when giving and receiving criticism?
15. Give examples of the four requirements for active listening or empathetic listening?
16. What are the three qualities or attitudes, when communicated to others, that improve relationships with people? Give at least five specific examples of how relationships improve when these qualities are practiced.

Key Terms

Active listening
Advising response
Assume (Assumptions)
Attentive listening
Closed questions
Communication
Communication barriers
Communication channels
Communication process
Decoding
Door openers
Double bind
Emotion-packed phrases
Empathetic listening
Empathy
Encoding
External noise
Feedback
Genuineness

Hearing
Hidden agenda
Ignoring while listening
Internal noise
Internal psychological filter
Interpretative response
Intimate distance
Judging response
Kinesics
Listening
Listening with the third ear
Minimal encourages
Nonverbal communication
One-way communication
Open questions
Paralinguistics
Paraphrase
Parroting
Parts of a communication transaction

Passive listening
Personal distance
Pretending while listening
Public distance
Questioning response
Reacting to others
Responding reflectively
Responding to others
Selective listening
Semantics
Social distance
Supportive response
Symbols in communication
Sympathy
Two-way communication
Understanding response
Verbal communication
"You" messages

??? Discussion ???

1. Discuss the causes for communication breakdown. In your opinion, what presents the biggest problem?
2. Many times nonverbal messages are more honest and revealing than what is verbally expressed. why? Give examples of nonverbal communication to support your answer.
3. Discuss some examples of semantics in your field of work—occupational jargon.
4. Is it possible to give constructive criticism without causing the other person to become defensive? How?
5. Of the techniques discussed for improving listening skills, which technique will be most difficult for you to use?
6. Of the six common styles of responding to others, which style of responding is the most difficult for you to use? Why?
7. Discuss any examples of cultural differences you have experienced in verbal or nonverbal communication.
8. Is it possible that the differences in communication styles of men and women, as discussed in this chapter, have more to do with basic personality styles, rather than gender?
9. What are the key qualities in the communication skills of others that impress you the most?

Name_____ Date _____

Personal Communication Self-Analysis

Purpose: To review how you perceive your personal communication.

Instructions: (1) Each line below contains four statements that represent a continuum going from "usually" to "rarely if ever." Place a checkmark on the line under the statement that best describes how you perceive your personal communication.

#4	#3	#2	#1
I usually listen carefully	I often listen carefully	I sometimes listen carefully	I rarely if ever listen carefully
I usually make sure I understand before I reply	I often make sure I understand before I reply	I sometimes make sure I understand before I reply	I rarely if ever make sure I understand before I reply
I usually describe how I'm feeling about what is being said	I often describe how I'm feeling about what is being said	I sometimes describe how I'm feeling about what is being said	I rarely if ever describe how I'm feeling about what is being said
I am usually very poised	I am often very poised	I am sometimes very poised	I am rarely if ever poised
I usually gesture freely when I talk	I often gesture freely when I talk	I sometimes gesture freely when I talk	I rarely if ever gesture freely when I talk
My face is usually an open book	My face is often an open book	My face is sometimes an open book	My face is rarely if ever an open book
I usually become defensive when my ideas are criticized	I often become defensive when my ideas are criticized	I sometimes become defensive when my ideas are criticized	I rarely if ever become defensive when my ideas are criticized
I am usually sensitive to the feelings of others	I am often sensitive to the feelings of others	I am sometimes sensitive to the feelings of others	I am rarely if ever sensitive to the feelings of others
I usually trust others	I often trust others	I sometimes trust others	I rarely if ever trust others

(2) Next, make a list below of the statements you checked as a #1 or a #2. Then, respond to the discussion questions.

Discussion

1. What areas on the self-analysis would you like to change? How?

2. Which area do you feel will be the most difficult for you to change or improve?

Gender and Communication

Purpose: To understand the gender differences in language and communication style so that communication can be more effective.

Instructions:
 I. Respond to the questions below, being as specific as possible.
 II. Divide into groups of five. Select a group spokesperson for the group. Each group member will share his or her responses to the questions below, with the spokesperson taking notes to present to the entire class.

Questions:
1. List five differences of how men and women communicate, listen, and understand various types of communication issues. (Women and men complete both responses.)

Women
Example: *They just want to talk about feelings and relationships*

Men
They just want to talk about sports and business events.

2. What would you suggest the "other sex" do to facilitate their communication with you? (Women complete women responses and men complete men responses.)

Women
Example: *I would like him to express his feelings more.*

Men
I would like her to become more interested in sports and cars.

3. What would you like the "other sex" to learn and understand about the way you communicate effectively? (Women complete women responses and men complete men responses.)

Women
Example: *I just want him to listen—
not try to solve my problems.*

Men
*I don't like to feel pressured into talking about
my feelings and problems.*

Discussion

1. What have you learned most about the communication style of men?

2. What have you learned most about the communication style of women?

3. What do you think you need to do to communicate more effectively with the "other sex?"

One Way/Two Way

Purpose: To demonstrate how descriptive communication can be interpreted differently by other people and also to show the superior functioning of two-way communication.

Instructions:

I. A sender is selected to give information to the class.

II. The sender is given a drawing, made up of designs of geometric figures. The participants are given a blank sheet of paper; they are instructed to label one side Diagram I and the other side Diagram II.

III. The sender turns his or her back to the rest of the group and tries to describe verbally how to reproduce the geometric model. This is Diagram I.

IV. Participants may neither ask questions nor give audible responses; participants may not talk or compare sketches with the other group members.

V. After 10 or 15 minutes, repeat the exercise with the sender facing his group, and giving directions for Diagram II. Participants should use the other side of their paper designated as Diagram II.

VI. Participants may ask any questions they desire. Senders may respond verbally, but no gestures, please.

VII. When Diagram II has been completed, the sender shows the participants the two diagrams, and they are to tell him or her how many figures they drew correctly.

NOTE: Instead of selecting one sender for the entire group, triads may be formed, with one student being the sender, one student being the receiver, and one student being the observer. The sender and receiver will place their desks or chairs back to back, with the observer nearby. The observer should record the length of time required for completing Diagram I and Diagram II. The observer will also give feedback to the sender and receiver when the diagrams are complete. For example, what contributed to the diagrams being accurate or inaccurate? Were there any unusual terms used by the sender? How long did it take to complete each diagram?

Discussion

1. What assumptions might you make about one and two-way communications? Which takes longer? Which is more accurate?

2. Explain which is more frustrating for the sender? For the receiver?

3. What parallels does this exercise have in your everyday life? Does this exercise tell you anything about the way you listen?

What Do You Communicate Nonverbally?

Purpose: To evaluate your nonverbal communication behavior and gain insight into how you can improve your silent language.

Instructions:

I. Before you begin, make a copy of the form on the next two pages.

II. Then, using the form, briefly in one or two sentences, evaluate what you perceive your nonverbal behavior reveals or says about you.

III. Then, give someone who knows you well a copy of the form and ask them to complete an evaluation of what they perceive your nonverbal behavior reveals about you.

IV. After your friend has completed his or her evaluation, compare the two evaluations of your nonverbal behavior. Then, list the areas where the greatest discrepancy occurs.

_____ **Evaluation of** _____ **Nonverbal Behavior**

a. **Facial expressions**

b. **Eyes**

c. **Vocal Qualities** (Rate of speech, pitch of voice, loud or soft tone of voice, and so on)

d. **Gestures and other body movements**

e. **Touching** (How much, how little)

f. **Personal space and distance** (How close does this person get to people when talking)

g. **The physical environment this person creates** (His or her home, room, office, inside of car, and so on)

h. **Clothing and personal appearance**

i. **Silence** (Does this person pause and think before he or she speaks; how much or how little does this person talk)

j. **Any other nonverbal behavior you wish to comment on**

k. **What nonverbal messages does this person display when he or she is feeling the following emotions:**

   1. Anger or irritation

   2. Boredom or indifference

   3. Happiness

   4. Sadness

   5. Worry, anxiety, or stress

Discussion

1. Why is it we oftentimes do not see ourselves as others see us?

2. What surprised you most about what you learned about yourself?

3. Do you feel there is a need to improve your nonverbal communication? In what areas?

4. Explain how your friend's perceptions in Item k compare with your own perceptions of how you verbally or nonverbally show these emotions? (It might be helpful to review your responses to the activity in Chapter 4: How I Express My Feelings.)

Empathetic Listening

Purpose: To develop an understanding of the importance of active listening.

Instructions:

I. Find a partner, then move to a place where you can talk comfortably. Designate one person as **A** and the other **B**.

II. Find a subject on the list below on which you and your partner apparently disagree, or you may select a current events topic, a philosophical or moral issue, or perhaps simply a matter of personal taste.

A. Abortion
B. Capital Punishment
C. Single Parenting
D. Teenage Pregnancy
E. Homosexuality
F. Euthanasia

G. Drug/Alcohol Abuse—
   How to prevent their use
H. Interracial Marriage
 I. Cohabitation
J. Ecology
K. Prison Reform

III. **A** begins by making a statement of the subject. **B**'s job is then to paraphrase the idea back, beginning by saying something like, "What I hear you saying is . . ." It is very important that in this step **B** feeds back only what he/she heard **A** say without adding any judgment or interpretation. **B**'s job is simply to understand here, and doing so in no way should signify agreement or disagreement with **A**'s remarks.

IV. **A** then responds by telling **B** whether or not his or her response was accurate. If there was some misunderstanding, **A** should make the correction and **B** should feed back his/her new understanding of the statement. Continue this process until you are both sure that **B** understands **A**'s statement.

V. Now it is **B**'s turn to respond to **A**'s statement, and for **A** to help the process of understanding by correcting **B**.

VI. Continue this process until each partner is satisfied that he/she has explained himself/herself fully and has been understood by the other person.

Discussion

1. As a listener how accurate was your first understanding of the speaker's statements?

2. How did your understanding of the speaker's position change after you used active listening?

3. Did you find that the gap between your position and that of your partner narrowed as a result of your both using active listening?

4. How did you feel at the end of your conversation? How does this feeling compare to your usual emotional state after discussing controversial issues with others?

5. How might your life change if you used active listening at home, at work, or with friends?

Name_____ Date _____

Are You an Active Listener?

Purpose: To assess your active listening skills and establish goals for improvement.

Instructions:

I. Before responding to the statements below, make a copy and have a person with whom you talk regularly answer these questions about you.

II. Select the response that best describes the frequency of your actual behavior. Place the letters A, U, F, O, or S on the line before each of the 15 statements.

Almost Always	Usually	Frequently	Occasionally	Seldom
A	U	F	O	S

_____ 1. I like to listen to people talk. I encourage them to talk by showing interest, by smiling and nodding, and so on.

_____ 2. I pay closer attention to speakers who are more interesting or similar to me.

_____ 3. I evaluate the speaker's words and nonverbal communication ability as they talk.

_____ 4. I avoid distractions; if it is too noisy, I suggest moving to a quiet spot, turning off the TV, and so on.

_____ 5. When people interrupt me to talk, I put what I was doing out of sight and mind and give them my complete attention.

_____ 6. When people are talking I allow them time to finish. I do not interrupt, anticipate what they are going to say, or jump to conclusions.

_____ 7. I tune people out who do not agree with my views.

_____ 8. While the other person is talking or the professor is lecturing, my mind wanders to personal topics.

_____ 9. While the other person is talking, I pay close attention to the nonverbal communications to help me fully understand what the sender is trying to get across.

_____ 10. I tune out and pretend I understand when the topic is difficult.

_____ 11. When the other person is talking, I think about what I am going to say in reply.

_____ 12. When I feel there is something missing or contradictory, I ask direct questions to get the person to explain the idea more fully.

_____ 13. When I do not understand something, I let the sender know.

_____ 14. When listening to other people, I try to put myself in their position and see things from their perspective.

_____ 15. During conversations I repeat back to the sender what has been said in my own words (paraphrase) to be sure I understand correctly what has been said.

Key for Scoring: For items 1, 4, 5, 6, 9, 12, 13, 14, and 15, give yourself: 5 points for each A, 4 for each U, 3 for each F, 2 for each O, and 1 for each S statement. Place the numbers on the line to your response letter. For items, 2, 3, 7, 8, 10, and 11 the score reverses: 5 points for each S, 4 for each O, 3 for each F, 2 for each U and 1 for each A. Place these score numbers on the lines next to the response letters. Now add your total number of points. Your score should be between 15 and 75. Place your score here _____ and on the continuum below.

Poor Listener   15 _____ 25 _____ 35 _____ 45 _____ 55 _____ 65 _____ 75 _____   Good Listener
Generally, the higher your score, the better your listening skills.

Note: To improve active listening, items 1, 4, 5, 6, 9, 12, 13, 14, and 15 should be implemented, whereas items 2, 3, 7, 8, 10, and 11 should be avoided.

Discussion

1. Explain how you did on the items to be implemented for improved active listening?

2. Explain how you did on the items to be avoided for improved active listening?

3. How did your perception of your listening skills compare to those of the individual who rated you? Do you agree or disagree?

4. After comparing your perception of your listening skills with those of the individual who rated you, in what areas do you feel you could improve to become a more effective active listener?

Interpersonal Communication

Learning Journal

Select the statement below that best defines your feelings about the personal value or meaning gained from this chapter and respond below the dotted line.

- **I learned that I . . .**   • **I was surprised that I . . .**

- **I realized that I . . .**   • **I was pleased that I . . .**

- **I discovered that I . . .**   • **I was displeased that I . . .**

· ·

continue on reverse

CHAPTER 6

Developing Close Relationships

Friendship

There is nothing in this whole world, Lord, like having one true, enjoyable, understanding friend. No one is ever so lonely that he doesn't have a friend. To find one, all you have to do is go out and help somebody. Now and then say to a friend, "I love you." Those words weren't meant only for sweethearts. They are just as significant, beautiful, and life-enhancing when said to a dear friend. A true test of friendship: If you died, which of your friends would you trust to clean out your drawers? When I talk, my friend listens. When my friend talks, I listen. That's one of the reasons we're friends. Friends are like bracelet charms. If you truly love and enjoy your friends, they are part of the golden circle that makes life good. If you want more friends, smile more! I've never known anyone who smiled a lot who didn't have a lot of friends. Friends are too precious to lose—even when they disappoint us. Lord, help me to forgive this friend—it is only because I need and love her. (And because I'd want her to forgive me!) Friends are worth forgiving. The heart has many doors, of which friendship is but one. Don't be too quick to bolt them.

Think about this...

Walt is a junior in college. He has had a lot of dates, but has never had a "real serious" intimate relationship with a member of the opposite sex. Walt has many close friends and is very active in school activities. He likes to ski, play tennis, watch Woody Allen movies, and listen to jazz. Walt would like to become a lawyer and is majoring in political science.

Sarah is a sophomore in college and has dated the same person since her junior year in high school. Sarah was a cheerleader and her boyfriend was captain of his football team. They seem to be "made" for each other. They had the same friends, went to dances together, and studied together. Sarah does not seem to have any other friends since she was always with her boyfriend. Sarah also seems to be depressed. There seems to be something missing in her life, but she is not sure what it is. Presently, Sarah's boyfriend is attending college in another state. She misses him, so she writes and calls him often.

Sarah would like to become a judge, so she is in a pre-law program with emphasis in history. She likes to play tennis and racquetball, water ski, and listen to jazz. Her boyfriend likes to play and watch football. Sarah only watches football if her boyfriend is playing. He likes ice hockey and plays basketball with the boys. He enjoys going to rock concerts. Her boyfriend is majoring in computer science. When Sarah and her boyfriend get together they are very active and busy, but they do not seem to really talk.

It's the first day of a new term and classes are just beginning. Walt walks into his European History class and sits down and notices an attractive female sitting three chairs away. It so happens that the attractive female is Sarah. Walt says to himself, "I would like to get to know her. Just looking at her makes my heart beat faster." Now the dilemma, how does he get to know her and what are the chances of him developing a close intimate relationship with her, especially since she already has a boyfriend?

We will continue following the development of this relationship throughout this chapter.

THE DEVELOPMENT OF A RELATIONSHIP

Relationships evolve, they do not just happen. They take *time* and *effort*. The first step in a relationship is *becoming aware* of the other person—*first impressions*. At this time we evaluate the person, using our past experience, prejudices, and stereotyping to make a judgment about whether or not to take the next step. Walt is impressed with Sarah's physical appearance—he perceives her as being attractive. Remember beauty is in the eye of the beholder, not all people would perceive her as beautiful. Now that Walt has *become aware* of Sarah he needs to decide how he is going to take the next step, that is *making contact,* or getting acquainted with her. This is a difficult step for many individuals.

What would you recommend for Walt to do in order to get to know Sarah? The *mere exposure phenomenon* may work in this situation (Moreland & Zajonc, 1982; Nuttin, 1987). The more familiar we are with someone or something, the greater the chance of liking them. The more Sarah sees Walt, the greater the chance of her interacting with him and liking him. Walt could improve his odds of *making contact* with Sarah by sitting in the chair next to her *(proximity)* or by making sure that he stands near the door everyday so she has to pass by him to enter the classroom *(exposure)*. Do not be too aggressive in this process or you may threaten the other person. During the first week or so, Walt may not even want to say anything—do not make it too obvious.

The third step is *disclosure*. As we become friends, we are more willing to disclose more about our personal lives—our hopes, dreams, and fears. As we begin to disclose information about ourselves, we are demonstrating to our partner that we trust them and they in turn will disclose to us. Thus, the relationship will become stronger and more intimate. As Walt begins to open up slowly to Sarah, and Sarah to Walt, the relationship will begin to develop. Walt could begin by asking Sarah questions about European History, then talk about school related subjects, ask about her hobbies and interests and tell her about his interests. As they continue disclosing information about themselves to each other, their interest in one another will continue to grow.

Do all the terms and concepts mentioned so far sound familiar? They should; we discussed all of them thoroughly in chapter one. This was a review of how a relationship develops over a period of time and now we will discover how the relationship will continue to evolve into a more intimate relationship.

> Be slow in choosing a friend, slower in changing.
>
> Benjamin Franklin

BECOMING FRIENDS

Friends play a very significant role in our lives. Throughout our life they are important to us. They may provide help in a time of need, praise in times of achievement, sympathy in a time of sorrow, support in a time of failure, and advice in a time of confusion. Without friends we are lonely. Friends provide us with the *emotional support* and *social ties* that are vital to our well being. A good friend will always be there when they are needed. We can rely on their support no matter what happens to us. They also provide us with a feeling of belonging and a feeling that we are part of a group. We need an identity and our friends help us in the development of finding who we are. Good friends satisfy these needs.

> If I don't have friends, then I ain't got nothing.
>
> Billie Holiday

Who do you consider your good friends? A good friend could be a family member, a boyfriend or girlfriend, a spouse, a work colleague, a teacher, a clergyman, a fellow member of a religious, social, recreational, or political group or any other person. Remember, the more "good" friends you have the more secure you will be. Research continues to suggest that having close relationships helps people adjust to stressful situations and buffers people from the ill effects of negative life events like: accidents, divorce, loss of a loved one, or family problems etc. (Cohen & Williamson, 1998).

What Is Your Definition of a Good Friend? A recent student poll at Tarrant County Junior College asked, "What values do you think are important in a friendship?" Here are a few of their responses:

● Trust, someone you can share a problem with. Someone who will be there for you and will know you're going to be there for them

What is a good friend?

A Definition of a Friend

"Friendship is the comfort, the inexpressible comfort of feeling safe with a person having neither to weigh thoughts nor measure words, but pouring all right out just as they are, chaff and grain together, certain that a faithful friendly hand will take and sift them, keep what is worth keeping and with a breath of comfort, blow the rest away."

George Eliot

True friendship is a plant of slow growth.

George Washington

. . . .

- Honesty
- Loyalty
- Acceptance, humor, sense of fun, honesty, mainly acceptance of each other
- Trust, keeping your word, loyalness, love, understanding, being able to trust him around your woman
- Trust is most important, reliability, acceptance, honesty. You can accept their faults as well as their good traits
- Trust

The responses from the 1996 survey in Texas are very similar to a 1979 survey of 40,000 readers of *Psychology Today* magazine. The readers were to indicate what qualities they valued in a friend. The results suggest that keeping confidences and loyalty were the most important factors in a good friend. If you review the responses given by the Tarrant County College students you will note that trust and loyalty were also the most mentioned. The next most important ingredients of friendships are warmth/affection and supportiveness. The respondents also indicated the importance of frankness and a sense of humor in a relationship. In another survey (Block, 1980) the respondents emphasized, as Carl Rogers did in Chapter 2, the importance of unconditional acceptance from a friend—*accept me as I am—not how you want me to be.*

Can You Trust Your Friends? If not, are they friends? Keeping confidence and trust are almost synonymous. Trust and respect is something people need to earn and not be given away lightly. There are three questions that need to be answered that will help us make decisions about whether to trust someone or not:

The man who trusts no others doesn't trust himself.

Napolean Hill

1. **How predictable is the individual?** A predictable person is someone whose behavior is consistent—consistently good or bad. An unpredictable person keeps us guessing about what might happen next. Such volatile people may make life interesting, but they do not inspire much in the way of confidence.
2. **Can I depend upon her or him?** A dependable person can be relied upon when it counts. One way to tell is to see how a partner behaves in situations where it is possible to care or not to care.
3. **Do I have faith in that person?** Through "thick and thin" you know you can rely on this person. They make us feel "safe."

Does Sarah trust Walt? Is he loyal? Is Walt Predictable? Can Walt Depend on Sarah? Is Walt being honest with Sarah? Are they friends yet? Only time will tell. They are still *getting acquainted.* It takes time for a relationship to grow and develop. What other factors are important in *becoming friends?*

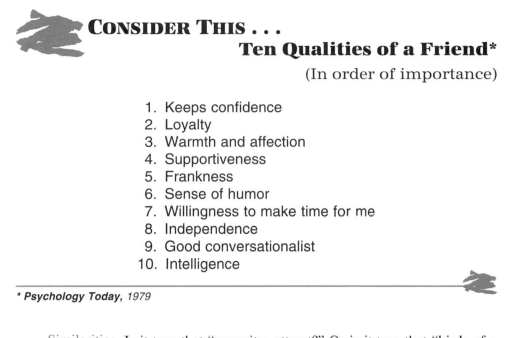

CONSIDER THIS . . .
Ten Qualities of a Friend*
(In order of importance)

1. Keeps confidence
2. Loyalty
3. Warmth and affection
4. Supportiveness
5. Frankness
6. Sense of humor
7. Willingness to make time for me
8. Independence
9. Good conversationalist
10. Intelligence

*** Psychology Today, 1979**

Similarities. Is it true that "opposites attract?" Or is it true that "birds of a feather flock together?" Look around, do most of your friends have different interests, beliefs, and political preferences than you, or are they similar? Research indicates that similarities attract. We tend to select friends who are similar to us in many different aspects, including ethnic background, social status, interests, income level, occupation, status, educational level, and political preferences (Hilton & von Hippel, 1996). Similarities are also important in the selection of a husband or wife. There is a correlation between length of marriage and the similarities between the two people. The more similarities there are between the two spouses, the longer the marriage tends to last.

Does Likeness-Lead-to-Liking? Why are we drawn to people who are similar to us? For one thing, people with similar interests and attitudes are likely to enjoy the same hobbies and activities. Even more important, however, we are more likely to communicate well with people whose ideas and opinions are similar to ours, and communication is a very important aspect of an enduring relationship. It is also reinforcing to be with similar people, for they confirm our view of the world, support our opinions and beliefs, and we in turn provide mutual reinforcement for each other.

The *likeness-leads-to liking* relationship holds true not only for college students but also for children and the elderly, for people of various occupations, and for those in other cultures. In a recent study, Susan Sprecher and Steven Duck (1994) put 83 student couples together on blind get-acquainted dates. They found that 16 percent of the couples who saw each other again were especially likely to see themselves as more similar than those couples that did not date again.

What would it be like if your friends always disagreed with you? You are a Republican and they are Democrats; you are pro-life and they are pro-choice; you are religious and they are not; you are conservative and they are liberal; you smoke and they do not; they like rock music and you like classical music; you like to participate in sports and they would rather smoke dope. Are you going to have fun together or is there going to be a lot of conflict? Research studies have found that there are two critical similarities that are important within a relationship; they are *similar beliefs* and *similar attitudes* (Taylor, et al. 2000). When considering a long term commitment between you and another person, ask yourself, what do we have in common? Are our beliefs and attitudes similar? If they are not, you may discover that over a period of time, conflict is more apt to develop between the two of you.

So, similarity breeds content. *Birds of a feather do flock together.* Surely you have noticed this upon discovering a special someone who shares your ideas, values, and desires—a soul mate who likes the same music, the same activities, even the same foods you do. So, how do I find someone who has something in common with me?

Where Do I Go to Find Friends? You need to go to those places where you will find other people who have similar interests and needs. *Proximity*, or physical nearness is a major factor in the development of friendships. When you were a young kid, most of your friends came from the local neighborhood where you lived, then from the local school you attended. This is what we mean when we say proximity—you get to know the people you are near or close to in regards to location. Proximity effects may seem self-evident, but it is sobering to realize that your friendship and love interests are shaped by seating charts in school, desks arrangements at the office or business, floor assignments in residence halls and closeness of your neighbors (Bersheid & Reis, 1998).

If you are lonely or do not have many friends and you want to find someone, where do you go to meet people? Where have you met most of your friends?

If you are not interested in religion, should you go to church to find your friends? If you do not drink and carouse, is the singles' bar the place to find your friends? If you like to dance, you go to dances. If you like sports, go to places where you will find other people who like sports. If you are interested in politics, go to political events that are of interest to you and you will find that you have something in common with the other people attending. These people will not come to you, you need to seek them.

> What about Walt and Sarah? Do they have anything in common? To begin, they are both taking European History, that is a good start. They are both in the pre-law program and enjoy studying history and political science. They both like to ski and participate in individual sports like tennis. After having coffee with Walt, Sarah thinks to herself, "Walt seems to be quite intelligent, he is very likable, I hope we get to meet again." They seem to have a lot in common—a lot more in common than Sarah and her present boyfriend. These similarities give Walt and Sarah a lot to talk about. Does Walt have a chance to start dating Sarah? Wait and see.

Do Opposites Attract? What about the saying *opposites attract?* They do for a period of time, until the novelty wears off, and then you will discover that these dissimilar beliefs, interests, and attitudes cause more conflict than attraction. You may find someone from a different culture exciting and interesting, primarily because of the novelty. You may interpret this interest as attraction, but over time you may discover that you do not have anything in common and the excitement and interest will wane.

Another interesting phenomenon is the fact that some people are initially and spontaneously repulsed by strangers who are very dissimilar to themselves (Rosenbaum, 1986). This is referred to as the *repulsion hypothesis*. Attitudes and values that contradict our own are physiologically arousing. Just as we implicitly

> There is no such thing as an uninteresting subject. There are only uninterested people.
>
> G.K. Chesterton

assume that people who are similar to us will probably like us and treat us well, so we implicitly assume that people who are very different from us will probably dislike us and treat us poorly. Thus, initial dissimilarities can cut a relationship short. Can you think of some examples where you have experienced this?

If you are someone who agrees with the pro-choice ideas toward abortion and you see someone you do not know at an anti-abortion protest, most of the time, you will have an immediate feeling of dislike for that person. If you are emotionally involved in environmental issues, such as save the old growth forest, and you encounter someone who is employed to cut the timber, you immediately have a dislike and maybe even a hatred for this person. If you see a car with a sticker on it that disagrees with your beliefs, what are your feelings toward the driver? Do you see how this hypothesis may influence our opinion of others?

But, what about people we know who have been married for years and seem to be totally different and seem to be happy together? Even though they seem to be opposites, they are very compatible. Why?

Do They Complement Each Other? People with complementary needs seem to be drawn to each other. You notice that one of your friends is very outgoing and her boyfriend is very shy. This does not seem consistent with the idea that similarities attract. Why do they get along so well? *We discover that differences in which one person's strengths compensate for the other person's weaknesses may lead to mutual attraction* (Drescher, 1979). Psychologists refer to this as *complementarity.* The personalities seem to complement each other. In most relationships each person supplies certain qualities that the other partner is lacking. Does your partner supply these missing characteristics?

Reciprocity. "Flattery will get you . . . everything or nowhere?" Which is true? What have you heard? The evidence on reciprocity indicates that we tend to like those who show that they like us and that we tend to see others as liking us more if we like them (Berscheid & Walster, 1978). Thus, there does seem to be an interactive process in which liking leads to liking and loving leads to loving.

If our self-esteem is low we are more susceptible to flattery, especially if the compliment is from someone of higher status. A person of high self-esteem may not be so easily swayed by positive treatment. Do you like to receive compliments? How do you feel about the person that is giving the compliments? Do they have a positive or negative influence on you? Do you now understand why some people seem to be greatly influenced by people who are nice to them, especially if that person is perceived as important to them?

> Walt has been complimenting Sarah a lot the last few weeks. He tells her how nice she looks, that he likes her dress, he likes her hair style, etc. Will this influence her feelings toward Walt, especially since she has been depressed lately? The story continues.

In his book *How to Win Friends and Influence People,* Dale Carnegie (1994) summarized six rules, that are still relevant today, that will help us win friends and influence people. Carnegie emphasized the use of praise and flattery.

We have discovered the importance of a friend and now we will see how the relationship evolves into a more intimate level as we begin the process of dating and mating.

> A real friend is one who walks in when the rest of the world walks out.
>
> Walter Winchell

> The average man is more interested in a woman who is interested in him than he is in a woman with beautiful legs.
>
> Marlene Dietrich

the other person. Unfortunately, both men and women admitted that they do not always tell the truth. What can you do to attract the opposite sex?

Do You Flirt? Is there an art to flirting? It seems as though some people are very good at it. What are they doing that you aren't doing to attract someone. Can I learn to flirt? Monica Moore at the University of Missouri (1998) has been interested in describing and understanding flirting and the role it plays in human courtship. Moore has observed and recorded many situations—in single bars and shopping malls—in order to study flirting, which she refers to it as *nonverbal courtship signaling.*

Both men and women flirt, women generally initiate a courtship. The woman signals her interest with glances that may be brief and darting, or direct and sustained. Often she smiles at the same time and gestures with her hands— often with an open or extended palm. Primping (adjusting clothing or playing with hair) is common. A flirting woman will also make herself more noticeable by sitting straighter, with stomach pulled in and breasts pushed out.

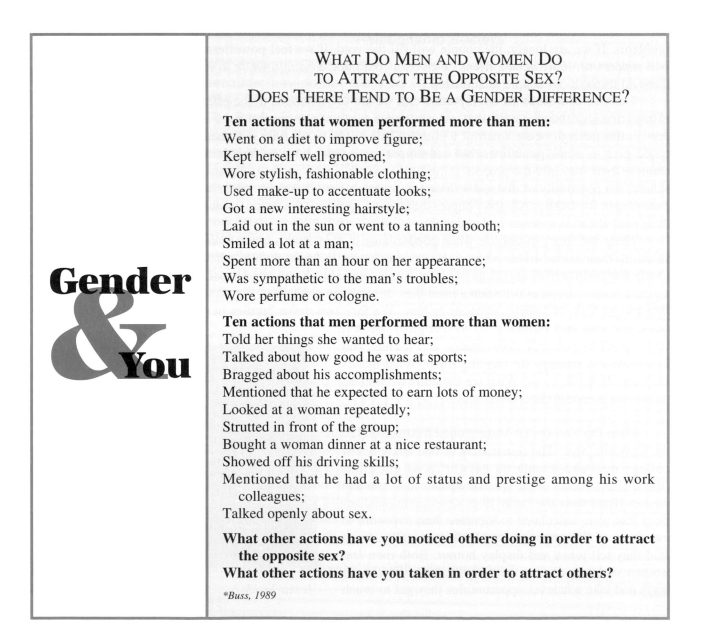

Gender & You

WHAT DO MEN AND WOMEN DO TO ATTRACT THE OPPOSITE SEX? DOES THERE TEND TO BE A GENDER DIFFERENCE?

Ten actions that women performed more than men:
Went on a diet to improve figure;
Kept herself well groomed;
Wore stylish, fashionable clothing;
Used make-up to accentuate looks;
Got a new interesting hairstyle;
Laid out in the sun or went to a tanning booth;
Smiled a lot at a man;
Spent more than an hour on her appearance;
Was sympathetic to the man's troubles;
Wore perfume or cologne.

Ten actions that men performed more than women:
Told her things she wanted to hear;
Talked about how good he was at sports;
Bragged about his accomplishments;
Mentioned that he expected to earn lots of money;
Looked at a woman repeatedly;
Strutted in front of the group;
Bought a woman dinner at a nice restaurant;
Showed off his driving skills;
Mentioned that he had a lot of status and prestige among his work colleagues;
Talked openly about sex.

What other actions have you noticed others doing in order to attract the opposite sex?
What other actions have you taken in order to attract others?

*Buss, 1989

Once contact is made and the couple is interacting, the woman increases the level of flirting. She orients her body toward his, whispers in his ear, and frequently nods and smiles in response to his conversation. More significantly, she touches the man or allows him to touch her. Women also use play behaviors to flirt. They tease, mock, hit, and tell jokes, not only to inject humor, but also to test the man's receptivity. Moore and other researchers indicate that flirting may be the single most important thing a woman can do to increase her attractiveness. Since the burden of making the first approach is usually the man's, men are understandably cautious and shy. Be careful in how you interpret her flirting. It does not always indicate that the woman is interested in sex. She flirts because she wants to get to know the man better; later she'll decide whether she wants to get serious. What do you do to get the attention of someone you are interested in?

What Makes Someone Desirable? What attracts men and women to their potential mate? In part, romantic attraction is a mystery. Scientists may not know everything about why people are drawn to the people that they are, but they know something. Every culture has standards for courtship and marriage. Without really thinking about it, most of us dutifully follow our cultural dictates. As we discussed the development of friendships and relationships in the previous pages of this chapter and in Chapter one, we will discover that the same characteristics that are important in finding friends are also very important in date and mate selection.

Most of us are looking for dates, mates, and friends who are similar to us (similarities). We seek out others who are about our own age, who are from the same socio-economic class, religion, and educational level. They can not be too tall or too short, too fat or too thin in comparison to us. Such preliminary screening cuts out a surprising number of potential partners. But most of us want more. Generally, we want someone who we perceive as good looking (physical attractiveness), personable, warm, a good sense of humor, someone we can trust, and who is intelligent. We also want someone whose views match our own. Other important variables that most of us also consider are reciprocity, personality fit, and most important, our own self-concept (self-confidence).

Mate Selection Throughout the World. Do people from different countries and different cultures look for the same traits when selecting a mate? The traits that people look for in a marriage vary around the world. In one recent large-scale study from thirty-seven countries and five islands, people varied in what they considered important in selecting a mate (Buss et al., 1990). Chastity was the most important factor in marital selection in China, India, Indonesia, Iran, Taiwan, and the Palestinian Arab culture. Adults from Japan and Ireland placed moderate importance on chastity. In contrast, adults in Sweden, Finland, Norway, the Netherlands, and Germany generally said that chastity was not important in selecting a marital partner. Researchers were surprised that men and women in the Netherlands, for example, do not care about chastity at all. Neither is virginity valued much in the Scandinavian countries such as Norway and Sweden. In China, however, virginity is indispensable in a mate—marrying a non-virgin is virtually out of the question.

Adults from the Zulu culture in South Africa, Estonia, and Columbia placed a high value on housekeeping skills in their marital preference. By contrast, adults in all Western European countries (except Spain, Canada and the United States) said that housekeeping was not an important trait in their partner.

What about religion? It plays an important role in marital preferences in many cultures. For example, Islam stresses the honor of the male and the purity of the fe-

> It is better to be beautiful than to be good. But . . . it is better to be good than be ugly.
>
> Oscar Wilde

How to . . .

. . . Meet Dates and Mates

Direct Approach

Select a few potential partners. Ask them out for coffee, lunch, to join a study group, to go on a hike, or so forth.

Be assertive, not aggressive. Do not be afraid to ask. Indicate interest to your potential dates and see how they respond.

Give compliments.

Ask questions that relate directly to them. People like to talk about themselves.

Indirect Approach

The best way to find a lover is to look for a friend. Most partners will say they were friends before they became lovers.

Have your friends introduce you to potential partners. Between 25% and 33% of men and women report that their most recent date was introduced to them by a friend.

Expose yourself. Go to parties, hang-out in the student center, arrange it so you sit in the middle of your classes—not in the corner—attend local activities, volunteer your services to local agencies, attend as many social activities as you can where there are other people and you are bound to meet people.

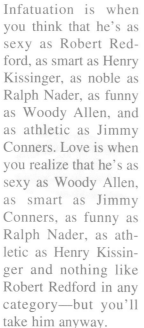

Infatuation is when you think that he's as sexy as Robert Redford, as smart as Henry Kissinger, as noble as Ralph Nader, as funny as Woody Allen, and as athletic as Jimmy Conners. Love is when you realize that he's as sexy as Woody Allen, as smart as Jimmy Conners, as funny as Ralph Nader, as athletic as Henry Kissinger and nothing like Robert Redford in any category—but you'll take him anyway.

Judith Viorst

Love is only a dirty trick played on us to achieve a continuation of the species.

W. Somerset
Maugham
1874–1965

siveness, typically generates greater emotion and power. As a result it can affect individuals more, having the potential to meet a broader sweep of human needs or to cause greater frustration and distress.

Is It Love or Infatuation? Have you ever looked at someone for the first time and said to yourself, "I think I'm in love?" Is there such a thing as _love at first sight?_ Research has found that we do not fall in love—we grow into love. Then, what is this feeling we are experiencing when we see this person?

Remember when Walt saw Sarah for the first time? It was the first day of class and Walt was fearful of having to take the European History class, because he had heard that this professor was one of the most difficult at the college. He was nervous and his heart was beating rapidly as he looked up and saw Sarah for the first time. Was it love? Walt thinks so. He attributed his physical arousal to Sarah and not to the fear of taking the class.

Positive or negative experiences that stimulate physical arousal, such as anxiety, nervous tension, excitement, heart palpitations, blushing, accelerated breathing, etc., may lead to the feeling of love if the labeling process is strong enough. A frightened person, an angry man, a jealous woman, or a euphoric individual is a potentially romantic person. If this emotionally aroused individual attaches these feelings to someone perceived as desirable, it will increase his or her attractiveness or feeling of love for that person. Once the person is aroused, all that remains is for the person to identify and label this complex feeling as love.

Many of you have experienced this but did not understand the process that created this feeling. Have you ever attended an event, such as a wedding, funeral, championship game, automobile race, or horror film where your body reacted by nervous tension (sweating, increased heart beat, butterflies in the stomach, etc.)? While this is all happening, your date reaches over to hold your hand and you look at your partner and feel that terrific rush within your body and attribute that feeling to your partner and not to the situation you are in at that time. *You know it must be love.* The event may be positive or negative and still create a positive feeling. While jogging, a young attractive person stops you to ask directions. Will you be more attracted to that person or to the person that asks you directions while you are waiting at a stop light on your way to work? While jogging your pulse rate has increased and your body is aroused due to the exercise, but you associate the physiological reaction to the other person and feel attracted to them. Is that feeling love or infatuation?

When you love someone, you love him as he is.

Charles Perry

What Is Love? This is a question people have been asking for years. Mass media, romantic novels, soap operas, songs, etc., have all been attempting to answer this question.

- Love is a many splendored thing
- All that the world needs is love
- Love makes the world go around
- I can't live without love
- How do I love thee, let me count the ways
- ◆ Love means never having to say you are sorry

Our lives seem to evolve around this subject. But, does anyone know what love is? Everyone seems to have their own definition of love. When your date says that he or she loves you, what does your date mean? Is it the same as when your mother or father says it to you? What is your definition of love? Before you continue on, take a few minutes and write down your definition of love. Share your definition of love with your friends and loved ones. Compare your definition with theirs.

We have found a definition of love that we would like to share with you. *When the satisfaction, security and development of another person is as important to you as your own satisfaction, security and development, love exists* (Harry Stack Sullivan, 1953). Using this definition of love, you will find that you can measure your love not only for your significant other, but your mother, father, siblings, friends, animals, and even inanimate objects. What do you think?

Love is moral even without legal marriage, but marriage is immoral without love.

Ellen Key

Myths About Love

True or False

T	F	1. True love lasts forever.
T	F	2. Love can conquer all.
T	F	3. Love is a purely positive experience.
T	F	4. When you fall in love, you'll know it.
T	F	5. When love strikes, you have no control over your behavior.

What are your answers to the above questions? These are some interesting myths about love that many of us have been agonizing over for years. Let us take a look at these myths and dispel some of the confusion regarding them.

> Love is the strange bewilderment which overtakes one person on account of another person.
>
> James Turber and
> E.B. White

1. *Does true love last forever?* It would be nice if love would last forever, but most of us have found that it does not. People who believe this myth may pursue love forever, looking for the ideal one that will bring complete happiness. This person will experience a lifetime of frustration. Would we have divorce if love lasted forever? It would be more realistic to view love as a wonderful experience that might be encountered on several occasions throughout life.

2. *Does love conquer all?* Many people believe that love and marriage will allow them to overcome (conquer) all their frustrations and problems in life. A supportive partner will help you solve many of your problems, but it does not guarantee success. Many people jump into relationships for this purpose, only to discover that the relationship creates additional problems.

3. *Is love a purely positive experience?* Mass media, television, romance novels, etc., are creating an unrealistic expectation that love is such a positive experience. In reality it can be a peak experience, but in contrast love can also bring intense negative emotions and great pain. As many of you know, a lover is capable of taking us to emotional peaks in either directions.

4. *Do you know when you are in love?* There is no physiological cue to tell us we are in love. So the emotional feeling and the cognitive interpretation is different for each of us. It is a state of confusion that many of us agonize over. It is normal to question our feelings toward another person. Remember, we grow to love someone gradually and usually do not fall in love.

5. *Do you behave irrationally when you fall in love?* Does love take control of your behavior? Some people stop eating, quit studying, are unable to concentrate on their job and avoid taking responsibility for their actions because they are in love. If you allow your heart to take control of your behavior, you

CONSIDER THIS . . .
What Do Men and Women Want in a Love Relationship?

What men like, in order of importance	What women like, in order of importance
Taking walks together	Taking walks together
Kissing	Flowers
Candle-lit dinners	Kissing
Cuddling	Candle-lit dinners
Hugging	Cuddling
Flowers	Declaring "I love you"
Holding hands	Love letters
Making love	Slow dancing
Love letters	Hugging
Sitting by the fireplace	Giving surprise gifts

*Livermore, 1993

may become vulnerable to irrational decisions about sexual involvement or long term commitments.

Love Is? Love is complex! Love is confusing! Most of you are aware of this. Love is difficult to measure and perplexing. People are yearning for it, will die for it, and even kill for it. But for some reason we have avoided studying it until the last few years. Psychologists are now doing research attempting to discover what love is. Robert Sternberg (1988) has developed a theory of love that includes three distinct components: 1) *passion,* an intense physiological desire for another person; 2) *intimacy,* the feeling that one can share all one's thoughts and actions with another; 3) *commitment,* the willingness to stay with a person through thick and thin, or for better or worse, or in sickness or health. Ideally, marriage is characterized by a healthy amount of all three components. Various combinations of these components result in quite different types of love. Figure 6.1 will demonstrate some of these. For example, Sternberg suggests that *romantic love* involves a high degree of passion and intimacy, yet lacks substantial commitment to the other person. *Companionate love* is marked by a great deal of intimacy and commitment but little passion. *Consummate love* is the most complete because it includes a high level of all three components. It is the most satisfying because the relationship is likely to fulfill many of the needs of each partner.

Walt can not think of anything but Sarah. "She's so wonderful, she's really pretty, I don't think I can live without her." What is Walt experiencing? Is it love yet? Early in a relationship it may only be passion. When love has only passion (without intimacy or commitment), it is often called "infatuation." We are infatuated with the other person when we cannot stop thinking about them and become physiologically aroused by touching, seeing, or even thinking of them.

Having a lot in common with Walt, Sarah has a warm comfortable feeling for him. She is concerned about his success and is willing to do whatever she can to help him succeed. Is this the intimacy stage? When love has only intimacy (without passion or commitment), we might be better off calling it "liking." This is when we enjoy being with our partner, respect them, and share with them. Would you call this love?

Does Sarah only like Walt or could it be something else? Sarah has been thinking more about the relationship recently, as time goes by she's considering the fact that this relationship could last forever. She would stay with Walt through "thick and thin." Is she getting more serious over the relationship? Is it love yet? When love has only commitment, it is "empty love." We display empty love when we remain in a relationship from which all passion and intimacy have gone, as unhappy couples do "for the sake of the children." Is this all that Sarah is experiencing?

Wait a minute! There may be more to Walt's and Sarah's relationship. What's missing? Take a look at the Triangle of Love (Figure 6.1). We notice that their relationship is maturing. There seems to be an equal mixture of intimacy, passion and decision/commitment and this is called consummate love—an ideal, but difficult to attain relationship. This is the type of relationship we should all be striving to reach. Do all cultures experience this? (See Focus on Diversity on page 297.)

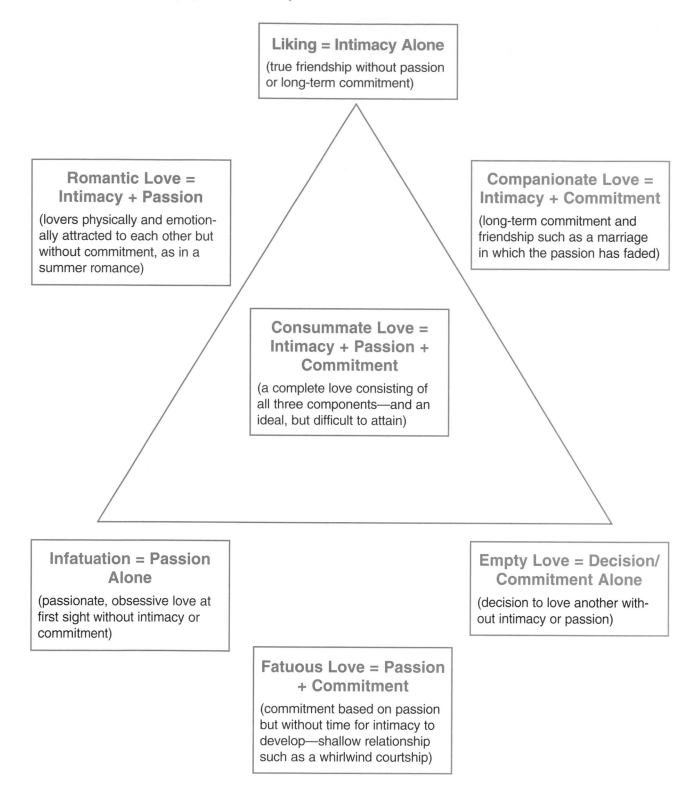

A Triangular Model of Love

Sternberg conceptualized love in the form of a triangle with three basic components: intimacy, passion, and decision/commitment. Love may be based primarily on one of these components, on a combination of two of them, or on all three. As shown in the figure, seven different types of relationships are possible, depending on how the components are combined.

(Adapted from Sternberg, 1988)

Figure 6.1. Is This What Love Is Made Of?

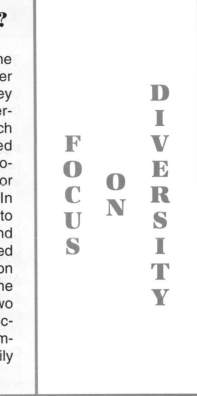

Is There a Cultural Influence on Love?

Cultural factors have a strong influence on the value of love. In the United States, love is crucial to a satisfying marriage. In the former Soviet Union, however, only 40 percent of the people say that they married for love; most did so because of loneliness, shared interests, or an unplanned pregnancy (Baron & Byrne, 1997). In research including two individualistic societies (Canada and the United States) and three collectivist societies (China, India, and Japan) romantic love is more likely to be considered an important basis for marriage in individualistic societies than in collectivistic ones. In many Asian societies the persons getting married are supposed to take into account the wishes of others, especially of parents and other family members. It is not unusual for marriages to be arranged by the respective families on the basis of such factors as occupation and status, not on the basis of love and the lover's free choice. The intense feelings of passionate love and the self-absorption of two lovers would be disruptive to the functioning of the group. In collectivist cultures, such as India and Japan, love is considered less important to a successful marriage than is the ability to resolve family conflicts (Matsumoto, 1994).

The Development of Love. Early in a relationship, passion is usually high, which may be one reason new love relationships and affairs are most intense. Intimacy, however, is not as high because the partners have not spent enough time together or shared enough experiences and emotions to be able to understand each other completely. Passionate love without intimacy creates a risk of misunderstanding and jealousy about any other person or activity that seems to interfere with the relationship. Early in the relationship, commitment also tends to be on the low side. It is interesting to note that these trends are true for most relationships including the married and unmarried, heterosexual and homosexual couples (Kurdek & Schmitt, 1986).

Over time passion seems to fade while intimacy and commitment grows stronger. According to Sternberg, passion is like an addiction: in the beginning a touch of the hand, a smile, even a mere glance will produce excitement. Gradually, however, one needs a greater dose of stimulation to get the same feeling. We habituate to the passion, and thus to continue this intense feeling for one another, *novel and significant stimuli* must be provided by each of the two individuals.

An understanding of the three components of love and the developmental process will help couples in the building of their relationship. A couple may want to schedule specific times each week, away from children and family, for a period of intimate sharing—a time to discuss problems as well as happy times. You may want to keep the passage burning by scheduling a weekend at the beach, buying your mate a special gift, taking them out to a special dinner, serving them breakfast in bed, etc. What else can you do to maintain the three components of love?

Love takes place in many different forms. Table 6.1 labels forms of love. Take a close look to see what forms you have experienced.

Passion is a fragile essence. It provides joy, excitement, delirium, and fulfillment—along with anxiety, suffering, and despair—for a short time. Companionship love is a heartier flavor. It can provide gentle friendship for life.

Walster & Walster

How to . . .

. . . Love and Be Loved

Never allow fear, anger, nor hate to take the place of love. When you discover these feelings, replace them with love.

Teach love to your children by approving of them. Praise them and each other.

Parents give and teach love by listening. The tone of voice, expression on your face, even the motion of your body teaches love.

Love is respect and consideration of others. Treat your children as little people, and they will respect and give love in return.

Guard your mental and physical health; both must be healthy to love.

Do not take each other (each member) for granted; always guard against too many "don't", "do", "won't" words.

Practice peace of mind with your children. Think of beautiful thoughts. Do not allow the mind to dwell on doubts. Fill your minds with positive thinking.

Teach by example. If you see someone standing alone be certain your children see you act with kindness toward that person. Hold your hands out to others, and your children will do so.

Fill your life with friendship. Reach out to others, gathering them into your family circle.

Appreciate nature. Take time with your family to enjoy the stars, the quiet of the night, the lake, the grass on the lawn—even an ant hill.

Touch and hug each other, and those you meet.

Be sincere. If you fill your heart with love, you will be loved.

> Marriage, to women as to men, must be a luxury, not a necessity; an incident of life, not all of it.
>
> Susan B. Anthony

people. Thus, they agree to begin a relatively long-lasting, more intimate relationship that to some extent excludes other close relationships. The couple agrees to depend on each other for the satisfaction of important needs, including companionship, love, and sex. The commitment may or may not include the decision to live together.

Making an agreement with another person to enter into a deeper, more exclusive, and lasting relationship is a crucially important life decision that must be made freely and with careful thought. Many individuals, consciously or unconsciously, feel pressured to enter into a relationship that they are not sure is good for them. Many people are not happy in their existing relationship or social situation, be it a bad home environment, an abusive mate, getting too old, being lonely, an alcoholic or addicted mate, etc., so they feel pressured to commit themselves to a new relationship as a means to escape the bad situation. A person who is pushed or pressured into a relationship will discover that their commitment is weaker and less enduring. If the commitment is made in defiance of pressure from parents or peers, the commitment may be very strong. As many of you know, if your parents were to tell you that you *cannot* date a specific person, you will do whatever it takes to make sure you will date them and be more committed to them. This phenomenon is known as *psychological reactance—the tendency to protect or restore one's sense of freedom or social control, often by doing the opposite of what has been demanded.* This is also known as the *Romeo and Juliet effect,* where their love was intensified, not weakened, by their families opposition. In summation, a commitment is likely to be strongest when it is arrived at freely and when it is cemented by taking action as a result of the commitment.

Marriage or ????? "Love and marriage go together like a horse and carriage." Are these lyrics from this popular old song true? People in love are eager to share their lives, their dreams and their goals with each other. How can they do this? What are their options? Today our society provides us with more options than we had in the past. But, some of these options may not be acceptable to our friends and family. So, what do we do, get married or live together?

Although alternatives to marriage are more viable than ever, experts still say that approximately ninety percent of us will marry at least once. During the past 25 years in the United States, the average age of marriage has risen steadily. The proportion of single women has doubled among twenty to twenty-four year-olds and nearly tripled among twenty-five to twenty-nine year-olds. During the same period, the number of couples living together outside marriage has quadrupled.

What About Premarital Sex? Despite centuries of religious and legal sanctions against premarital sex in many parts of the world, dramatic changes in sexual attitudes and behaviors have occurred in the last thirty years. Increasingly, sexual interactions have become a common and widely accepted part of a romantic relationship. The term premarital sex may become antiquated. More and more people are delaying marriage and premarital sex increasingly involves relationships between mature adults. Obviously, the emotional implications of sex between two fifteen-year-olds who still live with their parents and a pair of independent thirty-two year-olds are likely to be quite different. Many individuals are waiting until they are over thirty before marrying, should they be refraining from sex until they do get married? Is that realistic? Another problem with the term premarital sex is that it does not apply to homosexuals since they cannot legally get married. Is a couple that has been cohabiting for over seven years having premarital sex?

It is interesting to note, that the choice of sexual partners resembles other interpersonal choices, in that 90 percent of all sexual relationships involve partners of the same ethnic group, and 84 percent involve people who have the same educational background (MacDonald, 1995).

Physical intimacy is a defining characteristic of a romantic relationship. The more intimate the touch, the more it is perceived as an indication that the partner is committed to the relationship. As touch becomes more intimate and the couple moves toward petting and intercourse, both genders perceive greater commitment, but women interpret intimate contact as communicating much more about relationship commitment than men do.

Have STD's and Unwanted Pregnancies Influenced One's Sexuality? Incurable diseases and teenage pregnancies might be expected to result in decreases in premarital sexual activity, and some changes have, in fact, been reported, though not as much as you might guess. In the mid-1990s, the U.S. Centers for Disease Control and Prevention reported that the number of sexually active teenagers has leveled off at about 53 percent, and that more than half of these individuals regularly use condoms. As a result, there has been a slight decrease in the teenage birth rate and in the incidence of gonorrhea. The greatest behavioral changes, involving the use of safer sex practices and fewer partners, have however, been confined to those individuals most at risk for HIV infections—gays and prostitutes.

The fact that two human beings love each other does not guarantee they will be able to create a joyful and rewarding relationship. Their love does not automatically teach communication skills or effective methods of conflict resolution, or the art of integration of their love into the rest of their existence. Their love does not produce self-esteem; it may reinforce it but it cannot create it; still without self-esteem love cannot survive.

Nathaniel Branden

Should I Remain Single? Is this an option? Remaining single is becoming a more viable lifestyle. More and more people are remaining single. Furthermore, the negative stereotype of people who remain single, which pictures them as lonely, frustrated, depressed, odd, and unchosen is gradually disappearing.

Generally, single people do rate themselves as less happy than married people. However, the reported happiness of married people has declined steadily since 1972. In the meantime, the reported happiness for singles has increased (Steinhauer, 1995). A Norwegian study indicates that married individuals are better off than those who are unmarried—a lower suicide rate and higher self-reported feeling of well being than those who are unmarried—up until age thirty five to forty, but that after that, the advantages of being married rapidly decline (Mastekaasa, 1995). There is still substantial pressure in our society to marry. We are taught to believe that we are not complete until we have found our "other half" and entered into a partnership for life.

Should We Live Together Before Marriage? Cohabitation for many couples is the first step toward commitment with an informal sharing of domestic life. Cohabitation has become increasingly common, not only in the United States, but also in, most notably, Canada, Australia, France, and Sweden, as well as many other countries (Wilhelm, 1998). Overall, probably about half of all young adult North Americans cohabit for at least a few months. In 1997, there were slightly over 4.1 million unmarried couples living together in the United States. They represented about 7% of all couples (married or unmarried) sharing living quarters at that time. The cohabitation rate is about twice as high among African American couples as among caucasian couples. Fifty-five percent of male cohabitors and 41 percent of female cohabitors have never been married (U.S. Bureau of Census, 1990). Children live with about one cohabiting couple in three.

About one cohabitor in three is divorced. Divorced people are more likely to enter cohabiting relationships than people who never married. Apparently, the experience of divorce makes some people more willing to share their lives than their bank accounts—the second or third time around (Steinhauer, 1995).

Negative attitudes toward couples "living together" appears to be declining, though many people continue to disapprove of this practice. Cohabitation tends to be a relatively unstable way of life. Many cohabitors feel less commitment toward their relationship than married people do. About 40 percent of the cohabiting couples eventually marry. The majority of couples break up within three years. Termination of the relationship, not marriage, is the more likely outcome of cohabitation (Willis & Michael, 1994).

If We Live Together, Is Our Chance of Having a Successful Marriage Greater than Those Who Don't? Not only do many couples consider cohabitation a first step toward marriage; they also believe that cohabitation improves the chances of marital success. The research is inconclusive on this subject. Most people who live together and find that they are incompatible, separate before marriage. People who get married before living together and find that they are incompatible will generally work harder at trying to get the relationship to work before actually getting divorced. Recent evidence indicates that cohabitation does not

CONSIDER THIS . . .
Will Your Marriage Last Forever?

There is no foolproof recipe for lasting, happy marriages. Recent studies have provided us with some valuable clues as to what makes a happy and successful marriage (Klagsburn, 1985).

- Happily married couples spend a lot of focused time together doing what they both enjoy, much as they did in their courtship days before they married.
- They share many of the same values, such as the importance of physical intimacy, childrearing practices, religious beliefs, and morals.
- These couples exhibited a high degree of flexibility—they have the ability to accept change in their partners as well as changes in the nature of the married relationship.

Other factors that seem to be important predictors of marital success include:

- *Age at time of marriage*—couples who marry young have a higher divorce rate.
- *Socioeconomic class*—the frequency of divorce is higher in working and lower classes than in upper and middle classes (Raschke, 1987).
- *Length of courtship*—longer periods of courtship are associated with greater probability of marital success.
- *Family background*—people whose parents were unhappily married are more likely than others to have an unsatisfactory marriage (Teachman, Polonko, & Scanzoni, 1987).
- *Personality*—if one or both partners has a serious psychological or emotional disorder, problems will occur (Raschke, 1987).

---

strengthen marriage. In fact, the opposite seems true. In many studies in North America, as well as in Western Europe, marriages that are preceded by cohabitation typically are less happy and less durable. Couples who decide to cohabit are already at a higher risk of divorce than couples who do not, since they tend to be less conventional, less religious, and lower in status (DeMaris & Rao, 1992). A lot depends on the individual couple—especially their values.

Why Should I Marry? More than nine out of ten people eventually marry—most of them during their twenties and thirties. People tend to marry out of mixed motives—many of them unclear even to themselves. Now that marriage is no longer necessary for economic survival or the satisfaction of sexual needs, love has become the major rationale for getting married and staying married. Unfortunately, people sometimes marry for the wrong reasons: to become respectable, for money, for a regular sexual outlet, for status, or to make their parents happy. Even cohabiting couples may marry for the wrong reason. Just when the relationship begins to falter, marriage may be sought to save the relationship. It's a temporary "fix," because it does not solve the underlying conflicts.

Marriage is a risky proposition. In deciding to get married, people make a long range projection about the future of their relationship. Obviously, it is

Love is the only thing which gives value in life. It is the deepest, the greatest, the strongest reason for living.

Solar Frost

What are the chances of this marriage lasting? What do you think this couple needs to do to build a meaningful long-term marriage relationship?

difficult to predict thirty, forty, or even fifty years of commitment on the basis of one or two years of premarital interaction.

Psychology Today magazine (Lauer & Lauer, June, 1985) took a readers' poll asking them to list the most important reasons that made marriages last. It was interesting to note that they separated the responses by sex. The top seven out of fifteen choices were identical for the two sexes. The top seven reasons are listed in order of frequency:

1. My spouse is my best friend.
2. I like my spouse as a person.
3. Marriage is a long term commitment.
4. Marriage is sacred.
5. We agree on aims and goals.
6. My spouse has grown more interesting.
7. I want the relationship to succeed.

> Married couples who love each other tell each other a thousand things without talking.
>
> Chinese Proverb

Jeanette and Robert Lauer (1985) conducted a survey of 351 couples with enduring marriages to see what made their marriage a success. Couples were asked questions about their marriage, ranging from interests, hobbies, sex, money and attitudes toward their spouses, and reasons why their marriages had lasted.

The most frequently given reason for a lasting marriage is *having a positive attitude toward one's partner.* These individuals see their spouse as their best friend and they like him or her as a person. They are aware that their partner has faults, but their likable qualities more than offset their shortcomings. Many people stated that the present generation takes the marriage vows too lightly and are not willing to work at solving their problems. Marriage is a commitment and takes a lot of work. Both partners have to work at solving their problems. Another key ingredient to a lasting marriage is a mutual agreement about aims and goals of life, such as the desire to make the marriage last. A satisfying sex life is important, but this is not what makes the marriage last. Although there is a strong link between a couples' marital satisfaction and their perception of the quality of their sexual relationship, most of the couples surveyed said they almost always agree about sex and many are happy despite lack of such agreement (Fowers & Olson, 1989). A couple needs to learn to adjust and compromise.

MARITAL ADJUSTMENT

> Expect what is reasonable in others, not what is perfect.
>
> Anonymous

During courtship, many of us wear *"rose-colored glasses."* We tend to ignore or not notice our partners' faults. We tend to focus mostly on pleasurable activities and our partner's positive characteristics. But when people marry, they must face reality and the problems that they will encounter within this new relationship. Suddenly, marriage brings duties and obligations. One is no longer responsible for only oneself but now shares responsibility for two people and perhaps more if children arrive.

Furthermore, one's identity is changed with marriage. No longer are you simply you—you are now Sarah's husband, or Walt's wife, or Jon's mother or father. You become interdependent with others in your family and not indepen-

Are They Married?

At a California city college, a young woman was captured by a young man and his friends and taken to his home where he has sex with the unwilling woman. She calls the police, and they charge him with kidnapping and rape. However, the young man is shocked by her accusations. According to his culture, he believes he has married the young woman and thus is innocent of charges.

The couple in question were members of the Hmong community, in which marriage can be transacted when a young man takes a girl, often as young as fourteen years old, to his home and consummates the marriage. In exchange, the groom's family pays money—bride price—to the girl's family.

Zij poj niam (marriages by capture) is one of three accepted forms of marriage for these Laotian hill people. Of course, not all young women are unwilling partners in marriage by capture. Many are happy to continue the tradition, and they are proud to wear the white wrist band that shows that they are married women. On the other hand, as you can see, especially if the young woman has lived in the U.S. very long, it can cause conflict. Affected by American culture, many Hmong females no longer want to give up their independence, including social activities, schooling, future career, etc., for marriage. Many of these young women are now rebelling against this form of marriage.

While bride capture may seem strange to many of us, the Hmong are not unique in uniting couples in this manner. In Georgia, located between Europe and Asia, bride kidnapping (motatseba) still exists, and many unwilling females are still carried off by their suitors with no recourse.

By the way, for your information, considering the cultural components of this case, the judge agreed to allow the young man to plead to a lesser charge of false imprisonment. He ordered the male to pay a fine of $1,000 to the girl's family and to serve 90 days in jail (Dresser, 1996).

**WHAT DO YOU THINK SHOULD HAVE HAPPENED
IN THIS CASE?**

FOCUS ON DIVERSITY

dent. For some people this loss of independence may become a crisis, but for others this new identity may give them a new lease on life.

The changing nature of male and female roles creates problems for all types of couples as they settle down to live together. Even the most mundane tasks may become a problem. Who pays the bills? Who takes out the trash? Who cooks? Who will stay home and take care of the family? There is no such thing as a problem-free marriage. Successful marriages depend on the couples' ability to handle their problems.

What Are Your Expectations of Marriage? **When you get married what are your expectations of how life will be? Will marriage be a *"Bed of Roses?"* Will all your needs be met by your new spouse? Many people enter marriage with unrealistic expectations about how wonderful it's going to be (Sabatelli, 1988). People tend to create unreal ideas about what it is going to be like when they are married. We predict our future and have expectations about ourselves, our spouse, our children and our future. Mass media, magazines, novels, TV, etc. tends to romanticize marriage and mislead us into thinking that marriage is such an exciting and fulfilling institute. Romantic ideals lead us to expect so much from our mate and from our marriage that disappointment is likely. People who marry quickly are more likely to have unrealistic expectations of marriage and their mates and thus, they are more likely to experience more difficulty when reality sets in.**

Role Expectations. **What is the woman's role in married life? Is it different from a man's role? Should a man's and a woman's role be different? When a couple marry, they assume new roles, that of husband and wife. We all have developed our own expectations of how a wife or husband should behave. These expectations may vary greatly from one person to another. What happens if your expectations are different from your partners? Serious problems may occur. The more the two partners agree about marital roles, the more likely the marriage will last over a longer period of time.**

Where did you learn what the role of a husband or a wife should be? Most of us learned this from watching our parents through the process called *modeling*. But times are changing and other social forces are having an effect on our roles within a relationship. Careers are changing the timing of marriage and caretaking roles of the family. The women's movement has given women more options and has changed their perception of what their role is in a relationship. Marriage seems to be in a state of transition and consequently, most of us are in a state of confusion as to what role we should be playing.

It is imperative that couples discuss role expectations in depth before marriage. If they discover that their views are very different, they need to take seriously the potential for problems. Many people ignore gender-role disagreements, thinking they can "straighten out" their partners later on. But as we have all discovered, it is difficult to change our own behavior and more difficult to change someone else's behavior—especially their attitude.

While we are dating, and during the *honeymoon period, which can be any time from the wedding day to a year or so from that day,* many people do not see the people they love as they really are, but rather as they wish (expect) them to be. *We see what we expect to see, we hear what we want to hear—this is a psychological phenomenon of perception that can interfere with the way we perceive the world.* We tend to perceive only the positive characteristics of our partners and ignore the negative characteristics. In essence a person is in love with their own dreams and ideals and not with the person they marry. Living together day in and day out makes it only a matter of time until each partner is forced to compare ideals with reality.

The Honeymoon Is Over. One morning, after Walt and Sarah have been married for about a year, Sarah awakens and "realizes" that Walt is not the same man she married. She accuses him of changing for the worse. He is not as considerate and as kind to her as he was before. He does not pay as much attention to her. He doesn't enjoy going out all the time like they use to. He just wants to stay home. Walt insists,

of course, that he has not changed; he is the same person that she married and he enjoys quiet evenings at home alone with her.

This interaction may be signaling that the *"honeymoon"* is over for Walt and Sarah. This stage is very important in most marriages. It usually indicates that the unrealistic, overly high expectations about marriage and ones mate created by "love" are being reexamined. No one can live up to perfection. In a successful relationship it means that subjective perceptions are becoming more realistic and more objective. It also means that we are at last coming to know our mate as a real human being rather than as a projection of our expectations. Realizing the humanness of our partner allows us to relax, to be human as well and not feel that we have to live up to our partner's expectations. If my partner can make mistakes and be less than perfect, so can I, thank goodness.

After the *honeymoon period,* intensity diminishes and satisfaction with marriage generally dips, especially for wives. The most commonly cited reason for this change is the arrival of children. For most couples, the time and effort spent on parenting usually takes time away from the husband-wife relationship. Does this mean that marriages without children are more satisfying? This is a complicated question. In general, when both partners agree to postpone or decide not to have children, they tend to be much more pleased with each other than couples who have several young children.

What are some of the other issues and problems that a couple may encounter as they begin to face the reality of being married and functioning as a "twosome" rather than an individual? Now you need to consider your partners needs as well as your own while you interact and get involved in the world of work and leisure. An individual's job satisfaction and involvement can affect their own marital satisfaction, their partner's marital satisfaction, and their children's development and satisfaction.

Should the woman work after she gets married? Should she work after she has children? Should the husband stay at home with the children while the wife pursues a career?

Marriage and/or a Career. Men have been told that their career is of utmost importance in their lives, while women are still in a state of confusion as to what they are to do. Should they pursue a career or stay home and be a "mother" or do both? A successful career woman may experience role conflict and guilt over her strong work commitment. Many times finances make the decision for us. A woman may have to work to help provide for the family while still feeling guilty because she is not home taking care of the kids. There is not enough research evidence to draw any conclusions about the effects of wives' work on their marital satisfaction. But we do know that if a person is satisfied with their job, they will be happier at home. The reverse is also true, that if a person is satisfied with their marriage, they are more likely to be more effective on the job. If a person is highly committed to a satisfying career, they may have less time and energy to devote to their marriage and family. If a person has a high commitment to their marriage and their family, they will find time for both. It really depends on the person's commitment and values either to work or their marriage or both. Research indicates that there is no consistent differences in marital adjustment of male breadwinners versus dual career couples (Piotrowski, Rapport, & Rapport, 1987). It appears that marital satisfaction tends to be the highest when partners share similar gender-role expectations and when the wife's employment status matches her own expectations.

PARENTHOOD AND CAREER

It's not easy being a wife, mother, and having a career.

What does research on maternal employment indicate? In general, the research indicates that maternal employment is not harmful to children (Etaugh, 1974). In fact, there is evidence that maternal employment can have *positive* effects on children. Some studies have found that children of working mothers seem to be more independent, self-reliant, and responsible than children of non-working mothers. There seems to be a particular advantage for daughters of working mothers. They tend to perceive women as being very capable and independent individuals and thus, perceive themselves as being very competent and successful. They tend to be more successful in their academic endeavors and tend to exhibit higher than average career aspirations (Hoffman, 2000).

One common problem of two-paycheck families is the division of housework and child care, which usually has employed wives doing much more of the housework and child care than their employed husbands do. As you might expect, men who are better educated or younger tend to be more helpful around the house. Surprisingly, however, the more children a couple has the less likely they are to share equally in the household labor, even if both are working an equal number of hours outside the home (Haas, 1981). Thus, many employed mothers feel overworked and under appreciated. If a new mother quits her job to care for the children, she gives up an external source of self-esteem, social support, and status. However, most mothers who have left the work force believe that the sacrifices are worth it (O'Donnell, 1985).

Overall, research indicates that adults who combine all three roles—spouse, parents and employee—are healthier and happier than those who do not (Baruch, et al., 1983).

What other issues and concerns do married couples encounter as they strive to succeed in marriage?

What Do Most Couples Argue About? Is it sex, money, children, power, roles and responsibilities, jealousy, or extra-marital affairs? *Money* ranks as the single most common cause of conflict in marriage. Money not only influences a couples' lifestyle but also their feelings of security, self-esteem, confidence, and acceptance by others. Without money, families live in a constant state of stress, fearing the loss of jobs, illness, or household emergencies. Husbands tend to view themselves as poor providers, and their self-esteem may crumble as a result.

Neither financial stability nor wealth can ensure marital satisfaction. Even when financial resources are plentiful, money can be a source of marital strain. Quarrels about how to spend money are common and potentially damaging at all income levels (Pittman & Lloyd, 1988). Couples that tend to be more satisfied with their marriage engage in more joint decisions regarding their finances in comparison to couples that eventually divorced.

Examine the last sentence, and decide what underlies most problems in relationships—be it a marriage, a business relationship, or wherever two or more people interact.

Can a Bad Relationship Be Good? John Gottman (1995) has been studying love and marriage for the last twenty years. His research is threatening to turn much of current relationship therapy on its head. He contends that many aspects of marriage often considered critical to long-term success, such as how intensely people fight; whether they face conflict or avoid it; how well they solve problems; how compatible they are socially, financially, even sexually are less important than people and professionals once thought. Gottman believes that none of these things matter to a marriage's longevity as much as maintaining that crucial ratio of five-to-one.

What Is This Five-to-One Ratio? This is the difference between divorce and a positive long-term relationship according to Gottman—it is mind-boggling in its very simplicity. Satisfied couples maintain a five-to-one ratio of positive interactions to negative interactions in their relationship. It is hard to believe that the longevity of your relationship depends primarily on you being five times as nice to your partner as you are nasty to them. This may be surprising to you:

- Wildly explosive relationships that vacillate between heated arguments and passionate reconciliations can be as happy—and long lasting—as those that seem more emotionally stable. They may even be more exciting and intimate.
- Couples who start out complaining about each other have some of the most stable marriages over time, while those who do not fight early on are more likely to face the road to divorce.
- Fighting, whether rare or frequent, is sometimes the healthiest thing a couple can do for the relationship. In fact, blunt anger, appropriately expressed, "seems to immunize marriages against deterioration."
- Emotionally inexpressive marriages, which may seem like repressed volcanoes destined to explode, are actually very successful—so long as the couple maintains the five-to-one ratio in what they do express to each other. In fact, too much emotional catharsis among such couples can "scare the hell out of them," says Gottman.
- How warmly you remember the story of your relationship foretells your chances of staying together. In one study that involved couples telling about how their relationship evolved, psychologists were able to predict—with an astonishing 94 percent accuracy—which couples would be divorced within three years.
- Men who do housework are likely to have happier marriages, greater physical health, even better sex lives than men who do not (Hearing this, men may be running to find the vacuum cleaner).
- In happy marriages, there are no discernible gender differences in terms of the quantity and quality of emotional expression. In fact, men in happy marriages are more likely to reveal intimate personal information about themselves than women (When conflict erupts, however, profound gender differences emerge).

How to . . .

. . . Have a Happy Relationship

- **Learn to Calm Down**—Do not let the emotions take control of you. Do not over-react, wait, relax, take a walk, remove yourself from the stress event for a period of time until you have time to calm down and react logically. Once you have calmed down you can work on the other basic "keys" to improving their relationship.

- **Validate Your Partner**—Validation involves "putting yourself in your partner's shoes and imagining his or her emotional state." Let your partner know that you understand how he or she feels and why, even if you do not agree. You can also show validation by acknowledging your partner's point of view, accepting appropriate responsibility, and apologizing when you are clearly wrong. If this still seems too much of a stretch, at least let your partner know that you are trying to understand, even if you're finding it hard.

- **Learn To Speak And Listen Non-defensively**—This is tough, Gottman admits, but defensiveness is a very dangerous response, and it needs to be interrupted. One of the most powerful things you can do—in addition to working toward the ideal of listening with empathy and speaking without blame—is to "begin to apply praise and admiration into your relationship." A little positive reinforcement (appreciation) goes a long way toward changing the chemistry between couples.

- **Practice, Practice, Practice**—Gottman calls this "overlearning," doing something so many times that it becomes second nature. The goal is to be able to calm yourself down, communicate non-defensively, and validate your partner automatically—even in the heat of an argument.

Do you agree?

John Gottman

What do you think about the five-to-ratio? Should we be teaching couples how to apply this to their relationship?

COMMUNICATION PROBLEMS

Successful communication is the cornerstone of any relationship. Such communication must be open, realistic, tactful, caring, and valued. Maintaining this kind of communication is not always easy unless all the people involved are committed to the belief that good communication is important to life and marital satisfaction. This sounds simple, yet couples in marital trouble almost always list failure to communicate as one of their major problems. Basically, communication failures occur because one or perhaps both partners choose not to communicate or because of the lack of communication skills. You may want to refer back to the communication chapter and apply the material discussed in that chapter to improve upon your communication skills.

Many couples get so involved in the activities of everyday life—their career, their family activities and their outside interests—that they forget about the needs and interests of their spouse. Even though they spend time with their spouse they really do not communicate. If this seems to be true of your relationship, you may want to change this by *scheduling a time to communicate.* Tell your mate that you would like to take them out to dinner every Thursday night, even if it is to a fast food restaurant, so you have a time to sit down and talk. This is your time, do not take the kids or anyone else. You may want to write down things you want to talk about during the week so you won't forget about them. Many times a person will get to the scheduled session and say, "There's something I want to talk about, but I forgot what it was." You may want to schedule a weekend away from the family every few months so you can talk and plan for the future.

Fighting Fairly. Many couples state that their basic problem is that they fight all the time. Yet, rather than a problem, fighting is a normal part of a relationship. The problem is not whether one fights, but how one fights. Fighting is simply a matter of communication and all the principles of good communication skills apply here (See Chapter 7). If this is true of your relationship, you should learn to fight constructively and not destructively (Bach, 1971). Here are a few tips that might help.

Do not fight when you are emotionally upset:

- Slowly count to ten before saying what you may regret later;
- Take a walk around the block, exercise, or take a shower;
- If you can, you may want to sleep on it. Sleep can help relieve stress and frustration and when you awaken you can look at the problem more logically. This works only if your mate understands and does not become more upset because you do not seem to be concerned and are just sleeping.

Do not call your partner names:

- This makes them more upset.

Be specific, state exactly what the problem is that is bothering you:

- Do not *beat around the bush,* the other person may not know what the problem really is—your partner is not a mind reader.

Do not bring up past faults, mistakes, and problems:

- We can not change the past;
- Discuss only the immediate problem and what you are willing to do to solve the problem.

Fighting fairly and using problem solving techniques will enhance any relationship and keep it alive and growing. Failure to communicate clearly and fight fairly will usually cause disruption and the ultimate failure of intimate relationships.

FAMILY VIOLENCE

Physical violence is most apt to erupt in families lacking communication skills. Such families often can not talk to one another, do not listen to one another, and simply lack enough communication skills to make themselves understood. Children are often physically violent because they have not learned how to communicate. In a way adults who cannot communicate are like children and too often express themselves physically rather than verbally.

Family violence is difficult to measure and document because most of it occurs in the privacy of the home, away from public view and also goes unreported. Family violence includes child abuse, violence between spouses, sibling abuse, sexual abuse and parental abuse by children, especially elderly parents.

It is estimated that one out of every twenty-eight American children under the age of 14 was reported as abused or neglected in 1990. That is more than a million reported cases a year. Neglect is actually the most common form of maltreatment as well as the most destructive, causing more deaths, injuries, and long-term problems than abuse (Wolock & Horowitz, 1984). Some instances of neglect are blatant and horrifying; infants who are allowed to starve or freeze to death are examples. Others are less obvious, involving infants whose parents rarely hold, talk, or play with them or infants who are deliberately undernourished. Also, many childhood accidents (by far the greatest cause of childhood death and serious injury) can be traced to neglect.

The causes of family violence are many, including problems in the society (such as cultural attitudes toward women and children), in parents (such as drug addiction, alcoholism, and financial problems), and in the child (such as being a difficult child or being sickly). The most effective strategies should emphasize prevention and treatment rather than blame. In addition, any measures that help reduce stress and increase individuals' social support will make violence and abuse less likely. Remember, good communication skills underlie all good relationships.

It is actually easier than you think to avoid a violent or abusive relationship. Our problem is that we allow our emotions to take control of our behavior and not our common sense and intellect. Recent research has shown that in most relationships where violence has occurred, some form of abuse began during the *dating period.* If a person is abusive while the couple is dating, what are the chances of the person *not* being abusive when they are married? Not very likely! A person does not change overnight or as soon as they sign a marriage license. To the contrary, some people feel that the marriage license is a sign of ownership and they can now do whatever they want to their partner. If you are in an abusive relationship before marriage you may want to "think twice" before making a serious commitment to that person.

CODEPENDENCE

But, wait a minute, you know you can help that person. They need your help and you love them and you feel you can help them change. If you can get them to marry you it will be easier to help them change. This sounds like the beginning of a *codependent relationship—where one person has allowed another person's behavior (abuse, chemical addiction, etc.) to affect him or her, and who is obsessed with controlling that person's behavior* (Beattie, 1987). It is natural to want to protect and help the people we care about. It is also natural to be affected by and react to the problems of people around us. As the problems become more serious and remain unresolved, we become more affected and react more intensely to it. Does this sound like anyone you know?

- Have you become so absorbed in other people's problems that you do not have time to identify or solve your own?
- Do you care so deeply about other people that you have forgotten how to care for yourself?
- Do you need to control events and people around you because you feel everything around and inside you is out of control?
- Do you feel responsible for so much because the people around you feel responsible for so little?

Are You Codependent? If you or any of your friends answer yes to the above questions, you may be codependent. Whatever problem the other person has, codependency involves a habitual system of thinking, feeling, and behaving toward ourselves and others that can cause us pain. Codependent behaviors or habits are self-destructive, not only to themselves, but also to all their relationships. Most codependents have been so busy responding to other people's

CONSIDER THIS . . .
What Is Codependency?

- My good feelings about who I am stem from being liked by you.
- My good feelings about who I am stem from receiving approval from you.
- Your struggles affect my serenity. My mental attitude focuses on solving your problems or relieving your pain.
- My mental attention is focused on pleasing you.
- My mental attention is focused on protecting you.
- My mental attention is focused on manipulating you "to do it my way."
- My self-esteem is bolstered by solving your problems.
- My self-esteem is bolstered by relieving your pain.
- My own hobbies and interests are put aside. My time is spent sharing your interest and hobbies.
- Your clothing and personal appearance is dictated by my desires, because I feel you are a reflection of me.
- I am not aware of how I feel. I am aware of how you feel. I am not aware of what I want. I ask you what you want. If I am not aware, I assume.
- The dreams I have for my future are linked to you.
- My fear of rejection determines what I say and do.
- My fear of your anger determines what I say and do.
- I use giving as a way of feeling safe in our relationship.
- My social circle diminishes as I involve myself with you.
- I put my values aside in order to connect with you.
- I value your opinion and way of doing things more than my own.
- The quality of my life is in relation to the quality of yours.

problems that they have not had time to identify, much less take care of their own problems.

Can a codependent change? Yes, definitely. But as we have already learned, change is not easy—it takes a lot of work and effort on everyone's part. The first step toward change is awareness of the problem and the second step is acceptance. In order to become aware of what codependence is we need to know what the characteristics of a codependent are.

Codependency is many things. It is a dependency on people—on their moods, behavior, sickness or well-being, and their love. It is a paradoxical dependency. Codependents appear to be depended upon, but they are dependent. They look strong but feel helpless. They appear controlling but in reality are controlled themselves, sometimes by a disorder or illness such as alcoholism. If you find yourself in a codependent relationship, you may want to read some of the new literature and self-help books available at your local bookstores or seek professional help through the counseling office or mental health center near you.

During the courtship period and continuing throughout married life, there is an insecure feeling in many individuals when they fear the loss of affection of their partner, especially when they feel threatened by an outside source. That outside source may be a new baby, a new friend, a new career, etc. Let us take another look at Walt and Sarah.

> Walt has been working for a law firm for two years now and seems to be doing well. But the job is not as exciting as it originally was for the first two years. Walt is not considering changing jobs since he still knows that he could be a full partner within five years and that has been his goal for a long time.
>
> On the other hand, Sarah just changed jobs and is extremely excited about the new challenges and the new friends she is getting to know. Sarah is beginning to spend more and more time at work and more time socially with her new friends. Occasionally, she has been working late with a male colleague to complete a major project.

Jealousy is not a barometer by which the depth of love may be read. It merely records the degree of insecurity. It is a negative, miserable state of feeling, having its origin in a sense of insecurity and inferiority.

Margaret Mead

☞ CHECK THIS OUT . . .
Have You Ever Done This?

Have you ever called a lover unexpectedly just to see if he or she were where they were supposed to be?

Have you ever extensively questioned a lover about previous or present romantic relationships?

Have you ever listened in on a telephone conversation or secretly followed him or her?

Have you ever looked in your lover's personal belongings or wallet for unfamiliar names, phone numbers, etc. without them knowing?

Have you ever made nasty remarks or comments about someone who is better liked by your friends . . . who had possessions you wished to have . . . who was more attractive . . . who was more successful?

If you answered "yes" to many of the above questions, you may want to seek out help in working through jealousy and envy.

Walt comes home after work and Sarah's still working. He is used to having her companionship in the evenings. Walt's beginning to question Sarah about her late evenings and the fact she seems to be so happy recently and excited about life. He seems to be bored with his job and not too happy with the world around him. Walt's becoming suspicious of Sarah and her friends. What's happening in this relationship?

WHAT'S THE GREEN-EYED MONSTER?

Is Walt *jealous? Jealousy* is an emotion familiar to most of us, if not from direct experience, at least through the experience of friends, from novels, television and movies. *Romantic jealousy* carries the additional stress associated with the threat of losing an important relationship and often involves feelings of having been betrayed and perhaps deceived. Thus, this feeling of *romantic jealousy* provokes a host of negative feelings focused on the lover, the self, and the perceived rival. And it can be very destructive in a relationship.

In our culture, jealousy is manifested in a variety of petty ways. Margaret Mead said: "Jealousy is not a barometer by which the depth of love may be read. It merely records the degree of the lover's insecurity. It is a negative, miserable state of feeling, having its origin in a sense of insecurity and inferiority."

Is It Jealousy or Envy? *Jealousy* is defined as the thoughts and feelings that arise when an actual or desired relationship is threatened. *Envy* is defined as the thoughts and feelings that arise when our personal qualities, possessions, or achievements do not measure up to those of someone relevant to us. In general, society is more accepting of jealousy than envy, understanding the desire to protect lovers from rivals but not the begrudging of a friend's good fortune.

Researchers have suggested that jealousy and envy are rooted in low self-esteem or insecurities about self-worth. People with poor self-concepts are more likely to fear that the existing relationship is vulnerable to threat. Jealousy is also more likely to occur when people believe they are putting more into a relationship than their partner is; they have serious doubts about their partner's commitment. Men seem to respond differently to jealousy than women. Males seem less likely to admit they feel jealous but are more likely to express anger with themselves or toward the rival; females are more likely to react with depression and with attempts to make themselves more attractive to the partner.

Some people are more prone to get jealous than others. It appears that this jealous-prone disposition is primarily a function of poor self-esteem, feelings of insecurity about one's self-worth, or when there is less commitment from one partner (as when couples cohabi-tate instead of marry). After experiencing a jealousy-provoking situation, people feel even more insecure, unattractive, and dependent, making future jealous reactions even more likely (Radecki-Bush, Bush, & Jennings, 1988). One study indicated that single and divorced people were more likely than married to experience jealousy and to act on that feeling by calling lovers unexpectedly, listening in on their phone calls, and looking through their belongings (Salovey & Rodin, 1986).

Overcoming jealousy is not easy. Anything we can do toward becoming confident, secure individuals will help us cope with our own jealousy. We can try to learn what is making us jealous. What exactly are we feeling and why are

> Jealousy is not a barometer by which the depth of love may be read. It merely records the degree of insecurity. It is a negative, miserable state of feeling, having its origin in a sense of insecurity and inferiority.
>
> Margaret Mead

we feeling that way? We can try to keep our jealous feelings in perspective. We can also negotiate with our partner to change certain behaviors that seem to trigger our jealousy. Negotiations assume that we too are working to reduce our own unwarranted jealousy. Choosing partners who are reassuring and loving will also help reduce our irrational jealousies. Unfortunately, it is not as easy as it sounds to follow this advice because it is so often irrational, emotional, and unreasonable—and, at the moment of jealousy, all too often uncontrollable. It remains one of the puzzling components of love relationships.

During the last year of Walt's and Sarah's marriage, we find that Walt has been spending a lot of his spare time working on their computer, playing games and learning new programs. Sarah does not like to spend her time playing with some "dumb" computer when she could be exercising or interacting with people. When they first got married, Walt and Sarah seemed to have a lot in common: tennis, history, same friends and same goals, but now they seem to be growing apart. Sarah has her new job and new friends and Walt does not seem to be interested in either. All he seems to be interested in is his computer and watching sports on television.

GROWING APART

> There comes a time in some relationships when no matter how sincere the attempt to reconcile the differences or how strong the wish to recreate a part of the past once shared, the struggle becomes so painful that nothing else is felt and the world and all its beauty only add to the discomfort by providing cruel contrast.
>
> David Viscott

Relationships evolve and people evolve, but not always in the same direction. It is important that spouses allow each other room for personal growth. We need to recognize that it is unrealistic to expect one's partner to remain exactly the same forever. We all need personal time for the activities and hobbies that we enjoy that may not be of interest to our spouse. But at the same time, it is important to strive to maintain joint activities as well. Remember, there is a strong correlation between marital satisfaction and the amount of activities the two people have in common, especially leisure activities.

In Happiness and in Good Health, Till Divorce Do Us Part. Is this how the new marriage vows should read? As most of you know the number of divorces have increased rapidly over the last twenty years. Married adults are now divorcing two and one-half times as often as adults did twenty years ago, and four times as often as fifty years ago. Although there has been a modest decline in the divorce rate since the 1970's, nearly one-half of marriages end in divorce in the United States (Hetherington, et al., 1998). Martin and Bumpass (1989) project that if you include couples who separate permanently but never bother to file for divorce, two-thirds of today's marriages will result in marital dissolution. In the United States half of all divorces occur within five to seven years of marriage (Fisher, 1982). Is this what people are referring to when they say the "seven year itch?" Recent research indicates that most divorces may be happening sooner than that—more likely within the first five years.

What accounts for the rise in the divorce rate over the past years? One major factor, clearly, is that spouses today expect a great deal more from each other than spouses in the past. In earlier decades, earning the money was considered the man's responsibility, and housework and child care, the woman's. In addition, husbands and wives in the past usually did not expect to really understand each other; they generally assumed that masculinity and femininity are opposites, and that the sexes therefore are naturally a mystery to each other.

Who Divorces? Divorce rates vary by country, ranging from .01 percent of population annually in Bolivia, the Philippines, and Spain to 4.7 percent in the world's most divorce prone country, the United States. Divorce rates are higher among blacks than whites, among lower income couples, among those whose parents divorce (Kudek, 1993).

Worldwide divorce rates are increasing. To predict a culture's divorce rate it helps to know its values (Triandis, 1994). Individualistic cultures (where people are concerned about their own personal feelings and emotions and ask, "What does my heart say?") have more divorces than collectivistic cultures (where love includes obligation and people ask, "What will other people say?").

What kind of specific marital problems are preditive of divorce? Amato & Rogers (1997) found that infidelity, jealousy, foolish spending behavior and drug problems were the most consistent predictors of divorce.

Your marriage will have a greater chance of lasting if:

- You marry after the age of 22;
- You grow-up in a stable, two parent home;
- You dated for a long time prior to marriage;
- You are well and similarly educated;
- You have a stable income from a job you enjoy;
- You live in a small town or on a farm;
- You do not cohabit or become pregnant before marriage;
- You are religiously committed;
- You are of similar age, faith, and education.

None of these predictors, by themselves, is essential to a stable marriage, but the more you have, the greater the chance the marriage will last.

Today, marriage partners have a much more flexible view of marriage roles and responsibilities and are likely to expect each other to be a friend, lover, and confidant as well as wage-earner and care-giver.

Walt and Sarah have been married for eight years now. Walt believes in the "traditional" type of marriage, where there are male and

> After years of advising other people on their personal problems, I was stunned by my own divorce. I only wish I had someone to write to for advice.
>
> Ann Landers

When We Were in Love

Once upon a long ago when we were so in love,
    It seemed we'd never be apart, we're meant like hand in glove.
But years play tricks upon the young, and suddenly we're old,
    And though we love each other still, the fires of youth are cold.
The loving patience that we had is now in short supply,
    And keeping peace between us now is something we don't try,
The secret conversations we would have when night was deep,
    All about our hopes and dreams; and love instead of sleep,
We used to give each other comfort, sweet when we were sad,
    And face the world as man and wife; together things weren't bad.
But now our secret selves are hidden far away inside,
    Our little world of lovers young has withered up and died.
And though I'll love you always dear, it's not the same to me,
    Through all the lonely years ahead, apart we'll have to be.

as the children. In addition to learning how to live with one new person, which can be difficult enough for most people, one or both partners must also become accustomed to a ready made family. When the children are young, the stepparent has more opportunity to develop rapport and trust with the children. But when there are adolescents involved, it is more difficult for everyone involved. If the father too quickly assumes the authority as a parent, especially in matters of discipline, the stepchildren may resent it. Both parents must make allowances for their stepchildren's initial suspiciousness, jealousy, and resistance. One of the problems is that there are no rules or guidelines to assist stepparents in the process of building a happy blended family. When both parents develop a good working relationship, talking things out and cooperating on discipline and household chores, the blended family may do at least as well as intact families.

As we have previously noted, the traditional model of marriage has been undermined by many different changes within our culture. More and more people are selecting alternatives to marriage. Earlier in the chapter we discussed two alternatives, single life and cohabitation. Another alternative should be discussed.

Gay Relationships. Statistics indicate that there may be as many as twenty-five million gay people in the United States. Roughly 2 percent of the women and 4–5 percent of the men are exclusively homosexual (Laumann, et al., 1998).

The dynamics of a gay relationship do not seem to be any different than those in a heterosexual relationship. They are similar in terms of the forces that bring couples together, the factors that predict satisfaction with the relationship, and the problems couples face. Most of the material already discussed is relevant to gay couples.

The major problem that most gays encounter is the negative attitude about homosexuality in our society—especially now with people's attitude about AIDS. Most homosexual men and nearly all homosexual women prefer stable, long-term relationships. Promiscuity among gay men is clearly on the decline. Lesbian relationships are generally sexually exclusive. Gay relationships are characterized by great diversity. It is not true that gays usually assume traditional masculine and feminine roles. Both gays and heterosexual cohabitants may face opposition to their relationship from their families, and from society in general, and neither enjoys the legal and social sanctions of marriage.

As you read this, more and more states are considering giving more rights to non-traditional relationships, such as the same benefits married couples receive and also legally sanctioning these relationships.

The traditional model of marriage is being challenged by the increasing acceptability of additional alternatives. There are many more alternatives available to us now than we have had in the past. Some are considered acceptable to society and others are considered non-traditional or even unacceptable to others. Society and cultures change and evolve over time, not always for the best, but who are we to condemn others before we look into ourselves and accept ourselves as we really are.

Chapter Review

We are motivated not only to seek the company of others, but to form close and lasting relationships. The relationships you have are your greatest assets.

- Relationships evolve, they do not just happen. They take time and effort.
- The three steps involved in a relationship are:
  1. Becoming aware of the other person—first impression;
  2. Making contact or getting acquainted;
  3. Disclosure.
- Friends play a significant role in our lives. They provide us with *emotional support* and *social ties*. Without friends we experience loneliness.
- We are drawn to people who are similar to us. Research studies have found that similar beliefs and attitudes are the most important aspects of a relationship in order to keep a relationship together over a long period of time.
- In order to find friends, you must go to those places (proximity) where you will find other people who have similar interests and needs.
- The *repulsion hypothesis* indicates that many of us are repulsed by people whom we do not know and we perceive them as dissimilar to us.
- People with complementary needs tend to be drawn to each other—personality fit.
- We tend to like people who like us—reciprocity.
- We face two major hurdles in our quest for love and intimacy:
  1. to recognize what it takes to attract potential dates, mates, and friends; and
  2. to devise a strategy for meeting them.
- The most important factors people want in marital selection in China, India, Indonesia, Iran, Taiwan, and the Palestinian Arab culture is chastity. People from the Zulu culture in South Africa, Estonia, and Columbia placed a high value on housekeeping skills.
- Universally, both men and women want a mate who possesses emotional stability and maturity, dependability, a pleasing disposition, and good health.
- Men, worldwide, prefer wives who are younger than they are. Women in all cultures preferred husbands who were older—because men mature somewhat later than women and because older men often have access to more resources.
- Love is complex and confusing. Everyone thinks they know what love is.
- Harry Stack Sullivan has given us an excellent definition of love—"When the satisfaction, security, and development of another person is as important to you as your own satisfaction, security and development, love exists."
- Robert Sternberg has developed a theory of love that includes three components: passion—an intense physiological desire for another person; intimacy—the feeling that one can share all one's thoughts and actions with another; commitment—the willingness to stay with a person through thick and thin, etc.
- Cultural factors have a strong influence on the value of love. Romantic love is more likely to be considered an important basis for marriage in individualistic societies than in collectivistic ones.
- A recent study indicates that there are six types of love that many of us participate in: game-playing love, possessive love, logical love, altruistic love, companionate love, and exotic love.
- Psychological reactance is the tendency to protect or restore one's sense of freedom or social control, often doing the opposite of what has been demanded. This is also known as the Romeo and Juliet effect.
- Although alternatives to marriage are more viable than ever, over ninety percent of us will marry at least once. Individuals are waiting longer to get married.
- Cohabitation has become increasingly more common throughout the world. Couples who do decide to cohabit are at a higher risk of divorce than couples who do not.
- Most research indicates that the most important reasons to make a marriage last is: be your spouses' best friend, having similar beliefs, values and attitudes, exhibit a high degree of flexibility, having a positive attitude toward one's partner, and a couple needs to learn to adjust and compromise.

- The more two partners agree about marital roles, the more likely the marriage will last over a longer period of time. It is imperative that couples discuss role expectations in depth before marriage.
- Overall, research indicates that adults who combine all three roles—spouse, parent and employee—are healthier and happier than those who do not.
- Successful communication is the cornerstone of any relationship. Such communication must be open, realistic, tactful, caring, and valued. Physical violence is most apt to erupt in families lacking communication skills.
- John Gottman's research indicates that most relationships will be successful as long as the couple maintain the five-to-one ratio of positive responses to negative responses.
- A codependent relationship is where one person has allowed another person's behavior (abuse, chemical addiction, etc.) to affect him or her, and is obsessed with controlling that person's behavior.
- Jealousy is defined as the thoughts and feelings that arise when an actual or desired relationship is threatened, and envy as the thoughts and feelings that arise when our personal qualities, possessions, or achievements do not measure up to those of someone relevant to us.
- Divorce is two and one-half times more common than it was twenty years ago. It can have a devastating effect on the individuals involved, including the children. Over 80 percent of all divorced people will remarry.
- Statistics indicate that roughly two percent of all women and four to five percent of the men in the United States are homosexual.

"Real love" is loving what is real in your partner rather than what is desired. "Mature love" is being committed to the emotional and spiritual welfare of your partner as you are your own. A relationship is only as healthy as the people involved.

??? Questions ???

1. Discuss what is involved in the three steps in the development of a relationship.
2. What are the qualities of a good friend?
3. Explain the importance of similarities, proximity, complementarity, and reciprocity in the development of friendships.
4. What are the universal mate preferences shared by men and women?
5. Discuss the effective strategies for meeting dates and mates.
6. Discuss the difference between love and infatuation.
7. Describe Sternberg's theory of love.
8. Explain the six types of love described in the chapter.
9. Explain the phenomenon known as psychological reactance (the Romeo and Juliet effect).
10. Describe the positive and negative aspects of cohabitation.
11. What makes a happy and successful marriage?
12. Discuss how role expectations influence a relationship.
13. What do most couples argue about? Why?
14. Explain the five-to-one ratio. Why?
15. Explain how to fight constructively and not destructively.
16. What is a codependent relationship?
17. Describe the difference between jealousy and envy.
18. Explain the impact of divorce on the individuals involved, including children.
19. Describe the steps in divorce grief.

✎ Key Terms ✎

Altruistic love
Blended Families
Codependent
Cohabitation
Commitment
Communication
Companionate Love
Complementarity
Confidant
Consummate Love
Divorce
Empty Love
Envy
Exotic love

Fatuous Love
Five-to-one ratio
Friend
Game-playing love
Gay Relationships
Honeymoon Period
Infatuation
Intimacy
Jealousy
Liking
Living Together
Logical love
Loneliness (LTL)
Love

Lust
Marriage
Parenthood
Possessive love
Psychological reactance
Reciprocity
Remarriage
Repulsion hypothesis
Role Expectation
Romantic Love
Romeo and Juliet effect
Similarities
Singlehood

??? Discussion ???

1. Why do we need friends?
2. What is your definition of a good friend? Explain what a good friend is.
3. If you knew someone who was new to town, what would you recommend they do to find new friends?
4. Friendships satisfy needs. Study three relationships (friendships) that you currently have. What needs are they satisfying for you? Explain.
5. What is your definition of love? How do you know when you are in love?
6. What are the pro's and con's of cohabitation vs. marriage? Explain.
7. What are your experiences with jealousy? How should a person deal with a jealous lover?
8. Explain the role of the male and the role of the female in a married relationship. Are these roles different from how your parents viewed the role within their marriage? Explain.
9. What direct or indirect impact has divorce had on your life?
10. Explain codependence. Have you ever been in a codependent relationship? Discuss the relationship and explain how you could change the situation.

Roles and Expectations

Purpose: To discover the roles and expectations people have of themselves and other people in specific categories such as a spouse, parent, student, breadwinner, male, and female.

Instructions:

I. Select one of the three alternatives:
   1. Ask four to five married students (preferably, not from the class) to be on a panel. Have the students ask questions regarding roles and expectations in a marriage.
   2. Divide into groups of approximately six individuals (three females and three males would be ideal).
   3. Each student interviews six or more individuals, from different careers, from different socio-economic income levels, and/or different ethnic groups.

II. Discuss the following:
   The class may want to create their own questions or ask the questions listed below and then answer the discussion questions.
   1. What career have each of you chosen for yourself? What type of career is selected by the females; by the males? Are the careers sex-role oriented?
   2. What roles do you expect to play at home? Specify the tasks you are willing or not willing to do.
   3. What role will you take as a parent (full-time parent, half-time, change diapers, and so on).
   4. What role will you take as a breadwinner?

Discussion

1. Do you see evidence that today's college students subscribe to traditional sex roles or that they are free of such barriers to independent choice? Give examples.

2. What messages did you receive as you were growing up regarding specific expectations or behaviors appropriate to your gender?

3. How do you feel that your life would be different, if at all, if you were a member of the opposite sex? (Imagine, when you wake up tomorrow morning, you are the opposite sex) What would you do? How would you act? Would others relate to you differently? What would your expectations of yourself be? How would they change?

Name _____ Date _____

Are You Compatible?

Purpose: To discover whether you and your prospective mate or date are compatible.

Instructions: Answer the following questions with the appropriate number.

1 = Strongly agree
2 = Agree
3 = Neither agree or disagree
4 = Disagree
5 = Strongly disagree

1. We have similar religious beliefs and values. _____

2. We enjoy the same type of leisure activities. _____

3. We like each other's friends. _____

4. We enjoy each other's sense of humor. _____

5. We like to be with each other as much as we can. _____

6. We are willing to share whatever we have with each other. _____

7. We share our thoughts and feelings about even the most private topics. _____

8. We have similar political values and beliefs. _____

9. We are willing to listen to each other's problems and help resolve each other's problems. _____

10. We tend to agree on how to spend money and how to save money. _____

11. We support our partner's interest and activities even if they differ from our own. _____

12. Our personal lives, work schedules, sleep habits, outside interests and activities, fit together harmoniously. _____

13. We work well together in making decisions. _____

14. We are able to resolve conflict situations without getting too emotional or aggressive toward one another. _____

15. Our efforts to work out differences usually bring us closer together. _____

16. We desire the same level of openness. _____

17. We are able to work out a division of tasks and who is responsible for specific responsibilities. _____

18. We are both neat or disorderly, etc. _____

19. We enjoy the same type of vacations and travel. _____

20. We share pleasant feelings and unpleasant feelings about each other and our relationship. _____

Scoring: Add up your total score. The higher the score the less compatible you seem to be: between 60–80. The lower the score the more compatible you seem to be: between 20–40.

After you have completed the rating scale, answer the following questions:

1. Why is it important to have a lot in common with your mate?

2. How can you improve your relationship with your mate to make your relationship more compatible?

3. Do you think that two people who score high on this test could still be compatible? Explain.

Relationship Survey

Purpose: To develop an understanding of people's perception of different aspects of a relationship.

Instructions: You are going to do a survey. The class will decide whether you want to survey only students at your school or include people within the community.

I. The class, as a large group, may decide on the question or questions to be asked.

II. The questions should relate to the material in this chapter, such as:

What is love?

What is a friend?

What are the five most important qualities of a friend?

Should a couple live together before marriage?

What are the advantages and disadvantages of living together prior to marriage?

What are the most effective strategies to help someone find a date or mate?

III. Each student is to survey at least five individuals. (If you have 20 students in your class, you will end up with at least 100 responses)

Another alternative would be to do this as a group activity. Divide the class into groups of no more than four people per group. Each group may create their own question or questions. Each group member will ask at least ten different people the question or questions (If any of the group members has use of a computer (Internet), you may be able to get many more responses). Each group will compile the results and then discuss the answers with the rest of the class.

You may want to see if you can get the results of your survey published in your school newspaper or in your local newspaper.

Discussion

1. What did you learn from your results?

2. Do you think the results would be valuable information for other people to know about? Explain.

3. Did you get the answers that you expected? Explain.

4. Do you believe that surveys are good ways to get accurate information?

Name _____   Date _____

Mate Selection

Purpose: To identify the characteristics that are most important to you in selecting the person you wish to date or marry.

Instructions:

I. Rate each of the following factors according to their importance to you in selecting the person you would wish to marry (#1 = most important characteristic, #18 = least important characteristic).

Intelligence	Good looks
Emotional stability and maturity	Ambition and industriousness
Good financial prospects	Dependable character
Similar educational background	Good health
Social ability (friendly)	Similar political backgrounds
Similar religious background	Pleasing disposition
Desire for children	Neatness
Refinement	Chastity
Mutual love and attraction	Favorable social status or rating

II. List characteristics according to importance to you.

1.   10.

2.   11.

3.   12.

4.   13.

5.   14.

6.   15.

7.   16.

8.   17.

9.   18.

III. Divide into groups of three to four people. Discuss the following questions.
   1. How do the top four characteristics on your list differ from the other members of your group? Explain.

   2. Discuss why you think your top four characteristics are so important to you.

3. Do you think the importance of these characteristics would be different in different cultures or different socio-economic income levels?

4. After discussing these characteristics with the group, would you change the order of your list? Why or why not?

Rate-A-Mate

Purpose: To discover what is important to you and others in selecting a partner. What is important to you in selecting a prospective partner? What is important for other individuals in selecting a partner? How do you think people from other cultures would respond to this survey?

Instructions:

1. Take the survey individually to see what is important to you in a prospective partner. (Make a copy before you complete the survey)

2. Give the survey to one of your parents, or someone at least twenty years older than you.

3. As a group or individually, you may want to select individuals from other cultures or different socio-economic groups, or both.

4. If you are involved in a relationship presently, give this survey to your partner.

5. Take the survey again, but this time, circle the number as you see it relating to you. For example, give yourself a 4 if you feel your health is excellent, a 1 if you are not a good cook or housekeeper, etc.

Circle the number indicating the importance to you.

	Indispensable or extremely important	Very highly desired	Desired, but not terribly important	Irrelevant or unimportant
Good health	4	3	2	1
Good cook and housekeeper	4	3	2	1
Attractiveness	4	3	2	1
Pleasing disposition	4	3	2	1
Dependable character	4	3	2	1
Emotional stability	4	3	2	1
Desire for home and children	4	3	2	1
Refinement	4	3	2	1
Good financial prospect	4	3	2	1
Similar political background	4	3	2	1
Ambitious and industriousness	4	3	2	1
Chastity—No sexual intercourse before marriage	4	3	2	1
Sociable (friendly)	4	3	2	1
Favorable social status	4	3	2	1
Mutual interests	4	3	2	1
Similar educational background	4	3	2	1
Intelligence	4	3	2	1
Complementarity	4	3	2	1

Scoring: Add up your total score. If your score is within 15 points of another individual that took the survey there is a high probability that you will get along well. But, the important aspect to consider is that your score on each individual value is similar to the individuals who are important to you.

Discussion

1. How important is it for partners to have similar values? Can a couple be compatible with many dissimilar values?

2. Are your values different from a person twenty years older than you? What are the differences? Why do you think they have different values?

3. How do your values differ with people from different cultures and different socio-economic groups? Explain.

4. Do you think it should be important to have a partner whose score is similar to your score as you took the survey the second time (as #5 in the instructions stated)? Explain.

5. What did you learn from this experience?

Why People Get Divorced—Why People Get Married

Purpose:
- To better understand why people divorce and what it requires to choose to remain married.
- To get a better understanding of why people stay married.
- To discover if unmarried individuals perceive the reasons for divorce differently than divorced individuals.
- To discover whether unmarried, married, and divorced individuals have similar perceptions of why people stay married.

Instructions:

I. Interview four to six people who have been divorced, four to six people who have never been married, and four to six people who are married to find out why they feel divorce generally occurs. (You may want to use the form available at the end of this activity.)

II. Ask them what they would consider the major reason (in order of importance) for the high divorce rate in this country. (Ask the divorced individuals to make this judgment based on their own experiences.)

III. Ask them what they would consider the major reasons (in order of importance) for staying married.

IV. Divide into small groups or have a large class discussion.

Discussion

1. Do any individuals consider unrealistic romantic expectations to be a contributing factor for getting divorced? If so, what are they?

2. Do the divorced and the never-married people respond differently? If so, how would you characterize these differences? If not, why do you think people agree on the basic causes even when they have had very different experiences?

3. What seems to be the major reasons for divorce?

4. What seems to be the major reasons for staying married?

5. What could we do to prevent the high number of divorces in our society?

6. Did the exercise stimulate your thinking about yourself, your interpersonal style, and your relationships to your fellow group members? Why or why not?

Name: _____ **Date:** _____

Marital Status: _____ **Age:** _____

1. What would you consider the major reasons are for the high divorce rate in this country? (List in order of importance) Note: Divorced individuals will need to make this judgment based on their own experiences.

2. What would you consider the major reasons are for staying married? (In order of importance)

3. What do you think could be done to decrease the divorce rate in the United States?

Developing Close Relationships

Learning Journal

Select the statement below that best defines your feelings about the personal value or meaning gained from this chapter and respond below the dotted line.

- **I learned that I . . .**

- **I realized that I . . .**

- **I discovered that I . . .**

- **I was surprised that I . . .**

- **I was pleased that I . . .**

- **I was displeased that I . . .**

. . . .

continue on reverse

CHAPTER 7

Resolving Interpersonal Conflict

Arguments
Remind me
Of hot grease
In a skillet.

I can't
Control
Where it
Will pop next;

And if I don't
Stand back
Or turn the
Fire down.

I'll get
All splattered
And
Burned.

Delyn Dendy Harrison
Some Things Are Better Said
in Black and White.

*(Fort Worth, TX: Branch Smith, Inc., 1978.) *Used with permission.*

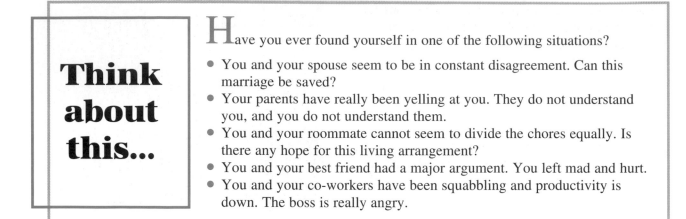

Think about this...

Have you ever found yourself in one of the following situations?

● You and your spouse seem to be in constant disagreement. Can this marriage be saved?
● Your parents have really been yelling at you. They do not understand you, and you do not understand them.
● You and your roommate cannot seem to divide the chores equally. Is there any hope for this living arrangement?
● You and your best friend had a major argument. You left mad and hurt.
● You and your co-workers have been squabbling and productivity is down. The boss is really angry.

Actually, the list could go on and on, but the fact is clear: when two or more people live or work closely together, for any length of time, a degree of conflict will be generated. Furthermore, the greater the emotional involvement and day-to-day sharing, the greater the potential for conflict. Although it is impossible to eliminate conflict, there are ways to manage it effectively. There is *hope* for healthier, stronger, and more satisfying relationships.

WHAT IS CONFLICT?

The word *conflict* comes from the Latin roots *com* meaning "together," and *figere* meaning to "strike." Common synonyms of conflict emphasize words like "struggle," "fight," "clash," and "sharp disagreements." Using these thoughts, Joyce Hocker and William Wilmot (1997) provide an interesting definition of conflict. Their idea is that *conflict* is an expressed struggle between at least two people who perceive the situation differently and are experiencing interference from the other person in achieving their goals. Author Jeffrey Rubin (1994) and his colleagues add some additional insights: *conflict* is a perception that one person's goals, plans, and aspirations are incompatible with another's.

What causes these struggles, interferences, and perceptions?

> Little things often become the major irritants of life.
>
> Robert Bolton

WHAT CAUSES CONFLICT?

Conflicts occur between people because people are different, think differently, and have different needs and wants. In fact, social psychologist Morton Deutsch (1973) believes that conflicts usually involve any of six basic types of issues: *1) control over resources, 2) preferences and nuisances, 3) values, 4) beliefs, 5) goals, and 6) the nature of the relationship between the partners.*

Perhaps the key word is *differentness,* because this is what causes conflict in human relationships. Differentness is a reality to reckon with, and the reality is that people enter relationships with differences in socioeconomic and cultural backgrounds, sex-role expectations, levels of self-esteem, ability to tolerate stress, tastes and preferences, beliefs and values, interests, social and family networks, and capacity to change and grow (Wright, 1999). And, add to these differences that many people are deficient in communication and conflict resolution skills and frequently have misunderstood styles of conflict management (Tannen, 1999). Therefore, it is easy to understand why *differentness* leads to disagreement and conflict.

THE REALITIES OF CONFLICT

Even though conflict is inevitable, it can have positive as well as negative effects. Thomas Gordan (1990), noted author and psychologist, explains this clearly:

What do you think these two people might be disagreeing about?

> A conflict is the moment of truth in a relationship—a test of its health, a crisis that can weaken or strengthen it, a critical event that may bring lasting resentment, smoldering hostility, psychological scars. Conflicts can push people away from each other or pull them into a closer and more intimate union; they contain the seeds of destruction and the seeds of greater unity; they may bring about armed warfare or deeper mutual understanding.

In our society conflict is often viewed negatively: It is "bad" to show anger, to disagree, or to fight. Some people look at conflict as something to avoid at all costs; but conflict is not necessarily bad—it exists as a reality of any relationship.

It would be a rare relationship if over a period of time one person's needs did not conflict with the other's needs. Authors Linda Hjorth and Maria Bakalis (1998) make a point by saying:

> With living and loving come risk and conflict. Human relationships cannot be put into a vacuum, void of difficulties and personal differences.

A quarrel between friends, when made up, adds a new tie to friendship, as experience shows that the callosity formed round a broken bone makes it stronger than before.

St. Francis De Salis

Every day of my life, I'm forced to add another name to the list of people who create problems for me!

Permanent List

_____

_____

_____

_____

List for Today

_____

_____

_____

_____

Since conflict is inevitable, coping with confrontations is one of the most critical of social skills. It's not the degree of conflict that sinks relationships, but the ways people resolve it. We must remember that conflict needs to be viewed from a problem-solving perspective. Often, solutions bring about change, and changes in a relationship should not be feared. Human relationships are dynamic and reflect the changes that accompany personal growth. Disagreements, if handled well, can help people know themselves better, improve language skills, gain valuable information, and cement their relationships (Marano, 2000). Constructive ways for resolving conflict will be discussed later in the chapter.

We will now discuss in more detail three common benefits of constructive conflict resolution (Duncan and Rock, 1993).

> *Most families today need more honest conflict and less suppression of feeling.*
>
> Gibson Winter

POSITIVE EFFECTS OF CONFLICT

Promotes Growth in a Relationship. **People who work through their conflicts can develop a stronger and more intimate relationship. They take the time to learn about each other's needs and how they can be satisfied. They take the time to clarify their feelings. They take the time to share, and in so doing, realize that dealing with problems can be an opportunity to know each other better.**

Allows for Healthy Release of Feelings. **When conflicts are resolved in constructive ways, both parties are able to air their feelings and leave the situation free of anger and hostility. For example, in a family conflict, unresolved anger and hostility can affect a person's performance at work or school. Likewise, unresolved anger and hostility in a work-related conflict is frequently brought home and may interfere with family and even social relationships. Talking things out and sharing what is going on are marvelous ways to relieve tension and anxiety.**

Increases Motivation and Self-Esteem. **When you have been able to resolve a personal conflict, or make a difficult decision, you naturally feel stronger and more motivated to tackle other struggles and difficult times. There is a real sense of pride and freedom when you join others and show respect for your rights and the rights of others. As a result, self-esteem is enhanced, and you are more motivated to take other interpersonal risks. In *Born for Love,* a remarkable book of challenging lessons in loving, Leo Buscaglia (1994) offers these thoughts:**

> Ideally, overcoming conflicts is all about adding new insights and acquiring new skills. When we approach obstacles as opportunities for making ourselves over, we not only find solutions, we also immeasurably enhance our general problem-solving abilities as well.

Cathy Birch (1999) in her book *Asserting Yourself,* stresses that conflicts can be turned into creative opportunities for more positive, healthy, and happy relationships. However, conflict can be destructive and result in negative outcomes, too.

People who work through their conflicts can develop a stronger relationship.

NEGATIVE EFFECTS OF CONFLICT

How we view conflicts and how we manage them can cause destructive outcomes. Johnson and Johnson (1989) outline two negative effects:

The Manner in Which We Approach Interpersonal Conflict. People generally view conflict with a belief that there must be a winner and a loser. It is human nature to want to win, just like it is human nature to not want to lose. When people approach a conflict situation with attitudes of winning and losing, a "tug of war" is often proclaimed. The net result is often one of disaster.

Larger Problems and Deeper Personal Resentments May Occur. Just because you avoid a conflict or fail to resolve a conflict does not mean the conflict is forever gone. It is likely to return again with much greater intensity. You may be less willing to cooperate if you have leftover anger or "bad" feelings from a previous confrontation. Failure to deal with conflict constructively can even "rob" you of a potentially satisfying relationship.

So far, we have been discussing the positive and negative realities of conflict. The question now is: How can we manage conflict in such a way as to minimize the risks and maximize the benefits? We will start by examining the makeup of a conflict situation. Perhaps we can then determine why some conflicts do not get resolved.

> Just as communication is the most important element in a relationship, arguments can be the most destructive element.
>
> John Gray

WHAT IS INVOLVED IN A CONFLICT SITUATION?

In order to resolve conflict, we must recognize that there are three elements to a conflict situation: *self, other person,* and the *issue.* (It should be noted here that the terms *self* and *other person* also mean individual or groups.) Any interpersonal conflict can be diagrammed like Figure 7.1.

Dealing with Self, Other Person, and the Issue. As we discover ourselves in a conflict, we are inside the circle of the situation with the other person and the issue. If the conflict is to be resolved constructively, all of these elements must be dealt with congruently. That means *your* feelings are important, the *other person's* feelings are important, and the *issue* is important. If any element is removed, the conflict cannot be resolved. According to Virginia Satir (1988) and Paula Englander-Golden and Virginia Satir (1990), our tendency is to:

Conflict Situation

Self (feelings)

Other Person (feelings)

Issue (What the conflict is about)

Figure 7.1

1. **Placate or conceal our own feelings** by saying statements like, "Yes, it was all my fault, I am sorry, forgive me." The placater tends to talk in an insinuating way, trying to please and apologize at the same time. When we placate, we remove the *"self"* from the conflict, leaving the *"issue"* and the *"other person."* Paula Englander-Golden and Virginia Satir (1990) in their stimulating book *Say It Straight,* personalize the result of placating: *When you placate, you cross out yourself. You believe that the other person's feelings and the issue are all that is important.* The situation then looks like Figure 7.2.

> Our marriage used to suffer from arguments that were too short. Now, we argue long enough to find out what the argument is about.
>
> Hugh Prather

2. **Blame the other person** by saying, "This is all your fault— can't you see where you messed up!" "You never do anything right!" The blamer is a fault-finder, a dictator, and a boss. When we do this, we remove the *"other person"* from the conflict, leaving the *"self"* and the *"issue."* Englander-Golden and Satir (1990) summarize the effect of blaming: *When you blame, you cross out the other person's feelings. You actually believe that your feelings are important, and the issue is important. However, the other person's feelings don't matter.* The diagram now changes to Figure 7.3.

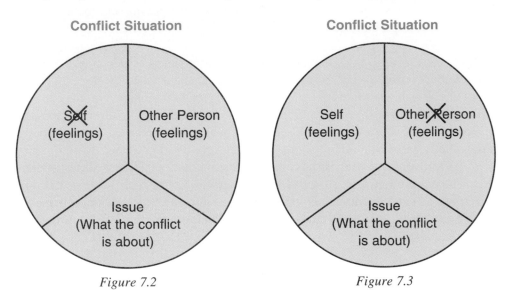

Figure 7.2	*Figure 7.3*

> We are not responsible for other peoples' behavior; we are responsible for our response to it. When something painful happens in our interactions, we have the responsibility to look at whatever part of the mess we contributed.
>
> Paula Englander-Golden and Virginia Satir

3. Be **super-reasonable** by delivering a factual lecture or sermon. For example, "You need to apply yourself more seriously if you want to get a decent job when you graduate. Read this article in last week's newspaper. It proves what I am trying to tell you." This is referred to as the *computer,* being very correct and logical, with no semblance of any feeling showing. This tends to remove *"both persons"* involved in the conflict, leaving only the *"issue."* Englander-Golden and Satir (1990) review the effect of being super-reasonable: *When you are super-reasonable, you cross out your feelings and the other person's feelings. You believe that the facts are the only thing that matters.* The conflict then looks like Figure 7.4.

4. **Hold the issue irrelevant** by saying, "Everybody has problems and disagreements. No big deal. Let's go get a pizza and go to the movie." This is frequently referred to as the *distractor,* with the goal being to respond in an irrelevant way to what anyone else is saying or doing. This removes the *"issue"* and *"both persons."* Englander-Golden and Satir (1990) explain the result of holding the issue irrelevant: *When you are irrelevant, you cross out the other person's feelings, your own feelings, and even the issue. Nothing matters!* The conflict situation now looks like Figure 7.5.

THE DIMENSIONS OF CONFLICT

From our previous discussion, it would be logical to conclude that there are two main dimensions of any conflict situation. We will refer to these as the *emotional* or *feeling* dimension and the *issue* dimension. If conflicts do not get resolved because we sometimes disregard the feelings of the people involved, as

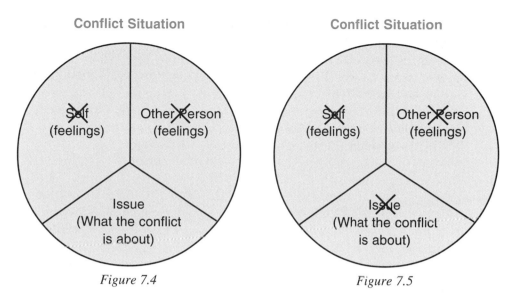

Figure 7.4   *Figure 7.5*

well as the issue involved, then there must be three important questions for us to answer.

First, how can we deal with the feelings of anger, distrust, defensiveness, resentment, fear, and rejection, which are often a part of a conflict situation?

Second, how can we deal with the issues of conflicting needs, preferences, values, and beliefs?

Third, do we deal with the issue dimension or the feeling dimension first?

THE EMOTIONS (FEELINGS) HAVE PRIORITY

It is sometimes difficult to separate the feeling dimension from the issue dimension. They frequently interact with each other. Issue conflict often generates into emotional conflict—anger, resentment, and so on. Emotional conflicts multiply the issues into additional differences over needs, goals, values, and beliefs.

Although it is vitally important to examine the tangible issues, most authorities agree that rational problem solving should usually be the second step.

Robert Bolton (1986), author and communication consultant, offers this advice: *"When feelings run high, rational problem solving needs to be preceded by a structured exchange of the emotional aspects of the controversy."* George Odiome (1974), a management consultant, confirms this thought: *"When a person is emotionally equipped for a brawl, he's very poorly equipped to get a problem solved."*

Let us look first at how we can deal effectively with the emotional content. Then, we will discuss the dif-ferent behavior styles and approaches used in conflict resolution. The chapter will be concluded with how to deal with the important tangible issues—referred to as *collaborative problem solving,* or the *win-win* approach to conflict resolution.

DEALING WITH THE EMOTIONAL DIMENSION

In order to deal with the emotional content of any conflict, Bolton (1986) believes it is important to remember the following rules of conflict resolution. You will recall that some of these principles were also discussed in Chapter 5.

While my emotions are throbbing with these fears, angers, and self-defensive urges, I am in no condition to have an open-minded, honest and living discussion with you or with anyone else. I will need . . . emotional clearance and ventilation . . . before I will be ready for this discussion.

John Powell

Rule 1: Treat the Other Person with Respect. You convey respect, or lack of respect by:

1. the way you look at the other person—do you approve or disapprove with various facial gestures?
2. the way you listen to the other person—do you maintain eye contact? do you appear bored with the conversation?
3. tone of voice used—do you speak in a harsh, loud tone?
4. selection of words—do you "put down" the other person?

Rule 2: Listen Until You Experience the Other Side. This can best be achieved by remembering Carl Rogers' (1995) communication rule discussed in Chapter 5: *Each person can speak up for himself only after he has first restated the ideas and feelings of the previous speaker accurately and to that speaker's satisfaction.* This means we try to understand the content of what the other person is saying, what the meaning is for him, and the feelings he has about it. It also means we actually try to step into the other person's shoes and look at the situation from his point of view.

Rule 3: State Your Views, Needs, and Feelings. After you have demonstrated respect for the other person and conveyed your understanding of his or her feelings and point of view, it is then time to express your feelings to the other person. This means you: 1) keep your message short, 2) avoid loaded words that may hurt or harm others, and 3) be honest and state the truth as it really is for you.

Do you deal with the emotional content as suggested above? When faced with a conflict, how do you handle it?

WHAT IS YOUR STYLE OF CONFLICT MANAGEMENT?

You are probably thinking that your style of conflict management depends on the conflict and who is involved. Although that is probably true, most people

How to . . .
. . . Master Interpersonal Conflict

Disagreements are inevitable, but they can be kept to a minimum and prevented from escalating into major blowups if you do not blame other people.

Think about the conflict before you react, then accept the challenge of changing yourself.

To master interpersonal conflict:

●   Understand why you feel and respond the way you do.
●   Observe how you respond when you are faced with conflict situations.
●   Feel the discomfort of not being in control of the situation.
●   Take responsibility for your actions.
●   Commit yourself to changing your behavior.
●   Find better ways to handle these types of situations.

have developed a characteristic style of managing conflicts. This style has emerged from our unique personality traits, as well as from what we learned growing up.

Think for a moment about how your parents managed conflicts. If your mother cried, sulked, or avoided confrontations, you may find yourself imitating her behavior. If your father yelled, intimidated, and dominated others with his anger, you may see some of these traits in your own pattern of conflict management. The question then is: How is your style of conflict management like and unlike those of your parents?

Actually, most of us go through life responding to conflict in a natural way that feels good to us. We may be unaware of our particular style and of even what methods we use to resolve interpersonal conflict. We may continue to use our approach whether it is appropriate or not.

Before we discuss the ways of responding to conflict, it might be beneficial to identify some interpersonal rights that each person has in interpersonal interactions, whether conflictual or not. Based on the writings of Smith (1985), Grasha (1995), and Davis, et al., (1998) the "Consider this" box below lists a sample of Basic Human Rights.

Now that you know some rights that each person has in interpersonal interactions, what would your answers be to these questions: Is it difficult for you to make your wishes known to others? Are you sometimes pushed around by others

> We do not understand an opposing idea until we have so exposed ourselves to it that we feel the pull of its persuasion.
>
> Dr. Richard Cabot

CONSIDER THIS . . .
Basic Human Rights

1. The right to say no to a request without feeling guilty
2. The right not to give people reasons for every action you take
3. The right to ask other people to listen to your point of view
4. The right to ask others to correct errors they made that affect you
5. The right to change your mind
6. The right to ask other people to compromise rather than get only what they want
7. The right to ask others to do things for you
8. The right to persist in making a request if people will not respond the first time
9. The right to be alone if you wish
10. The right to maintain your dignity in relationships
11. The right to evaluate your own behavior and not just listen to evaluations that others offer
12. The right to make mistakes and accept responsibility for them
13. The right to avoid manipulation by other people
14. The right to have and express your own feelings and opinions
15. The right to get what you pay for
16. The right to ask for information from professionals
17. The right to choose not to assert yourself
18. The right to set your own priorities
19. The right to be successful
20. The right to be treated with respect

> The test of a man or woman's breeding is how they behave in a quarrel.
>
> George Bernard Shaw

Smith, (1985); Grasha, (1995); Davis, et al. (1998)

A person's individual rights in any relationship are the same rights he enjoyed before he even knew the other person existed. Rights are not to be bargained for: They simply exist. A relationship's task is to recognize and protect the rights of both parties.

David Viscott

because of your own inability to stand up for yourself? Do you ever push others around to get what you want? Do you speak your thoughts and feelings in a clear, direct manner, without judging or dictating to others? Do you use clean fighting or dirty fighting techniques in resolving your conflicts? The answers to these questions characterize your behavior style in responding to conflict.

BEHAVIOR STYLES

Now, we will return to our earlier question: How do you respond to conflict? George Bach (1989), a leading authority on conflict resolution and communication skills, has indicated that people tend to deal with conflict by using clean fighting or dirty fighting techniques. Dirty fighting techniques can weaken relationships and cause much pain, resentment, and hostility. Table 7.1 shows some of the ways that people engage in dirty fighting behavior to resolve conflicts.

There are basically three behavior styles we use in handling opposition and responding to conflict. These have been classified as *passive* (also known as nonassertive), *aggressive, and assertive*. We will now discuss the behaviors, belief systems, advantages, disadvantages, and when it might be appropriate to use each style.

Table 7.1   Dirty Fighting Techniques

THE KITCHEN SINKER—throws in everything that has been a problem instead of dealing with the specific conflict at hand.	**THE BACK STABBER**—after agreeing to a solution fails to carry out or express different opinions to parties outside the conflict.	**THE BLAMER**—is concerned with assigning guilt or placing blame for the conflict, rather than resolving it.
THE AVOIDER—pretends the conflict does not exist and refuses to deal with it in an open manner.	**THE STAMP COLLECTOR**—stores up days or months of hurt feelings and resentment and "cashes" them all in at once.	**THE MARTYR**—attempts to change the other person's behavior through a guilt-trip, hoping the other person will feel some responsibility for the martyr's pain.
THE ARMCHAIR PSYCHIATRIST—attempts to read the other person's mind, making sure to tell the other person why he or she is doing "whatever" they are doing.	**THE JOKER**—refuses to take the fight seriously, laughing at the other person, making a joke, or even avoiding the conflict.	**THE WITHHOLDER**—intentionally denies what the other person wants—sex, affection, approval, or anything else that makes life more pleasant for the other person.
THE IRRITATOR—intentionally expresses resentment by doing something that really annoys the other person: smacking gum loudly, turning up the TV too loud, and so on.	**THE TRAITOR**—openly encourages attacks from outsiders or refuses to defend the partner when he or she is being put down by others.	**THE HUMILIATOR**—uses intimate knowledge of the other person to "hit" below the belt. This is usually a sensitive issue the other person is trying to overcome.

Bach, (1989)

Passive Style

You may respond to conflict situations by *avoidance.* That is, you may remove yourself from the situation by leaving, shutting up, placating, concealing your feelings, or postponing a confrontation until a better time (Hocker & Wilmot, 1997).

Behavior Description: When you behave passively, sometimes referred to as *submissively,* you are usually emotionally dishonest, indirect, and self-denying. You are likely to listen to what has been said and respond very little. Because you do not express your honest feelings, needs, values, and concerns, you actually allows others to violate your space, deny your rights, and ignore your needs. More importantly, you actually demonstrate a lack of respect for your own needs and rights.

Belief System: The message of a submissive person is, "I should never make anyone uncomfortable or displeased except myself. I'll put up with just about anything from you; my needs and my feelings don't matter, you can take advantage of me."

Advantage: You usually do not experience direct rejection or get blamed for anything. Others may view you as nice, selfless, and easy to get along with. This approval from others is extremely important to you.

Disadvantage: You are taken advantage of and may store *up a heavy load of resentment and anger.* You do not get your needs met and other people do not know what you want or need. Consequently, passive people lack deep and enduring friendships. They frequently lose the love and respect of the people they were busy making sacrifices for.

When to Use: When neither the goal nor the relationship is very important, it may be wiser to just avoid the conflict.

> Are there genuinely nice, sweet people in the world? Yes, and they get angry as often as you and I. They must—otherwise, they would be full of vindictive feelings, which would prevent genuine sweetness.
>
> Theodore Rubin

Aggressive Style

You may respond to conflicting situations by *fight.* That is, you *move against* another with the intent to hurt. In his book *Human Aggression,* Green (1991) refers to the aggressive style as *domination.*

Behavior Description: You may literally, or verbally attack another person. Typical examples of aggressive behavior are fighting, blaming, accusing, threatening, and generally stepping on people without regard for their feelings, needs, or ideas. You may be loud, abusive, rude, and sarcastic. You are in this world to intimidate and to overpower other people.

Belief System: The message of an aggressive person is, "I have to put others down in order to protect myself; I must exert my power and control over others. This is what I want; what you want is of lesser importance or of no importance at all."

Advantage: Other people do not push the aggressive person around, so they seem to wind up getting what they want. They tend to be able to protect themselves and their own space. They *appear* to be in control of their own life and even the lives of others.

> Cutting comments create hostility.
>
> Haim Ginott

Disadvantage: In the process of gaining control, the other person in the interaction frequently feels humiliated, defensive, resentful, and usually hurt. Others do not want to be around you, and you wind up with an accumulation of enemies. This causes you to become more vulnerable and fearful of losing what you are fighting for: power and control over others. Therefore, you may create your own destruction.

When to Use: When your goal is important and the relationship involved is considerably less important, you may want to move against your opposition.

Assertive Style

You may respond to conflicting situations by *moving toward*. That is, you move toward your opposition until you are either closer together or on the same side. In *The Encyclopedia of Conflict Resolution*, Heidi and Guy Burgess (1997) indicate this style is used in *cooperative (collaborative) problem solving*, with some negotiation and compromise along the way.

Behavior Description: You behave assertively when you stand up for yourself, express your true feelings, and do not let others take advantage of you. However, you are considerate of others' feelings. Actually, assertion is a manner of acting and reacting in an appropriately honest manner that is direct, self-respecting, self-expressing, and straightforward. You defend your rights and personal space without abusing or dominating other people. Joseph Telushkin (1996), in his powerful book, *Words That Hurt, Words That Heal,* expresses these thoughts:

> In a dispute with someone, you have the right to state your case, express your opinion, explain why you think the other party is wrong, even make clear how passionately you feel about the subject at hand. But these are the only rights you have. You do not have a moral right to undercut your adversary's position by invalidating him or her personally. It is unethical to dredge up past information about the person—information with which you're most likely familiar because of your formerly close association—and use it against that person.

Assertive people simply talk about things in such a way that others will listen and not be offended, and they give others the opportunity to respond in return (Birch, 1999).

Belief System: The message of the assertive person is, "I respect myself, and I have equal respect for others, too. I am not in this world to conform to others' expectations, and likewise, they are not in this world to conform to my expectations."

Advantage: You generally get more of what you want without making other people mad. You do not have to feel wrong or guilty because you ventilated your feelings—you left the door to communication open. Consequently, effective confrontation is mutually acceptable. From this, you develop more fulfilling relationships. Also, because you exercise the power of choice over your actions, you are in a much better position to feel good about yourself. Therapist Herbert Fensterheim (1975) shares this thought: *"The extent to which you assert yourself determines the level of your self-esteem."*

Be fair with others, but then keep after them until they are fair with you.

Alan Alda

Why?*

Why is it we always seem to fight?
Why is it we sleep apart every night?
Why is it our attempts at talking, all seem to escalate quickly into so many
  screams?

WHY?

Why is it you turn a deaf ear to my plea?
Why is it your view I refuse to see?
Why is it your feelings I try hard to hurt?
Why is it you retaliate and treat me like dirt?

WHY?

Why is it you say "always"
and "everytime," too?
Why is it I say the same things to you?
Why is it my faults you so readily see, and yours I point out so rapidly?

WHY?

Why is it so easy for me to make you cry?
Why is it that you tell me "Oh, just eat dirt and die!"
Why is it we can try again to start each day anew?
With just four simple little words,
the words I DO LOVE YOU?

WHY?

Bob Crawley, 1988

*(Used with permission of Bob Crawley, Fort Worth, Texas, 1988).

Disadvantage: As you become more open, honest, and direct, you also take some real risks in how others will perceive you. Some people have difficulty with these kinds of exchanges; therefore, you may experience some hurts and disappointments in some of your relationships.

When to Use: When both the goal and the relationship are important to you, the most appropriate approach is to move toward your opposition.

Now that we have discussed the three behavior styles, it might be helpful to note the characteristics of the assertive and nonassertive person. Table 7.2 lists these characteristics. Then, we will look at the three styles in action. The *passive, aggressive,* and *assertive* styles are illustrated in the following examples of a woman who wants help with the house.

> Sarcasm is dirty fighting.
>
> George Bach

THE STYLES IN ACTION

Passive Style:

Margret: Excuse me, but would you be a sweetie and pick up your clothes in the bathroom?
Charles: I'm reading the paper.
Margret: Oh, well, all right.

Table 7.2   Characteristics of the Nonassertive and the Assertive Person

Nonassertive Person

He confuses the goal of being liked with being respected.

He is conditioned to fears of being disliked or rejected.

He is unable to recognize the difference between being selfish in the bad sense and in the good sense.

He allows others to maneuver him into situations he does not want.

He is easily hurt by what others say and do.

He feels inferior because he is inferior. He limits his experiences and does not use his potential.

Assertive Person

He acts in a way that shows he respects himself, is aware that he cannot always win, and accepts his limitations.

He strives, in spite of the odds, to make the good try. Win, lose or draw, he maintains his self-respect.

He feels free to reveal himself: "This is me. This is what I feel, think, and want."

He can communicate with people on all levels—strangers, friends, and family. Communication is open, direct, honest, and appropriate.

He has an active orientation to life. He goes after what he wants—in contrast to the passive person who waits for things to happen.

Analysis: The statement "Oh, well, all right" only rewards Charles for postponing Margret's request. Margret certainly does not get what she wants. She probably feels sorry for herself and may pay him back by giving him the "silent treatment" over dinner.

Aggressive Style:

Margret: I've got another thing to tell you. I've had it with picking up after you and trying to keep this house straight. You either pitch in and help me, or I'm quitting this nonsense.

Charles: Now, calm down, I'm reading the paper.

Margret: Did your mother just "wait" on you and treat you like a king? You don't give a flip about anything around this house, as long as you get to read the daily news whenever you want.

Charles: Now, don't start in on me about my mother.

Margret: All you do is come home and relax in the easy chair and grab the paper.

Charles: Shut up! What's wrong with you?

Analysis: The opening statement is an attack, and Margret "relives" hostilities of earlier annoyances. Interactions such as this clearly have no winner, because aggressive behavior hurts another person, creates resentment, and guarantees resistance to change.

Assertive Style:

Margret: I would like for you to pick up your clothes in the bathroom.
Charles: I'm reading the paper.
Margret: I would feel much better if we shared in keeping the house straight. You can read the paper when we're done straightening the house.
Charles: I'm almost finished with the sports section.
Margret: Well, I can start the wash. Will you help me when you are through reading the sports section?
Charles: Sure!

> **Analysis:** Assertive behavior does not aim to injure but to solve an interpersonal problem. Assertive requests include a specific goal and the willingness to negotiate a mutually agreeable plan to solve the problem.

It would be unreasonable to expect people to use assertive behavior exclusively. There are times when it is wise to be passive and just give in to others; there are times when it is necessary to aggressively defend your rights; there are times when being assertive does not succeed in obtaining its goal. Bolton (1986) views the effects of the three behavior styles in this way:

> My observation of others and my personal experience leads me to believe that more of a person's needs will be satisfied by being consistently assertive than by submissive (passive) or aggressive behavior. In most circumstances, assertive behavior is the most appropriate, effective, and constructive way of defending one's space and fulfilling one's needs.

Would you like to be more assertive in dealing with interpersonal conflicts and other difficult situations? We will begin by discussing the different types of assertive expressions you may need to make.

LEARNING TO BE ASSERTIVE

The main goal of assertiveness training is to help people express their thoughts, feelings, and rights in a way that respects those of others. As you learn to do this, it is important that you become aware of the different types of assertive expressions (Atwater & Duffy, 1998).

Basic assertion is learning to stand up for your rights or express your feelings, such as saying, "Pardon me, I'd like to finish what I was saying."

Another type of assertiveness is *learning to express positive feelings,* such as, "I really liked the way you cleaned the car." Do you have difficulty in giving compliments, as well as receiving them? Some people do.

You may have to use an *escalating type of assertion when people fail to respond to your earlier request.* An example here would be, "This is the third time I'm going to tell you. I don't want to change insurance companies."

Then, there are time when you need to express *negative feelings.* The *"I" message, frequently referred to as the focal point of learning to be assertive,* is a way of expressing yourself effectively before you become angry and act in self-defeating ways.

Only I am responsible for my behavior. Only I can change what I do. However, when I change my behavior, I may give the other person in the relationship the opportunity to evaluate his behavior and perhaps modify it.

John Narciso and
David Burkett

The "I" Message. According to Thomas Gordon (1990), an "I" message has four parts: 1) an objective, nonjudgmental description of the person's behavior in specific terms, 2) how I feel about this, 3) the concrete effects on me; and 4) what I would prefer the person do instead. Let us look at each part.

1. **An objective, nonjudgmental description of the person's behavior in specific terms.** There are four guidelines to help you deliver an effective behavior description.

   First, describe the person's behavior in specific terms, rather than fuzzy, unclear words. For example,

Specific	Fuzzy
When you frequently call after 11 o'clock at night . . .	When you frequently call me late at night . . .

   The person you are angry with may have a different idea of what late means. Therefore, if you want your needs to be met, you will need to give the exact time you consider too late to receive a phone call.

   Second, do not add your thoughts and perceptions about the other person's motives, attitudes, character, and so on. It is human nature to describe another person's behavior by stating what you think the other person intended. This causes defensiveness, whereas describing what a person actually did creates an atmosphere for further communication.

   Third, make your behavior description an objective statement, rather than a judgment. Assertion messages avoid character assassinations, blame, sarcasm, or profanity.

   Fourth, behavioral descriptions should be brief as possible. The longer your message is, the more likely you will not be heard and understood. Also, there is less tendency for others to judge and evaluate when you keep your message simple. One sentence is ample, too.

2. **How I feel about this.** Once you have identified what your real feelings are, you must take the responsibility for your own feelings. This means you say, "I feel angry or disappointed," rather than "You made me feel angry or disappointed." Continuing with the late-night calls as an example, we now have the following:

   When you call me after 11:00 o'clock at night, I feel angry.

3. **The concrete effects on me.** People may not be aware of how their behavior is affecting you. In most instances, they are not deliberately trying to annoy or frustrate you. Once they become aware of how their behavior affects you, they are usually more considerate. Our example now becomes:

   When you call me after 11:00 o'clock at night, I feel angry, because I am awakened by your calls at least twice a week.

4. **What I would prefer the person to do instead.** Simply stated, this means that you use "I" messages and tell others what behavior you would like for them to substitute the next time a similar exchange occurs. Be sure and express your

> When people won't let you alone, it's because you haven't learned how to make them do it.
>
> David Seabury

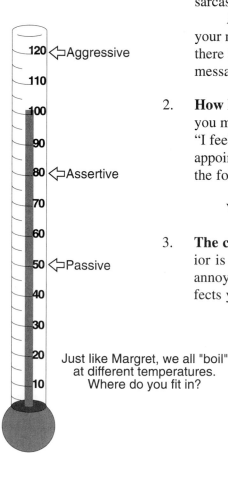

Just like Margret, we all "boil" at different temperatures. Where do you fit in?

Table 7.3   Examples of "I" Messages

Nonjudgmental description of person's behavior	My feelings about it	Concrete effects on me	What I would prefer the person to do
1. When you call me after 11:00 o'clock at night . . .	I feel angry . . .	because I am awakened by your call at least twice a week.	I would like you to call before 10:00 o'clock, except in an emergency.
2. When you are late picking me up from school . . .	I feel frustrated . . .	because I waste a lot of time waiting for you.	I would like to be picked up on time.
3. When you do not put your dirty clothes in the hamper . . .	I feel irritated . . .	because it makes extra work for me when I do the wash.	I would like you to put your dirty clothes in the hamper each day.
4. When you borrow my car and bring it home on "empty" . . .	I feel annoyed . . .	because I have to get gas before I can even go to work.	I would like you to re-fill the tank with as much gas as you use.

request in one or two simple sentences. It is important to be firm, specific, and kind. Our example now looks like this:

> When you call me after 11:00 o'clock at night, I feel angry, because I am awakened by your call at least twice a week. I'd like you to call before 10:00 o'clock, except in an emergency.

To be sure that you understand each part of the "I" message, review the examples in Table 7.3. You will notice that these "I" messages do not attack or blame the other person. Instead "I" messages are a way of expressing your sincere feelings and requests in a way that encourages others to listen and cooperate.

SUGGESTIONS FOR DELIVERING AN ASSERTIVE "I" MESSAGE

Alberti and Emmons (1995) offers three suggestions for improving the success of assertive "I" messages.

Write and practice your message before delivering it. This will give you an opportunity to review two important questions: 1) Is it likely to arouse defensiveness in the other person? 2) Are you likely to get your needs met with this assertion?

Develop assertive body language with your "I" Message. In order to assure that your verbal message is congruent with your nonverbal behavior, you will need to (Review Chapter 5 for more details):

- maintain direct eye contact
- maintain an erect body posture
- speak clearly, firmly, and have sufficient volume to be heard
- emphasize your message with appropriate gestures and facial expressions
- do not whine or have an apologetic tone to your voice.

Don't be sidetracked by the defensiveness or manipulation of others. This can be accomplished by using the *broken-record technique*—calmly repeating your point without getting sidetracked by irrelevant issues. Some examples might be:

- Yes, but . . .;
- Yes, I know, but my point is . . .;
- I agree, but . . .;
- Yes, but I was saying . . .;
- Right, but I'm still not interested.

Remember, persistence is one of the keys to effective assertion. One of the main reasons why people do not get their needs met when they assert is because they give up or give in after the first defensive or manipulative response of the other person.

So far, we have discussed the passive, aggressive, and assertive behavior styles used in interpersonal conflict. Added to these different behavior styles are two powerful variables that affect the way people manage conflict: gender and culture. We will now discuss each of these factors.

> Peace cannot be kept by force. It can only be achieved by understanding.
>
> Albert Einstein

GENDER AND CONFLICT MANAGEMENT

You will recall that in Chapter 5, we discussed the different communication styles that men and women use. We indicated that males are likely to speak and understand a language of "status and independence," while females are likely to speak and understand a language of "connection and intimacy." These different communication styles obviously lead to different approaches in dealing with conflict.

Gender Differences. Actually, these differences can be seen in childhood. For example, males are more likely to be aggressive, demanding, and competitive, while females are more cooperative.

Psychologist Jacqueline Sachs (1987) and her colleagues studied children from preschool to early adolescence and found some interesting patterns. For example, boys try to get their way by ordering one another around: "Lie down." "Get off my steps." "Gimme your arm." Girls, on the other hand, are more likely to make proposals for action, using the words "let's" and "we": "Let's go find some," "Let's ask her," "Do you have any bottles?" or "Let's go around the restaurant." Furthermore, guys tend to tell each other what role to take in pretend play ("Come on, be a doctor"); girls more often ask each other what role they want ("Will you be the patient for a few minutes?"), or make a joint proposal ("We can both be doctors"). Also, boys often make demands without offering an explanation ("Look, man. I want the pliers right now"). Girls, however, often give reasons for their suggestions ("We gotta clean them first . . . cause they got germs"). Girls simply attempt to influence what the others do without telling them what to do. Deborah Tannen (1991) views this difference in childhood language as being the different social structures of girls and boys, and women and men:

> In the hierarchical order that guys and men find or feel themselves in, status is indeed gained by telling others what to do and resisting being told what to do. But girls and women find or feel themselves in a community that is threatened by conflict, so they formulate requests as proposals rather than orders to make it easy for others to express other preferences without provoking a confrontation. If a man struggles to be strong, a woman struggles to keep the community strong.

These differences often persist into adulthood. M. J. Collier's (1991) survey of college students revealed that regardless of cultural background men and women view conflicts in contrasting ways. (See "Gender & You" box below.) From this study, female students described men as being concerned with power and more interested in content than relational issues. By contrast, women were described as being more concerned with maintaining the relationship during a conflict. Do you agree or disagree with what the college students said?

Learning Flexibility. Tannen (1991) suggests that when one's habitual style is not working, trying harder by doing more of the same will not solve problems. She advises men and women to adopt some flexibility in their styles. For example, women who avoid conflict at all costs would be better off if they learned that a little conflict will not kill them. And, men who habitually take oppositional stances would be better off if they broke their addiction to conflict. After all, because people are different, not only in gender but in cultural background, differences in attitudes toward verbal opposition will persist among friends, lovers, and fellow workers. Frustration can be reduced by simply realizing that what seems like unfair or irrational behavior may just be the result of a different style in approaching conflict.

> We meet naturally on the basis of our sameness and grow on the basis of our differentness.
>
> Virginia Satir

PHRASES USED TO DESCRIBE MALE AND FEMALE CONFLICT STYLES

M. J. Collier's (1991) study of college students revealed that men and women viewed conflicts in the following ways. What do you think about what the students said?

Men	Women
The most important thing to males in conflict is their egos.	Women try to solve problems without controlling the other person.
Men don't worry about feelings.	Women are more concerned with others' feelings.
Men are more direct.	Women are better listeners.

Do you agree or disagree?

Gender & You

FOCUS ON DIVERSITY

How Would You Handle this Cultural Conflict?

The husband would typically try to confront his wife verbally and directly *(as is typical in the United States)*, leading her to either become violently defensive or withdraw completely from the discussion. She, on the other hand, would attempt to indicate her displeasure by changes in mood and eye contact *(typical of Chinese culture)* that were either not noticed or uninterpretable by her husband. Thus, neither "his way" nor "her way" was working and they could not see any realistic way to "compromise."

Fontaine, (1999)

CULTURE AND CONFLICT MANAGEMENT

Different cultures often define and deal with conflict in different ways. When individuals from different cultures face a conflict, their normal, habitual communication patterns may not blend smoothly. An example of the challenge faced by an American husband and his Chinese wife is illustrated above (Fontaine, 1999). What do you think this couple can do to more effectively deal with conflict? With their cultural differences, will they be able to find a conflict style that is comfortable for them both?

Ting-Toomey (1994) suggests that the way in which people manage conflict varies depending on their cultural background. That is, high-context and low-context cultures manage conflict quite differently.

High-Context Cultures. These cultures value self-restraint, avoid confrontation, rely heavily on nonverbal systems, and give a great deal of meaning to the relationships between communicators. Preserving and honoring the face of the other person is a prime goal, and communicators go to great lengths to avoid any communication that might risk embarrassing a conversational partner. The Japanese, Chinese, Asian, and Latin-American cultures are examples of high-context cultures. Japanese, for example, are reluctant to say "no" to a request. They will probably respond with, "Let me think about it for a while," which anyone familiar with Japanese culture would recognize as a refusal (Adler and Towne, 1999).

Low-Context Cultures. These cultures use more explicit language, are more direct in their meanings, rely less on nonverbal systems, and stress goals and outcomes more than relationships. Examples include the German, Swedish, American, and English cultures. Individuals in low-context cultures manage conflict more directly. They are more confrontational and more goal oriented rather than being relationally focused, and they are less concerned about "saving face." Therefore, conflict in low-context cultures is more open, volatile, and threatening than high-context conflict (Gudykunst and Ting-Toomey, 1988).

Let's get back to our example of the American husband and the Chinese wife. The husband from a low-context culture and the wife from a high-context culture were simply responding to their cultural learning of how to deal with conflict. For example, when indirect communication (that used by the wife) is a cultural norm, it is unreasonable to expect more straightforward approaches to succeed (that used by the husband). Can the husband learn to be cautious in his straightforward approach and more attuned to his wife's nonverbal signals? Can the wife be more verbally direct without relying so much on her nonverbal signals to express her real feelings?

One thing is for sure, a mutual understanding about their cultural attitudes towards verbal conflict may result in less frustration in the future. Yes, conflicts will still arise, but at least they can be arguing about real conflicts of interest rather than fighting styles.

METHODS OF CONFLICT RESOLUTION

When you approach a conflict situation, you can choose to *avoid* the situation, *fight* with the use of power and force, or *move toward,* using negotiation skills (Adler & Rodman, 1999).

Win-Lose. One approach to conflict resolution is that one person gets his or her way, and the other does not. For example, Linda and Tom have a conflict-of-needs situation about where to build the swimming pool. Let us look at their interaction:

Tom: I've decided we will build the swimming pool to the right of the patio.
Linda: What do you mean, you've decided! I want to build it to the left of the patio.
Tom: That's a stupid idea, then we will have to move all the shrubs.
Linda: Well, first of all, I'm not stupid, because the contractor can do that for us.
Tom: I make the money around here, and I'm not paying for the shrubs to be moved.
Linda: Well, okay, if that's what you say.

> **Analysis:** Tom decides what the solution should be and announces it to Linda. Obviously, Tom hopes Linda will accept his idea. When Linda doesn't, Tom uses persuasion to get Linda to "give in." However, this fails, so Tom tries to get compliance by employing his aggressive, power, control, and authoritarian techniques to get his way. *Power* is the distinguishing characteristic in win-lose conflict resolution, since it is necessary to defeat an opponent to get what you want.

Although Tom and Linda both wanted their way, Tom, the person satisfied, was inconsiderate and disrespectful to the needs of Linda. He was issue oriented. Consequently, Linda felt defeated, angry, and resentful at Tom for not considering her feelings.

Lose-Lose. In the win-lose type of conflict resolution, Linda was very unhappy with the outcome, but Tom was "happy as a lark." In the lose-lose type of conflict resolution, neither party is happy with the outcome. Let's listen to Linda and Tom again.

Hatred is never ended but by love, and a misunderstanding is never ended by an argument but by tact, diplomacy, conciliation, and a sympathetic desire to see the other person's viewpoint.

Buddha

Behavior is a mirror in which everyone shows his image.

Goethe

Conflicts occur between people because people are different, think differently, and have different needs and wants.

Tom: I've decided we will build the swimming pool to the right of the patio.
Linda: What do you mean you have decided! You're not the only one who lives here, you selfish jerk!
Tom: You are too stupid to understand we can't put the pool where the shrubs are.
Linda: I'm not stupid! You are just too stupid to understand the contractor will do it for us.
Tom: I'm the one who makes most of the money here, you fruitcake! I'm not paying the contractor to move 100 shrubs.
Linda: Then, we won't even build a pool, Mr. Penny Pincher deluxe!

> Let us begin anew, remembering on both sides that civility is not a sign of weakness.
>
> John F. Kennedy

Analysis: Linda decides she will be more aggressive this time. Very quickly, she starts verbally attacking Tom. There is no way that Tom is going to take this, so he reciprocates and verbally attacks Linda. She comes back for more of the same. . . . Tom comes back for more of the same . . . Linda leaves angry and hostile, with the issue never resolved. Tom is angry and hostile, with the issue never resolved.

Linda and Tom both lose. They both forgot the feelings of each other; they both forgot the issue.

Win-Win. In this approach to conflict resolution, conflicts are resolved with no one winning and no one losing. Both win because the solution must be *acceptable to both.* Let's see how Tom and Linda handle the swimming pool issue this time.

Tom: Will tonight after dinner be a convenient time with you for us to talk about where we can build the swimming pool?
Linda: That will be fine!
Tom: Good, let's both be thinking of some possible locations.
Linda: That's a great idea.

After Dinner

Tom: What are your ideas and how do you feel about this?
Linda: I see three possible locations—to the left of the patio, the right of the patio, or in the middle. What are your ideas?

Resolution

Today we had a meeting
like so many other times.
At once we started listing what
we saw as each other's crimes.
But there was one thing different
on this bright and wondrous day.
We'd sworn till all had been resolved
we would not walk away.
The first ground rule that we laid down
was different from before.
We agreed we would not scream and shout
nor storm out of the door.
We then agreed right then and there
that we would "fairly" fight.
We would not call each other names
nor take a "psychic" bite.
The little things we could concede
that we could live without.
We tore them into little bits
and then we threw them out.
Upon our individual slips
of paper we did write,
the concessions each of us would make
to help to end the fight.
And then upon another sheet
we wrote what it would take,
to finally happy once again
each of us to make.
We then exchanged the papers
and to both of our surprise,
we each had written just one thing
for the other's eyes.
And now we are together
but not as before.
For we learned a lesson
to carry us evermore.
The lesson was so simple
that things are easy to solve,
when we sit down together
our problems to resolve.

Bob Crawley, 1989

Used with permission of Bob Crawley, Fort Worth, Texas, 1989.

Tom: Well, I've been thinking of those, too. Let's talk about the pros and cons of all three. Let's hear your ideas first.

Linda: Ok, the left side would be a prettier view from the bedroom; the right side would be more convenient for the kids, but we wouldn't have a view from the house; the middle would be a prettier view from the den. What are your ideas?

Tom: The left side would be more expensive, since we would have to move 100 or more shrubs; the right side would really be more convenient for the kids; the middle would give a nice view from the house, I guess. I really had not thought about the middle as a possibility.

Linda: Those shrubs really do look nice from the bedroom, and we can save a lot of money by not having to move all those shrubs. The kids can probably adjust to a few feet of inconvenience.

Tom: The kids will be gone in a couple of years anyway, and their convenience won't be a factor then. I'm getting to like the middle more and more.

Linda: Why don't we tentatively think about building the pool in the middle, and then each of us can think about this for a week.

Tom: That sounds good. Can we talk about this again next Monday night?

Linda: Sure!

> Things are not usually all good or bad, all right or all wrong. Life is just not that simple. The answers and solutions we seek usually lie somewhere between the opposites. When we insist on seeing things as only black or white, we are further removed from understanding; further isolated from truth. Giving in does not imply giving up any more than being flexible is a sign of lacking conviction. Most often, by being willing to give a little, we get more than we ever dreamed.
>
> Leo Buscaglia

Analysis: Tom asks Linda to participate with him in a joint search for some solution acceptable to both. Tom and Linda both offer possible solutions. They critically evaluate them and eventually make a decision on a final solution acceptable to both. No selling of the other is required after the solution has been selected, because both have already accepted it. No power is required to force compliance, because neither is resisting the decision.

One of the strong advantages to this type of conflict resolution is that Linda is more motivated to carry out a decision that she has participated in making than she is a decision that has been imposed upon her. Also, Tom and Linda feel better about themselves and each other. Neither feel defeated; neither feel hostile. Tom and Linda resolve their conflict by dealing with each other's feelings and the issue, too. From the examples of Tom and Linda, it is easy to see that the win-win method of conflict resolution is clearly superior to the win-lose and lose-lose method.

STEPS FOR WIN-WIN CONFLICT RESOLUTION

Earlier in this chapter we stated that there were three elements in a conflict situation—*self, other,* and the *issue.* We also stated that if the conflict situation is to be resolved constructively, all of these elements—the *feelings* and *emotions* of both individuals, plus the *tangible issue* involved—must be dealt with congruently.

You have already learned how to deal with the *feelings* and *emotions* involved in a conflict situation. You saw how Linda and Tom listened to the feelings of each other and how they dealt with the tangible issue, too.

Let us look more closely at the exact steps used in the win-win approach to interpersonal conflict resolution.

Many authorities have written on the no-lose or win-win approach to conflict resolution. However, win-win problem solving works best when it follows a seven-step approach, based on the writings of Douglas Stone, et al., (1999) and Thomas Gordon (1990). The steps are:

1. **Define the Problem in Terms of Needs, Not Solutions.** This is the critical point where you need to decide what it is you want or need. We generally

define a problem in terms of solutions—what will satisfy our need. This really leads to win/lose results—one person gets what he or she wants, and the other loses what he or she wants. For example, let's consider this exchange between David and John.

David: I need the car to go to the library and study.
John: I need the car to go to the out-of-town basketball game.

David and John have both defined their goal in terms of solutions. They each want to get what they want—the car. Actually, David and John both had a need for transportation, and the family car was the solution.

A useful key to identify a *need* is to fill in the following blank "I need . . ." with a statement of the goal, not the solution. For example, "I need some kind of transportation (the goal), but I do not have to use the family car (John and David's original solution).

Sometimes your needs may not be as clear as the example above. In these cases, either think about your *needs* alone before approaching the other person, or talk to a third party who may be able to help you separate your thoughts. Do not forget to explore all the reasons you are dissatisfied as well as the relational issues that may be involved.

2. **Share Your Problem and Unmet Needs.** Once you have defined your problem and unmet needs, it is time to share them with the other person. Remember, no one can be expected to meet your needs unless they know why you are upset and what you want. There are two guidelines to remember in this step:

First, *be sure to choose a time and place that is suitable.* Frequently, destructive fights often start because the initiator confronts the other person who is not ready. Unloading on a tired, busy person is likely to result in your concerns not being heard or given much attention. Furthermore, it is important that you are calm and have time to discuss what is bothering you. Bringing up issues of concern when you are angry, overly upset, or in a hurry frequently causes you to say things you really do not mean. Making a date to discuss what is bothering you increases the likelihood of a positive outcome.

To discover needs, we try to find out why the person wants the solution he/she initially proposed. Once we understand the advantages that a solution has for them, we have discovered their need.

Robert Bolton

Remember: There does not have to be a winner and a loser

You might say, "Something's been bothering me. When would be a convenient time for us to talk about it?"

Second, *be sure and use "I" messages and the assertive techniques* you have already learned in this chapter. You will remember that the most important part of the "I" message is to describe how your partner's behavior affects you—not attach blame or labels.

The final part of this step is to confirm your partner's understanding of what he or she heard.

3. **Listen to the Other Person's Needs.** Once you are sure the other person understands your message, it is now time to find out what he or she needs to feel satisfied about the issue. Remember, if you expect some help in meeting your needs, it is only fair that you be willing to help the other person meet his or her needs. Thinking back about the exchange between David and John, John might say, "Now that I've told you that I need a way to go to the library to study, tell me what you need to feel okay about this situation with the family car." David might say, "I also need a way to the out-of-town basketball game." Be sure to review the listening skills discussed in Chapter five and be prepared to listen actively to your partner. It is also important to check your understanding of your partner's needs before going any further. You might say, "Now, do I understand correctly that you need . . .?"

You are now ready to arrive at a shared definition of the problem that expresses *both needs*. Try to state both sets of needs in a one-sentence summary of the problem. For example, David and John might conclude, "We both need a way to go where we want or need to go, and we only have one car."

4. **Brainstorm Possible Solutions.** Once the problem is adequately defined, the search for possible solutions begins. You might suggest, "What are some things we might do?"

Roger Fisher and William Ury (1992), two Harvard law professors, give some important guidelines to assist in the brainstorming session:

- *seek quantity rather than quality.* Think of as many solutions as possible. Do not evaluate, judge, or belittle any of the solutions offered. This will come in the next step.
- *avoid ownership of a solution.* It is important to not get involved with your solution and my solution. Build upon each other's solutions by adopting an attitude: These are *our* solutions.
- *list every possible solution.* The final result should be a long list of possible ideas and solutions. Since each idea needs to be considered, it is advisable for all solutions to be written down. Otherwise, a good idea may get lost.

5. **Evaluate the Possible Solutions and Choose the Best One.** *Check Possible Consequences.* Now it is time to evaluate the solutions in terms of how they best meet the mutually shared goals. You want to evaluate how each solution meets each partner's needs and then arrive at a final understanding of which solution satisfies the most goals. However, sometimes it is easier and less time-consuming to initiate these four guidelines:

- ask the other person which solution he or she feels best solves the mutual shared goal. Be sure his or her needs are met.

- state which solution looks best to you. Be sure your needs are met.
- see which choices are congruent with yours and the other person.
- together, decide on one or more of the solutions. If you took the time to carefully examine each other's needs when you began your conflict resolution, several of the same solutions will generally be selected by both people.

It is extremely important that each person is satisfied with the final solution. Remember, people are generally more motivated to work on resolving a problem if they are not manipulated or pressured into deciding on the best solution.

The final aspect of this step is to *consider the possible consequences of your final solution or combination of solutions.* Sometimes it is helpful to ask, "What is the worst thing that could happen by choosing this solution?"

6. **Implement the Solution.** It is extremely important that you agree on exactly how the solution will be implemented. Your solution will only be effective if you mutually agree *on who does what and by when.*

Because people are forgetful, it is usually desirable to write out the agreement that was reached, being sure to include the details of *who will do what by when.* The written agreement should be viewed as a reminder to both parties about exactly how the solution will be implemented.

7. **Evaluate the Solution at a Later Date.** Just like you made a date to begin talking about your problem and unmet needs, it is also important to make a date and review the progress of your final solution. This is an opportunity to "check back" with each person to see how the solution is working for each person. Is the mutually shared goal being met? If changes need to be made, now is the time to discuss what is on your mind.

Personal Problem Solving. It is important to note here that a modification of the win-win approach to interpersonal conflict resolution can also be used in personal problem solving. Hammond (1998) and his colleagues provide these steps:

- Identify and define the conflict.
- Generate a number of possible solutions.
- Evaluate the alternative solutions.
- Decide on the best solution.
- Evaluate the solution at a later date.

When people join together and take the time to find a solution acceptable to both, most problems that occur between them can be resolved with a high degree of success. However, the win-win approach to conflict resolution is not a panacea for all life's problems. There are some occasions when this method will not work, or when another approach is more fitting.

WHEN CONFLICTS CANNOT BE RESOLVED

Sometimes, the most well-thought-out plans do not always work. Despite your best intentions and most dedicated efforts, not all conflicts can be worked

> Consider how hard it is to change yourself and you'll understand what little chance you have of trying to change others.
>
> Jacob M. Braude

through. In *Beyond Blame*, Jeffrey Kottler (1996), a professor of counseling and educational psychology, describes three occasions when conflicts may not be resolved: differences in basic beliefs, values, and past issues; struggles where there is no solution; and situations out of our control. The authors would like to add one more—when things have to be a certain way. Look more closely at these.

Differences in Basic Beliefs, Values, and Past Issues. There are times when two people are so different in their basic beliefs and values, and in the ways they perceive the world, that conflict between them is unavoidable, no matter what they do. Is there a person in your life with whom you have to work or associate with frequently who has completely different political or religious orientations from you? Or, what about some unresolved family issues with a relative from the past that can never really be laid to rest completely? Perhaps you have tried and tried to see each other's point of view, but you still disagree, and each party leaves feeling angry or hurt.

You may just have to face a reality of life: agree to disagree when you discuss certain topics. When two people feel as differently about things as you do, conflict is the logical result. And in order to resolve your difficulties, one of you would have to abandon a position that is a fundamental part of your very being or thinking. You can both resolve to respect each other, however, for your right to have your own beliefs, values, and ways in which you each perceive the world, or what may have happened in the past. You can also learn to *tread lightly around each other.* With this attitude and commitment, you can progress to no longer blaming the other person for the way he or she is, nor blaming yourself for the problems. When two people reach an understanding of the differences in orientation, you and the other person can reduce the intensity of your struggles so that you both stop allowing yourselves to feel angry or hurt when you deal with one another.

Struggles Where There Is No Solution. The reality of life is that there is no guarantee that any particular human struggle has a solution, and certainly not a "best" one that can be determined easily. Look at this example:

> Maria has just received the call from the doctor. Her mother has a progressive case of Alzheimer's disease and now must move in with Maria and her husband, Hector. The sick mother is verbally abusive and demanding to Hector, and oftentimes even to Maria. There are no other family members to help with the sick mother, and finances are tight, making it impossible to send the mother elsewhere. Added to these difficulties are cultural values related to taking care of aging parents. They have no choice but to all live together, knowing that harmony among them is out of the question.

What can Hector and Maria do? They can partition off the house as much as possible, giving them and the sick mother as much privacy as possible. Hector and Maria can support one another as they try to enforce some limits. However, they still have to live with a certain degree of conflict in their home. There is no solution to this situation other than to learn to endure the situation in such a way that they minimize its effect on their relationship.

Situations Out of Our Control. Have you ever had to deal with a situation in which you believed that if only you worked harder, if you knew more, or were more highly skilled, then you could make things better? What would you do in the following situation?

> After 25 years of a stable, happy marriage, Jenny started drinking heavily. Their only child has finished college and was financially independent. George had talked to Jenny about her problem, and they had been to numerous counseling sessions. Jenny said she wanted to quit drinking, but she did little to help herself. So, the drinking continued. George had been an extremely responsible father and husband and felt that he could, or should, be able to do something to help Jenny with her problem. Divorce was the last thing George wanted to consider.

Is there anything that George can do to "fix" the problem? In life, it is critical to recognize realistically what is within your power to change and what is not. George needs to come to accept that not everyone really wants to change, no matter what they might say. Sometimes the payoffs of a person's dysfunction and behavior are too attractive, or they just do not want to do the hard work that is involved. Rather than not blaming Jenny or himself for the situation, George can take inventory of all the things that he has tried that has not worked, and rather than repeating them, try something else. Perhaps George may need to separate himself from Jenny for a period of time and let Jenny decide what she wishes to do for herself. George can choose to take up a new hobby, or interest, with friends who can be supportive of him during this time. He can build a new life for himself; George cannot "fix" Jenny's problem—only Jenny can.

When Things Have to Be a Certain Way. Have you ever wanted someone to change to meet wants or expectations you believe are important? "If only they would . . . things around here would be so much better." Consider the following situation, assuming you are the roommate who wants "things around here to be better."

> There is growing tension between you and your roommate. She has an 8:00 o'clock class and gets up before you do and eats a breakfast muffin and orange juice at your kitchen table. Your roommate continues to leave her dirty plate, glass, and crumbs on the table. You clean your side of the table and put your dishes in the dishwasher when you leave for school. This is just essential—the way it is supposed to be! You are irritated and decide to discuss this with your roommate, knowing that she is quite good about cleaning her side of the table when she gets in from class and sharing in the other chores around the apartment. Your roommate listens to your concerns and indicates a willingness to change. However, the problem continues, and you become more and more irritated.

What are your options? You can clean up her side and run the risk of having to do more of the cleaning chores around the apartment, you can get another roommate, you can decide to live by yourself, or you can decide to not let the dirty dishes bother you so much.

When you live and work with other people, it is only natural that differences in the *way some things should be done* can create problems. The reality of life is, however, that if you want *some things* to be a *certain* way, then it is unrealistic to think that other people will necessarily do what you believe is *essential*. Thinking otherwise is a guarantee for conflict and stress to exist. In our example, the problem is yours—your roommate is happy and just trying to get to class on time. In other words, the person who is bothered by the problem is the person who needs to correct the problem.

Review the options discussed above and decide what to do, but remember—*when you believe something must be done a certain way and at a certain time, you need to do this task perfectly, and to your satisfaction.* Sometimes, we all need to learn to live with less than what we want! Chapter eight will discuss in more detail the stress involved in placing unrealistic demands and expectations on other people.

Chapter Review

When any two people live or work closely together, conflict is bound to occur just because people are different, think differently, and have different needs and wants that sometimes do not match.

- Conflict is an expressed struggle between at least two people who perceive the situation differently and are experiencing interference from the other person in achieving their goals.
- Conflicts usually involve any of six basic types of issues: 1) control over resources, 2) preferences and nuisances, 3) values, 4) beliefs, 5) goals, and 6) the nature of the relationship between the partners.
- Constructive resolution of conflicts can promote growth in a relationship, allow for a healthy release of feelings, and increase motivation and self-esteem.
- Two negative effects of conflict can be: the manner in which we approach interpersonal conflict (believing there must be a winner and a loser), and larger problems with deeper personal resentments may occur.
- In order to resolve conflict, we must recognize that there are three elements to a conflict situation, and each must be dealt with. These elements are your feelings, the other person's feelings, and the issue— what the conflict is about.
- The two dimensions of any conflict situation are the emotional or feeling dimension, and the issue dimension. In order to prevent emotional conflicts from multiplying the issue(s) into additional differences, it is wise to deal with the emotional, or feeling, dimension first.
- In dealing with the emotional dimension, it is helpful to remember three rules: 1) treat the other person with respect, 2) listen until you experience the other side, and 3) state your views, needs, and feelings.
- The three behavior styles used in handling opposition and responding to conflict are 1) passive—also known as nonassertive, 2) aggressive, and 3) assertive. The assertive approach is generally the most appropriate, effective, and constructive way of responding to conflict.
- There are several types of assertive expressions: basic assertion, learning to express positive feelings, and an escalating type of assertion when people fail to respond to your earlier request.
- The "I" message is frequently referred to as the focal point of learning to be assertive—expressing yourself effectively before you become angry and act in self-defeating ways. The four parts of the "I" message are 1) an objective, nonjudgmental description of the person's behavior in specific terms, 2) how I feel about this, 3) the concrete effects on me, and 4) what I would prefer the person do instead.
- When delivering an assertive "I" message, it is helpful to remember these suggestions: Write and practice your message before delivering it, develop assertive body language with your "I" message, and do not be sidetracked by the defensiveness or manipulation of others.
- Added to the different behavior styles used in interpersonal conflict are two powerful variables that affect the way people manage conflict: gender and culture. Regardless of cultural background, men and women view conflicts in contrasting ways. Likewise, high-and low-context cultures manage conflict quite differently.
- When you approach a conflict situation, you can choose to avoid the situation (Win-Lose), fight with the use of power (Lose-Lose), or move toward your opposition, using negotiation skills (Win-Win).
- Win-Win problem solving works best when it follows a seven step approach: 1) define the problem in terms of needs, not solutions, 2) share your problem and unmet needs, 3) listen to the other person's needs, 4) brainstorm possible solutions, 5) evaluate the possible solutions and choose the best one— check possible consequences, 6) implement the solution, and 7) evaluate the solution at a later date.
- Personal problem solving can be facilitated with the following steps: 1) identify and define the conflict, 2) generate a number of possible solutions, 3) evaluate the alternative solutions, 4) decide on the best solution, and 5) evaluate the solution at a later date.
- There are some occasions when the Win-Win approach to conflict resolution may not work. Possible occasions can include: differences in basic beliefs, values, and past issues; struggles where there is no solution; situations out of our control; and when things have to be a certain way.

How you resolve your interpersonal conflicts is the single most important factor in determining whether your relationships will be healthy or unhealthy, mutually satisfying or unsatisfying, friendly or unfriendly, deep or shallow, or intimate or cold.

??? Questions ???

1. Define conflict and what causes conflict.
2. Why is conflict generally viewed negatively? What are the positive and negative effects of conflict?
3. Explain the three elements involved in a conflict situation. Why must we deal with all three elements congruently?
4. What are the two main dimensions of any conflict situation? Which dimension should be dealt with first? Why?
5. Explain the three rules to remember in dealing with the emotional dimension.
6. What are the three behavior styles used in handling opposition and responding to conflict? Explain the behavior description, belief system, advantages, disadvantages of each style, as well as when each style should be used.
7. List at least ten Basic Human Rights?
8. Explain the characteristics of the nonassertive and the assertive person.
9. What is the focal point of learning to be assertive? List and write an example of each of the four parts of an "I" message.
10. When delivering an "I" message, what three suggestions should you remember?
11. What are at least three different ways in which men and women view and deal with conflict?
12. Explain the different approaches high- and low-context cultures use in conflict resolution.
13. List and give examples of the three methods you can use in conflict resolution.
14. What are the seven steps to use in Win-Win conflict resolution? What are the steps to be used in personal problem solving?
15. Explain four possible occasions when conflict may not be resolved.

🔑 Key Terms 🔑

Aggressive	Domination	Move Against
Assertive	Feeling Dimension	Moving Toward
Avoidance	High-Context Culture	Passive
Blamer	"I" Message	Placater
Broken-Record Technique	Issue Dimension	Submissive
Collaborative Problem Solving	Lose-Lose	Win-Lose
Conflict	Low-Context Culture	Win-Win
Distractor		

??? **Discussion** ???

1. What kinds of differentness in others cause you the greatest interpersonal conflict?
2. What situations do you find most difficult to respond to with assertive behavior?
3. Which of the dirty fighting techniques is the most difficult for you to deal with?
4. Generally speaking, have your conflicts made your relationships stronger or weaker? Why?
5. Which one of the parts of the "I" message is most difficult for you to remember to use?
6. Discuss any personal experiences you have had with the different approaches high-and low-context cultures use in conflict resolution.
7. Do you agree that men and women view and deal with conflict differently? Why or why not?
8. Do you disagree with any of the Basic Human Rights? If so, explain.
9. Is the Win-Win approach to conflict resolution too good to be true?

Personal Conflict Resolution

Purpose: To review your style of conflict management.

Instructions:

I. Respond to the following questions:

1. Describe the last "fight" or conflict you had with a friend or family member.

2. What was your goal in the conflict?

3. What do you think the other person's goal was in the conflict?

4. Describe how you responded to the conflict—passively, assertively, or aggressively.

5. Describe how the other person responded to the conflict—passively, assertively, or aggressively.

6. Was the conflict resolved by the win-lose, lose-lose, or win-win method? Explain how the method was used.

Discussion

1. What does this event tell you about your style of conflict management?

2. What can you do to improve your approach to conflict resolution?

How Did Your Parents Handle Conflict?

Purpose: To review your parents' style of conflict management and to determine in what ways you may be presently imitating their behavior.

Instructions:

I. Respond to the following questions:

    1. How did your mother deal with interpersonal conflict?

    2. How did your father deal with interpersonal conflict?

    3. How is your style of conflict management like and unlike those of your parents?

      MOTHER:

      Like:

      Unlike:

FATHER:

Like:

Unlike:

4. What bothered you most about your parents' style of conflict management?

MOTHER:

FATHER:

5. What did you admire most about your parents' style of conflict management?

MOTHER:

FATHER:

II. After you have responded to the previous questions, divide into groups of four and share your answers or have an open class discussion.

Discussion

1. What does this tell you about the power of learning by imitation?

2. Why is it that we continue to imitate behavior we saw in our parents but also disliked?

Name_____ Date_____

Understanding the Passive, Aggressive, and Assertive Styles

Purpose: To practice composing passive, aggressive and assertive responses to real life situations.

Instructions:

   I. After each situation, compose a passive, aggressive and assertive response.

  II. Then, share your responses in an open class discussion or divide into small groups of four students.

    1. You have just paid for your dinner at one of your favorite restaurants. However, you suddenly realize that your change is a dollar short.

      Passive Response:

      Aggressive Response:

      Assertive Response:

    2. You are relaxing with the paper after a long day. Your spouse rushes in and hands you a list of food items and says, "I never thought you would get here. Quick, pick these up from the store."

      Passive Response:

      Aggressive Response:

      Assertive Response:

    3. Your teacher lost the test you handed in and says you must take the test again.

      Passive Response:

      Aggressive Response:

      Assertive Response:

4. Your roommate has not been doing his or her share of chores around the apartment.

   Passive Response:

   Aggressive Response:

   Assertive Response:

5. While you wait patiently for the clerk to finish with the customer ahead of you, another customer comes in and the clerk waits on him before you.

   Passive Response:

   Aggressive Response:

   Assertive Response:

Discussion

1. Which responses were the most difficult for you to compose: The passive, aggressive, or assertive?

2. Would others who know you well, say you are more passive, aggressive, or assertive in dealing with conflicts and problem solving? Explain.

Name _____ Date _____

The Assertiveness Inventory*

Purpose: To assess your strengths and weaknesses in being assertive and to establish goals for improvement.

Instructions:

I. Respond to the following questions by drawing a circle around the number that describes you best.

   For some questions, the assertive end of the scale is at 0, for others at 4.

   Key:

   0 means no or never
   1 means somewhat or sometimes
   2 means average
   3 means usually or a good deal
   4 means practically always or entirely

1. When a person is highly unfair, do you call it to their attention? 0 1 2 3 4
2. Do you find it difficult to make decisions? 0 1 2 3 4
3. Are you openly critical of others' ideas, opinions, behavior? 0 1 2 3 4
4. Do you speak out in protest when someone takes your place in line? 0 1 2 3 4
5. Do you often avoid people or situations for fear of embarrassment? 0 1 2 3 4
6. Do you usually have confidence in your own judgment? 0 1 2 3 4
7. Do you insist that your spouse or roommate take on a fair share of
    household chores? 0 1 2 3 4
8. Are you prone to "fly off the handle?" 0 1 2 3 4
9. When a salesperson makes an effort, do you find it hard to say "No" even
    though the merchandise is not really what you want? 0 1 2 3 4
10. When a latecomer is waited on before you are, do you call attention to the
    situation? 0 1 2 3 4
11. Are you reluctant to speak up in a discussion or debate? 0 1 2 3 4
12. If a person has borrowed money (or a book, garment, thing of value) and
    is overdue in returning it, do you mention it? 0 1 2 3 4
13. Do you continue to pursue an argument after the other person has had
    enough? 0 1 2 3 4
14. Do you generally express what you feel? 0 1 2 3 4
15. Are you disturbed if someone watches you at work? 0 1 2 3 4
16. If someone keeps kicking or bumping your chair in a movie or a lecture,
    do you ask the person to stop? 0 1 2 3 4
17. Do you find it difficult to keep eye contact when you are talking to
    another person? 0 1 2 3 4
18. In a good restaurant, when your meal is improperly prepared or served,
    do you ask the waiter/waitress to correct the situation? 0 1 2 3 4
19. When you discover merchandise is faulty, do you return it for an adjustment? 0 1 2 3 4
20. Do you show your anger by name-calling or obscenities? 0 1 2 3 4

*From *Your Perfect Right: A Guide To Assertive Living* (Sixth Edition) © 1995 by Robert E. Alberti and Michael L. Emmons. Reproduced for Velma Walker by permission of Impact Publishers, Inc., P. O. Box 1094, San Luis Obispo, CA 93406. Further reproduction prohibited.

21. Do you try to be a wallflower or a piece of the furniture in social situations?.............. 0 1 2 3 4
22. Do you insist that your property manager (mechanic, repairman, janitor) make repairs, adjustments or replacements which are his or her responsibility? 0 1 2 3 4
23. Do you often step in and make decisions for others? 0 1 2 3 4
24. Are you able openly to express love and affection?... 0 1 2 3 4
25. Are you able to ask your friends for small favors or help?............................. 0 1 2 3 4
26. Do you think you always have the right answer? 0 1 2 3 4
27. When you differ with a person you respect, are you able to speak up for your own viewpoint? 0 1 2 3 4
28. Are you able to refuse unreasonable requests made by friends? 0 1 2 3 4
29. Do you have difficulty complimenting or praising others? 0 1 2 3 4
30. If you are disturbed by someone smoking near you, can you say so? 0 1 2 3 4
31. Do you shout or use bullying tactics to get others to do as you wish? 0 1 2 3 4
32. Do you finish other people's sentences for them? 0 1 2 3 4
33. Do you get into physical fights with others, especially with strangers? 0 1 2 3 4
34. At family meals, do you control the conversation? 0 1 2 3 4
35. When you meet a stranger, are you the first to introduce yourself and begin a conversation? 0 1 2 3 4

II. **Analyzing Your Results:** When you complete the Inventory, you'll probably be tempted to add up your total score. Don't! It really has no meaning, since there is no such thing as a general quality of assertiveness. The authors of the inventory suggest the following steps for analysis of your responses to the Assertiveness Inventory:

1. Look at individual events in your life, involving particular people or groups, and consider strengths and shortcomings accordingly.

2. Look at your responses to questions 1, 2, 4, 5, 6, 7, 9, 10, 11, 12, 14, 15, 16, 17, 18, 19, 21, 22, 24, 25, 27, 28, 30, and 35. These questions are oriented toward nonassertive behavior. Respond to these questions:

   A. Do your answers to these items tell you that you are rarely speaking up for yourself? How do you feel about what you have learned about yourself?

3. Look at your responses to questions 3, 8, 13, 20, 23, 26, 29, 31, 32, 33, and 34. These questions are oriented toward aggressive behavior. Respond to these questions:

   A. Do your answers to these questions suggest you are pushing others around more than you realized? How do you feel about what you have learned about yourself?

Discussion

Most people confirm from completing these three steps that assertiveness is situational in their lives. No one is nonassertive all the time, aggressive all the time, assertive all the time! Each person behaves in each of the three ways at various times, depending upon the situation. It is possible that you have a characteristic style that leans heavily in one direction. Reread each question on the Inventory and carefully analyze your answers. Look specifically at four aspects (situations, attitudes, obstacles, and behavior skills) of the information and respond to the questions below:

1. What *situations* give you trouble? Which can you handle easily?

2. What are your *attitudes* about expressing yourself? For example, do you feel you have a "right" to be assertive? Why or why not?

3. What *obstacles* are in the way of your assertions? For example, are you frightened of the consequences, or do other people in your life make it especially difficult? Who?

4. Are your *behavior skills* (eye contact, facial expression, body posture) intact? Can you be expressive when you need to?

5. What specific goals do you need to set for yourself in learning to be more assertive?

4. **Situation:** The teacher had promised to return your test on Monday. It is now Friday and you still don't know how you did.

   "I" Message:

5. **Situation:** A friend borrows your English book and promises to return it the next day. She doesn't bring it back.

   "I" Message:

6. Make up a situation and make an "I" Message to go with it.

   Situation:

   "I" Message:

III. Now, divide into groups of four and share your assertive messages. Members of the group will give each person feedback on his or her assertive messages.

IV. Correct any errors in your assertive messages and try to practice giving "I" Messages during the next week.

Discussion

1. What errors, if any, did you find in your assertive messages?

2. Do you think you will be able to practice any of these assertive messages in the next week? Explain how.

3. What will your biggest problem be in learning to be assertive?

4. How do you plan to overcome this problem?

Personal Problem Solving

Purpose: To learn how to apply the five steps of personal problem solving.

Instructions:

1. Write out the details of one of your conflicts as related to a personal problem you are trying to solve. Then analyze and write your responses to the steps of personal problem solving on the next page, making sure to decide on a date when you will complete step five.

2. Share your responses to the five steps with an individual you respect and trust (or this could be done in small group). Ask this individual to give you feedback on your responses. Make notes of the individual's feedback as you progress through the five steps.

Five Steps of Personal Problem Solving: (Complete individually—by yourself)

1. Identify and define the conflict.

2. Generate a number of possible solutions.

3. Evaluate the alternative solutions. (List pros and cons to each possible solution in #2 above).

            Pros   Cons

4. Decide on the best solution.

5. Evaluate the solution at a later date. (Make a commitment when you will evaluate the effectiveness of the solution decided in #4 above).

Discussion

1. Why did you select the particular individual to share this problem with?

2. What, if any, helpful feedback did you receive from the person you shared your problem with?

Name _____ Date _____

Resolving Interpersonal Conflict

Learning Journal

Select the statement below that best defines your feelings about the personal value or meaning gained from this chapter and respond below the dotted line.

- **I learned that I . . .**
- **I realized that I . . .**
- **I discovered that I . . .**

- **I was surprised that I . . .**
- **I was pleased that I . . .**
- **I was displeased that I . . .**

. . . .

continue on reverse

Managing Stress and Wellness

What is the true picture of your life? Imagine that there is an hourglass on your desk. Connecting the bowl at the top with the bowl at the bottom is a tube so thin that only one grain of sand can pass through it at a time.

That is the true picture of your life, even on a super-busy day. The crowded hours come to you always one moment at a time. That is the only way they can come. The day may bring many tasks, many problems, strains, but invariably they come in single file.

You want to gain emotional poise? Remember the hourglass, the grains of sand dropping one by one.

James Gordon Gilkey

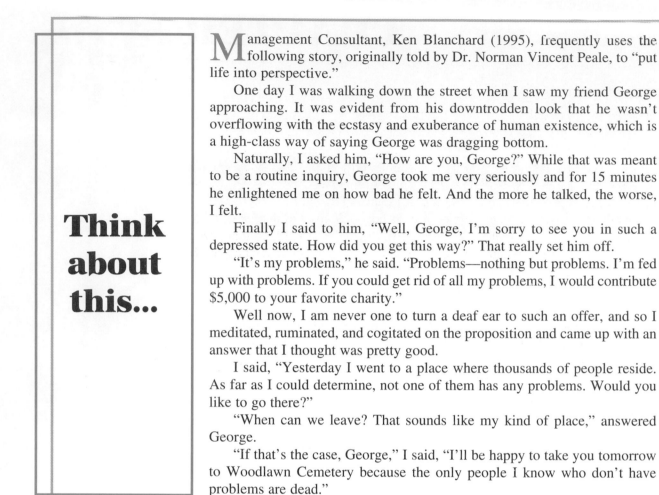

Think about this...

Management Consultant, Ken Blanchard (1995), frequently uses the following story, originally told by Dr. Norman Vincent Peale, to "put life into perspective."

One day I was walking down the street when I saw my friend George approaching. It was evident from his downtrodden look that he wasn't overflowing with the ecstasy and exuberance of human existence, which is a high-class way of saying George was dragging bottom.

Naturally, I asked him, "How are you, George?" While that was meant to be a routine inquiry, George took me very seriously and for 15 minutes he enlightened me on how bad he felt. And the more he talked, the worse, I felt.

Finally I said to him, "Well, George, I'm sorry to see you in such a depressed state. How did you get this way?" That really set him off.

"It's my problems," he said. "Problems—nothing but problems. I'm fed up with problems. If you could get rid of all my problems, I would contribute $5,000 to your favorite charity."

Well now, I am never one to turn a deaf ear to such an offer, and so I meditated, ruminated, and cogitated on the proposition and came up with an answer that I thought was pretty good.

I said, "Yesterday I went to a place where thousands of people reside. As far as I could determine, not one of them has any problems. Would you like to go there?"

"When can we leave? That sounds like my kind of place," answered George.

"If that's the case, George," I said, "I'll be happy to take you tomorrow to Woodlawn Cemetery because the only people I know who don't have problems are dead."

Stress is like spice—in the right proportion it enhances the flavor of a dish. Too little produces a bland, dull meal; too much may choke you. The trick is to find the right amount for you.

Donald Tubesing

Did this story "put life into perspective" for you? Certainly it is true that fewer health, financial, family, work, or social problems would make life more secure and satisfying. However, not having any problems or any stress would you leave you with no choices in life, which would be dull and uninteresting. A certain number of problems and stresses can be stimulating. While some stress is good and necessary, excessive stress can create physical problems and/or behavioral changes.

Do you know that you have the power within yourself to modify both the amount of stress in your life and your reaction to it? Some of you may need to make only a few minor adjustments in your daily life for stress to become more constructive and manageable. Some of you will have to make some radical external changes (for example, change jobs) or internal changes (such as change some of your social requirements and/or attitudes).

Most people, who with courage and support undertake such changes, have only one regret: They did not do it sooner. We would like to encourage you to begin considering what adjustments you may need to make in your daily life for stress to become more constructive and manageable.

Let's begin by discussing what stress is and what causes it.

WHAT IS STRESS?

Even though there is no widely accepted definition of stress, the following viewpoints are worthy of consideration. Hans Selye (1978) studied stress for over 40 years. He considered stress to be a general response by an organism in reaction to any of a number of environmental events. Selye (1978) defines *stress as the rate of wear and tear within the body*. Martin and Osborne (1993) conclude that *stress* can refer to (1) challenging and potentially threatening events and situations; (2) our immediate reactions to those situations; and (3) our body's long-term physical reaction to continuing, threatening events and situations. Dan Taylor (1989; 1990), a stress management consultant in Arlington, Texas, defines *stress* as the mismatch between an individual's coping skills and the demands of his or her environment. From these definitions, the authors conclude that *stress* arises when the perceived demands of a situation exceed the perceived capabilities for meeting the demands.

> Successful activity, no matter how intense, leaves you with comparatively few "scars." It causes stress but little distress.
>
> Hans Selye

Which of the following would you call stressful?

1. Building a new home
2. Being audited by the IRS
3. Getting a promotion
4. Sitting in a dentist's chair for braces
5. Getting married
6. Taking an exam

All of these six life events are stressful because they require us to adapt and change in response to them, which taxes our mental and physical adaptive mechanisms. Because positive or pleasurable events, such as getting a new home, can require as much adaptation on our part as negative or painful events, like being audited by the IRS, they can be equally stressful.

As Stanford psychiatrist David Spiegel says, *"Living a stress-free life is not a reasonable goal. The goal is to deal with it actively and effectively"* (Cowley, 1999). Is there a difference between good stress and bad stress?

TYPES OF STRESS

Hans Selye (1974) has described and labeled four basic types of stress:

1. **Eustress** is defined as good stress or short term stress that strengthens us for immediate physical activity, creativity, and enthusiasm. It is characterized as short-lived, easily identified, externalized, and positive. Two examples would be an individual who experiences short-term stress by psyching up for the hundred-yard dash, and an individual who is really excited about beginning a new project at work. The secret of positive stress is a sense of control. When we can make choices and influence the outcome of a situation, we meet the challenge successfully and return to a normal level of functioning relatively quickly. This is the happy feeling of "I did it!"

2. **Distress** is negative or harmful stress that causes us to constantly readjust or adapt. Distress occurs when we feel no control over outcomes; we see few or no choices; the source of stress is not clear; the stress is prolonged over a period of time, or several sources of stress exist simultaneously. However,

not all negative events cause psychological distress. According to Lazarus and Folkman (1984), distress arises only when the stressor makes demands on the individual that exceed the individual's ability to cope. Therefore, distress is accompanied by feelings of tension, pressure, and anxiety rather than the concerted energy of eustress.

3. **Hyperstress** or overload occurs when stressful events pile up and stretch the limits of our adaptability. An example would be an individual who goes through a divorce, loses a parent, and then has a serious illness, all in the same year. It is when we have to cope with too many changes at once or adapt to radical changes for which we are not prepared that stress can become a serious problem.

4. **Hypostress** or underload occurs when we are bored, lacking stimulation, or unchallenged. This type of stress frustrates our need for variety and new experiences. For example, having a job that does not have new challenges can cause constant frustration. This is considered negative stress. Hans Selye (1974) believes that people who enjoy their work, regardless of how demanding it may be, will be less stress-ridden than people who are bored with a job that makes few demands or is too repetitive. It is not the stress itself that is enjoyed but instead the excitement or stimulation of the anticipated rewards. If you are involved in something you like, you are much more likely to handle frustration, pressure, or conflict effectively. This kind of stress is just not as "stressful."

We have seen that some stress is necessary to give our lives variety and to challenge us to grow and expand our abilities, but too much stress, or the wrong kind, or at the wrong time, becomes debilitating.

As important as it is to understand what stress is, it is even more important to understand where the stress originates. When you determine what stress means for you, you have a choice of dealing with it more effectively or eliminating it completely.

CAUSES OF STRESS

Is it other people, your job, too many things to do, your financial situation, pressure, illness? Stress consists of an event, called a stressor, plus how we feel about it, how we interpret it, and what we do to cope with it.

Common stressors include:

- the setting in which we live
- other people
- places we go
- our daily routine
- family members
- our job
- time—too little, too much
- money
- school
- dating
- our given health condition
- a spoken word

> If you want the rainbow, you have to put up with the rain. It's the same with life. In most lives there are dark and bright spots; there is joy and there is sorrow. The few people who have never known adversity invariably don't have lives that are as rich and satisfying as those who have. If you can handle it, adversity makes you stronger. It also makes you a kinder and more empathetic person. At the end of a life without adversity, it's hard to find a rainbow.
>
> Dolly Parton

- a certain event
- a simple thought

Life Events. Two words best relate to the actual cause of stress: *change* and *threat.* Either or both can disturb the psyche. When workers lose their job, that is a significant change and usually a threat to their ego, self-esteem, and even the material aspects of their life. Similarly, the loss of a spouse is a major change and may pose many different threats.

On the other hand, there are positive events such as marital reconciliation and retirement which can also create changes and threats that must be faced. The changes that result from positive events, however, are generally not as difficult to cope with as the changes that result from negative ones.

Changes and threats often fall into three possible categories (Taylor, 1989; 1990):

1. **Anticipated Life Events.** Examples might be graduation from high school and entering college, a job promotion, marriage, birth, and retirement.
2. **Unexpected Life Events.** Some examples might be a serious accident, separation from a spouse or someone we love, sudden death of a loved one, divorce, and financial problems.
3. **Accumulating Life Events.** This would include a dead-end job, traffic, deadlines and pressures, and on-going conflict with friends or family members.

As you can see, some of the changes and threats above are major and some may be described as just the everyday circumstances of life. What about the daily hassles of living?

Daily Hassles. In recent years, researchers have found that everyday problems and the minor nuisances of life are becoming increasingly significant forms of stress. Richard Lazarus (1993), a leading psychologist who studies emotions and stress, calls these irritating and frustrating incidents that occur in our everyday transactions with the environment—*daily hassles.*

What about your own life? What are the biggest hassles? Are any of the following everyday problems or nuisances stressful for you: misplacing or losing things, having too many tasks to do, wasting time, or worrying about meeting high achievement standards? The ten most frequent hassles derived from Lazarus and his colleagues' study of college students are listed in Table 8.1.

While traumatic life events such as the death of a loved one, or the loss of one's job, are stressful and exert adverse effects on health, the minor hassles of daily life—perhaps because of their frequent, repetitive nature—may sometimes pile up until they eventually overwhelm you (Seta, et al., 1991). Whatever their relative importance, both traumatic life events and daily hassles are important sources of stress for many individuals. Remember, stress eventually adds up.

Now, we have a question for you. What causes some people to be devastated and others motivated by the same event? After all, change by itself does not necessarily lead to stress reactions in all individuals (Naune, 2000).

The Power of Our Thoughts. Dan McGee (Taylor and McGee, 1990) teaches his clients that stress is caused by the interaction between the events in a person's environment and how he or she interprets these events. Modern stress theory

Have you ever felt that it's the little things in life that get you down? Daily hassles may have a greater effect on our moods and health than do the major misfortunes of life.

Richard Lazarus

Life is full of interruptions; this is just another one.

Dr. Ronny Crownover

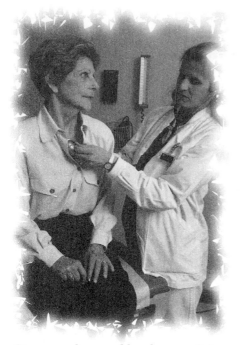

Stress can be a problem because it is linked to a number of illnesses and visits to family doctors.

these stages of chain of reactions to stress the *general adaptation syndrome*. We will discuss each of these reactions.

The Alarm Stage. Your body recognizes the stressor and prepares for fight or flight, which is done by a release of hormones from the endocrine glands. These hormones cause an increase in the heartbeat and respiration, elevation in the blood sugar level, increase in perspiration, dilated pupils, and slowed digestion. According to Dr. Walter B. Cannon of the Harvard Medical School, you then choose whether to use this burst of energy for fight or flee.

The Resistance Stage. This is a period of recovery and stabilization, during which the individual adapts to the stress. Consequently, the individual does what he or she can to meet the threat. Although it is true that the level of bodily arousal is not as high as it was in the alarm stage, it does remain higher than usual. This is nature's way of giving us greater protection against the original stressor. Coping responses are often strongest at this point. Because the individual attempts to do what is necessary to meet the threat, the most effective behavior of which the person is capable of often comes forth. Often, people are so overwhelmed in the alarm stage that they simply cannot function. However, if there is effective functioning, it occurs in the resistance stage.

The Exhaustion Stage. Stress is a natural and unavoidable part of our lives, but it becomes a problem when it persists and becomes long term. Continuous stress will not enable the important *resistance* step to take place, and you will go from step one, *alarm,* directly to step three, *exhaustion.* When you remain exhausted because of continual exposure to stress, you become more receptive to physiological reactions and behavioral changes.

Stress can be a problem because it is linked to a number of illnesses (Baron and Byrne, 1999). It has been estimated that close to 90% of visits to primary care physicians are for stress-related problems. And, recent research indicates fully 40% of employee turnover is stress-related (Epstein, 2000). Furthermore, absenteeism in the workplace shot up 25% from 1997 to 1998. Increasingly, it's stress (Stone, 1999). Stress can lead to such physiological responses as increased heart rate and blood pressure. If prolonged, these changes can be dangerous, sometimes leading to *psychosomatic* or *psycho-physiological disorders* that are real physical disorders in which stress and emotional reactions play a part (Kaplan, 1998).

What are these reactions and changes?

PHYSICAL EFFECTS OF STRESS

John Powell (1990) says, *"We do not bury our emotions dead—they remain alive in our subconscious minds and intestines to hurt and trouble us."* Review Table 8.2—Physical Effects of Stress for some examples of the "trouble" that can result (Miller and Smith, 1994; Davis et al., 1998).

These physical problems are your body's natural way of telling you that there is too much stress and tension in your life, and most of us have a special physical organ or target area that let us know when the stress is too great. Do you know what your special target area is? Once you have learned to tune into your own signals, you will be able to recognize stress when it starts, before it takes a toll on your body.

BEHAVIORAL EFFECTS OF STRESS

Another measuring tool for you to help recognize excessive stress in yourself and others is through behavioral changes. Review these changes in Table 8.2 Behavioral Effects of Stress.

Evaluate this list in relationship to your own life and add any other behavioral changes you may experience that are not included here. This list can help you recognize imbalance and disharmony within and without, and that recognition is necessary if you are to effect a positive change for yourself.

Now that you know how to recognize physiological and behavioral effects of stress, is there anything else you need to be aware of?

Table 8.2 Effects of Stress

Physical

Headaches	Rapid heart rate
Dermatitis	Impotence
Ulcers	Indigestion
Asthma	Diarrhea
Colitis	Stomach aches
Common colds	Fatigue
Skin rashes	Aching back and limbs
Allergies	Neck and shoulder tension
Hyperventilation	Excessive sweating
Vaginal discharges	Blurry vision
Dizziness	Burning stomach
Muscle spasms	Vomiting
Hypertension	Delayed menstruation

Behavioral

Nervous tics	Clammy skin
Door slamming	Withdrawal
Fist clenching	Depression
Insomnia	Irritability
Tears	Acts of violence
Frowning	Impatience
Hair twisting	Changed eating habits
Jaw tightening	Changed drinking habits
Nail biting	Changed smoking habits
Grinding of teeth	Worry
Temper tantrums	Boredom
Apathy	Visible fears

Miller & Smith, (1994); Davis et al., (1998)

PERSONALITY TYPES

Are you a stress seeker or a stress-avoider? How do you perform under pressure? Is it possible to respond to the normal pressures and stress of life with vitality, meaning, and joy? What kind of lifestyle do you prefer to live: rushed, relaxed, or somewhere in between?

Research has indicated that there are basically three personality types in relation to stress, with each type differing in their abilities to effectively handle stress. These types are *Type A, Type B,* and a combination of Type A and Type B. What behavioral characteristics do these types have?

Type A. There has been a tremendous amount of research directed toward determining the correlation between heart disease and emotional stress. Among the findings is evidence that there is an association between coronary artery and heart disease and a complex of emotional reactions which have been designated *Type A Behavioral Pattern* (Friedman & Rosenman, 1981). These researchers found that almost all of their cardiac patients had in common a competitive, aggressive, ambitious, and stressful lifestyle.

Recent research on the link between Type A behavior and coronary disease indicates, however, that the association is not as strong as Freedman and Rosenman thought. Attention is focusing on hostility and anger-prone tendencies. People who are *hostile,* or consistently *turn anger inward,* appear to be more likely to develop heart disease (Allan & Scheidt, 1996).

Here are some other characteristics of the Type A behavioral pattern:

- A drive to succeed, coupled with impatience, irritability, and aggressiveness
- Trouble relaxing and is restless
- Perfectionist and seeks results *now*
- Feelings of pressure even when relaxed
- A constant clock watcher
- Ignores fatigue while doing strenuous work
- Thrives on stress; his or her work is never done
- Only happy with a vigorous, fast-paced lifestyle
- Time pressures frequently create frustration and sometimes hostility
- May appear nervous, scattered, and hyper
- Eats fast, walks fast, and talks fast

> One striking thing we have discovered is that there are two main types of human beings: "racehorses" and "turtles."
>
> Hans Selye

Are you . . .

a racehorse

a turtle

or somewhere in between?

What kind of lifestyle do you prefer to live: rushed, relaxed, or a balance between the two?

Furthermore, Dr. James Blumenthal (1999), professor of medical psychology at Duke University Medical Center, suggests that Type A people have a strong need to control events in their lives, including the behavior of people around them. Dr. Blumenthal also indicates that one reason Type A people suffer so much from life stress is they have difficulty accepting what they can and cannot control.

Type B. This behavior pattern (Friedman & Rosenman, 1981) is the opposite of the Type A. Type B people are seldom harried by the need to be involved in an ever-increasing series of activities in a continually decreasing amount of time. Here are some other characteristics of Type B people:

- Serious but easy going
- Patient and relaxed
- Enjoys leisure and opportunities to experiment and reflect
- Prefers a peaceful, steady, quiet, and generally tranquil lifestyle
- Not easily irritated
- Are less competitive than A's
- Slower paced; feels no need to hurry
- May appear lethargic, sluggish, and bored
- Is a stress avoider; may avoid new challenges
- Speaks slow, walks slow, eats slow
- Sometimes lacks the excitement, enthusiasm, and dynamism needed to perform at peak levels under pressure

> The time to relax is when you don't have the time for it.
>
> The Best of Bits & Pieces

Sensible, enjoyable exercise is nature's anti-stress reaction remedy.

Type B people may have a tremendous drive, but they may not take the risks necessary for big rewards. When they do take the risks, their drive is coupled with time to ponder leisurely and weigh alternatives. It may sound like Type B people do not have a lot of stresses. However, if they are in a Type A environment that requires a great deal of structure, this can be very stressful to them.

Which Type Are You? Most of us are either Type A or Type B, with varying degrees of Type A and B. It is estimated that about 40 percent of the population is Type A and 60 percent is Type B (Paulus, et al., 1999).

You will be given an opportunity to complete a personality type inventory at the end of this chapter. Like most stress inventories, this one is somewhat flawed because it does not give enough weight to individual differences. Be sure and take this into consideration when you look at your scores.

Actually, each of us is really the best judge of ourselves, and we can gradually develop an instinctive feeling that tells us whether we are running above or below the stress level that suits us best. Do you know what your normal stress endurance level is? We encourage you to examine your own behavior in relation to stress, because the key to effective stress management is recognizing when stress becomes more debilitating than stimulating.

In the following section, we will discuss some negative and debilitating techniques of coping with stress.

> When we finally come to learn that many things come to all of us that we cannot do anything about, we shall have put a broad and sturdy plank into the foundation of our philosophy.
>
> Grove Patterson

NEGATIVE AND DEFENSIVE COPING

Coping refers to active efforts to master, reduce, or tolerate the demands created by stress (Weiten and Lloyd, 1999). When we cope, we consciously think and make a decision to deal with the problems we face. However, we may cope in negative ways. We may drink too much, eat too much, worry too much, or even abuse medication and drugs. See "Consider This" below for additional negative copers.

Sometimes the stress, frustration, and conflict of dealing with these problems interferes with our ability to maintain a healthy self-concept. We become extremely sensitive to threats to our ego. We will do almost anything to avoid, escape, or shield ourselves from the anxieties elicited by these threats.

In order to protect our feelings of self-esteem and self-respect, we may unconsciously resort to various distortions of reality, frequently referred to as *defense mechanisms* (Freud, 1936).

Defense mechanisms do not eliminate the problems that are the cause of anxiety, but they help us to hide or disguise our feelings and temporarily deal with anxiety or stress. Defense mechanisms have two primary characteristics. *First, they distort and deny reality. Second, they operate unconsciously, so that we are unaware that we are using them.*

Following is a discussion of some of the more commonly used defense mechanisms:

Rationalization is perhaps the most widely used defense mechanism, because we all feel a need sometimes to explain our behavior. When the explanations of-

CONSIDER THIS . . .

Negative Copers*

Alcohol:	Drink to change your mood. Use alcohol as your friend.
Denial:	Pretend nothing is wrong. Lie. Ignore the problem.
Drugs:	Abuse coffee; aspirin/medications. Smoke pot. Pop pills.
Eating:	Keep binging. Go on a diet. Use food to console you.
Fault Finding:	Have a judgmental attitude. Complain. Criticize.
Illness:	Develop headaches/nervous stomach/major illness. Become accident prone.
Indulging:	Stay up late. Sleep in. Buy on impulse. Waste time.
Passivity:	Hope it gets better. Procrastinate. Wait for a lucky break.
Revenge:	Get even. Be sarcastic. Talk mean.
Stubborness:	Be rigid. Demand your way. Refuse to be wrong.
Tantrums:	Yell. Mope. Pout. Swear. Drive recklessly.
Withdrawal:	Avoid the situation. Skip school or work. Keep your feelings to yourself.
Worrying:	Fret over things. Imagine the worst.

Have you ever used any of these copers?

*Reprinted with permission from Structured Exercises in Stress Management, *Volume II*, Nancy Loving Tubesing and Donald A. Tubesing, Editors. © 1995 Whole Person Press, P. O. Box 3151, Duluth, MN 55803, (218) 728-6807.

fered are reasonable, rational, and convincing—but not real reasons—we say a person is *rationalizing*. Rationalization unconsciously provides us with reasons for behavior we ourselves find somewhat questionable. We frequently see this defense mechanism used in schools and universities. Every teacher is familiar with a rather amazing phenomenon that occurs whenever a test is scheduled. An incredible number of disasters sweep through the area. An amazing number of grandparents, mothers, fathers, aunts, uncles, relatives, and pets become ill or die. Alarm clocks do not work and cars will not start.

Repression is the exclusion of painful, unwanted, or dangerous thoughts and impulses from the conscious mind. However, these thoughts and impulses continue to influence our behavior. They may be the cause of our "forgetting" an appointment with the doctor or, "inadvertently" working so late that we cannot go to the meeting we felt uncomfortable attending.

Projection is when we attribute our own feelings, shortcomings, or unacceptable impulses to others. An individual is suspicious of her boyfriend. She thinks he is dating other women and is overcome with the feeling of jealousy. The young woman's feeling of anxiety comes from her unconscious desire to date others.

Reaction formation is a defense in which impulses are not only repressed, they are also controlled by emphasizing the opposite behavior. A person who has strong sexual desires that are considered immoral joins The Association to Eliminate Pornography. By joining this organization, the individual is able to avoid his or her undesirable feelings by acting out a behavior opposite from the real impulse or feelings.

Sublimation is when we redirect our basic desires toward a socially valued activity. An example is the hostile individual who was beaten by a parent and later finds a productive outlet in establishing an organization for victims of child abuse. Although this is certainly a valued activity and may provide a degree of comfort for the individual, he or she may have been able to accomplish more by directing hostility toward changing and strengthening the laws for child abuse criminals.

Displacement is when the person redirects strong feelings from one person or object to another that seems more acceptable and less threatening. Your boss gets mad at you, but you cannot release your feelings on your boss, so you go home and yell at your spouse. Your spouse gets mad at your child, so your child kicks the dog and the dog bites you. These are all examples of displacement. Substitute objects are rarely as satisfying as the original objects, but they are less anxiety arousing.

Defense mechanisms are designed to help us escape the pain of anxiety in stressful situations. Most of us would have difficulty maintaining our mental health without resorting to such defenses. However, the trouble is that these defenses can become common patterns of behavior for reacting to problems and stress.

Do you have a habit of using any of these defense mechanisms? Think of it like this: the more aware you are of the defense mechanisms you use and why you use them, the more likely will be your attempts to face your stressful situations in an open and honest manner. It is important for you to remember that although defense mechanisms offer you short-term relief, your discomfort quickly returns. Why? Your problem has not been solved!

> The world breaks everyone and afterward many are stronger at the broken place.
>
> Ernest Hemingway

Speaking of problems for a moment, is there a difference in how men and women cope with problems and the normal stresses of living? Does cultural background have any influence in what events are perceived as most stressful? Let us look further at these two questions.

GENDER, CULTURE AND STRESS

As we have already discussed, individuals have different levels of tolerance for stress. Some seem to thrive in situations in which others feel uncomfortably stressed. Also, some individuals actually seem to seek out stressful situations. As a result of these differences, methods of coping with stress vary accordingly.

Gender and Stress. One of the major differences between men and women is how they cope with stress. Men become increasingly focused and withdrawn, while women become increasingly overwhelmed and emotionally involved. It is these differences in coping styles which can lead to friction in relationships. Review the "Gender and You" box below taken from John Gray's (1992) bestseller, *Men are from Mars, Women are from Venus.*

Without understanding their differences, Mary and Tom will grow further apart. When a man has problems, or is under stress and cannot find a solution, he copes by doing something else to disengage his mind from the problems of the day, like reading the newspaper, playing a game, or tinkering with his car. He will focus on solving his problems at a later date, and during this time, he temporarily loses awareness of everything else. However, when a woman becomes upset, or is stressed by her day, to find relief, she copes by seeking out someone she trusts and then talks in great detail about the problems of her day or whatever potential problems she may see on the horizon. Through exploring her feelings in this process, she gains a greater awareness of what is really bothering her. Although she would like to talk with her husband, she frequently finds that he attempts to help her find a solution to her problems. After all, that is what he would do, solve his problem himself.

In another one of Dr. Gray's (1993) popular books, *Men, Women and Relationships,* the suggestion is made for men to just listen to women's problems, without giving advice. Remember, talking is a woman's natural and healthy way of reacting to stress, and if she feels she is being heard, her stress will seem much less. On the other hand, women need to let men disengage and ponder their own problems, and when they have discovered the solution for themselves, they will then share some of "what has been going on with them" and possibly even report their personal solution(s). Remember, quiet concentration, without an immediate need to talk, is a man's natural and healthy way of reacting to stress.

> If women resent men's tendency to offer solutions to problems, men complain about women's refusal to take action to solve the problems they complain about.
>
> Deborah Tannen

When Tom comes home, he wants to relax and unwind by quietly reading the newspaper. He is stressed by the unsolved problems of his day and finds relief through forgetting them.

His wife, Mary, also wants to relax from her stressful day. She, however, wants to find relief by talking about the problems of her day. The tension slowly building between them gradually becomes resentment.

Tom secretly thinks Mary talks too much, while Mary feels ignored.

Four ethnic groups—Caucasian, African-American, Hispanic, and Asian-American—estimate how stressful they would expect to find events in three different domains:

Academic Domain: Older African-Americans and Hispanics perceived more stress than older Asian-Americans. Older Hispanics perceived significantly more stress than older Caucasians.

Financial Domain: Both African-American and Hispanic individuals felt more stress in meeting events than did either Caucasian or Asian-American individuals.

Personal Domain: African-American men perceived greater stress in the personal domain than did African-American women. Young Caucasian women perceived more stress in this domain than did older Caucasian women.

Pliner & Brown, (1995)

FOCUS ON DIVERSITY

Getting back to Mary and Tom, do you think Mary can learn to let Tom have a little time to unwind from the day before she tries to talk with him? Do you think Tom can learn to just *listen* and try to *understand* Mary's problems?

Culture and Stress. Who you are is a factor in what you may find stressful and how stressed you feel. For example, Judith Pliner and Duane Brown (1995) surveyed 229 students (123 females and 106 males) from four ethnic groups (white, African-American, Hispanic, and Asian-American) who were asked to estimate how stressful they would expect to find events in three different domains: academic, financial, and personal. Responses to the survey, summarized above in Focus on Diversity, indicate that an individual's ethnic background is associated with what that person appraises as stressful.

Studies such as this imply that although some events are inherently stressful for everyone, many other events are appraised as stressful or not according to an individual's ethnic background, gender, and conditioning (Dawis and Fruehling, 1996).

Perhaps it is now time to answer this question: How can I cope when I have so many problems and so many stressors?

WHAT EFFECTS THE WAY INDIVIDUALS COPE WITH STRESS

It seems that some individuals are stress resistant and others are more susceptible to the harmful effects of stress. What accounts for the difference in the way different individuals cope with stress? Dr. Lyle Miller and Dr. Alma Smith (1994) give an interesting view in their book, *The Stress Solution:*

People are quite different from one another in their susceptibility to stress. Some are like horses, and some are like butterflies. The horses tolerate great amounts of stress without faltering or breaking stride; the butterflies fall apart under the slightest demand or pressure. Whether you're a horse or a butterfly depends on several ingredients: your physical constitution, how well you take care of yourself, and your resources for coping with stress. The tougher you are, the more you can take. If you have a stress-prone constitution, are lazy about exercise, eat poorly, abuse stimulants, don't get enough sleep, or don't use your coping resources, you don't stand much chance against stress.

Hardiness. One characteristic that seems to distinguish stress-resistant people from those who are more susceptible to its harmful effects is known as *hardiness*. Actually, this term refers to a cluster of characteristics rather than just one. Stress researcher Suzanne Kobasa's (1984) findings suggest that hardy people seem to differ from others in three respects:

● *Commitment* (rather than alienation)—they have deeper involvement in their jobs and other life activities.
● *Control* (rather than powerlessness)—they believe that they can, in fact, influence important events in their lives and the outcomes they experience.
● *Challenge* (rather than threats)—they perceive change as a challenge and an opportunity to grow rather than as a threat to their security.

While some studies have replicated Kobasa's findings (Ouellette, 1993), others have questioned whether or not all the characteristics of hardiness identified by Kobasa are important in helping people to resist stress reactions. For example, researcher S. C. Funk (1992) believes that *commitment* and *control* are more important than viewing life as a challenge. Which of these three elements is important to you in resisting stress? You may recall in Chapter 3 that an optimistic outlook was discussed as a major ingredient for achieving success in various personal endeavors.

One thing seems fairly certain: stress-hardy people manage their lives by managing themselves. Wayne and Mary Sotile (1996) in a *Psychology Today* article, summarize stress-hardy people in this way:

> They deal with stress from the inside out, controlling their own attitudes, coping tendencies, and relationship dynamics in order to maintain their emotional well-being.

While there may not be complete agreement with Kobasa's research findings, there is little doubt but that such research has stimulated further studies on how personality affects people's health and their tolerance of stress. Some of these findings point to the role of an optimistic outlook in stress tolerance.

Optimism or Pessimism. *Optimism* is defined as a general tendency to envision the future as favorable. In contrast, *pessimism* may be defined as a general tendency to envision the future as unfavorable. Research suggests that optimists cope with stress in more adaptive ways than pessimists (Scheier and Carver, 1992). For example, optimists are more likely to engage in action-oriented, problem-focused coping. They are more willing than pessimists to seek social support, and they are more likely to emphasize the positive in their appraisals of stressful events. For the person who expects to achieve success, stress may be viewed as

Are you a horse or a butterfly? . . .

an obstacle to be overcome rather than as an obstacle that cannot be hurdled. Consequently, pessimists are more likely to deal with stress by giving up or engaging in denial.

Are you a horse or a butterfly? Do you believe you can influence important events in your life and the outcomes you experience? Do you perceive change as a challenge or a threat to your security? What choices do you have when confronted with stressful events and situations?

Three Coping Options. Actually, we have three different options when we are confronted with stressful events and situations. According to Taylor and McGee (1989, 1990), we can:

1. **Change Environments.** We might choose to move to another city, change jobs, separate from our spouse, and so on.
2. **Change the Environment.** We can often work to improve the situation that is causing us so much stress.
3. **Change Me (Improve My Coping Skills).** William James once said, *"The greatest discovery of our generation is that men can alter their lives by altering the attitudes of their mind."* This is especially important to remember in relation to stress because, as we stated earlier, *it is not really the event that causes stress, it is our reaction to it—our attitude.*

Our reaction to any event, stressful or not, depends on our thoughts and feelings about what happened or what should have happened. Earlier in this chapter, we stated that most often, the greatest source of stress is the tremendous pressure and anxiety we create internally with our own thoughts and feelings. We also indicated that we would discuss how to deal with stressful thoughts and feelings. We are now ready to do this.

Your response to an event is based on your thought, which is in control, since the quality of your thought is based on your beliefs, prejudices, and attitude.

Dale Rink

DEALING WITH STRESSFUL THOUGHTS AND FEELINGS

Have you ever said, "I can't help the way I feel?" You want to feel calm when taking tests, but you still get butterflies in your stomach. You want to feel confident when talking to your teacher about a "bad" grade, but you still feel nervous. You do not want to be afraid of heights, but you cannot keep yourself from feeling scared. It is almost like you have no control over your feelings. These feelings are just automatic responses to certain stressful events and people in your life.

Consequently, you may say that these events or people cause you to feel the way you do. After all, touching your hand to a hot burner causes pain, so why can't people and certain events cause you stress? Let us diagram two events and see what is happening. See box at bottom of page.

By now, you are still convinced that certain events and other people cause you to feel the way you do. The authors will not argue with you that touching your hand to a hot burner really does cause pain. However, we can not agree that talking to your teacher really causes you to have tense, stressful feelings. Here's why!

Who listens when you are stressed? Is it your spouse, friend, child, or your dog?

THE POWER OF SELF-TALK

Rational emotive therapist Albert Ellis (1980) indicates that the event of talking to your teacher does not cause you to feel tense and stressed. Instead it is your beliefs, or what you say to yourself *(self-talk)* about talking to your teacher that causes you to feel tense, nervous, and stressed.

Ellis (1980) believes that a great deal of our stress is unnecessary, and that it really comes from faulty conclusions we have made about the world. It is really our interpretations, *what we say to ourselves about our experiences,* that creates the debilitating emotions of anxiety, anger, and depression, as discussed in Chapter four.

Let us examine the theory of Dr. Ellis by looking at an example he frequently gives at the Institute for Rational-Emotive Therapy in New York:

> Assume you walk by your friend's house, and he sticks his head out the window and calls you a bunch of nasty names. You would probably become angry and upset with your friend.

In a real sense, through our own self-talk, we are either in the construction business or the wrecking business.

Dorothy Corkville

Activating Event	Causes	Consequences or Feelings
Touching your hand to a hot burner	causes	physical pain
Talking to your teacher	causes	stressful, tense feelings

Now let's imagine that you were walking by a mental hospital, rather than your friend's house, and your friend is a patient in the hospital. This time, he yells at you, calling you the same ugly names. What would your feelings be? Would you be as angry and upset now that you know he is not normal and does not live in his house? Probably not!

Actually, the activating event (being called nasty names) was identical in both cases, but your feelings were very different because you were saying something very different to yourself.

In the first example, you were probably saying things like, "He shouldn't call me those nasty names! That's really awful! I'll pay him back!"

However, in the second example, you might be telling yourself something like, "Poor sick John. He can't help what he is doing." Instead of feeling angry, you were probably feeling a degree of sympathy for your friend.

It is easy to see that your *different beliefs (interpretations and thoughts)* about the events determined your feelings. Let us look at the diagram below of your two emotional experiences: A + B = C.

Ellis (1993) and cognitive therapist Aaron Beck (1993, 1991) stress that our extreme, debilitative and stressful emotions are due largely to our *irrational beliefs*—what we say to ourselves.

Do you have some of the irrational beliefs outlined in Table 8.3? What is the difference between rational and irrational beliefs? Perhaps we need to examine this further.

> It is always better to proceed on the basis of a recognition of what is, rather than what ought to be.
>
> Stewart Alsop

WHAT IS THE DIFFERENCE IN IRRATIONAL AND RATIONAL BELIEFS—SELF-TALK

Sometimes, *self-talk,* what we say to ourselves about an event or situation is irrational. It does not even make sense, but we believe that it is true. *The ingredient that makes a belief irrational is that it cannot be scientifically verified. There is no empirical evidence or proof to support the belief.*

Irrational beliefs (self-talk) result in inappropriate emotions, behaviors, and more stress. Inappropriate emotions and behaviors are those that are likely to thwart an individual's desired goals. As we discussed in Chapter four, when annoyance turns into anger or disappointment turns into depression, an individual is likely to be unsuccessful in achieving his or her goals. Consequently, the individual feels stressed.

> Your most important irrational pathway is musturbation—or you're devoutly following the tyranny of the shoulds.
>
> Albert Ellis

A	+	B	=	C
		Thoughts		**Consequences**
Activating Event	+	**or beliefs**	=	**or feelings**
Being called names		My friend shouldn't do this		Angry, upset
Being called names		My friend must be sick		Pity, sympathy

On the other hand, *rational beliefs (self-talk)* are those beliefs that result in appropriate emotions and behaviors. Appropriate emotions and behaviors are those that are likely to help an individual attain desired goals. Consequently, the individual feels less stress. It is important to remember that even negative emotions (such as disappointment, concern, etc.) can be appropriate. *The ingredient that makes a belief rational is that it can be scientifically verified. There is empirical evidence or proof to support the belief.*

We will now examine the characteristics of irrational and rational self-talk: What makes sense and what doesn't? What objective evidence can be provided to support your self-talk—your beliefs?

CHARACTERISTICS OF IRRATIONAL AND RATIONAL SELF-TALK

As you can see from Table 8.3, almost all irrational self-verbalizations include Should Statements, Awfulizing Statements, and Overgeneralizations. David Burns (1999) refers to these irrational self-verbalizations *as a twisted form of absolutist thinking.* We will now look at these individually.

Should Statements. These are absolutistic demands or moral imperatives that the individual believes must occur. Individuals tend to express their shoulds in three areas: *I should, you should, and the world should. Should statements also contain words such as ought, have to, and must.*

Have you ever made statements similar to the ones below?

> Helen **should not** be so inconsiderate.
> John **should** be a better teacher.
> People **ought** to be at meetings on time.
> I **have to (must)** make an "A" on the next test.

These statements all imply that other people and things in your world need to be as you want them to be. This is really unreasonable.

True, it would be more pleasant if Helen were more considerate; it would be helpful if John were a better teacher; it would be beneficial if people were at meetings on time; it would be nice to make an "A" on the exam.

Think about it like this: Does it really make sense that a person *should* or *should not* do something? Where can you find objective proof that a person *should* or *should not* do something? Is not it reasonable that people can actually do or choose not to do whatever they want. What evidence or proof can you provide that you *must* make an A on the test? Are you going to die if you do not make an A?

It is perfectly rational for us to wish that people would behave differently and that things in our world would be as we want them to be. It is even okay to change what can be changed and accept those things that cannot be altered. It is unreasonable, however, for you to expect that other people or the world will ever meet your unrealistic expectations. Reality is reality! Failure to accept this reality can result in your life being filled with disappointments and *more stress.* Albert Ellis (1993), author of *How To Stubbornly Refuse to Make Yourself Miserable About Anything—Yes, Anything,* has an interesting insight:

The way one interprets and evaluates reality is the key to one's emotional and mental health.

Albert Ellis

Long ago I made up my mind to let other people have their own peculiarities.

David Grayson

Table 8.3   Rational and Irrational Beliefs

Albert Ellis (1998) has identified some common irrational beliefs. The rational belief is listed next to the irrational belief.

Irrational Belief	Rational Belief
It is a dire necessity for me to have love and approval from peers, family, and friends.	It is desirable to win the approval of others for practical purposes. It is productive to concentrate on giving rather than receiving love.
I must be competent, adequate, achieving, and almost perfect in all that I undertake.	It is better to accept oneself as a fallible human being who makes mistakes. It is more important to do your best than to be perfect.
When people act badly or unfairly, they should be punished or reprimanded. They are bad people.	Individuals may engage in inappropriate acts. It is useful to try to help them change or to just accept them as they are.
It is awful, horrible, and catastrophic when people and things are not the way I want them to be.	It is too bad that life isn't always the way I'd like it to be. It makes sense to try to change those things that can be changed and to accept those things that can't be altered.
Human unhappiness is caused by external events and individuals have little or no ability to control their unhappiness.	Emotional disturbance is caused by our attitudes about events, and we can reduce our misery by working hard to change our irrational beliefs.
I should be anxious about events or things in the future that are unknown or dangerous.	One can neither predict nor prevent unknowns in the future. It is better to change what can be changed and accept the inevitable when it is beyond our control.
It is easier to avoid than to face life's difficulties and responsibilities.	The easy way out is usually more difficult in the long run.
Human beings must be dependent on others and have someone strong on whom to rely.	Although it is helpful to turn to others for advice or feedback, making your own decisions is ultimately the better path toward accomplishing your aims.
My present problems are a result of my past history. Because I have this past, my problems must continue to endure.	Just because something affected me in the past, there is no reason that it must continue to affect me in the future. I can learn from past experiences.
There must be a perfect solution to this problem, and it is awful if I can't find it.	Some problems are insoluble. Even where solutions exist, it is likely that no solution will be perfect.
The world should be fair.	We live in an unfair world. It is more productive to accept what we can't change and to seek happiness despite life's inequities.
I should be comfortable and without pain at all times.	Few things can be achieved without pain. Although pain is uncomfortable, it can be tolerated.

1. **Monitor Your Emotional Reactions.** Try to describe what you are *feeling* as accurately as possible. Say, "I feel angry, depressed, fearful, hurt, jealous, sad, worried." Because it is possible to experience more than one negative emotion at the same time, be sure and write down all the unpleasant feelings that you are having.

2. **Describe the Activating Event.** Write down your perception of the event or whatever seemed to trigger the events that led to your unpleasant feelings and your present stressful condition. It may be something that someone did; it may be something you need to do but are afraid of doing; it may be a series of several small unpleasant happenings, and you have just had too much!

3. **Record Your Self-Talk.** What are you saying to yourself that is causing you to feel angry, depressed, and so on? What are you thinking or what is going through your head? What are you worried about? When you think about . . . (the activating event) . . ., how do you make yourself depressed or angry? Becoming aware of your self-talk may be difficult at first, but with practice, you can learn to do so.

4. **Dispute Your Irrational Beliefs.** It is now necessary for you to go back to step 3 and do three things: 1) decide whether each statement is a rational or an irrational belief; 2) explain why the belief does or does not make sense; and 3) write some different statements that you can say to yourself in the future to prevent yourself from having such debilitative emotions and experiencing such stress. For example, let us say that you are the type of person who overgeneralizes about the consequences of failing a test. You think such irrational thoughts as:

   "Why do I always mess up?"
   "This is going to be terrible"

A man is hurt not so much by what happens, as by his opinion of what happens.

Montaigne

Some effective coping statements might include:

   "I'm not going to think about failing."
   "I'm going to concentrate on being successful; that's better than getting nervous."
   "I'm going to take three deep breaths, relax, calm down, and practice positive thinking; then I'll start to work on the exam."

The activity, Identifying and Disputing Self-Talk and Beliefs, will give you an opportunity to review and practice this four-step process.

Now that you know how to identify and dispute the irrational beliefs that have been causing you stress, we will now discuss some additional ways of managing stress.

20 TIPS FOR MANAGING STRESS

Following is a list of several suggestions that may help you live with stress, whether it is an occasional mild upset, which most of us experience, or one that is more lasting and severe. Table 8.4 also gives some additional positive coping strategies.

Table 8.4   Positive Copers*

Diversions

Getaways:	Spend time alone. See a movie. Daydream.
Hobbies:	Write. Paint. Remodel. Create something.
Learning:	Take a class. Read. Join a club.
Music:	Play an instrument. Sing. Listen to the stereo.
Play:	Play a game. Go out with friends.
Work:	Tackle a new project. Keep busy. Volunteer.

Family

Balancing:	Balance time at work and home. Accept the good with the bad.
Conflict Resolution:	Look for win-win solutions. Forgive readily.
Esteem Building:	Build good family feelings. Focus on personal strengths.
Networking:	Develop friendships with other families. Make use of community resources.
Togetherness:	Take time to be together. Build family traditions. Express affection.

Interpersonal

Affirmation:	Believe in yourself. Trust others. Give compliments.
Assertiveness:	State your needs and wants. Say "No" respectfully.
Contact:	Make new friends. Touch. Really listen to others.
Expression:	Show feelings. Share feelings.
Limits:	Accept other's boundaries. Drop some involvements.
Linking:	Share problems with others. Ask for support from family and friends.

Mental

Imagination:	Look for the humor. Anticipate the future.
Life Planning:	Set clear goals. Plan for the future.
Organizing:	Take charge. Make order. Don't let things pile up.
Problem Solving:	Solve it yourself. Seek outside help. Tackle problems head-on.
Relabeling:	Change perspectives. Look for good in a bad situation.
Time Management:	Focus on top priorities. Work smarter, not harder.

Physical

Biofeedback:	Listen to your body. Know your physical limitations.
Exercise:	Pursue physical fitness. Jog. Swim. Dance. Walk.
Relaxation:	Tense and relax each muscle. Take a warm bath. Breathe deeply.
Self-Care:	Energize your work and play. Strive for self-improvement.
Stretching:	Take short breaks through your day.

Spiritual

Commitment:	Take up a worthy cause. Say "yes." Invest yourself meaningfully.
Faith:	Find purpose and meaning. Trust God.
Prayer:	Confess. Ask forgiveness. Pray for others. Give thanks.
Surrender:	Let go of problems. Learn to live with the situation.
Valuing:	Set priorities. Be consistent. Spend time and energy wisely.
Worship:	Share beliefs with others. Put faith into action.

*Reprinted with permission from Structured Exercises in Stress Management, *Volume 2, Nancy Loving Tubesing and Donald A. Tubesing, Editors* © 1995 Whole Person Press, P. O. Box 3153, Duluth, MN 55803, (218) 728-6807.

God grant me the serenity to accept the things I cannot change, courage to change the things I can, and the wisdom to know the difference.

Reinhold Niebuhr

1. **Work Off Stress.** If you are angry or upset, try to do something physical such as running, gardening, playing tennis, or cleaning out the garage. Working the stress out of your system will leave you much better prepared to handle your problems.

2. **Have Fun.** Part of the zest for life that minimizes the adverse effect of stress is enjoyment. Do something each day that you really enjoy, whether it is reading your favorite book or magazine, having lunch with a friend, watching your favorite TV program, taking a walk, playing your musical instrument, or having fun with some kiddie-toy collection. Authorities agree that people who preserve their sense of fun are better equipped to solve problems, think creatively and manage stress (Fox, 1999).

3. **Talk It Out.** When something is bothering you, talk it out with someone you trust and respect such as a friend, family member, clergyman, teacher, or counselor. Sometimes another person can help you see a new side to your problem and thus, a new solution.

4. **Give in Occasionally.** If you find yourself getting into frequent quarrels with people, try giving in once in awhile instead of fighting and insisting that you are always right. You may find others beginning to give in, too.

5. **Do Something for Others.** If you find that you are worrying about yourself all the time, try doing something for somebody else. This helps get your mind off yourself and can give you a sense of well-being.

6. **Have Some Real Close Friends.** Having true friends that you do not need to fear criticism from, and whom you can talk freely to, is important. Friends who are accepting are not a threat to your ego. Without at least one such friend, a person is forced into emotional isolation, which in itself is a stress, and one that usually produces adverse responses.

Strategies to . . .

. . . MANAGING STRESS

- Work it off
- Have fun
- Talk it out
- Give in occasionally
- Do something for others
- Have some real close friends
- Eat sensibly
- Get organized
- Rehearse
- Do it now
- Learn to say "No"
- Learn to accept what you cannot change
- Avoid self-medication
- Live a balanced life
- Get enough sleep and rest
- Make yourself available
- Shun the "Perfect" urge
- Develop a regular exercise program
- Take care of yourself
- Learn to relax

7. **Eat Sensibly.** Try to have balanced meals and pay close attention to the habit of eating "junk foods." Do not starve yourself to lose weight. Watch excessive sugar and caffeine. Think of your body as a car. If you do not put oil, gas, and water in your car frequently, it will quit running. So will your body if you abuse it with improper eating habits.

8. **Get Organized.** Plan, schedule, take notes, and keep good files. Organizing the daily nitty-gritty of life reduces stress. Save your memory for more creative and pleasurable things.

9. **Rehearse.** When you are facing a situation that you know will be stressful to you, rehearse it. Either mentally or with a friend, anticipate what might occur and plan your response. Being prepared reduces stress.

10. **Do It Now.** Do your most difficult or most hated task at the beginning of the day when you're fresh; avoid the stress of dreading it all day. Procrastination breeds stress!

11. **Learn to Say "No."** Say no when your schedule is full: to activities you do not enjoy; to responsibilities that are not really yours; to emotional demands that leave you feeling drained; to other people's problems that you cannot solve.

12. **Learn to Accept What You Cannot Change.** If the source of stress is beyond your control at the present, try your best to accept it until you can change it or it changes itself. This is much better than spinning your wheels and getting nowhere.

13. **Avoid Self-Medication.** There are many chemicals such as alcohol and other drugs that can mask stress symptoms, but they do not help you adjust to stress itself. Also, many are habit-forming and can cause more stress than they solve; consult with your doctor before you decide to use them. It is important too, that the ability to handle stress comes from within you, not from externals.

14. **Live a Balanced Life.** Make time for what is important to you. Work and school are important, but they are not the only important areas in your life. What about time with your family and friends? What about time for a hobby? Stop and ask yourself, "Am I spending too much time on one important area of my life and forgetting the others?"

15. **Get Enough Sleep and Rest.** Lack of sleep can lessen your ability to deal with stress by making you more irritable. If stress continually prevents you from sleeping, you should inform your doctor.

16. **Make Yourself Available.** Many of us have the feeling that we are being left out, slighted, neglected, or rejected. Often, we just imagine that others are feeling this way about us, when in reality they are eager for us to make the first move. Instead of withdrawing and feeling sorry for yourself, get involved.

17. **Shun the "Perfect" Urge.** Some people expect too much from themselves and are in a constant state of worry and anxiety because they think they are not achieving as much as they should. No one can be perfect in everything, so decide which things you do well and put your main effort into these. Next, give the best of your ability to the things you can not do as well, but don't be too hard on yourself if you do not excel at these tasks (Basco, 1999).

18. **Develop a Regular Exercise Program.** Like most things, including stress, there is an optimal amount. A sensible exercise program can begin with a short daily walk that is gradually increased. To avoid excess physical stress,

Keeping in good physical shape is an important antidote to stress overload, but it's not the cure.

Michael Cavanagh

you need to develop your own program gradually and then maintain it constantly. There is increasing evidence that regular, sensible exercise causes a number of important chemical changes in the body. It helps to eliminate depression. It helps to alleviate anxiety. Sensible, enjoyable exercise is nature's antistress reaction remedy. Experts consider aerobics to be an excellent release.

19. **Take Care of Yourself.** If you do not, no one else will. Don't say, "I don't have time." You have got all the time there is—24 hours a day—so begin today by choosing some stress reduction techniques that will divert your attention from whatever is causing you stress.

20. **Learn to Relax.** You can learn to counteract your habitual reaction to stress by learning to relax. Relaxation gives you more energy and normalizes your physical, mental, and emotional processes. Consequently, you are more equipped to handle the stresses in your life.

THE RELAXATION RESPONSE

Would you like to try a deep breathing and relaxation exercise now? One of the best studied stress relievers is the relaxation response, first described by Harvard's Herbert Benson, M.D. more than twenty years ago (Carpi, 1996). Its great advantage is that it requires no special posture or place. You can use this relaxation response even if you are stuck in traffic, when you're expected at a meeting. Or, you can use this response if you are having trouble falling asleep because your mind keeps replaying over the events of the day. Are you ready?

> Things usually turn out best for people who make the best of the way things turn out.
>
> Art Linkletter

- Sit or recline comfortably. Close your eyes if you can, and relax your muscles.
- Breathe deeply. To make sure that you are breathing deeply, place one hand on your abdomen, the other on your chest. Breathe in slowly through your nose, and as you do you should feel your abdomen (not your chest) rise.
- Slowly exhale. As you do, focus on your breathing. Some people do better if they silently repeat the word *one* as they exhale; it helps clear the mind.
- If thoughts intrude, do not dwell on them; allow them to pass on and return to focusing on your breathing.

Although you can turn to this exercise any time you feel stressed, doing it regularly for 10 to 20 minutes at least once a day can put you in a generally calm mode that can see you through otherwise stressful situations.

Was Dr. Benson correct? Do you feel more relaxed?

Obviously, not all of these coping strategies and stress-management techniques are applicable to everyone. So take a long, hard look at your own personal life style, and try to make a good evaluation as to what factors are adding stress to your life, particularly negative stress. Perhaps, you will even find yourself falling into the category of Type A behavior. Then, select the specific strategies that fit your personal situation and make a commitment to do whatever is necessary to reduce the negative stress in your life or at least learn to better cope with it effectively.

Chapter Review

Even if it were possible to go through life without stress, we really would not want to, because stress is what prepares us to handle things we are unfamiliar with, or things that appear to threaten us. Without a doubt, some stress challenges us to think creatively and to find innovative solutions to problems.

- Stress is the rate of wear and tear within the body.
- There are four basic types of stress: eustress (good or short term stress), distress (negative or harmful stress), hyperstress (overload), and hypostress (underload).
- Stress consists of an event, called a stressor, plus how we feel about it, how we interpret it, and what we do to cope with it.
- Two words best relate to the actual cause of stress: change and threat. Changes and threats often fall into three possible categories: 1) anticipated life events, 2) unexpected life events, and 3) accumulating life events.
- Daily hassles—irritating and frustrating incidents that occur in our everyday transactions with the environment—may sometimes pile up until they eventually overwhelm us.
- Modern stress theory agrees that what causes us stress is not what happens to us but how we perceive what happens to us.
- The body has a three-stage reaction to stress: alarm, resistance, and exhaustion. These stages of chain of reactions to stress are called the general adaptation syndrome.
- Stress can be a problem because it is linked to a number of illnesses. There are both physical and behavioral effects of stress.
- Research has indicated that there are basically three personality types in relation to stress—Type A, Type B, and a combination of Type A and Type B.
- There are both negative and defensive techniques of coping with stress. Some commonly used defense mechanisms in coping with stress are: rationalization, repression, projection, reaction formation, sublimation, and displacement.
- Although some events are inherently stressful for everyone, many other events are appraised as stressful or not according to an individual's culture, gender, and conditioning.
- Hardy people seem to deal more effectively with stress. They are more likely to demonstrate the attitudes of commitment, control, and challenge when dealing with stressful situations. Optimistic people are more likely to cope with stress in more adaptive ways than pessimists.
- Three options, when confronted with stressful events and situations, are 1) change environments, 2) change the environment, and 3) change me—improve my coping skills.
- One of the most effective ways of dealing with stressful thoughts and feelings is to watch our self-talk—what we say to ourselves about our experiences or what is happening to us.
- Self-talk can be irrational, resulting in inappropriate emotions, behaviors, and more stress. Self-talk can also be rational, resulting in appropriate emotions, behaviors, and less stress.
- Almost all irrational self-verbalizations contain should statements, awfulizing statements, and overgeneralizations.
- Irrational beliefs that create feelings of stress can be improved by using a four-step process: 1) monitoring your emotional reactions, 2) describing the activating event, 3) recording your self-talk, and 4) disputing the beliefs which are irrational.
- There are numerous strategies for learning to live with stress. It is important to select the specific strategies that fit your personal situation and to which you can make a commitment for coping and dealing with the stress in your life.

Handled well, stress is a positive force that strengthens us for future situations. But handled poorly, or allowed to get out of hand, stress becomes harmful and can lead to physical, mental, or emotional problems.

Therefore, it is extremely important not only that we recognize stress, but that we learn how to handle it, live with it, and make it work for us.

??? Questions ???

1. What is stress, and give examples of the four basic types of stress.
2. Define the term stressor, and explain what else stress consists of.
3. What two words best relate to the actual cause of stress? Explain the three categories that changes and threats often fall into.
4. Explain what your daily hassles consist of.
5. In relation to the power of our thoughts, what causes some people to be devastated and others motivated by the same event?
6. Explain the three-stage reaction to stress.
7. How does stress affect you physically as well as behaviorally?
8. Explain the characteristics of the Type A and Type B personality behavior patterns. Which personality type are you?
9. List and define some of the more commonly used defense mechanisms. What are the two primary characteristics of defense mechanisms? What are at least five other negative ways of coping with stress?
10. In relation to stress, explain the different coping styles of men and women.
11. Explain the extent that Caucasian, African-American, Hispanic, and Asian American cultures perceive stressful events which might be in the academic, financial, and personal domains.
12. List and explain the three characteristics of hardy people? How do optimistic and pessimistic people differ in their reaction to stressful events?
13. Explain the three options possible when confronted with stressful events and situations.
14. What is the difference in irrational and rational beliefs—self-talk? Name and give examples of the three self-verbalizations frequently found in irrational beliefs—self-talk. How could these same examples be worded into rational beliefs—self-talk?
15. Identify and explain the four-step process for disputing irrational beliefs?
16. List at least ten positive "copers," or tips, for managing stress.

🗝 Key Terms 🗝

Alarm Stage	Hardiness	Reaction Formation
Coping	Hyperstress	Repression
Daily Hassles	Hypostress	Resistance Stage
Defense Mechanisms	Irrational Belief	Self-talk
Displacement	Optimism	Stressor
Distress	Pessimism	Sublimation
Eustress	Projection	Thought-stopping
Exhaustion Stage	Psychosomatic Disorder	Type A
General Adaptation	Rational Belief	Type B
Syndrome	Rationalization	

??? **Discussion** ???

1. What is your personal definition of stress?
2. Discuss the types of situations that are most stressful to you?
3. What are some examples of daily hassles in your environment?
4. What can you do to alleviate some of the stress, as well as daily hassles, in your life?
5. How does stress affect you physically, as well as, behaviorally?
6. Discuss this statement: Modern stress theory agrees that what causes stress is not what happens to us but how we perceive what happens to us.
7. In relation to stress, how do Type A and Type B personalities create difficulties in relationships with others?
8. Discuss the differences in the way men and women cope with stress.
9. What techniques do you personally use to manage stress?

Name_____ Date _____

Where Does the Stress Come from in Your Life?

Purpose: To discover where the sources of stress are in your life.

Instructions:

I. You need to keep track of any stressful event that occurs in your life for a one-week period of time. Each day at approximately 10:00 A.M., 6:00 P.M., and 10:00 P.M. write down each of the stressful events that occurred to you during the previous period of time.

II. Use the following form:

Day	Time	Stressful Event	Type of Stress (Indicate whether the event involves conflict, hassle, change, frustration, or some combination.)	Your Reaction

Discussion

1. Specifically, what areas are causing you the greatest amount of difficulty?

2. Specifically, what lifestyle changes are you willing to make in order to more effectively cope with stress?

Name _____ Date _____

How Much Can You Take?

Purpose: To help you become more aware of stress-producing events in your life, whether negative or positive, and to demonstrate the correlation between cumulative stress and major health changes.

Instructions:

I. Each participant is to individually fill out the Social Readjustment Rating Scale by transferring to "Your Event" column, the value of each stressful event you have experienced in the past 12 months. For example, if you have been fired from your job, you would place 47 in "Your Event" column.

II. Total "Your Event" column.

III. Become aware of what your chances are of experiencing a major health change in the next two years:

> 0–150 points   = 1 in 3 chance
> 150–300 points = 50-50 chance
> Over 300 points – almost 90 percent chance

IV. Divide into groups of four or five to discuss the results of each individual's scale.

Social Readjustment Rating Scale

Life Changes	Value	Your Event
FAMILY:		
Death of a Spouse	100	_____
Divorce	73	_____
Marital Separation	65	_____
Death of a close family member	63	_____
Marriage	50	_____
Marital Reconciliation	45	_____
Major change in health of family member	44	_____
Pregnancy	40	_____
Addition of new family member	39	_____
Major change in arguments with spouse	35	_____
Son or daughter leaving home	29	_____
Trouble with in-laws	29	_____
Spouse starting or ending work	26	_____
Major change in family get-togethers	15	_____

---

*Holmes, T. H. and Rahe, R. H. "The Social Readjustment Rating Scale," from JOURNAL OF PSYCHOSOMATIC RESEARCH, No. 227. Reproduced by permission from Pergamon Press Ltd., Headington Hill, Oxford, England.

Name _____   Date _____

Type A and Type B Behavior*

Purpose: To help you identify individual personality characteristics that would indicate Type A or Type B behavior.

Instructions:

 I. Rate yourself as to how you typically react in each of the situations listed below by circling one response for each question.

 II. Find your total score by adding together the circled number response of each question.

 III. Determine whether your behavior is primarily Type A or Type B according to the following scale:

1– 47	Extreme Type B
48– 94	Type B
95–141	Both Type A and Type B
142–188	Type A
189–235	Extreme Type A

In general: a score greater than 120 is Type A and a score less than 120 is Type B

	Always	Frequently	Sometimes	Seldom	Never
1. Are you punctual?	5	4	3	2	1
2. Do you work under constant deadlines?	5	4	3	2	1
3. Do you indulge in competitive hobbies?	5	4	3	2	1
4. Do you like routine household chores?	5	4	3	2	1
5. Do you prefer to do a task yourself because others are too slow or can't do it as well?	5	4	3	2	1
6. Do you work while you are eating, in the bathroom, etc.?	5	4	3	2	1
7. Do you walk fast?	5	4	3	2	1
8. Do you eat hurriedly?	5	4	3	2	1
9. Are you patient and understanding?	5	4	3	2	1
10. Do you carry on several lines of thought at the same time?	5	4	3	2	1
11. Do you interrupt others when they talk about subjects that don't interest you?	5	4	3	2	1

---

*Mirabal, Thomas E. "Identifying Individual Personality Characteristics." Reproduced by permission from Synergistic Training Systems, Inc., Dallas, Texas.

	Always	Frequently	Sometimes	Seldom	Never
12. Do you pretend to listen to others when they talk about subjects that don't interest you?	5	4	3	2	1
13. How often does time seem to pass rapidly for you?	5	4	3	2	1
14. How often do you look at your watch?	5	4	3	2	1
15. Do you feel vaguely guilty when you relax and do absolutely nothing for several hours/days?	5	4	3	2	1
16. How often do you become exasperated when standing in line at movies, restaurants, etc.?	5	4	3	2	1
17. Do you ever find that you cannot recall details of the surroundings after you left a place?	5	4	3	2	1
18. How often are you preoccupied with getting materialistic things?	5	4	3	2	1
19. Do you use a relaxed, laid back speech pattern?	5	4	3	2	1
20. How often do you attempt to schedule more and more in less and less time?	5	4	3	2	1
21. How often do you feel aggressive, hostile, and compelled to challenge people who make you feel uncomfortable?	5	4	3	2	1
22. Do you accentuate your speech, talk fast?	5	4	3	2	1
23. How often do you gesture by clenching your fists, banging your hand on the table, pounding one fist into the palm of the other hand, clenching your jaw, grinding your teeth, etc.?	5	4	3	2	1
24. Do you prefer respect and admiration to affection?	5	4	3	2	1
25. Do you listen well and attentively?	5	4	3	2	1
26. Do you evaluate the activities of yourself and others in terms of numbers (e.g., minutes, hours, days, dollars, age)?	5	4	3	2	1

	Always	Frequently	Sometimes	Seldom	Never
27. How often do you play to win?	5	4	3	2	1
28. How often do you stay up late to socialize?	5	4	3	2	1
29. How often are you angry?	5	4	3	2	1
30. Do you go out of your way to conceal your anger?	5	4	3	2	1
31. How often are you dissatisfied with your present position or promotional progress?	5	4	3	2	1
32. Do you daydream a lot?	5	4	3	2	1
33. Do you participate in numerous organizations?	5	4	3	2	1
34. Did you ever attend night school?	5	4	3	2	1
35. How often do you go to a doctor?	5	4	3	2	1
36. Do you ever "sigh" faintly between words?	5	4	3	2	1
37. How often do you come to work even when you are sick?	5	4	3	2	1
38. How often is your laughter a grim, forced chuckle?	5	4	3	2	1
39. Do/would you avoid firing people?	5	4	3	2	1
40. How often are you genuinely open and responsive to people?	5	4	3	2	1
41. How often do you go to bed early?	5	4	3	2	1
42. If you smoke, do you prefer cigarettes as opposed to a pipe or cigar?	5	4	3	2	1
43. How often do you salt your meal before tasting it?	5	4	3	2	1
44. How often do you exercise?	5	4	3	2	1
45. Do you ever combine vacations with business?	5	4	3	2	1
46. How often do you work late?	5	4	3	2	1
47. How often do you hum, fidget, or drum your fingers while not involved in an activity?	5	4	3	2	1

Total Points _____

Discussion

1. Did the results of this exercise make you aware of any Type A behavior pattern in your own personality? Were you surprised?

2. What are some of the dangers of Type A behavior?

3. Is it possible to change from Type A to Type B? How?

4. Would you want to change your behavior patterns if you could?

Name_____ Date _____

Irrational and Rational Self-Talk

Purpose: To focus on how irrational and rational self-talk can be used in common, practical events and situations.

Instructions:

I. For each situation below, consider how you would feel and what you might say to yourself. Then, write an irrational and a rational belief about each situation.

II. Be prepared to share your responses in a class discussion or in small groups of four or five students.

Situation	Irrational Self-Talk	Rational Self-Talk
1. You have to give a 5-minute speech in your college class. **(Example)**	1. **This is terrible. I just can't bear having to give this speech.**	1. **This is going to be difficult. I will work hard and be as successful as I can be.**
2. You didn't meet a very important work deadline.	2.	2.
3. A friend canceled a date with you.	3.	3.
4. You are criticized publicly in class or at work.	4.	4.
5. You're having a final exam in your most difficult class.	5.	5.
6. You have just had a major "blow-up" with your fiancee.	6.	6.
7. You were laid off from your job.	7.	7.
8. Write your own situation.	8.	8.

Discussion

1. Was it easier for you to write the irrational or the rational self-talk and beliefs? Why?

2. How many times did you use *should, should not, must, ought, have to?*

3. How many times did you write awfulizing statements?

4. How many times did you make overgeneralizations?

5. How do you think irrational self-talk contributes to a common situation becoming more stressful?

Name _____ Date _____

Identifying and Disputing Self-Talk and Beliefs

Purpose: To identify irrational beliefs, consequences of those beliefs, and then dispute and challenge those beliefs, to improve emotional functioning.

Instructions:

I. Think of a recent situation in which you had negative feelings that caused you to be emotionally upset.

II. Next, review the examples below and write your responses to each category.

1. Write down the facts of what happened—the activating event. Be sure to write down only the objective facts; do not include your subjective, personal value judgments.

EXAMPLE:

My husband came in and told me he wanted a divorce because he wanted to marry a woman at the office where he works.

YOUR EVENT:

2. Write down and number your self-talk about the event. This includes your subjective value judgments, assumptions, beliefs, and predictions that you said to yourself.

EXAMPLE:

1. If he marries her, I won't be able to stand it.
2. He should not have done this to me and the children. He is a sick person.
3. I trusted him so much.
4. Everybody will think I am a complete fool.
5. Why didn't he tell me before now. I just wish he would have done this.

YOUR BELIEFS:

1.

2.

3.

4.

5.

3. Identify the consequences of your self-talk and beliefs. Label your feelings with words such as depressed, angry, hurt, afraid, jealous, and insecure.

   EXAMPLE:

   I felt hurt and angry.

   YOUR CONSEQUENCES:

4. Dispute your beliefs and self-talk. For each sentence in Number 2 of this exercise, decide whether what you have written is a rational or irrational belief. Explain why it is rational or irrational and write some alternative rational self-talk.

   EXAMPLE:

   1. I am being irrational. I won't like it one bit if he marries her, but I am sure I can stand it. After all, I do want to keep on living. I am just telling myself I can't stand it.
   2. This is irrational. He really can do whatever he wants—he can get away with this. I cannot control what he or anyone else does. I wish this had not happened, but I will try to concentrate on loving the children and being an effective parent.
   3. I chose to trust him. This is rational. After all, I loved him and trusted him. I cannot imagine loving John and not trusting him. It is only natural that I would feel some hurt, but I will be okay. I just need some time.
   4. I am overgeneralizing. This is irrational. I am not a complete fool. I'm not even sure what a complete fool really is. Who is everybody, anyway? It is best that I not concern myself with what other people think. I really have more important things to be concerned with.
   5. Of course I wish he had told me before now. It is very rational for me to desire this. He chose not to do so, what else can I say?

YOUR DISPUTES:

1.

2.

3.

4.

5.

Discussion

1. Was it difficult for you to decide which of your beliefs were rational or irrational?

2. Was it difficult for you to write some alternative self-talk to your irrational statements?

3. Do you believe that your self-talk about your emotional situation caused you to have emotional pain?

4. How do you feel about the situation now?

Managing Stress and Wellness

Learning Journal

Select the statement below that best defines your feelings about the personal value or meaning gained from this chapter and respond below the dotted line.

- **I learned that I . . .**
- **I realized that I . . .**
- **I discovered that I . . .**

- **I was surprised that I . . .**
- **I was pleased that I . . .**
- **I was displeased that I . . .**

. . . .

continue on reverse

Meaning and Values

I have been able to function as a catalyst,
trying to bring to our awareness that we can
only truly live and enjoy and appreciate life
if we realize at all times that we are finite.
Needless to say I have learned these lessons
from my dying patients—who in their suffering
and dying realized that we have only NOW—
"so have it fully and find what turns you on,
because no one can do this for you!"

Elisabeth Kübler-Ross

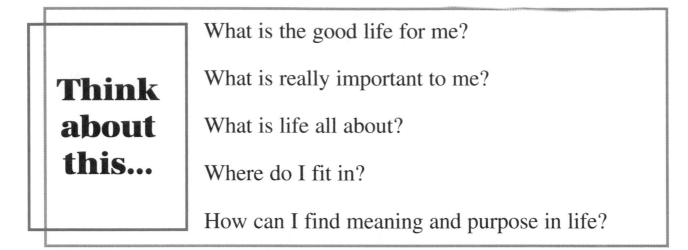

Think about this...

What is the good life for me?

What is really important to me?

What is life all about?

Where do I fit in?

How can I find meaning and purpose in life?

Have you ever asked yourself any of these questions? These and similar questions are being heard with increasing frequency in modern society.

Today, people are confronted by many more choices than in previous generations. It is no longer uncommon for people to change careers (or even spouses) two or three times in a lifetime; the choice of pursuing a college education or vocational training is now the norm, rather than the exception; and the "dual career marriage/family" is increasing in numbers each year. Then, there are choices concerning premarital sex, the fear of AIDS, and even the experimentation with drugs.

There was a time when children grew up knowing to a far greater extent than we, what roles they would play in adult life, where they would live, and what they would believe in. They did not have to choose who and what they would be. Actually, these issues were decided before they were born.

Today, the recent increase in violent crimes by young people has created a multitude of questions. It just seems that young people are plunging into a whole world of influences, values and enticements (Okrent, 1999). And, it is for this reason that people are asking more value questions. In order to begin to find answers to these questions, we need first of all to be able to identify what values are.

> Things have the value that we ourselves have the capacity to give them.
>
> Nikos Kazantzakis

WHAT ARE VALUES?

For just a few minutes, consider the following analogy: If you were going to build a new home, one of the first considerations would be to decide upon your house plan. After having carefully studied your house plan and having made the necessary adjustments, you would have your house plan converted into a blueprint. This blueprint would serve as a guide for the construction of your new home. For example, the choices and decisions concerning the layout of the kitchen, the placement of doors and windows, the design of electrical outlets, and so on, would be in accordance with this blueprint—the plan or guide for your new home.

Could it be possible that we also have a blueprint or guide concerning the choices and decisions we make in our way of living? Is there a relationship between this *blueprint* or *guide* and our values?

Authors have written extensively about the meaning of the term value(s). For example, a *value* is the degree of importance we attach to various beliefs, ideas, objects, or things (Milliken, 1997). Hunter Lewis (1990) defines *values* in this way:

> Although the term value(s) is often used loosely, it should be synonymous with personal beliefs about the "good", the "just", and the "beautiful", personal beliefs that propel us to action, to a particular kind of behavior and life.

We could conclude then that our values give rise to our personal goals and tend to place limits on the means we shall use to reach them (Rathus and Nevid, 1999).

Thinking of the term value(s) in the above ways, now review the following "Consider This" box for a partial listing of some typical values. Which ones are important to you? Which ones propel you to action or to a particular kind of behavior and life?

Because we have many values, it is, therefore, appropriate to speak of our set of values or our value system. A set of values is more than just a set of rules and regulations. Instead, it is the underlying system of beliefs about what is important in life to a person. Actually, our value system represents the blueprint or guideline for the choices and decisions we make throughout our life. Still true today, Kluckhohn (1956) explains these choices and decisions:

> What is a value system? First of all, it is yours, and it is unique because you are one-of-a-kind. It is your code of ethics by which to live. It is your "behavior-bible." It is what guides your life.
>
> Helen Johnson

 CONSIDER THIS . . .
Twenty-One Typical Values

- Being honest and trustworthy
- Having a family and staying close to them
- Being financially and materially successful
- Being independent
- Feeling safe and secure
- Having plenty of leisure time
- Dressing in style
- Having friends
- Having a religious or moral code
- Being in good health
- Having a special love relationship
- Having a fulfilling career
- Being approved of and liked by others
- Having self-respect and pride
- Being of service to others
- Learning and getting an education
- Being productive and achieving
- Loving others and being loved
- Living a long, healthy life
- Belonging to a chosen group
- Living in a world of peace

Every individual operates according to a system of values, whether it is verbalized and consistently worked out or not. In selecting goals, in choosing modes of behavior, in resolving conflicts, he is influenced at every turn by his conception of what is good and desirable for him. Although everyone's value system is in some degree unique, an individual's values are usually grounded in the core values of his culture. . . . Depending on his conception of what is desirable and good in human life, he selects certain goals over others and patterns his behavior according to standards of what he believes to be right and worthwhile. The way a man carries on his business activity, the kind of relationships he has with his wife and children and with his friends, the degree of respect he has for other individuals (and for himself), his political and religious activity—all these reflect the individual's values, though he may scarcely have thought them through.

Actually, as Elliot (1991) explains, *"everything we do, every decision we make and course of action we take is based on our consciously or unconsciously held beliefs, attitudes, and values."*

An excellent test to determine the intensity of your conscious or unconscious values is to notice how strongly you feel about an idea or thought. For example, how would you react to these issues: abortion, drug abuse, and euthanasia? If you have a strong conviction on any of these issues, it is highly likely that aspects of your value system are being revealed.

TYPES OF VALUES

Milton (1985) classifies values into two broad categories: *moral values* and *nonmoral values*. In his book, the terms *moral* and *nonmoral* are used without any religious connotations.

Moral Values. These values have to do with right and wrong, good and evil. They form the basis for judgments or moral responsibility and guide such ethical behavior as telling the truth, keeping agreements, and not injuring others. Character traits such as honesty, loyalty, and fairness are often associated with moral values. Moral statements often contain words such as *must, ought, should, never,* and *always.*

Non-moral Values. These values have to do with tastes, preferences, and styles. They relate to what is desirable and undesirable, as opposed to what is right and wrong or good and evil. Non-moral values carry no sense of obligation. There is no moral responsibility connected with accepting or rejecting a non-moral value.

The traits associated with non-moral values tend to be personality traits like charm, shyness, or cheerfulness, as opposed to character traits like honesty or fairness. The activities that come out of non-moral values are merely preferred, not dictated: going to the ballgame instead of to a movie, reading a book instead of watching television.

Non-moral values are a lot more plentiful than moral values, because they are expressions of your attitudes toward all sorts of objects, concepts, and expe-

Morals and ethics are not a religion. They are logical, sensible principles of good conduct that we need for a peaceful, productive society.

The Best of Bits & Pieces

It is easier to fight for one's principles than to live up to them.

Alfred Adler

riences: cars, paintings, art, knowledge, pleasure, democracy, history, sports, hobbies, and so on. Statements of non-moral values often contain the same words as statements of moral values, but examination shows that the words are not meant in an absolute, normative sense.

Without a doubt, values are highly operative in our life. Have these values *just always been there,* or do we gradually acquire them, as if through familial and cultural osmosis?

HOW DO VALUES DEVELOP?

Throughout your life, you have, in all probability, heard many *life messages:* "Life is . . .", "Success is . . .", "The most important thing is . . ." transmitted to you by parents, peers, and society in general.

We are not born with values, but we are born into cultures and societies that promote, teach, and impart their values to us. We learn to be what we are.

Shoulds and Should Nots. Basically, the years of adolescence are extremely important for the learning and development of values (Worchel and Goethals, 1998). Most psychologists concur that we first acquire the cognitive understanding of right and wrong by observing the behavior of the people most important to us, usually (and hopefully) our parents (Begley and Kalb, 2000). Actually, our first goals and ambitions will be drawn from this frame of reference. During the first few years of our life, we lacked the knowledge and maturity to evaluate our value orientation.

As we entered school, however, parental influence was combined with the influence of peers, teachers, and public media. We had one set of *shoulds* and *should nots* from our parents. The church often suggested a second. Our friends and "peer group" offered a third view of values. And then, the chaos of value conflicts: values from opposing political groups; militancy of left or right; the values of different cultures and social classes; the influence of Hollywood, popular magazines, television, the "net," and advertising claims (Kerschenbaum, 1994). As a side note, with recent research indicating that many young people spend thirty to forty hours a week in front of the TV set, and the internet there continues to be great concern about the influence of television, the "net" and advertising claims on values formation (Reece and Brandt, 1999).

With all of this additional information we began to question and reevaluate our original value orientation. Much of this questioning was revealed through testing the *shoulds* and *should nots.* Therefore, actual experience became very real in the forming of our value system. For some people, this reevaluation period occurred during the adolescence period, early adulthood, or maybe even later.

Individuation. How old were you when you reevaluated your original value system? Were you 18, 20, 25, or . . .? Regardless of the exact time, examining and acquiring your personal set of values was, or is, the birth of your

> Life is a succession of lessons which must be lived to be understood.
>
> Helen Keller

What kinds of values do children learn from their families?

What values need to be considered when choosing a college or university?

own individuality. In fact, Carl Jung (1923) one of the early psychoanalysts, called the process of becoming an individual—individuation.

Individuation refers to the separation from our family system and the establishing of our identity based on our own experiences, rather than merely following our parents' dreams. Although individuals may accept many of their parents' values, to genuinely individuate they must choose these values freely rather than automatically incorporating them into their personality.

The values we place upon different aspects of our environment have an effect upon how we view things and how we function. In other words, an act viewed as right or wrong, moral or immoral will depend upon the frame of reference of the perceiver. As a result, something that one person considers worthwhile and desirable may appear exactly the opposite to another person. Do we, therefore, tend to judge other people's actions by our own standards—our values?

What else influences the development of our values?

THE INFLUENCE OF OTHER FACTORS

Other important factors are influential in the formation of our value system. Some of these are religious beliefs, attitudes, prejudices, and stereotypes.

CONSIDER THIS . . .
Possible Life Messages

- "Life is to have things: your own home, enough money for an emergency, security for old age."
- "Life is to get ahead, to prove yourself, to make people respect you."
- "Success in life is judged by how popular you are—by how many people love you."
- "You are worth only what you are worth in God's eyes."
- "Success in life is spelled: M-O-N-E-Y."
- "Life is for having good times."
- "If you've got your health, you'll be all right."
- "Education is what is important. They can take everything away from you except your mind."
- "Life is for loving and sharing with others."

What messages did you hear about the nature and purposes of life? Have you had any conflicts between what you heard and in what you now actually believe?

Religious Beliefs. What is a belief? A *belief* is the acceptance of some thought, supposition, or idea. This belief may be in a God, or in Gods, or even in some form of spirituality. Studies show that most Americans want spirituality, but perhaps not in religious form. In the 1990's and as we enter the millennium, it appears that Americans are becoming more expressively spiritual (Elkins, 1999). In fact, M. Scott Peck (1998), in *Further Along The Road Less Traveled,* notes that he likes to speak of *"spirituality"* rather than *"religiosity."* Peck goes on to indicate that every major religion of the world has similar ideas of love, the same goal of benefitting humanity through spiritual practice, and the same effect of making their followers into better human beings.

In some form or another, religion and established moral codes are found in all cultures and societies. A commitment toward a chosen moral code helps to define our purpose in life, gives meaning and direction in life, and thus, becomes an integral part in shaping our value system.

Attitudes. *Attitudes* are positive or negative orientations toward a certain target. For example, you have attitudes toward specific persons (parents, children, teachers), as well as toward groups of people (blacks, whites, male ministers, female ministers). You also have attitudes toward things or targets such as food, movies, holidays, or marriage.

The attitudes you have today have been acquired throughout your life. How did you acquire them? You may have acquired some of your attitudes by hearing parents, family, friends, and teachers express positive or negative attitudes toward certain issues or people. The mass media, including advertising, may also be responsible for shaping some of your attitudes. The attitudes you have formed through your own direct experience are strongest, however, and they are also more resistant to change (Hetherington, 1996).

> The meaning of things lies not in the things themselves, but in our attitude towards them.
>
> Antoine de Saint Exupery

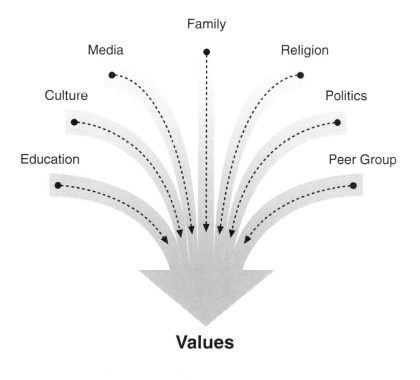

Values

Values come from many sources.
What source has had the greatest influence
in the development of your value system?

More than likely, your positive attitudes are a result of positive experiences, and your negative attitudes are a result of negative experiences. Whatever you learned in these experiences is likely to take the form of *expectations* later in life. It is just natural to expect the same or similar results from similar situations. Consider these statements:

I'm not going to get married again; if I did, it would just probably end in another divorce.

Tom's mother is so different from Frank's mother—certainly not what I expected from a mother-in-law.

I'm sure I can work for Mrs. Jones; I've worked for another female, and we got along just great.

Reject and condemn prejudice based on race, gender, religion, or age.

Martin Luther King, Jr.

How has the influence of religion or spirituality influenced the development of your value system?

As you can see in these examples, the attitudes were formed from prior *experiences* and *expectations.* Is it possible that your prior experiences and expectations are shaping the attitudes and values you presently hold? If so, do you need to reevaluate these attitudes and values? Remember, the stronger an attitude is, the more difficult it is to change. Why? Because your emotions are involved.

Prejudices. A *prejudice* is a preconceived opinion, feeling, or attitude, either positive or negative, that is formed without adequate information. For example, you may have a negative prejudice towards the black English teacher who is going to teach your class next semester. Although you have not had this teacher before, you have heard statements made by other students, and you have already formed your opinion. It is only when you are actually in this teacher's class that you can make a justified opinion. Why? Prejudices are often unjustified attitudes. And, sometimes these attitudes extend to entire groups of people.

Actually, there are three components to a prejudice (Myers, 1999). They are as follows:

- To hold certain *beliefs* against members of a group—*"Indians are mostly alcoholics."*
- To *feel* negatively toward them—*"I despise Jews."*
- To be inclined to *act* negatively toward them—*"I wouldn't hire a Mexican."*

Prejudice is being down on what we are not up on.

John Stevens

It is interesting to note that our strongest negative emotions are often reserved for groups rather than individuals. As Gordon W. Allport (1954) commented in his classic book, *The Nature of Prejudice, "anger is customarily felt toward individuals only, whereas hatred may be felt toward whole classes of people."*

Stereotypes. When we allow our prejudiced attitudes to make *generalizations* by categorizing an object, person, or situation, we are guilty of *stereotyping.* As psychologist Jack Dovidio (1998) of Colgate University notes: *"we create stereotypes to explain why things are the way they are and stereotypes don't have to be true to serve a purpose."* For example:

Women are emotional.

Latin Americans are a hot-headed race.

Mothers-in-law are bossy and interfering people.

There are just a bunch of hypocrites at *that* church.

According to these examples, if you are a woman, a Latin American, a mother-in-law, or if you go to *that* church, you have now been given a label. You are not thought of as an individual—you are a member of the group and, of course, you have *their* similar characteristics.

Pause for a minute and just ask yourself these questions: What prejudices and stereotypes do I have? What are they based on? Do I really want to have these values?

At this point, you may find it helpful to review the "Focus on Diversity" box, Breaking Down Barriers, for some suggestions on dealing with prejudices and stereotypes.

> To know one's self is wisdom, but to know one's neighbor is genius.
>
> Minna Antrim

WHAT ARE MY VALUES?

At the present time, what things are most important to you in your life? Is your career of primary importance? How about your school work and/or the training for your future career? How about the time you spend with your family? Do you have outside leisure interests, community activities, or volunteer work?

As Shames (1989) confirms, there are always many factors in your life that compete for your time and attention. Actually, what you value most often determines how you will spend your time. When you decide to work late on a repeated basis rather than go home to dinner, this is a value decision. If you gave up a movie in order to study for a test, this is also a value decision. When you decide to go out with some friends rather than attend your son's baseball game, this is another value decision.

You are always making value decisions, and an awareness of what values are most important to you can help you to live a more harmonious and less stressful life. When you know which values have a higher priority, you can more eas-

> It's good to have money and the things money can buy, but it's good to check once in a while and make sure you haven't lost the things that money can't buy.
>
> George Horace Lorimer

Breaking Down Barriers

To reduce your prejudices and use of stereotypes, these steps may be helpful:

1. Admit your prejudices and biases and try to understand them.
2. Identify the stereotypes that reflect your prejudices and attempt to modify them.
3. Identify the actions that reflect your prejudices and modify them.
4. Avoid judging differences, view diversity as a strength.
5. Attempt to learn about cultures that differ from your own.

Are you willing to test, adapt, and change your perceptions?

Johnson, (2000) and Corey, et al., (2000)

FOCUS ON DIVERSITY

ily make life's major and minor decisions. We'll have more to say about prioritizing values a little later, but for now, think of your own values as you read the following results of a Personal Value Assessment Survey.

Gender and You. 1,273 students in Human Relations classes at Tarrant County College-Northeast Campus—were asked to complete the Personal Value Assessment in the activities section at the end of this chapter. They were then asked to prioritize their top five values. Values frequently mentioned, but not prioritized by the 1,273 students, were as follows:

> What do I believe? To what extent am I ready to live up to my beliefs? How far am I ready to support them? We all create the person we become by our choices as we go through life.
>
> Eleanor Roosevelt

- Happiness
- Good health
- A stable marriage
- Close family and close friends
- Living according to strong moral values
- Happy love relationship
- Stable life
- Fulfilling career
- Religion
- Children

From the more commonly mentioned values, the final results on the next page, actually reveal the top six prioritized values. You will also be given an opportunity to complete this activity, and you might want to compare your results with these findings.

Desiderata*

Go placidly amid the noise and haste, and remember what peace there may be in silence. As far as possible without surrender be on good terms with all persons. Speak your truth quietly and clearly; listen to others, even the dull and ignorant; they too have their story.

Avoid loud and aggressive persons, they are vexations to the spirit. If you compare yourself with others, you may become vain and bitter; for always there will be greater and lesser persons than yourself. Enjoy your achievements as well as your plans.

Keep interested in your own career, however humble; it is a real possession in the changing fortunes of time. Exercise caution in your business affairs; for the world is full of trickery. But let this not blind you to what virtue there is; many persons strive for high ideals; and everywhere life is full of heroism.

Be yourself. Especially, do not feign affection. Neither be cynical about love; for in the face of all aridity and disenchantment it is perennial as the grass.

Take kindly the counselor of the years, gracefully surrendering the things of youth. Nurture strength of spirit to shield you in sudden misfortune. But do not stress yourself with imaginings. Many fears are born of fatigue and loneliness. Beyond a wholesome discipline, be gentle with yourself.

You are a child of the universe, no less than the trees and the stars; you have a right to be here. We are all children of God. We are made in His image and likeness. This being the case, we must treat everyone with the respect, dignity, thoughtfulness, and consideration that this situation commands. And whether or not it is clear to you, no doubt the universe is unfolding as it should.

Therefore be at peace with God, whatever you conceive Him to be, and whatever your labors and aspirations, in the noisy confusion of life keep peace with your soul. With all its sham, drudgery, and broken dreams, it is still a beautiful world. Be careful. Strive to be happy.

*Found in Old Saint Paul's Church, Baltimore, MD; dated 1692.

TOP SIX PERSONAL VALUES

In Human Relations classes at Tarrant County College-Northeast Campus 1,273 students—62% females and 38% males—reveal their top personal values:

Females	**Males**
1. Stable marriage	1. A happy love relationship
2. Close family and close friends	2. Happiness
3. Happiness	3. Financially stable
4. Good health	4. A fulfilling career
5. Living according to strong moral values	5. Good health
6. A fulfilling career	6. Close family and close friends

How do your top five values compare with what the male and female students said?

Gender & You

Do Values Change? Your values do change as you go through the various life stages. As children, your highest value might have been play and having fun; as adolescents, perhaps it was peer relationships; as young adults, it may be relationships with the opposite sex, and as adults your highest value may be your family and the work you do. For many older people, service to others and enjoying leisure time is often the highest value.

If you are currently seeking some change in your career or lifestyle, it may be due in part to the fact that some of your values may have changed. What was important to you in the past may be less important now. You may want to devote greater attention in your life to new things or to some of the things you did not have as much time for in the past.

Do you see any changes in your personal set of values over the past five or ten years? Has there been any change in the kinds of values you consider to be important in your life? You will be given several opportunities in the activities at the end of this chapter to review your values, past and present.

We have already stated that because we are unique individuals, something that one person considers a value might not be a value to another person. For example, we all want a feeling of security. However, your idea of what makes you feel secure may differ remarkably from that of other people. Some people may equate security primarily with money; others may equate security with education, religion, or close family relationships. Sometimes a combination of all these types of security are desired. The order of importance then becomes a matter of value.

> The cost of a thing is the amount of what I call life which is required to pay for it, immediately or in the long run.
>
> Henry David Thoreau

CLASSIFYING YOUR PERSONAL VALUES

Your values may be *abstract (intangible)* or *specific (tangible)*. For example, one may value such entities as a car, helping others, knowledge, career, security, close relationships with family and friends, an education, religious or spiritual growth, social interactions, material possessions, money, being an honest person,

CONSIDER THIS . . .
Your Values–Some Hard Questions

You probably do not have the answers to these questions on the tip of your tongue. They require some thought and discussion. They will lead you to a better understanding of your values.

1. If you were independently wealthy, what would you do with your life?
2. What issues are of deep concern to you regarding your home, campus, community, church, state, country, or world?
3. If you were independently wealthy, to what causes would you contribute?
4. After your death, what would you like people to say about you? How would you like to be remembered?

___

> It is a law of human life, as certain as gravity: To live fully we must learn to use things and love people . . . not love things and use people.
>
> John Powell

freedom, creativity, and so on. What are some of your intangible and tangible values?

Value Orientations. Your interests, attitudes, and behavior often indicate whether your value system is oriented mainly toward *things, ideas, or people* (Reece and Brandt, 1999). A person who is willing to work hard and save to obtain material objects or even a large bank account may be *thing-oriented.* On the other hand, some people have a zest for working with ideas, theories, and concepts. They enjoy devising strategies and creating solutions to complex problems. We might say that these individuals have an *idea-oriented* value system. However, if you truly enjoy working and being with other people, your value system may be *people-oriented.*

It is highly possible that a combination of these three value orientations may be desired. However, one of these value orientations is probably at the core of your value system, even though you may not be aware of how your behavior is reflected in this particular value orientation. Where do your values fit in? Perhaps the real question is—what do you direct your life toward acquiring?

CLARIFYING YOUR PERSONAL VALUES

Clarifying our values is a crucial aspect of self-development (Rathus and Nevid, 1999). Sometimes important choices in life are made on the basis of peer pressure, unthinking submission to authority, or the power of propaganda. We may even guide our lives by what others expect of us, instead of what we truly believe is right. Many times, thoughts and expectations of society and others largely influence our value system. Thus, our value orientation becomes other-directed rather than self-directed. The obvious result is a feeling of being very insecure and easily threatened in our valuing process.

When we become conscious of our own personal value system and how it functions, we can begin to manage our own value system rather than allowing others to manage it. Hunter Lewis (1990) in his thought-provoking book *A Question of Values,* emphasizes the importance of managing our own value system:

People need to think about their own values, think hard about them, think for themselves. Personal values really do matter. Without functioning values, we can hardly live at all, much less lead a purposeful and satisfying life.

How do we discover what our true values are?
Values clarification is a process that helps people arrive at an answer. Simon, et al., (1995) shares this thought:

It is not concerned with an ultimate set of values (that is for you to decide), but it does stress a method to help you determine the content and power of your own set of values. It is a self-audit, and an inventory of soul and spirit. It is a tool to help you freely decide between alternatives or among varied choices. It is a methodology to help you make a decision, to act, to determine what has meaning for you.

According to Simon et al., (1995), the process of clarifying values involves choosing, prizing and acting. See accompanying box.

> To describe a man's philosophy is to say how he orients himself to the world of his experiences, what meanings he finds in events, what values he aspires to, what standards guide his choices in all that he does.
>
> Abraham Kaplan

How to . . .

. . . Clarify Values

Choosing:
Freely;
from alternatives;
after thoughtful consideration of the consequences of each alternative.

Prizing:
Cherishing, prizing, and being happy with the choice;
willing to affirm the choice publicly.

Acting:
Doing something with the choice, taking action;
acting repeatedly, in some pattern of life.

Simon, et al., (1995)

Before something can be a *full,* true value, it must meet all seven of the above criteria. Simon et al. (1995) suggest that there are three levels involved in the criteria: *choosing* relies mainly on the cognitive or thinking area: *prizing* relies on the affective or feeling area; and *acting* relies on the behavioral areas. When we have a *full value,* our thoughts, feelings, and actions are in agreement; what we think, say, feel, and do are in agreement and are evident in our lives.

Let us look at the seven criteria a little more closely.

Choosing freely means we consciously and deliberately make the choice ourselves. There is no pressure to believe what our parents taught us. An example of choosing freely would be when you have been raised and taught that there is only one religion worthy of your belief, and you later decide that your beliefs are more in line with another religious faith. Even if you end up choosing the same religious faith which your parents hold, that becomes a full value for you because you make the personal choice to follow that faith.

> Life is an endless process of self-discovery.
>
> Dave Gardner

Choosing from alternatives means there are options. If there are no alternatives, there is no freedom of choice. For example, you really cannot value breathing, of itself, because there is no choice involved; a person must breathe to live. However, you can value mountain air, or a special breathing technique, such as yoga.

Choosing after considering the consequences means you ask yourself, "What would be the result of the alternatives of my choice?" This gives you the opportunity to choose with thoughtful consideration, and not on impulse. Many of the problems which we have are the result of impulsive, poorly thought-out decisions, or action taken without regard for ourselves or others. For example, sometimes people impulsively decide to get a divorce and then later realize they are not happy with their "quick" decision.

Cherishing and feeling happy about the choice means that it influences your behavior in some way, and you do not mind spending your time on this value. For example, if you value being thrifty and you need to buy a new VCR, you will spend a considerable amount of time researching and comparing prices. When you finally get your VCR, you will be satisfied and content that you "got the best buy."

Publicly affirming a value means you are willing to tell others about it. Some people even crusade for their values. For example, if you value a particular political ideology, you may be seen campaigning for the politician who holds the same value. Remember, you have the right to publicly affirm your values, but you do not have the right to impose your values on others. This interferes with their freedom of choice.

Doing something about a value means taking action. Full values are those things which we work for, do something about, and take action on. Thus, what a person does reflects his or her values. For example, you will read literature that supports your values; you will join clubs or organizations whose members share your values and whose goals correspond to your values.

Acting repeatedly means there is a life pattern that is evident, and the stronger the value, the more it influences your life. There is a consistency of action which manifests itself in all aspects of your life: in dress, in friends selected, in the place you live, in leisure time, in what you read, in your career, in the selection of your spouse, and how you spend your time and money.

In summary, a value that is freely chosen from alternatives whose consequences have been thoughtfully considered, of which we are proud and happy to the point that we publicly take a stand, and that we act upon with repetition and consistency is a full value.

Some authorities add an eighth criterion as the natural outgrowth of the other seven: **A value enhances a person's total growth.** If a value has been affirmed as a full value by having met the seven preceding criteria, it follows as a matter of course that value will contribute to and enhance the person's total growth toward the goals and ideals that he has chosen for himself. We are more likely to continue choosing, prizing, and acting upon those values that help us to grow in our lives and that help us to achieve the goals which we have set for ourselves.

What about those values we simply say are important to us?

Do what you value;
value what you do.

Sidney Simon

VALUE INDICATORS

Most of us have partial values that are in the process of being formed. Partial values, or *value indicators,* include desires, thoughts not acted on, opinions, interests, aspirations, goals, beliefs, attitudes, feelings, convictions, activities, daydreams (Rokeach, 1973). For example, we may say that we have a certain goal, but we are not working toward it. Also, we may say that we have an interest in learning to play bridge, but we have never taken the time to act on that interest.

We have already stated that the way we use our money and time is a strong value indicator. For example, John may say he values very highly the importance of reading and keeping up in "his thinking." However, if you asked him how much time he spends reading each week or when he last bought a good book, you may be surprised to discover that he does not even remember. It has been said before that a simple process in determining the strength of a value is to ask a person or family to describe how they spend their money. Generally speaking, the more money they spend on something, the greater the value is to people.

From the preceding, it is easy to see that we can find out what our real values are by examining our *actual behaviors—the way in which we invest our time, money, energies, and resources.* Consequently, in order to better understand your real values, you might want to apply the following four tests to your value orientation (Rokeach, 1973):

1. **The Choice Test.** What do I do in situations involving a choice?
2. **The Time Test.** How much time and energy am I willing to spend on the value?
3. **The Sacrificial Test.** What satisfaction am I willing to forego on behalf of the value?
4. **The Emotion Test.** How much satisfaction or guilt do I experience when I am true to my value or when I violate it?

The most important thing to remember is that to claim a value, you must act in accordance to what you say you believe. Otherwise, you will be on a seesaw, going up and down and back and forth between "what is" and "what should be" in your life.

> If you can bring your actions and the time you spend in your life more into harmony with your values, you will feel more in control of your life and more satisfied with the decisions you make.
>
> Fred Hecklinger

VALUES TESTING THROUGH GOAL SETTING

From the discussion above, we might conclude that values may either be *conceived (stated)* or *operative (real).* Many individuals have conceived values

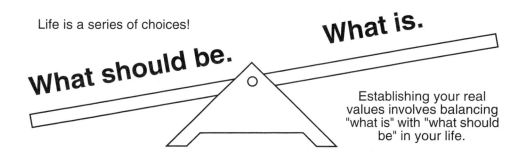

Life is a series of choices!

What should be.   What is.

Establishing your real values involves balancing "what is" with "what should be" in your life.

but do not bother to implement them. *Operative* values are the ones we work on (Sicard, et al., 1994). You will be given several opportunities in the activities at the end of this chapter to evaluate your stated or real values. We would encourage you to give special attention to the results of the activity: What Do You Value?

A direct relationship exists between our value structure and our motivation. That is, what we value we will be motivated to work toward achieving. This is not to say that what we say we value will necessarily motivate us. Many students say, "I value a college education." Yet, they do not obtain one, because on the emotional level of valuing, it is less important than other values. Their behavior indicates that something else is more valuable to them right now.

One way of clarifying our stated or real values is by testing our values through *priority ranking*. This is a process whereby an individual takes inventory of his or her values, examines them, and puts them in order of their importance. Next, the individual is asked to set a goal in relation to his or her stated top values. For example, let's look at the following illustration. (You will be given an opportunity to test this illustration for yourself in the activity: Values Testing Through Goal Setting).

Mrs. Smith, a community college counselor, described her top values as follows:

1.   My professional career
2.   My personal growth and awareness
3.   My family
4.   My friends

Using her top values, Mrs. Smith decided to set a goal to write all the local high schools and see whether they needed any of her college's catalogues, brochures, and so on. The following week came, and Mrs. Smith had not written any letters. When Mrs. Smith was asked what she had really done in the past week, she said "I took my little boy to the zoo and museum." The next week Mrs. Smith decided she would really get those letters written. Once again, she had not completed her goal. Instead, she had made clothes for the other family members. After talking with Mrs. Smith in a group discussion, it soon became evident that her family was really of more value than her profession. She admitted that she really had wanted to quit her job and have another child. However, she felt her husband needed her to work. Finally, she was able to admit her priority to her husband. It wasn't too long before Mrs. Smith made plans to terminate her job; she was pregnant. Mrs. Smith admitted that her "professional career" was not one of her top four values.

By testing her values through goal setting, Mrs. Smith's behavior demonstrated that something else (her family) was more valuable to her and more motivating to her than her stated top value.

Mrs. Smith had actually listed a *should* value in her priority list rather than an *actual* or *want* value. Her priority ranking did not really change her value as much as it helped them to become clearer. Actually, Mrs. Smith's *should* value was not motivating enough to be valuable to her. Setting a goal in relation to one's values and achieving that goal, simply indicates the importance of that value to the individual.

Everything can be taken from a man but one thing: The last of his freedoms—to choose one's attitude in any given set of circumstances, to choose one's own way.

Viktor E. Frankl

WE LEARN TO VALUE WHAT WE SUFFER FOR

Why does a child who has to work to earn money value his or her bicycle more than the child who is given a bicycle? Why are members of cults so dedicated to their organizations? These questions and many others may be answered by taking a look at cognitive dissonance, the mental pain of inconsistency, and justifying a sacrifice.

Cognitive Dissonance. What is cognitive dissonance, and how does it affect our values, beliefs, and attitudes? We are all motivated to maintain consistency within ourselves. We do not normally hold values, beliefs, or attitudes that are mutually incompatible or dissonant with each other, nor do we behave in ways contradictory to our values or attitudes. Although people differ in the amount of inconsistency they can tolerate, a basic assumption of *cognitive dissonance theory* is that inconsistency is intolerable to an individual.

The concept of cognitive dissonance was introduced by Leon Festinger (1957) to account for reactions to inconsistencies in attitudes and beliefs. According to this theory, when two or more cognitions such as beliefs, opinions, and the things we know about various types of behavior, people, objects, or circumstances are in disagreement (dissonance), a state of tension results. This inconsistency (dissonance) motivates the individual to adjust these cognitions so as to reduce the dissonance and thereby reduce the tension.

The Mental Pain of Inconsistency. When there is dissonance between attitudes and behavior, the individual may modify attitudes rather than behavior.

To illustrate these points, suppose that a cigarette smoker is aware of the dangers of smoking to his or her health but continues to smoke. The individual is faced with two dissonant cognitions: "I enjoy smoking, or smoking is harmful." The *dissonance theory* predicts that such an inconsistency would produce an uncomfortable state that would motivate the individual either to give up smoking or change his or her ideas about the risks involved in continuing to smoke. In cases such as this, we typically find the individual expressing one of the following ideas:

- "I enjoy smoking and it is worth it."
- "No one in our family has ever had cancer."
- "A person can't always avoid every possible dangerous situation and still continue to live an enjoyable life."
- "Perhaps even if I stopped smoking I would put on weight, which is equally as bad for one's health."

Thus, Festinger suggests that continuing to smoke is, after all, consistent with the person's ideas about smoking.

Although the individual may have stated that he or she would like to give up smoking, the person's inability to do so resulted in rationalizing some facts to support his or her belief system and to match the person's behavior. Now the tension is somewhat relieved. However, it has been suggested by some authorities that the individual may have to deal with his or her true feelings and behavior again.

Can you think of ways cognitive dissonance and the mental pain of inconsistency might apply to difficulties in losing weight or in breaking a substance abuse habit?

We write our own destiny . . . we become what we do.

Madame Chiang Kai-Shek

If you do not live the life you believe—you will believe the life you live.

Why does a person continue to smoke when they know it is harmful to their health?

It's important for people to know what you stand for. It's equally important that they know what you won't stand for. Above all, you better not compromise yourself; it is all you got.

Janis Joplin

Justifying a Sacrifice. To answer the questions asked earlier, as we have observed through cognitive dissonance, an individual is motivated to justify his or her behavior. A child who has to work to earn money to buy a bicycle will value it more because he or she put more effort into getting it. Cult members, just as other members of groups and organizations, will generally experience some type of initiation process that will take a lot of effort on the individual's part. After putting in all this effort, the individual has to justify why he or she suffered or worked so hard in order to be a member of the cult or organization. As a result of all this, the individual will generally become a very dedicated member of this group as a means of justifying why he or she went through this process.

As a student, most of you would admit that you value a class you succeed in that takes more effort than a class you succeeded in that was considered "easy." As you can see from these examples, *we learn to value what we suffer for* (Aronson, 1999).

LIVING WITH YOUR VALUES

This is a confusing world to live in. At every turn, we are forced to make choices about how to live our lives. Consider these questions: What is your philosophy of life? What would be included in your system of personal ethics? What do you do when you are confronted with confusion and conflicts regarding your values and ethics?

 CONSIDER THIS . . .
Value-Oriented Conflicts

It's the action, not the fruit of the action, that's important. You have to do the right thing. It may not be in your power, may not be in your time, that there'll be any fruit. But that doesn't mean you stop doing the right thing. You may never know what results come from your action. But if you do nothing, there will be no result.

Gandhi

- Maybe John and I should live together before marriage. Wouldn't this help us know if we're really compatible?
- Does religion have some meaning in my life, or is it nothing more than a series of outmoded traditions and customs?
- What will my family and friends think and say if Jane and I get a divorce? We've always been the model couple.
- Should I go back to work or college when the kids all get in school, or should I be a full-time Mom and homemaker?
- How can I really enjoy working and living and avoid getting into the rat race for the convertible and the house in the suburbs?
- Do I really need to take that career promotion and be gone from home most of the time, or would it be better to stay with my current job and be home with the family?
- Should I quit school and get a job? I'm tired of living in poverty. I can always get an education later.
- Should I buy a new car or save my money?
- What occupation shall I choose, so that I don't spend my life like so many others who dislike the jobs they go to every morning?
- Do I want children? Being a parent is kind of frightening to me.

**Which of these value-oriented conflicts present
a problem for you?**

Personal Ethics. As you think about the questions above, one thing is certain, your personal system of ethics is based on the values and attitudes you practice in your daily living. Actually, your system of personal ethics becomes an attempt to reconcile what *ought to be* with *what is.* Each of us, relying on our set of personal ethics, must decide what is *right* or *wrong* for us. There are many alternatives, but each of us can *choose* our direction in life.

Stephen Covey (1990), in his highly popular book, *The 7 Habits of Highly Effective People,* is concerned about some of the choices currently being made. He indicates that prior to World War I, people governed their lives by values like "integrity, humility, fidelity, temperance, courage, justice, patience, industry, simplicity, modesty, and the Golden Rule." Today, however, people are likely to be unsure of what a few of these words mean, and they are likely not to understand how they might apply to their lives.

Covey analyzes the changes in human interaction since about the time of World War I as a result of a focus on behavior and personality rather than character. What has been important has been having the right kind of personality defined by the right techniques. These techniques and a positive mental attitude shaped what Covey has called the *personality ethic.* Life influenced by the personality ethic involves having the right images and doing the right things—being good parents, using proper workplace protocol, showing concern for others, etc.

While there is nothing wrong with good image and good behavior, Covey reminds his readers that such behavior can lead people to lose sight of the character ethic. The *character ethic* is a style of living based *first* and *foremost* on prioritized principles and values rather than on techniques. Thus, these identified principles and values guide behavior. Consequently, Covey encourages his readers to return to the character ethic. After all, who can really dispute principles and values such as honesty, respect, integrity, etc?

Psychologist Lawrence Kohlberg (1981), who studied moral development and elements of the character ethic for many years, reminds us that *"the highest level of moral functioning requires us to use ethical principles to define our own moral standards and then to live in accord with them."* Ideally, our choices will be made on the basis of the values and *ethics*—our standards of conduct or behavior—we hold (Thompson, 1990).

Confusion and Conflict. Being human, sometimes we may experience confusion and conflict.

> Watch your thoughts;
>   they become words.
> Watch your words;
>   they become
>   actions.
> Watch your actions;
>   they become habits.
> Watch your habits;
>   they become
>   character.
> Watch your character;
>   it becomes your
>   destiny.
>
> Frank Outlaw

Life

The adventure of life is to learn.
The purpose of life is to grow
The nature of life is to change.
The challenge of life is to overcome.
The essence of life is to care.
The opportunity of life is to serve.
The secret of life is to dare.
The spice of life is to befriend.
The beauty of life is to give.
The joy of life is to love.

William Arthur Ward

What are your value priorities? It is important to understand what you will not compromise.

Perhaps one of the most difficult things to do is to establish for ourselves a consistent set of values (Pojman, 1998). If we go against a value, we feel bad. Inconsistencies in our values make us unhappy; they make us feel guilty. If we allow inconsistencies to become a habit, we become hypocrites. Hypocrites are people who do not act on the values they claim to hold. If we usually live up to our values, we are happy, satisfied people with consistent value systems.

It is true that we cannot always satisfy our values; many compromises must be made, because value conflicts are likely to appear when two or more people get together. Therefore, we need to learn when we can afford to give up and compromise values and when we cannot. It is best not to compromise values of high priority. Values that are not so important may be compromised without destroying our self-concept, as well as our personal ethics. Actually, satisfied, happy people are people who do not compromise their most important values but are willing to compromise their less important values.

Perhaps the question is really—*What is most important to me?* In making value compromises, therefore, it is very important that we understand our priorities. It is this understanding that helps us define our purpose and give meaning to our life. Controversial radio icon, Dr. Laura Schlessinger (1998), puts it quite simply: *"ultimately, we decide the course of our lives by the ethical decisions we make."*

THE IMPORTANCE OF MEANING AND PURPOSE

Viktor Frankl, a European psychiatrist, dedicated much of his professional life to the study of meaning in life. According to Frankl (1978), what distinguishes us as humans is our *search for purpose.* The striving to find meaning in our lives is a primary motivational force. Humans are able to live and even die for the sake of their ideals and values. Frankl (1963) is fond of pointing out the wisdom of Nietzsche's words: *"He who has a why to live for can bear with almost any how."* Drawing on his experiences in the death camp at Auschwitz, Frankl asserts that inmates who had purpose or a meaningful task in life had a much greater chance of surviving than those who had no sense of mission (Corey and Corey, 2000).

As human beings, it is our challenge and our task to create our own meaning. No one can do this for us. We encourage you to take some of the wisdom from William Ward's *"Life"* and begin to practice them each day.

Yalom (1980) reviewed a number of studies of the role of meaning in people's lives and described the following results:

- A person's lack of a sense of meaning in life is related to the existence of emotional and behavioral disorders; the less the sense of meaning, the greater the degree of personal disturbances.
- A positive sense of meaning in life is associated with having a set of religious beliefs.
- A positive sense of meaning is associated with possessing values relating to the betterment of humanity and an interest in the welfare of others.

Something to do, someone to love, and something to hope for, are the true essentials of a happy and meaningful life. No matter how rich you are, if you lack one of these essentials, life's true fulfillment will not be yours. No matter how poor you are, if you possess all three of these, you can build a satisfying existence for yourself.

David Goodman

- A positive sense of meaning is associated with a dedication to some cause and with having a clear set of life goals.
- Meaning in life is not to be seen as a static entity but should be viewed in a developmental perspective. The sources of meaning differ at various stages in life, and other developmental tasks must precede the development of meaning.

Along with Frankl, Yalom concludes that humans require meaning to survive: To live without meaning and values provokes considerable distress, and in its severe form it may lead to the decision for suicide. Jourard (1971) confirms this by making the following point:

> People decide to live as long as they experience meaning and value in life, but they may decide to die when meaning and value vanishes from life.

Dr. Barry Schwartz (2000), professor of psychology at Swarthmore College, in his review of social psychologist David Myer's latest book, *The American Paradox: Spiritual Hunger in an Age of Plenty*, discusses additional insights about the importance of meaning and purpose. He notes that in some respects freedom and opportunity have simply made us more miserable than ever. For example, even though wealth is at an all time high, we have less happiness, more depression, more fragile marital relationships, less communal contentment, more crime (even after the recent decline), and more demoralized children. It seems that we walk aimlessly through life—searching, searching, searching for "what's the meaning." Incidentally, we will discuss the research on happiness in the next chapter.

Corey and Corey (2000) summarize the importance of meaning and purpose:

> Humans apparently have a need for some absolutes in the form of clear ideals to which they can aspire and guidelines by which they can direct their actions.

Do you have clear ideals to which you can aspire and guidelines by which you can direct your actions? Do you have meaning and purpose in your life?

Do you value patriotism enough to be willing to fight for your country?

Chapter Review

A well-defined value system is basic to personal motivation, self-determination, and a lifestyle with meaning. Actually, our value system should be the control point of our life, helping us to choose the direction and course we will take.

- A value is the degree of importance we attach to various beliefs, ideas, objects, or things.

- Milton classifies values into two broad categories: moral values—right and wrong, good and evil; nonmoral values—tastes, preferences, and styles.

- We are not born with values, but we are born into cultures and societies that promote, teach, and impart their values to us. We first gain our value orientation from the "significant others" in our lives, with the years of adolescence being extremely important for the learning and development of values. During this time, we test the shoulds and should nots coming from peers, school, media, and advertising influences.

- Individuation is the separation from our family system and the establishment of our own identity based on our own experiences and values.

- Other factors influencing the formation of our value system include religious beliefs, attitudes, prejudices, and stereotypes. The three components to a prejudice are: to hold certain beliefs against members of a group, to feel negatively toward them and to be inclined to act negatively toward them.

- Because we live and work in a multicultural world, it is extremely important that we be willing to view diversity as a strength and to test, adapt, and change our perceptions as we interact with others.

- Our values do change as we go through various stages of our life.

- Values may be classified as abstract (intangible) or specific (tangible).

- Our interests, attitudes, and behavior often indicate whether our value system is oriented mainly toward things, ideas, or people.

- Values clarification is a process that helps individuals discover their true values. The process of clarifying values involves choosing freely from alternatives, prizing and or affirming the choice publicly, and acting repeatedly in some pattern of life.

- Value indicators or partial values are values still in the process of being formed. How we use our time and money are often strong value indicators. Four tests to apply to your value orientations include: (1) The choice test, (2) the time test, (3) the sacrificial test, and (4) the emotion test.

- Values are either conceived-stated values, or operative-real values we work on. One way of clarifying our stated or real values is by testing our values through priority ranking and then setting a goal in relation to the stated top values. Should values are not motivating enough to be truly valuable long-term to a person.

- According to the cognitive dissonance theory, when two or more cognitions such as beliefs, opinions, and the things we know about various types of behavior, people, or circumstances are in disagreement (dissonance), a state of tension results. This inconsistency (dissonance) motivates the individual to adjust these cognitions so as to reduce the dissonance and thereby reduce the tension. Often, attitudes, rather than behavior, are modified. Quite simply, we are motivated to justify our behavior. We frequently learn to value what we suffer for.

- One of the most difficult tasks we face is living with our values—there are so many choices to make. Since World War I, there has been a focus on behavior and personality—the personality ethic—having the right kind of personality defined by the right techniques. Prior to World War I, there was a focus on the character ethic—a style of living based first and foremost on prioritized principles and values.

- In making value compromises, it is extremely important that we remember our priorities.

- As human beings, we have a need for clear ideals to which we can aspire and guidelines by which we can direct our actions. Thus, it becomes our challenge and our task to create our own meaning and purpose.

The real values in life are those we have actually experienced. Thus, what we say we believe in is sometimes significant; what we really do is where the significance lies.

??? **Questions** ???

1. Explain what the term "value" means.
2. Define and give examples of the two broad categories Milton classifies values into.
3. Explain how we develop values. Define the term individuation and explain its significance in the development of our value system.
4. List and give examples of the three components to a prejudice.
5. Explain at least three things you can do to break down barriers in dealing with prejudices and stereotypes.
6. Define and give personal examples of abstract (tangible) and specific (tangible) values.
7. List and explain the three possible value orientations. Give examples of the value orientation more descriptive of your lifestyle.
8. Define values clarification, and explain the process of clarifying values.
9. List and give examples of the four tests to apply to your value orientations. Explain at least two strong value indicators.
10. Explain the difference between conceived values and operative values.
11. Explain the process of values testing through goal setting. What is the difference in a should value and an actual I want value?
12. Explain the cognitive dissonance theory, using a personal example, if possible. How does justifying a sacrifice relate to the concept of cognitive dissonance?
13. Distinguish between the personality ethic and the character ethic.
14. What is the most important thing to remember when considering whether to make value compromises?
15. Explain the role and significance of meaning in an individual's life.

🗝 **Key Terms** 🗝

Acting
Attitudes
Belief
Character Ethic
Choosing Freely
Cognitive Dissonance
Conceived Values
Ethics
Full Value
Idea-Oriented Value System

Individuation
Intangible Values
Moral Values
Non-Moral Values
Operative Values
People-Oriented Value System
Personality Ethic
Prejudices
Prizing

Stereotyping
Tangible Values
Thing-Oriented Value System
Value
Value Indicators
Value System
Values Clarification

??? **Discussion** ???

1. What have been some of the factors that have influenced the development of your value system? Which factor has been of the greatest significance?
2. What are some differences between your value system of today and that of five or ten years ago?
3. Two strong value indicators were discussed: how we spend our money and how we spend our time. Which one is a greater indicator?
4. Discuss any prejudices and stereotypes you have personally experienced.
5. How can we minimize prejudice and stereotyping in our society? How would you compare prejudicial attitudes today compared to 10–20 years ago?
6. What is your perception of the value assessment survey of college students discussed in this chapter?
7. What are some of your partial values or value indicators which are in the process of being formed?
8. Have you ever applied the cognitive dissonance theory to one of your stated values? If so, explain how you changed your belief system to "match" your behavior.
9. How would you describe your personal ethics? How would you describe your philosophy of life?

Name _____ Date _____

Self-Inventory

Purpose: To understand and evaluate your value system for personal goal setting.

Instructions:

I. For each statement below, indicate the response that most closely identifies your beliefs and attitudes. Use this code:

>5 = Strongly agree
>4 = Agree in most respects
>3 = Undecided
>2 = Disagree in most respects
>1 = Strongly disagree

_____ 1. Because of the demands and expectations of others, it is difficult for me to maintain a true grasp of my own identity.

_____ 2. At this particular time, I have a sense of purpose and meaning that gives me direction.

_____ 3. I have evaluated and questioned most of the values I now hold.

_____ 4. Religion gives a source of meaning and purpose to my life.

_____ 5. I generally live by and proclaim the values I hold.

_____ 6. I have a close idea of who I am and what I want to become.

_____ 7. I let others influence my values more than I'd like to admit.

_____ 8. The majority of my values are similar to those of my parents.

_____ 9. Generally, I feel clear about what I value.

_____ 10. My values and my views about the meaning of life have changed a great deal during my lifetime.

_____ 11. The way I use my time right now reflects my personal values.

_____ 12. I have a clear picture of "my philosophy of life."

_____ 13. I must admit that I have some prejudices and stereotypes that are currently part of my value system.

_____ 14. The way I spend my money right now reflects my personal values.

_____ 15. The values that I presently believe in are the ones I want to continue to live by.

II. Responses may be shared in small groups or just viewed as a personal inventory.

Discussion

1. Would you like to change your responses to any of the questions? Which ones, and to what numerical degree?

2. What goals would you like to set to ensure that the desired responses occur?

Name _____ Date _____

Tracing Values Through My Life

Purpose: To review the importance of early learning on your value system.

Instructions:

I. Below is a list of common value areas. Remember and record what you learned/were told as a young person and what was important about each of these values; for example, money: I was told to save my money and not be a "spendthrift." I learned to manage money well so I would be able to have things I wanted or needed.

II. Next, indicate whether this early value is still important (I) or not important (NI).

III. Lastly, look through the list as a whole and rank the areas 1–12 in how important they are to you today: 1 is most important and 12 is least important.

Value Area	What I Learned/ Was Told as a Child	Current Importance	Ranking
Education/ new knowledge			
Health—emotional and physical well-being			
Money/Possessions			
Love/Affection			
Religion/Morals/Spirituality			
Achievement/Recognition			
Helping Others			

Value Area	What I Learned/ Was Told as a Child	Current Importance	Ranking
Marriage/Family			
Friendships			
Security			
Work/Career			
Leisure Time			

IV. Have your values changed over the past 5–10 years? Are things that were important then not as important now? Have other things taken on greater importance? In what ways have your values changed? List those things that have become more important and those that have become less important to you. (Feel free to use value areas other than the ones listed in this activity.)

More Important	Less Important
_____	_____
_____	_____
_____	_____
_____	_____

Discussion

1. Are you surprised at the changes you see or don't see? What insights did you get from this exercise?

2. How do you think your parents would have ranked the 12 values?

3. Give examples of how you are living your life today to reflect your four most important values?

    1.

    2.

    3.

    4.

4. What values do you want to model to your children?

What Do You Value?

Purpose: To identify what you "really" value in everyday life.

Instructions:

I. Write down the three things that you most value in life, such as your family, education, religion, money, boyfriend or girlfriend, and so on.

    1.

    2.

    3.

II. Identify at least two days within a week, a normal work or school day and a day that you have more freedom to choose what you like to do, such as a weekend day. During each of those two days, write down what you do every two hours within a 24-hour day, including sleep.

    Day One _____

Day Two _____

III. Review your daily diary. How much time did you spend doing those things you stated that you value in Instruction I?

Discussion

What you do in your everyday life demonstrates what you really value in life. Did you spend only ten minutes with family and five hours watching television? What does that tell you about your values?

1. Based on your diary, time-wise, what do you value most (list 1, 2, 3, and 4)?
    1.
    2.
    3.
    4.

2. How do the activities in your daily diary compare to what you stated your values to be?

3. What can you do in order to allow your behavior to follow your values (change your values or your behavior)? How are you going to change?

4. What did you learn from this activity?

Name _____ Date _____

Personal Value Assessment*

Purpose: To identify your values through priority ranking.

Instructions:

I. The following is a list of personal values. Go through this list and rate the personal values in terms of their importance to you. Place a check (✓) mark in the category that best represents your feelings about how important the personal value is to you. (Exercise continues through the next 3 pages).

Personal Value	Very Important	Moderately Important	Somewhat Important	Not Important
Good health				
Having close friendships				
Having a close family				
A fulfilling career				
A long life				
A stable marriage				
A financially comfortable life				
Independence				
Being creative				
Participating in an organized religion				
Intimacy with another				
Having children				
A variety of interests and activities				
Freedom to create my own lifestyle				
Having a house				
A happy love relationship				
Fulfilling careers for me and my spouse				
Contributing to my community				

*Fred Hecklinger and Bernadette Black, *Training for Life* (Dubuque, Iowa: Kendall/Hunt Publishing Co., 2000), pp 46–48. Used with permission.

Personal Value	Very Important	Moderately Important	Somewhat Important	Not Important
Abundance of leisure time				
Happiness				
Ability to move from place to place				
A life without stress				
Strong religious values				
A chance to make social changes				
To be remembered for my accomplishments				
Helping those in distress				
Freedom to live where I wish				
A stable life				
Time to myself				
Enjoyment of arts, entertainment and cultural activities				
A life without children				
A life with many challenges				
Opportunity to be a leader				
Opportunity to fight for my country				
A chance to make a major discovery that would save lives				
A good physical appearance				
Opportunity to establish roots in one place				
Opportunity for physical activities				
An exciting life				
A chance to get into politics				

Personal Value	Very Important	Moderately Important	Somewhat Important	Not Important
To live according to strong moral values				
Opportunity to teach others				
To write something memorable				
A chance to become famous				
To help others solve problems				
To make lots of money				
Others:				

II. In the space below, list at least ten of your most important personal values from your Personal Values Assessment.

1. _____   6. _____

2. _____   7. _____

3. _____   8. _____

4. _____   9. _____

5. _____   10. _____

III. In the space below, list your top five personal values in order of priority, with number one as the most important.

1. _____   first priority

2. _____   second priority

3. _____   third priority

4. _____   fourth priority

5. _____   fifth priority

Discussion

1. Does your life right now reflect your values? Is the time you spend consistent with your priorities?

2. If the time you spend in your life right now does not reflect your personal values, how can you change your life so that the time you spend is more in keeping with your values?

3. Are there some parts of your life that you would like to change but that you cannot right now? If so, what is your timetable for bringing your lifestyle more into harmony with your values?

Multicultural Panel Discussion

Purpose: To learn to value and respect fundamental differences among cultures and ethnic groups.

Instructions: Using the diverse populations within your classroom, your instructor will select multicultural, ethnic, and gender-mixed members from the class to participate in a panel discussion of the topics below. Instructors are encouraged to allow time for questions from the class members.

Topics:

I. Attitudes, beliefs and values concerning:

Dating/personal relationships

Marriage (within culture; outside of culture; interracial marriage)

Divorce

Family life (including extended families)

The purpose and meaning of life

Education

Work/Careers

Social involvement

Religion, worship, spirituality, moral codes

Death and funerals

Government enforced laws

Leisure time

Male roles/female roles

II. Customs and practices about:

Holiday celebrations (religious and other)

Weddings and funerals

Appearance (clothing, shoes, or other attire)

Gift-giving and charity

Food, alcohol, or drugs (differences in types, use or misuse of)

III. Miscellaneous concerns:

What would you like the class members to understand most about your culture or ethnic group?

Discussion

1. What did you learn as a result of this panel discussion?

2. Explain any prejudices or stereotypes you may have previously held that you perceive differently as a result of this panel discussion.

3. Are there any questions that you would have liked to ask but didn't feel comfortable asking? If so, what are the questions?

Name _____   Date _____

Values Testing Through Goal Setting

Purpose: To test values through priority-ranking.

Instructions:

   I. List your top four values in order of their importance to you.

      1.

      2.

      3.

      4.

   II. Set a goal in relation to your stated top value. (Priority-ranking #1)

      MY GOAL:

   III. Make a list of what you can do during the next two to three weeks that will help you reach your goal.

   IV. After a two or three week period, evaluate what progress you have made toward your goal. Write below what all you did toward your goal or what you did instead of working on your goal.

V. Evaluate your goal by answering the discussion questions below.

Discussion

1. What did your behavior during the two or three week period demonstrate was important to you?

2. Is your #1 value a *should* or *actual I want* value?

3. What did you learn about yourself as a result of this activity?

Name _____ Date _____

Meaning and Values

Learning Journal

Select the statement below that best defines your feelings about the personal value or meaning gained from this chapter and respond below the dotted line.

- I learned that I . . .
- I realized that I . . .
- I discovered that I . . .

- I was surprised that I . . .
- I was pleased that I . . .
- I was displeased that I . . .

. . . .

continue on reverse

CHAPTER 10

Where Do I Want To Go with My Life?

My advice is to live your life. Allow that wonderful inner intelligence to speak through you. The blueprint for you to be your authentic self lies within. In some mystical way the microscopic egg that grew to be you had the program for your physical, intellectual, emotional, and spiritual development. Allow the development to occur to its fullest; grow and bloom. Follow your bliss and be what you want to be. Don't climb the ladder of success only to find it's leaning against the wrong wall. Do not let your age limit your future growth as a human being.

Bernie Siegel
Love, Medicine, and Miracles

Think about this...

For just a few minutes, we are going to share an analogy with you we recently heard at a Life Planning workshop, based on the work of authors Fred Hecklinger and Bernadette Black, 2000.

Compare your journey through life to a train trip. You are constantly moving ahead, with stops along the way. With every mile and every new passenger, the train changes just a small amount. For every new person you meet or new experience you have, you change a bit. Just as the train will take on new passengers, employees, and supplies and will eventually let them go, so will you take on new interests, friends, and skills. Some of them you will choose to keep and others you will let go. But just as the train keeps going, remaining basically the same, so do you keep going. You are changed by your experiences, but you always come back to you and you must make the decisions that significantly alter your journey through life.

Just as a train goes through tunnels, around curves, and encounters bumpy tracks, slowdowns and detours, your journey through life will be marked by both smooth and rough travel. At times the direction in which you are headed may not seem very clear. But a course is there, just as the train tracks are there. You may end up going in circles at times, but you still keep moving. Whenever you come to a junction and have to decide which track to take, you must make a decision. Some of these decisions can significantly alter the direction of your life. You run your life, just as an engineer runs a train. You will be responsible for making many decisions. You must invest time and energy on this journey, but the rewards should be well worth your investment.

You are now on your journey and have already been through many stations or experiences on the way. Do you like the direction that your life is taking? Do you feel that you have control over where you are going? You must decide whether to take charge of your trip and be the engineer or simply be a passenger on your train, letting others make the critical decisions for you.

The authors believe you have the right and power to make choices about your life. Furthermore, we believe that your long-range happiness is guaranteed when you decide to direct and plan your own life. "But, isn't this all just a little bit frightening?" you might ask.

> Nobody can go back and start a new beginning, but anyone can start today and make a new ending.
>
> Maria Robinson

LEARNING TO TAKE RISKS

If you are ever going to get serious about life planning, you will have to take risks. There is simply no way you can grow without taking chances, because everything you really want in life involves taking a risk. To live a creative, interesting, challenging, and successful life, you have to gamble, take some risks, and experiment. (Johnson, 2000).

David Viscott (1988) defines *risk* in this way:

> To risk is to loosen your grip on the known and the certain and to reach for something you are not entirely sure of but believe is better than what you now have, or is at least necessary to survive.

Basic Law of Life. Howard Figler (1999), a life-planning specialist at the University of Texas at Austin, gives the following advice to his students:

> One-half of knowing what you want in life is knowing what you are willing to give up to have what you want. This translates into a basic law of life: For everything you get in life, you also have to give up something.

Think about the truth of this. For example, if you go to college to further your education and career opportunities, you have to give up some time for study and going to class; if you take a job promotion in another state, you have to give up the security of your friends and familiar places; if you get married, you have to give up some of your independence; if you decide to have children, you have to give up some of your personal time; if you decide to lose some weight, you have to give up some of your high-calorie snack foods; and if you decide to retire from the world of work, you have to give up a higher paycheck.

As you can see, in every risk, there is some unavoidable loss, something that has to be given up to move ahead. However, life is full of many risks and changes. Dr. Spencer Johnson (1998), author of the best seller, *Who Moved My Cheese?* reminds readers: *"change isn't everything; it's the only thing. Embrace change, don't fight it."*

To live an interesting, challenging, and successful life, you have to gamble, take some risks, and experiment.

Many people are terrified by any possible loss and try to avoid all risks. However, this is really the surest way of losing. Why would you lose if you didn't take risks?

David Viscott (1988) gives us the answer:

> If you do not risk, risk eventually comes to you. If a person postpones taking risks, the time eventually comes when he will either be forced to accept a situation that he doesn't like or to take a risk unprepared. . . . If you continually shun any risk, you become comfortable with fewer and fewer experiences. . . . Your world shrinks and you become rigid. . . . Your life has no direction but is only a reaction to what the world presents to you.

It seems beneficial, therefore, to review some suggestions for more effective risk taking. David Johnson (2000), professor of Educational Psychology at the University of Minnesota, offers some considerations in the "How to" box on the next page.

Therefore, the purpose of life planning is not to eliminate risks but to be certain that the risks you take are the right ones, based on careful thought (Boles, 1999). The question then becomes, how can I find direction for my life?

WHAT MOTIVATES YOU?

The old saying "Where there's a will, there's a way" means that if you want—really want—to do something, you will find a way to do it. In other words,

Life is not a spelling bee, where no matter how many words you have gotten right, if you make one mistake you are disqualified. Life is more like a baseball season, where even the best team loses one-third of its games and even the worst team has its days of brilliance. Our goal is not to go all year without ever losing a game. Our goal is to win more than we lose, and if we can do that consistently enough, then when the end comes, we will have won it all.

Harold Kushner

How to . . .

. . . Take Risks Effectively

1. Take risks often.
2. Start small. Small risks, with small penalties for failure, may be attempted first. If successful, you will increase in both self-confidence and knowledge and, therefore, can take on bigger risks.
3. The most appropriate risk is one in which there is a fifty-fifty chance of success or failure. This means that on the average, you will fail half of the time and succeed half of the time.
4. Prepare for your risks. Do not try to swim the English Channel without studying how it is done, practicing, getting into shape physically, and obtaining the proper equipment and support systems. The more experienced and better equipped you are, the more likely that your risk will succeed. You can control the outcome of your risks by being prepared and well-informed.

Johnson, (2000)

you must be motivated to act. The stronger your motivation, the more likely you are to accomplish your purpose. The weaker your motivation, the less likely you are to reach your goal.

What is it that causes a person to consider getting a college degree, becoming more financially responsible, seeking the company's sales award, or planning the direction of their life?

Needs and Motives. Let us look at the definition of these two words: *Need* is a lack of something desirable or useful; to be in want. *Motive* is something (a need or desire) that causes a person to act. Actually, the two words are very closely related. When we find ourselves in *need* of something, we begin to search for it. Therefore, the *need* gives us a reason to act—*a motive.*

If all the air were suddenly sucked out of the room you are in right now, what would happen to your interest in reading the remaining pages of this chapter for your final exam? You would not care about reading and studying for a final exam and getting a credit in your last college course; you would not care about anything except getting air. Survival would be your only motivation.

But now that you have air, it does not motivate you. Stephen Covey (1996) calls this one of the greatest insights in the field of human motivation: *Satisfied needs do not motivate. It's only the unsatisfied need that motivates.*

Psychologists have said that there is a reason for everything a person does. Therefore, what are some of the needs that lead people to different types of action?

Fundamental Human Needs. In *First Things First,* Stephen Covey (1996) discusses the essence of human needs being captured in the phrase: *"to live, to love, to learn, and to leave a legacy."* Specifically, these four human needs are:

1. *To live* is our *physical* need for such things as food, clothing, shelter, economic well-being, and health.

> Happiness is a man's greatest achievement: it is the response of his total personality to a productive orientation toward himself and the world outside.
>
> Erich Fromm

2. *To love* is our *social* need to relate to other people, to belong, to love, to be loved.
3. *To learn* is our *mental* need to develop and to grow.
4. *To leave a legacy* is our *spiritual* need to have a sense of meaning, purpose, personal congruence, and contribution.

Although we will refer to these needs again when we discuss what goals you would most want to accomplish, these needs are believed to be fundamental to human fulfillment. If these basic needs are not met, we feel empty and incomplete.

MASLOW'S HIERARCHY OF NEEDS

Perhaps the most widely accepted category of human needs was presented by Abraham Maslow (1987). It might help us to understand Maslow's theory of human motivation by referring to how we reach the top of a ladder—*one step at a time.* Maslow feels that before we can "blossom" and grow toward self-actualization, the top of the ladder, we progress through certain steps. His theory of the stepladder, better known as *Maslow's Hierarchy of Needs,* might look something like Figure 10.1.

Basically, Maslow believes that there are certain survival needs that must be met before we can become concerned with the satisfaction of other needs. We will now examine *Maslow's Hierarchy of Needs.*

Physiological Needs. These biological needs include food, water, and air, which are essential to our physical well-being. Hence, they are often referred to as our *primary needs* because they keep us alive.

Safety and Security Needs. When our physiological needs have been satisfied, the safety needs are the next most important step on the hierarchy. Safety and security needs include a reasonably orderly and predictable way of life, a savings account, shelter, insurance policies, etc.

Fundamental Human Needs:
"to live, to love, to learn,
and to leave a legacy."

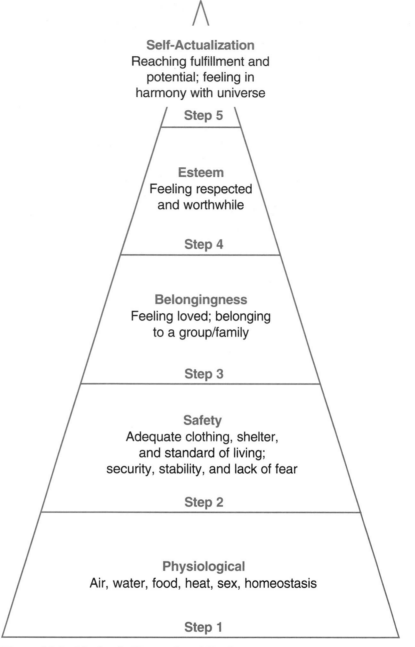

Figure 10-1. Maslow's Hierarchy of Needs

Love and Belonging Needs. If our physiological needs are satisfied and our safety needs have been reasonably fulfilled, needs for love, affection, and belonging are the next step on the hierarchy. Love and belonging needs drive us to seek meaningful relationships with others. We seek acceptance, approval, and a feeling of belonging in our social relationships. Companionship and friendship are very important in satisfying this need to love and be loved.

Esteem Needs. Maslow believes that if people have their survival, safety, and affection needs met, they will develop a sense of appreciation for themselves. This sense of appreciation may be nothing more than the development of self-confidence, which strengthens our self-esteem—our self-worth. We need to experience some degree of success to feel that we have achieved something worthwhile.

Self-Actualization Needs. The last step on the hierarchy represents the fullest development of our potentialities. Some writers believe that *self-actualization* is the need for self-fulfillment—to fulfill oneself as a creative, unique individual according to his or her own innate potentialities. It has been said that we develop and use only about *10 to 15 percent* of our potential mental ability. Therefore, only a small percentage of people achieve what they are really capable of doing.

There are degrees of achievement of self-actualization, however. One person might feel that complete fulfillment is being the ideal mother. Another person might satisfy this need by setting an occupational goal and reaching it. Actually, self-actualization is a matter of interpretation, and we have the right to decide what constitutes our satisfaction of this top step on the hierarchy.

Maslow's (1993) last book, *The Further Reaches of Human Nature,* contains some specific suggestions for increasing our self-actualization. Those suggestions are listed in the following "How to" box.

Where are you on the ladder? It is important that we realize that this stepladder of needs is somewhat flexible. All people do not fulfill their needs in the order that Maslow gives; there are some exceptions. For example, some people may feel that self-esteem is more important than belonging and love. Furthermore, many of us move around on the ladder, as we strive to satisfy several needs together.

How do you go about satisfying the needs and wants in your life?

> I long to accomplish a great and noble task, but it is my chief duty to accomplish small tasks as if they were great and noble.
>
> Helen Keller

How to . . .
. . . Increase our Self-Actualization

1. Experience life fully, be alive and absorbed with what you are doing at the moment.
2. Learn to trust your own judgment and feelings in making life choices, such as marriage and career.
3. Be honest with yourself and take responsibility for what you do.
4. Whenever possible choose growth, rather than safety or security.
5. Recognize your defenses and illusions, and then work to give them up.
6. Even though peak experiences are transient, keep the aspiration of these moments of self-actualization alive in your everyday thoughts and actions.
7. Remember that self-actualization is a continual process; it is never fully achieved.
8. Commit yourself to concerns and causes outside yourself, because self-actualization comes more as a by-product of developing your full capacities than the egocentric pursuit of growth itself.

From Maslow The Further Reaches of Human Nature *(1993)*

PLAN YOUR LIFE LIKE YOU WOULD A VACATION

Richard Boles (1983), in his workshops on Life Planning, frequently refers to our lives being divided into three periods. The first period is that of *getting an education;* the second period is that of *going to work and earning a living or working in the home and community;* and the third and last period is that of *living in retirement.*

One of Boles concerns is that these periods have become more and more isolated from each other. He makes a statement you may find somewhat surprising:

> Life in each period seems to be conducted by those in charge without much consciousness of . . . never mind, preparation for . . . life in the next period.

Why Plan? If you really want to take an active part in satisfying the needs and wants of your life, you need a plan or an outline that will direct you toward your ultimate goal. The dictionary says *a goal is an aim or purpose—a plan.* You would not think of going on a vacation without some plans or goals for your trip. After all, you might get lost. Are you trying to play the game of life without goals by moving from different periods of your life without any plans or any direction?

If this describes the picture of your life right now, read the following words of Maxwell Maltz (1987) carefully:

> We are engineered as goal-seeking mechanisms. We are built that way. When we have no personal goal which we are interested in and means something to us, we have to go around in circles, feel lost, and find life itself aimless and purposeless. We are built to conquer our environment, solve problems, achieve goals, and we find no real satisfaction or happiness in life without obstacles to conquer and goals to achieve. People who say that life is not worthwhile are really saying that they themselves have no personal goals that are worthwhile. Get yourself a goal worth working for. Better still, get yourself a project. Decide what you want out of a situation. Always have something ahead to look forward to.

In short, we might say that goals give purpose and meaning to our lives; they give us something to aim for, something to achieve. Remember, the reason you make plans for your vacation is so you will reach your destination and have a good time in the process. Achieving what we want out of life is much like climbing to the top of a ladder. We do not leap to the top of the ladder; we have to take a few steps at a time. As the steps on a ladder lead to the top—the goal—our plan for achieving what we want out of life must have steps, too. Otherwise, we will be unable to climb.

After you reach the top, can you quit? No! Goals become self-extending. We do not achieve a goal and suddenly feel comfortable and just quit. You do not get to your vacation destination and quit either. There are things you want to do, and then you have to get back home, too. Rather, we achieve one goal and then find that another fills its place. This is the way we continue to grow and get what we want out of life.

The Responsibility Is Yours. It is your responsibility to build the road to your own enrichment; you must lay the foundation. David Campbell (1990), in his thought-provoking book, *If You Don't Know Where You're Going, You'll Probably End Up Somewhere Else,* likens life to a never-ending pathway, which has many side roads or paths in the form of options which confront us along that road; these side roads or paths have gates which are open or closed to us. When we come to each new option, there are two factors that determine whether we continue on the same path, or take a new direction: one is *credentials,* and the second is *motivation.*

Most people most of the time make decisions with little awareness of what they are doing. They take action with little understanding of their motives and without beginning to know the ramifications of their choices.

M. Scott Peck

Planning is bringing the future into the present so that you can do something about it.

Alan Lakein

If you have the credentials (such as education, training, skills), you have an option available to you and may choose or not choose to take a new path. If you do not have the credentials, the gate remains closed at that point even if you are extremely motivated. In other words, no matter how much you may want that option, if you have not prepared for it, it is not going to be available to you.

Where will you be in five/ten/twenty years? You may not know, but you probably have some dreams and ideas. Planning today will help you to go where you want to go, just like you want to get to your vacation destination, rather than drift along relying on luck or fate. Remember, do not forget to keep your options open.

Because we live in a world of change, the fulfillment of our needs may vary from the experiences we encounter. A death of a spouse, for example, may threaten our security needs. Furthermore, as we grow and understand ourselves more clearly, our needs and wants probably change, too. In *Be All That You Are,* James Fadiman (1986) notes that goals can serve as a coping strategy throughout our entire lives:

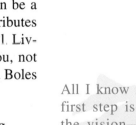

Where will you be in five/ten/twenty years?

> Since we are changing, having goals is a way for us to direct that change. Since we have no choice but to be older, we can choose how we intend to grow older. We can also choose to have better health or worse, more freedom or less, greater income or less, more relationships or fewer.

Without a doubt, goals help us control the direction of change in our lives. We may have to ask ourselves quite often, "Where am I on the stepladder? What are my goals? What are my plans for reaching these goals?"

SETTING YOUR GOALS: WHAT DO YOU WANT?

What do you want to achieve? It is important that you get to the "heart of yourself" and answer this question. Whatever is satisfying and worthy can be a goal for you to accomplish. Therefore, no goal is *too insignificant* if it contributes to your sense of achievement. It cannot be small; only you can make it small. Living each day fully is just as important as writing a book. At any rate, you, not anyone else, must be impressed with the goals you set for your life. Richard Boles (2000) confirms this statement:

> You have got to know what it is you want, or someone is going to sell you a bill of goods somewhere along the line that can do irreparable damage to your self-esteem, your sense of worth, and your stewardship of the talents that God gave you.

Authors Covey (1996), Roger-John and McWilliams (1991), and Ziglar (1998) write of at least seven different kinds of goals:

- physical
- financial
- spiritual
- career
- family
- mental
- social

All I know is that the first step is to create the vision—that creates the *want* power.

Arnold Schwarzenegger

How to . . .

. . . Set successful goals

Your goals must be your own
The goal must not be in conflict with one's personal value system
Goals need to be specific and written down
Start with short-range goals
Goals must be realistic and attainable
Goals should contain specific time deadlines

> *I don't know the key to success, but the key to failure is trying to please everybody.*
>
> Bill Cosby

Do you have any needs, wants, or desires that could be worked on in any of the seven goal areas? Think about some of these possibilities:

- Would you like to lose some weight or improve your appearance in some way? Would you like to start a personal physical fitness program?
- Would you like to meet some new people? Would you like to do some volunteer work for non-profit organizations or become more involved in your community?
- Are you satisfied with your spiritual life? If not, what could you do to improve that element in your life?
- Have you been thinking of further developing your skills and capacities? What would you like to accomplish while you are in college?
- Do you need to spend more time with your family? Do you need to reestablish a relationship with a distant family member?
- Is your financial management what it needs to be to provide for necessities and some of your wants? How can you save to buy that new car next year?
- Would you like an enjoyable, satisfying job? Have you thought of planning to make an appointment with a counselor at your school and begin some serious career counseling?

Do your teammates help you reach your goals?

As you can see, the list of possibilities is just endless. You know what some of your wants and needs are. Are you ready to select one or more of the seven goal areas and begin to establish some serious goals? When? What is wrong with today? Do not procrastinate. There will never be a completely convenient time.

CONTRIBUTORS TO SUCCESS

There are countless definitions of what success really is. Success has often been referred to as the *progressive realization of a worthwhile, predetermined personal goal* (McCullough, 1997). For example, some people define success in terms of money and material possessions. Others may feel success is found in personal relationships. Then, there are some people who believe that developing their potential in work or some particular interest defines success. We might conclude that *success is setting a goal and achieving that goal, whatever that goal may be.*

What actually contributes to success?

A Sense of Direction. If we do not know where we are going, we will certainly end up elsewhere. There will, no doubt, be conflicting wants and needs. However, we need to establish priorities and make choices. *A philosophy of life*—or rules for living and values in life—is basic to the direction we choose. Successful people know the direction in which they are moving, and why they are going there. A unified purpose, whatever that may be, gives meaning to our existence, and you already know from Chapter 9 how important this is.

Life is like a piano. What you get out of it depends on how you play it.

How to . . .

. . . Achieve success

Contributors to Success

A sense of direction
A feeling of self-confidence
A healthy mental attitude
A belief in perseverance
An understanding of others

Live all you can; it is a mistake not to. It doesn't so much matter what you do in particular, so long as you have had your life. If you haven't had that, what have you had?

William James

A Feeling of Self-Confidence. If we desire to be successful, a belief in our abilities and our worth as a human being is extremely essential. Most of our actions, feelings, behavior, and even our abilities are consistent with the degree of self-confidence we have. Surely, we have all experienced failures, as well as successes in life. However, if we allow our failures to rule our life, we will never be able to realize our full potential. We are all imperfect. To be successful, we must learn to accept that our blunders, as well as our successes, are a part of us. Our blunders should only be remembered as guides to learning. Johnson (2000) makes this profound statement:

> A basic tenet of all individuals who wish to succeed in any endeavor is "I have to be willing to fail." You cannot learn, you cannot improve your interpersonal effectiveness, you cannot build better relationships, and you cannot try new procedures and approaches unless you are willing to accept your mistakes. You need the ability to fail. Tolerance for failure and the ability to learn from it are very specific characteristics of any highly successful person.

In order to succeed, you must know what you are doing, like what you are doing, and believe in what you are doing.

Will Rogers

Success is to be measured not so much by the position that one has reached in life as by the obstacles that one has overcome while trying to succeed.

Booker T. Washington

Don't Quit

When things go wrong, as they sometimes will,
When the road you're trudging seems all uphill,
When the funds are low and the debts are high,
And you want to smile, but you have to sigh,
When care is pressing you down a bit—
Rest if you must, but don't you quit.

Life is queer with its twists and turns,
As everyone of us sometimes learns,
And many a fellow turns about
When he might have won had he stuck it out.
Don't give up though the pace seems slow—
You may succeed with another blow.

Often the goal is nearer than
It seems to a faint and faltering man;
Often the struggler has given up
When he might have captured the victor's cup;
And he learned too late when the night came down,
How close he was to the golden crown.

Success is failure turned inside out—
The silver tint of the clouds of doubt,
And you never can tell how close you are,
It may be near when it seems afar;
So stick to the fight when you're hardest hit,—
It's when things seem worst that you mustn't quit.

Certainly, feelings of successful achievement are the greatest motivation for continued success. We have all heard the statement that we can do whatever we think we can. Thus, we will never experience success unless we have confidence in ourselves. Because your performance is directly tied to the way you see yourself, real confidence in yourself is always demonstrated by action.

A Healthy Mental Attitude. The one word that influences our life more than any other is *attitude*. This word actually controls our environment and our entire world. Actually, our life is what our thoughts make it. If we think happy thoughts, we will be happy. If we think miserable thoughts, we will be miserable. If we think sickly thoughts, we will be ill. If we think failure, we will certainly fail. Successful people succeed because they think they can attain their goal.

Failure, rejection, and mistakes are the perfect stepping stones to success.

Dr. Alan Goldberg

Certainly, a healthy mental attitude does not imply a pollyanna attitude toward all our problems. It simply means that we approach our problems and goals with a positive attitude. A negative attitude defeats us before we even start to work on our goals. On the other hand, a positive attitude enables us to take action toward facing our problems and obtaining our goals. Mamie McCullough (1997), author and motivational speaker, defines a positive and a negative attitude in this way: A positive attitude says, *"I can";* a negative attitude says, *"I can't"* or *"I won't."* Behavioral researcher, Shad Helmstetter (1990), offers this thought-provoking statement:

 ## CONSIDER THIS . . .

The value of courage, persistence, and perseverance has rarely been illustrated more convincingly than in the life story of this man (his age appears in the column on the right):

Failed in business	22
Ran for Legislature—defeated	23
Again failed in business	24
Elected to Legislature	25
Sweetheart died	26
Had a nervous breakdown	27
Defeated for Speaker	29
Defeated for Elector	31
Defeated for Congress	34
Elected to Congress	37
Defeated for Congress	39
Defeated for Senate	46
Defeated for Vice President	47
Defeated for Senate	49
Elected to President of the United States	51

That's the record of Abraham Lincoln!

No one, not one single person who was ever born on the face of this earth, was born to fail—or to automatically succeed. Through life—we tend to make choices to fail or succeed.

A Belief in Perseverance. In the game of life, you have to put something in before you can take anything out. After all, is not this what you also have to do with your checking account? Successful people *itch* for a lot in life, but they are willing to *scratch* for what they want. Therefore, we must determine how much time we are willing to give and what sacrifices we are willing to make towards the attainment of our goals. The magic word to success has been referred to as *work*—working hard and long to accomplish goals. The late Sam Walton (1993), founder of the Wal Mart stores, had this to say about perseverance:

My life has been a trade-off. If I wanted to reach the goals I set for myself, I had to get at it and stay at it every day.

We need to remember that to give up is to invite complete defeat. Some people, *quit* before they have given themselves a chance to succeed. People with a true belief in perseverance work toward their goals when encouraged and work harder when discouraged. It is very easy to give up, but much harder to continue, especially when "the going gets rough." However, nothing worthwhile has ever been accomplished the easy way.

> Let me tell you the secret that has led me to my goal. My strength lies solely in my tenacity.
>
> Louis Pasteur

> ## Press On
>
> Nothing in this world can take the place of persistence.
> Talent will not; nothing is more common than unsuccessful men with talent.
> Genius will not; unrewarded genius is almost a proverb.
> Education will not; the world is full of educated derelicts.
> Persistence and determination alone are omnipotent.
>
> Calvin Coolidge

The only place where success comes before work is in the dictionary.

Vidal Sassoon

An Understanding of Others. More than likely our goals will involve other people. As a matter of fact, it is dangerous to make goals without carefully considering the effects they could have on your family. Remember, *you do have to work around and with these folks.* Furthermore, you want to take them with you down the road to your successes.

It is important, therefore, that we learn to understand what their needs are, how they feel, and how to interact with them. Learning the art of human communication is vitally important to achieving success. Successful people rarely make it completely on their own; they have generally been encouraged by others.

In essence, people who are successful in reaching their goals have *direction, dedication, discipline, and a super positive attitude.*

But, will you have enough time to develop these qualities of success?

THE TIME IN YOUR LIFE

Time presents a problem to all of us. Alec Mackenzie (1997), a time-management expert, offers some interesting insights:

> You can't save it and use it later.
> You can't elect not to spend it.
> You can't borrow it.
> You can't leave it. Nor can you retrieve it.
> You can't take it with you, either.

But . . .

Time is always with you—and you can lose it or use it—the choice is up to you. However, sometimes we get up-tight about "time." These frustrations of time are largely due to your attitudes toward time. Many of these attitudes are based on false assumptions (Douglas and Douglas, 1993).

For example, you have been told that to be successful you must *learn to manage your time.* This is impossible. You cannot *manage time.* It is frustrating to think you can manage something over which you have absolutely no control. But you can learn to manage *yourself.*

Another false assumption is saying, "I don't have time to do that." Probably not so. You have the time. You just do not choose to spend it in that manner. It is probably an unpleasant task that you would rather not do. That's okay. But why blame time?

Thoughts on Time

Time is the inexplicable raw material of everything. With it, all is possible, without it, nothing. The supply of time is truly a daily miracle, an affair genuinely astonishing when one examines it.

You wake up in the morning, and lo! your purse is magically filled with twenty-four hours of the unmanufactured tissue of the universe of your life! It is yours. It is the most precious of possessions. . . . No one can take it from you. And no one receives either more or less than you receive.

You have to live on this twenty-four hours of daily time. Out of it you have to spin health, pleasure, money, content, respect, and the evolution of your immortal soul. Its right use, its most effective use, is a matter of the highest urgency and of the most thrilling actuality. All depends on that. Your happiness—the elusive prize that you are all clutching for, my friends—depends on that.

If one cannot arrange that an income of twenty-four hours a day shall exactly cover all proper items of expenditure, one does muddle one's whole life indefinitely. . . .

We never shall have any more time. We have, and we have always had, all the time there is.

> Your future success depends on getting yourself to do what you have to do even when the "I don't want to" thoughts and "I don't feel like" feelings get in your way.
>
> Bits and Pieces

Or how about, "She has more time than I do." Everybody has the same amount of time. But everybody spends it doing different things by choice or habit.

Time Management Is Really Self-Management. There are several ways of looking at exactly how much time we have. For example, each of us has *twenty-four hours—1,440 minutes a day, 10,080 minutes a week, or 8,760 hours a year* to spend, invest, or fritter away. We spend time doing the maintenance tasks of life—working, eating, sleeping, and so on. We invest time in learning, creating or loving. These time "investments" continue to pay dividends in personal satisfaction, career advancement, or fond memories. Sometimes we fritter away valuable time in activities we do not really enjoy and soon forget. Often, this is caused by our inability to say "No!" (Lakein, 1996).

Remember, you should be the master of time and not let it master you. Discovering your *time wasters* is the key to managing yourself in relation to time. The word *time waster* can be defined to mean anything preventing you from achieving your objectives most effectively. Most time wasters are self-generated. For example, do you ever procrastinate—put things off until it's too late or no longer matters? You might be surprised to learn that *procrastination* is one of the most common time management problems, or time wasters.

Establishing Priorities. Take a moment and reflect on this question: What one thing could you do in your personal and

Discovering your time wasters is the key to managing yourself in relation to time.

professional life that, if you did on a regular basis, would make a tremendous positive difference in your life? Now, reflect on this question: How much time are you spending in this area or on this activity?

People who accomplish the most do so not because they have more time, but because they use their time more wisely. They know that planning and goal setting are the keys to successful time management.

Stephen Covey (1990), author of the best seller, *The 7 Habits of Highly Effective People,* teaches participants in personal leadership training groups that the essence of effective time and life management is to organize and execute around *balanced priorities.* Covey then asks his participants to consider the following: If you were to fault yourself in one of three areas, which would it be:

1.   The inability to *prioritize*
2.   The inability or desire to *organize* around those priorities
3.   The lack of *discipline* to execute around them, to stay with your priorities and organization

Covey says that most people believe that their main fault is *discipline.* However, Covey believes the basic problem is that people's *priorities have not become deeply planted in their hearts and minds.* In *First Things First*, Covey (1996) summarizes the importance of priorities with these words:

> Putting first things first is an issue at the very heart of life. Almost all of us feel torn by the things we want to do, by the demands placed on us, by the many responsibilities we have. We all feel challenged by the day-to-day and moment-by-moment decisions we must make regarding the best use of our time.

> Anything less than a conscious commitment to the important is an unconscious commitment to the unimportant.
>
> Stephen Covey

How to . . .

. . . Waste Time

- Procrastination
- Personal disorganization
- Lack of planning
- Poor communication
- Commuting and/or traffic delays
- Lack of self-discipline
- Not setting deadlines
- Inability to say No!
- Watching TV
- Talking on the telephone
- Meetings
- Excessive errands
- Attempting too much at once
- Leaving tasks unfinished
- Drop-in visitors

Which of these timewasters create a problem for you? Which do you have control over?

Decisions are easier when it's a question of "good" or "bad." We can easily see how some ways we spend our time are wasteful, mind-numbing, even destructive. But for most of us, the issue is not between the "good" and the "bad," but between the "good" and the "best." So often, the enemy of the best is the good.

Using time effectively is dependent on *your daily identification of priorities of the important things you have to do or want to do.* You must decide what the important objectives are in your life and then establish priorities every day in relation to these objectives.

CULTURE AND THE ORGANIZATION OF TIME

Let us assume that you have arranged to meet one of your friends for lunch at 12:30 P.M. The friend has not arrived at 12:45; 1:00, or even 1:15. Now, answer these questions: What time did you arrive? Were you "on time?" How long would you wait for your friend before you started to feel worried or annoyed?

In most parts of the United States and Canada, you would have been there pretty close to 12:30 and not waited much past 1:00. That is because these countries, along with northern European nations, are what Edward T. Hall (1990) calls *monochronic cultures:* Time is organized into linear segments in which people do one thing "at a time." Actually, the day is divided into appointments, schedules, and routines, and because time is a precious commodity, people do not like to "waste" time. In such cultures, therefore, it is considered the height of rudeness (or status) to keep someone waiting.

However, the farther south you go in Europe, South America, and Africa, the more likely you are to find *polychronic cultures*. In these cultures, time is organized along parallel lines. People do many things at once, and the demands of friends and family supersede those of the appointment book. As a matter of fact, people in Latin America and the Middle East think nothing of waiting all day, or even a week, to see someone. The idea of having to be somewhere "on time," as if time were more important than a person, is unthinkable.

The differences in time orientation between the two cultural styles is summarized in the Focus on Diversity box on the following page.

> What, of all things in the world, is the longest and the shortest, the swiftest and the slowest, the most neglected, and the most regretted, without which nothing can be done: TIME.
>
> Voltaire

CREATING HARMONY IN YOUR LIFE

Think about the last time you heard a symphony orchestra play and then answer these questions: Just by chance, was there one instrument that was given so much emphasis the others simply were not heard? Was there one instrument that seemed "out-of-synch"? Or, were all the instruments playing in a harmonious melody?

What does a symphony orchestra have to do with your life? The important areas in your life, to which you devote your time and energy, do not exist in isolation but are very much like a symphony orchestra playing. Individual instruments (like work) sound fine, but when combined into a symphony (your life), the effect on your whole life is then multiplied. Could it be possible that you have not found a harmonious melody to play with all of the important areas in your life? Could it be possible that you might have one important "instrument" that has been

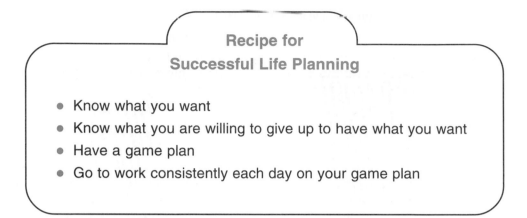

**Recipe for
Successful Life Planning**

- Know what you want
- Know what you are willing to give up to have what you want
- Have a game plan
- Go to work consistently each day on your game plan

In essence, in life there are tradeoffs. There is a price to pay for what is important to you. You and you alone must decide what your trade-offs will be.

EFFECTIVE LIFE PLANNING:
IT'S ALL UP TO YOU!

If it is to be; it is up to me.

Fortune Cookie

The key to successful life planning is the *willingness to take responsibility for ourselves.* It is indeed possible for us to take control of our lives in the midst of the forces around us. In a life situation, we have three choices: *change it, enjoy-tolerate it, or leave it.* To *change it,* we must change our behavior, goals, or circumstances. If we choose to *enjoy* it, we must recognize that it is our choice to stay with it, for whatever set of reasons. Then, if we choose to *leave our life situation,* we must find another environment for our energies. We must remember that feeling forced to stay with our life situation and hating it is not a viable and productive alternative.

There are many opportunities for us to grow, to find interesting work, and to vary our lives. Actually, the freedom and opportunity to realize our potential are relatively rich and available to a relatively large proportion of people. However, we must choose to actively pursue the possibilities we do have. We cannot wait for "good things" to happen to us; we have to make them happen.

Because goals give direction and purpose to our life, goal setting should be a continuous activity throughout our lifetime. What happens in life planning is that we pause frequently to reevaluate ourselves, our goals, and our performances. As we improve in the understanding of ourselves, our wants, our needs, and our goals may change. If we are careful in assessing our potentials, needs, and wants, we will be able to set more realistic goals and keep our chair of life in balance.

With this thought in mind, there are some questions you can ask yourself about the arena of life and work planning. See Check this out.

If we, from time to time, apply these questions to our personal objectives, our lives will be more effective, satisfying, and of course, more in balance.

But, what exactly makes a person feel satisfied and fulfilled? Have you ever asked yourself these questions: "Is there a secret to happiness?" "What would really make me happy?" We will conclude this chapter with a discussion of happiness and well-being.

☞ CHECK THIS OUT . . .

Who Am I? This seems like such a simple question. However, this is a very complex and difficult question to answer cogently. Knowledge of yourself must be organized and properly focused in order to contribute to practical progress.

What Am I Up To? This question implies what is really going on with you right now, what are you trying to get done right now, and what are your needs and motives right now.

Where Am I Going? Obviously, this question relates directly to effective goal setting. At this point, you may have to take an inventory of your priorities—what means the most to you right now. Also, you might want to take a look at where you have been versus what you want to be doing in the near future.

What Difference Does It Make Anyhow? The difference lies in the degree of happiness and fulfillment you are experiencing in your life. You can be happy and fulfilled, or miserable and stifled. You choose who you become.

Super, (1980)

HAPPINESS AND WELL-BEING

The question of what makes a person happy has been the subject of much speculation and increasingly more research studies. Americans have a peculiar relationship to happiness. On the one hand, we consider happiness a right, and we do everything in our power to try to possess it, most particularly in materialistic form. However, materialistic comforts by themselves have not led to lasting happiness. Having reached that conclusion, we do not often see another way and retreat into our comforts, barricading ourselves from what appears to be a hostile and threatening world. And, we continue to crave a happiness that seems both deserved and yet out of reach.

What Is Happiness? Psychiatrist, Dr. Mark Epstein (1995), believes that one reason we have so much trouble attaining happiness is that we do not even know what it is. For example, the very ways in which we seek happiness actually block us from finding it. Our first mistake is in trying to wipe out all the sources of displeasure in our lives. Actually, pleasure and displeasure are two sides of the same coin. We cannot have one without the other, and trying to split them off from each other only mires us more deeply in our own dissatisfaction.

Happiness, therefore, is not easy to define. Dr. Epstein (1995) offers the following definition of *happiness: "We confuse happiness with a life uncluttered by feelings of anxiety, rage, doubt, and sadness. But happiness is something entirely different. It's the ability to receive the pleasant without grasping and the unpleasant without condemning."*

Social psychologist David G. Myers reviews thousands of recent studies conducted worldwide in search of the key to happiness in his book, *The Pursuit of Happiness.* Dr. Myers (1993) defines *happiness* in this way: *"It is a 'pervasive' sense that life is good—a state of well-being that outlasts yesterday's moment of elation, today's buoyant mood, or tomorrow's feeling of sadness."*

> Happiness is easy. It is the letting go of unhappiness that is hard. We are willing to give up everything but our misery.
>
> Hugh Prather

Psychologists and researchers frequently refer to happiness as *subjective well-being (SWB)* and are exploring it in their labs, often teaming with neuropsychiatrists to locate centers for happiness in the brain. One discovery is that happy people show more electrical activity in the left frontal lobe of the brain, while those who tend toward sadness or depression show more right frontal lobe activity (Myers, 1996).

MYTHS ABOUT HAPPINESS

Additional work needs to be done in refining and redefining studies of who has SWB, who does not, and why, and how to help those who do not have enough. In the process, researchers are overturning many cherished myths and coming up with surprising new findings:

- **Happiness is not an illusion or a delusion.** SWB can be measured on finite scales and is just as real as its opposite number, depression. People who define themselves as satisfied are supported in their belief by friends and family who concur. Happiness is evident in practically everything they do.
- **Happiness and marriage go together.** Despite the booming divorce rate, "most people are happier attached than unattached," says Dr. Ed Diener (1991), researcher from the University of Illinois. Married people appear to be happier because they are less lonely than singles and enjoy more supportive relationships. Also, marriage offers two roles, spouse and parent, that enhance self-esteem and happiness.
- **Happiness knows no gender.** An analysis of 146 SWB studies showed a less than one percent difference in happiness between the sexes (Myers, 1993; 1996). This contradicts the popular belief that women are sadder than men. Although it is true that women are twice as likely as men to suffer from depression and anxiety, men have five times their rate of alcoholism and antisocial personalities—which evens out the happiness equation.

What do men and women feel enhances their happiness? *U.S. News* and the advertising agency Bozell Worldwide Inc. polled 1,009 American adults in 1995 and asked them to name the three things that most contribute to their quality of life. John Marks (1995) summarizes the gender results in the following "Gender and You" box.

- **Happiness doesn't depend on age.** No particular stage of life is less happy than any other; not the tumultuous teenage years, not the "midlife crisis" period, not even the waning decades of old age. This was born out by a worldwide survey of almost 170,000 people, conducted in the late 1980's and reported by Ronald Inglehart (1990), Ph.D., of the University of Michigan and author of *Culture Shift in Advanced Industrial Society.*
- **Wealth does not beget happiness.** Contrary to what most people think, it appears that those in all walks of life feel pretty much the same. As Dr. Myers points out, although our individual buying power has doubled since the 1950's, in 1990 just as in 1957, only one in three Americans told the University of Chicago's National Opinion Research Center that they were "very happy." *"So, we're twice as rich, yet we're no happier,"* says Dr. Myers (1996).

A happy person is not a person in a certain set of circumstances, but rather a person with a certain set of attitudes.

Hugh Downs

QUALITY-OF-LIFE ENHANCERS

U.S. News and the advertising agency Bozell Worldwide Inc. polled 1,009 American adults in 1995 and asked them to name the three things that most contribute to their quality of life. Americans cited these factors: (Marks, 1995)

Men

1.	Job/career satisfaction	32%
2.	Relationship with family	28%
3.	Money I earn from job/financial independence	18%
4.	Good health	12%
5.	Where I live (city/state/urban/suburban/rural)	11%
6.	Religion/spirituality	11%
7.	Relationship with spouse/significant other	10%
8.	Relationship with friends	10%
9.	Education level	8%
10.	My home	7%

Women

1.	Relationship with family	33%
2.	Job/career satisfaction	28%
3.	Good health	19%
4.	Religion/spirituality	18%
5.	Money I earn from job	17%
6.	Relationship with children	14%
7.	Relationship with friends	12%
8.	Where I live (city/state/urban/suburban/rural)	10%
9.	Relationship with spouse/significant other	9%
10.	My home	8%

What three things would contribute most to your quality of life?

Gender & You

And in a survey of the *Forbes* 100 wealthiest, Dr. Diener (1985) found that the privileged are not much happier, overall, than working-class folk. Money may become an avenue for something bigger and better—a way to keep score and compare. For example, you may have a lovely home, but if it sits next door to a neighbor's mansion, it may be a source of more dissatisfaction than happiness. Even striking it rich does not seem to have the effect of boosting a person's happiness. Studies of lottery winners reveal that the sudden euphoria experienced upon winning quickly wears off. What is important, though, is having enough money to buy life's necessities.

WHO IS HAPPIEST?

Drs. Diener (1991), Myers (1993; 1996) and their fellow SWB researchers have pinpointed a number of traits that seem to be shared by happy people:

- **Self-Esteem.** Happy people like themselves. A healthy self-esteem is positive yet realistic and provides a less fragile foundation for enduring joy. Hand-in-hand with self-esteem go personal identity and having a sense of purpose, accomplishment and achievement.
- **Optimism.** Happy people are hope filled and are confident they can make things better, even when they have failed or experienced rejection in some endeavor. People who expect the best are the happiest, and they are also healthier and less vulnerable to illness.
- **Extroversion.** Happy people are more outgoing, more cheerful, and high-spirited. Extroverted people are more involved with people, have a larger circle of friends, engage in rewarding social activities, experience more affection, and enjoy greater social support.
- **Personal Control.** Happy people believe that they choose their own destinies. You will recall from our discussion in Chapter 3, individuals with an "internal locus of control" participate in determining the contents of their lives and live more happily. Summarizing the University of Michigan's nationwide surveys, Angus Campbell (1981) commented that *"having a strong sense of controlling one's life is a more dependable predictor of positive feelings of well-being than any of the objective conditions of life we have considered."*

Other ingredients to happiness. Having a strong spiritual faith, having close, supportive friendships and marriages, and having work and other activities that enhance our identity and absorb us into flow appear to be additional ingredients to happiness. Being really happy, according to psychologist Mihaly Csikszentmihalyi (1997), is *living in a state of flow*—that is, being totally absorbed in an activity, whether at work or play. *Flow* goes beyond mere contentment; it entails active participation, a sense of mastery, and the use of all or most of your skills. Using too few skills generates boredom, which Dr. Csikszentmihalyi warns, may be the biggest threat to happiness.

WAYS TO BE HAPPY

Have you ever thought, I will be happy when this semester is over and I make an "A" in my psychology class, or when I get a new job, or the perfect someone with whom to share my life. But, would you like to start making happiness a habit right now? In her books, *Simple Abundance* and *The Simple Abundance Companion,* Sarah Breathnach (1998, 2000), writes of our need to adopt a new state of mind about happiness. She encourages us to stop thinking that things outside our control will bring us happiness.

Certainly, the semester being over and making an "A" in psychology, getting a new and exciting job, or finding that special someone can make us feel—at least momentarily—happier. But the magic seeds of contentment are planted deep within us—our outlook on life. Although the pursuit of happiness is an inalienable right guaranteed by the Declaration of Independence, we have to be willing to pursue it.

In *Notes on How to Live in the World and Still be Happy,* Hugh Prather (1986) says, *"You must make the effort—the struggle to be happy now—and not first gain what you need in order to be happy."* Dr. Myers (1996, 2000) agrees

---

Often people attempt to live their lives backwards: they try to have more things, or more money, in order to do more of what they want so that they will be happier. The way it actually works is the reverse. You must first be who you really are, then, do what you need to do, in order to have what you want.

Margaret Young

Happiness is having a sense of self—not as a feeling of being perfect but being good enough and knowing that you are in the process of growth, of achieving levels of joy. It's a wonderful contentment and acceptance of who and what you are and a knowledge that the world and life are full of wondrous adventures and possibilities.

Leo Buscaglia

How to . . .

. . . Achieve Happiness

Savor the moment. Live in the present and take advantage of treasured moments and events that occur every day.

Take control of your time. Happy people set big goals, then break them into small, doable daily bits.

Reprogram the mind. Happy people work to control their emotions by thinking more positively than negatively.

Leave time for love. Having—or developing—an enriching and fulfilling relationship with another person.

Act happy. Happy people are self-confident, optimistic and extroverted. Even if you do not feel that way, act happy.

Do not vegetate. Get involved in something that utilizes your skills, rather than engaging in self-absorbed idleness.

Get moving. Aerobic exercise is an antidote to depression and anxiety.

Get rest. Happy people exude vigor, but they also reserve time for sleep and solitude.

Give priority to close relationships. People with close friends, spouses, and significant others cope better with stresses such as bereavement, job loss, illness, etc., so seek friendship and do not shy away from commitment.

Take care of the soul. Faith cannot insure immunity from sadness, but it can nudge you along on the road to happiness.

Myers (1996, 2000)

Life can't give me joy and peace; it's up to me to will it. Life just gives me time and space; it's up to me to fill it.

by saying, *"happiness is less a matter of getting what you want—money, possessions, success, etc.—than of wanting what you have."* He offers ten steps to happiness, culled from his own and other psychologists observations of how happy people live. See "How to" box above.

Ultimately, genuine happiness can only be realized once we commit to making it a personal priority in our lives. In *How to Get What You Want and Want What You Have: A Practical and Spiritual Guide to Personal Success*, John Gray (1999) reminds readers that you can get what you want—without struggling for it—if three elements are present in your outlook: *Desire for more in your life, Confidence that you can get what you want,* and *Appreciation for what you already have.* In fact, he believes that if any of these elements is missing, you may achieve some external success—but you won't be happy. He sums it up this way:

> Without strong desire, your life will lack passion—and power.
> Without confidence, you won't have the courage to persist.
> And, if you can't appreciate what you have, your achievements
> will feel hollow.

Chapter Review

If you are going to get serious about life planning, you will have to take risks. The purpose of life planning is to be certain that the risks you take are the right ones, based on careful thought.

- The Basic Law of Life is related to risk taking in that, for everything you get in life, you also have to give up something.

- Needs and motives cause us to consider life planning. One of the greatest insights in the field of human motivation is that satisfied needs do not motivate. It's only the unsatisfied need that motivates.

- Four fundamental human needs, according to Stephen Covey, are to live, to love, to learn, and to leave a legacy.

- Abraham Maslow's Hierarchy of Needs is based on the principal that there are certain survival needs that must be met before we can become concerned with the satisfaction of other needs. The hierarchy of needs includes: physiological, safety and security, love and belonging, self-esteem, and self-actualization, the fullest development of our potentialities.

- Our lives are divided into three periods: 1) getting an education, 2) going to work and earning a living or working in the home and community, and 3) living in retirement. It is important that we consider each period when we consider life planning. A plan is a goal, or aim for satisfying the needs and wants of your life. In short, goals give purpose and meaning to our lives.

- Authorities generally write of at least seven different kinds of goals: physical, financial, spiritual, career, family, mental, and social.

- Some guidelines or criteria for identifying personal goals and making them work are: your goals must be your own, the goal must not be in conflict with one's personal value system, goals need to be specific and written down, start with short-range goals, goals must be realistic and attainable, and goals should contain specific time deadlines.

- Success might be defined as the progressive realization of a worthwhile, predetermined personal goal. Contributors to success are: a sense of direction, a feeling of self-confidence, a healthy mental attitude, a belief in perseverance, and an understanding of others.

- A basic tenet of all individuals who wish to succeed in any endeavor is "I have to be willing to fail." And, the magic word to success has been referred to as "work"—working hard and long to accomplish goals.

- You cannot manage time, but you can learn to manage yourself within the time you have. Discovering your time wasters—anything preventing you from achieving your objectives most effectively—is the key to managing yourself in relation to time. The essence of effective time and life management is to organize and execute around balanced priorities. When we either direct too little or too much time to the important areas in our life, our chair of life is out of balance.

- In monochronic cultures time is organized sequentially, and schedules and deadlines are valued over people. In polychronic cultures time is organized horizontally, and people tend to do several things at once and value relationships over schedules.

- The key to successful life planning is the willingness to take responsibility for ourselves. As we take control of our lives in various situations, we have three choices: change it, enjoy—tolerate it, or leave it.

- Four questions to ask yourself about the arena of life and work planning are: 1) who am I, 2) what am I up to, 3) where am I going, and 4) what difference does it make anyway.

- One mistake people commonly make in seeking happiness is to try to wipe out all the sources of displeasure in their life, but we cannot have one without the other. Happiness is a sense that life is good—a state of well-being that outlasts yesterday's moment of elation, today's buoyant mood, or tomorrow's feeling of sadness.

- Several myths about happiness are: happiness is not an illusion or a delusion, happiness and marriage go together, happiness knows no gender, happiness does not depend on age, and wealth does not beget happiness.
- Several traits that seem to be shared by happy people are: self esteem, optimism, extroversion, and personal control. Having a strong spiritual faith, having close, supportive friendships and marriages, and having work and other activities that enhance our identity and absorb us into the flow appear to be additional ingredients to happiness. Living in a state of flow is being totally absorbed in an activity, whether at work or play, with a sense of mastery, and the use of all or most of one's skills.
- We can learn to adopt a new state of mind about happiness: making the effort to be happy now, rather than first gaining what we want or need in order to be happy.

Remember, you are in control of what you want to achieve in life and how you are going to accomplish your goals.

??? **Questions** ???

1. Explain what the Basic Law of Life means and how it applies to risk-taking.
2. Explain how needs and motives cause us to consider life planning or take various directions for our life. In the field of human motivation, which needs motivate, and which needs do not motivate?
3. Explain the four fundamental human needs, as outlined by Stephen Covey.
4. Explain the concept of Maslow's Hierarchy of Needs. List and discuss the needs at each level in the hierarchy.
5. According to Richard Boles, into what three periods are our lives divided. Explain how these three periods should be considered in life planning. Discuss the purpose of goal setting?
6. List at least five different kinds of goal areas, as discussed in the text.
7. Discuss the guidelines or criteria for identifying personal goals and making them successful.
8. Explain the contributors to success. What is the magic word to success?
9. Identify and explain the significance of the basic tenet of all individuals who wish to succeed in any endeavor.
10. Explain why it is impossible to manage time. What is the essence of effective time and life management? Explain the chair of life concept. Is your chair of life in balance or out of balance—why?
11. Distinguish between monochronic and polychronic cultures in relation to the way time is organized.
12. Identify and explain the key to successful life planning. What three choices do we have as we learn to take control of our lives in various situations?
13. Discuss four questions you can ask yourself about the arena of life and work planning.
14. Define happiness, and discuss why pleasure and displeasure are "two sides of the same coin."
15. Discuss at least five myths of happiness.
16. Discuss the traits that seem to be shared by happy people. What other ingredients lead to happiness? Explain the term, "living in a state of flow," as it relates to happiness.
17. Explain how we can learn the happiness habit. List and discuss at least six steps to happiness.

🐿 Key Terms 🐿

Basic Law of Life
Chair of Life
Esteem Needs
Flow (Living in a state of)
Goals
Happiness

Love and Belonging Needs
Maslow's Hierarchy of Needs
Monochronic Cultures
Motive
Need
Physiological Needs

Polychronic Cultures
Risk
Safety and Security Needs
Self-Actualization Needs
Success
Time waster

??? Discussion ???

1. What risks are you afraid of taking right now in your life?
2. What are you going to have to give up to have what you want?
3. What do you think are the basic needs and wants of human beings?
4. Identify some of the needs and wants you have established right now in your life. What are you now doing to satisfy them?
5. Of Maslow's five basic needs, which one seems most important for you to satisfy right now?
6. What does success mean to you?
7. What determines success in our society?
8. Discuss this statement: Each of us becomes what we think about.
9. What is your greatest time waster? How much of your time do you spend in this activity?
10. Diagram and discuss your chair of life. Is it in balance? If not, why?
11. What is your definition of happiness?
12. Discuss this statement: if you can't appreciate what you have, your achievements will feel hollow.

Your Life's Activities

Purpose: To demonstrate how your activities make up your life.

Instructions:

I. Divide the circle on the left, as a pie, into parts that represent your current life. Label each part: for example, home life, work, personal, education, leisure, and whatever else represents your current life.

II. Divide the circle on the right into parts that represent your life three years ago. Use the same labeling as in the first circle or add others as needed.

III. For the third circle, divide it in a way that represents the ideal way you'd like your life to be. Label each part as in previous circles.

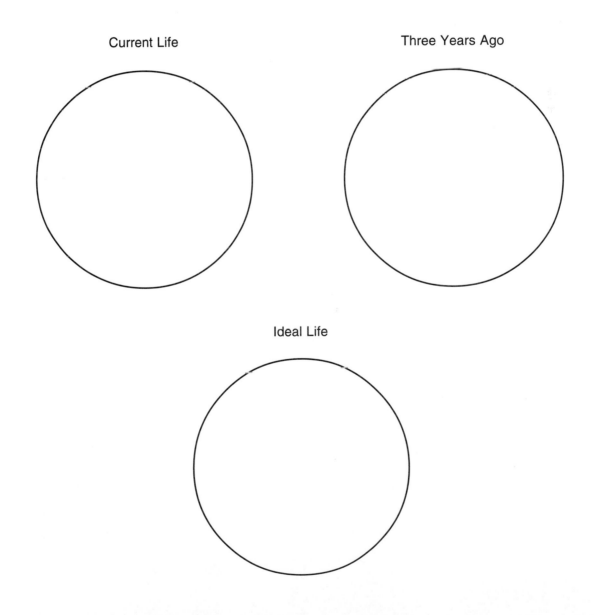

Current Life

Three Years Ago

Ideal Life

IV. Complete the answers to the questions below and be prepared to discuss them in small groups.

Discussion: Let us compare and contrast the three circles.

1. What is keeping your present circle of activities from being like the ideal circle?

2. What can you do within the next six months to make the ideal circle like your real life?

3. Is your ideal circle realistic for you? Why or why not?

4. What did you learn about yourself from this activity?

What Do You Want?

Purpose: To establish three sets of goals and to examine what you are really working toward accomplishing.

Instructions:

I. Write down what goals you would like to accomplish in the following areas. If you do not have a goal in a particular area, that is okay. You decide.

FAMILY:

1.

2.

PHYSICAL:

1.

2.

MENTAL:

1.

2.

SOCIAL:

1.

2.

RELIGIOUS:

1.

2.

FINANCIAL:

1.

2.

CAREER:

1.

2.

II. Next, select the three things you want most to accomplish within the next six months.

1.

2.

3.

III. Now, select from your goals the three things you want most to accomplish in the next year.

1.

2.

3.

IV. Now, select your three most important life goals.

1.

2.

3.

V. Now, write down anything, large or small, you have done within the past month to accomplish any of these goals.

Discussion

1. Are you presently working toward what you say is important to you? If not, why?

2. Do you really want these things?

3. Review the seven areas of possible goals and write down what goals you really want to start working on now.

Name _____ Date _____

Lifeline

Purpose: To take a look at where you have been, where you are, and where you want to go.

Instructions:

I. On a piece of heavy poster board or construction paper, start with the year in which you were born and depict the significant experiences and people who have helped shape your life.

II. Your lifeline will be dated in terms of the years these significant experiences or people appeared in your life.

III. Make notations above or below each year to remind you of exactly what occurred.

IV. When completed, your lifeline will appear like a graph: "highs and lows," "hills and valleys," and "steady" periods of your life. You may use pictures, words, or whatever you wish to depict these significant time periods in your life.

V. The last dot on your lifeline should be on a "hill," a high point in the future. Fantasize and jot some words down to describe what you would like to have happening in your life in the next five or ten years. What will you be doing, where will you be, and who will be with you?

VI. After you have completed your lifeline, you will divide into small groups and explain your lifeline. Be prepared to give a ten-minute presentation.

Discussion

1. How do you feel about the quality of your life at the present time?

2. What experiences are primarily responsible for where you are today?

3. What experiences are primarily responsible for what you want to accomplish in the future?

4. What goals are implied as you picture yourself five to ten years in the future?

Name_____ Date _____

My Future Autobiography

Purpose: To think about the quality of your life and to demonstrate that you still have a life ahead with which to do whatever you choose.

Instructions:

I. In the space below, write at least a two or three paragraph autobiography for yourself. Include things that you would like to have said or written about you near the end of your life. Write about things that you would like to accomplish and what contributions you want to make. Write about what character strengths you want to have and what qualities you want to develop.

II. Have someone else read your autobiography and complete the first discussion question.

VI. Review your autobiography and your lifeline and list the tentative goals implied in each activity.

VII. Review your responses to the activity "What Do I Want" and your responses to the previous questions in this activity and write down at least three goals that you want to start working on now. Consider the following questions before listing your goals.

Is this a goal I really want to achieve?
Is it realistic; that it can be achieved?
Does this goal contradict any of my basic values?
Do I have the personal strengths to achieve this goal?
Do I need and have the support of my family?

MY GOALS:

1.

2.

3.

Name _____ Date _____

Goal Project

Purpose: To develop a plan of action for what you want to accomplish.

Instructions:

I. From the previous exercise, select two goals and develop a plan of what you can do this next year to achieve these goals.

Goal Number One

1. I want to _____

   _____

2. What obstacles must I overcome?

3. How do I plan to overcome these obstacles? Be specific.

4. What behaviors must I change?

5. How do I plan to change these behaviors? Be specific.

6. When will I achieve this goal? Be specific.

Goal Number Two

1. I want to _____

   _____

2. What obstacles must I overcome?

3. How do I plan to overcome these obstacles? Be specific.

4. What behaviors must I change?

5. How do I plan to change these behaviors? Be specific.

6. When will I achieve this goal? Be specific.

Discussion

1. How do you feel about the goal project you have just completed?

Where Do I Want To Go With My Life?

Learning Journal

Select the statement below that best defines your feelings about the personal value or meaning gained from this chapter and respond below the dotted line.

- **I learned that I . . .**

- **I realized that I . . .**

- **I discovered that I . . .**

- **I was surprised that I . . .**

- **I was pleased that I . . .**

- **I was displeased that I . . .**

. . . .

continue on reverse

# References

Chapter 1

Adler, R., & Towne, N. (1999). *Looking Out/Looking In,* 8th Ed. Ft. Worth, Tx: Harcourt Brace.

Argyle, M. and Henderson (1987). "The Rules of Friendship." *Journal of Social and Personal Relationships,* 211–237.

Baron, R. (1986). "Self-Presentation in Job Interviews: When There Can Be 'Too Much of a Good Thing.'" *Journal of Applied Social Psychology,* 16, 16–28.

Bhawuk, D.P.S. (1990). "Cross-Cultural Orientation Programs." In R. Brislin (Ed.). *Applied Cross-Cultural Psychology,* 325–346. Newbury Park, CA: Sage.

Berscheid, E., Dion, K., Walster, E. and Walster, G. W. (1971). "Physical Attractiveness and Dating Choice: A Test of the Matching Hypothesis. *Journal of Experimental Social Psychology,* 7, 173–1789.

Berscheid, E. and Graziano, W. (1979). "The Initiation of Social Relationships and Interpersonal Attraction." In R. L. Burgess and T. L. Hustom (Eds.). *Social Exchange in Developing Relationships.* New York: Academic Press.

Berscheid, F. (1974). "Physical Attractiveness." In L. Berkowits (Ed.). *Advances in Experimental Social Psychology.* 7. New York: Academic Press.

Berscheid, E., Snyder, M., & Omato, A., (1989). Issues in studying close relationships: Conceptualizing and measuring closeness. Hendrick (Ed.), *Review of personality and social psychology.* 10. Newbury Park, CA: Sage.

Brislin, R. (1999). *Understanding Culture's Influence on Behavior.* Orlando, FL: Harcourt Brace College Publishing.

Brooks-Gunn, J. and Watkins, M. (1989). "Recognition, Memory and the Mere Exposure Effect." *Journal of Experimental Psychology: Learning, Memory and Cognition,* 156, 968–976.

Buckhout, R. (1980). "Nearly 2,000 Witnesses Can Be Wrong." *Bulletin of Psychonomic Society* 16, 307–310.

Carducci, B. & Zimbardo, P., (1995). "Are You Shy?" *Psychology Today,* 28, 6.

Cline, R.J. (1986). The effects of biological sex and psychological gender on reported and behavioral intimacy and control of self-disclosure. *Communication Quarterly* 34, 41–54.

Cozby, P.C. (1973). "Self-Disclosure: A Literature Review." *Psychological Bulletin.* 79, 73–91.

Craig, G.J. (1998). *Human Development,* (5th ed.). Englewood Cliffs, N.J.: Prentice-Hall.

Daluiso, V.E. (1972). Self-disclosure and perception of that self-disclosure between parents and their teenage children, *Dissertation Abstract International* 33, 420B.

Delerga, V., Metts, S., Petronia, S. & Margulis, S.T. (1993). *Self-Disclosure.* Newbury Park, CA: Sage.

Dill, J.C., & Anderson, C.A. (1998). Loneliness, shyness, and depression: The etiology and interrelationships of everyday problems in living. In T. Joiner & J.C. Coyne (eds.) *Recent advances in interpersonal approaches to depression.* Washington, D.C. American Psychological Association 575–576.

Dion, K. and Berscheid, E. (1974). "Physical Attractiveness and Peer Perception Among Children." *Sociometry,* 37, 1–12.

Dion, K.L. and Dion, K.K. (1987). "Belief in a Just World and Physical Attractiveness Stereotyping." *Journal of Personality and Social Psychology.* 52, 775–780.

Dovidio, J.F. and Gaertner, S.L. (Eds.). (1986). *Prejudice, Discrimination, and Racism.* New York: Academic Press.

Eagly, A., Ashmore, R., Makhijani, M., & Longo, L. (1991). "What is beautiful is good, but . . . ; A meta-analysis review of research on the physical attractiveness stereotype." *Psychological Bulletin,* 110, 109–128.

Feingold, A. (1992). "Good looking people are not what we think." *Psychological Bulletin,* 111, 304–391.

Fiske, S.T. (1993). Social cognition and social perception. *Annual Review of Psychology,* 44, 155–194.

Frank, M.G. and Gilovich, T. (1988). "The Dark Side of Self and Social Perception: Black Uniforms and Aggression in Professional Sports." *Journal of Personality and Social Psychology,* 54, 74–85.

Goldstein, H.S., Edelberg, R., Meier, C.F., & Davis, L. (1991). "Suppressor effects in the relations of psychological variables to resting blood pressure." *Psychological Reports,* 69, 283–288.

Jourard, S.M. (1971). *The Transparent Self.* (2nd Ed.). Princeton, N.J.: Van Nostrand.

Kiley, D. (1999). *Living together, feeling alone.* New York: Prentice-Hall.

Kraus, L.A., Davis, M.H., Bazzini, D., Church, M. and Kirchman, C.M. (1993). "Personal and social influences on loneliness: The mediating effect of social provisions." *Social Psychology Quarterly* 56, 37–53.

Krull, D.S., & Dill, J.C. (1998). Do smiles elicit more inferences than do frowns? The effect of emotional valence on the production of spontaneous inferences. *Personality and Social Psychology Bulletin,* 24, 289–300.

Levinger, G. and Snoek, D.J. (1972). *Attraction in Relationships: A New Look at Interpersonal Attraction.* Morristown, NJ: General Learning Press.

Lewis, R.A. (1978). Emotional intimacy among men. *Journal of Social Issues,* 34, 108–121.

Major, B., Carrington, P.L., & Carnevale, P.J.D. (1984). "Physical attractiveness and self-esteem: Attribution for praise from an other-sex evaluator." *Personality and Social Psychology Bulletin,* 10, 43–50. (645)

Miller, R.S. and Lefcourt, H.M. (1982). "The Assessment of Social Intimacy." *Journal of Personality Assessment,* 46, 514–518.

Moreland, R. and Beach, S. (1992). "Exposure effects in the classroom: development of affinity among students." *Journal of Experimental Social Psychology.* Volume 28, May 1992 (3255–276).

Moreland, R. and Zajonc, R. (1982). "Exposure Effect in Person Perception: Familiarity, Similarity and Attraction." *Journal of Experimental Social Psychology.* 18, 395–415.

Page, R.M., & Cole, G.E., (1991). "Loneliness and alcoholism risk in late adolescence: A comparative study of adults and adolescents." *Adolescence,* 26, 925–930.

Perlman, D. & Peplau, L.A. (1998). Loneliness. *Encyclopedia of Mental Health* (Vol. 2, 571–581). New York: Academic Press.

Pingitore, R., Dugoni, B.L., Tindale, R.S., & Spring, B. (1994). "Bias against overweight job applicants in a simulated employment interview." *Journal of Applied Social Psychology,* 79, 909–919.

Priest, R., & Sawyer, J. (1967). Proximity and peership: Bases of balance in interpersonal attraction. *American Journal of Sociology,* 72, 633–649.

Rosenfeld, L.B., (1981). *Self-disclosure and small group interaction, In Small Group Communications* (5th ed.). R.S. Cathcart and L.A. Samovar, eds. Dubuque, IA: Wm. C. Brown.

Rosenthal, R. and Jacobson, L. (1968). *Pygmalion in the Classroom.* New York: Holt, Rinehart and Winston.

Rothbart, M. and Park, B. (1986). "On the Confirmability and Disconfirmability of Trait Concepts." *Journal of Personality and Social Psychology,* 50, 131–142.

Schultz, P.W., & Oskamp, S. (2000). *Social Psychology: An applied perspective.* Upper Saddle River: Prentice Hall.

Solomon, M., (1987, December). Standard issue. *Psychology Today,* 30–31.

Steinberg, N., (1993, February). "Astonishing love stories" (from an earlier United Press International report) *Games,* 47.

Sullivan, H.S. (1953). *The Interpersonal Theory of Psychiatry.* New York: Norton

Thornton, B., & Moore, S. (1993). "Physical attractiveness contrast effect: Implications for self-esteem and evaluations of the social self." *Personality and Social Psychology Bulletin,* 19, 474–480.

Weiss, R.S. (1974). "The Provisions of Relationships." In Z. Rubin (ed.). *Do Unto Others: Joining, Molding, Conforming, Helping, Loving.* Englewood Cliffs, NJ.: Prentice-Hall.

Wortman, D.B., Adosman, P., Herman, E. and Greenberg, R. (1976). "Self-Disclosure: An Attributional Perspective." *Journal of Personality and Social Psychology,* 33, 184–191.

Zimbardo, P. (1990). *Shyness,* What It Is, What to Do about It. Reading, MA: Addison-Wesley.

Zimbardo, P.G. (1987). *Shyness,* New York: Jove.

Chapter 2

Adler, A. (1998). What Life Could Mean to You. Boston: Little Brown.

Allen, L., & Majidi-Ahi, S. (1989). "Black American children." In J.T. Gibbs & L.N. Huang (Eds.), *Children of color.* San Francisco, CA: Jossey-Bass.

Bandura, A. (1986). Social Foundation of Thoughts and Action: A Social-Cognitive Theory. Englewood Cliffs, NJ: Prentice-Hall. 434–435.

Bandura, A. (1996). "Failures in self-regulations: Energy depletion or selective disengagement." *Psychological Inquiry,* 7, 20–24.

Baumgardner, A.H., Kaufman, C.M. and Levy, P.E. (1989). "Regulating Affect Interpersonally: When Low Self-Esteem Leads to Greater Enhancement." *Journal of Personality and Social Psychology.* 56, 907–921.

Briggs, D.C. (1975). *Celebrate Your Self. Enhancing Your Own Self Esteem.* New York: Doubleday.

Brooks-G. & Lewis, M. (1975). "Mirror Image Stimulation and Self-Regulation in Infancy." Presented at the meeting of the Society for Research in Child Development. Denver, CO.

Brown, J.D. (1991). "Accuracy and Bias in Self-Knowledge." In C.R. Snyder and D.F. Forsyth (Eds). *Handbook of Social and Clinical Psychology: The Health Perspective.* New York: Pergammon Press.

Copeland, J., (1993). "Motivational approaches for expectancy confirmation." *Current Directions in Psychological Science,* August, 117–119.

Dunning, D., Leuenberger, A. & Sherman, D. (1995). "A new look at motivational inferences: Are self-serving theories of success a product of motivational forces?" *Journal of Personality and Social Psychology,* 69, 58–68.

Eder, R.A., & Mangelsdorf, S.C. (1997). The emotional basis of early personality development implications for the emergent self-concept. In R. Hogan, J. Johnson, & S Briggs (Eds), *Handbook of personality psychology* 209–324. San Diego: Academic Press.

Erikson, E. (1950/1993). *Childhood and Society,* (2nd ed.). New York: W.W. Norton.

Feldman, R.S. (2000). *Development Across the Life Span.* Upper Saddle River, New Jersey: Prentice-Hall.

Festinger, L., (1954), *A theory of social comparison processes.* Human Relations, 7, 117–140.

Frankl, V. (1998). *Man's Search for Meaning.* New York: Washington Sq. Pr.

Freud, S. (1920). *New Introductory Lectures on Psychoanalysis.* New York: Norton.

Freud, S. (1936). *The Problems of Anxiety.* New York: Norton.

Harris, T. (1969). *I'm OK—You're OK.* New York: Harper & Row.

Hermans, H. (1996). "Voicing the self: From informational processing to dialogical interchange." *Psychological Bulletin,* 119, 31–50.

Jarrett, M. & Lethbridge, D. (1994). "Looking forward, looking back: Women's experience with waning fertility during mid-life." *Qualitative Health Research,* 4, 370–384.

Levinson, D. (1986). *The Seasons of a Man's Life.* New York: Ballantine Books.

Levinson, D. (1986). "A conception of adult development." *American Psychologist,* 41, 3–13.

Levinson, D. (1996). *The season's of a woman's life.* New York: Knopf.

Majors, R. and Billson, J.M. (1992). *Cool Pose: The Dilemmas of Black Manhood in America.* Lexington, MA: Lexington Books.

MacArthur Foundation, (1999). *Research network on successful midlife development.* The John D. and Catherine T. MacArthur Foundation, Vero Beach, FL.

Maslow, A. (1969). *The Healthy Personality.* New York: Van Nordstrand Reinhold.

Maslow, A.H. (1971). *The Farther Reaches of Human Nature.* New York: Viking Press.

McCrae, R.R. & Costa, P.T. Jr. (1987). Validation on the five-factor model of personality across instruments and observers. *Journal of Personality and Social Psychology,* 52, 81–90.

McCrae, R.R. & Costa, P.T. Jr. (1990). *Personality in adulthood.* New York: Guilford Press.

McCrae, R. & John, O. (1992). An introduction to the give-factor model and its application. *Journal of Personality,* 60, 175–215.

McKay M., & Fanning, P. (1997). *Self-esteem.* Oakland, CA: New Habinger.

Mischel, W., & Shoda, Y. (1997). "A cognitive affective system theory of personality: Reconceptualizing situations, dispositions, dynamics, and invariance in personality structures." *Psychological Review, 102,* 246–268.

Mischel, W. (1998). Introduction to Personality (8th Ed.) New York: Holt, Rinehart, and Winston.

Myers, D. (1999). *Psychology.* New York: Worth.

Newman, M. and Berkowitz, B. (1990). *How to Be Your Own Best Friend.* New York: Ballantine Books.

Ozer, D.J. & Reise, S.P. (1994). Personality assessment. *Annual Review of Psychology,* 45, 357–388.

Roberts, P., & Newton, P. (1987). "Levinsonian studies of women's adult development." *Psychology and Aging,* 2 (2), 154–163.

Rogers, C. and Stevens, B. (1972). *Person to Person: The Problems of Being Human.* New York: The Pocket Book.

Rogers, C. (1995). *On Becoming a Person: A Therapist's View of Psychotherapy.* Boston, MA: Houghton Mifflin.

Satir, V. (1975). *Self Esteem,* Berkeley, CA: Celestial Arts.

Satir, V. (1988). *New Peoplemaking.* Palo Alto: Science and Behavior Books.

Sheehy, G. (1996). *New Passages: Mapping Your Life Across Time.* Knopf.

Sullivan, H. (1953). *The Interpersonal Theory of Psychiatry.* New York: Norton.

Triandis, H.C. (1994). *Culture and social behavior.* New York: McGraw-Hill.

Viorst, J. (1998). *Necessary Losses.* New York: Fawcett Gold Medal Books.

Virgil, J.D. (1988). "Group Processes and Street Identity: Adolescent Chicano Gang Members." *Ethos,* 16, 421–445.

Chapter 3

Axelrod, S. and Apsche, J. (1983). *The Effects of Punishment on Human Behavior.* New York: Academic Press.

Bandura, A. (1986). *Social Foundations of Thought and Action: A Social-Cognitive Theory.* Englewood Cliffs, NJ: Prentice-Hall.

Bandura, A. (1997). "Self-Efficacy." *The Harvard Mental Health Letter.* March, 4–5.

Carver, C.S., Ironson, G., Wynings, C., Greenwood, D., et al. (1993). *Coping with Andrew: How coping responses relate to experience of loss and symptoms of poor adjustment.* Paper presented at the annual meeting of the American Psychological Association, Toronto.

Cohn, L. (1991). "Sex Differences in the Course of Personality Development: A Meta-Analysis." *Psychological Bulletin.* 109, 252–266.

Hockenbury, D.H., & Hockenbury, S.E. (1999). *Psychology.* New York: Worth.

James, W.H., Woodruff, A.B. and Werner, W. (1965). "Effects of Internal and External Control Upon Changes in Smoking Behavior." *Journal of Consulting Psychology,* 29, pp. 184–186.

Joseph, R.A., Markus, H.R. and Tafarodi, R.W. (1992). "Gender and Self-Esteem." *Journal of Personality and Social Psychology.* 63, 391–402.

Langer, E.J. (1983). *The Psychology of Control.* Beverly Hills, CA: Sage.

Lefcourt, H.M. (1985). *Locus of Control: Current Trends in Theory and Research.* Hillsdale, N.J.: Erlbaum.

Lefton, A.L. (2000). *Psychology.* Needham Heights, MA: Allyn & Bacon.

Mayer, F.S., & Sutton, K. (1996). *Personality: An integrative approach.* Upper Saddle River, NJ: Prentice-Hall.

Mischel, W., & Shoda, Y. (1998). Reconciling dynamics and disposition. *Annual Review of Psychology,* 49, 229–258.

Myers, D. (1993). *The Pursuit of Happiness.* New York: Avon Books.

Rotter, J.B. (1966). "Generalized Expectancies for Internal Versus External Control for Reinforcement." *Psychological Monographs.* 80, No. 609.

Rotter, J.B. (1990). "Internal versus external control of reinforcement: A case study of a variable." *American Psychologist,* 45 (4), 489–491.

Seligman, M.E.P. (1998). *Learned Optimism.* New York: Knopf.

Seligman, M.E.P. (1992). *Helplessness: On Depression, Development and Death.* San Francisco, CA: Freeman.

Skinner, B.K. (1972). *Beyond Freedom and Dignity.* New York: Knopf.

Solomon, M. (December, 1987). "Standard Issue." *Psychology Today.* 30–31.

Stajkovic, A.D., & Luthans, F. (1998). Self-efficacy and work related performance: A meta-analysis. *Psychological Bulletin,* 124(2), 240–261.

Watson, D.C. and Tharpe, G.G. (1997). *Self-Directed Behavior: Self-Modification for Personal Adjustment.* Pacific Grove, CA: Brooks/Cole.

Watson, J.B. and Rayner, R. (1920). "Conditioned Emotional Reactions." *Journal of Experimental Psychology*, 3, 1–14.

Weiten, W., & Lloyd, A.L. (2000). *Psychology Applied to Modern Life*. Belmont, CA: Wadsworth.

Chapter 4

Adler, R. and Towne, N. (1999). *Looking Out Looking In*. Fort Worth, TX: Harcourt Brace.

Atwater, E. (1998). *Psychology for Living: Adjustment, Growth and Behavior Today*. Englewood Cliffs, NJ: Prentice-Hall, Inc.

Bandura, A. (1976). "On Social Learning and Aggression." *Current Perspectives in Social Psychology*. New York: Oxford University Press.

Beck, A.T. (1991). "Cognitive Therapy: A 30-Year Retrospective." *American Psychologist*, 46, 368–375.

Begley, S. (1999). "Why the Young Kill." *Newsweek*. May 3, 33–35.

Burns, D. (1999). *Feeling Good: The New Mood Therapy*. New York: Avon Books.

Buscaglia, L. (1982). *Living, Loving and Learning*. New York: Holt, Rinehart and Winston.

Carlson, R. (1997) *Don't Sweat the Small Stuff . . . and it's all small stuff*. New York: Hyperion.

Cline, F.W. and Fay, J. (1998). *Parenting with Love and Logic: Teaching Children Responsibility* (audiocassette). Evergreen, CO: Love and Logic Press.

Dickenson, D. and Johnson, M. (1993). *Death, Dying and Bereavement*. Newbury Park, CA: Sage.

Dishion, T.J. (1990). "The Family Ecology of Boys' Peer Relations in Middle Childhood." *Child Development*, 61, 874–892.

Ekman, P. (1992a). "Are There Basic Emotions?" *Psychological Review*, 99, 550–553.

_____(1992b). "Facial Expressions of Emotion: New Findings, New Questions." *Psychological Science*. 3, 34–38.

Ellis, A. (1999). *How to Control Your Anxiety Before it Controls You?* North Hollywood, CA: Wilshire Books.

Ellis, A. and Harper, R. (1998). *A Guide to Rational Living*. CA: Wilshire Books.

Emery, G. and Campbell, J. (1987). *Rapid Relief from Emotional Distress*. New York: Ballantine Books.

Enright, R. (1996). "Forgiveness: Serious Stuff or Fluff?" *Psychology Today*, 29, 12.

Enright, R., North, J., and Tutu, D. (1998). *Forgiveness*. Wisconsin: University of Wisconsin Press.

Freeman, A. and De Wolf, R. (1993). *The 10 Dumbest Mistakes Smart People Make and How to Avoid Them*. New York: Harper-Collins Publishers.

Freud, S. (1936). *The Problems of Anxiety*. New York: Norton and Norton, Inc.

Fromm, E. (1956). *The Art of Loving*. New York: Harper and Row Publishers, Inc.

Gaylin, W. (1989). *The Rage Within: Anger in Modern Life*. New York: Avon.

Gibbs, N. (1995). "The EQ Factor." *Time*. October 2, 60–68.

Ginott, H. (1985). *Between Parent and Child*. New York: The MacMillan Company.

Goleman, D. (1995). *Emotional Intelligence*. New York: Bantam Books.

Grollman, E. (1995). *Living When a Loved One Has Died*. New York: Beacon Press.

Gudykunst, W.B. and Young, Y.K. (1996). *Communicating with Strangers*. New York: McGraw-Hill.

Harris, M.B. (1994). "How Provoking! What Makes Men and Women Angry?" *Journal of Applied Social Psychology*. 23, 199–211.

Izard, C.E. (1993). "Four Systems for Emotion Activation: Cognitive and Noncognitive Processes." *Psychological Review*, 100, 68–90.

Jourard, S. (1973). *Personal Adjustment*. New York: The MacMillan Company.

Jung, C.G. (1923). *Psychological Types*. New York: Harcourt Brace.

Kalish, R.A. (1985). *Grief and Death, Caring Relationships*. (2nd Ed.). Monterey, CA: Brooks/Cole.

Kübler-Ross, E. (1997). *Death: The Final Stage of Growth*. New York: Simon & Schuster.

Kushner, H. (1994). *When Bad Things Happen to Good People*. New York: Avon Books.

_____(1997). *How Good Do We Have to Be*. Canada: Little, Brown & Co.

Labi, N. (1999). "The Grief Brigade," *Time*. May 17, 69–70.

Larsen, E. (1992). *From Anger to Forgiveness*. New York: Ballantine Books.

Lazarus, R.S. and Folkman, S. (1991). "Cognition and Motivation in Emotion." *American Psychologist*. 46, 352–367.

Lerner, H.G. (1997). *The Dance of Anger*. New York: HarperCollins.

May, R. (1967). *Man's Search for Himself*. New York: W. W. Norton and Co.

Menninger, K. (1980). "Feelings of Guilt," *DHEW Publication* No. (ADM) 78–580.

Morris, W.N. (1990). *Mood*. New York: Springer Verlag.

Plutchik, R. and Conte, H. (1996). *Circumplex Models of Personality and Emotions*. American Psychological Association. Washington, DC.

Powell, J. (1995). *Why Am I Afraid to Tell You Who I Am?* Allen, TX: Tabor Publishing.

Roger-John and McWilliams, P. (1994). *Life 101*. Wilton, CT: Consolino & Woodward.

Rogers, C. (1972). *On Becoming a Person*. Boston, MA: Houghton-Mifflin.

Salovey, P. and Mayer, J. (1990). "Emotional Intelligence," *Imagination, Cognition, and Personality*. 9, 185–211.

Schachter, S. and Singer, J. (1962). "Cognitive, Social and Psychological Determinants of Emotional States." *Psychological Review*, 69: 379–399.

Simon, S. and Simon, S. (1991). *Forgiveness: How to Make Peace With Your Past and Get on With Your Life*. New York: Warner Books.

Smedes, L. (1996). *Forgive & Forget: Healing the Hurts We Don't Deserve*. New York: Harper Collins Paperback.

Tavris, C. (1989). *Anger: The Misunderstood Emotion*. New York: Simon and Schuster, Inc.

Viorst, J. (1998). *Necessary Losses*. New York: Fawcett Columbine.

Viscott, D. (1990). *The Language of Feelings.* New York: Pocket Books.

Wallace, P. and Goldstein, J. (1999). *An Introduction to Psychology.* New York: McGraw-Hill.

Weiten, W. (1999). *Psychology-Themes and Variations.* Pacific Grove, CA: Brooks/Cole.

Welshons, J. (1999). *Awakening from Grief: Finding the Road Back to Joy.* New York: Open Heart Publications.

Wood, S. and Wood, E. (1999). *The World of Psychology.* Needham Heights, MD: Allyn & Bacon.

Chapter 5

Adler, R., Rosenfeld, L. and Towne, N. (1998). *Interplay—The Process of Interpersonal Communication.* Ft. Worth, TX: Harcourt Brace.

Barker, L., Edwards, C., Gaines, C., Gladney, K. and Holley, R. (1981). "An Investigation of Proportional Time Spent in Various Communication Activities by College Students." *Journal of Applied Communication Research.* 8: 101–109.

Baruth, L.G. and Manning, M.L. (1998). *Multicultural Counseling and Psychotherapy: A Lifespan Perspective.* New York: Macmillan.

Blanchard, K. and Johnson, S. (1993). *The One Minute Manager.* New York: The Berkley Publishing Group.

Blum, D. (1998). "Face it." *Psychology Today.* 31: 32–29.

Bolton, R. (1986). *People Skills.* New York: Simon and Schuster, Inc.

Buscaglia, L. (1990). *Loving Each Other: The Challenge of Human Relationships.* New York: Holt, Rinehart and Winston.

Cline, F.W. and Fay, J. (1998). *Parenting with Love and Logic: Teaching Children Responsibility* (audiocassette). Evergreen, CO: Love and Logic Press.

Cohen, R.L. and Borsoi, D. (1996). "The Role of Gestures in Description Communication: A Cross-sectional Study of Aging." *Journal of Nonverbal Behavior,* 20: 45–64.

Covey, S. (1990). *The 7 Habits of Highly Effective People.* New York: Simon and Schuster, Inc.

Covey, S. (1992). *Principle-Centered Leadership.* New York: Simon and Schuster, Inc.

De Vito, J.A. (1997). *The Interpersonal Communication Book.* Reading, MA: Addison Wesley.

Drakeford, J. (1967). *The Awesome Power of the Listening Ear.* Waco, TX: Word Publishing.

Dresser, N. (1996). *Multicultural Manners.* New York: John Wiley and Sons, Inc.

Eckman, P. and Friesen, W. (1984). *Unmasking the Face: A Guide to Recognizing Emotions from Facial Clues.* Englewood Cliffs, N.J.: Prentice-Hall, Inc.

Englander-Golden, P. and Satir, V. (1990). *Say It Straight.* Palo Alto, CA: Science and Behavior Books, Inc.

Everett, F., Proctor, N. and Cartmela, B. (1997). "Providing Psychological Services to American Indian Children and Families." In D. R. Atkinson, G. Morten, and D. W. Sue (Eds.) *Counseling American Minorities.* Dubuque, IA: Wm. C. Brown.

Fast, J. (1988). *Body Language.* New York: M. Evans.

Garrison, M. and Bly, M. (1997). *Human Relations.* Needham Heights, MA: Allyn & Bacon.

Gordon, T. (1990). *Parent Effectiveness Training.* New York: New American Library.

Gray, J. 1992. *Men Are From Mars, Women Are From Venus.* New York: Harper Collins.

Groder, M. (1997). "All About Criticism." *The Bottom Line,* 18: 13–14.

Hall, E.T. (1992). *The Hidden Dimension.* Garden City, NY: Anchor Books.

Halonen, J. and Santrock, J. (1999). *Human Adjustment.* Dubuque, IA: Brown and Benchmark.

Hamilton, C. (2000). *Communicating for Results.* Belmont, CA: Wadsworth Publishing Co.

Harrison, D.D. (1978). "Word Power" in *Some Things Are Better Said in Black and White.* Fort Worth, TX: Branch Smith, Inc.

Harrison, R. (1970). "Nonverbal Communication: Exploration into Time, Space, Action, and Object." *Dimensions in Communication: Readings.* Edited by James Campbell and Hall Harper. Belmont, CA: Wadsworth Publishing Co.

Heslin, R. and Alper, T. (1983). "Touch: A Bonding Gesture." *Nonverbal Interaction.* Ed. J.M. Wiemann and R.P. Harrison. Beverly Hills, CA: Sage Publishing Co.

Hoffman, G. and Graiver, P. (1983). *Speak the Language of Success.* New York: G. P. Putnam's Sons.

Horn, S. (1996). *Tongue Fu! How to deflect, Disarm and Defuse Any verbal Conflict.* New York: St. Martins Griffin.

Johnson, D. (2000). *Reaching Out.* Needham Heights, MA: Allyn and Bacon.

Mayeroff, M. (1990). *On Caring.* New York: Harper and Row.

Mehrabian, A. (1968). "Communication without Words." *Psychology Today.* 9: 53.

Mehrabian, A. (1980). *Public Places and Private Spaces.* New York: Basic Books.

Menninger, K. and Holzman, P. (Editor) (1995). *Theory of Psychoanalytic Technique.* Northvale, NJ: Jason Aronson.

Miller, S., Wackman, D., Nunnally, E. and Saline, C. (1981). *Straight Talk.* New York: Rawson Wade Publishing Co.

Milliken, M.E. (1997). *Understanding Human Behavior.* Albany, New York: Dalmar Publishers, Inc.

McNeill, D. (2000). *The Face.* New York: Back Bay Books.

Rogers, C. (1957). "The Necessary and Sufficient Conditions of Personality Change." *Journal of Counseling Psychology.* 22: 95–110.

Rogers, C. (1995). *On Becoming a Person: A Therapist's View of Psychotherapy.* Wilmington, MA: Houghton Mifflin.

Satir, V. (1976). *Making Contact.* Millbrae, CA: Celestial Arts.

Sperry, L. (1975). *Skills in Contact Counseling.* Reading, MA: Addison Wesley.

Tannen, D. (1991). *You Just Don't Understand.* New York: Ballantine Books.

Tannen, D. (1992). *That's Not What I Meant.* New York: Ballantine Books.

Tavris, C. and Wade, C. (1999). *Invitation to Psychology.* New York: Longam Publisher.

Telushkin, Joseph. (1998). *Words That Hurt, Words That Heal.* New York: William Morrow and Company, Inc.

Weiss, L. and Cain, L. (1991). *Power Lines.* Dallas, TX: Taylor Publishing Co.

Birch, C. (1999). *Asserting Yourself: How to Feel Confident About Getting More From Life.* New York: How To Books, Ltd.

Bolton, R. (1986). *People Skills.* New York: Simon and Schuster, Inc.

Bower, S.A. and Bower, G.H. (1991). *Asserting Your Self.* Massachusetts: Addison-Wesley.

Burgess, H. and Burgess, G. (1997). *Encyclopedia of Conflict Resolution.* Santa Barbara, CA: ABC-Clio.

Buscaglia, L. (1994). *Born for Love.* New York: Ballantine Books.

Collier, M.J. (1991). "Conflict Competence within African, Mexican, and Anglo-American Friendships," in *Cross-Cultural Interpersonal Communication.* S. Ting-Toomey and F. Korzenny, (Eds.) Newbury Park, CA: Sage.

Davis, M., Eshelman, E.R. and McKay, M. (1998). *The Relaxation and Stress Reduction Workbook.* Oakland, CA: New Harbinger Publications.

Deutsch, M. (1973). *The Resolution of Conflict.* New Haven: Yale University Press.

Duncan, B.L. and Rock, J.W. (1993). "Saving Relationships: The Power of the Unpredictable." *Psychology Today.* January/February.

Englander-Golden, P. and Satir, V. (1990). *Say It Straight.* Palo Alto, CA: Science and Behavior Books, Inc.

Fensterheim, H. (1975). *Don't Say Yes When You Want to Say No.* New York: David McKay.

Fisher, R. and Ury, W. (1992). *Getting To Yes: Negotiating Agreement without Giving In.* Boston, MA: Houghton, Mifflin.

Fontaine, G. (1999). "Cultural Diversity in Intimate Intercultural Relationships," in D.D. Cahn, *Conflict in Intimate Relationships.* New York: Guilford.

Gordon, T. (1990). *Parent Effectiveness Training.* New York: New American Library.

Grasha, A. (1995). *Practical Applications of Psychology.* Reading, MA: Addison Wesley.

Green, R. (1991). *Human Aggression.* Pacific Grove, CA: Brooks/Cole.

Gudykunst, W.B. and Ting-Toomey, S. (1988). *Culture and Interpersonal Communication.* Newbury Park, CA: Sage.

Hammond, J., Keeney, R., and Faiffa, H. (1998). *Smart Choices: A Practical Guide to Making Better Decisions.* Cambridge, MA: Harvard Business School Press.

Harrison, D.D. (1978). *Some Things Are Better Said in Black and White.* Fort Worth, TX: Branch Smith, Inc.

Hjorth, S. and Bakalis, M. (1998). *Who Do You Think You Are: Interpersonal Interactions.* Englewood Cliffs, New Jersey: Prentice Hall, Inc.

Hocker, J. and Wilmot, W.W. (1997). *Interpersonal Conflict.* New York: McGraw Hill.

Johnson, E.W. and Johnson, R.T. (1989). *Cooperation and Competition: Theory and Research.* Edina, MN: Interaction Book Co.

Kottler, J. (1996). *Beyond Blame.* San Francisco: CA: Jossey-Bass.

Marano, H. (2000). "The Eight Habits of Highly Popular People." *Psychology Today.* 33: 78.

Odiome, G. (1974). *Objectives-Focused Management.* New York: Amacom.

Phelps, S. and Austin, N. (1997). *The Assertive Woman: A New Look.* San Luis Obispo, CA. Impact Publishers.

Rogers, C. (1995). *On Becoming a Person: A Therapist's View of Psychotherapy.* Wilmington, MA: Houghton Mifflin.

Rubin, J., Pruitt, D., and Kim, S. (1994). *Social Conflict: Escalation, Stalemate and Settlement.* New York: McGraw-Hill.

Sachs, J. (1987). "Young Children's Language Use in Pretend Play." *Language, Gender, and Sex in Comparative Perspectives,* ed. by Susan Philips, Susan Steel, and Christine Tanz. Cambridge: Cambridge University Press.

Satir, V. (1988). *The New Peoplemaking.* Palo Alto, CA: Science and Behavior Books.

Smith, M. (1985). *When I Say No I Feel Guilty.* New York: Bantam Books.

Stone, D., Patton, B., and Heen, S. (1999). *Difficult Conversations.* New York: Viking Press.

Tannen, D. (1991). *You Just Don't Understand.* New York: Ballantine Books.

Tannen, D. (1999). *The Argument Culture: Stopping America's War of Words.* New York: Ballantine Books.

Telushkin, J. (1996). *Words that Hurt, Words that Heal.* New York: William Morrow and Company, Inc.

Ting-Toomey, S. (1994). "Managing Conflict in Intimate Intercultural Relationships," in *Conflict in Personal Relationships,* D. D. Cahn, Ed. Hillsdale, NJ: Erlbaum.

Wright, D. (1999). *Personal Relationships.* Mountain View: California. Mayfield Publishing Co.

Chapter 8

Alan, R. and Scheidt, S. (Eds.). (1996). *Heart and Mind.* Washington, D.C.: American Psychological Association.

Baron, R. and Byrne, D. (1999). *Social Psychology.* Needham Heights: MA: Allyn & Bacon.

Basco, M. (1999). "The Perfect Trap." *Psychology Today.* 32: 30–34.

Beck, A.T. (1991)."Cognitive Therapy: A 30-Year Prospective." *American Psychologist.* 46, 368–375.

Beck, A.T. (1993). *Cognitive Therapy and the Emotional Disorders.* New York: New American Library.

Bernard, M.E. (1991). *Using Rational Emotive Therapy Effectively: A Practitioner's Guide.* New York: Plenum.

Blanchard, K. "Nothing but Problems," in Cranfield, J. and Hanse, M. (Eds.) (1995). *A 2nd Helping of Chicken Soup for the Soul.* Deerfield Beach, FL: Health Communications, Inc.

Blumenthal, James (1999). "How to Take Control of Your Life and Say Good-bye to Stress," in *Best of Internal Medicine.* Chicago, IL: American Medical Association.

Burns, D. (1999). *The Feeling Good Handbook.* New York: William Morrow and Co.

Carpi, J. (1996). "What to do about Stress." *Psychology Today,* 28:2, 34–40.

Cowley, Geoffrey (1999). "Stress Busters: What Works." *Newsweek.* June 14: 60–61.

Davis, M., Eshelman, E.R. and McKay, M. (1998). *The Relaxation and Stress Reduction Workbook.* Richmond, CA: New Harbinger Publications.

Dawis, R. and Fruehling, R. (1996). *Psychology: Realizing Human Potential.* St. Paul, MN: Paradigm.

Ellis, A. (1993). *How to Stubbornly Refuse to Make Yourself Miserable about Anything—Yes, Anything.* New York: Carol Publishing Group.

Ellis, A. (1980). "Overview of the Clinical Theory of Rational-Emotive Therapy." R. Greiger and J. Boyd (Eds.). *Rational Emotive Therapy: A Skills-Based Approach.* New York: Van Nostrand Reinhold.

Ellis, A. and Harper, R. (1998). *A Guide to Rational Living.* Hollywood, CA: Wilshire Books.

Epstein, Robert (1999). "On the Real Benefits of Eustress." A conversation with Hans Selye. *Psychology Today Reader.* Dubuque, Iowa: Kendall/Hunt Publishing Co.

_____(2000). "Stress Busters." *Psychology Today.* 33: 30–36.

Fox, Jasmine (1999). "Adults Just Wanna Have Fun." *Psychology Today.* 32: 12.

Freud, S. (1936). *The Problems of Anxiety.* New York: Norton.

Friedman, M. and Rosenman, R.H. (1981). *Type A Behavior and Your Heart.* New York: Fawcett.

Funk, S.C. (1992). "Hardiness: A Review of Theory and Research." *Health Psychology,* 11 (5), 335–345.

Gray, J. (1992). *Men are from Mars Women are from Venus.* New York: Harper Collins.

Gray, J. (1993). *Men, Women and Relationships.* New York: Harper Paperbacks.

Hallowell, Edward (1997). "Why Worry." *Psychology Today.* 30: 34–40, 66–70.

Kanner, A., Coyne, J., Schaefer, C., and Lazarus, R. (1981). "Comparison of Two Modes of Stress Measurement: Daily Hassles and Uplifts Versus Major Life Events." *Journal of Behavioral Medicine,* 4 (13), 1–39.

Kaplan, P. (1998). *The Human Odyssey-Life Span Development.* St. Paul, MN: West Publishing Co.

Kobasa, S. (1984). "How Much Stress Can You Survive?" *American Health,* September, 64–77.

Lazarus, R.S. (1993). "From Psychological Stress to the Emotions: A History of Changing Outlooks." *Annual Review of Psychology,* 44, 1–21.

Lazarus, R.S. and Folkman, S. (1984). *Stress Appraisal and Coping.* New York: Springer Publishing Co.

Martin, G. and Osborne, J. (1993). *Psychology Adjustment and Everyday Living.* Englewood Cliffs, NJ: Prentice Hall, Inc.

McKinnon, W., Weisse, C.S., Reynolds, C.P., Bowles, C.A. and Baum, A. (1989). "Chronic Stress, Leukocyte Subpopulations and Humoral Response to Latent Viruses." *Health Psychology.* 8, 389–402.

Miller, L.H. and Smith, A.D. with Rothstein, L. (1994). *The Stress Solution.* New York: Pocket Books.

Naune, James (2000). *Psychology: The Adaptive Mind.* Belmont, California: Wadsworth/Thomas Learning.

Ouellette, S. (1993). "Inquiries into Hardiness." in L. Goldberger and S. Breznitz (Eds.), *Handbook of Stress: Theoretical and Clinical Aspects* (2nd ed.). New York: Free Press.

Paulus, P., Seta, C., and Baron, R. (1999). *Effective Human Relations: A Guide to People at Work.* Needham Heights, MA: Allyn & Bacon.

Pliner, J. and Brown, D. (1995). "Helpers among Students from Four Ethnic Groups." *Journal of College Student Personnel,* 26, 147–157.

Powell, J. (1995). *Why Am I Afraid to Tell You Who I Really Am?* Allen, TX: Tabor Publishing.

Scheier, M. and Carver, C. (1992). "Effects of Optimism on Psychological and Well-Being: Theoretical Overview and Empirical Update." *Cognitive Theory and Research,* 16 (2), 201–228.

Selye, H. (1982). "History and Present Status of the Stress Concept." In L. Goldberger and S. Breznitz (Eds.). *Handbook of Stress: Theoretical and Clinical Aspects.* New York: Free Press.

Selye, H. (1974). *Stress without Distress.* New York: J. B. Lippincott Co.

Selye, H. (1978). *The Stress of Life.* New York: McGraw-Hill.

Seta, J., Seta, C., and Wang, M. (1991). "Feelings of Negativity and Stress: An Averaging-Summation Analysis of Impressions of Negative Life Experiences." *Personality and Social Psychology Bulletin,* 17, 376–384.

Simon, S.B. (1989). *Getting Unstuck: Breaking Through the Barriers to Change.* New York: Warner.

Sotile, W. and Sotile, M. (1996). "The New Frontiers of Happiness." *Psychology Today,* July/August, 50–55.

Stone, Brad (1999). "Get a Life." *Newsweek.* June 7: 68–69.

Taylor, D. and McGee, D. (1990). *Stress Management Workshop Series.* Metro-McGee Associates, Inc. Arlington, TX.

Tubesing, N.L. and Tubesing, D.A. (1995). *Structural Exercises in Stress Management.* Volume II. Duluth, MN: Whole Person Press.

Wallis, E. (1986). "Stress: Can We Cope?" *Time,* 6, 48–54.

Weiten, W. and Lloyd, M. (1999). *Psychology Applied to Modern Life: Adjustment in the 90's.* Pacific Grove, CA: Brooks/Cole Publishing Co.

Wolpe, J. (1992). *The Practice of Behavior Therapy.* Elmsford, NY: Pergamon Press.

Chapter 9

Allport, G.W. (1954). *The Nature of Prejudice.* Reading, MA: Addison-Wesley.

Aronson, E. (1999). *The Social Animal.* New York: W. H. Freeman.

Begley, S. and Kalb, C. (2000). "Learning Right from Wrong." *Newsweek,* March 13: 30–32.

Corey, G. and Corey, M. (2000). *I Never Knew I Had a Choice.* Pacific Grove, CA: Brooks Cole Publishing Co.

Corey, G., Corey, C., and Corey, H. (1997). *Living and Learning.* Belmont, CA: Wadsworth.

Covey, S.R. (1990). *The Seven Habits of Highly Effective People.* New York: Simon and Schuster, Inc.

Elkins, D. (1999). "Spirituality—It's What's Missing in Mental Health." *Psychology Today,* 32: 45–48.

Elliot, C. (1991). *With Integrity of Heart: Living Values in Changing Times.* New York: Friendship Press.

Festinger, L. (1957). *A Theory of Cognitive Dissonance.* Stanford, CA: Stanford University Press.

Frankl, V.E. (1963). *Man's Search for Meaning.* New York: Washington Square Press.

Frankl, V.E. (1978). *The Unheard Cry for Meaning.* New York: Bantam.

Grasha, A., and Kirschenbaum, D. (1980). *Psychology of Adjustment and Competence.* Cambridge, MA: Winthrop.

Hecklinger, F. and Black, B. (2000). *Training for Life.* Dubuque, IA: Kendall/Hunt Publishing Co.

Hetherington, C. (1996). *Celebrating Diversity.* Duluth, MN: Whole Person Associates.

Johnson, D. (2000). *Reaching Out.* Needham Heights, MA: Allyn and Bacon.

Johnson, H. (1998). *How Do I Love Me?* Salem, WI: Sheffield Publishing Co.

Jourard, S. (1971). *The Transparent Self: Self-Disclosure and Well-Being* (Rev. Ed.). New York: Van Nostrand Reinhold.

Jung, C. (1923). *Psychological Types.* New York: Harcourt Brace.

Kirschenbaum, H. (1994). *100 Ways to enhance Values and Morality in Schools and Youth Settings.* Needham Heights, MA: Allyn & Bacon.

Kluckhohn, F. (1956). "Value Orientations." In *Toward a Unified Theory of Human Behavior: An Introduction to General Systems Theory.* Ed. R.R. Grinker, Sr. New York: Basic Books, Inc., Publishers.

Kohlberg, L. (1981). *The Philosophy of Moral Development: Moral Stages and the Idea of Justice.* San Francisco: CA: Harper & Row.

Lewis, H. (1990). *A Question of Values.* New York: Harper and Row.

Milliken, M.E. (1997). *Understanding Human Behavior.* Albany, NY: Delmar Publications, Inc.

Milton, W. (1985). *Values Clarification Workshop.* Dallas, TX.

Myers, D.G. (1995). *Psychology.* New York: WH Freeman & Co.

Okrent, D. (1999). "Raising Kids Online: What can Parents Do?" *Time.* 153: 38–43.

Paul, A. (1998). "Where Bias Begins: The Truth about Stereotypes." *Psychology Today.* 31: 53–55.

Peck, M. (1998). *Further Along the Road Less Traveled.* New York: Simon & Schuster.

Pojmon, L.P. (1998). *Ethics: Discovering Right and Wrong.* Belmont, CA: Wadsworth.

Rathus, S. and Nevid, J. (1999). *Adjustment and Growth.* Fort Worth, TX: Holt, Reinhart and Winston, Inc.

Reece, B. and Brandt, R. (1999). *Effective Human Relations in Organizations.* Boston, MA: Houghton Mifflin Co.

Rokeach, M. (1973). *The Nature of Human Values.* New York: The Free Press.

Schlessinger, L. (1998). "Dr. Laura Wants you to Stop Whining." *Psychology Today.* 31:29.

Schwartz, Barry. (2000). "Waking Up from the American Dream." *Psychology Today.* 32:74.

Shames, L. (1989). *The Hunger for More: Searching for Values in an Age of Greed.* New York: Time Books.

Sicard, G., Moorman, R., Nichols, C., and McNair, J. (1994). *Individuals in Transition.* Dubuque, IA: Kendall/Hunt.

Simon, S., Kirschenbaum, H., and Howe, L. (1995). *The Classic Guide to Discovering Your Truest Feelings, . . .* Revised Ed. New York: Warner Books.

Thompson, B.L. (1990). "Ethics Training Enters the Real World." *Training.* October, 1990.

Worchel, S. and Goethals, G. (1998). *Adjustment: Pathways to Personal Growth.* Englewood Cliffs, NJ: Prentice-Hall, Inc.

Yalom, I.D. (1980). *Existential Psychotherapy.* New York: Basic Books.

Chapter 10

Ash, M.K. (1995). *Mary Kay: You Can Have It All (Lifetime Wisdom from America's Foremost Woman Entrepreneur).* Roseville, CA: Prima Publishers.

Boles, R.N. (1983). *The Three Boxes of Life.* Berkeley, CA: Ten Speed Press.

Boles, R.N. (2000). *What Color Is Your Parachute?* Berkeley, CA: Ten Speed Press.

Breathnach, S. (1998). *Simple Abundance.* New York: Warner Books.

Breathnach, S. (2000). *The Simple Abundance Companion.* New York: Warner Books.

Campbell, A. (1981). *The Sense of Well-being in America.* New York: McGraw Hill.

Campbell, D. (1990). *If You Don't Know Where You're Going, You'll Probably End Up Somewhere Else.* Niles, IL: Thomas More Press.

Colson, J. and Eckerd, J. (1991). *Why America Doesn't Work.* Dallas, TX: Word Publishing.

Covey, S. (1996). *First Things First.* New York: Fireside.

Covey, S. (1990). *The 7 Habits of Highly Effective People.* New York: Fireside.

Csikszentmihalyi, M. (1997). "Finding Flow." *Psychology Today.* 30: 46–48.

Diener, E. and Gallagher, D. (1991). "Response Artifacts in the Measurement of Subjective Well-being." *Social Indicators Research,* 24, 35–56.

Diener, E., Horwitz, J. and Emmons, R. (1985). "Happiness of the Very Wealthy." *Social Indicators Research,* 16, 263–274.

Douglas, M. and Douglas, D. (1993). *Manage Your Time, Manage Your Work, Manage Yourself.* New York: AMACOM.

Epstein, M. (1995). "Opening up to Happiness." *Psychology Today.* 28:4, 42–46.

Fadiman, J. (1986). *Be All That You Are.* Seattle, WA: Westlake Press.

Figler, H. (1999). *The Complete Job Search Handbook.* New York: Owl Books.

Gray, J. (1999). *How to Get What You Want and Want What You Have: A Practical and Spiritual Guide to Personal Success.* New York: HarperCollins.

Hall, E. and Hall, M. (1990). *Understanding Cultural Differences.* Yarmouth, ME: Intercultural Press, Inc.

Hecklinger, F. and Black, B. (2000). *Training for Life.* Dubuque, IA: Kendall/Hunt Publishing Co.

Helmstetter, S. (1990). *Choices.* New York: Pocket Books.

Inglehart, R. (1990). *Cultural Shift in Advanced Industrial Society.* Princeton NJ: Princeton University Press.

Johnson, D. (2000). *Reaching Out.* Needham Heights, MA: Allyn and Bacon.

Johnson, S. (1998). *Who Moved My Cheese?* New York: G. P. Putnam's Sons.

Lakein, A. (1996). *How to Get Control of Your Time and Your Life.* New York: New American Library.

MacKenzie, A. (1997). *The Time Trap: The New Version of the 20 Year Classic on Time Management.* New York: AMACOM (Division of American Management Association).

Maltz, M. (1987). *PsychoCybernetics.* Englewood Cliffs, NJ: Prentice Hall, Inc.

Marks, J. (1995). "Time Out." *U. S. News.* 119:23, 85–96.

Maslow, A. (1987). *Motivation and Personality.* Reading, MA: Addison Wesley.

Maslow, A. (1993). *The Further Reaches of Human Nature.* New York: Arkana (Viking).

McCullough, M. (1997). *I Can, You Can Too!* Nashville, TN: Thomas Nelson Publishers.

Myers, D. (1993). *The Pursuit of Happiness.* New York: Avon.

Myers, D. (1996). Interview: "The Mystery of Happiness." *ABC News Special,* April 15, 1996.

Myers, D. (2000). *The American Paradox: Spiritual Hunger in an Age of Plenty.* New Haven, CT: Yale University Press.

Peck, M.S. (1998). *The Road Less Traveled.* New York: Simon and Schuster, Inc.

Prather, H. (1986). *Notes on How to Live in the World and Still be Happy.* New York: Doubleday.

Roger-John and McWilliams, P. (1991). *Do It.* Los Angeles, CA: Prelude Press.

Siegel, B. (1990). *Love, Medicine, and Miracles.* New York: Harper & Row.

Super, D.E. (1980). "A Lifespan, Lifespace Approach to Career Development." *Journal of Vocational Behavior,* 16, 30.

Viscott, D. (1988). *Risking.* New York: Pocket Books.

Walton, S. (1993). *Made in America.* New York: Doubleday.

Ziglar, Z. (1998). *Over the Top.* Nashville, TN: Thomas Nelson Publishers.

Glossary

Acting   A process of clarifying values, whereby an individual follows a pattern of taking action on a chosen value.

Active Listening   Seeing the expressed idea or problem from the speaker's point of view.

Adolescent Identity Crisis Stage   One of Levinson's developmental stages occurring between the ages of 17 and 22; characterized as the period of searching for personal, career, and social identity, along with the need to become independent from parental influences.

Advising Response   Responding to others by offering a solution.

Agreeableness   One of the "big five" dimensions of personality: ranges from good-natured, cooperative, trusting at one end to irritable, suspicious, uncooperative at the other.

Aggression   Any behavior that is intended to hurt someone, either verbally or physically.

Aggressive   Moving against another with an intent to hurt.

Alarm Stage   The stage where the body recognizes the stressor and prepares for fight or flight, which is done by a release of hormones from the endocrine glands.

Altruistic Love   Sacrificing for the sake of love.

Anger   The feeling of extreme displeasure, usually brought about by interference with our needs or desires.

Annoyance   A mild form of anger.

Anxiety   An unpleasant, threatening feeling that something bad is about to happen; the basis of the fear is not generally understood.

Assertiveness   Response to conflicting situations that involves standing up for yourself, expressing your true feelings, and not letting others take advantage of you; however, assertiveness involves being considerate of others' feelings.

Assume or Assumptions in Communication   To accept as fact without any evidence of proof.

Attentive Listening   One of the four levels of normal listening; paying attention and focusing energy on the words that are being said.

Attitudes   Positive or negative orientations toward a certain target.

Attribution Error   The tendency to overemphasize internal explanations of other people's behavior.

Attribution Theory   An explanation that suggests we frequently overestimate the influence of an individual's personality and underestimate the impact of his or her situation.

Autonomy vs Doubt   Erikson's psychosocial crisis at the second stage of the human life cycle; the two- and three-year-old develops independence and self-reliance in proportion to positive parental encouragement and consistency of discipline.

Avoidance   Response to conflicting situations that involves being passive and removing yourself from the conflict.

Basic Law of Life   For everything you get in life, you also have to give up something.

Behavioral Contract   An agreement (commitment) made to change your behavior.

Belief   The acceptance of some thought, supposition, or idea.

Blamer   A fault-finder, a dictator, and a boss.

Blended Families   A family system consisting of stepchildren and stepparents.

Blind Self of Johari Window   Information about you of which you are unaware but is easily apparent to others.

Broken-Record Technique   Calmly repeating your assertive message without getting sidetracked by irrelevant issues.

Categorizing   Placing people into groups—by race, sex, physical attractiveness, height, etc.

Catharsis   An emotional release through talking.

Chair of Life   An analogy, representing four valuable parts of life. The "chair" (our life) can either be in balance or out of balance, based on the amount of time we devote to each of these important parts of life.

Character Ethic   A style of living based on principles and values rather than on techniques.

Choosing Freely   Consciously and deliberately making a value choice without any pressure from significant others.

Classical Conditioning   A type of learning in which a neutral acquires the capacity to evoke a response that was originally evoked by another stimulus.

Closed Questions   Questions that often result in yes, no, or a very short response.

Codependent   A dependency on people—on their moods, behavior, sickness, well-being, and their love.

Cognitive Dissonance   A concept (theory) that accounts for reactions to inconsistencies in attitudes and beliefs.

Cognitive-Physiological Theory of Emotions   A theory emphasizing the interaction between a person's thoughts and his or her physiological arousal.

Cognitive Restructuring   The process of modifying thoughts, ideas, and beliefs.

Cognitive Theory   Our mental processes turn our sensations and perceptions into organized impressions of reality.

Cohabitation   A situation in which couples live together outside of marriage.

Collaborative Problem Solving   The win-win approach to conflict resolution whereby conflicts are resolved with no one winning and no one losing. Both win because the solution must be acceptable to both.

Collectivism   Putting group goals ahead of personal goals and defining one's identity in terms of the groups to which one belongs.

Commitment   A joint decision to begin a relatively long-lasting, more intimate relationship that to some extent excludes other close intimate relationships.

Communication   The process of conveying feelings, attitudes, facts, beliefs, and ideas between individuals, either verbally or nonverbally, and being understood in the way intended.

Communication Barriers   Things that stop, block, prevent, or hinder the communication process.

Communication Channels   The medium through which a message passes from sender to receiver.

Communication Process   A process involving three parts: 1) a sender of the message, 2) a receiver of the message, and 3) the content of the message.

Companionate Love   Commitment and intimacy, but no passion.

Complementarity   One person's strengths compensate for the others weaknesses.

Conceived Values   Stated values not acted on.

Conditioned Response (CR)   A learned reaction to a conditioned stimulus that occurs because of previous conditioning.

Conditioned Stimulus (CS)   A previously neutral stimulus that has, through conditioning acquired the capacity to evoke a conditioned response.

Confidant   A significantly close personal friend with whom one can safely share one's deepest concerns and joys.

Conflict   An expressed struggle between at least two people who perceive the situation differently and are experiencing interference from the other person in achieving their goals.

Conflicting Stimuli   Things that are in conflict with your beliefs and values.

Conscientiousness   One of the "big five" dimensions of personality: ranges from well-organized, careful, responsible at one end to disorganized, careless, unscrupulous at the other.

Consequences   The results of your behavior—positive reinforcement, negative reinforcement, or punishment.

Consummate Love   Commitment, intimacy, and passion.

Coping   Refers to active efforts, either positive or negative, to master, reduce, or tolerate the demands created by problems and/or stress.

Cultural Display Rules (in emotions)   Norms about when, where, and how much individuals from different cultures should show emotions.

Daily Hassles   Irritating and frustrating incidents that occur in our everyday transactions with the environment.

Debilitative Emotions   Emotions that prevent a person from functioning effectively.

Decoding   The process in which a receiver attaches meaning to a message.

Defense Mechanisms   Behavior patterns used to protect one's feelings of self-esteem and self-respect.

Delight   The earliest pleasant reaction (emotion), appearing in the form of smiling, gurgling, and other babyish sounds of joy.

Desensitization   Method of behavioral modification whereby the individual's fear of an object or person is replaced by relaxation.

Displacement   A defense used when the person redirects strong feelings from one person or object to another that seems more acceptable and less threatening.

Distractor   An individual who responds in an irrelevant way to what anyone else is saying or doing.

Distress   Negative or harmful stress that causes a person to constantly readjust or adapt.

Divorce   A complete, legal breaking up of a marriage.

Domination   An aggressive technique of resolving conflict, characterized by moving against another with the intent to hurt.

Door Openers   Short responses inviting the other person to share his/her ideas, judgments, or feelings.

Double Bind in Communication   A situation in which the nonverbal message contradicts the verbal message.

Ego   The rational, logical, and realistic part of the personality that attempts to maintain balance between the id and superego.

Emotional Attachments   Feelings that there is someone around to take care of us or help us out.

Emotional Debt   A condition of imbalance in which feelings are trapped instead of expressed.

Emotional Intelligence   Qualities such as self-awareness, impulse control, persistence, zeal and self-motivation, empathy, and social deftness that mark people who excel in real life.

Emotion-packed Phrases   Phrases when combined with different mood levels that can cause an individual to verbally react in inappropriate ways.

Emotions   Feelings that are experienced.

Empathetic Listening   The fifth level, known as the highest form of listening to others; listening with the intent to understand. (See active listening and the understanding response.)

Empathy   The ability to "feel with" another person, to sense what that person is feeling in an emotionally arousing situation.

Empty Love   A form of love that includes commitment, but no intimacy or passion.

Encoding   The process of putting thoughts into symbols—most commonly words.

Envy   The thoughts and feelings that arise when our personal qualities, possessions or achievements do not measure up to those of someone relevant to us.

Esteem Needs   The need to feel worthwhile, which is often satisfied by maintaining a healthy self-image, through status, prestige, a good reputation, or titles; also referred to as one of Maslow's Hierarchy of Needs.

Ethics   Our standards of conduct or behavior.

Eustress   Good stress or short-term stress that strengthens individuals for immediate physical activity, creativity, and enthusiasm.

Exhaustion Stage   In a three-stage reaction to stress the stage in which continuous stress will not enable the important resistance step to take place, and an individual will go from step one, alarm, directly to step three, exhaustion.

Exotic Love   Sheer physical excitement and sexual pleasure.

Expectations   The perceived possibilities of achieving a goal.

Exposure Effect   A phenomenon which states the more we are exposed to novel stimuli, a new person, or a new product, our liking for such stimuli increases.

External Locus of Control   A characteristic of individuals who see their lives as being beyond their control; they believe what happens to them is determined by external forces—whether it be luck or fate, or other people.

External Noise   Includes such elements in the physical environment as temperature, a show on television, music on a stereo, loud traffic, or any other external event or distracting influences.

Extraversion   One of the "big five" dimensions of personality: ranges from sociable, talkative, fun-loving at one end to sober, reserved, cautious at the other.

Facilitative Emotions   Emotions that contribute to effective functioning.

Fatuous Love   Commitment and passion, but no intimacy.

Fear   The feeling associated with expectancies of unpleasantness.

Feedback   The process by which the sender clarifies how his or her message is being received and interpreted.

Feeling Dimension   The emotional aspects of any conflict situation.

First Impressions   One of the factors that seems to influence our social perceptions. (See Social Perceptions.)

5-to-1 Ratio   A five-to-one ratio of positive interactions to negative interactions is vital to a happy relationship.

Flow (Living in a state of)   Being totally absorbed in an activity, whether at work or play, with a sense of mastery, and the use of all or most of one's skills.

Forgiveness   A healing process involving six stages, whereby painful past experiences are put into perspective and one gets on with life, unencumbered by excess emotional baggage.

Friend   A person attached to another by respect or affection.

Full Value   A value that meets all of the criteria that have been established by Value Clarification theorists.

Game-Playing Love   Treating love like a game or sport.

Gay Relationships   Homosexual relationships.

General Adaptation Syndrome   The stages of chain of reactions to stress.

Generativity vs Self-Absorption   Erikson's psychosocial crisis at the seventh stage of the human life cycle; conflict between concern for others and concern for self.

Genuineness   This means being honest and open about one's feelings, needs, and ideas—being what one really is without front or facade.

Getting Established Stage   One of Levinson's developmental stages occurring between the ages of 22 and 28; characterized by establishing oneself in a career, getting married, and having a family.

Getting Settled Stage   One of Levinson's developmental stages occurring between the ages of 33 and 40; characterized as the period of establishing ourselves in society, solidifying our family life, and becoming successful in the world of work.

Goals   An aim or purpose—a plan.

Good Grief   The process of working through the stages of grief so that it becomes a positive growth experience.

Grief and Bereavement   To be deprived of someone or something very important; sometimes referred to as mourning.

Grief-Work   The process of freeing ourselves emotionally from the deceased and readjusting to life without that person.

Guilt   The realization of sorrow over having done something morally, socially, or ethically wrong.

Happiness   A sense that life is good—a state of well-being that outlasts yesterday's moment of elation, today's buoyant mood, or tomorrow's feeling of sadness.

Hardiness   A cluster of characteristics that seem to distinguish stress-resistant people from those who are more susceptible to its harmful effects. These characteristics are commitment, control, and challenge.

Hate   May be thought of as intense anger felt toward a specific person or persons.

Hearing   The physiological sensory process by which auditory sensations are received by the ears and transmitted by the brain.

Hidden Agenda   Entering a conversation or situation with a special interest in mind, a grudge that we are wanting to bring into the open, or even a "chip on our shoulder."

Hidden Self of Johari Window   Information and personal feelings that you keep hidden from others.

High-Context Culture   Those cultures which value self-restraint, avoid confrontation, rely heavily on nonverbal systems, and give a great deal of meaning to the relationships between communicators. Examples are the Japanese, Chinese, Asian, and Latin American cultures.

Honeymoon Period   Anytime from the wedding day to a year or so from that day.

Hostility   A mild form of anger/hate directed to a specific person or group.

Hyperstress   An overload that occurs when stressful events pile up and stretch the limits of a person's adaptability.

Hypostress   An overload that occurs when a person is bored, lacking stimulation, or unchallenged.

"I" Message   A message that describes the speaker's position without evaluating others.

Id   The part of the personality composed of the basic biological drives that motivate an individual.

Idea-Oriented Value System   A value system categorized by someone who has a zest for knowledge; someone who likes to think, imagine, and intellectualize.

Identity vs Role Confusion   Erikson's psychosocial crisis at the fifth stage of the human life cycle, in which the 12- to 18-year-old adolescent must integrate his experiences to develop a sense of ego identity.

Ignoring while Listening   One of the four levels of general listening, better known as not really listening at all.

Impression Management   Our conscious efforts to present ourselves in socially desirable ways.

Individualism   Putting personal goals ahead of group goals and defining one's identity in terms of personal attributes rather than group memberships.

Individuation   The establishment of one's identity, based on experiences, rather than following parent's dreams.

Industry vs Inferiority   Erikson's psychosocial crisis at the fourth stage of the human life cycle; the 6- to 11-year-old whose curiosity is encouraged develops a sense of industry, as opposed to the child whose curiosity is disparaged and who develops a sense of inferiority.

Infatuation   An irrational feeling or passion for someone or something. Passion, but no commitment or intimacy.

In-group—Out-group Bias   Refers to our tendency to perceive people differently depending on whether they are members of our in-group or out-group.

Initial Response Level   Every response of the targeted behavior that occurs within a specific period of time prior to conditioning.

Initiative vs Guilt   Erikson's psychosocial crisis at the third stage of the human life cycle; the 4- or 5-year-old either is encouraged to go out on his own or is restricted in his activities.

Intangible Values   Abstract values such as knowledge, religious, or spiritual growth.

Integrity vs Despair   Erikson's psychosocial crisis at the eighth stage of the human life cycle; a response that depends on how an old person remembers his life.

Intense Emotions   Emotions that are debilitative—they disrupt our overall functioning.

Interactional Possibilities   Considering the situation and the possible options before making a response.

Internal Locus of Control   The state in which individuals who feel that what happens to them and what they achieve in life is due to their own abilities, attitudes, and actions.

Internal Noise   Includes such things as a headache, lack of sleep, daydreaming, preoccupation with other problems, or even a preconceived idea that the message is going to be unimportant or uninteresting.

Internal Psychological Filter   A filter through which all information received is processed. This filter consists of prejudices, past experiences, hopes, and anxieties.

Interpersonal Relations   Our interactions with others—how they relate to us and how we relate to them.

Interpretative Response   A response in which the receiver tries to tell the sender what his or her problem really is and how the sender really feels about the situation.

Intimacy   The feeling that one can share all of one's thoughts and actions with another.

Intimacy vs Isolation   Erikson's psychosocial crisis at the sixth stage of the human life cycle; the young adult either is able to relate to others or feels isolated.

Intimate Distance   One of Hall's four distance zones, ranging from skin contact to 18 inches.

Irrational Beliefs   Beliefs that result in inappropriate emotions and behaviors.

Issue Dimension   Conflicting needs, preferences, values, and beliefs involved in a conflict situation.

Jealousy   The state of demanding complete devotion from another person; being suspicious of a rival or of one believed to enjoy an advantage.

Johari Window   A model that describes the relationship between self-disclosure and self-awareness.

Judging Response   A response that shows that the receiver is making a judgment about the motive, personality, or reasoning of the sender.

Kinesics   The science of study of nonverbal communication.

Learned Helplessness   The assumption—based on past failures—that one is unable to do anything to improve one's performance or situation and gives-up.

Learning   A relatively permanent change in behavior as a result of experience or practice.

Liking   A fondness or preference for someone or something. Intimacy, but no commitment or passion.

Listening   An intellectual and emotional process that integrates physical, emotional, and intellectual inputs in a search for meaning and understanding.

Listening with the Third Ear   Listening to what is said between the lines and without words, what is expressed soundlessly, and what the speaker feels and thinks.

Living Together Loneliness (LTL)   The results of a perceived discrepancy between expected and achieved contact has been identified.

Logical Love   Treating love as a practical down to earth decision.

Loneliness   A feeling of longing and emptiness, which is caused by the lack of emotional attachments and/or social ties.

Lose-Lose   An approach to conflict resolution whereby neither party is happy with the outcome.

Love   When the satisfaction, security, and development of another person is as important to you as your own satisfaction, security, and development (Harry Stack Sullivan); also referred to as the desire to see another individual become all they can be as a person—with room to breathe and grow.

Love and Belonging Needs   The need to feel loved, included, and accepted; this need usually assumes importance after the safety and survival needs have been met; also referred to as one of Maslow's Hierarchy of Needs.

Low-Context Culture   Those cultures which use more explicit language, are more direct in their meanings, rely less on nonverbal systems, and stress goals and outcomes more than relationships. Examples are the German, Swedish, American, and English cultures.

Lust   An intense physiological attraction for another person.

Marriage   A close union of two people who decide to share their lives, dreams, and goals with each other.

Maslow's Hierarchy of Needs   The arrangement of needs in order of basic importance as established by Abraham Maslow: physiological needs, safety needs, belongingness and love needs, esteem needs, and self-actualization needs.

Matching Hypothesis   A concept that proposes that people of similar levels of physical attractiveness gravitate toward each other.

Mere-Exposure Effect   The more familiar we become with someone or something the more accepting we will become.

Midlife Crisis   Occurring somewhere between the ages of 40 and 45; may be characterized by a painful and disruptive struggle with one's identity and satisfaction of personal needs.

Midlife Transition Stage   One of Levinson's developmental stages occurring between the ages of 40 and 45; characterized as the period when individuals realize their life is half over and they reevaluate their life and what they want out of the remainder of their life.

Mild Emotions   Emotions that are facilitative—they assist us in preparing for the future, solving problems, and in doing what is best for us.

Minimal Encourages   Brief indicators to the speaker indicating that the receiver is still listening.

Mixed Emotions   Emotions that are combinations of primary emotions. Some mixed emotions can be expressed in single words (that is awe, remorse), whereas others require more than one term (that is, embarrassed and angry, relieved and grateful).

Modeling   Imitating a behavior one observes.

Monochronic Cultures   Cultures in which time is organized sequentially; schedules and deadlines are valued over people.

Moods   A general feeling tone.

Moral Values   Values having to do with right and wrong, good and evil.

Motive   Something (a need or desire) that causes a person to act.

Move Against   Being aggressive and responding to conflicting situations with the intent to hurt.

Moving Toward   Responding to conflicting situations by moving toward your opposition until you are either closer together or on the same side.

Need   A lack of something desirable or useful; to be in want.

Negative Reinforcement   Anything that increases a behavior by virtue of its termination or avoidance.

Neurotic Anxiety   Anxiety experienced when the quality of the threatening experience is blown out of proportion to the actual danger posed, and to the point that the anxiety hinders daily functioning.

Neuroticism   One of the "big five" dimensions of personality: ranges from calm, secure and self-satisfied at one end to anxious, insecure, self-pitying at the other.

Neutral Stimulus (NS)   Classical conditioning begins with a stimulus that does not elicit a response. The neutral stimulus will eventually become the conditioned stimulus (CS).

Non-Moral Values Values having to do with tastes, preferences, and styles.

Nonverbal Communication Messages expressed by other than linguistic means.

Novel Stimuli People, places, or things that are new, different, unique, or original.

Observational Learning Learning that occurs when an individual's behavior is influenced by the observation of others—modeling.

One-Way Communication Communication in which a receiver provides no feedback to a sender.

Open Self of Johari Window An area that represents information, feelings, and opinions that you know about yourself and that others know about you.

Open Communicator One who is willing to seek feedback from others and to offer information and personal feelings to others.

Openness Trust and mutual sharing of information and feelings.

Openness Trait One of the "big five" dimensions of personality: ranges from imaginative, sensitive, intellectual, at one end to down-to-earth, insensitive, crude at the other end.

Open Questions Questions that provide space for the speaker to explore his or her thoughts.

Operant Conditioning Conditioning based on the principle of reinforcement; the consequences of a response determine whether that response will persist.

Operant Level The number of responses prior to conditioning or baseline of behavior prior to conditioning.

Operative Values Real values implemented in our lifestyle.

Optimism A general tendency to envision the future as favorable.

Optimistic Explanatory Style Using external, unstable, and specific explanations for negative events.

Paralinguistics Nonlinguistic means of vocal expression: tone, rate, pitch, and so on.

Paraphrase Stating the essence of the other person's spoken words in your own words.

Parenthood The role of being a mother or father.

Parroting To repeat exactly the speaker's words.

Parts of a Communication Transaction Six steps commonly referred to as the idea, encoding, transmission, receiving, decoding, and understanding.

Passive Avoiding or removing yourself from the conflicting situation by leaving, shutting up, placating, concealing your feelings, or postponing a confrontation until a better time.

Passive Listening See One-way Communication.

People-Oriented Value System A value system categorized by someone who truly enjoys working and being with people.

People Perception The study of how we form impressions of others.

Perceptual Awareness Process The means by which we interpret or misinterpret the world around us.

Personal Distance One of Hall's four distance zones, ranging from 18 inches to 4 feet.

Personality Ethic A style of living based on having the right image and doing the right things, defined by the right kind of special techniques and a positive mental attitude.

Personality Fit The process of being attracted to another person because the differences in one person's strengths compensate for the other person's weaknesses.

Personal Self Image The part of the self that includes physical, behavioral, and psychological characteristics that establish uniqueness.

Pessimism A general tendency to envision the future as unfavorable.

Pessimistic Explanatory Style Using internal, stable, and global explanations for negative events.

Physical Attractiveness Our perception of the beauty of another person.

Physiological Needs Our most basic and fundamental needs, such as food, water, sleep, clean air to breathe, exercise, and sex; also called our primary or survival needs; also referred to as one of Maslow's Hierarchy of Needs.

Placater An individual who conceals his or her own feelings.

Polychronic Cultures Cultures in which time is organized horizontally; people tend to do several things at once and value relationships over schedules.

Positive Reinforcement Anything that increases a behavior by virtue of its presentation.

Possessive Love Wanting to bind the partner to an enduring relationship.

Pot of Self Worth   Virginia Satir's view of how much self-worth we have at any given time; the amount in the pot is constantly changing based on the different experiences we have, as well as the feedback we get from others.

Prejudices   A preconceived opinion, feeling, or attitude, either positive or negative, which is formed without adequate information.

Preparation Anxiety   Anxiety that helps individuals get energized to deliver their best, such as mild tension before going for a job interview.

Pretending while Listening   One of the four levels of normal listening. Some examples are "Yeah. Uh-huh. Right."

Primacy Effect   Occurs when the first impression carries more weight than subsequent information.

Primary Emotions   Basic emotions identified by R. Pluchick as joy, acceptance, fear, surprise, sadness, disgust, anger, and anticipation; identified by Gary Emery and James Campbell as mad, sad, glad, and scared.

Primary Reinforcer   A reinforcer to which we respond automatically, without learning (food, drink, heat, cold, pain, physical comfort or discomfort).

Prizing   Cherishing and being happy with the choice (value), as well as being willing to affirm the choice (value) publicly.

Projection   A defense mechanism used when an individual attributes their own feelings, shortcomings, or unacceptable impulses to others.

Proximity   Geographical nearness, location.

Psychological Reactance   The tendency to protect or restore one's sense of freedom or social control, often by doing the opposite of what has been demanded.

Psychosomatic Disorders   Real physical disorders in which stress and emotional reactions play a part. (This is sometimes called psychophysiological Disorders).

Public Distance   One of Hall's four distance zones, ranging outward from 12 feet.

Punishment   Anything that decreases a behavior by virtue of its presentation.

Questioning Response   A response that indicates that the receiver wants to probe the sender for additional information and to discuss the issue further.

Rage   Uncontrolled, intense anger and implies that the anger is expressed through violent physical activity.

Rational Beliefs   Beliefs that result in appropriate emotions and behaviors.

Rationalization   A defense mechanism consisting of reasonable, rational, and convincing explanations, but not real reasons.

Reacting to Others   A situation in which the emotional, feeling, and irrational characteristics of a person are communicated.

Reaction Formation   A defense mechanism in which impulses are not only repressed, they are also controlled by emphasizing the opposite behavior.

Real Self   The person you really are, not who you think you are; a situation in which the belief system is accurate, rather than distorted.

Reciprocal Determinism   The interacting influences between, person, behavior, and environment.

Reciprocity   The tendency to like individuals who tend to like us.

Reinforcement   The effect of applying reinforcers.

Reinforcers   Pleasant or unpleasant stimuli that strengthen behavior.

Remarriage   Marrying for the second, third, or subsequent time.

Repression   A defense mechanism consisting of the exclusion of painful, unwanted, or dangerous thoughts and impulses from the conscious mind.

Repulsion hypothesis   People are initially, spontaneously repulsed by strangers who are very dissimilar to themselves.

Resentment   Chronic anger resulting from unresolved anger at an injustice.

Resistance Stage   The period of recovery and stabilization, during which the individual adapts to the stress.

Responding Reflectively   Paraphrasing the essence of the speaker's content and mirroring back to the speaker the emotions which he/she is communicating.

Responding to Others   A situation in which the rational, thinking, logical part of a person is communicated.

Risk   To reach for something you are not entirely sure of but believe is better than what you now have, or is at least necessary to survive (David Viscott).

Role Confusion   An uncertainty experienced by individuals during the ages of 12 and 18 about who they are and where they are going.

Role Expectations   Beliefs about a man and woman's roles in marriage.

Romantic Love   A form of love that includes intimacy and passion, but no commitment.

Romeo & Juliet Effect   Same as psychology reactance—when love is intensified not weakened, by their families opposition.

Safety and Security Needs   The need to protect oneself from danger and to keep safe from harm; on a psychological level, safety needs might relate to safety and security, such as finding and keeping a job; also referred to as one of Maslow's Hierarchy of Needs.

Search for Meaning   Viktor Frankl's idea that our task in life is to create a life that has meaning and purpose.

Secondary Reinforcers   Stimuli to which we have attached positive or negative value through association with previously learned conditioned reinforcers.

Selective Listening   One of the four levels of normal listening, known as hearing only certain parts of the conversation.

Self-Actualization   The fulfillment of one's own completely unique potential.

Self-Actualization Needs   The need for self-fulfillment; the need to become all that one is capable of becoming; also referred to as one of Maslow's Hierarchy of Needs.

Self-Awareness   The capability to reflect and decide and become aware of our responsibility for choosing the way we live and thus influence our own destiny.

Self-Control   A person's sense of their ability to control their own behavior.

Self-Disclosure   The process of deliberately revealing information about oneself that is significant and that would not normally be known by others.

Self-Discovery   The process of getting to know yourself as a person—the person within yourself.

Self-Efficacy   Our belief about our ability to perform behaviors that should lead to expected outcomes.

Self-Esteem   An overall evaluation of oneself, whether one likes or dislikes who one is, believes in or doubts oneself, and values or belittles one's worth.

Self-Evaluation   How you compare yourself with others.

Self-Fulfilling Prophecy   A prediction or expectation of an event that makes the outcome more likely to occur than would otherwise have been the case.

Self-Image   A mental blueprint of how we see ourselves and how we feel about ourselves.

Self-Perception   How you evaluate your "self"—physically and psychologically.

Self-Serving Bias   A person's tendency to evaluate their own behavior as worthwhile, regardless of the situation.

Self-Talk   A person's beliefs or what they say to themselves.

Self-Validation   Disclosing information with hopes of obtaining the other persons approval.

Self-Worth   Virginia Satir's idea that our individual worth is our perception of what happens between people and inside people.

Semantics   The study of the meaning and changes of meaning in words.

Shyness   The feelings, physical reactions, and thoughts that create a state of anxiety, discomfort, and inhibition.

Significant Others   The important people in our lives.

Significant Stimuli   Anything directly related to another person's needs, wants, interests, and desires.

Similarity   The process of selecting friends because of comparable interests, income level, educational beliefs, and so on.

Singlehood   The decision not to marry.

Situational Shyness   Specific environmental circumstances that develop feelings, physical reactions, and thoughts that create a state of anxiety, discomfort, and inhibition.

Social Comparison   How a person evaluates themselves in relation to others.

Social Control   Revealing personal information may increase your control over other people and sometimes over the situation.

Social Distance   One of Hall's four distance zones, ranging from 4 to 12 feet.

Social Learning Theory   The theory that suggests that personality development occurs through observational learning.

Social Perception   The way we perceive, evaluate, categorize, and form judgments about the qualities of people we encounter.

Social Ties The feeling that we are part of a group or have an identity.

Stages of Grief Work The process of freeing ourselves emotionally from a "loss," readjusting to life without the cause of this loss, resuming ordinary activities, and forming new relationships; the stages are identified as denial, replacement or searching activity, anger, depression, and acceptance.

Stages of Psychosocial Development Eight stages of Erikson's human life cycle; the stages are trust versus mistrust, autonomy versus doubt, initiative versus guilt, industry versus inferiority, identity versus role confusion, intimacy versus isolation, generativity versus self-absorption, and integrity versus despair.

Stepfamilies Remarriages involving children from one or both spouses.

Stereotyping A process of making generalizations by categorizing an object, person, or situation.

Stress The nonspecific response of the body to any demand placed on it, whether that demand be real, imagined, pleasant, or unpleasant.

Stressor A stressful event.

Sublimation A defense whereby an individual redirects their basic desires toward a socially valued activity.

Submissive An individual who behaves passively in a conflicting situation.

Success The outcome of setting a goal and achieving that goal, whatever that goal may be.

Superego The part of the personality that consists of our values, morals, religious beliefs, and ideals of our parents and society; sometimes referred to as our conscience.

Supportive Response A response that shows the receiver's intent is to reassure, comfort, or minimize the intense feelings of the sender.

Suppression A defense mechanism in which people are conscious of their emotions, but deliberately control rather than express them.

Symbols in Communication Such things as the selection of words, tone and pitch of voice, nonverbal method, or even types of supportive materials.

Sympathy The ability to feel for another person.

Tangible Values Specific values such as a car or money.

Target Behavior The goal you have set for yourself—your behavioral goal.

Thing-Oriented Value System A value system categorized by someone who works hard and saves money to obtain material objects or even a large bank account.

Thought-Stopping Concentrating on the unwanted thoughts and, after a short time, suddenly stopping and emptying the mind of all stressful thoughts.

Time Waster Anything preventing you from achieving your objectives most effectively.

Trait A relatively stable and consistent personal characteristics.

Trust vs Mistrust Erikson's psychosocial crisis at the first stage of the human life cycle; the subsequent response of a person to the way he is treated as an infant.

Two-Way Communication An exchange of information in which the receiver deliberately provides feedback to a sender.

Type A Behavioral Pattern A behavioral pattern characterizing individuals who live a competitive, aggressive, ambitious, and stressful life style.

Type B Behavioral Pattern A behavior pattern characterizing individuals who live a more relaxed and less hurried lifestyle.

"You" Messages Messages creating a feeling of blame and accusation.

Unconditional Positive Regard The situation in which love is given freely and does not depend on any specific aspects of behavior.

Unconditioned Response (UCR) An unlearned reaction to an unconditioned stimulus that occurs without previous conditioning.

Unconditioned Stimulus (UCS) A stimulus that evokes an unconditioned response without previous conditioning.

Understanding Response This response indicates that the receiver is seeking to fully understand what the sender is actually saying. This is the most effective way of responding to others and requires the skills of active listening, sometimes referred to as empathetic listening. (See active listening and empathetic listening).

Unknown Self of Johari Window Information about you that is unknown to self or others.

Value The personal worth placed on an object, thought, or idea.

Value Clarification A process that helps people distinguish between full values and partial values.

Value Indicators   Partial values, such as desires, thoughts not acted on; opinions, interests, aspirations, goals, and so on, that are in the process of being formed.

Value System   The personal blueprint or guidelines for one's life, based upon one's values.

Verbal Communication   The expression of words; language.

Wavering and Doubt Stage   One of Levinson's developmental stages occurring between the ages of 28 and 33; characterized as the period of evaluating "what we are doing and where we are going."

Win-Lose   An approach to conflict resolution whereby one person gets his or her way, and the other does not.

Win-Win   An approach to conflict resolution whereby conflicts are resolved with no one winning and no one losing. Both win because the solution must be acceptable to both.

Index